Britain and the Balance of Power
in North America 1815–1908

Britain and the Balance of Power in North America

1815–1908

Kenneth Bourne

Lecturer in International History, London School of Economics
Visiting Lecturer in History, University of California, 1966–67

University of California Press

Berkeley and Los Angeles

1967

Contents

List of Maps

Preface

This book is not a history of Anglo-American relations; nor is it even a history of British policy towards the United States. It is rather an attempt to follow one particular theme in British policy – the problems raised by thinking about and planning for the possibility of a future war with the United States, and their general influence upon official British policy towards the United States. I have therefore made no attempt to re-examine in any detail the records of British foreign policy as contained in the Foreign Office files. Some occasional forays into that material have been necessary; but generally speaking I have relied on the existing monographs. The conventional approach to the history of Anglo-American relations has been exhaustively written. H. C. Allen's *Great Britain and the United States: a History of Anglo-American Relations (1783-1952)* (London, 1954) presents the essentials of the story in an admirably comprehensive volume. To it should be added for the period 1895–1903 Charles S. Campbell, Jr, *Anglo-American Understanding, 1898–1903* (Baltimore, 1957); A. E. Campbell, *Great Britain and the United States, 1895–1903* (London, 1960); R. G. Neale, *Britain and American Imperialism, 1898–1900* (St Lucia, Queensland, 1965); and J. A. S. Grenville, *Lord Salisbury and Foreign Policy; the Close of the Nineteenth Century* (London, 1964). These volumes have been concerned, principally or in part, with the so-called 'rapprochement' in Anglo-American relations at the end of the nineteenth century and have suggested many important modifications to the classic thesis expounded by Lionel M. Gelber, *The Rise of Anglo-American Friendship* (London, 1938). In contrast to these works the other major area of revision in recent years has been the War of 1812. Reginald Horsman, *The Causes of the War of 1812* (Philadelphia, 1962), and Bradford Perkins, *Prologue to War: England and the United States, 1805–1812* (Berkeley, 1961), examine the origins of the war in both Britain and America. J. Mackay Hitsman, *The Incredible War of 1812: a Military History* (Toronto, 1965), is the most recent work on the conduct of the war. Bradford Perkins, *Castlereagh and Adams: England and the United States, 1812–1823* (Berkeley, 1964), emphasizes wartime diplomacy, the peace negotiations and the aftermath of the war. By concentrating on the decline of hostility rather than the rise of friendship I have made a different approach to the history of the period between the two crucial phases which have so preoccupied recent writing in this field. In doing so I do not mean to suggest that the emphasis placed on the common features of British and American politics and society, the importance of their economic relations, and their interchange of ideas, culture and people has been wrong; only to remind the historian that statesmen are inclined to be preoccupied with power and that for a very long time British statesmen, like their counterparts on the other side of the Atlantic, tended to see a special danger and a special hostility in Anglo-American relations. The policy and measures into which they were led by this preoccupation and the way in which they eventually reversed their attitude towards American power are at least as deserving of attention.

In contrast to the wealth of literature on Britain's foreign policy in the nineteenth century, her defence policy has been generally neglected, though there are now signs of a new interest in the subject. As a general introduction to the subject of imperial defence W. C. B. Tunstall's chapters in *The Cambridge History of the British Empire*, vols. II and III, are useful. A more recent book on an important aspect of the subject is Donald C. Gordon, *The Dominion Partnership in Imperial Defense, 1870–1914* (Baltimore, 1965). On the military side there is really nothing worth mentioning which takes a general look at extra-European problems. The navy is much better served. I have found C. J. Bartlett's *Great Britain and Sea Power, 1815–1853* (Oxford, 1963) particularly useful, as also of course A. J. Marder's *The Anatomy of British Sea Power: a History of British Naval Policy in the Pre-Dreadnought Era, 1880–1905* (New York, 1940), and *From the Dreadnought to Scapa Flow: the Royal Navy in the Fisher Era, 1904–1919*, vol. I, *The Road to War, 1904–1914* (London, 1961). On British defence policy in North America there are a number of relevant books. The naval bases of Bermuda, Esquimalt and Halifax all have monographs of varying quality: Roger Willock, *Bulwark of Empire: Bermuda's Fortified Naval Base, 1860–1920* (privately published, Princeton, N.J., 1962); F. V. Longstaff, *Esquimalt Naval Base: a History of its Work and its Defences* (Victoria, 1941); Harry Piers, *The Evolution of the Halifax Fortress, 1749–1928* (Halifax, 1947), and T. H. Raddall, *Halifax, Warden of the North* (Toronto, 1948). But first and foremost among Britain's defence problems in North America was Canada. On this subject I must acknowledge a considerable debt to the work of the Canadian military historian, Colonel C. P.

Stacey. Among many articles of real importance his classic revisionist piece, 'The Myth of the Unguarded Frontier, 1815–1871', *American Historical Review*, lvi (1950–51), 1–18, is the essential starting-point for the study of this subject. On a much larger scale his *Canada and the British Army, 1846–1871; a Study in the Practice of Responsible Government* (London, 1936) contains a wealth of information and good sense. A revised edition published by the University of Toronto Press in 1963 adds a few notes and brings the bibliography up to date. Stacey's theme is rather different from mine and is confined to a shorter period. So far as manuscript sources are concerned it is based entirely on materials available in Canada. My concern has been rather with Britain's defence policy as seen and made in Whitehall. With few exceptions, therefore, I have been happy to rely on Stacey's work for the Canadian side and to concentrate on the very substantial materials available in London. Without Stacey's guidance, however, I could probably not have found my way at all among the records of the Colonial and War Offices which, with those of the Admiralty also preserved in the Public Record Office in London, provide one of my two main kinds of source.

My approach to the mass of relevant material in the Public Record Office has not been to attempt the impossible task of examining everything; but to concentrate on periods of crisis in Anglo-American relations and to follow up other special investigations made by the service departments into the more important problems of North American defence. The correspondence of the secretaries of state with their overseas governors and military commanders and the principal files of the engineers and ordnance contain a vast amount of material relating to the defence of North America, Bermuda, British Columbia, and the West Indies. Especially useful among the War Office papers were the secretary's in and out letters (W.O. 1 and W.O. 6) and Ordnance 'Miscellanea' (W.O. 55). For the period after 1855, when the War Office parted company with the Colonial Office, much less has survived of a more strictly military nature. Some of the 'principal' War Office papers, and especially those deemed worthy of printing, were collected together in a special series (W.O. 33). But this was a small fraction of the whole and for the most part correspondence has disappeared in some crazy 'weeding' fever. The surviving files of the Military Intelligence Department (W.O. 106) to some extent compensate for the deficiencies in the documentation of the later period. Fortunately the Colonial Office records have suffered nothing like the same fate and its correspondence continues to be rich in material relating to defence. The principal files of the Admiralty also appear to be substantially complete.

Particularly useful have been the occasional 'case' volumes in 'Miscellaneous' series. Thus Adm. 7/624 contains important material on the 'Lakes and Rivers of Canada', 1861–62; Adm. 7/625 and 626 on special investigations of Canadian naval defences in 1845–46; and Adm. 7/712 is a collection of intelligence material on the U.S. Navy in the period 1826–52. The files of the main series of the Board of Admiralty papers, Adm. 1 and 2, however, have been somewhat disappointing. The secretary's correspondence with the commanders-in-chief on the Pacific and North American stations has been useful for supplying details of naval strength and the condition of bases – actual or prospective – and for the practical measures taken during specific crises. But it tends to throw up little discussion of naval strategy and imperial defence. Nor is this gap at all filled by correspondence between the service departments and between them and the Foreign and Colonial Offices.

To fill this gap I have had recourse to a large body of private papers. Among those of a more strictly naval and military character I have found the papers of Admiral Sir Thomas Byam Martin (in the British Museum) and Admiral Sir Alexander Milne (in the National Maritime Museum, Greenwich) extremely useful. But my main purpose in using so many collections of private papers has been to illuminate the relationship between Britain's defence and foreign policies in regard to North America. Until late in the century it was in cabinet alone that this vital connection was systematically made and in the absence of any other form of documentation for cabinet discussions the private papers of the ministers have been vital. Indeed in the long mid-Victorian period in particular one cannot but be impressed with the knowledge and industry of British ministers on this as on so many other subjects. The first decade or so after 1815 has suffered rather too much at the hands of auctioneers and collectors. I have found a few pieces of interest among the papers of the second earl of Liverpool in the British Museum and among the collections of George Canning's and the second Viscount Melville's letters in the William Clements Library, Ann Arbor, Michigan. But searches among the papers of Lord Castlereagh at Mount Stewart, County Down, and the third Earl Bathurst at Cirencester Park, Gloucestershire, revealed nothing new. In these circumstances the papers of Admiral Sir Thomas Byam Martin proved particularly important in filling in some of the earlier gaps concerning naval policy in Canada. Similarly the various series of Wellington's published correspondence – *Despatches, Correspondence, and Memoranda of Field Marshal, Arthur Duke of Wellington* (London, 1867–70), and *Supplementary Despatches*, etc. (London, 1858–65) – were very useful for land defences in the same period. For the long period of crisis in Anglo-American relations from the mid 1830s to the late 1860s there is a rich harvest in the many available collections of leading cabinet ministers. The collections which have proved of most value to me are those of the third Viscount Palmerston (in the British Museum and in those formerly at Broadlands, Romsey, Hampshire, and now temporarily with the National Register of Archives in London); Sir Robert Peel, the fourth earl of Aberdeen, and W. E. Gladstone (in the British Museum).

In the last part of this study the nature of the sources changes. New kinds of official source come to the fore and private papers almost disappear. This is in part due to the fact that soon after the end of the American Civil War real crises in Anglo-American relations tended to recede and almost all thoughts of war with the United States to disappear from the private correspondence of leading ministers. At the same time a bureaucratic professionalism, and military bureaucracy in particular, overtook Britain as well as other western nations. In 1873 and 1886 respectively there appeared the Military and Naval Intelligence Departments. About the same time too came the first real attempts to provide an integrated system of defence planning for the empire. Out of the Russian scare of 1878 there eventually emerged in 1885 the permanent Colonial Defence Committee, followed in 1891 by the Joint Naval and Military Committee, in 1895 by the Cabinet Defence Committee, and finally in 1902 by the Cabinet Committee of Imperial Defence. None of these bodies – not even the last – ever succeeded in providing a real policy-making machinery; perhaps it was never seriously intended that they should do so. But, so far as documentation is concerned, they did supply the kind of interdepartmental consideration and review that was so clearly lacking in the first two-thirds of the century. In Part 3 therefore I tend to use private papers comparatively little and to follow instead the systematic files of the Colonial Defence Committee and the Committee of Imperial Defence preserved in the cabinet documents series in the Public Record Office.

Occasionally the reader will notice that I have extended my investigations to the American side of the picture. Originally I hoped to examine this side of things much more thoroughly. My experience in the archive collections in the United States, however, soon convinced me that the surviving material was too fragmentary and too scattered. With some reluctance therefore I have made only such limited use of American material as may help to test the validity of British speculations.

For their kindness and help in making available all these collections, and others mentioned in the footnotes, I owe a great debt to large numbers of individuals on both sides of the Atlantic. I must thank in particular the staffs of the Public Record Office and the British Museum in London, and of the National Archives and the Library of Congress in Washington, D.C. Mr A. W. H. Pearsall of the National Maritime Museum at Greenwich gave me most helpful assistance both with the manuscript collections in his care and with many problems of naval history. The staff of the Public Record Office of Northern Ireland, with Viscountess Bury's gracious permission, examined for me the papers of Lord Castlereagh at Mount Stewart, County Down; Lord Bathurst kindly permitted a similarly fruitless search in the papers at Cirencester Park, Gloucestershire. For permission to make such extensive use of the Palmerston papers at Broadlands I owe a great debt to the late Countess Mountbatten of Burma. Lastly I have to acknowledge the gracious permission of Her Majesty the Queen to make use of material from the Royal Archives at Windsor.

Research for this book has extended over more than a decade. In 1955–56 I enjoyed a rare freedom to pursue it with the aid of Research Fellowships from the Institute of Historical Research in the University of London and from Reading University. The London School of Economics has naturally helped in many ways – not least with generous leaves of absence and with financial support at a moment of apparent crisis. To the Rockefeller Foundation, the British Association for American Studies and the Fulbright Commission, I owe a year's travel and research in the United States and Canada. My friend Dr C. J. Bartlett of Queen's College, Dundee, read part of the manuscript and made helpful suggestions. The final stages of preparing the manuscript for publication have been aided by a generous grant from the University of California at Davis, and by the efforts of two of my research students, located appropriately on either side of the Atlantic: Mr Gareth Davies of the London School of Economics and Mr J. M. Armstrong of the University of California. I wish also to thank my colleagues, my friends, and my family for the patience and tolerance they have shown towards me while this book struggled to materialize. To Professor W. N. Medlicott, whose help and encouragement I have enjoyed for nearly twenty years, I owe more than I know how to acknowledge.

Davis, California　　　　　　　　　　　　　KENNETH BOURNE
November 1966

Part 1

The Defence of British North America after the War of 1812

I

The Royal Navy and the Great Lakes

Great Britain emerged from the European wars in 1815 with the greatest territorial and commercial empire the world had ever seen, as undisputed mistress of the seas, and, after Waterloo especially, as a by no means contemptible power on land. Her naval power was more impressive on paper than in reality; many of the 214 ships of the line and the 792 cruisers she possessed in 1815 were utterly useless and thereafter she found it difficult to maintain even a hundred ships of the line. But given the destruction and neglect of other navies the Royal Navy was nevertheless unassailable.[1] Yet this did not mean that government or public enjoyed complete security; for to the increased sense of vulnerability that inevitably accompanied the growth of wealth were soon added the fear of social upheaval at home and the expansion of Russia and the revival of France abroad. The ambitions of these two powers remained, throughout the century, Britain's principal foreign fears; but across the Atlantic there existed a special and not unrelated problem in the growing power of the United States.

The war with the United States, also brought to an end in 1814 – 15, was a distinctly subsidiary affair when contrasted with the titanic struggles in Europe; but in its very mixed fortunes it was a lasting blot on Britain's naval and military record, and in political and strategic significance it provided some very worrying lessons. The fortunes – or rather misfortunes – of that war, from the capture of the invading American army at Detroit in August 1812 to the British disaster at New Orleans in January 1815, were due primarily to chance and incompetence. Yet for the British the strategic conditions of the war were clear enough. On the seas they had a mercantile trade, highly vulnerable to the privateers and other raiders which the Americans could fashion out of a merchant marine second only to the British.[2] In North America

---

[1] For the size and efficiency of the Royal Navy in and after 1815 see C. J. Bartlett, *Great Britain and Sea Power, 1815–1853* (Oxford, 1963), pp. 21–8.

[2] Mahan estimated that the British lost about 1,350 merchant vessels to American privateers in the three years of the war; he reckoned annual losses to the French at an average of 500 over the twenty-one years of the war: A. T. Mahan, *Sea Power in its Relations to the War of 1812* (two vols., Boston, 1905), ii. 242.

they had a colony over 2,500 miles distant from the mother country, its population and local resources grossly inferior to those of its hostile neighbour and concentrated in the interior of the continent in a relatively narrow strip along the water frontier of the St Lawrence and Lakes Ontario and Erie.

Both circumstances emphasized the importance of communications. On the ocean Great Britain had a naval strength and a system of island bases with which she could ultimately safeguard her own trade, blockade the enemy, and harass his cities. But none of this would be aimed at conquest – the United States was already too large, the absence of a single centre of wealth and power too frustrating for that – and the attacks upon both New Orleans and Washington had been intended only as raids.[1] On the land frontier both sides had suffered enormously from weak and primitive communications; but Britain's difficulties promised to be militarily more persistent. Canada's communications in the interior and with the United Kingdom were both imperfect and, from a military point of view, highly vulnerable. The best means of communication was by water, along the St Lawrence from the sea to the Great Lakes. By this route even the largest vessels could, in good weather, reach Quebec; but from that place up river nature placed some very hazardous obstacles in the way. In favourable conditions reasonably large vessels, even frigates, could reach Montreal, but after that the rapids of the St Lawrence reduced water transport only to the various types of flat-bottomed craft, and the Niagara Falls prevented even these from passing into Lake Erie. No useful naval force, therefore, could as yet be introduced from the sea onto the upper St Lawrence and the lakes. If the British wanted such a force they had to build one on the spot, or rather, as they had had to do in the recent war, build three – one for Lake Champlain, one for the upper St Lawrence and Lake Ontario, and one for the upper lakes. And although those supplies and reinforcements which had successfully eluded American privateers and safely negotiated 2,500 miles of ocean from Europe, could pass up to Lake Ontario by water and by portage to Lake Erie, their journey was difficult, expensive, and, being for a considerable distance very near or even upon the frontier, liable to attack and interruption by the enemy. Between December and April, when ice completely closed the water communication, any aid to Canada would have to face the additional expense, difficulty, and hazard of the overland route from Halifax or St John. There was a rough and ready route

[1] Bradford Perkins, *Castlereagh and Adams: England and the United States, 1812–1823* (Berkeley and Los Angeles, 1964), p. 141.

mapped out through New Brunswick but it too lay for a great part of its length perilously close to the frontier and in the recent war the British had found it necessary to cover it by the occupation of a large part of Maine.[1] As a result of the war then the British in London as well as in Canada at last perceived the vital importance for all military operations, offensive or defensive, of improving communications in North America and taking special measures to command the lakes and inland waters.

So far as the material results of the war were concerned, neither side could claim substantial victory. The Americans secured none of the objectives with which they had entered the war, either by force of arms or by the peace treaty. Canada remained in British hands and maritime rights and impressment were left untouched. Moreover, by the end of the war the British were in possession of a large if peripheral portion of New England and, more important, were exercising an increasing stranglehold on America's maritime trade.[2] But whatever might have been the long-term effects upon the economy of New England and the loyalty of its Federalist inhabitants – both already cracking in 1814 – the blockade compared most unimpressively with the American victories in individual naval duels and in winning the final battles of the war at Plattsburg and New Orleans. The Americans had much the more glamorous successes and by publicizing these they were able in national mythology and tradition to turn a weary survival into a more colourful victory. Even if they had not conquered Canada or made Great Britain retreat over maritime rights they had successfully checked the greatest of the powers and had even emerged with the advantage from the peace negotiations at Ghent. They had, in particular, established once and for all their security against British intrigues with the Indians.

For the British neither the war nor the peace could provide any such satisfaction – real or illusory. The vast damage done to their mercantile marine seriously impaired the credit of the blockade; above all, there had been no Trafalgar and no Waterloo but only humiliation in so many naval engagements and in the last great battles of the war. These failures engendered a sense of frustration and bitterness in public

[1] See Map 2, p. 107. In 1813 it had taken a New Brunswick regiment nearly four weeks to march on snowshoes from Fredericton to Quebec: A. L. Burt, *The United States and British North America from the Revolution to the Establishment of Peace after the War of 1812* (New Haven, 1940), p. 341.

[2] According to E. F. Heckscher, *The Continental System* (London, 1922), p. 146, U.S. exports (smuggling apart) fell from $38,530,000 in 1812 to $6,930,000 in 1814 and imports in the same period from $77,030,000 to $12,970,000.

opinion corresponding to the fillip given by the war to Anglophobe nationalism on the other side of the Atlantic. In England the effects probably did not constitute any great change of feeling, but rather a new and wary circumspection. The patent importance of Anglo-American trade remained a permanent and restraining, if not always pacifying, factor. Thus the Tory prime minister addressed the House of Lords in 1820: 'Of all the powers on earth, America is the one whose increasing population and immense territory furnish the best prospects for British produce and manufacture. Every man, therefore, who wishes prosperity to England, must wish prosperity to America.'[1] But though far from silenced, the exponents of Anglo-American commercial interdependence and ties of consanguinity, were nevertheless checked in their insistence upon an especially friendly relationship. Typical of the now more cautious state of feeling was the way in which injured self-esteem sought to excuse itself by claiming the parenthood of American successes. 'Despicable in the Cabinet, ridiculous in the field, upon the waves they retain the blood and spirit almost of Englishmen', commented *The Times* after Perry's victory on Lake Erie.[2]

Feelings were rather worse in the United States where the war was certainly not the side issue that it was for Britain and where it was closely associated with a deep political and sectional rift. The collapse of the Federalists seemed to follow inevitably upon the successful ending of the war and the triumph of Anglophobia was consolidated in the pursuit of a nationalist policy designed to lessen the economic dependence upon British manufactures. But while the shock administered to British pride and the flattery bestowed upon American enterprize naturally tended all the more to alienate the two peoples, Anglo-American enmity after two wars found its loudest expression less in action and policy than in what John Quincy Adams called the 'warfare of the mind' – the campaign of casual or deliberate mutual denigration in speech and writing that so marked the first half of the nineteenth century. The need for economy and some measure of grudging respect dictated a rather different course for the policy of governments. In the United States congressional resistance to the increase of the Federal power and, at first, the drive for new inroads into the commercial system of the British Empire checked an extreme nationalist policy for the time being. In Britain enmity similarly failed to capture official policy, especially while Castlereagh was foreign secretary.

[1] *Hansard's Parliamentary Debates*, 2nd series, i. 575.
[2] *The Times*, 7 Oct. 1813, quoted by B. Perkins, p. 37.

It had clearly been the looming dangers in Europe as well as war weariness and financial difficulty at home that had brought the government so readily to a disappointing peace in 1814, and it was essentially the same considerations which dictated a postwar policy of caution in relations with America. Castlereagh was certainly not preoccupied with American affairs, but when he turned to them he saw to it that the spirit as well as the letter of the peace treaty was preserved and that the inevitable incidents of peace did not incline to hostility and war. Intrigues with Indians, whether on the frontiers of Canada or in the Floridas, were forbidden and disavowed; trade was at least restored to its former state; and satisfactory *modi vivendi* were reached over the fisheries and territorial disputes. Official British policy therefore appeared essentially conciliatory and this met a measured, if surprised, response from across the ocean; the spirit, if not the substance, of Anglo-American relations seemed to improve considerably in the years immediately following the Peace of Ghent.

This improvement in Anglo-American relations, however, remained 'always fragile and subject to popular attack, often undermined by effusions of publicists and editors'.[1] Soon, in the mid 1820s, it was to be strained almost to the limit, not as statesmen on both sides had feared by the issue of impressment,[2] but by the collapse of the Spanish empire in America and, more briefly, by the threat of renewed commercial warfare. The motives behind British policy moreover did not reflect a simple, sentimental view of Anglo-American relations. Castlereagh was conciliatory not out of affection but out of common sense. This clearly emerges from the interview he had with Stratford Canning shortly before the latter left to take up his post as minister at Washington in August 1820. Canning's notes of the advice he was given about England's general policy read:

Pacific – conciliatory – forbearing – cannot oppose them with success on inferior local points – national animosity a considerable part of their strength, and therefore in our interest to soften or abate it – By their own

---

[1] B. Perkins, p. 282.

[2] For example, Madison to Monroe, 28 Nov. 1818: 'Impressment and peace, it must now be evident, are irreconcilable' (G. Hunt, *The Writings of James Madison* [9 vols., New York, 1900–10], viii. 418); and Liverpool to Castlereagh private and confidential, 26 Sept. 1816: 'If satisfactory arrangement on this subject cannot be effected, I am persuaded we never shall be engaged in a maritime war with any Power without it leading to a war with the United States of America.' (F.O. 5/119. Foreign Office and other departmental papers in the Public Record Office in London will be referred to in their conventional abbreviated form.)

confession, made during the discussions on the fisheries, they would *for the present* give up to us on any point for which we were ready to go to war, but a continued thwarting they would not brook – we are extending ourselves to the East, why should we be jealous of their doing the same on their own ground? – In angry discussing we have all to lose, as they are always ready to go to the furthest in insolence – once committed, we cannot recede, and hence the great delicacy of treating with them; but when it is not worth our while to call out our whole strength, they must always have an advantage over us.[1]

Behind Castlereagh's policy there lurked no real conception of a major clash of interest between the two powers, nor – though such thoughts were by no means absent from some sections of opinion – the animosity 'inspired', so John Quincy Adams thought, 'by the two deepest and most malignant passions of the human heart – Revenge and Envy'.[2] But there was an apprehension, derived principally from recent experience, of the special dangers of a war. 1812 was seen as a stab in England's back, treacherously delivered during a desperate crusade against the tyrant of Europe, and this was a view which the Americans' hostile and suspicious attitude towards British policy certainly did nothing to dispel. The fact was that Britain's presence on the American continent was of infinitely greater importance to the United States than to Britain herself, involving directly the general security of the Union as well as being a constant reminder of Britain's role in the revolutionary and national development of the state. This understandable though certainly not harmless factor only radical opinion in Britain generally seemed to appreciate; for most other people the American attitude appeared to present a constant threat, all the more sinister in its utter injustice to Great Britain.

No less worrying to British governments was the apparent unwillingness of the British public properly to resist the threat, even when it had broken into actual war. They could recall that in 1814, with victory apparently achieved in Europe, they had still been unable to concentrate the country's enmity and power upon the United States. Cobbett's prophecy that 'nothing will ever make an American war popular in England' seemed fully confirmed.[3] Then, too, there was the unfortunate conduct of the war itself – in particular the shocking if ultimately

[1] Notes of an interview of 27 July 1820 in the Stratford Canning papers in the P.R.O., F.O.352/62. Sir Charles Webster's appreciation of Castlereagh's American policy (*The Foreign Policy of Castlereagh, 1815–1822* [2nd edn., London, 1934], pp. 437–53) is rather superficial. For a more judicious appreciation, see B. Perkins, pp. 199–202.

[2] Quoted by B. Perkins, p. 176.   [3] *Ibid.*, p. 10.

ineffective American success on the seas, and the British inability either to defend completely so long a land frontier or successfully to invade the enemy's. Past experience as well as future fears and the uncertain results of conciliation all suggested, then, not merely caution in foreign policy but also precaution in naval and military preparation.

The suspicion on both sides that Ghent was, as John Quincy Adams put it, 'a truce rather than a peace', led each side to keep a special watch on the other's naval and military activities. For the Americans the border and in particular the Great Lakes were of the first importance in this respect. As early as 29 August 1815 Adams was reporting pessimistically from London on an imminent increase of the British force on the lakes.[1] The British, on the other hand, were particularly sensitive to the development and activities of the United States Navy. This was partly a matter of pride and prestige arising out of the humiliating naval defeats of the war but it was also due to a realistic awareness of the damage that the American navy, regular or privateering, had done and could again do to British trade, and to a genuine respect for the quality of the American ships and their crews. The growth of the American navy they almost automatically tended to connect with the prospect of a new war. *The Times* editorial, commenting on the Ghent peace, predicted 'the speedy growth of the American navy, and the recurrence of a new and more formidable war'.[2] Thus while no particular notice seems to have been taken of the proposal to keep the peacetime American army at four times its prewar strength – it was after all, though slowly carried out, a reduction from the wartime strength of 38,000 to a mere 10,000 men[3] – the news of the American navy bill of 29 April 1816, looking forward to the construction of nine 74-gun line-of-battle ships, twelve 44-gun frigates, and three steam batteries for coast defence, was greeted in London with considerable concern. The minister in Washington kept a close eye on the progress of the naval programme; and espionage proper was also not overlooked.[4]

These investigations certainly seemed to suggest that it was not merely an insincere defence of the naval estimates of 1816–17 that led, as Adams reported, to 'the prospect of a new war with the United

[1] Burt, p. 388.
[2] Quoted by S. E. Morison and H. S. Commager, *The Growth of the American Republic* (4th edn., New York, 1950), i. 445.
[3] The figure was further reduced, in 1820, to 6,000 and this without the proposed provision for reserves.
[4] Charles Bagot to Castlereagh, 'separate and secret', 4 June 1816, F.O. 5/114 pt. II; for an amusing letter from one British spy, see Capt. Charles Hamilton Smith to Earl Bathurst, 20 May 1817, C.O. 42/177.

States [being] distinctly held up by the ministers and admitted by the opposition as a solid reason for enormous and unparalleled expenditure and preparation in Canada and Nova Scotia'. It is not at all surprising to find a lord of the Admiralty declaring in these debates of March 1816 that 'bumboat expeditions and pinchbeck administrations would no longer do for Canada'; but Castlereagh too warned of the 'great and growing military power' of the United States.[1] British concern moreover was not at all confined to parliamentary manœuvres or even to American waters. In 1815 the government made an apparently friendly gesture in allowing Decatur's squadron to use Gibraltar as a base against Algiers; but at the same time they decided not to reduce their own squadron in the Mediterranean below the strength of the American, and, indeed to apply that rule to every station.[2] Admiral Sir David Milne, who was later to assume the command on the Halifax station, in fact adopted a very hostile attitude indeed to the Americans:

The Americans and Algerines . . . are going to war, and nothing would give me so much pleasure as to hear of the Yankees getting a good thrashing. I almost think it would be good policy for some of the European powers to join the Algerines and destroy the American squadron; for their entering into this petty warfare is only to form a navy and keep their ships employed; and which at no very distant period may give trouble enough, particularly to Great Britain.

When reminded by a friend of the special importance of good Anglo-American relations he agreed

that it is the interest of this Government and America to be on the most intimate footing possible; but the people of America have a hatred and jealousy towards Great Britain it is impossible to describe. But I even think that we ought to sacrifice a good deal to keep up that amity and concord so much the interest of both countries. But I most sincerely wish to see their naval power nipt in the bud, for if ever they get it to any extent they will give us trouble enough and none of our West Indian possessions would be safe.

Milne kept to this opinion right to the end of his brief command in America thinking, as he wrote in the autumn of 1818, that war would 'come to pass some years hence'. Milne had had to delay assuming the American command until early in 1817. One reason for the delay, ironically enough, was his appointment as second in command of the

---

[1] J. Q. Adams to secretary of state, 30 Mar. 1816, W. C. Ford, ed., *Writings of John Quincy Adams* (New York, 1915), v. 550–5.
[2] B. Perkins, p. 165.

expedition by which Lord Exmouth finished off the Americans' 'petty warfare' against Algiers. An earlier reason for the delay, and one more seriously concerned with the duties of his American command, was a series of very difficult consultations in Whitehall about the special problems of the defence of Canada's inland frontier.[1]

That the war had forced a considerable change in the British government's attitude to the interior defence of North America was made very clear in some of their proposals at Ghent. Before the war, while local commanders had constantly worried and complained, Whitehall had tended to regard Canada as a convenient base of attack upon the United States. In the first instructions to the peace commissioners, on the other hand, Castlereagh looked to the establishment of a new frontier south of the Great Lakes and the St Lawrence and to the acquisition of a large part of Maine. These proposals reflected an unjustified belief in the strength of England's bargaining position and the outcome of the final battles of the war but they were based too upon a realistic appreciation of the weakness of the existing line of frontier. Exclusive possession of the inland waters would vastly increase the security of the border and existing lines of communication; the acquisition of parts of Maine would provide and protect a good land communication between Quebec and the sea which could be used in winter when the St Lawrence route was closed by ice. Forced to retreat from these extreme demands by the firmness of the Americans and the pessimism of their military advisers, the government's demands subsided to the creation of an Indian buffer state, the limitation of American armaments on the lakes, and finally to the *status quo ante bellum*. It was even tacitly assumed from the peace negotiations that there would be an end to the British contacts with American Indians which were thought to be so profitable in peace and so useful in war. Shortly afterwards Castlereagh did issue express orders to this effect.

The only opportunity for the improvement of Great Britain's military position left to diplomacy seemed to lie in the bargains to be made in the various boundary commissions agreed to by the treaty; but so complex and so intractable were most of the boundary problems that the most crucial strategic questions concerning the frontier remained to be settled in the crises of the 1840s. Nevertheless, the ingenuity of the diplomats was not utterly exhausted in the immediate postwar

[1] Milne to George Home, 24 and 31 May 1815, 26 Jan., 17 Sept., and 14 Nov. 1818, Historical Manuscripts Commission, *Report on the Manuscripts of Col. David Milne Home of Wedderburn Castle, N.B.* (London, 1902), pp. 168 and 175–6.

period for they soon revived the idea of a limitation of armaments on the lakes.[1]

The end of the war had left both sides in hot pursuit of an armaments race on the lakes, and each beginning to indulge in the construction of even the largest types of vessel. The British had already in commission a 112-gun vessel, the *St Lawrence,* and each had two three-decker battleships on the stocks, the American ships, *Chippewa* and *New Orleans,* being possibly the largest warships then in existence.[2] To go on in such a manner in peacetime would have been dangerous and, in view of the urgent need for economy on both sides, perhaps even impossible. This the Americans were first to admit. On 27 February 1815, ten days after the Senate had ratified the treaty of Ghent, the House passed an act authorizing the president to reduce the fresh-water establishment to the size necessary for revenue purposes, though the armament and other equipment of the vessels sold or laid up was to be 'carefully preserved'. As a result work was stopped on the two three-deckers at Sackett's Harbor (though the uncompleted ships were housed over at a cost of $25,000), and by late 1816 all the American vessels were laid up or dismantled save for a brig of eighteen guns and three small schooners used for transport.

Any hopes that the Americans had of setting an example to the British and encouraging harmony as well as economy were soon dashed by reports from their minister in London, John Quincy Adams, of an apparent determination on the British side actually to increase their armaments on the lakes. If the reduction were not to be utterly one-sided, therefore, Secretary of State Monroe had to conclude some definite agreement with the British. The idea of such an agreement was not by any means new. It seems first to have been raised by John Adams at the Paris negotiations of 1782 and, at the suggestion of Alexander Hamilton, John Jay proposed it unofficially to Grenville in 1794. But on neither of these occasions had the British responded and at Ghent they had thought rather of an agreement which would exclude only American armaments and so ensure permanent command of the lakes to themselves. Now, in November 1815, Monroe raised the matter again, with the British chargé d'affaires in Washington and through

[1] For the diplomatic negotiations of the lakes armaments agreement the following account draws mainly on Burt, pp. 387–95. The older, standard work is J. M. Callahan, *The Neutrality of the American Lakes and Anglo-American Relations* (Baltimore, 1898). For some new information, see B. Perkins, pp. 87 and 239–44.

[2] C. P. Stacey, 'The Myth of the Unguarded Frontier, 1815–1871', *American Historical Review,* lvi (1950–51), 9.

Adams in London. At first the British response appeared as unpromising as ever. When Adams approached him on 25 January 1816 Castlereagh was friendly but cautious. Both had already been hard at work smoothing over various minor but nonetheless irritating and potentially dangerous incidents arising out of the contact between haughty naval officers on the lakes and both knew how useful such an agreement might therefore be. But Castlereagh now knew enough about Britain's weakness in Canada to make him pause. He agreed that 'keeping a number of armed vessels parading about the Lakes in time of peace . . . would be absurd' and that 'everything beyond what is necessary to guard against smuggling is calculated only to produce mischief'. 'But you know', he told Adams, 'we are the weaker party there. Therefore it was that we proposed at Ghent that the whole Lakes should belong to one party.' What Castlereagh meant was that the Americans' greater local resources would give them the advantage in any arms race on the lakes, whether it took place in peacetime or upon the actual outbreak of war. Any reciprocal agreement therefore would not balance the naval position but ensure the United States advantage. Moreover, while Castlereagh promised to consult his government and assured him that they would reciprocate the 'pacific dispositions' of the United States, Adams was quite convinced that the American proposal would not be accepted and two months later, at the end of March, the bombastic references in the debates on the naval estimates utterly confirmed him in this opinion. But Adams was wrong.

The British government's public concern about the lakes, though certainly not entirely false, had probably been exaggerated in parliament in order to encourage the passage of the estimates. These were safely through when Adams next raised the matter with Castlereagh on 9 April and he found the foreign secretary very willing to negotiate. Taken utterly by surprise it was now Adams's turn to hedge. He had to plead lack of instructions and these, in view of his recent pessimistic reports, it seemed unlikely he would get for some time. They agreed therefore that the new British minister, Sir Charles Bagot, should take up the matter directly in Washington. In the meantime, they arranged between themselves a gentlemen's agreement, though this suffered the usual fate of such unwritten agreements in that it was differently recorded by the two gentlemen concerned. Adams deemed it to be a mutual disavowal of all new armaments on the lakes, while Castlereagh considered that it bound Britain only 'to keep in commission the smallest number [of vessels] compatible with the ordinary routine of the peace establishment'. Moreover, when

Castlereagh wrote to Bagot on 23 April instructing him to open negotiations he expressed a preference for a similarly vague and informal understanding, suggesting that it would be 'an easier course for both' governments 'to act in the spirit of confidence and of abstaining from exertion in that quarter than to reduce their system to positive stipulations'. But his preference was very mildly stated and Bagot was permitted to negotiate for a definite agreement. He was also told that while not empowered to conclude anything he was to keep in touch with the authorities in Canada who would be told to 'frame their measures' according to the information he supplied about American intentions.

In Washington, in the meantime, Monroe had already been roused to action by Adams's pessimistic reports and he had reopened discussions with Bagot on 2 May. Like Castlereagh, Bagot began by pouring cold water on the secretary of state's proposals on the familiar ground of their one-sided effect and when pressed, like Adams, pleaded lack of instructions. He reported, however, that Monroe was prepared to meet the objection about mutual disarmament giving the potential command to the United States by permitting both parties to lay down keels and to take other precautionary measures.

There may have been little significance in the differences between the American and British versions of the gentlemen's agreement or in the apparent preference for a vague general understanding in the instructions to Bagot; but these features probably had something to do with a serious discrepancy between Castlereagh's policy and the actions contemplated by the Admiralty. The government had begun the peace in 1815 with no intention whatever of allowing the Canadian border to fall once again into the neglect it had suffered in the period before 1812. This did not mean that the existing force on the lakes was to be kept up in its entirety, let alone increased as Adams had mistakenly believed. The wartime commander on the lakes went so far as to declare that so great was the vulnerability of the St Lawrence supply line and so superior were the Americans' shipbuilding resources that 'the preservation of the province of Canada by means of a Naval force on the Lakes, will, in my opinion, be an endless, if not futile undertaking'. Of the recent war he commented: 'tho' much has been done by the mutual exertions of *both Services*, we owe as much if not more to the perverse stupidity of the enemy; the impolicy of their plans; the disunion of their Commanders, and lastly, between them and their minister of war, the fatal, and, fortunate for us, mistaken confidence they placed in the attachment, of the Canadians to their cause.' But bowing to Melville's 'superior judgment' on the necessity of a squadron he recommended that to be of any use they must have 'a very large Military and Naval establishment' and a secure passage for supplies by opening up the Ottawa and Rideau Rivers.[1] The Admiralty did not intend to give up the struggle. Orders went out to the commissioner at Kingston dockyard, Captain Robert Hall, to reduce the civil establishment as early as 4 January 1815. But there was no intention of breaking up the squadron; it was rather to be reformed and reconstituted after the most thorough investigation.[2]

In March 1815 Captain W. F. Owen was ordered to the lakes for the purpose of making 'Surveys and Reports on the Naval Defence of Canada', and to help his brother, Commodore Sir Edward Owen, now in command of the squadron, make appropriate recommendations.[3] Commodore Owen's principal recommendations, concerning improvements in water communications, fortifications, and sites for naval establishments, as well as the war strength of the proposed squadron, were conveyed in a series of despatches between June and November 1815.[4] Apparently it was not until the end of the following May that they were given any thorough consideration. Possibly the delay was due to a wish to bring together for consultation in Whitehall not only Sir David Milne and the newly designated commander on the lakes, Captain Hall, but also Commodore Owen himself. By May, however, the estimates had been safely if narrowly passed and there were signs that the Admiralty's enthusiasm for large expenditure in Canada had waned. But the change was not a precipitate one. At a meeting on 31 May Milne was concerned to find that the government still intended 'to expend large sums of money there in making canals, roads, wharves, etc.'; but a significant advance in the direction of economy had already been made in that it was apparently intended to keep up only the frames of vessels. Whether this was due to anything beyond the peculiar tendency of Canadian timber to decay is not clear but Milne himself was inclined to think that 'it would be better for this country if it were quit of Canada altogether', and a fortnight later his doubts do seem to have been shared by the government:

[1] Commodore Sir James Yeo to Melville, 30 May 1815, Adm. 1/2738.
[2] Navy Board to Hall, 4 Jan. 1815, Adm. 106/2488.
[3] Adm. to W. F. Owen, 27 Mar. 1815, Adm. 2/166.
[4] E. Owen to Adm., nos. 36, 37, 48, 82 and 83, 30 June, 3 and 15 July, 25 and 28 Nov. 1815. The last encloses a comprehensive paper of 'Observations on the defence of the Lake Frontier', 5 Nov. 1815, and all of these despatches are best seen together with numerous papers relating to W. F. Owen's surveys in Adm. to C.O., 6 July 1817, C.O.42/171.

I expected my orders yesterday [he wrote on 13 June], but was told I must now wait until the papers we have been busy at the Admiralty with be laid before Lord Bathurst [the secretary for war and colonies]. Ministers are, I believe, much at a loss how to act with respect to Canada. If we are to keep up our establishment there and be ready to act against the Americans, the expense will be so enormous that the country cannot afford it. . . . There will arise many disputes, the Americans claiming islands and water passages that it is impossible for us to grant without throwing our frontier, particularly the Niagara one, quite open to them. . . . From what I have seen it would be lucky for this country to be well rid of it. It is certainly a fine country but too distant for us to defend against so powerful a neighbour.[1]

There was no chance of the government taking such an extreme course and it is unlikely that Milne meant it seriously; but clearly opinion was moving in a more economical direction and one therefore more favourable to the American suggestions about limitation of armaments. Yet the decisions finally arrived at by the Admiralty on 6 July aimed not only at the maintenance of a fair-sized force on the lakes, but also at large expenditure generally on defence in Canada. On that day the Admiralty at last sent Owen's principal reports to the Colonial Office with general expressions of approval, and a few days later Hall got instructions to maintain in commission on the lakes a force of ten sloops and schooners. At the same time Hall was told that he would be getting orders to build six gunboats for service on the Grand River and the St Clair River and Lake.

Rather more interesting were the special measures contemplated to meet Great Britain's decided disadvantage on Lake Erie. Owen had turned to this problem in his report of 25 November and had then suggested that the best course would be to build for service on that lake vessels similar to the *Princess Charlotte* (later renamed *Burlington*) on Lake Ontario, but of somewhat lighter draught. Like that vessel, the new ones, though called corvettes (i.e. flush-deck vessels with a single deck of guns), should be constructed so as to allow the ready addition of a further deck of guns in the event of imminent hostilities. On 6 July Croker, the secretary of the Admiralty, began a series of investigations with the comptroller, Sir Thomas Byam Martin, Hall, and the surveyor of the navy, to see if the scheme were practicable.[2] On 17 July 'immediate and secret orders' were formally given to the Navy Board

[1] Milne to George Home, 1 and 13 June 1816, *MSS. of Col. Milne Home*, pp. 169–70.
[2] Adm. to Byam Martin, 6 July 1816, and to Hall, 11 July, Adm. 3/262.

to give secret instructions to Commissioner Sir Robert Hall to take measures immediately on his arrival for collecting Timber and Stores for the construction and equipment of four ships on Lake Erie, of the same class as the *Princess Charlotte,* now called the *Burlington* on Lake Ontario, and to cause the said ships to be set up, so soon as the spot on which the Naval establishment on Lake Erie is to be formed shall be decided upon; and to be put in such a state, that they may be completed with despatch whenever circumstances may render it necessary.[1]

That it was intended to deceive the Americans is beyond any shadow of doubt:

It seems almost unnecessary [wrote Byam Martin to Hall] to advert to the importance of a most strict and guarded secrecy upon a matter so deeply regarding the interest of H.M. Service and the success of his arms in the event of a renewal of hostilities; for it is by this deception with respect to our naval strength that we can best hope to obtain an early superiority over the American Force.[2]

Quite how far the deception was supposed to extend, in particular whether it really included the arrangements being made by the diplomats, is not clear. Technically the Admiralty's actions did not constitute a breach of Castlereagh's version of the 'gentlemen's agreement'; and while they hardly conformed to the spirit of the instructions sent to Bagot on 23 April, no new commitment had yet been made and in the meantime, on 15 June, there had arrived in London Bagot's account of his conversation with Monroe of 2 May, in which the secretary of state had seemed to offer to exclude keels, and keels were not so very much less than frames. Confusion might also have added accidentally to the appearance of deceit. Interdepartmental communications were far from perfect and the presence of the first lord, Melville, in the cabinet may not have compensated much for the deficiency.[3] Certainly events in Canada were soon to reveal that there had been a breakdown of communication, and to suggest that the Admiralty was simply unaware of Castlereagh's April arrangements with Adams and Bagot. But even if in the summer of 1816 there was no deliberate intention, by the government as a whole or by the Admiralty alone, to mislead the Americans over the proposed agreement, a certain ambiguity lingered over the Admiralty's plans long after a final agreement, and one which did forbid new construction, had been concluded in 1817.

[1] Adm. to comptroller, 17 July 1816, Adm. 106/3575.
[2] Byam Martin to Hall, 15 July 1816, Byam Martin papers, B[ritish] M[useum] Add[itional] MS. 41,400.
[3] He was not a member of the 'inner' cabinet which at this time embraced only Liverpool, Castlereagh, and Bathurst (Webster, pp. 15 and 35).

Bagot had received the foreign secretary's instructions of 23 April on 3 July and having failed to persuade Monroe to accept an informal and vague arrangement, agreed early in August to pass on to London what eventually formed the substance of the final agreement of April 1817. Each side was to restrict its force on the lakes to four vessels – one on Lake Champlain, one on Lake Ontario, and two on the upper lakes – and each vessel was to be of not more than 100 tons and mounting not more than one eighteen-pounder cannon; all other armed vessels were to be dismantled; and the agreement might be terminated by either party after giving notice. Bagot had no authority to conclude a final arrangement and so in the meantime it was thought best to make a provisional arrangement. This gave some difficulty since, Monroe claimed, after Congress's orders of February 1815 the United States now had no force on the lakes and an agreement merely to suspend building would consolidate Great Britain's temporary advantage. They agreed therefore that Bagot would supply a list of the British force, which the naval officer in command would be ordered not to increase, and that any American force should be confined to the same standard.[1]

Bagot's report of the August agreement reached London in the middle of September and at the end of the month Castlereagh wrote giving his warm approval but saying that the matter would require 'some consideration' and that a final answer would have to wait until the cabinet, then much scattered, could reassemble. In fact it was not until four months later, on 31 January 1817, that Castlereagh did reply authorizing the conclusion of an agreement on the terms suggested and it was not until 28 and 29 April that an exchange of notes finally confirmed what, through an interim change of control at the State Department, became known as the Rush-Bagot agreement.[2]

If London appeared to be pleased with what had been done, the reaction was very different in Canada. When Sir Edward Owen was recalled, he had turned over command to Captain W. F. Owen, but the brother, too, was soon recalled, and as Hall had not yet arrived, the summer of 1816 found yet a fourth officer, Commander W. Baumgardt, temporarily in command. Whether or not these rapid changes were the cause, Bagot's letter of 14 August communicating the provisional agreement and asking for a statement of force caught both Captain

[1] Burt, pp. 391–2. The provisional agreement was formally completed on 4 and 7 November, when they actually exchanged lists. These, showing the condition and armament of all ships on the lakes, are conveniently reprinted by Burt, p. 392, n. 55. The British list, however, was supplied before Hall arrived in Canada with the orders mentioned above, pp. 16–17.   [2] Burt, p. 394.

Owen, who had not yet left Canada, and Baumgardt totally unprepared. In spite of the authority which Castlereagh's instructions of 23 April had given Bagot, and in spite of the assurance to the contrary in those instructions, neither Owen nor Baumgardt had heard a word on the subject from the Admiralty. As neither of those officers had any instructions about increasing the squadron, however, only the matter of the list was of any immediate significance and this Baumgardt felt able to supply. This did not stop Owen making a protest to the Admiralty. Equality of armaments, he insisted, would have an unequal effect upon the two parties and it would be Great Britain who would be at the disadvantage if war did break out, because she lacked the local resources for the rapid assembly of a makeshift force on the lakes. A naval force on the lakes, moreover, was her only effective means of defence, whereas it was not the Americans' only means of attack. Even in peacetime such a measure would be a false economy: it would force the British army to rely on the merchant marine for transport and, as so much of this was in the hands of Americans, all the more upon their good faith. Nor was the arrangement likely to remove jealousy. It might please the Americans, but in Canada jealousy and, worse, disloyalty, would be stimulated by fear. For all purposes, then, strength would be better than trust; the good faith of Americans he considered a very 'feeble foundation'.[1]

On 16 September, soon after Owen wrote this, Hall arrived at Kingston to take over the command. Hall ought to have been in a better position to know what the government's policy was. It had, after all, been the consultations about the lakes question which had delayed his leaving London and he it was who brought to Canada the various Admiralty instructions of July. Yet these apparently did not include complete, if any, guidance about what Bagot had been instructed to do at Washington, for when Hall learned of what had passed between Bagot and Baumgardt he wrote home expressing surprise and concern. Bagot, he gathered, had pledged Great Britain not to undertake any further construction under the impression that she was already greatly superior on the lakes; but in this the minister was totally wrong, having apparently 'altogether forgotten the events of the late war which have thrown into the hands of the Americans our Squadrons both on Erie and Champlain'. Bagot, of course, had not forgotten anything; but had, rather, taken into account what he understood to be the condition of the two

[1] Bagot to E. Owen, secret and confidential, 14 Aug., Baumgardt to Bagot, 5 Sept., and W. F. Owen to Baumgardt, 3 Sept. 1816, P[ublic] A[rchives of] C[anada], M[anuscript] G[roup] 24/A/13, Bagot papers, i. 24–8 and 77–86.

forces. Hall, however, had different ideas about the sort of arrangement that should be made and the sort of man who should conclude it: an arrangement 'to prevent all squabbling (if 'tis an object to keep peace with the blackguards) and reduce our expense . . . should be made on our part by a person acquainted with nautical matters or otherwise the Yankees will outwit him. I hope they have not Mr B[agot]; but a young man of fashion is little calculated to deal with Americans.' He did not therefore feel at all bound by any pledge Bagot had given![1]

It is not surprising that Hall went out to Canada without full instructions and apparently ignorant of the negotiations with the Americans for, in London, the comptroller, Melville's close collaborator and the man through whom Hall's more secret instructions were being routed, seems to have been no better informed. Byam Martin replied to Hall on 2 December that while respectfully pointing out any consequent inconveniences he was not to oppose Bagot's instructions since it must be *presumed* that he was obeying the government's wishes, and even this reserved and uncertain reply had first to be checked with Melville.[2] When in the middle of May 1817, therefore, Hall heard from Bagot of the arrangement finally agreed upon, it was an understandable exaggeration for him to claim still to have heard 'nothing' from the Admiralty. He did however conform to the agreement and call in for dismantling all his force save for one schooner of the agreed tonnage and armament on each lake. A few days later he at last got his orders from the Admiralty; but if he had been concerned at what Bagot had done he was astonished by what the government now proposed. He was, he complained to Bagot, ordered 'to pay off the whole of H.M.'s vessels on the lakes, and place them in a state of ordinary. . . . This reduction is much greater than I could have anticipated; for in place of leaving a small vessel of 100 tons in each lake, we are reduced to a

[1] Hall to Adm., 25 Sept. 1816, Adm. 1/3443, and Hall to Byam Martin, 27 Sept. 1816, Byam Martin papers, B.M.Add.MS.41,400.
[2] Byam Martin to Melville and to Hall, 2 Dec. 1816, Byam Martin papers, B.M.Add.MS.41,400. There is no sign in the Admiralty papers that the F.O. had asked them to instruct their officers in North America to follow Bagot's guidance about the lakes. It may well be that there was some confusion with almost simultaneous instructions about the fisheries. On 24 April 1816, the day after the instruction about the lakes, Bagot was sent a second despatch suggesting a *modus vivendi* about the fisheries and also undertaking to have the British naval officers ordered to accommodate their actions in this matter to what Bagot told them (F.O. 5/113). This the Admiralty were asked to do in a letter from the F.O. on 18 May (F.O. 5/118) and appropriate orders were sent out (Adm. to Rr. Adm. Griffith [Halifax], 22 May, Adm. 2/1583). No mention was made of the Great Lakes question in either letter.

boat's crew on the civil establishment. If the measures of the American Government are equally pacific, there is undoubtedly no chance of collision to be apprehended.'[1]

What had happened in London was no doubt a clearing up of confusion after Castlereagh's promised reassembly of the cabinet to consider Monroe's proposals. Castlereagh wrote to Bagot on 4 February 1817 to tell him that the government were at last ready to accept the agreement. Ten days before that the Admiralty had written to Bathurst suggesting that, subject to the state of Anglo-American relations being satisfactory, the whole of the force on the lakes be placed in ordinary.[2] They were ready to go so far beyond the requirements of the agreement, the Admiralty said, because of the continued pressure for economy. The naval estimates had passed in 1816, but only just, and the demands for economy had not at all subsided. And now, as the prospect of next year's estimates grew nearer, popular disturbance and agitation were again increasing and once more emphasized the need for concentration on matters nearer home. It was, moreover, all the more easy to call a halt to military expenditure in North America since it had not as yet proceeded very far.

The Colonial and War Office does not seem to have approached the defence question in 1815 as systematically as the Admiralty, but there was plenty of experience from the war, and individual officers enough to supply useful reports and suggestions, from a former engineer officer of the King's German Legion, Captain de Gaugreben, to a future secretary of state, General Sir George Murray.[3] The military authorities in Canada, moreover, closely cooperated with the naval surveys and

[1] Hall to Bagot, 18 May and 4 June 1817, P.A.C., M.G. 24/A/13, Bagot papers, i. 110 and 112.
[2] Burt, p. 394, n. 57, and Adm. to C.O., secret and immediate, 25 Jan. 1817, C.O. 42/176.
[3] H. R. Holmden, ed., 'Baron de Gaugreben's Memoir on the Defence of Upper Canada', *Canadian Historical Review*, ii (1921), 58–68. Murray administered Upper Canada for only a few months, hurrying back to Europe in a vain attempt to take part in the Waterloo campaign. In that brief period, however, he spent most of his time investigating Canadian defence. Some of his observations, on military settlers, a naval base on Lake Huron, and on the seat of government, he conveyed in a letter and accompanying memorandum to Melville, 27 March 1815. G. S. Graham, 'Views of General Murray on the Defence of Upper Canada, 1815', *Canadian Historical Review*, xxxiv (1953), 158–65. A more elaborate 'Memorandum respecting Canada, 1815', he possibly kept back until the Maine boundary crisis (see below, p. 115, n. 1). For a lively treatment of the Canadian militia question see Lt.-Col. G. Macdonell to Bathurst, April 1817, C.O. 42/177. Macdonell was lately Inspecting Officer of the militia and had 'managed the principal branch . . . of the secret service' in Canada.

proceeded with a number of measures of immediate and obvious utility, particularly works at Quebec and Kingston.

None of these measures had got very far before the government in London began to have second thoughts. One factor making delay advisable was that the boundary commissions set up by the peace treaty had not yet finished their work. No final plan of defence could be adopted while the exact line of frontier remained unsettled and in any case it was best not to draw the attention of the Americans to Britain's interest in positions whose title had not yet been conceded. But the main obstacle was the priority of naval requirements on the lakes. The principal lessons of the war seemed to emphasize naval defence, and until the Admiralty had completed its investigations no general plan could be adopted by the government. On 10 October 1815, therefore, the colonial secretary, Lord Bathurst, had ordered a complete suspension of all military defence works; and the effort in Canada was concentrated instead on having plans and estimates prepared for future works, on the Niagara frontier where the Americans had recently strengthened their own fort, and at Isle aux Noix to counter the American forts at Rouse's and Windmill Points on the northern tip of Lake Champlain.[1]

With the decisions of July 1816, however, the groundwork of defence policy had at last been laid and the Admiralty had clearly looked to a resumption of active preparation in Canada. It was with a view to this that they had sent Owen's principal reports to the Colonial Office on 6 July, pointing generally to the various works thought necessary for the improvement and protection of the water communications. They drew particular attention to the need to establish and protect a naval base in the entrance to the Grand River on Lake Erie, to have a new fort at Isle aux Noix to command the northern exit from Lake Champlain, and to provide for the protection of York (Toronto). These papers in turn had been passed for opinion to the governor in Canada, General Sir John Sherbrooke, and to the Treasury. The latter's response was perhaps inevitable: the information contained in them was 'imperfect'; the estimates were incomplete, only that for Isle aux Noix – £86,726 13s. 4d. – being properly specified; and from the many works recommended it was clear that there would be an expenditure of 'many hundred thousand pounds'. On 15 October 1816 the Treasury at length

[1] Owen to Adm., no. 36, 30 June 1815, enclosed in Adm. to C.O., 6 July 1816, C.O. 42/171; Drummond to Bathurst, no. 117, 12 April 1816, C.O. 42/166; and various papers in Ordnance to C.O., 30 April 1816, C.O. 42/169.

replied to the Colonial Office that while 'fully aware of their great importance', the imperfections of the reports, the enormous expenditure they envisaged, and not least the present urgent need for economy led them to conclude that 'none of [the measures] appear to be of such urgent and immediate necessity that they may not be dispensed with at least for the present'.[1]

By the beginning of 1817, then, Treasury parsimoniousness had combined with Colonial Office uncertainty and the policy of the Foreign Office to bring the Admiralty's preparations in North America to an abrupt halt. 'The Ministry', wrote Milne at the end of January when he was at last about to take up his command after the diversion to Algiers, 'are so much alarmed that they are reducing the expenditure of the Navy as much as possible. All the frigates are to be taken from the Newfoundland station, and some of the ships from me, and the vessels on the lakes of Canada are to be paid off and only a few men left to take charge of them.'[2]

The opportunity offered by the negotiation with the Americans seemed all the more tempting in view of the peculiar difficulties involved in the naval establishment on the lakes. It was both extraordinarily expensive and extremely difficult to make efficient. By the end of 1816 Byam Martin reckoned that in wages and allowances alone its cost was running at over £28,000 a year.[3] Even Hall contributed to the arguments in favour of economy; indeed he was complaining of his predecessors' extravagance from the very first. Captain F. W. Owen, he complained, had had 'little feeling for the pocket of Mr Bull', and had left behind him both confusion and expense – including even a band of musicians made up from French prisoners of war; while in his extensive plans and recommendations of the previous year, Sir Edward Owen, he found, had 'calculated too largely'. Like Yeo and Milne before him he was worried by the great difficulty of defending Canada, and he too wondered if it was worth it: 'These Lakes will be a millstone round our necks and indeed the colony is scarcely worth the expense.' But like the others he also had an unfriendly view of Anglo-American relations. So having demonstrated his personal disinterestedness by offering to forgo a third of his salary, he put forward his own scheme.

[1] Adm. to C.O., 6 July 1816, C.O. 42/171; Treasury minutes in bundle 15,604, T 1/1564; and Treasury to C.O., 15 Oct. 1816, T 28/47, f. 214. Sherbrooke's detailed opinions on the naval reports are in his despatch no. 68 to Bathurst, 16 Dec. 1816, C.O. 42/167.

[2] Milne to Home, 29 Jan. 1817, *MSS. of Col. Milne Home*, p. 172.

[3] Byam Martin to Melville, 23 Dec. 1816, Byam Martin papers, B.M.Add.MS., 41,394.

What worried him about the situation presented to him by the joint efforts of the Admiralty and Bagot was not so much the complete decommissioning of the squadron. If squabbles with the Americans had to be avoided, he would have preferred an agreement for both sides to lay up all ships and stores, keeping only a battalion of marines at Kingston to take care of the ships and get them ready in an emergency. It was, rather, the ban on construction he so disapproved. For this impeded the preparation for what he and everyone else believed to be the only practical method of operating in wartime on the lakes. American incompetence apart, Britain's only chance, he thought, would be to take immediate offensive action against the Americans' bases at the very commencement of war. These were, in addition to Plattsburg which was possibly too obvious for him to bother to mention, Sackett's Harbor on Lake Ontario, Erie on Lake Erie, and Fort Gratiot at the head of the River St Clair. Sackett's Harbor he seems to have regarded primarily as a problem for the army, though their present force was 'insufficient' to attack the fortifications. Lakes Huron and Erie, however, were a naval problem, and a very difficult one in view of the superiority of local American resources and the lack of communications with Lake Ontario and the sea. It was proving impossible, moreover, to find a satisfactory site for a naval base on Lake Erie, because of the shallowness of the coastal waters. Sir Edward Owen had recommended the mouth of the Grand River, but even there they would need a pier and Hall rightly did not think the expense would be tolerated. Amherstburg, the only other suitable site, was clearly much too near the Americans. On Lake Huron, however, a good site, far from the Americans, had been chosen for a naval base at Penetanguishene. What Hall proposed to do therefore was, as he put it, 'to play our next game' on that lake. Immediately upon the outbreak of war a force should go out from Penetanguishene to harass the posts and settlements the Americans were at this time constructing in a thin line through the Michigan territory, and thus distract American forces from other and, to the British, more dangerous areas. This force should not hesitate in 'encouraging and letting loose the Indians' among the Americans. They might be 'expensive and uncertain auxiliaries', but it was against such scattered and detached posts that they were most effective. If it were objected that this was 'a savage idea ... alas! every sentiment of humanity is forgotten in the advantage or glory of our Country, and really the Americans of the Lakes are worse than savages'. The ships, moreover, should be of light draught so that, having taken Fort Gratiot, they might force the passage of the St Clair into

Lake Erie. Thus, in peacetime, there need be no base and no force upon that lake except a schooner for military transportation; on Lake Huron, however, proper preparation at Penetanguishene, including the disguised 'corvettes' formerly ordered for Lake Erie, would become all the more important.[1]

If Hall really feared that the arrangements with the Americans threatened even these secret preparations he was wrong; the threat came from a quite different direction. Byam Martin mentioned the secret orders about the 'corvettes' in the first letter he wrote to Hall after the decision to confirm the arrangement made between Bagot and Monroe and after the Admiralty's orders to lay up the entire squadron. He pointed out that they were at odds with the agreement, but he did not cancel them. He simply said that the Admiralty had reached no decision on what they should now do. He went on to become perhaps even more ambiguous:

You have a great deal to do [he told Hall], and much responsibility as to the constant readiness of the ships in every respect [he was here referring to the force generally and not merely the 'corvettes']; – the great thing is arrangement both as to materials for equipment and the knowing how to procure men, but I trust it will be many years before there is any occasion to make any such hustle, and at any rate let us be careful that no offence is given on our part.[2]

No final decision about the ships had been made even by the spring of 1819 when Hall died and the commissioner at Kingston, Captain Robert Barrie, took over the command. It was certainly not that the possibility of hostilities with the United States had been utterly rejected. These the Admiralty thought were 'highly improbable', with the 'amicable relations at present subsisting' between the two countries. Nevertheless they did 'consider it their duty to provide for such a contingency on the Lakes', and, in view of the difficulty of communications with Canada, to give the governor-general authority to issue war orders to Barrie in an emergency.[3] No mention was made of the 'corvettes' in these secret orders; indeed the day before Byam Martin was ordered

[1] Hall to Byam Martin, 27 Sept., 7 and 10 Oct. 1816, and 10 June 1817, *ibid.*, Add.MS.41,400.
[2] Byam Martin to Hall, 28 Mar. 1817, *ibid.*, Add.MS.41,394.
[3] The Admiralty wrote first on the subject to Barrie on 25 May 1819 ('secret', Adm. 2/1692); but said they would postpone sending the precautionary orders to Canada until Bagot, who was now giving up the legation in Washington, had returned to London and given his advice. The orders were not drawn up and put into the governor's safe keeping until 17 April 1820 (*ibid.*). On 6 April 1822 they were amended to authorize the call-up of all R.N. officers in Canada (*ibid.*).

to tell Barrie to be 'extremely careful not to infringe in any way' the agreement of 1817.[1] That did not mean they had been overlooked or countermanded. It was rather that the especially secret device of communicating upon them only through the comptroller himself was still being employed. On 10 April the following year Byam Martin wrote to Barrie to ask if he had found the old secret orders of 1816 among Hall's papers and to say that he would be advising the Admiralty to have the frames of the 'corvettes' laid by to season.[2]

In spite of all this and whatever the intentions of the Admiralty or government may have been, it is not in fact clear that the 1817 agreement was actually broken by the British. Byam Martin's letter of 10 April 1820 possibly seems to imply that the frames existed by that date, and if this was so their construction must have been in breach of the agreement, for Hall's letters to the comptroller make it reasonably clear that he had not begun work on the vessels by the spring of 1817. It is very doubtful, however, if any work at all was done on the vessels. The orders had in the first place been conditional on the selection of a naval base on Lake Erie where they were to be constructed, and no such site was ever chosen. Hall intended that the work should be transferred to Penetanguishene, but because of the approaching winter he did not propose to begin on that base either until the spring of 1817.[3] Before long, however, he had decided that, even though not actually commissioned, these vessels must be both built and launched, since frames could so easily be destroyed by the enemy if war broke out.[4] But Byam Martin thought that Hall's arguments about using Penetanguishene as the wartime base for both Lakes Huron and Erie, though otherwise 'incontrovertible', held two major flaws: was it certain that the ships would be able to force the passage of the St Clair in the face of American opposition and, once there, what base would they have on Lake Erie?[5] Furthermore, by the time the comptroller was talking to Barrie in 1820 about having the frames laid by to season, serious doubts were again attacking the whole approach to the lakes question.

Barrie had brought to the Admiralty's attention the rapid decay that was already affecting the laid up ships of the old squadron in a series of letters in the autumn of 1819 and Byam Martin was now beginning

[1] Draft instruction to Byam Martin, 24 May 1819, Adm. 3/262.
[2] Byam Martin to Barrie, 10 April 1820, Byam Martin papers, B.M.Add.MS. 41,395.
[3] Hall to Byam Martin, 27 Sept. 1816, *ibid.*, Add.MS.41,400.
[4] Hall to Byam Martin, 7 and 10 Oct. 1816, *ibid.*, Add.MS.41,400.
[5] Byam Martin to Hall, 28 Mar. 1817, *ibid.*, Add.MS.41,394.

to worry that their 'dilapidated state ... made them entirely unprepared for any hostile movement on the part of the Americans'. This
made the huge cost of the establishment – nearly £47,000 in 1820 – seem
all the more alarming. In salaries and allowances alone the landlubbered
officers, seamen, and marines had cost about £28,000 in that year;
while other expenditure, on materials for repair in particular, absorbed
an additional £20,000. In April 1820 Byam Martin had promised
Barrie that the Admiralty would consider the whole problem 'very
shortly'. Two years later a decision had still not been reached, and in
March 1822 the comptroller proposed a totally new establishment
in order to effect 'a very considerable saving and to provide for the
prompt equipment of a flotilla in the event of a sudden war with the
United States'. This seems to have been accepted in substance. The
bases at Isle aux Noix and at Penetanguishene were to be maintained
on a reduced scale with a captain and a lieutenant respectively; Lake
Erie was to continue to have no establishment at all, and as it was
expensive to move stores up to Kingston, and this place was also exposed to a *coup de main*, the stores depôt was to be moved to Montreal.
At Kingston there should be 'an active, intelligent officer as Resident
Commissioner' and three sets of warrant officers ready to commission
three vessels. There should also be one or two other officers whose
duty it would be to supply information and be generally useful in the
event of war. Most important of all was the maintenance of a serviceable
fleet by a regulated programme of repairs. To repair first some of the
gunboats and then other vessels up to the limits of the 1817 agreement,
there were to be a master shipwright and his assistants with a budget of
£2–3,000 a year. In addition, the frames for two or three ten-gun
brigs should be kept in home yards in constant readiness for the lakes.
The total annual expenditure was to be some £12,000.[1]

Barrie at once protested that this provision was inadequate but
Byam Martin had already warned him that 'the very small sum granted
by Parliament for naval purposes rendered this measure unavoidable
however inconvenient it may prove in the event of a war, of which I
think there is no chance for some years to come'. He admitted that
Barrie's objections were 'manifestly founded upon good sense and
sound policy', and promised to press them, but he repeated that
proposals to increase expenditure 'touch us in a very sensible part'.
Two years later Barrie was writing home that the money voted had
been enough only for very slow progress and that his shipwrights

[1] Byam Martin to Barrie, 10 April 1820, to Melville, 6 Mar. 1822, and to
Barrie, 7 Mar. and 5 April 1822, Byam Martin papers, B.M. Add.MS.41,395.

could reckon on managing to repair only one frigate in three years. In fact he had only one small vessel fit for service. He warned, moreover, that so bad was Canadian timber that even if repaired and housed over these vessels would not last many more years.[1] Again there was a long delay until, eighteen months later, the British found themselves with something of a war scare on their hands.

In an attempt to break into the exclusive British mercantile system, the Americans had begun in 1817 a campaign of retaliatory economic legislation and, in spite of substantial British concessions, had so maintained it that it looked eventually as if another 1812 were looming up. Already, towards the end of 1818, Admiral Milne was writing: 'My successor, I think, may have a troublesome time of it, for we cannot remain long in our present political situation with America. I give till next June, either to have a commercial treaty or a war.'[2] Milne's forecast was a little precipitate for the crisis did not really come to a head until July 1826, when orders in council closed the West Indian ports absolutely to American ships. From the summer of 1826, however, with Canning refusing to discuss the matter with the Americans and with President Adams refusing to yield, tension remained at a fairly high level until after Canning's death in August 1827 and Adams's defeat in the presidential election of 1828. As late as May 1827 General Sir James Kempt, the lieutenant-governor of Nova Scotia, was writing that 'it does not appear that our Government are disposed to *bend* to Jonathan in any thing. Mr Canning will not depart from the Position which he has taken up, and the American people are mortified and grieved at the indiscretion and folly of their own Rulers in *not* accepting in time of the liberal terms which were offered to them. . . .'[3] In July 1827 C. R. Vaughan, the friendly British minister in Washington, still found it necessary to remind his government that while threats might be in order, actual war would be both futile and disastrous in view of the impossibility of conquest and the importance of Anglo-American trade.[4] The surviving evidence of British moves and calculations is

[1] Martin to Barrie, 5 April and 10 Aug. 1822, Byam Martin papers, B.M. Add.MS.41,395. Barrie's report of 1 Nov. 1824, referred to in Byam Martin to Melville, *ibid.*, Add.MS. 41,396.
[2] Milne to Home, 14 Nov. 1818, *MSS. of Col. Milne Home*, p. 176.
[3] Kempt to Sir Thomas Cochrane, 6 May 1827, Cochrane MSS., National Library of Scotland, 2269.
[4] 'Effects or result of war between the United States and Great Britain, July 1827', C. R. Vaughan papers, All Souls College Library, Oxford. His personal views of Anglo-American relations are characteristically expressed in a private letter he wrote to Lord Holland, 11 Sept. 1827: 'I look forward to the influence of your opinion being felt in our relations with this country, as I cannot see that

nevertheless very thin and scrappy. A senior officer went out to examine American naval yards and ships in the autumn of 1826 and there followed an especially systematic collection of information from various sources on the United States Navy.[1]

In all this Byam Martin seems to have played a very large part. He wrote an important letter to Admiral Sir George Cockburn 'regarding . . . preparations against any American call'; but this has not come to light perhaps, as Cockburn said, because it was 'meant to be kept as quiet and secret as the nature of the thing will admit of'.[2] What has survived is a comparison of the American and British navies which was read at a meeting of the cabinet and which Byam Martin had sent to Melville on 25 July 1826. What they found worrying in this comparison was not so much American superiority in numbers of large frigates as the greater fire power of some of the battleships. To match the American ships' armament they immediately ordered the construction or rebuilding of ten first-rates. At the same time the comptroller reminded Melville of the letter he had written about the Canadian lakes on 24 May.[3]

In this letter Byam Martin had at last taken up the complaints Barrie had made in November 1824 in order to emphasize the unsatisfactory state of affairs on the lakes. He referred in particular to Great Britain's inferior facilities for the establishment of a squadron on the outbreak of war. It was reckoned that there might be as many as five hundred shipwrights available locally, but their work was rough, expensive, and unsatisfactory, and certainly did not compare with the Americans' resources for rapid construction and conversion in an emergency. The opening of the Erie canal in October 1825, moreover, gave the Americans a relatively safe and easy means of supplying a

---

either Party could derive the least possible advantage from the most successful war. I am anxious to see removed out of our way, the many disputed points of boundary and Commerce which repeated negotiations, since the separation of the two countries have left unsettled. Yet it is not easy to get rid of the mutual distrust, which is evident in all our transactions, which shows itself in a nice adjustment of equivalents; and the American tenacity has introduced into our diplomacy the spirit of the Counting House' (Holland House papers, B.M.Add. MS.51,616).

[1] 'A Tour of 2,000 miles of the U.S.A. commencing Oct. 16 1826 and ending Nov. 23 1826 by Capt. F. Fead, R.N.', Adm. 1/4364. This was entered in a special volume (Adm. 7/712) and there followed a series of entries relating to American naval matters. The entry book continued in use for this purpose right down to 1852.

[2] Cockburn to Croker, 28 Aug. 1826, Croker papers, William Clements Library, Ann Arbor, Michigan.

[3] Byam Martin to Melville, 25 July 1826, Byam Martin papers, B.M.Add.MS. 41,396. What appear to be notes of the reading of this paper in cabinet have also survived in the Huskisson papers, B.M.Add.MS.38,766. See also Bartlett, p. 33.

force on the lakes and even of shipping frames from New York. The new British communication between Lakes Erie and Ontario, the Welland canal, would also be useful for moving stores when it was completed. But these still had to be got up into Canada in the first place:

the experience of the last war has shown the enormous expense and difficulties, with which we have to contend in sending out supplies of seamen, artificers, etc. etc., for the first operations of war on the Lakes, and the precariousness of the succour which the mother country can afford owing to the St Lawrence not being navigable for several months of the year, and the interruptions from the cruisers of the Americans.

Local resources and local conditions alike, then, made the 1817 agreement favour the Americans:

That which would be a wise, provident, and politic course on the part of the Americans during Peace, as relates to the Lakes Force, wd. be the reverse as regards this country. A war upon the Lakes is completely a war in their own country, backed by the ready and never failing help of the various naval ports and seamen of the United States – while our Lake operations must under the best circumstances, rest upon a first supply of seamen and artificers from this country, and a constant succession of them to supply the casualties arising from various causes. So circumstanced, the Americans wisely abstain from all the expense of preparation during Peace, seeing that it is wholly unnecessary; – but it is only by making use of the leisure of peace that we can hope to diminish the natural disadvantages under which we are placed.[1]

Quite what should be done to adjust the balance Byam Martin did not say. He mentioned only that to prepare part of the existing force for service in two or three years would cost an additional £25,000 a year, bringing the total to about £40,000. Barrie, who had been waiting in London for a decision at least since May, apparently had a scheme for keeping frigates at Quebec and a limited establishment at Kingston to act in an emergency. The latter alone it was estimated would cost nearly £60,000 a year and perhaps for this reason nothing was done beyond the commissioning of a single schooner, the *Cockburn*, in 1827.[2] There the matter seems to have rested until April 1830 when Byam Martin again pressed Barrie's proposals, and in particular that these should include steam vessels. In his paper of 24 May 1826 he had already noted that the American navy had some and that these would be of 'great advantage' on the lakes. Now he repeated his argument and

[1] Byam Martin to Melville, 24 May 1826, Byam Martin papers, B.M.Add.MS. 41,396.
[2] Adm. to Barrie, secret, 14 June, 11 and 23 Aug. 1826, Adm. 2/1694; Byam Martin to Croker, 2 Sept. 1826, Byam Martin papers, B.M.Add.MS. 41,396; and Stacey, 'Myth of the Unguarded Frontier', p. 13.

Barrie added: 'I think it more than probable that in any future war with the United States of America, steam vessels equipped for the purpose of war will be in general use on the Lakes, and that we should be prepared (on the spot) with the *necessaria* for the equipment of steam vessels.'[1] However, with the change of government in November 1830 and the departure of first Melville and then Byam Martin in the following year, the Admiralty swung even more definitely in the direction of economy. By February 1831 the 'enormous' expenditure of £18–20,000 a year and the huge amount of stores to the value of £180,000 they were inclined to think were 'applied to no useful purpose in peace, while . . . wholly inadequate to the preparation of an efficient naval force for war'. That this was so Byam Martin's own remarks in 1826 they believed had already made clear:

If then the statement be correct, and their Lordships entertain not the slightest doubt of its accuracy, that the ships now at Kingston are unfit for service, their repair expensive, their speedy decay certain, their future use most doubtful, it is high time to come to a decision whether we should continue to keep up the semblance of a fleet while the only reality is the cost; or whether it would not be the wiser plan to follow the example of the Americans and seize the favourable opportunity, which the moment of profound peace affords, of putting an end to a large and useless expense by withdrawing or at least reducing to the lowest possible scale, our naval establishments in Canada, and thus showing to the Americans the sincerity of the pacific policy of our Government. . . . This country can scarcely hope to look forward to any permanent and beneficial result from engaging in *naval* warfare on the Lakes of Canada; . . . the expediency therefore of keeping up a dockyard at Kingston can only be considered in reference to the degree of naval co-operation which may be necessary for assisting in the defence of the Canadian frontier, and not with any view of again undertaking offensive operations on a scale of that magnitude which was adopted in the last war, against a country possessing the resources and the superior local advantages now enjoyed by the United States.

They proposed, therefore, to abandon all idea of keeping in repair a large fleet but, so as not to appear openly to throw doubt upon 'the firm determination of the Mother Country to defend those great and important Colonies to the utmost', to maintain a limited establishment such as would in an emergency 'afford the means, aided by the resources of the Country, of speedily equipping and arming a flotilla of

[1] Byam Martin to Melville, 1 April 1830, enclosing his memorandum, 'Canada. A Statement of the several subjects connected with the establishment which require the decision of the Lords Commissioners of the Admiralty', together with some additional comments by Barrie, Byam Martin papers, B.M.Add.MS. 41,398.

gunboats, steam vessels and other craft, fit to navigate the Lakes, and, if need be, of putting together the frames of vessels that may be built at Quebec and Montreal, and sent up to Kingston by the Rideau canal'. What they wanted was merely sufficient officers under Barrie to maintain stores, buildings, and wharves, and a number of frames, but not machinery, for steam gunboats.[1] In 1831 the vote for repairs was discontinued and during 1832 most of the vessels disposed of. Nor did the economy drive stop there. By the end of 1833 the Admiralty was pointing to a growing emphasis on military rather than naval means for the interior defence of Canada and to the improvements in fortifications and communications as justification for 'breaking up altogether' the naval establishment on the lakes. With the consent of the Colonial Office the establishment was almost completely closed down in 1834. Two clerks remained, at Kingston and Montreal, to look after the stores until 1836 or 1837, and at last in 1837–38, with a vote of £200 for 'contingent expenses on breaking up the establishment', the 'enormous expense' was reduced finally to nothing.[2]

It was the overwhelming need for economy that had compelled the moves towards the 'disarmament' agreement of 1817 and this Admiralty and Foreign Office alike had shared. What the Admiralty clearly did not share was that degree of calculated good sense – rather than sentimental good will – that marked Castlereagh's approach to Anglo-American relations. In their case, rather, a sense of peculiar difficulty and disadvantage on the lakes had inclined them to deception. For a time confusion had disguised the exact proportions of the gulf between diplomacy and deceit, but ultimately the unrelenting drive for economy, together with the results of delay and decay, forced a degree of disarmament not only far beyond that envisaged by the agreement but also beyond that actually applied by the Americans.[3]

[1] Adm. to Navy Board, 23 Feb. and 23 Mar. 1831, Adm. 2/1694.
[2] Stacey, 'Myth of the Unguarded Frontier', pp. 13–14.
[3] The Americans had also found expense and decay too much for the maintenance of the force permitted. In 1821 the annual cost of the three naval bases – at Erie, at Sackett's Harbor on Lake Ontario, and at Whitehall on Lake Champlain – was over $33,000, and that for Sackett's was, at $15,000, one of the most expensive of any American yard, being second only to Boston. Yet by 1820 they had only two vessels in commission and by the next year decay had so advanced in those laid up that twenty were reckoned unworthy of repair. In 1825–26, therefore, the yards were closed down save for a caretaker establishment, and all the ships sold except the *Chippewa* and *New Orleans*, two three-decker battleships on the stocks at Sackett's Harbor. The *Chippewa* was sold in 1834 but the *New Orleans* was ordered to be preserved for frontier defence and remained on the U.S. Navy list until 1882. (Stacey, 'Myth of the Unguarded Frontier', p. 14.)

2

Wellington and the Fortification of North America

The increasing emphasis on the land defences of the Canadian frontier to which the Admiralty referred in 1834 in order to help justify the complete breaking up of the naval establishment reflected a significant departure from the opinion of 1815. At that time the emphasis had been rather the reverse and all military works had been suspended until the completion of a plan of defence based squarely upon naval command of the lakes. This suspension was supposed to be temporary, but the postwar economy drive of 1816–17 had threatened to make it permanent: 'economy, approaching even to parsimony, was the panoply of peace', declared one critic of the army estimates.[1] In March 1816 it had been intended to maintain in British North America, including Bermuda, a garrison of 9,500 British regulars, a considerably larger number than before the war; by the end of the same year the number had fallen to 8,000, half of them in the Canadas, and the emphasis placed once more upon the improvement of the militia and the adoption of a policy of military settlement along the frontier and lines of communication.[2]

Paradoxically, the decline in naval preparation had the effect of countering the economy drive and renewing attention to the land defences. Thus Wellington, who before the end of the war in 1814 had been so insistent upon the necessity of superiority on the lakes, was forced a few years later – and by the naval investigations themselves – to abandon a directly naval approach to the problem: 'the pains which Sir Edward Owen has taken to survey these lakes and rivers, and to point out the places at which loaded boats and vessels might take shelter and might receive protection from works and troops, show the difficulty, nay, the impossibility of executing such a system.'[3]

[1] *Hansard's Parliamentary Debates*, xxxiii. 333 (Wellesley, 15 Mar. 1816).
[2] *Annual Register, 1816*, p. 97; C.O. to duke of York, 27 Dec. 1816, C.O. 323/185; C. P. Stacey, 'The Myth of the Unguarded Frontier, 1815–1871', *American Historical Review*, lvi (1950–51), 9.
[3] 'Memorandum on the Defence of Canada', addressed to Bathurst, 1 Mar. 1819, *Despatches, Correspondence, and Memoranda of Field Marshal, Arthur, Duke of Wellington* (5 vols., London, 1867–1870), i. 39; cf. Wellington to Liverpool, 7 and 9 Nov. 1814, *Supplementary Despatches etc.* (12 vols., London, 1858–65), ix. 422 and 425–6.

Opinion was already moving in this direction when the question of the land defences in Canada was suddenly resumed in the summer of 1818 by reports from the new governor-in-chief, the duke of Richmond, of the 'very bad state' of the fortifications at Quebec. The citadel, he reported, was already incapable of withstanding a siege what with the weakness of its garrison and the constant encroachment of private buildings upon the glacis. Now there rose the further threat of a plan to lay out a large part of the Heights of Abraham as a suburb. What was needed was a new citadel such as his military advisers recommended on Cape Diamond: 'It strikes me that without some strong place of this sort it will be almost impossible to defend ourselves against a dashing enemy. The Garrison is so weak at this moment that we should have to trust almost entirely to the Militia, and however zealous they may be, they could not at the beginning of a war be all equal to the Regulars.'[1] Then, after his inspection of the frontier, there followed in November the first comprehensive, though outline, report on the general question of Canadian defence since the abortive investigations of 1815. This pointed to the importance of preserving Quebec and Kingston as the keys of the two provinces and Montreal as the depôt for the militia and the commanding point of communication between the Canadas.

The measures Richmond proposed in order to secure these positions were modest indeed by contrast with what had passed and what was yet to come. To prevent an enemy capturing Montreal and thus making an attack upon Quebec in its present state 'an easy undertaking', he recommended his advisers' plan to concentrate the defences on the island of St Helen. This done the enemy would then have to make his principal attack from Lake Champlain down the River Richelieu – a course which the extensive preparations at Rouse's Point proved the Americans had first in view.[2] The posts on that river at St John, Chambly, and Sorel might all serve to delay the enemy's advance and gain the time so peculiarly valuable in the Canadian winter, but only a strong work at the head of the river at Isle aux Noix – at an expenditure of about £10,000, 'a trifling sum' – could make that advance impossible. For the defence of Kingston field works would do, provided the num-

---

[1] Richmond to C.O., no. 6, 11 Aug. 1818, C.O. 42/179; see also Richmond to Bathurst, private, 11 and 21 Aug. 1818, Historical Manuscripts Commission, *Report on the Manuscripts of Earl Bathurst* (London, 1923), pp. 450–1 and 454.
[2] This line of attack was settled upon in the final American plan of campaign for 1815, but the end of the war prevented its prosecution: see C. P. Stacey, 'An American plan for a Canadian campaign: Secretary James Monroe to Major-General Jacob Brown, Feb. 1815', *American Historical Review*, xlvi (1940–41), 348–58.

bers of troops on either side were not too unequal, but nothing could be done about establishing them until an emergency allowed martial law to displace the settlements already planted among their proposed positions. So far as the lakes were concerned, any attempt to contest the superiority of the Americans he considered 'manifestly hopeless', unless they had some 'fortunate success' in an attack upon Sackett's Harbor, the only offensive operation he recommended other than one against Fort Niagara. Otherwise they would have to wait for help to arrive from England. But, he warned, if the Americans did their business properly, the line of communication between Upper and Lower Canada would be cut within three days of hostilities. The only answer to this was the establishment of a supply route to the rear of the frontier, from Montreal along the Ottawa and Rideau Rivers to Kingston. A survey of the route had just been completed and the cost reckoned at £20,000. This vital improvement apart the whole emphasis of Richmond's remarks was upon the necessity of delaying tactics against the enemy, so as to give time for reinforcements and supplies to arrive from England. For this, defence works and improved lines of communication were not the only necessity: 'without the hearty co-operation' of the militia on the flanks and rear of the advancing enemy, 'the ultimate defence of Canada must be hopeless'.[1]

By the time this report arrived in England, Wellington had returned from France and in January 1819 had entered the cabinet as master-general of the Ordnance. He was therefore readily available for consultation and at Bathurst's request he submitted his views in a memorandum of 1 March 1819. Wellington throughout strongly endorsed Richmond's opinions, differing only in points of detail and adding some important remarks about the defending army, offensive operations, and communications. The invading enemy force he estimated at a maximum of 5,000 regulars and 3,000 militia and Indians; even if the Americans could assemble more, which he doubted, their army would then be too unwieldy and would be forced to retire. To meet such a force he reckoned would require a defending army of 5,000 regulars and there would have to be two such field armies, one in each of the principal areas of attack. One would be placed near the Rideau whence it could march to cover the Richelieu line of attack upon Quebec and Montreal or to aid Kingston and the area of Lake Simcoe. The other would be stationed between Hollands and Grand Rivers to cover York (Toronto), Kingston, and the Niagara frontier. In addition,

---

[1] Richmond to Bathurst, no. 13, 19 Nov. 1818, C.O. 42/179.

garrisons of 1,000 at Quebec, and 500 each at Montreal, Kingston, Penetanguishene, and along the Rivers Rideau and Niagara would bring the total force of British regulars to 13,500. Offensive operations on any large scale he wrote off as abruptly now as he had done in 1814:

In considering this system I have laid aside, as impracticable, the notion of attacking the United States on this frontier. I have never yet seen any plan of attack upon that power which was at all likely to answer the purpose; but I am certain that an attack could not succeed made from this frontier, in which we are frozen up for five months of the year, and on which the enemy have, and must continue to have, the naval superiority.

What rather captured Wellington's attention was the improvement of communications for the effective supply of the army: namely, the Ottawa and the Rideau scheme, the completion of a canal at Lachine to pass the St Lawrence rapids above Montreal and give access to the Ottawa River, and a canal or railway to Lake Simcoe by the Black and Rideau Rivers. Properly executed, these schemes would not only provide more secure routes for the movement and supply of the army but might also permit the establishment of naval superiority on Lake Huron.[1]

As a result of the pressure from the two dukes, work on the land fortifications and military communications in North America was resumed at once in 1819. In that year work was begun on a new fort, Fort Lennox, at Isle aux Noix, and by 1825, not Richmond's 'trifling sum' of £10,000, but £57,688 had been spent on it. In the same year began the construction of some 'bombproof' storehouses to make a defended supply depôt on St Helen's Island which had been acquired in 1817. There was also some attention to the fortifications and barracks at Kingston. But the largest undertaking of this kind was a new citadel at Quebec, built between 1820 and 1831 at a cost of some £236,500 to the British taxpayer. No less important were the improvements carried out on the lines of communication. The imperial government made a contribution of £12,000 to the construction of the Lachine canal which was finished in 1826 and the army itself undertook the canalization of the Ottawa in 1819.[2]

These constituted a major – and expensive – step forward in the fortification of the Canadian frontier but they were far from complete, not least in the still relatively open state of Montreal and the slow progress of the canal improvements. In the 1820s, however, the defence

[1] 'Memorandum on the Defence of Canada', addressed to Bathurst, 1 Mar. 1819, *Despatches, Correspondence, and Memoranda of . . . Wellington*, i. 36–44.
[2] Stacey, 'Myth of the Unguarded Frontier', pp. 3–5.

of North America received another large impulse. This second phase had its origins primarily in the climax brought to the Latin American question after Castlereagh's death and the French invasion of Spain in 1822–23. The principal fear was of France and French designs upon the West Indies, especially Cuba, and in his search for help Canning even turned in the summer and autumn of 1823 to the United States. But he succeeded only in emphasizing the almost ideological gulf still dividing the two English-speaking nations and in reawakening their mutual suspicions about each other's designs on the former Spanish Empire. To the Americans Canning's approaches to their minister in London appeared suspiciously equivocal; to the British President Monroe's reaction in his famous Message of 2 December seemed disappointingly isolationist and even offensive. Canning also emphasized and probably deliberately exaggerated their differences in order to overcome the opposition of the king and some of the cabinet to his policy in Europe and America. Canning's bombastic personality therefore noisily revived the sort of verbal warfare which Castlereagh had been so careful to restrain. Then, in 1826, there was added an apparently more substantial crisis of Anglo-American economic warfare. Out of what was primarily a European crisis in 1823 then, apprehensions of American ambitions quickly replaced those about France and military attention extended rapidly from the West Indies to North America generally.

Suspicion of American ambitions towards Cuba had led to the strengthening of the British naval force in the West Indies at the end of 1822, and the landing of marines to suppress the privateers who were such a nuisance to British trade and so convenient an excuse for American intervention. In 1823–25 mysterious French naval moves in the vicinity led to the squadron being increased again, and at a time of great strain upon the navy generally, to no less than twenty vessels exclusive of small craft, principally by the addition of two battleships.[1] It was also with France in mind that attention was turned at the same time to the land defences of the various naval and military positions in the West Indies. After the end of the French and American wars in 1815, these had been divided into two military commands, one in

---

[1] J. F. Rippy, *The Rivalry of the United States and Great Britain over Latin America 1808–1830* (Baltimore, 1929), pp. 79–87. There is also some interesting but incomplete cabinet and other correspondence on these matters in the collections of the William Clements Library, Ann Arbor, Michigan: Sir George Cockburn to Croker, 1 Dec. 1822 (Croker MSS); Liverpool to Melville, 21 Oct. 1823 (Melville MSS); Melville to Canning, 19 and 28 Oct. 1823, and Canning to Melville, 22 Oct. 1823 (Canning MSS).

Jamaica and the other covering the Windward and Leeward islands Trinidad, and Berbice (British Guiana), with its headquarters at Barbados. In March 1816 it had been intended to have 4,000 men in the Jamaica command and 9,000 in the other; but by the end of the year the latter figure had dropped to 6,800.[1] In 1824 there were about 3,000 British regulars in Jamaica and over 4,000, together with nearly 1,000 men of the West Indian regiment, scattered about the other possessions. This was a situation which ensured neither efficiency nor economy, being related only to the incidental military works and naval facilities inherited from the eighteenth century. But a commission of engineers under Colonel Sir James Carmichael Smyth, specially sent out to the West Indies by Wellington in the autumn of 1823, found no reason to depart from this system and merely recommended the reduction of the Barbados division to a peace strength of 300 artillery and 3,700 infantry (the war strength was to be 565 and 7,900 respectively). A headquarters garrison and reserve of 1,200 infantry at Barbados apart, their recommendations still envisaged a dispersal in units of between 50 and 600 men among some eleven posts. The 3,000 infantry in Jamaica they proposed to leave, mainly for reasons of internal security. In neither case did the commission make any explicit reference to the United States, but this was largely because they had not had time to visit the islands which would be more immediately concerned in any war with that power – Bermuda and the Bahamas.[2]

The increasing strain in Anglo-American relations, however, led to Smyth's commission being sent out again in the summer of 1825, this time to review the defences of North America itself. Their report, dated 9 September 1825, surveyed some nine hundred miles of frontier from Maine to the Lake Huron end of the River St Clair, but naturally concentrated on the anticipated American invasion routes: down the Richelieu from Lake Champlain; upon Kingston from Lake Ontario; and from Lake Erie upon the rear of a force defending the Niagara frontier. The measures they advocated to meet these dangers were by no means novel. In general they followed the lines of Wellington's own 1819 recommendations and were intended to complete the work already begun at Quebec and Isle aux Noix. Thus extensive works were recommended for Halifax, Montreal, Kingston, and along the Niagara frontier, as well as the development of a secure winter road across New

[1] *Annual Register, 1816*, p. 54; C.O. to duke of York, 27 Dec. 1816, C.O. 323/185.
[2] Reports of the commission of engineers on the defences of the West Indies, 20 Jan. 1824, and of Jamaica, 9 Feb. 1824, W.O. 55/1828.

Brunswick and the completion of the second and more expensive leg of the Ottawa River and Rideau connection between Montreal and Kingston. The total cost of these works was estimated at £1,646,218 – a considerable underestimate as it turned out.

Where the commissioners went far beyond Wellington's old plan was in their support of major offensive operations. So far as the interior of the continent was concerned, they were reasonably circumspect. Like Wellington, they suggested various minor operations to destroy the Erie canal and harass and delay the enemy's advance but these they considered 'but a petty mode of warfare, and not suited to the character and dignity of His Majesty's arms'. Evidently they thought a more dashing and worthy adventure could be found in pushing an army down from the head of Lake Champlain to Waterford in western Pennsylvania, thus preventing any invasion of Canada along the line of the St Lawrence. But they were also well aware that 'such a movement would probably . . . be reckoned too enterprising and hazardous', and since geography prevented any other such operation from Canada, they looked elsewhere for some means of striking a 'blow . . . which would be sensibly felt by the Government of the United States'. The Federal government, they pointed out, depended for its revenue upon the customs and 'if, therefore, their external commerce can be effectually and completely suspended, the Government from want of means to pay the expenses of a war, . . . must be compelled to make Peace upon the Terms imposed by that Power which can control the navigation'. So they suggested a measure which 'if conducted with secrecy and promptitude could not fail of success, and would be a more effectual blow than any operation which could be undertaken from Canada'. This was the occupation of Long Island and Staten Island by a force of 5,000 men who 'could never be dislodged' and who would then provide a perfect base for the blockade of New York and 'a very considerable extent of the American coast'. In this way they would be able 'not only to deprive the American Government of all revenue arising from the commerce of so important a place; but to prevent any Ships of War sailing from thence for the annoyance of the Trade of His Majesty's Subjects'.[1]

The various recommendations for the improvement of communications and the building of fortifications Wellington pressed on the

---

[1] 'Report to his Grace the Duke of Wellington . . . relative to H.M.'s North American Provinces', 9 Sept. 1825, W.O. 55/1551/7. The Report is summarized, with extensive quotations, in J. J. Talman, 'A Secret Military Document, 1825', *American Historical Review*, xxxviii (1932–33), 295–300.

government with determination if not enthusiasm, endeavouring in particular to counter both their pessimism and their parsimony by stirring their conscience:

As on the one hand, I do not entertain the smallest doubt that if the communications and works proposed by the Committee are carried into execution, His Majesty's dominions in North America ought to be, and would be, effectually defended and secured against any attempt to be made upon them hereafter by the United States, however formidable their power, and this without any material demand upon the military resources of the country; so on the other, I am convinced that if these, or some measures of this description, are not adopted, and if measures are not taken at an early period, to manifest the determination of the King's Government to hold this dominion at all events, we cannot expect the inhabitants, upon whose loyal and gallant exertions we must in the end depend for their defence, will do otherwise than look for the security of their lives and properties to a seasonable submission to the United States.

Even by the greatest exertion of the military resources of His Majesty's Government in time of war, these dominions could not be successfully and effectually defended, without the adoption of the greatest part of the measures proposed; but if they are all adopted, and attention is paid to the militia laws in these countries, and care taken to keep alive a military spirit among the population, the defence of these dominions ought not to be a more severe burden upon the military resources of the empire in war, than such defence as was made proved to be during the late war.[1]

The duke's firmness proved a poor match for the pressure being brought to bear on the government by the vociferous exponents of retrenchment and the application of Smyth's recommendations was hesitant and piecemeal. How to deal with the problem gave the government great concern between 1826 and 1828 in particular. At first they proposed to ask parliament for a grant of £100,000 in the session of 1826–27, half for the Ottawa and Rideau canals and half for the works at Kingston and Halifax. Wellington's desire for secrecy and the Treasury's pessimism, however, forced the government to limit expenditure for the present to some £25,000 for the canals, since these came under the Colonial Office and could be authorized in advance by the secretary of state without previous reference to parliament. In the meantime the whole defence plan was to be submitted secretly to a select committee of the House of Commons who it was hoped would first give general approval and then from time to time recommend to parliament grants to carry the scheme into execution.

Meanwhile both estimates and actual expenditure grew astronomically. By the time it came to approach parliament in the spring of 1828,

[1] Wellington to Bathurst, 6 Dec. 1825, *Despatches, Correspondence, and Memoranda of . . . Wellington*, ii. 573.

£56,000 had already been taken up for the work on the canals, another £56,000 was going to have to be sought for the coming year, and the estimate of the total expense required had risen from Smyth's £169,000 to a minimum of £474,000. At length in 1835, three years after the completion of the work, it was reported that a total of no less than £1,069,026 had been paid by the imperial government for the canal improvements in Canada. This figure included the work done on the Ottawa leg before 1826 and, perhaps, the contributions to the Lachine and Welland canals.

In the meantime work on fortifications was limited almost entirely to the pre-1826 projects for Quebec and Isle aux Noix. But while only £5,000 had been spent on assembling materials at Kingston, much detailed work had been done on plans and by 1828 the estimates for Smyth's fortification projects had risen considerably as well. For these the commission had reckoned on an expenditure of a little less than £1,500,000. By 1828 the figure had risen to over £1,600,000 for the Canadas and over £240,000 for the Maritime Provinces.[1] It had been difficult enough to keep the estimates down even to this level. Early in 1827 the governor of New Brunswick had tried to draw attention to what he considered to be the Smyth commission's neglect of several important places in his command, only to be resisted by Smyth and demolished by Wellington.

There is nothing so ill-judged, on general principles [said the duke] as to carry a *System of Defence* to the extreme frontier of a country which can be entered at all points. St Andrews and the Island of Grand Manan may be in themselves important points, and it may eventually be necessary to occupy those points with defence works to enable the militia and colonial troops to maintain them. But these posts must not be considered as points in the general defence system of the province.[2]

[1] The principal papers on this subject are printed in Wellington's *Despatches, Correspondence, and Memoranda*, vol. iii: Wellington, 'Memorandum on the Parliamentary grants for the works of defence in British North America', 31 Jan. 1826 (pp. 79–80); Hardinge, 'Memorandum upon the works in North America', 17 Feb. 1826 (p. 80); Wellington, 'Minute on Canals and Public Works in Canada', 15 June 1826 (pp. 335–8); V. G. Ellicombe, 'Memorandum relative to the money required for the works of defence and water communications in the Canadas, in consequence of the Commissioners' Report', 1 Mar. 1828 (pp. 81–2). See also C. P. Stacey, *Canada and the British Army, 1846–1871; a Study in the Practice of Responsible Government* (Toronto, 1963), pp. 14–15.

[2] Wellington, 'Minute on the observations of Major General Sir Howard Douglas and Major General Sir James Carmichael Smyth on the Defences of the Province of New Brunswick', April 1827, Wellington's *Despatches, Correspondence, and Memoranda*, iii. 615. Douglas's and Smyth's 'observations' are printed in *ibid.*, iii. 521–8 and 604–5.

In any case the unsettled state of the New Brunswick frontier question made it impossible to come to any detailed decisions in that area, including even the important question of the communications between Quebec and Halifax.[1] An attempt to revive schemes of general emigration in aid of defence he also successfully resisted, on the grounds that there were already enough inhabitants if the present recommendations were carried out, and that further *premature* migration would create a disloyal population.[2] So far as the Smyth commission's principal recommendations were concerned, Wellington stuck to his original endorsement and he firmly defended the whole plan in the evidence which he gave before the House of Commons select committee in March 1828. Asked 'what would be the probability of defending Canada if neither the water communication nor the works mentioned in these estimates were executed?', he replied:

I should say that the defence of Canada would be impossible. I have never been in that country, but I must add that I have been astonished that the officers of the army and navy employed in that country were able to defend those provinces last war; and I can attribute their having been able to defend them as they did only to the inexperience of the officers of the United States in the operations of war, and possibly likewise to the difficulty which they must have found in stationing their forces, as they ought to have done, upon the right bank of the St Lawrence.[3]

Wellington was now prime minister, but in view of both the rise in the estimated expense and the improvement in Anglo-American relations after the death of Canning, it is not surprising that even his government should have considered it discreet to adhere to the parliamentary tactics of 1826. They got the Board of Ordnance to divide the proposed works into three classes, and asked parliament to grant money in the first instance only for those considered necessary at once, the citadels of Halifax and Kingston.[4] Even so, the amount asked for, £330,000, was severely criticized in the House of Commons and it was never found expedient to apply for the money for the second and third groups of works. Still, by 1840 Canada had received – and moreover at the expense of the home government – the great citadel of Quebec, extensive works at Kingston and Isle aux Noix, the Ottawa and Rideau canal, and numerous minor works, as well as contributions

[1] Wellington to Smyth, 10 Aug. 1826, Wellington's *Despatches, and Correspondence, and Memoranda*, iii. 373-4.
[2] Wellington to F. Robinson, 20 Oct. 1826, *ibid.*, iii. 432-7.
[3] 'Evidence of Field Marshal his Grace the duke of Wellington on the Defences of British North America', 15 April 1828, *ibid.*, iv. 389-97.
[4] *Idem*, and Stacey, *Canada and the British Army*, p. 15.

to canal improvements undertaken on colonial responsibility. In the other conditions he considered essential to the successful defence of Canada, Wellington had to face greater disappointments. Instead of two field armies of 5,000 British regulars each and a total British garrison of about 13,500 in the Canadas alone, there were on the eve of the Canadian rebellion in 1837 only about 5,000 in the whole of British North America. Instead of an organized and properly trained force of 40,000 Canadian militia, there was by 1840 merely a vast paper force of nearly 250,000 embracing the entire male population between the ages of eighteen and sixty. In 1829 those up to forty had been separated into an 'active' force, but even this remained totally untrained, being required merely to muster once a year. And, of course, the naval force on the lakes had entirely disappeared in 1834.

While preparations in North America proceeded slowly and never came anywhere near meeting the full recommendations of the principal naval and military experts, they did nevertheless go some considerable way towards providing by the early 1840s the material basis for a *general* plan of operations. Upon this plan there was an apparent consensus of opinion. There was, in the first place, general agreement that operations on the frontier must be defensive and designed to resist, dissipate, and defeat the invading efforts of the enemy; in short to prevent the Americans' conquest of Great Britain's North American dominions, and not to undertake a British conquest of the United States. To this extent the prospective operations in Canada resembled very much a holding operation, with forts and posts to hold off or delay the enemy on his principal lines of attack, falling back if necessary ultimately upon the keys of the system of communications. Indeed, with such an insufficient garrison it was always felt desirable, if domestic political circumstances in Canada permitted, to concentrate the forces in as few places as possible even in peacetime, lest another outbreak of war should catch them in small and scattered detachments where they could be reduced piecemeal.[1]

The frontier itself was not quite as vulnerable as it sometimes looked. The region of the western lakes remained relatively remote, wild, and unpopulated. More worrying was the St Lawrence strip, in which by far the greater part of Canada's population and resources was concentrated. It was almost everywhere vulnerable to American raids, but was open to large scale attack for the purpose of permanent conquest only in a few, possibly no more than three, areas: from Lake Champlain

[1] See, for example, Sherbrooke to Bathurst, private and confidential, 10 Oct. 1816, C.O. 42/167.

43

down the Richelieu River to Quebec or Montreal; generally upon the Niagara frontier; and from Lake Ontario upon Kingston. This limitation considerably reduced the disadvantages under which the British generally suffered; but however much it promised to confine the American lines of advance it still did not offer any real prospect of holding the country generally secure from attack and depredation. Much as the United States was hampered in the pursuit of an efficient and effective military effort by the peculiar characteristics of its political institutions and social habits, still no one could expect that the Americans would not be able to mount an ultimately overwhelming offensive.

The American ability to launch such an attack had been very greatly enhanced in the two decades after 1815 by the rapid development of a system of road, canal, and railway communications leading from the heart of the Atlantic seaboard to the very threshold of the Canadas. Against such an attack neither the delaying tactics of the British nor even the climate could hope to be completely successful. In view of this it was clearly the British plan that, while the American occupation of a large part of the provinces should be made as uncomfortable as possible by the activities of whatever militia forces could be assembled, the main defensive effort would consist in hanging on to the keys of the system of communications within the Canadas and with the Maritimes and Great Britain. With the regulars successfully holding on to Kingston, Montreal, and Quebec, and with militia raids harassing the flank and rear, the Americans could never consolidate their grip on the provinces and the British could always look forward to large reinforcements in the spring when the thaw once more opened communications. The question of timing was all important. Winter would probably help the American advance by land, provided that it proceeded quickly and succeeded easily, while it would prevent all chance of British reinforcement; but it would also stop the Americans undertaking the only kind of siege operations likely to overcome the massive defences of the principal fortresses. The best chance of American success, therefore, was at the very last moment of winter to advance across the frozen St Lawrence and, when the thaw came, be ready to seize these fortresses before the British had time to move up any reinforcements.

The British, unlike the Americans, were thought to have little chance of introducing troops into the Canadas in winter when the St Lawrence was closed by ice. There was still no satisfactory route overland. The Smyth commission had recommended two. One went from Quebec to Fredericton, a distance of 365 miles, 110 of them along the line of the

St Lawrence, but then eastward for thirty-six miles across very difficult country to Lake Temiscouata and thence along the Madawaska and St John river valleys. The other, from Quebec to Halifax, a distance of 660 miles, was the Matapediac route, and going by the Miramichi and Restigouche Rivers to the Bay of Chaleur was more remote from the frontier and had therefore been favoured by Sir James Kempt.[1] The commission had advised that the second at least, being mainly in quite unsurveyed country, should be left to the natural process of time and the provincial legislature of Nova Scotia; but they had recommended the expenditure of £40,000 to complete the first. Both were in fact left to the intermittent and incomplete attentions of the local civil authorities. By the 1840s only the Temiscouata route was in regular use and this lay for a considerable part of its length so perilously close to the border that it was bound to be cut in the event of war. The unsettled boundary disputes in the north-east, moreover, made it quite uncertain that it would remain in British hands in peace, let alone in war.

During spring and summer the position was much better. The comparative invulnerability of the maritime ports – because of the presumption of general and local British naval superiority and the impracticability of a major land attack across the very difficult country of the New Brunswick border – ensured to Great Britain command of the St Lawrence as far as Quebec. But no further. Beyond that point battleships could not navigate and frigates could not reach beyond Montreal. By 1840 improvements to the St Lawrence canals were permitting the passage of small steamers but not any useful class of warship. In any case the Americans were bound to cut the river above Montreal or even between that city and Quebec by commanding the passage with guns on the south bank if not by actual invasion. In the rear there was, admittedly, Wellington's major achievement, the Rideau and Ottawa canal system, but this was designed to carry military stores and could admit only the smallest class of gunboats. Even this route was not entirely secure as it could be cut by a dash upon one or more of its locks.

There was no question, then, of tapping Great Britain's immense naval power for service on the lakes; all reliance must be placed on what could be done locally. In view of this, the Rush-Bagot agreement and the subsequent running down of the naval establishment to its closure in 1834 marked the absolute abandonment of any plans for taking the

[1] See map 2, p. 107.

45

major offensive in the provinces. Clearly the most that was envisaged below Montreal, or even Quebec, was limited operations strictly in aid of the army's supply and transportation and perhaps bold strikes at the enemy's more exposed bases. But there was unlikely to be much opportunity for the latter unless the Americans were extraordinarily careless. Even Wellington's expensive ideas did not extend to an offensive. He had repeatedly written off such a project as impractical and foolhardy in view of Britain's disadvantage in local resources and the length of communications with the homeland. It was, on the other hand, the duke's hope that by the improvement of the interior lines of water communication, it would be possible to pass both army and naval forces from lake to lake, asserting local superiority wherever they went. Even this was a useless dream. By the late 1820s a civil canal, the Welland canal, had opened water communication between Lakes Erie and Ontario; but its capacity was very limited and the work so poorly executed and maintained, its profits so small, that it was soon in a state of utter disrepair. In any case its extremely vulnerable position, so near the Niagara frontier, would have made it useless in war. The communication with the western lakes that the duke hoped would be opened by extending the Ottawa River passage to Lake Simcoe and Penetanguishene was never undertaken; nor was the alternative he urged from Kingston via the Bay of Quinte to Lake Simcoe, at a cost of over £200,000. In any case the forces that the Americans would have needed to command and block the exits of such narrow passages would probably not have seriously diminished their general superiority.

Naval and military planning alike emphasized the purely defensive posture of the British in the Provinces. At best it was hoped that the Americans might commit errors similar to those of the opening campaigns of the two previous Anglo-American wars; in that case British tactics would have increased immensely the consequent drain on American morale and material. At worst most of the country would have to be abandoned – though not without such resistance as the militia, sustained by the lesser British posts, could put up. But they would have to hold on to a few principal centres and to the lifeline with Great Britain. Through this lifeline massive reinforcements would ultimately be poured to undertake the reconquest of the provinces when circumstances moved more decisively in Great Britain's favour.

True, such an abandonment would seriously damage Great Britain's prestige and encourage not only the United States but also the latter's potential allies in Europe, France and Russia, perhaps even jolt them into the war. It might well, too, alienate the loyalty of the Canadians, especially if they ever got wind of the intention beforehand. But even if, as some pessimists believed, the British might not be able to hold on to Kingston, Montreal, and Quebec, defeat in Canada would not lose the war generally. Britain's weakness in Canada lay primarily in her inability to overcome distance – within Canada and between Canada and Great Britain – by the application of her principal asset – an immense sea power. Elsewhere her prospects were much better.

Just as in the immense Canadian hinterland, settlement in the first half of the nineteenth century was largely confined to a relatively narrow strip along one side of the St Lawrence, so was a large part of American population, trade, and resources concentrated in the coastal cities of the Atlantic, not least in the vital commercial ports of Boston, New York, Philadelphia and Baltimore. Immediately available for operations against them the British had in the waters of the western Atlantic a very impressive proportion of their fleet. In January 1816, after the rearrangements following the end of the wars in Europe and America, the British still had no less than four squadrons and forty-five warships in American waters, excluding the Canadian lakes and the Brazils station. On the Halifax and Newfoundland stations together there were sixteen ships, including a battleship and two frigates; on the Leeward Islands station fourteen ships, including a battleship and three other large vessels; and on the Jamaica station, fifteen ships, including three frigates. By January 1817 the total force had fallen to thirty-three but included three battleships. By 1825 the battleships had been recalled and the squadrons combined into two, the North American and the West Indian; but there were still a powerful cruiser and a frigate on the former and another cruiser and six frigates on the West Indian station. In 1830 the two squadrons were joined under a single command but in January 1838, shortly before the growing crisis in North America compelled a rapid increase, the strength of the new squadron was still more than twenty-seven vessels, including a third rate battleship and four frigates.[1] There were some special problems to overcome – the coastal waters were uncomfortably shallow – but the Atlantic cities and their trade were clearly pretty well at the mercy of these squadrons operating from such convenient bases as Halifax and Bermuda. Hence the very special attention given in these same years to the improvement of these two naval bases.

The defences of Halifax had fallen into considerable decay by the time Smyth's commission came to report upon them in 1825. But

[1] These figures are based on the official lists in Adm. 8, supplemented for the years 1815–21 where the lists are lacking, by *Steel's List of the Royal Navy*.

47

following their recommendations work on a great new citadel was ordered to begin with a vote of £15,000 in 1828 and by 1861, following additions to the scheme officially completed in 1856, some £233,882 had been spent on the fortifications.[1] Protected on the seaward side by these defences and to the landward by the difficulty of the country and the distance from the border and possessing a large and deep harbour, Halifax naturally became one of the navy's principal bases. It was well placed as a point of disembarkation for the men and supplies coming from Europe to the North American colonies, as a dock and yard for the general maintenance of the fleet in the north-western Atlantic, and being only 340 miles from Portland, Maine, for offensive operations against the coast of New England.

The Smyth commission had not had time to visit Bermuda in either of its American investigations of 1823 and 1825, but the second report's references to offensive operations in the vicinity of New York clearly pointed to that island's peculiar importance in a war with the United States. In the debates of March 1816 the government's naval spokesman had declared: 'With respect to the force at Bermuda, it formed the great security of Canada, and was a point from which a British fleet might sweep the whole extent of the coast of North America.'[2] Already, early in 1817, the drastic reductions contemplated on the Canadian lakes had led Byam Martin to express an apprehension of Great Britain being ultimately driven out of North America and to a shift of emphasis to Bermuda, where he hoped the navy would find a secure careening base for operations against the Atlantic frontier of the United States. Investigations and reports had continued during the next few years and in 1821 it had been decided to spend up to £20,000 a year on the improvement of the dockyard and its defences.[3]

In September 1823 came another extensive report from the officer in command of the Royal Engineers on the islands, followed, in 1828, by even more enthusiastic recommendations from the naval commander-in-chief in the West Indies. By this time the destruction of the citadel at Havana and the opening up of a direct trade between Great Britain and South America had considerably decreased the strategic and commercial importance of Port Royal, Jamaica. Bermuda,

[1] George F. Stanley, *Canada's Soldiers, 1604–1954* (Toronto, 1954), p. 183.
[2] *Hansard's Parliamentary Debates*, xxxiii. 581.
[3] Capt. J. M. Lewis, resident commissioner at the Bermuda yard, to T. Byam Martin, 9 Feb. and 27 Mar. 1817, and Martin to Lewis, 19 April 1819, Byam Martin papers, B.M.Add.MS.41,394; Martin to John Taff, master-shipwright at Bermuda, 27 April 1821, *ibid.*, B.M.Add.MS.41,395.

on the other hand, was relatively secure from hurricanes and had a generally better climate. With its extensive refitting facilities and a harbour capable of receiving the largest ships, it had already become the general depôt for the Western Atlantic. Particular stress was placed upon Bermuda's importance in a war with the United States; it was only 640 miles from the Chesapeake and its smallness and isolation made it ideal for the preparation of secret operations against the American coast. There was some need, however, to provide against a *coup de main* because of the increased strength of the American navy and various new works of defence and an increase in the war garrison to between 1,200 and 1,500 men were consequently recommended. In 1826, Melville and Wellington agreed upon a general scheme of defence for the Bermudas, concentrating the dockyard on Ireland Island, and providing barracks for 400 infantry and a brigade of artillery on Main Island, and a series of forts on St George's Island.[1]

The experience of the War of 1812 alone would have ensured that the vulnerability of their coastline was as clear to the Americans as it was to the British. Then Baltimore and New Orleans had escaped miraculously, but Washington had not, and its fate Smyth had intended New York should share in the next war. This the Americans well knew as an official report of 1840 made clear:

The object may be to lay a great city under contribution or to destroy one of the naval depots, or to take possession of one of our great harbors. . . . It was estimated that in the great fire in the city of New York in the year 1835 the property destroyed within a few hours, was worth upwards of $17,000,000, although the fire was confined to a very small part of the city and did not touch the shipping. Is it easy then to estimate the loss that would accrue from the fires that a victorious enemy could kindle upon the circuit of that great city when no friendly hand could be raised to extinguish them? Or is it easy to overrate the tribute such a city would pay for exemption from that calamity? Can we value too highly the pecuniary losses destruction of one of the great naval yards would involve, and the loss beyond all pecuniary value of stores and accommodations indispensable in a state of war and that a state of war can hardly replace?[2]

[1] Major T. Blanchard, 'Report on the Defences of Bermuda', 1 Sept. 1823, W.O. 55/1551/(3); Adm. Sir Charles Ogle (c.-in-c., Halifax) to duke of Clarence, private, 20 Sept. 1828, Melville papers, Clements Library. For a most useful account of Bermuda's development as a naval base see Roger Willock, *Bulwark of Empire: Bermuda's Fortified Naval Base, 1860–1920* (privately published, Princeton, N.J., 1962).

[2] Report no. 1 of a board of engineers, 'On the defence of the Atlantic frontier from the Passamaquoddy to the Sabine', in the secretary of war's *Report on Military and Naval Defences*, 24 April 1840, Senate Report no. 451, 26th Cong[ress], 1st sess[ion], vol. vii.

The problem of the frontiers, both land and water, had compelled expensive attention by the United States from the very first days of peace. Acts of 3 March 1815 and 29 April 1816 provided $400,000 and $838,000 for fortifications; in 1816 a board of engineers, assisted by the French General Bernard, was appointed to work out a vast comprehensive scheme; and between 1816 and 1829 $8,250,000 was voted for the fortifications. Of this comparatively little was spent on the northern line, partly because of the priority of the Indian 'frontier' and partly because of the relative sense of security on the Canadian border. Only on Fort Niagara and, until October 1818 when they were found by the boundary commission to lie within Canadian territory, on Rouse's and Windmill Points on the invasion route from the northern tip of Lake Champlain, was there any large expenditure in the decade after the end of the war.[1] Instead most of the money went towards the construction of a massive system of fortifications on the Atlantic and Gulf coast, the most notable being Fortress Monroe in Hampton Roads. But such a vast undertaking was bound to meet a fate similar to that which frustrated all of Wellington's schemes. In 1821 Congress intervened to secure the supervision of each work in turn, instead of making general appropriations, and the whole programme inevitably ground almost to a halt. President Jackson tried unsuccessfully to revive it in the 1830s but it took the crises of the 1840s and more especially the Civil War itself to bring the scheme to a virtual completion.

At the end of 1837 it was reported that all the fortifications on the maritime frontier were 'incomplete, unfinished, and unarmed', all of them being in need of extensive and costly repairs: 'There is not a fortress on our long line of sea defences capable of resisting an armed brig, not one that may not be taken by a small force and some of them from their quasi-insular position, if captured, may be occupied permanently during the continuation of a war, or are only to be retaken at the cost of much blood and treasure.'[2] Nor were there sufficient troops to man even these imperfect works. After the reduction to 6,000 regulars in 1821, the authorized establishment of the regular army had crept up to about 7,000 by the beginning of 1838, principally by the addition of cavalry. Even this number proved very difficult to raise, the actual strength in 1835 being little more than 4,000. And with Indian troubles like the Seminole war occupying the major part of

[1] Stacey, 'Myth of the Unguarded Frontier', pp. 5–8.
[2] Secretary of war's *Report on the Protection of the Frontiers*, 9 Jan. 1838, Senate Doc[ument] no. 88, 25th Cong., 2nd sess., vol. i.

the army for some six years from the end of 1835 most of the inland and frontier posts remained virtually defenceless: 'every post on the Atlantic from Maine to the Sabine is without a single company to garrison it or to take charge of the public property', reported General Macomb in November 1837.[1] Even if they had been properly completed and garrisoned the Atlantic forts would have drawn off forces for offensive operations on the Canadian frontier. In any case they could never have promised total immunity from attacks by concentrated naval forces, which would be morally at least as damaging and materially much more damaging than any British reverses in Canada. The only way of effectively fending off such attacks – as well of course as protecting American overseas trade – would be by the construction of a large navy, and this the United States was not able to do until the Civil War.

British apprehension about the American navy, arising out of her unfortunate experience in the recent war and the American navy bill of 1816, had reached its height in the 'crisis' of 1826. Thereafter, while the American need for economy and the difficulty of obtaining seamen made their effort level off and decline, the British pushed on with their naval programme, a large part of which was specifically designed to cope with the American problem. By 1829 the British had regained confidence in their battleships and, by 1838, though still inferior in numbers of large frigates, they felt they could cope with these vessels too.[2]

If, then, in spite of colossal expenditure and Wellington's persistent demands for more, the British position in Canada remained highly vulnerable, the balance was adjusted very substantially in her favour on the Atlantic coast. But this did not mean that the British could win the war in the Atlantic any more than the Americans could win it in Canada. Blockade and bombardment, generally now held to have been of secondary importance even against Germany in the twentieth century, could not have ruined the United States materially – at least not after the first decade of the nineteenth century. And the authoritative opinion of the duke of Wellington, effectively reinforced by the disaster of New Orleans, was that an invasion on a large scale was out of the question. The only prospect of complete success for any or all of these was through the moral collapse of the American people and the defection of a large

[1] 'The Major General of the Army to the Secretary of War, November 1837', enclosure no. 7 to the secretary of war's report accompanying the president's *Annual Message*, 4 Dec. 1837, Ex[ecutive] Doc. no. 3, 25th Cong., 2nd sess., vol. i.

[2] For comparisons of American and British naval strength in these years, see C. J. Bartlett, *Great Britain and Sea Power, 1815–1853* (Oxford, 1963), pp. 31–4, 70–4, and 125.

section of the Union. Otherwise a war-weary stalemate was the most likely result. So long as the sweet fruits of real victory were so difficult to obtain, the automatic damage to mutual trade that war would bring was certainly a deterrent, though because of the concern of men with prestige and power and the perversity of chance, probably not such an absolute one as is usually asserted in this case. To avert the stalemate, as well as to achieve their independent political and economic ends, what each sought was a change in the balance of power in North America.

3

Manœuvring for Power

In the first two decades after the peace of Ghent the plans made in anticipation of a new war with the United States were intensive and the expenditure committed to works of defence enormous. But no scheme was ever completed and even if one had been it is unlikely that it would have inspired complete confidence. It was natural then that the patent military weakness of the British position in Canada should give additional force to that growing body of opinion in nineteenth-century Britain which, on economic grounds at least, opposed the retention of colonies in general and awkward Canada in particular. This feeling was not to reach its climax until about the middle of the century but even from the first it was by no means entirely confined to those whom Palmerston was later to call 'theoretical gentlemen'.[1] Indeed it extended, as has been seen, to some of the principal military figures.

In January 1815 Castlereagh had congratulated his prime minister on the 'auspicious and seasonable event' of the American peace, and on their country's 'being released from the millstone of the American war'.[2] Only a year later even the peacetime establishment on the lakes had become, in Commissioner Hall's opinion, 'a millstone round our necks, and indeed,' he continued, 'the colony itself is scarcely worth the the expense'.[3] In the same year Admiral Sir David Milne had remarked that Canada was 'certainly a fine country, but too distant for us to defend against so powerful a neighbour', and he could not therefore 'help thinking that it would be better for this country if it were quit of Canada altogether'.[4] But on military grounds alone there was at

---

[1] Palmerston to Newcastle, 7 Nov. 1861, Palmerston papers, B.M.Add. MS.48,582.

[2] Castlereagh to Liverpool, 2 Jan. 1815, Wellington's *Supplementary Despatches*, ix. 523.

[3] Hall to T. Byam Martin, 7 Oct. 1816, Byam Martin papers, B.M.Add.MS. 41,400.

[4] Milne to Home, 13 and 1 June 1816, Historical Manuscripts Commission, *Report on the Manuscripts of Col. David Milne Home of Wedderburn Castle, N.B.* (London, 1902), p. 169.

least one very large objection to withdrawal. 'On my journey [to Vienna]', wrote Castlereagh in October 1814, 'I had an opportunity of looking into our system towards America for years past, as well as the growing value of Canada, and I trust we shall never again commit the egregious folly of spoiling America by acts signally unjust to our own subjects and to all foreign powers. I have certainly acquired by those researches a very increased notion of the value of our North American provinces to us as a naval power.'[1]

What Castlereagh was referring to was, of course, the Maritime Provinces' traditional role as the 'nursery of British sea-power'. In those provinces there lay not only an alternative, if inferior, source of naval supplies, but, what was to have more lasting importance, a reserve of seamen and ships in their extensive merchant and fishing marine and in the great naval arsenal of Halifax one of the very few large harbours on the Atlantic coast of North America capable of sheltering the largest ships. Early in the century Canadian timber, though vastly inferior to English oak, was a vital alternative supply now that the English forests had been ruined: 'It can almost be said that Canadian pines and oaks sustained the Navy during its long struggle with the Napoleonic Empire.'[2] The conversion to steam propulsion and then to iron construction very much lessened the general importance of the provinces to Britain's naval power, but not that of Halifax. In the first half of the century neither Halifax nor Bermuda had entirely satisfactory docking facilities for the larger warships, and while Bermuda got a floating dock in 1869, Halifax had to wait until 1889 for a large dry dock. But Bermuda had to import almost all its water and food supplies. Halifax, on the other hand, had a supply of coal in the Nova Scotian mines at Pictou. In any case, as with so many of Great Britain's insular possessions, even anti-colonial opinion had to admit that in this case too what was of comparatively little value to the mother country might be of immense value to a potential enemy.

This would certainly be the case with the United States and their naval power. They lacked not only offshore bases and, until vast improvements had been carried out, sufficient deep-water harbours on the Atlantic coast, but also, through the very prosperity of their merchant marine, enough men to man even a small peacetime navy. In wartime, it was estimated in 1837, their present resources of seamen

[1] Castlereagh to Bathurst, 4 Oct. 1814, Historical Manuscripts Commission, *Report on the Manuscripts of Earl Bathurst* (London, 1923), pp. 295–6.
[2] R. G. Albion, *Forests and Sea Power: the Timber Problem of the Royal Navy, 1652–1862* (Cambridge, Mass., 1926), p. 346.

might permit a total force of fifteen battleships, twenty-five each of frigates, sloops, and steamships, and twenty-five smaller vessels. This was a very respectable force, but as the American secretary of war pointed out at the time, it hardly bore comparison with the war strengths of the British and French navies.[1] This problem at least the acquisition of the British North American colonies would solve; and for that reason, if for no other, their fate was pressed upon the attention of both governments as the crisis over the Maine boundary loomed up in the late 1830s. For some it went much further than this. To the quartermaster-general of the American army, General T. S. Jesup, the colonies were not only a vital resource of naval power but also the key to the continental security of the United States. In British hands they formed an integral part of that worldwide system of trade and shipping by which she dominated all the nations of the earth. Together with her other island possessions in American waters they formed 'great outworks whence she projects her missiles (ships of war) upon the wings of every wind, and maintains . . . a cross fire upon the whole surface of the globe'. So far as the United States was concerned Great Britain's North American possessions,

bearing heavily upon our flank and rear; and the influence which [they] are capable of exercising over the Indians upon our western frontier and the Texan and Mexican states render their geographical position a most powerful check upon us. If she retain these colonies she may add the force of Texas and Mexico to her own. These states can never possess naval power; they must therefore rely on alliances with some great maritime power for the protection of their valuable and growing commerce. We have adopted the maxim, whether wisely or not time must determine, of non-interference, under any circumstances, with the affairs of other nations. That protection then which they would gladly receive from us but which we are precluded by our settled policy from affording them, Great Britain will readily extend to them and in a war with us, they will be so much added to her force on the weakest flank of our country. Her colonies, therefore, and their consequent influence are a guarantee to her against our commercial, maritime, and political ascendancy, so long as she holds them.[2]

At the same time, Jesup went on, it was the United States who alone threatened the defensive system of the British Empire. The American watch on Cuba withheld from Great Britain the last great link in her network of island bases and on the northern frontier the United States

[1] Secretary of war's *Report on the Protection of the Frontier*, 9 Jan. 1838, Senate Doc. no. 88, 25th Cong., 2nd sess., vol. i.
[2] Jesup to Poinsett, 21 Mar. 1839, Selected Confidential Letters Received by the Secretary of War, United States National Archives, Record Group 107.

had a fortunate strategic advantage. 'British naval power is vulnerable only in its contact with us; and it requires but an ordinary store of sagacity to perceive that the principal pillar of that power [the trade and fisheries of the North American colonies] is within our grasp.' Once the conquest was accomplished he expected the United States not only to achieve real continental security but also to build up dramatically her wealth and power.

Our maritime resources would be more than doubled. We should be forever freed from Indian difficulties; and Texas and Mexico in all offensive operations against us would be passive, if not powerless: our means of defence would be doubled because our northern frontier would be shortened more than one half, and the resources for its protection augmented in a proportionate degree. In the same ratio that the power of the United States would then be increased, would the maritime preponderance, resources, and political influence of Great Britain be diminished.[1]

Jesup was writing in the heat of a crisis threatening imminent war and he was anxious to impress upon his masters both the dangers of too feeble a military preparation and the real opportunities of a great effort. On the other side too there was a similar impression, equally exaggerated no doubt, but equally endowed with an element of truth. A former adjutant-general of the Canadian militia summed the matter up in characteristic, if somewhat hysterical language:

All the Naval Powers of Europe would do well to prevent the Americans becoming supreme on the Ocean – For, even now, they would willingly overthrow every Monarchical Govt. with which they are likely to come into contact . . .

1st   The Americans dread a standing Army, lest it may endanger their liberties.

2nd   They desire, ardently desire, to become a great Naval Power.

3rd   They never can become such without the possession of the North American colonies.

4th   Having them, England would be deprived of them, and with losing them she would soon lose the Fisheries and West Indian Possessions and soon after nearly all her Naval Power.

5th   The United States would then lord it over the high seas: her Northern States, having the British Provinces, would lord it over the Southern States – would exclude British manufactures from all the States – would cultivate their own northern manufactures and take the cotton of the Southern States – would seduce to their shores English artisans, and

[1] Jesup to Poinsett, 21 Mar. 1839, Selected Confidential Letters Received by the Secretary of War, United States National Archives, Record Group 107.

would soon supplant many English fabrics in other Countries, as they now do in the articles of coarse cotton cloth. In fifty years, perhaps in half that time, the United States would thus cause the downfall of Great Britain, if Great Britain does not this very year, 1838, take the most decided preventive measures to secure her Colonies, and to withhold the advantages hitherto so easily, so lavishly, extended to the American People, by coining money and extending mercantile credit, to the several States, their banks, and their merchants. I fear that all these loans and credits will be lost to England.[1]

From a naval point of view, then, it was as necessary to hold the Maritime Provinces as it was the West Indies, and for this the possession of the interior was also essential. On this Wellington's opinion was authoritative and categorical: 'The abandonment of Canada', he told the House of Commons select committee in 1828, 'would occasion the loss of New Brunswick and Nova Scotia.'[2] Even if there had not been any material or military objects in view – and certainly, Halifax apart, those mentioned had substantially declined by the middle of the century – pride, prestige, and even a sense of obligation to the colonists would still have impeded, if not prevented, withdrawal. This was a theme constantly employed, and in a manner difficult to oppose, by Wellington himself: 'In considering this subject', he had suggested to Bathurst in 1825, 'I entreat your Lordship to observe, that it is impossible . . . to withdraw from these dominions. Whether valuable or otherwise, which can scarcely be a question, they must be defended in war.'[3]

Given that British North America had to be preserved from invasion and annexation by the United States, but also that a really effective system of interior defences was probably illusory and certainly intolerably expensive, Great Britain had either radically to improve her relations with the United States or seek to adjust in her favour the balance of power in the Americas. What she did of course was to pursue both objectives. But very few – not even Castlereagh – were inclined to be optimistic about the first. It was rather in the overall expansion of British North America – in wealth, in population, and in territory – that

---

[1] Postscript of 22 June to 'A Sketch or outline of my opinions on the Political State of the British Provinces in North America', by James FitzGibbon, Toronto, 18 June 1838, W.O. 55/1551 (7b). See also, the several papers pressed by Sir Frederick Lamb upon his brother, the prime minister, and upon the foreign secretary: Lamb to Melbourne, 26 Jan. 1838, and to Palmerston, 28 Feb. 1838, Broadlands papers.

[2] 'Evidence of . . . Wellington on the Defences of British North America', 15 April 1828, *Despatches, Correspondence, and Memoranda*, iv. 393.

[3] Wellington to Bathurst, 6 Dec. 1825, *ibid.*, ii. 572–5.

the greatest opportunities seemed to lie. 'The security of the country', the Admiralty argued in support of the running down of the lakes establishment in 1831, 'will depend on the growing prosperity of Canada, not on public expenditure.'[1]

Even before the end of the war in 1814 the government had initiated schemes of assisted immigration. General Murray had pressed the idea of settling discharged soldiers on the strategic frontier in 1815; and in the early years of peace special measures had been taken to settle enrolled pensioners in the vicinity of Fort Malden at Amherstburg and to recruit labourers to build the Rideau canal.[2] But military settlement as a whole was a doubtful and temporary expedient. Already in 1820 Castlereagh was complaining to Stratford Canning: 'In general, [it is] pretty clear that the Colonial Office is neither prepared to give up Canada, nor has it any settled system for making it sufficiently strong to serve as a counterbalance to the United States.'[3] By 1826 even Wellington was having doubts about the effects of military settlement on the loyalty of the rest of the population and about the same time parliament refused to have anything further to do with financing emigration schemes. Rather more promising, at first, was the prospect of a major adjustment in the relative populations of the United States and Canada through the general process of immigration. In 1812 the white population of British North America was about a tenth of that in the United States, 600,000 as against 6 million. After the war, with special assistance from both government and private sources, the number of emigrants going direct from the United Kingdom to the British colonies in North America in 1818 overtook the number going to the United States and with few exceptions was maintained at a higher rate until the mid 1830s. In and after the 1840s, however, the number of British migrants to the United States leaped ahead of the number going to the colonies, averaging twice as many in the 1840s and about four times as many over the century. So although the white population of British North America had risen to about 1½ million by 1837, continued migration from British, as well as other European and even Canadian, sources ensured that the population of the United States kept well ahead. In 1851 the population of Canada had barely reached 2½ million;

[1] Adm. to Navy Board, 23 Feb. 1831, Adm. 2/1694.
[2] Helen I. Cowan, *British Emigration to British North America* (Toronto, 1961), pp. 40–64; G. S. Graham, 'Views of General Murray', *Canadian Historical Review*, xxxiv (1953), 158–65; George F. G. Stanley, *Canada's Soldiers, 1604–1954* (Toronto, 1954), pp. 186–7.
[3] Notes of an interview of 27 July 1820 in Stratford Canning papers, P.R.O., F.O. 352/62.

while that of the United States was still nearly ten times as great. By the end of the century the figures had grown to about $5\frac{1}{2}$ million and nearly 80 million respectively.[1]

Hardly any more successful was the early competition for territory. Just as the Quebec Act had sought to protect the fur trade from the disturbing westward thrust of American pioneers and settlers so, after independence, British military power and diplomacy had tried between 1783 and 1814 not only to preserve that trade but also to contain American expansion and better protect Canada, first by pushing the frontier southwards and then by the establishment of an Indian buffer state. After the military and diplomatic defeats of 1814, however, they had to fall back upon a more modest policy, namely in manœuvring for the advantage in the various lengths of boundary still left undefined or in need of revision. Some of these concerned crucial military issues in the defence of British possessions. Thus the north-eastern boundary, through New Brunswick to the St Lawrence, involved the whole question of communications from the sea to the Canadas, and the St Lawrence and Great Lakes line that of the interior water communication. In neither of these issues did the British achieve much success. In 1822 the Ghent boundary commissioners defined the boundary line along the St Lawrence and the lakes in such a manner that the Americans secured with Barnhart Island the command of the river passage from two sides between Montreal and Kingston, and, in Drummond Island, what was, according to the governor-general, Dalhousie, 'the only safe anchorage in the western half of Lake Huron'.[2] On the north-eastern boundary where the American claim thrust a deep wedge towards the north, there were even more important issues at stake: 'The extent of the territory in dispute is not without some degree of interest,' commented Stratford Canning in 1823 or 1824, 'but the objects of real importance are to remove the American frontier as much as possible from the line of the St Lawrence, to open a direct communication between Canada and New Brunswick, and to exclude the Americans from a valuable position on Lake Champlain.'[3]

[1] Based on figures in Cowan, p. 288; H. C. Allen, *Great Britain and the United States* (London, 1954), pp. 39 and 103–5; and J. B. Brebner, *North Atlantic Triangle* (New Haven, 1945), p. 296.

[2] Adm. to Barrie, secret, 12 Mar. 1823, Adm. 2/1693; Dalhousie to Bathurst, private, 14 Nov. 1821, C.O. 42/187. The British in fact kept possession of Drummond Island until late in 1828; but by that time they had concluded it was too distant to be a secure base in wartime: Dalhousie to C.O., no. 23, 12 June 1826, C.O. 42/209; Kempt to C.O., no. 1, 6 Oct. 1828, C.O. 42/217.

[3] Undated memorandum in the Stratford Canning papers, F.O. 352/59. See map 2, p. 107.

Canning's last reference was to the one substantial advantage (the acquisition of Grand Manan Island apart) which fell to the British from the work of the boundary commission. In 1818 it had discovered that the American fortifications at the head of Lake Champlain were really within British territory. As a result the Americans had to abandon a work which was apparently 'the most formidable the United States had ever erected on the border', and waste an investment that already amounted to about $113,000. By 1825 the central tower was reported to be 'in a state of ruin'.[1] The British however were not sure that they wanted the position. Military opinion in 1824 inclined to think that the Americans should not be allowed to have it; but the diplomats rightly suggested that there might be even more important points on the frontier for which Rouse's Point could be used as a bargaining counter.[2] Smyth's commission pointed out that the American claims on the frontier would interrupt the overland communication through New Brunswick and, more important in their view, bring the Americans to within eleven miles of the St Lawrence below Quebec. It is not surprising that on such a crucial question the boundary commission deadlocked in 1822. John Quincy Adams was perfectly willing to bargain, but domestic interests objected and he had to refuse the British offer of 1824 to exchange Rouse's Point and the navigation of the St Lawrence for the intercolonial road.[3] In 1827 the question was submitted to the arbitration of the king of the Netherlands and his simple decision, dividing the disputed territory in half, was acceptable to the British since it gave them at least a safe overland communication with Quebec.[4] But Maine again objected and the Americans had to reject the award.

Further west, from the lakes to the Pacific Ocean, where no frontier and little settlement existed, a quite different issue was involved – the possession of a vast area of possibly rich land and a potential connection across the sea with the riches of the East. Castlereagh had allowed a

[1] C. P. Stacey, 'The Myth of the Unguarded Frontier, 1815–1871', *American Historical Review*, lvi (1950–51), 8.
[2] See e.g., S. Canning to Huskisson, private, 6 May 1824, Huskisson papers, B.M.Add.MS.38,745, enclosing the opinions of General Murray and General Mann; Huskisson to Wellington, private, 30 July 1824, *ibid.*, B.M.Add.MS. 38,746; Dalhousie to Wellington, 23 Aug. 1824, enclosing the opinion of General Beckwith, Dalhousie microfilms, P[ublic] A[rchives of] C[anada, Ottawa], M[anuscript] G[roup] 24/A/12; Huskisson's memorandum on Rouse's Point, May 1824, *Despatches, Correspondence, and Memoranda of . . . Wellington*, ii. 264; and Wellington's draft instructions to the Smyth commission, 11 April 1825, *ibid.*, ii. 436–46.
[3] Samuel Flagg Bemis, *John Quincy Adams and the Foundation of American Foreign Policy* (New York, 1949), pp. 473–8.
[4] William IV to Palmerston, 17 Jan. 1831, Broadlands papers.

substantial advantage to slip through his fingers in 1818 when he let the Americans reoccupy Astoria on the Columbia River. In the same year, by the treaty settling the frontier westward from the Lake of the Woods to the Rockies, Great Britain was shut off forever from the Mississippi. The area between the mountains and the ocean, the Oregon territory, however, he would not so easily surrender and a temporary arrangement was made leaving it open to free settlement by both sides for ten years. When congressional pressure forced Adams to reopen the question in the 1820s he met not the conciliatory Castlereagh but an angry Canning and Canning resisted the American demands on characteristic grounds:

1st That the ambitious and overbearing views of the States are becoming daily more developed, and better understood in this country.

2nd That the Trade between the Eastern and Western Hemispheres, direct across the Pacific, is the trade of the world most susceptible of rapid augmentation and improvement. Between China and Mexico it is now going on largely. . . . We cannot get into this trade on account of the monopoly of the E[ast] I[ndia] C[ompan]y. But ten years hence that monopoly will cease; and though at that period neither you nor I shall be where we are to answer for our deeds, I should not like to have my name affixed to an instrument by which England would have foregone the advantages of an immense direct intercourse between China and what may be, if we resolve not to yield them up, her boundless establishments on the N.W. Coast of America.[1]

The most that could be got out of Canning therefore was the renewal of the 'joint occupation' agreement in 1827 for a further twenty years.[2]

So far as the northern frontier was concerned then, the British had little cause for satisfaction about the outcome of the two decades following the end of the war in 1814. For the present their disappointment was tempered to some extent by American forbearance over the larger issues. But there were warnings enough about the distant future. The world, John Quincy Adams had declared at a cabinet meeting in November 1819, must be

familiarized with the idea of considering our proper dominion to be the continent of North America. From the time when we became an independent people it was as much a law of nature that this should become our pretension as that the Mississippi should flow to the sea. Spain had possessions upon our southern and Great Britain upon our northern

---

[1] Canning to Liverpool, 7 July 1826, E. J. Stapleton, ed., *Some Official Correspondence of George Canning* (London, 1887), ii. 71–5.

[2] For these negotiations see F. Merk, *Albert Gallatin and the Oregon Problem: a Study in Anglo-American Diplomacy* (Cambridge, Mass., 1950).

border. It was impossible that centuries should elapse without finding them annexed to the United States.[1]

British North America, Americans like Adams tended to believe, would fall to their dominion without much effort; monarchy could not flourish on the American continent. To the south it had already wilted; but the Spanish empire's dying agonies nevertheless brought immediate, and serious dangers for the still feeble United States. Certainly there were opportunities as well as dangers: the Louisiana Purchase, the penetration of the Mississippi valley, and the acquisition of the Floridas all helped enormously to increase territory, improve trade communications, and pacify the Indians on the border. But in the transfer of Louisiana to Napoleonic France in the first instance in 1800, and in British intrigues, official and unofficial, in and immediately after the war of 1812, lay ominous warnings about the continental security of the United States and her pretensions to future empire.

After she had secured her immediate territorial objectives by the Floridas treaty of February 1819 the United States principal preoccupation in the Latin American question was to prevent the substitution for a collapsing Spanish rule of another and stronger European rival, British, French, or Russian. For a time a common opposition to the Latin American policy of the continental powers obscured the mutual suspicions of Britain and the United States. Thus in 1803 fear of Bonaparte's empire being extended to the American continent had taken priority over jealousy of the United States and had led the British government to approve and assist the transfer of Louisiana to the Americans.[2] Then in the first years after the end of the war in 1814, Castlereagh had acquiesced in the American penetration of the Floridas in the hope of averting a more serious crisis in Spanish-American relations. As the European 'Concert' began to crumble the United States sense of weakness and Great Britain's isolation even brought them close to formal and active cooperation in the Spanish American question. But though obscured, their mutual suspicion was never quite concealed. Castlereagh displayed the utmost forbearance when in 1818 General Jackson celebrated his unauthorized excursion into Spanish Florida by hanging two rather dubious British subjects. Nonetheless he had substantial reservations about the whole affair:

[1] C. F. Adams, *Memoirs of John Quincy Adams* (Philadelphia, 1874–77), iv. 439.
[2] See B. Perkins, *The First Rapprochement: England and the United States, 1795–1805* (Philadelphia, 1955), pp. 166–70.

Were Great Britain to look to its own interests alone, and were that interest worth asserting at the present moment, at the hazard of being embroiled with the United States [he told Bagot in 1817], there can be no question that we have an obvious motive for desiring that the Spaniards should continue to be our neighbours in East Florida rather than that our West Indian possessions should be so closely approached by the territory of the United States, but this is a consideration which we are not prepared to bring forward in the discussion at the present moment in bar to a settlement between Spain and North America.[1]

And in spite of the apparently overriding consideration of conciliation between Spain and the United States, he had in fact already warned Adams in 1815:

No; if it is supposed that we have any little trickish policy of thrusting ourselves in there [i.e. in Florida] between you and Spain, we are very much misunderstood indeed. You shall find nothing little or shabby in our policy. We have no desire to add an inch of ground to our territories in any part of the world . . . military positions may have been taken by us during the war of places which you had taken from Spain, but we never intended to keep them. Do you only observe the same moderation. If we should find you hereafter pursuing a system of encroachment upon your neighbours what we might do defensively is another consideration.[2]

These words applied even more to Cuba, 'the Turkey of transatlantic politics, tottering to its fall, and kept from falling only by the struggles of those who are contending for the right of catching her in her descent', as one English newspaper aptly described the island in 1825.[3] The interest of each side was clear. Adams wrote to the minister in Madrid in 1823:

Cuba, almost in sight of our shores, from a multitude of considerations, has become an object of transcendant importance to the commercial and political interests of our Union. Its commanding position, with reference to the Gulf of Mexico and the West Indian seas, the character of its population, its situation midway between our Southern coast and the island of Santo Domingo, its safe and capacious harbor of the Habana, fronting a long line of our shores destitute of the same advantages, the nature of its production and of its wants, furnishing the supplies and needing the returns of a commerce immensely profitable and mutually

---

[1] Castlereagh to Bagot, 10 Nov. 1817, C. K. Webster, *The Foreign Policy of Castlereagh, 1815–1822* (2nd edn., London, 1934), pp. 448–9.

[2] *Memoirs of John Quincy Adams*, iii. 289–90.

[3] Quoted by J. M. Callahan, *Cuba and International Relations* (Baltimore, 1899), p. 17.

beneficial, give it an importance in the sum of our national interests with which that of no other foreign territory can be compared and little inferior to that which binds the different members of the Union together.[1]

Canning more briefly but just as pointedly had written a year earlier: 'The possession by the United States of both shores of the channel, through which our Jamaica trade must pass, would . . . amount to a suspension of that trade, and to a consequent total ruin.'[2] It mattered little that the Americans believed their acquisition of the island lay in the very distant future, if indeed it ever was to be theirs, or that Great Britain had no such ambition at all. Mutual suspicions abounded and each kept a close watch on the other. Attempts at mutual self-denying guarantees in 1823–26 broke down on the very suspicions that inspired them.[3]

When, in the spring and summer of 1823, the crisis of the Spanish question and his isolation from the other European powers had made Canning look about for a friend to comfort him, he had prefaced his approaches to the American minister with the most effusive references to the 'mother and daughter' relationship of Great Britain and the United States. After the apparent rebuff from Monroe and the virtual disappearance of the threat from France he had moved once more into a mood of hostility more characteristic than the banquet platitudes with which he had regaled the American minister. In a real sense Monroe's famous message was a prohibition of a European balance of power in America and Canning's reaction shows how well he knew it. Almost at once he increased his pressure upon his colleagues for a more active policy in Latin America. Certainly recognition of the new republics and the very busy diplomacy that ensued were designed to preserve and improve England's trading position. But the letters and memoranda with which foreign secretary and prime minister bombarded their cabinet colleagues at the end of 1824 reflect a grave concern with a threat from the United States which was supposedly naval and political as well as commercial: 'I am conscientiously convinced', the prime minister wrote to one of the most obstinate members of his cabinet, 'that if we allow these new states to consolidate their system and their policy with the United States of America, it will in a very few years

[1] W. C. Ford, ed., *Writings of John Quincy Adams* (New York, 1913–17), vii. 369.
[2] Memorandum for the cabinet, Nov. 1822, J. H. Latané, *The United States and Latin America* (Garden City, N.Y., 1920), pp. 93–4.
[3] J. F. Rippy, *The Rivalry of the United States and Great Britain over Latin America, 1808–1830* (Baltimore, 1929), pp. 87–8.

prove fatal to our greatness, if not endanger our safety.'[1] What he meant by this he and Canning spelled out in a series of memoranda[2]:

The great and favourite object of the policy of this country, for more than four centuries, has been to foster and encourage our navigation, as the sure basis of our maritime power. In this branch of national industry the people of the United States are become more formidable rivals to us than any other nation which has ever yet existed. . . . The views and policy of the North Americans seem mainly directed towards supplanting us in navigation in every quarter of the globe, but more particularly in the seas contiguous to America.

Let us recollect that, as their commercial marine is augmented, their military marine must proportionally increase. And it cannot be doubted that, if we provoke the new states of America to give a decided preference in their ports to the people of the United States over ourselves, the navigation of these extensive dominions will be lost to us, and it will, in a great measure, be transferred to our rivals.

Let us remember, then, that peace, however desirable, and however cherished by us, cannot last for ever. Sooner or later we shall probably have to contend with the combined maritime power of France and of the United States. The disposition of the new States is at present highly favourable to England. If we take the advantage of that disposition, we may establish through our influence with them a fair counterpoise to that combined maritime power.

Let us not, then, throw the present golden opportunity away, which, once lost may never be recovered.

And in another memorandum shortly afterwards the argument developed:

The other and perhaps still more powerful motive is my apprehension of the ambitions and ascendancy of the U.S. of Am. It is obviously the policy of that Govt. to connect itself with all the Powers of America in a general Trans-Atlantic league, of which it would have the sole direction. I need not say how inconvenient such an ascendancy may be in time of peace, and how formidable in case of war.

I believe we now have the opportunity (but it may not last long) of opposing a powerful barrier to the influence of the U.S. by an amicable connection with Mexico, which from its position must be either subservient to or jealous of the U.S. In point of population and resources it is at least equal to all the rest of the Spanish Colonies; and may naturally expect to take the lead in its connections with the powers of Europe.

[1] Liverpool to Wellington, 8 Dec. 1824, Charles Duke Yonge, *The Life and Administration of Robert Banks, second earl of Liverpool* (London, 1868), iii. 305.
[2] The memoranda of November-December 1824 from which the two following passages are quoted are printed respectively in Yonge, iii. 297–304, and in Harold Temperley, *The Foreign Policy of Canning, 1822–1827* (London, 1925), pp. 550–5. The authorship of both is uncertain but Temperley argues convincingly that if not actually written by Canning they express what are clearly his ideas.

It was avowedly with these objects in view that Canning steered his government into a policy of recognition and intervention in Latin America, after the recession of the French and Russian threats in 1823. This policy, and particularly the decision to recognize Mexico in 1825, he claimed, would defeat 'the great danger of the time . . . a division of the World into European and American, Republican and Monarchical; a league of worn-out Govts. on the one hand, and of youthful and stirring Nations with the Un. States at their head, on the other'.[1]

So far as the immediate future was concerned each side grossly exaggerated the danger from its rival. Beyond the Floridas and Texas the United States had no urgent territorial objective; her domestic problems and her sense of material weakness abroad saw to that. Britain, though far stronger, had equally limited objectives; she certainly desired no territory and even in trade wanted equality of opportunity, not a commercial monopoly. The general policy of both, therefore, was essentially defensive and the character of their rivalry in Latin America was skirmishing rather than anything else. This applied even to so sensitive a spot as Cuba. In the Caribbean the British had such a multiplicity of bases that their main problem was to know how to defend what they already had. The 7,500 troops garrisoning the West Indian and Jamaican commands in August 1827 Wellington considered sufficient only for purposes of internal security.[2] The Americans, on the other hand, were badly off for bases. In 1822 they established a small refitting base at Key West in Florida and in 1824 began to develop Pensacola as a base. Both measures the British naturally connected with a supposedly active intention on the Americans' part to acquire Havana.[3] British policy in the Caribbean therefore was primarily defensive, keeping an eye on the Americans, trying to tie their hands by formal diplomatic arrangements, and removing all excuse for intervention by curbing the activities of Spanish pirates operating from Cuba. To the Americans Great Britain's activities looked selfishly ambitious rather than merely obstructive. Some of the English press certainly advocated the seizure of the island in 1823 and some army and navy officers found the idea both attractive and practical.[4] Canning

[1] Canning to Frere, 8 Jan. 1825, Gabrielle Festing, *John Hookham Frere and his Friends* (London, 1899), pp. 267–8.

[2] 'Memorandum on the proposed reduction of the army', 4 Aug. 1827, *Despatches, Correspondence, and Memoranda*, iv. 105–18.

[3] C. J. Bartlett, *Great Britain and Sea Power, 1815–1853* (Oxford, 1963), p. 70, note 1.

[4] Rippy, pp. 83–4, and Cockburn to Croker, 21 Feb. 1823, Croker papers, William Clements Library, Ann Arbor, Michigan.

himself may even have played momentarily with some scheme at the end of 1826 when a quarrel loomed up over Spanish policy towards Portugal; but his intention was probably only a naval attack, not permanent occupation.[1] In the Caribbean, then, British moves were limited to watching the Americans – and, of course, the French.[2]

Elsewhere the Americans would have had rather more justification for their suspicions, if the British had been able to find any potential base for which it was worth risking a quarrel with some other power or, worse, stimulating similar activities on its part. In the South Atlantic and on the Pacific coast, the British had no permanent base to support their squadrons. The Brazils squadron had to use a storeship anchored permanently in Rio, and when it was separated in 1837 the Pacific squadron had to establish its headquarters in similar fashion at Valparaiso. The Admiralty were therefore quite definitely interested in the Falkland and Hawaiian Islands, to both of which they believed Great Britain had some legitimate claim. But it was not clear that the latter could provide a suitable harbour, and in 1824 it was decided only to safeguard British interests by the appointment of a consul and by the visits of warships. At the same time the navy had orders to object if others attempted to seize the islands and if necessary to assume a protectorate.[3] The measure appeared in good time. In 1825 the first American squadron appeared in the Pacific and in 1826 an American warship paid its first visit to Honolulu. By 1836 the Americans had aroused considerable suspicion and a British admiral was forecasting their imminent annexation of both Hawaii and Tahiti.[4] Meanwhile the search continued for some alternative on the Pacific coast, including even San Francisco, which the government had surveyed in 1827 and again in 1839.[5] The Falklands, too, even Wellington hesitated to occupy, for fear of stimulating French and American rivalry and in 1829 it was decided to act only in anticipation of some aggressive move by either of those powers.[6] Nevertheless the islands were occupied in 1833.

[1] Canning to Liverpool, most secret and confidential, 6 Oct. 1826, Stapleton, ii. 144.
[2] A Swedish offer to sell the island of St Bartholomew in 1833 was met with a complete lack of interest: F.O. and C.O. to Adm., 11 and 14 Mar. 1833, Adm. 1/4251.
[3] Adm. to F.O., 5 July 1824, and Adm. to Capt. Lord Byron, 14 Sept. 1824, Adm. 2/1693; J. I. Brookes, *International Rivalry in the Pacific Islands, 1800–1875* (Berkeley and Los Angeles, 1941), pp. 49–50. When Lieutenant Wilkes reported for the U.S. on his Pacific exploring expedition of 1838, he too found the Hawaiian islands unimpressive as a naval base: *ibid.*, p. 65.
[4] *Ibid.*, pp. 61 and 64.
[5] N. A. Graebner, *Empire on the Pacific* (New York, 1955), pp. 68–9.
[6] Bartlett, p. 82.

The failure of the American government to invoke the Monroe Doctrine against the British occupation of the Falklands is notorious. Whatever the reason, it certainly symbolized the fading away of the supposed American threat and signalled the consolidation of British power and influence in Latin America. Within a few years after 1823, through the able and persistent efforts of British diplomacy and equally through the ineptitude of many of the American representatives, whatever danger there was had been completely averted. The United States had secured some favourable response over maritime rights but no more territory, and the futility and shallowness of any 'Transatlantic League' policy had been exposed at the congress of American states at Panama in 1826. By 1830 British influence and commerce reigned supreme almost everywhere. Already by February 1826 even Canning was saying:

The avowed pretension of the United States to put themselves at the head of the confederacy of all the Americans and to sway that Confederacy against Europe is *not* a pretension identified with our interests, or one that we can countenance or tolerate. It is, however, a pretension which there is no use in contesting in the abstract, but we must not say anything that seems to admit the principle.[1]

Canning's language, no doubt, was coloured and his hostility exaggerated as much by his cabinet difficulties as by a sense of affronted self-esteem. To persuade some of his colleagues, and not least the king, to commit themselves to the recognition of Latin American republics, he had had to make the situation sound much worse than it was. After his death in 1827 the temper of Anglo-American relations cooled rapidly. But if the spirit of Anglo-American relations under President Jackson and Prime Minister Wellington appeared to evince some special sympathy between generals, Wellington privately was still not reassured: 'I cannot avoid to feel a little anxiety respecting the existing state of the world, and the bout of fever in which our [French] neighbours are', he wrote to the secretary for war in September 1828. 'I consider that whenever we go to war at all we shall recommence the contest in America. Have you ever looked at the state of the American [i.e. British-American] militia laws?'[2] Friction between Spain and Mexico in 1828–30 found not only Wellington but even one of his less bellicose colleagues, Peel, still very apprehensive both of French intrigue and of

[1] Canning to Vaughan, 18 Feb. 1826, Temperley, p. 158.
[2] Wellington to Murray, private, 22 Sept. 1828, Murray papers, P.R.O., W.O. 80/2.

'the chance of the United States finding a good pretext for its interference and under pretence of putting down piracy, or a servile insurrection, getting possession of Cuba'.[1] Canning's attitude then had not been
merely a passing phase of fictitious or even personal hostility which had
evaporated with his death in 1827. What had happened rather was that
the threat of American expansion had been kept more quietly in check.
Moreover, even though much of the extravagance of Canning's language
in his pronouncements upon American affairs had been due to the
necessity of overawing a particularly obstinate opposition to his policies
in cabinet and at court, its memory survived to bequeath to his successors, and to Palmerston especially, a convenient manner of interpreta-
tion that was to do much to intensify the hostility of the 1840s and 1850s.

In the interval between Canning's death and the crises of the 1840s
general British opinion of the United States seriously deteriorated.
While the Reform Act agitation intensified the Tory drive to vilify
American 'mobocracy' in the 1830s, the apparent decline of political
life in the United States in the same period tended to alienate even the
moderate Whigs.[2] Among the critics' common observations was one
which gave encouragement to anti-American opinion, if despair to the
radicals. This was the apparent growth of sectionalism since Jackson's
accession to the presidency. The Americans' difficulties, with money,
militia, and the New England Federalists, in the war of 1812–14 had
already demonstrated both that government's ill-suitedness to the
efficient prosecution of war and the very fragility of the Union itself.
In spite of the political consolidation that had followed the news of
Ghent, Vaughan, the British minister, could still observe in 1827 that
'their form of govt. provides but a feeble executive to carry a country
through the exigencies of war', and that it was 'with reason that an
opinion is generally entertained in Europe of the instability of the
Union between these states so jealous of the distinct and separate
sovereignty which they exercise within the limits of their own territories'.[3] Vaughan had then gone on to say that there was 'in this

[1] Wellington to Aberdeen, 31 July 1829, and Peel to Aberdeen, private and
confidential, 13 Feb. 1830, Aberdeen papers, B.M.Add.MSS.43,057 and 43,061.
Peel had felt the same when the Eastern crisis loomed up in the previous year:
'Here then is a prospect of war, in which we are pretty nearly singlehanded against
Europe – and the "right of search" – and General Jackson ready to embroil
us in two months after its commencement, with the United States' (Peel to
Aberdeen, private, 23 Aug. 1829, ibid., B.M.Add.MS.43,061).
[2] David Paul Crook, *American Democracy in English Politics, 1815–1850*
(Oxford, 1965), p. 203.
[3] 'Effect or result of war between the United States and Great Britain, July
1827', C. R. Vaughan papers, All Souls College Library, Oxford.

strange and motley population, in which is to be found emigrants from every part of Europe, . . . a certain infusion of the good sense and steadiness of the English character which has made a right judgement predominate, at the very moment perhaps when the world at large was predicting confusion'. But the social and political tensions and crises of the 1830s suggested that this was no longer the case.

It seemed, then, that a really effective balance of power might be established in North America through the disintegration of the Union itself. At its most extreme this view promised to solve virtually all the problems of Great Britain's American policy. Alexander Baring, Lord Ashburton, who had a considerable interest, personal as well as commercial, in the prosperity of the United States and was to make a notable contribution to good Anglo-American relations in 1842, privately had little affection for that 'fickle democracy'. The Americans made 'troublesome neighbours' with whom 'nothing [was] more easy than to get into war . . . any morning with a very good cause'. 'But before you get into Cabul', he went on, 'you should consider how you are likely to get out again.'[1] He was worried of course by the immense damage that such a war would do to England's trade and finance: 'I always feel afraid of discussion with that people because I know their arrogance and I know that our weavers and spinners will bring upon us the most humiliating disgrace after the first six months of any conflict.' Thus while he was one of those who believed that 'our safety in our mixed government much depends on showing up the dark side of democracy', he also insisted that one must be careful not to give offence. 'Jonathan is the vainest and most thin skinned of mortals and an offensive article in a leading English review or a foolish bragging passage in . . . speech might . . . bring about war', he warned an anti-American publicist in 1838.[2] War, moreover, would have precisely the wrong effect in tending to consolidate the United States and in arousing all their latent power: 'If you want to continue that state of chaos

[1] Ashburton to Croker, 13 Feb. 1843, Croker papers, Clements Library.

[2] Ashburton to Croker, 22 March 1842, *ibid*. Ashburton was criticizing the draft of an article for the *Quarterly Review* (lxi, no. 122, 'The Ballot'). A few years later Ashburton cautioned him again, this time on the subject of his own American negotiations: 'I feel an anxiety about your writing because your temper, pretty good on most subjects, is irritable on everything connected with Jonathan and it is from pamphlets, periodicals, and journals that the great danger of an explosion arises. They are in truth the great disturbers of the informed world. They rule as we know to our cost in Paris but between mother and child in the new and old world the danger is infinitely increased. An article in the *Quarterly* or a sarcasm of Mr Dickens is read with intense sensitiveness in all parts of the Union' (13 Feb. 1843, Croker papers, Clements Library).

leave the wild beast alone, and when he approaches you walk if you can on the other side of the way.'[1] Ashburton was inclined to believe it would best suit Great Britain's interests to get out of the Americans' way not only in Texas but even in Canada. On the one hand, the recent rebellion in that colony suggested that Great Britain would be well rid of it. On the other, 'the American Union is always in danger and the danger will increase as ambition swells the Leviathan's back. Texas and Canada added, and a split will be inevitable'.[2] Such a view, at first at least, had little appeal for full-blooded British foreign secretaries; but it was always there as a convenient excuse and consolation for inaction and even diplomatic defeat.

When two rebellions, in Texas in 1835–36 and in Canada in 1837, enflamed the Anglo-American 'frontier' both in the south and in the north, they raised for each side apparent opportunities as well as dangers. All the old issues of competition and hostility on the boundary from Maine to Oregon were revived and their settlement made more urgent. With the addition of the newly enlarged issue to the south, however, the prospective improvement of a military frontier widened into a more crucial confrontation between the British balance of power policy and what was soon to become known as the Manifest Destiny of the United States. As it happened British policy concentrated at first on the problems of the northern frontier. The possible opportunity in Texas for improving the southern barrier against the expansion of the United States and perhaps opening a widening breach into the Union itself was by no means overlooked, but it was feebly pursued. Certainly it crumbled before an expansionism which now revived and drove in all directions more powerfully than ever before or since. In the north and north-west not only were all the unsettled boundary issues stirred up, but monarchy and European intrusion generally seemed on the brink of destruction. In the west and south the American transcontinental empire appeared on the verge of realization. For the British the drive of American *Manifest Destiny* brought dangers more critical even than the border crises in the north. Gradually it involved all the other keys in the balance of power, and as it moved from Texas, California, and Mexico, and out again to Cuba and Hawaii, British resistance stiffened.

[1] Ashburton to Bagot, private, 11 May 1842, Bagot papers, P.A.C., M.G. 24/A/13, vol. ii, pt. 1.
[2] Ashburton to Croker, 22 Mar. 1838, Croker papers, Clements Library.

Part 2

The Crises, 1836–1862

4

Texas and Maine, 1836–1842

In March 1836 resistance to the régime of Santa Anna in Mexico culminated in the declaration of Texan independence. In September a plebiscite voted overwhelmingly in favour of joining the United States and in August the following year the formal proposal was made. For the moment the growing sectional conflict in the States prevented the move, and talk of annexation subsided until 1842. But the continued threat of Mexican attack forced the Texans to turn to Great Britain for support. They probably hoped that this move would also frighten United States opinion into a more cooperative attitude. In 1837 a Texan agent arrived in England to seek the recognition already granted by the United States in March. But doubts about the nature of the new state and, above all, a desire not to prejudice their ability to mediate with Mexico stopped the British government short of such a decision. In November it was decided to recognize the independence of Texas but further difficulties held up the formal conclusion until June 1842. In response, the American government itself revived the annexation project in the following year. By the end of 1843 Great Britain and the United States appeared to be moving into open conflict on the southern frontier of the Union.

In the north the frontier had been enflamed by the outbreak of rebellion against the British régime in Canada in November 1837. Before the end of the year recruiting for the revolt had already begun on the American side of the border, and a Canadian government force had crossed the Niagara River and burned the American ship, *Caroline*, which had been used to supply the rebels. In the United States the monarchy in North America was at first deemed to be approaching its inevitable fate and sympathy for the rebels was widespread and noisy. Secret societies, like the 'Sons of Liberty' and the 'Hunters Lodges', were formed with the avowed object of revolutionizing Canada and promoting republican institutions, and with their aid several attacks were staged from across the border into Canada during 1838. The rebels' popularity, the limitations on his constitutional powers, and the weakness of the available military forces made it difficult for President Van Buren to take really effective action against these illegal activities. But General Winfield Scott nevertheless did very good work on the frontier, dashing about with his force to check the raids. All of those which did break through were easily repulsed and as the revolt petered out in the second half of 1838 American opinion generally began to appreciate that most Canadians did not wish to join the Republic. But however much each government wished to avoid war, both realized how delicate was the situation on the border. Any incident, like the burning of the *Caroline*, might lead to war; indeed, one of the secret societies, the Canadian Refugee Relief Association, had such an object in mind when in May 1838 some of its members burned the British steamboat, *Sir Robert Peel*. While the Hunters kept this dangerous situation alive on the Canadian border throughout 1839, the still unresolved Maine boundary dispute flared up again in the same year with clashes between local inhabitants and local authorities and with military forces on both sides apparently moving to a conflict. For a time General Scott's intervention and good sense on the part of both governments managed to damp down the crisis here too. But from the end of 1838 into the early 1840s the whole northern frontier remained in a dangerous state of excitement and uncertainty. Any incident might have brought war and such an incident threatened to arise in November 1840 when Alexander McLeod, a British citizen supposed to have been involved in the *Caroline* affair, was arrested in New York State on the capital charges of murder and arson.[1]

The coincidence of the two revolts in Texas and Canada in 1836 and 1837 did not immediately bring out the full force of the movement which was later to become known as Manifest Destiny, and correspondingly, no real alarm was at first expressed in the policy of the British government. Both countries were involved in other difficulties and, for that reason as well as others, too anxious for conciliation to run headlong into a major international crisis. Still the frontiers of the United States were now generally at issue and both sides recognized from the first the potential dangers and opportunities. Texas had after all been one of the areas of Anglo-American contest in Latin America in the 1820s and England's local representatives had constantly sought to counter and defeat United States penetration and expansion into the area. In the summer of 1836 voices were raised in parliament against the extension of slavery, and the loss of Mexico's richest mining

[1] This summary of the crisis on the Canadian boundary is based on Albert B. Corey, *The Crisis of 1830–1842 in Canadian-American Relations* (New Haven, 1941).

assets and the command of the Caribbean to the United States. In reply the foreign secretary, Lord Palmerston, agreed that the United States could not be allowed to 'pursue a system of aggrandizement' and that their annexation of Texas would be a question 'which ought seriously to engage the attention of the House and of the British public'.[1] But Palmerston never developed a really active policy with regard to Texas. He worked reasonably hard at encouraging a settlement between Mexico and Texas, recognizing throughout that reconquest was out of the question. In 1839 he even talked of the advantage of such a barrier between Mexico and the United States on the one hand, and, on the other, of the danger of driving Texas into the Union.[2] But this was clearly an attempt to persuade the reluctant Mexicans to come to terms with the rebels. Not until November 1840 did he conclude commercial and other treaties with the new state and even then he was apparently so unafraid of, or so uninterested in, the danger of driving Texas into the arms of the United States that when he left office a year later ratification was still being held up in an attempt to secure Texan agreement to a slave trade treaty as well.[3] In part, Palmerston's comparative indifference was due to some concern for British relations with Mexico and, after the annexationists' failure in August 1837, to the improbability of any early admission to the Union. Texas never caught his imagination as a promising area for his statecraft. This he made clear in a letter he wrote to a cabinet colleague in October 1837:

. . . We cannot pretend to exert much influence on the destiny of Texas; & have little to do, but to watch the course of events.

Mexico will not reconquer Texas; we must see whether the Band of outlaws who occupy Texas will be able to constitute themselves into such a community as it would be decent for us to make a Treaty with – At all events it would not do for us to make a Treaty with a self denominated State, till events had proved that such a state could permanently maintain its independence.

Perhaps when the Texians no longer fear Mexico, their wish for admission into the Northern Union may diminish. That admission would be objected to by the Northern States who are not slave holders, & by the cotton growers of the southern states. . . . The latter Parties would view with jealousy the superior fertility of the Texas soil; & would fear that if that soil were brought into full cultivation the Price of Cotton would be lowered by the increased production of it; & that they should not make proper interest upon the Capital they have invested in their own cotton lands.

[1] See E. D. Adams, *British Interests and Activities in Texas, 1838–1846* (Baltimore, 1910), pp. 16–17.

[2] *Ibid.*, pp. 29–30.   [3] *Ibid.*, pp. 54–9 and 67.

To us perhaps it does not very much signify what becomes of Texas, though in a Political view it would be better that Texas should not be incorporated with the Union; commercially it would make little difference. But we may be pretty sure that if it should suit the Two States to unite, their union would not be prevented by a Commercial Treaty between us and Texas. I told Iturbide the Mexican chargé d'affaires the other day when he wanted us to help Mexico against Texas, that the Mexicans behave so ill to us, & the North Americans so honestly that as far as our Commercial Interests are concerned we should have no objection to see the whole of Mexico belong to the United States. He laughed and said perhaps I was right.[1]

Given that British anxieties and British forces were soon diverted in a succession of grave crises in Europe and Asia – the first Afghan War (1839–42), the second Egyptian crisis (1839–41), and the Opium War (1839–42) – it is no wonder that even Palmerston was reluctant to waste much time on Texas. In the end he was moved to speed up the treaty negotiations only by the news that France – as well as the United States, Belgium, and Holland – had already recognized the new state.

I cannot believe [the Texan agent at once took the opportunity to write to him] that it is your Lordship's wish to have another 'Mahomet Ali' on the Shores of the Gulf of Mexico, under the influences of a most friendly and politic alliance with your jealous neighbour – not too in the shape of an ignorant, ferocious & licentious Barbarian, but in the embodied form of a free, civilised & valiant people, speaking your own language, & pushing with the steadiness & invincibility of British bravery, the sceptre of Conquest, over regions which dwarf into absolute insignificance the whole of Egypt & her relations, past, present, & to come.[2]

Although it had taken years for Palmerston to act on Texas, it was hardly to be expected that there would be similar forbearance about the dangers looming on the borders of British North America. As it had been decided not to send out any army reinforcements to Canada in the previous summer, the Canadian rebellion found the number of British regulars in North America in January 1838 still about 4,500 and of these only some 2,000 were in Canada. During 1838 over 10,000 militia and volunteers were brought into active service in the Canadas and in 1839 the figure rose to over 21,000. In September 1838 30,000 stand of arms were sent out from England to supplement the 9,000 already at Quebec. But the realization that even these would be insuffi-

[1] Palmerston to T. Spring Rice (chancellor of the Exchequer), private (copy), 9 Oct. 1837, Broadlands papers.
[2] General Hamilton to Palmerston, 8 Oct. 1840, Broadlands papers. For Palmerston's quick reaction see his letter to Russell, 18 Oct., *ibid.*

cient to cope with the rebellion had led the government in December 1837 to prepare to raise the force in North America to 10,000 men, exclusive of artillery, as soon as the season permitted. In February 1838 news of the *Caroline* incident led them to add a further two regiments. In December the same year they promised another three or four regiments in view of the activities of the secret societies. By the spring of 1839 the number of regulars in the Canadas alone had risen to over 10,500, and a year later to nearly 11,500, including two battalions of guards.[1] Meanwhile, in January 1838, the army asked the Admiralty whether they could establish a small naval squadron, perhaps recruited in Canada, to cruise on the St Lawrence between Montreal and Quebec. In February Captain Sandom, R.N., arrived to reform the naval establishment in Canadian waters. By January 1839 he had purchased or hired three small steamboats and 'a few' gunboats for Lake Ontario, three large steamboats and three schooners for Lake Erie, and one or two other vessels for use elsewhere. By the end of the year he was able to claim: 'I have by dint of perseverance formed a little navy and my establishment is reckoned to be four hundred men exclusive of artificers – at present two commanders, nine lieutenants, fifteen mates etc. I have four steamboats, some schooners, gunboats and rowboats.'[2] At the same time the force on the North American and West Indian station rose significantly. On 1 January 1838 there were twenty-seven vessels on the station; by 1 June the number had risen to thirty-six, and by 1 November to forty-one, principally by the addition of steamships, but also of some large vessels.[3]

These were all very impressive increases in British military strength in North America and though aimed primarily at suppressing the rebellion and pacifying the border they also reflected a growing apprehension of war with the United States. British officials in North America had almost from the very beginning expressed the fear that such a war would come. As early as February 1838 Lieutenant-General Sir John Colborne, the governor of Lower Canada and commander-in-chief of the army in the Canadas, was insisting that 'the placing of a respectable army of occupation in the Canadas for a year or perhaps

[1] Corey, pp. 66–7 and 104–6; Jackson to Fitzroy Somerset, 1 Dec. 1842, W.O. 1/538, gives a useful table of the forces in Canada, 1838–42.
[2] Corey, pp. 69 and 108–10; Sandom to Colchester, private, 26 Jan. and 15 Sept. 1839, and 13 Feb. 1846, Colchester papers, P.R.O. 30/9/2, pt. 2, 30/9/2, pt. 1, and 30/9/6, pt. 1.
[3] Adm. 8/118. The reinforcement may have had as much or more to do with the French blockade of Mexico in 1838 (C. J. Bartlett, *Great Britain and Sea Power, 1815–1853* [Oxford, 1963], p. 118).

longer would be . . . best calculated to prevent war with the United States'.[1] Colborne, however, continued to believe in the anxiety of the American government to avoid war.[2] Sir George Arthur, the lieutenant-governor of Upper Canada, was just as eager that the army should be strengthened, and much more certain that it would be needed against the United States. 'I quite agreed with you that the American Government must be anxious to avoid war with us,' he wrote to Colborne in April 1838, 'but how are they to help it if the People will it?' At this time he believed war would come 'at no distant period'; by February 1839 that it could 'scarcely be avoided'; and in spite of the frequent lulls in the crisis he continued to forecast war.[3] Throughout he found his position as the guardian of one of the British Empire's most vulnerable frontiers distinctly uncomfortable:

I have restrained and shall endeavour to restrain attempts in this quarter, to make reprisals in the United States; not because I feel that the making them would be unjustified; but because this is obviously not the place in which such a course could be effectually taken. I may by the conflagration of Detroit, Buffalo, Lewiston and Ogdensburg awaken the partially dormant hostilities of America; but I cannot check it by producing the serious consequences of a marine war, and attack upon the great Atlantic cities. . . .

This Canadian contest in my opinion, cannot end without an American war. It is probable however, that our Government cannot be easily persuaded of the futility of all attempts to conciliate the United States, until the thin veil, which is now spread over American Politics is withdrawn. In the meantime, however, I shall have discharged my duty by declaring, in the most exposed and defenceless portion of the empire, that, I believe, war is inevitable, unless the American Government can be induced by strong remonstrances on the part of England, not only to *profess amity* but to *enforce it*.[4]

This letter was one of several Arthur wrote privately to Henry Stephen Fox, the minister in Washington, and in him Arthur found a fellow spirit. As early as the end of November 1837 Fox was advising that reinforcements to Canada should not be sent via the easier route through United States territory for fear of arousing popular interest:

[1] Colborne to Sir Colin Campbell (lieutenant-governor of Nova Scotia), private, 21 Feb. 1838, Fox papers, P.R.O., F.O. 97/18 (H. S. Fox was British minister at Washington).
[2] Colborne to Arthur, private, 24 Mar. and 11 May 1838, C. R. Sanderson, ed., *The Arthur Papers* (Toronto, 1943), i. 65–6 and 118.
[3] Arthur to Colborne, private, 5 April 1838, to J. F. Love, 14 Feb. 1839, and to various correspondents, 1839–40, *ibid.*, i. 71, and ii. 45, 109, 149–50, 197, 212, and 393.
[4] Arthur to Fox, confidential, 15 Nov. 1838, Fox papers, F.O. 97/18.

If the game that has been played towards Texas, or anything approaching to it, were attempted with respect to Canada, the two countries might be driven into a war, in despite of the best intentions on the part of the supreme government. I repeat, that I do not think there is at present any disposition amongst the people of the U.S. to interest themselves in the quarrel of the Canadian malcontents . . . but the continuance of this state of indifference is of such incalculable value that we cannot too studiously avoid anything which might tend however remotely to disturb it.[1]

By the new year he had become less sanguine about the American attitude. Hitherto, he wrote to Colborne, he had felt that the United States government was behaving very well in very difficult circumstances and that both parties desired friendship with Great Britain. But recent American assistance to the rebels had made him apprehensive of war and though the immediate danger seemed to have pretty well passed, it had left a nasty taste. The United States had given every *outward* appearance of doing their best, but Fox was no longer satisfied with their conduct. 'Upon a full consideration, I am unavoidably brought to the conviction that this Government both wished and expected the Canadian rebellion would succeed.' What they were looking to, he warned, was the annexation of Canada to the United States.[2] By March 1838 he believed 'the crisis of immediate danger' was over and even that the chances were 'clearly in favor' of peace but 'the final settling of accounts, for what has passed, [might] yet lead to discussions between the two governments, of the most extreme importance and of great hazard to the preservation of peace'. Hence he wrote to the commander-in-chief of the North American squadron:

I do not desire to excite unnecessary alarm: but I would venture, confidentially, to recommend to Your Excellency, so to regulate the situation of your squadron, as to render it most available in the event of war breaking out, suddenly, between Great Britain and the United States. You will agree with me, looking to what happened in former times, that if we should unfortunately be forced into a war with the Americans, it would be of immense importance for us to be enabled to commence that war by an astounding blow upon their navigation and commerce.[3]

A year later he was still urging preparation.[4] Evidently he would have preferred the naval preparations to be a little more apparent for he complained as diplomats are wont to:

The worst obstacle which meets me tacitly at every step in my course of

[1] Fox to Sir John Harvey (lieutenant-governor of New Brunswick), 30 Nov. 1837, Fox papers, F.O. 97/17.   [2] Fox to Colborne, 19 Jan. 1838, *ibid.*
[3] Fox to Adm. Sir Charles Paget, secret and confidential, 15 Mar. 1838, *ibid.*
[4] Fox to Adm. Sir Thomas Harvey (Paget's successor), 30 July 1839, *ibid.*

duty here, is the impression upon the minds of the Americans that we are not in earnest in our resolution to retain the North American Provinces; and it unfortunately does not rest with any of Her Majesty's servants on this side of the Atlantic, to remove that impression.[1]

Considering the large numbers of troops poured into Canada by this time both Fox and Arthur were being rather unfair to their masters. But opinion in England, both government and press, did remain for a long time impressed with the conciliatory behaviour of the American government and with the distracting crises elsewhere in the world. Only *The Times* and the *Morning Herald* as yet apparently 'betrayed a marked anti-American bias'.[2] In March 1838 Lord Stanley spoke in the House of Commons of 'the candid, honorable, and handsome manner', in which the American government had conducted itself.[3] And though less fulsome, the attitude on the government side was very similar. Thus the reinforcements ordered to North America in December 1837 were designed to crush the rebellion and pacify the border rather than prepare for war with the United States. After February 1838 the government resisted demands for further troops on the grounds that there were already enough for these tasks and that more would unnecessarily alarm the United States and strain Anglo-American relations. Only in December did reports of the activities of the Hunters Lodges really arouse the apprehension of the government. On 11 December the colonial secretary, Lord Glenelg, wrote to Colborne promising a further three or four regiments.[4] Even so the prime minister was still inclined to follow a more conciliatory line. The conduct of the American government, Melbourne thought, was satisfactory so far as it went; and rather than make a martial display he suggested to Palmerston on 15 December that the two governments might make some mutual arrangement to quieten things on the frontier:

I am aware that it is a very delicate matter, in as much as it touches the internal law and the constitution, and I am aware also that we do not

[1] Fox to Arthur, private, 30 Aug. 1839, Fox papers, F.O. 97/17. Like his famous uncle Fox had a reputation for good living. Perhaps what he most resented at this time therefore was the sort of advice Palmerston attached to one of his instructions on the Maine boundary question: 'I hope you will ... cultivate the Americans as much as you can. Much may be accomplished by frequent, & constant Social Intercourse with Men with whom public Business is to be transacted; and Sir C. Vaughan not only made himself personally popular by his Habits of easy Intercourse with the leading Persons at Washington but he acquired thereby facilities for the Transaction of Business which he would not otherwise have had – he lived the life of the Place where he lived and found great Advantage from doing it' (Palmerston to Fox, 6 April 1839, Fox papers, F.O. 97/19).
[2] Corey, p. 86.   [3] *Ibid.*, p. 86, note 15.   [4] *Ibid.*, pp. 66–7 and 105–6.

stand so free from the same sort of conduct as to enable us to complain with very good grace. We have by no means been able, nor indeed always willing to restrain our subjects from interfering in the internal affairs of other countries, and I have always thought that this practice of subjects making war, whilst Governments were at peace was very inconvenient in itself and would lead to greater inconveniences – anything therefore that we can do must be done amicably. I think we should make great allowance for the situation of the American government and particularly that we shall if possible abstain from any violation of their territory.[1]

But by the end of the month Glenelg had persuaded the prime minister that Colborne was right and that 'the question of peace or war depends upon our showing ourselves in earnest in this matter'.[2]

Strangely enough it was Palmerston who responded least among the principal ministers to the alarmist reports from North America. He was naturally more interested in affairs in Europe and the East and hitherto his relations with the United States had been peculiarly friendly. It was only a short while ago, in the Franco-American quarrel of 1834–36, that he had acted as the peacemaker in America.[3] When, during 1831–32, Van Buren had been minister in London, Palmerston seems to have been on very good terms with him; so much so, indeed, that the American later went out of his way to correct the impression of Palmerston's prejudice against the United States and on the contrary to affirm his 'genial and conciliatory disposition'.[4] In the present difficulties Palmerston's attitude had from the beginning been one of quiet confidence both in the pacific disposition of the American government and in the efficacy of British firmness. 'The land jobbers of Maine must learn to be more reasonable,' he wrote to Fox in November 1837, 'and they will become so, when they find that we do not care for their swagger; that

---

[1] Melbourne to Palmerston, 15 Dec. 1838, Broadlands papers. The suggestion for an 'arrangement' arose out of the American government's statement in October that it would be unable to deploy a sufficient force to prevent the Hunters' invasion. Fox had therefore suggested the American government give advance sanction for any violations of their territory resulting from Canadian reprisals or 'hot pursuit'. On 15 December Palmerston sent him instructions to make such a proposal, but Fox had already approached the American government and been repulsed (Corey, pp. 107–8).

[2] Melbourne to Howick (secretary at war, later third Earl Grey), 30 Dec. 1838, Grey of Howick papers, microfilms in P[ublic] A[rchives of] C[anada], M[anuscript] G[roup] 24/A/10, reel 3 (A 405).

[3] C. K. Webster, 'British Mediation between France and the United States, 1834–36', *English Historical Review*, xlii (1927), 58–78.

[4] John C. Fitzpatrick, ed., *The Autobiography of Martin Van Buren* [American Historical Association Annual Report for 1918, vol. ii] (Washington, 1920), pp. 465–6. For a general description of the early phase of Palmerston's American relations, see Herbert C. F. Bell, *Lord Palmerston* (2 vols., London, 1936), i. 230–47.

we are resolved to keep the whole [of the disputed territory], till an amicable arrangement is made; and that we are quite strong enough to do so. The Central Government must see & feel that Maine puts forward an unjustifiable pretension and the union is not likely to choose to involve itself in war to please a few speculators in Maine.'[1] So far as the American difficulties were concerned it was the Maine boundary rather than the Canadian rebellion that occupied him and this he believed he had safely disposed of for a year or two by an agreement he made with the Americans at the end of 1838 for a new joint commission to survey and determine the frontier.[2] The agreement was not as effective as he had hoped and in the new year clashes on this part of the frontier culminated in what was called the 'Aroostook War'. 'If the People of Maine will not listen to the President, & persist in their present Intentions of settling in the disputed Territory and of taking forcible Possession of it, they must be expelled by Force of Arms, let the consequences be what they may', he warned Fox in April.[3] But though firm he continued to be reassured by the Van Buren administration's conciliatory policy and, not less important, by their apparent neglect of naval preparation for war.[4] A year later, he still had 'no

[1] Palmerston to Fox, 19 Nov. 1837, Fox papers, F.O. 97/19.

[2] See his memorandum for Melbourne, 'The exact State of the N. American Boundary Question . . .', 4 May 1840, Broadlands papers. Palmerston admitted in a letter of 20 Oct. 1839 to Russell that while the survey scheme would delay a settlement for a year or two it would also in the meantime 'keep things quiet'. Russell evidently objected to this delay and on 25 Oct. 1839 Palmerston replied: 'I believe you are quite right about the feeling of Van Buren and Clay towards England, though probably any President would find that it is the interest of the United States to remain at Peace with England. But do not suppose that I wish to *decide* to defer a settlement of the Boundary question for two years – on the contrary I should be delighted to settle it in two days; but there are two parties concerned in the matter, and though nothing would be easier than to settle the question at once, if we were to choose to give up the whole territory to the Americans, yet if we mean to keep that which rightly belongs to us, and which I believe will turn out to be, very nearly all we have ever claimed, there are but two ways of doing so, the one by going to war and forcing the Americans to give us what we ask, the other by negotiation and proving to the Americans that we are justly entitled to what we ask. The first mode is out of the question, and the latter requires time.' Hence he arranged the survey for the latter case; but the commissioners would not be able to complete a survey before the end of 1840 and so there could be no settlement until 1841. Actually no joint commission was ever appointed, and the British one, with which Palmerston insisted on going ahead, reported back in the spring of 1840. (Palmerston to Russell, 20 and 25 Oct. 1839, Russell papers, P.R.O. 30/22/3D; see also Bell, i. 251–2.)

[3] Palmerston to Fox, 6 April 1839, Fox papers, F.O. 97/19.

[4] He had asked Fox in the spring of 1838 for information about the American navy's 'movements and preparations', and Fox had replied on 17 May 1838 that the Americans were less prepared for war than at any time since 1814 and quite overawed by Britain's strength (Corey, p. 102, note 1). At the same time Congress

fear of war arising out of this Question if we act with ordinary Prudence':

The great mass of the Union do not care two straws about it, and even in the state of Maine the outcry is a factitious one raised by a few land jobbers & speculators; and Maine herself would think Twice before she engaged in actual hostility with us upon this matter. The Maine men talk very big, and encroach readily enough when unresisted; but they will stop whenever they are opposed. The states of the Union are in a Condition of general Bankruptcy, and that does not give a fancy for maritime war to a nation who live by commerce and who have made no naval Preparations whatever for a Fight by sea. Moreover Maine is the only state, with the Exception perhaps of New Hampshire, that has any direct Interest whatever in this Question. But Van Buren has recently purchased the Consent of Maine to allow this question to be dealt with exclusively by the Central Govt., and this gets rid of Danger of local Collisions. Maine incurred a Debt for the equipment of her militia last year, *and she cannot pay it*; and Van Buren has undertaken that it shall be paid by the Central Govt., if Maine will leave to that Govt. the Disposal of the Question. But is it likely that Maine would undertake an expensive war, when she cannot pay even the cost of a short Demonstration last year?[1]

What most tended to maintain Palmerston in this attitude was the growing crisis over Mahomet Ali's claims in the Mediterranean. In June 1839 the Turkish armies had been decisively defeated by the Egyptians at Nezib; in July the great powers moved in concert to settle the eastern question; but in March of the following year Thiers assumed office in Paris, and by July 1840 Palmerston was well launched on the course that led to Acre and the breach with France. In October 1839 he was already suggesting the government might spare 'a ship or two' from the West Indies. And just as his concentration upon the crisis in Europe led him to play down the crisis in America, so Lord John Russell, who had recently moved to the Colonial Office and who led the dissatisfaction with Palmerston's anti-French line, sought to reverse the emphasis. In October 1839 Russell was suggesting that affairs on the Canadian border were more pressing than Turkey and Egypt and objecting both to any reduction of the fleet in American waters and to Palmerston's delaying tactics over the Maine boundary question. During the following summer he continued to press his differences with Palmerston, and in September was threatening his

---

had severely mutilated an attempt to increase the army, providing in July 1838 for an increase of 4,650 instead of the 6,650 asked (*ibid.*, pp. 58–60). Some repairs were carried out on the frontier fortresses in 1838 and 1839 but a major attempt to revive the fortification scheme was not made until July 1840, the necessary bill being passed in September (*ibid.*, p. 151).

[1] Palmerston to Lansdowne, 25 April 1840, Broadlands papers.

resignation and predicting war with both France and the United States.[1] But by the end of 1840, though many difficult negotiations lay ahead, Palmerston's eastern policy had been brought to a triumphant climax by the fall of Thiers and the capture of Acre. When the news of McLeod's arrest arrived in England the foreign secretary was relatively free at last to acknowledge the existence of a crisis in America.

In December Fox was reporting the American government's insistence that it could not interfere with the jurisdiction of the New York courts, and in the new year came the news of the first, abusive debate in Congress.[2] On 9 February 1841 Fox was sent official instructions to demand McLeod's release and if this were refused and McLeod were condemned and executed Fox was to quit Washington, at the same time telling the governor-general of Canada and the naval commanders on the American station what had happened.[3] The 'substance' of this latter part of his instructions Fox was also to communicate to the president 'confidentially, but not officially', and lest there remained the slightest possibility of misunderstanding, Palmerston also communicated privately with both the American minister in London, Andrew Stevenson, and with Fox himself. 'Speaking not officially but as a Private Friend', Palmerston told Stevenson that 'if McLeod is executed there must be war'; and Fox was to disabuse the president and the secretary of state of any illusions they might have about States' Rights in matters of jurisdiction and foreign relations:

... if any harm should be done to McLeod the indignation and resentment of all England will be extreme. Mr Van Buren should understand this, and that the British nation will never permit a British subject to be dealt with as the people of New York propose to deal with McLeod, without taking a signal revenge upon the offenders. McLeod's execution would produce war, war immediate and frightful in its character because it would be a war of retaliation and vengeance.

It is impossible that Mr Forsyth can wish to bring upon the two countries such a calamity, and we can have no doubt that he will prevent it. He must have the means of doing so, or else the Federal Union exists but in name.[4]

[1] Palmerston to Russell, 17, 20, and 25 Oct. 1839, and Russell to Melbourne, 26 April and 20 Sept. 1840, Russell papers, P.R.O. 30/22/3.

[2] Corey, pp. 131–2.

[3] Palmerston to Fox, nos. 4 and 5, 9 Feb. 1841, C.O. 42/382 (where the correspondence on the McLeod affair is conveniently brought together in a cabinet print).

[4] Palmerston to Fox, 9 Feb. 1841, Evelyn Ashley, *The Life and Correspondence of Henry John Temple, Viscount Palmerston* (2 vols., London, 1879), i. 408.

With Palmerston taking the prospect of war more seriously the government at last moved in the direction of military preparations which would be effective for war with the United States rather than merely for the pacification of the border. Such preparations certainly seemed urgent. In December 1838 there had been 3,200 regulars in the Jamaica command, including five British and one West Indian infantry battalions. But to replace the troops moved up from the Maritime Provinces into Canada two of the British battalions had been removed and by May 1839 the command was considered 'dangerously weak'.[1] Nor were the fortifications in any state to compensate for the weakness in men. In 1841 the garrison of the Bahamas numbered only three hundred instead of the agreed five hundred and the principal fort was in a poor state.[2] Of the Windward and Leeward Islands generally the officer commanding the troops commented: 'With very few exceptions the Defences of this Command are very much out of repair; and of 109 pieces of ordnance at St Lucia and Dominica, 50 are quite unserviceable.'[3] Even Bermuda, which opinion unanimously asserted was of vital importance in an American war and likely to be the immediate object of an attack if improperly defended, still awaited the completion of the works approved under the scheme of 1826.[4]

The Bahamas were hardly important enough any longer, it seems, to deserve attention unless war actually broke out,[5] but Russell had not been by any means idle with places like Bermuda. On assuming the Colonial Office in September 1839 he had found himself presented with various questions relating to colonial defence which he thought

---

[1] Printed 'Minute on the present state and demands of the British Army serving on Colonial stations', May 1839, C.O. 537/155.

[2] Col. Cockburn to C.O., 17 April 1841, W.O. 1/579.

[3] Lord Vivian (master-general) to Sir Frederick W. Mulcaster (inspector-general of fortifications), 25 Feb. 1841, W.O. 46/36.

[4] See, e.g., J. W. Croker to Russell, private and confidential, 13 March 1841, Russell papers, P.R.O. 30/22/4A. In July 1839 Fox had reported that the Americans believed the population were not loyal to their British connection, the islands having once been formally part of Virginia. Consequently, he suggested, the Americans' 'course of aggrandisement is even more likely to be attempted by political intrigues and encroachments, than by open assault' ('Précis of some despatches and papers relating to the defence of the Bermuda Islands', April 1840, C.O. 537/155; the papers referred to may be found in W.O. 44/505). An American spy who was in Bermuda in 1841 reported very differently: 'The inhabitants are well satisfied with their government and anticipate great spoils in the event of war with the United States' (Albert Fitz to Secretary of State Webster, 21 July 1842, Despatches of Special Agents, vol. xii, 1836–42, General Records of the Department of State, U.S. N[ational] A[rchives], R[ecord] G[roup] 59).

[5] Minute on Cockburn to C.O., 17 April 1841, W.O. 1/579.

ought not to be left to 'desultory settlement' and to review them he had appointed a special departmental committee.[1] One of the positions to which their attention was first turned was Bermuda and by May 1840 it had already been decided to press on with the 1826 scheme, with modifications to meet attacks by steam ships, and, when barracks were ready, to increase the garrison at once to two full battalions as the 1826 scheme had always intended.[2] Work still seemed to take an inordinate amount of time but an American spy at least was impressed with what had been done by the middle of 1841. The garrison, he reckoned, totalled about '1,500 men in a high state of efficiency'; and the works, though incomplete, already mounted over a hundred powerful guns and promised 'to be one of the most impregnable fortresses in the western hemisphere'. The defence works in the British West Indies, however, including those in Jamaica, he thought were all 'fast going to decay', and he understood that the principal reliance for defence would be placed upon the fleet.[3] In 1840 and 1841 Russell was trying to make room in the estimates for a barracks for half a battalion of infantry at Woodstock in New Brunswick to check any American force advancing from Houlton against the Temiscouata road.[4] In the Canadas there was no real question about the necessity of keeping up a large force of regulars for internal security even if not everyone was convinced of the need to guard against foreign war. Throughout 1840 and 1841 Russell kept the force of regulars in Canada at about 11,500 men and in August 1841 even managed to secure the formation of a local regiment, the Royal Canadian Rifles.[5]

With naval forces Russell had rather less success, no doubt because of the enormous demands made by Palmerston's policy in the eastern Mediterranean. By the beginning of 1840 the force on the North American station had already fallen from its peak of forty-one vessels in the summer of 1839 to twenty-eight, none of them a battleship.[6] On the lakes he was a little more successful. One of the old vessels preserved at Kingston, the brig *Niagara*, formerly *Netley*, was commissioned, and

---

[1] Russell to Vivian, private, 14 Sept. 1839, Russell papers, P.R.O. 30/22/3D.
[2] Committee to C.O., 12 May 1840 and C.O. to Treasury, 23 May 1840, W.O. 1/596. In April 1840 the garrison consisted of only a company each of artillery and engineers and 487 infantry: 'Précis etc.', C.O. 537/155.
[3] Fitz to Webster, 21 July 1842, *loc. cit.*
[4] Various correspondence in W.O. 1/537.
[5] His original scheme had been to form a battalion of veterans but this was dropped as it might be impossible legally to require them to cross the frontier. The principal purpose was, however, still to check desertion (*ibid.*).
[6] Return of 1 Jan. 1840, Adm. 8/119.

though this was really only an unseaworthy hulk, by September 1841 Sandom had a force of four steamships and a schooner on the lakes. One of the 500-ton steamboats, *Minos*, had been specially built for this purpose in 1840 and was in itself a considerable breach of the 1817 agreement.[1] Nevertheless in February 1841 the Admiralty had ordered the construction of two more steamboats on the lakes.[2] Thereafter Sandom kept up his pressure to meet the growing danger of war. 'The Americans are braggarts,' he wrote home in April, 'and would easily be brought to their bearings if promptness in action, and ample means were resorted to.' In February he was asking for another twenty gunboats, armed with eighteen or twenty-four pounders, for Lake Ontario and for the Rivers Niagara and St Lawrence; in April for the enlargement of the Welland canal so that his force could pass from Kingston into Lake Erie; and in the same month for his ninety marines and three hundred seamen to be increased to eight hundred and twelve hundred respectively. But the Admiralty had had enough and could find no more room in the estimates for the lakes; even Arthur felt the Welland scheme unworthwhile at £250,000.[3]

Rather more difficult than any of these questions was that of the still far from complete fortification of the Canadian frontier. Until 1840 the government in London and Colborne in Canada had both been thinking in terms of a protection against filibuster attacks from the United States. In March 1839 Colborne had proposed the establishment of a line of posts along the border designed to protect the frontier at its weakest points. In September Russell had rejected this scheme in favour of the supposedly cheaper alternative of military settlements, but two months later when Colborne, now Lord Seaton, submitted a revised scheme, Russell pressed it upon the Board of Ordnance.[4] Seaton's new scheme

[1] An Admiralty statement of 13 Sept. 1841 shows the lakes force as the *Niagara*, two steam vessels, *Traveller* and *Experiment*, and the schooner, *Montreal*, at Kingston, and two steam vessels, *Minos* and *Toronto*, on Lake Erie. There was another schooner, *Bullfrog*, in a defective state at Port Colborne on Lake Erie. (Adm. to W.O., 13 Sept. 1841, W.O. 1/537.)
[2] Adm. to C.O., 8 Feb. 1841, C.O. 42/482. These were the *Mohawk* and *Cherokee*.
[3] Sandom to Colchester, 6 April 1841, Colchester papers, P.R.O. 30/9/2 pt. 1; Sandom to Lord Sydenham (governor-general of Canada), 8 Feb., Sandom to Adm, 5 April, Adm. to C.O., 26 March, and minute of 29 May 1841, C.O. 42/482.
[4] Colborne to Glenelg, 18 Mar., and Russell to C. P. Thomson (Lord Sydenham), 7 Sept. 1839, Corey, pp. 148–9; Seaton to Russell, 30 Dec. 1839, enclosing 'Memoranda respecting the defence of Upper Canada with reference to the present state of the Province and the Hostility of the American Patriots', and James Stephen (colonial under-secretary) to R. Byham (under-secretary at the Ordnance), 13 Jan. 1839, in 'Papers relative to the Fortifications and Defences of Canada', confidential, 'printed solely for the use of the Cabinet', n.d., W.O. 1/536.

proposed to spend £240,000 on the erection of barracks and permanent defence works at a few of the more vulnerable places on the frontier, particularly on the Niagara frontier and the Richelieu River. He had already spent £40,000 on the barracks and now it was agreed to spend another £20,000 a year on the defence works. When these and the works still going on at Quebec, Halifax, and Kingston were completed, the most important parts of the old 1825 scheme would have been accomplished. But as proper plans and estimates had not yet been prepared and as nothing could be done during the winter in any case, the vote was postponed until the estimates for 1841–42.[1]

By this time Seaton's successor as commander-in-chief in Canada, Lieutenant-General Sir Richard Jackson, had had time to review the military situation and he was rather more impressed than his predecessor with the need to provide for war with the United States. The Americans, he pointed out in a memorandum of March 1840, at present had only 12,000 regular soldiers and these were barely adequate to cope with the frontiers and the Indian war in Florida. But in November 1839 the secretary of war had proposed to construct new works on the northern frontier, to reorganize the militia, and to build barracks for their concentration in places that appeared well selected to support attacks on Canada. Jackson admitted that financial embarrassments would probably check these plans but he believed them significant enough to require countermeasures. What worried him most was the exposed position of Montreal, 'the key and capital of the Canadas', as Smyth had called it. But Smyth's project was hopelessly expensive and instead of about £350,000, Jackson now proposed the expenditure of a mere £45,000 on a number of less ambitious works on the island of Montreal and along the Richelieu invasion route.[2] Russell supported this proposal to the extent of suggesting an expenditure of £25,000 in the current year but the master-general of the Ordnance successfully evaded the issue by stating that Jackson's proposals were insufficiently detailed and that the engineers already had enough on their hands without trying to prepare further estimates for the present year: 'The Master-General and Board therefore think nothing more can be done in the present case than has already been called for. The city of Montreal is no doubt of very great importance, but they are of opinion it will be better to

---

[1] Vivian to Russell, 4 March, Stephen to Byham, 11 March, and Byham to Stephen, 3 April 1840, in 'Papers relative to the Fortifications and Defences of Canada', n.d., W.O. 1/536.

[2] Jackson's 'Memorandum upon Montreal and its immediate frontier', enclosed in Thomson to Russell, 26 Mar. 1840, *ibid.*

devote our means to covering its frontier by good works than to attempt surrounding the city itself by a chain of posts such as the statement contemplates.'[1] Russell, however, went ahead and asked that Jackson be directed to prepare a more detailed plan.[2]

Jackson's new memorandum, dated November 1840, was as long and detailed as the Ordnance could possibly demand, and it was based professedly upon the authority not only of Smyth's and Wellington's earlier opinions but also on new evidence from the American government. On 12 May the secretary of war had presented to Congress a 'Report upon the National Defences and National Boundaries' in which, Jackson thought, American policy had been clearly exposed as aiming at the construction of a number of forts designed 'not only for defense . . . but to act offensively with decisive effect' both from the head of Lake Champlain and along the whole northern frontier. To meet this danger the completion of the old fortification scheme based on Smyth's report was in Jackson's opinion the best recourse, and should be proceeded with if at all possible. In the meantime he would have to rely on troops rather than fortifications. At present these numbered 11,000 rather than the 13,000 recommended by Wellington and the number of volunteers was only 2,500. To bring the available field force to 20,000 and to provide local defence forces at the principal cities Jackson therefore suggested an immediate increase of the volunteers. But he did not propose to make the old American error of accumulating an unwieldy mass of undisciplined and untrained militia. To support these forces he also proposed the immediate prosecution of a modified system of fortifications costing at a rough estimate less than £800,000 instead of the amount of over £2,300,000 which it was now reckoned would be needed to complete the existing fortification plans. Jackson's scheme, however, did not include the Maritime Provinces and the protection of the vital intercolonial road.[3]

These proposals the inspector-general of fortifications, Sir Frederick Mulcaster, was prepared to treat as 'valuable revisions' of the existing scheme, though he disagreed over many points of importance. But the master-general was not at all enthusiastic, believing that on such an open frontier the main reliance must be placed on the loyalty of the population rather than expensive works. He recommended that they should for the

---

[1] Stephen to Byham, 24 April, and Byham to Stephen, 4 May 1840, in 'Papers relative to the Fortifications and Defences of Canada', n.d., W.O. 1/536.

[2] Russell to Thomson, 9 May 1840, *ibid*.

[3] Jackson to Sydenham, 14 Nov. 1840, enclosing 'Memorandum upon the Canadian Frontier', Nov. 1840, *ibid*.

present confine themselves to the schemes for Kingston and Quebec and those additions at St John, Niagara, and Amherstburg which Seaton had proposed in 1839. It would be time enough to think of countering new American works when Congress showed any disposition to act upon the report mentioned by Jackson.[1] But on 22 February Russell wrote to ask for Wellington's opinion. 'The objects to be kept in view', he said were those stated by the duke himself in 1825.

These are, 1. The defence of the province, with no greater demand upon the military resources of this country than were made during the last war with the United States of America. – 2. Such a disposition of our military means as may encourage and call forth the spirit of the loyal inhabitants of the Queen's North-American Provinces. – 3. Such support to the peaceable population as may induce them to rely on the continual protection of the Queen, and the exertion of the resources of the British Empire in case of invasion.

And while Russell went on to admit the difficulty of the problem in face of American power and possible disaffection among Canadian subjects and to warn against the construction of forts which would require large garrisons and weaken the army in the field, he also commented:

Still, with the Duke of Wellington's sanction to the opinion that these provinces may be defended without any material demand upon the military resources of the country [i.e. in regular troops beyond the 13,000 mentioned in 1825], I have no hesitation in saying that we are bound in honour, and entitled in reason, to maintain the Queen's authority by all the means most likely to be successful.[2]

In reply Wellington, supported by the commander-in-chief, Lord Hill, naturally resorted to the recommendations of the Smyth commission, and in particular to the canal and road improvements he had continually pressed. So far as concerned the immediate prosecution of substantial works, especially the fortification of Montreal, both experts came down heavily on Jackson's side.[3] In April Russell proposed to the cabinet that Jackson's scheme should be adopted in its entirety and a vote of £80,000 be sought in the current year. He also suggested that the government should spend £15–20,000 a year to promote emigration to Canada.[4]

[1] Vivian to Russell, 18 Feb. 1841, enclosing Mulcaster to Vivian, 4 and 8 Feb. 1841, in 'Papers relative to the Fortifications and Defences of Canada', n.d., W.O. 1/536.
[2] Russell to Hill, 22 Feb. 1841, *ibid.*
[3] Hill to Russell, 8 April 1841, enclosing Hill to Wellington, 5 Mar., with his own 'Considerations on the Defence of Canada', and Wellington to Hill, 7 April, with the duke's memorandum of 31 Mar., *ibid.*
[4] Memorandum of April 1841, Russell papers, P.R.O. 30/22/4A.

In the meantime alternating reports of good and bad news had kept the McLeod question in a state of worrying uncertainty. In March 1841 came a change of administration in the States; but also news of the refusal to release McLeod on bail. But the uncertainty and not least Daniel Webster's appointment as secretary of state allowed Palmerston to return to his preoccupations in the near east. In July the Straits convention was signed and late in August Palmerston was making reassuring speeches in the House of Commons about the state of Anglo-American relations. In any case Melbourne's government was tottering to its fall. At the end of August it resigned and on 3 September Peel assumed office with Aberdeen as foreign secretary.

When he accepted office on 3 September Aberdeen did so in the firm intention of restoring the good relations with the Orléans monarchy which he had first established in 1830 and which he, like many others among Whigs as well as Tories, believed Palmerston had so ruthlessly and so unnecessarily destroyed. About relations with the United States the new government was not so sure. After all the cabinet included Wellington and in May he had thought war very probable.[1] The Tories generally had been quite unconvinced by Palmerston's deflation of the American crisis in August and in September arrived news of another incident upon the border that might be expected to enflame American opinion. The new government was puzzled that in so critical a matter no instructions could be found telling the naval and military commanders in North America what to do in the event of McLeod being executed and Fox leaving Washington. On 4 September the new colonial secretary, Lord Stanley, wrote to his predecessor asking what secret instructions had been given.[2]

Presumably they had not found the orders the Admiralty had sent to Sir Thomas Harvey early in March and it was probably to these that Russell's reply now drew their attention. These merely required the Admiral to keep in touch with Fox and the governor-general and 'to conform . . . as much as possible to their wishes'.[3] Fox at least was

---

[1] Wilbur Devereux Jones, *Lord Aberdeen and the Americas* (Athens, Ga., 1958), p. 10.

[2] Stanley to Russell, private and confidential, 4 Sept. 1841, together with a semi-official letter of the same date, Russell papers, P.R.O. 30/22/4B.

[3] Adm. to Harvey, no. 52, secret, 3 Mar. 1841, Adm. 2/1696. The Admiralty was hardly to blame for the ambiguity. The Colonial Office had simply forwarded the Foreign Office correspondence and asked 'their Lordships to give such instructions to the Admiral commanding on the North America and West Indies station as shall correspond with the views of Her Majesty's Government on this subject' (C.O. to Adm., most confidential, 3 Mar. 1841, C.O. 42/483).

dangerously prone to violent outbursts against the Americans. And it was pretty clear how he would interpret Palmerston's instructions of 9 February to keep the naval and military officers informed – especially in view of Palmerston's private letter of the same day.[1] With such ambiguous instructions as he had received, Harvey, or his successor, Sir Charles Adam, might do too little or too much, and if Fox had anything to do with it it would probably be the latter. On 6 September therefore the cabinet decided to authorize the governor-general, Sydenham, in the event of McLeod's execution and Fox's departure from Washington, or even only 'if the situation on the frontier required it', to keep two regiments at Halifax which had been about to return home but to forbid the commencement of hostilities without further orders.

As an additional safeguard new instructions were sent to Fox on 28 September that he was not to leave Washington in the event of McLeod's conviction and that he should do so without further instructions only if McLeod were actually executed.[2] These instructions did

[1] See above, p. 86.

[2] Cabinet memorandum no. 5, 6 Sept. 1841, Derby papers microfilms, P.A.C., M.G. 24/A/15, reel 2, Cabinet memoranda, 1841–45; C.O. to Sydenham, confidential, 10 Sept. 1841, C.O. 42/483; F.O. to Fox, no. 1, 28 Sept. 1841, F.O. 5/358. Fox had understood his instructions of 9 Feb. to mean that he was not to leave Washington unless McLeod were executed; but the new government's caution was nonetheless justified. Fox had, as he said, been 'under the impression, that both the military and naval commanders had orders to commence hostilities immediately upon receiving from me such notice of my departure' (Fox to Jackson, confidential, 25 Oct. 1841, Fox papers, F.O. 97/17). And though Jackson had had no such orders he too now revealed that in that event he would have commenced hostilities, believing the withdrawal of a minister to be tantamount to war (Peel to Stanley, private, 1 Nov., and Stanley to Peel, private, 2 Nov., Peel papers, B.M.Add.MS.40,467). The Americans appear to have been under a similar impression. On 30 Sept. Fox had an 'extraordinary intimation, privately and personally', from President Tyler that if McLeod were executed he would try and avert war by preventing Fox's departure, by refusing a passport and if necessary by force, so as to give the British government time to consider the case more fully. Fox at once wrote to the naval and military commanders that his detention in such a case was not to be regarded as obliging them 'to suspend the execution of the measures which you may have been directed by Her Majesty's Government to take' (Fox to Adm. Sir Charles Adam, secret and confidential, 5 Oct. 1841, Fox papers, F.O. 97/17; and Corey, p. 144). Peel commented that 'the object which the President professes to have in view would be better answered by the immediate compliance with Mr Fox's demand for passports, and the simultaneous despatch of a special mission to this country conveying whatever explanations or offers of reparation the President may have in contemplation' (Peel to Queen Victoria, 28 Oct. 1841, A. C. Benson and Viscount Esher, eds., *The Letters of Queen Victoria . . . 1837–1861* [3 vols., London, 1907], i. 446).

not mean that the new government was more optimistic than its predecessor; only that it was more cautious. By the middle of September
the prime minister was apparently already thinking of offensive operations against the American coast, and at his request Stanley personally
instructed an army officer on 17 September to spy out the defences of
the Atlantic ports.[1] By 20 September Peel was worried enough to ask
Stanley to look to the defences of Bermuda.[2] By 17 October he had
decided to summon a meeting of some of his cabinet colleagues to
consider the '*possibility*' that some immediate and decisive demonstration on our part may be necessary'. He did not mean by this that the
measures should 'partake of the character of menace', but that as 'war
may be inevitable . . . the decision upon war or peace . . . beyond our
control', they 'ought to take measures which, without diminishing the
hopes of peace, may be suitable to the alternative of war'.[3] It had already
been decided to send out the new governor-general of Canada, Sir
Charles Bagot, in a battleship, as 'a very useful way of having a great
ship in these waters without running the least risk of giving offence';
and to hold another ready to go out to Bermuda. Now, at Peel's suggestion, four more battleships were to be kept ready at Gibraltar, and it
was proposed also 'gradually to collect such heavy frigates and steamers

---

[1] Stanley to Peel, private, n.d. (but between 26 and 30 Nov. 1841), Peel papers,
B.M.Add.MS. 40,467. Copies of Lt. H. D. Fanshawe's three reports from the
U.S., dated 15 Oct., 30 Nov., and 14 Dec. 1841, are in Adm. 7/626 (though the
first is here wrongly dated 1846). They deal respectively with Boston and the
harbours immediately to the north, with New York, and with the principal
harbours between Boston and New York. He reported that at present there were
no guns mounted at Boston and the only opposition to a naval attack would
therefore have to be by the American fleet. When the defences planned were
complete the port would be unassailable but it would then still be possible for
troops to approach by good roads from the harbours to the north unless their
poor defences were also improved. New York had few troops in the vicinity and
its fortifications were in part dilapidated and not fully armed. The ports in
between he revealed as in more or less the same imperfect condition. The whole
suggested that attacks would be quite practicable for the present though
there were active plans to improve the defences generally. He warned, however,
against any over-confidence in the collapse of American morale: 'The feeling of
the people of Boston has always been remarkably pacific and friendly towards
Great Britain and they are conscious of their unprepared state for war, and
unhesitatingly declare their weakness: but in the event of hostilities, they would
join with energetic spirit in support of the General Government.'
[2] Peel to Stanley, 20 Sept. 1841, cited by W. D. Jones, 'Lord Ashburton and
the Maine Boundary Negotiations', *Mississippi Valley Historical Review*, xl
(1953–54), 478.
[3] Peel's 'Memorandum sent to the Earl of Aberdeen, Lord Haddington, and
Lord Stanley', 17 Oct. 1841, C. S. Parker, *Sir Robert Peel from his Private
Papers* (London, 1891–99), iii. 387–8.

as are available without any extraordinary preparation in the neighbourhood of Plymouth'.[1]

Meanwhile the United States too had been turning its active attention once more to external defence. In November 1837, thinking of the Maine boundary dispute as well as Indian troubles, General Scott had recommended various increases in the regular army, but the principal preoccupation of the American government remained for some time the pacification of the border. Not until the news of the Aroostook 'war' arrived in Washington early in March 1839 did the government really turn with any serious purpose to the question of war with Great Britain. Joel Poinsett, the secretary of war, at once summoned the chiefs of the various military bureaux of the War Department in Washington and asked them to think over the best way of preparing for such a war.[2] Chief among the recommendations made by these experts was the raising as quickly as possible of a force of 50,000 twelve-month volunteers and a million six-month militia, and their organization for training in a number of military districts under the command of specially suited regular officers. Beyond this most of the replies were vague and some of them quite brief. But while they differed about details, especially about the precise distribution of the available forces, they were, by and large, in agreement about concentrating the maximum number of regulars upon the northern frontier. A nucleus of regulars, especially artillery and cavalry, would have to remain, but, these apart, the occupation of the posts on the Indian frontier in the west, the conduct or rather containment of the war against the Seminoles in Florida, and even the garrison of the forts on the Atlantic seaboard would have to be left to the volunteers. The last, in particular, would certainly be

[1] Lord Haddington (first lord of the Admiralty) to Peel, private, 13 Sept. 1841, and Peel to Wellington, confidential, 18 Oct., Peel papers, B.M.Add.MS. 40, 456.

[2] Poinsett evidently put his questions to chiefs of bureaux, probably verbally, on 7 Mar. 1839. The replies, dated between 11 and 21 Mar., are collected together in Selected Confidential Letters Received by the Secretary of War, U.S.N.A., R.G. 107. This file also includes a series of letters from Winfield Scott about affairs on the border, March 1839–Sept. 1841, and one of Gaines's letters, 22 Mar. 1839, about his defence schemes; there is a series of letters from Gaines to Poinsett on the subject of the defence of New Orleans, which recur almost daily for the last week of Mar. 1839 (Letters Received by the Chief of Engineers, S–621/1839, R.G. 77). Jesup's 'Memoranda' for the secretary of war, in the collected replies of the chiefs of bureaux, are accompanied by a long letter to Poinsett, 21 Mar. 1839, reflecting on the policy and power of Great Britain (see above, pp. 55–6). There are copies of this interesting letter in both collections of Jesup papers in the Library of Congress and in the William Clements Library, Ann Arbor, Michigan.

unpopular and would expose the seaboard trade and cities to great hazard. The forts themselves might well be quickly improved and manned sufficiently to hold off attacks by warships. Against landings by troops however they would be far from completely effective and for their general defence the seaboard states would have to rely on large but inexperienced militia armies.

General J. R. Fenwick, commanding the 4th Artillery, warned that in the Chesapeake at least they ought to take special precautions against disasters more terrible even than they had suffered by the burning of Washington in 1814. General Gaines, the commander of the western district, was already taking advantage of the crisis to write almost daily to the secretary of war, stressing once again his old scheme of steam battleships for the coastal harbours and railways for the rapid movement of large numbers of militia to threatened points. Without such measures, he warned, New Orleans would be utterly exposed to attack and 'nothing but a miracle can save our principal seaports from destruction or pillage'. But Gaines, and the military advisers in general, were agreed that the largest possible number of regulars must be concentrated on the northern frontier. Here there was some fear that the Indians would be tempted to join in the war; 'An Indian cannot be neutral', commented Colonel Abert, the chief of the Bureau of Topographical Engineers, 'his moral as well as his physical organization is against it. If not with us he will be opposed to us.' Most expected the Indians to join the British but Jesup, the quartermaster-general, evidently expected to have the help of some 10,000 on the northern frontier.

Of the attitude of the French population of Canada the Americans were a little uncertain. All insisted upon their disaffection from the British but no one assumed an immediate uprising. Jesup seems to have thought they would first have to be reassured by substantial American victories over the British garrison and seduced by the formation of a provisional government of their own. But the chief factors here were on the one hand the presence of an unusually large and imposing force of British troops and, on the other, the generally advantageous position of the Americans. This advantage moreover lay in their good position for taking the offensive, whether to prevent any advance by the enemy or with a view to the conquest of Canada. And offensive operations suggested not a line of fortifications but a few secure bases of operation, as at the head of Lake Champlain or Sackett's Harbor, and, against so large a force of British troops, not an advance by hordes of ill-trained and unreliable militia but by as many as possible of the regular army.

The most comprehensive and detailed paper was Jesup's, perhaps because he was the most impressed with the ultimate implications of the crisis.[1] His idea was to concentrate on the northern frontier no less than ten of the fourteen regiments of regulars, about 9,000 men, together with 45,000 volunteers and 500,000 militia. Of these some would make attacks on the Detroit and Niagara frontiers, as diversions or to seize important lines of communication, like the Welland canal. But the major operation on the Canadian frontier would be an attack by two armies, each of about four regiments of regulars, 10,000 or 15,000 volunteers and a large number of militia, and operating respectively against Montreal from the head of Lake Champlain and between that lake and Sackett's Harbor. It looks as if Gaines would have seriously disagreed with this part of Jesup's plan. He urged his old 1813 scheme to establish forts and, now, steam batteries at some point on the St Lawrence above Quebec. By this means British communications with the interior would be cut off and Canada's resistance would 'wither away' without the Americans even having to establish a naval force on the lakes. Unless it was prepared to sally out in force, the British garrison in Quebec would be bottled up and starved out. Most seem to have agreed that there was no likelihood of major operations by either side on the Maine frontier. Jesup, however, proposed that another four regular regiments, 16,000 volunteers and a large force of militia should operate in two lines to cut the New Brunswick road and advance upon Halifax. With this base in American hands British naval operations against the trade and coast of the United States would be seriously hampered and the Americans strategically poised for the conquest of the West Indies.

Clearly once the necessary forces were raised Poinsett's advisers were confident of ultimate success on the Canadian frontier and a success, as Jesup for example insisted, worth even the very damaging attacks they would have to bear at sea and on the Atlantic and Gulf coasts. But what *was* crucial was the interval of unpreparedness while the volunteers and militia were raised and trained. According to Abert this would dictate an initial policy of 'caution' on the frontier. No one directly forecast complete disaster.[2] But Poinsett himself certainly made

[1] For Jesup's views on this, see above, pp. 55–6.
[2] Later on, however, Brigadier-General Wool, the commander of the Eastern District, insisted that such was the state of the fortifications, the scarcity of artillery, and the demoralization of the regular army that war would have been disastrous at any period up to the end of 1840 (Wool to Scott, 13 Nov. 1841, Letters sent by the Eastern Division, vol. 31, pp. 68–84, Records of the U.S. Army Commands, U.S.N.A., R.G. 98).

no bones about the seriousness of the immediate conditions, when, after digesting these various replies from his advisers, he came to review the situation for the president. He was anxious, no doubt, to impress upon Van Buren the necessity of rapid preparation; but with such gloomy facts, no exaggeration was required.

The administration itself and Poinsett in particular had already tried hard enough to improve the nation's defences. In January 1838, when Scott had been ordered to the frontier to control filibustering, it had been found that he had neither the material nor the legal resources to ensure the success of even that limited undertaking. The neutrality laws were most unsatisfactory; the available naval and military forces ridiculously small. They had one small revenue cutter for service on the lakes and they were able to hire a few steamers.[1] But while the paper strength of the army stood at about 8,000 the actual strength was not much more than 5,000, and most of these were still bogged down in Indian wars, all the artillery and nine of the thirteen regiments of infantry being engaged in Florida.[2] So even while still thinking primarily in terms of pacifying the frontier the administration had found it necessary in January 1838 to seek not only new neutrality legislation but also a wholesale reorganization of the army and its increase to 15,000 men. But the reorganization was almost completely denied and the new establishment ultimately obtained in July was limited to 12,500 officers and men. Now, in April 1839, it was still over 3,000 men short of its authorized strength and by far the greater part was still fighting the Indians in Florida. Poinsett thought he would have little trouble completing the regular army's establishment during 1839; but the act enabling him to raise volunteers had expired in the previous March and in the same year Congress had rejected his revolutionary scheme for forming an active militia of 250,000 men. Instead all that he could hope to maintain with the small sums voted for defences was about 3,000 volunteers. No less worrying was the general state of the defences. After the rejection of the last major review in 1836, financial crises and other political preoccupations had continued to starve the coastal and frontier forts; and though congressional interest in the northern frontier had revived at the end of 1837 and had been pressed by Poinsett himself early in 1838, only relatively small appropriations had been made. In sum, Poinsett reported, too little had been spread too thinly over too many positions.[3]

[1] J. M. Callahan, *The Neutrality of the American Lakes and Anglo-American Relations* (Baltimore, 1898), p. 95. [2] Corey, p. 57.
[3] Poinsett to Van Buren, 12 April 1839, Van Buren papers, Library of Congress, series ii, vol. 35.

In place of forts on the sea coast little could be expected from the navy. In March orders went out to make ready both ships and yards; and in the same month Congress did empower the president to raise a naval force for the defence of the lakes and coast and authorize the construction of three new ocean-going steamers, two of which, *Missouri* and *Mississippi*, were laid down during that year. But by November the navy's total force of ships built, building, and worthy of repair, still boasted only the steamship *Fulton II*, eleven battleships, fourteen frigates, and twenty-one sloops. Of the larger vessels, moreover, only a few were actually in commission and many of these scattered in distant squadrons.[1] At the same time new plans and estimates on both the fortifications and the navy were called for; but so much did the experts disagree and so vast was the problem that the next year was taken up almost entirely by lengthy reports and recommendations. At last, in January 1840 came the navy's plan to provide no less than forty steamers for the protection of the coast, and in addition, for the sea-going fleet, the maximum number of warships for which it was reckoned seamen could be found in the event of war, that was to say twenty-five battleships, thirty frigates, thirty sloops, and twenty-five smaller vessels in addition to the forty steamers. With the works necessary for the dockyards the total expenditure they estimated would be needed to complete this fantastic programme was no less than $56 million.[2] In April followed the long reports of the Board of Engineers on the fortifications recommending the completion of a modified scheme also at a total cost of $56 million.[3] And in May came Poinsett's comprehensive *Report upon the National Defence*, combining the principal features of the naval and military reports.[4] Notable among his recommendations was the provision of the three new forts at the head of Lake Champlain and the four new barracks on the frontier which, as Jackson, the British commander, had noted, Poinsett had already pressed for in his annual report of 30 November 1839. They were now freely referred to as facilitating offensive operations against Canada.[5]

---

[1] Orders of 21 and 24 March 1839, Department of the Navy, Naval Records Collection of the Office of Naval Records and Library, U.S.N.A., R.G. 45, area file 7; Callahan, p. 100; *Report on Military and Naval Defences*, 24 Jan. 1840, Senate Doc. no. 120, 26th Cong., 1st sess., vol. iii.

[2] *Report on Military and Naval Defences*, 24 Jan. 1840, *loc. cit.*

[3] *Report on Military and Naval Defences*, 24 April 1840, Senate Rep. no. 451, 26th Cong., 1st sess., vol. vii.

[4] 12 May 1840, House Doc. no. 206, 26th Cong., 1st sess., vol. vi.

[5] House Doc. no. 2, 26th Cong., 1st sess., vol. i.

Poinsett's report had been preceded in March 1840 by alarmist outbursts in Congress and a special memorandum by General Scott on the state of British forces and works on the other side of the border.[1] But in spite of all the excitement the prosecution of the national defences was again held up by the cooling off of the crisis and still more by the diversion of a particularly bitter presidential election. Not until March 1841, when the new administration came in and found itself faced with Palmerston's threat about the McLeod trial, did interest centre once again on the defence question. Under his existing powers the president increased the number of officers nearly as much during the year as in the whole of the preceding twenty years. Congress at once authorized the construction of three medium-sized steamers; and work also began on the *Princeton*, the third of the large steamers authorized in March 1839, and the first screw-driven warship in the world.[2] But these were very small increases in such a crisis and in any case could have no effect in the event of an early war. A Navy Department memorandum at the time reckoned that out of those already in service, building, or fit to repair, they could assemble in two or three months a total force of nine battleships, fourteen frigates, and fifteen sloops. Of the large steamships only the *Fulton* was more or less ready and she was limited to the harbour service for which she had been built. The other two begun in 1839, the *Missouri* and *Mississippi*, would be finished by October but would not get their engines until the following summer. There were in addition, under the old naval programme, a large number of the frames of various classes of vessel distributed among the principal Atlantic ports; but the only frames actually completed were for four battleships, seven frigates, and six sloops, and there was in any case a serious shortage of guns.[3] The most pressing concern however was the weakness of the force immediately available for the protection of the coast, many of the larger vessels in commission being in service with distant squadrons. In July approval was given for the establishment of a 'home' squadron to consist of the two steamers, *Missouri* and *Mississippi*, two frigates, three sloops, and two smaller vessels.[4] At the same time a new fortification bill was at last presented to Congress which emphasized coastal defences. But public

---

[1] Corey, pp. 151–2, and Callahan, pp. 103–7.

[2] Harold and Margaret Sprout, *The Rise of American Naval Power, 1776–1918* (Princeton, 1939), pp. 116–17 and 125.

[3] 'Memorandum handed to the Secretary', 7 Mar. 1841, Letters to the Secretary of the Navy, vol. 7, p. 19, Records of the Board of Navy Commissioners, 1815–42, Naval Records Collection of the Office of Naval Records and Library, U.S.N.A., R.G. 45.   [4] Sprout, pp. 117–18.

concern about the northern frontier led to amendments looking to that area too. The final act as it emerged in September 1841 made a total appropriation of nearly $2¼ million and included sums for new forts at Niagara, Oswego, and Lake Champlain, barracks at Buffalo, and $100,000 for steamers on Lake Erie.[1]

Clearly throughout this period of crisis the United States were ill-prepared for war with Great Britain. Yet the American experts seem to have agreed with the British that once they had managed to concentrate a large part of the regular force on the northern frontier the advantage would be almost all theirs in that area. Indeed the very subordinate place occupied by that portion of the frontier in the fortification bill of 1841 and the comparatively small amounts – only $260,000 for steamers, forts, and barracks out of nearly $2¼ million – ultimately voted in September show how confident they felt in that area. In March General Swift, formerly chief engineer of the United States Army and since 1829 the civil engineer in charge of harbour improvement on the Great Lakes, had gone off on a confidential mission to spy out British preparedness in North America and though impressed with the strength and quality of the British regulars, he nevertheless seemed confident still in his own side's ability to press on with the established strategy: to cut the British communications above and below Montreal and more especially by a major attack upon the St Lawrence from the head of Lake Champlain.[2] On the lakes they had no force but General Scott confidently expected to obtain the command of most of them, including perhaps even Lake Ontario, by the rapid conversion of the larger merchant ships, most of which were in American hands. The Navy Department had neglected to assemble a supply of guns for them locally but it seems that even if the army had had none available in their arsenals at Albany and Rome there was a variety of ordnance in the navy yard at New York which could have been moved up by the Erie canal.[3]

The Americans were in similar agreement with the British about the vulnerability of their position on the seas and on the Atlantic coast.

[1] Corey, p. 153, and Callahan, pp. 110–14.

[2] General Joseph G. Swift to Col. J. J. Abert, Chief of Topographical Engineers, confidential, 19 May, 16 July, and 28 Oct. 1841, Records of the Office of the Chief of Engineers U.S.N.A., R.G. 77. Abert's report of 23 Mar. and his letter to the secretary of war, John Spencer, 28 Oct. 1841, show that this mission had been secretly decided upon in March between the president, Abert, Scott, and Spencer's predecessor, John Bell.

[3] Scott to Bell, 15 Sept. 1841, copy, Seward papers, University of Rochester; Seward to Webster, 22 Sept., Simms (acting secretary of the navy) to Webster, 23 Sept., Callahan, pp. 117–18.

The orders given to the Mediterranean squadron when war appeared imminent in March 1841 make it clear that the squadrons in foreign waters would have harassed British shipping only for so long as they could elude the far greater fleets of the enemy and would then have run for home. Then American overseas trade would have been left to the mercy of the enemy.[1] In the meantime the coastal trade and the Atlantic cities would have been subjected to the assaults of superior British seapower. A secret investigation of the defences of British possessions in the Caribbean at this time possibly suggests that their generally neglected defences might have inspired some thoughts of desultory attack but the British concentration on Bermuda which the report also made unmistakably clear promised no good in view of the American weakness in their home waters.[2] No one of any sense in the United States, any more than in England, expected a successful invasion or conquest, nor naturally was there any lack of confidence in an ultimate victory, but the damage that they would suffer was awesome enough. The large demands that the secretary of the navy came to make towards the end of the year must have encouraged him to exaggerate; but his warnings were sufficiently well founded in the tactics actually contemplated by the British to be worth repeating:

Free Governments, which are necessarily more embarrassed in their councils, and slower in their action, than those which are not bound to observe the necessary *forms* of free government, have a peculiar interest to guard their soil from invasion. The nature of our institutions presents a very strong appeal upon this point. A war between the United States and any considerable maritime Power would not be conducted at this day as it would have been even twenty years ago. It would be a war of incursions, aiming at revolution. The first blow would be struck at us through our own institutions. No nation, it is presumed, would expect to be successful over us for any length of time in a fair contest of arms upon our own soil; and no *wise* nation would attempt it. A more promising expedient would be sought in arraying what are supposed to be the hostile elements of our social system against one another. An enemy so disposed, and free to land upon any part of our soil which might promise

[1] Capt. Isaac Hull, commanding the Mediterranean squadron, to the secretary of the navy, nos. 367 and 368, 24 and 25 Mar. 1841, Letters received by the Secretary of the Navy from Captains, Naval Records Collection of the Office of Naval Records and Library, U.S.N.A., R.G. 45. One of the principal ships in the squadron, the frigate *Brandywine*, in fact ran so fast for home that before the news of the passing of the immediate crisis could catch up with her she had reached New York. Explanations had to be given in Congress and the captain was reprimanded.
[2] Albert Fitz to Webster, 21 July 1842, *loc. cit.* Fitz's instructions have not been found but he certainly went out before Nov. 1841.

success to his enterprise, would be armed with a four-fold power of annoyance. Of the *ultimate result* of such incursions, we have no reason to be afraid; but even in the best event, war upon our own soil would be the more expensive, the more embarrassing, and the more horrible in its effects, by compelling us, at the same time, to oppose an enemy in the field, and to guard against attempts to subvert our social systems.

Heretofore, we have found in the shallowness of many of our waters security, to a certain extent against invasion by sea. So long as maritime wars were conducted in vessels of large size and great draught, we had little to apprehend from them except at a few points, and those were susceptible of adequate defence on land. But this security can no longer be relied on. The application of steam power to vessels of war, and the improvements which have recently been made in artillery, are destined to change the whole system of maritime war. Steamboats of light draught, and which may easily be transported across the ocean in vessels of a larger class, may invade us at almost any point of our extended coast, may penetrate the interior through our shallow rivers, and thus expose half our country to hostile attacks. The celerity with which these movements could be made, the facility with which such vessels could escape, and the promptness with which they could change the point of attack, would enable an enemy, with a comparatively inconsiderable force, to harass our whole seaboard, and to carry all the horrors of war into the securest retreats of our people. The effect of these incursions would be terrible everywhere, but in the southern portion of our country they might, and probably would, be disastrous in the extreme.

It is obvious that a war thus conducted must be successful to a very great extent, in spite of all the defences on land which we could contrive. Nothing less than the conversion of half our country into a military garrison, could protect us against it. Such is the exposed condition of our country, such is the character of our institutions, and such the position of our people, that a population of twice our present number, under the best possible military organization, would avail us but little. Whilst the combined Powers of the world could not subdue us, even a secondary naval Power could avoid our land defences, set our armies at defiance, and prosecute against us a war intolerably harassing, and disastrous.[1]

Meanwhile McLeod had at last been brought to trial in Utica, New York, and in spite of all British and American fears, on 12 October he was acquitted by a jury's verdict. On 30 October the news arrived in England and, as Stanley told the queen, 'happily rendered unnecessary the adoption of any measures of a hostile character'.[2] On 12 November Jackson reported that he had released the two regiments whose relief from Nova Scotia had been held up by the crisis.[3] But though warlike

[1] *Annual Report of the Secretary of Navy*, 4 Dec. 1841, House Doc. no. 2, 27th Cong., 2nd sess., vol. i.

[2] Stanley to Queen Victoria, 30 Oct. 1841, Queen Victoria's papers, Royal Archives, Windsor B3/61.

[3] Jackson to Stanley, 12 Nov. 1841, W.O. 1/536.

preparation pretty well ceased, this did not mean that interest in the defence problems of North America disappeared from view; only that they passed once more into the hands of diplomatists. Late in December Peel and Aberdeen, fearful that Fox was too 'thoroughly imbued with a feeling of hatred to the United States' to promise any favourable results from his negotiations, committed the task of settling the various outstanding issues of Anglo-American relations to Lord Ashburton.[1]

The most urgent question for Ashburton to settle was that of the Maine boundary and here the important thing, matters of pride and prestige apart, was to obtain a safe military communication through New Brunswick. Of this Aberdeen was well aware; but neither he nor Ashburton was prepared to hold out for merely military advantage. Aberdeen wrote privately to Ashburton to say 'that the importance of a successful result is so great as almost to justify any sacrifice compatible with the safety of the North American Provinces'.[2] Ashburton had already formed a similar view of his mission:

My task is not an easy one [he told Bagot]. I have to deal with a critical and jealous public and I hold it to be important on this and all the other objects of my negotiation here to make such a settlement as shall satisfy the honourable and reasonable portion of it. No slight advantages to be derived from contrivance and cunning can for a moment be placed in comparison with those to be derived from leaving as a result of my negotiation a reciprocal feeling of respect and harmony.[3]

What worried him most, he commented a fortnight later, was 'the danger of letting the soldiers have their own way in this matter'.[4]

On 8 February Ashburton had been sent off from London with instructions giving him a very wide latitude, but on the same day Wellington had intervened to remind the cabinet of the important military considerations involved. Consultations with the military experts then revealed some apparently serious differences of opinion. Sir George Murray, now master-general of the Ordnance, wanted to protect the Temiscouata road by pushing the boundary to the south of the St John River. Sir James Kempt, Murray's immediate predecessor and formerly governor of Nova Scotia (1820–28) and administrator

---

[1] Peel to Aberdeen, private, 17 Nov. 1841, Aberdeen papers, B.M.Add.MS. 43,061. For this mission and for special attention to its military aspects, see W. D. Jones, 'Lord Ashburton and the Maine Boundary Negotiations', *Mississippi Valley Historical Review*, xl (1953–54), 477–90.

[2] Aberdeen to Ashburton, 2 July 1842, *ibid.*, p. 485.

[3] Ashburton to Bagot, 16 April 1842, Bagot papers, P.A.C., M.G. 24/A/13, vol. ii, pt. i.

[4] Ashburton to Aberdeen, private, 26 April 1842, Aberdeen papers, B.M.Add. MS.43,123.

of Canada (1828–30), naturally insisted on the utility of the alternative route via the Bay of Chaleur which he had mapped out long ago, and which was usually called after him. But both roads approached the St Lawrence below Quebec where American claims to the north and west of the St John also threatened to cut or command them. On the value of the respective roads the military advisers might continue to disagree but on the desirability, moral as well as military, of keeping the Americans out of sight of Quebec even Aberdeen and Wellington could unite. Ashburton's instructions were therefore changed so as to require him to seek an improvement of the line of frontier in the vicinity of Quebec and the lower St Lawrence in return for British concessions in the valley of the St John.[1] For a while Ashburton persisted in making full use of the latitude which Aberdeen's earlier private letters had appeared to give him but ultimately he was forced to come round pretty well to what the British generals he scorned had asked for. This was largely because of the emotional value to the Americans of the Madawaska settlements in the valley of the St John. But it was also because the military bargain proposed by Aberdeen's new instructions happened to suit the demands of the American military advisers as well.

On the strategic significance of the areas in dispute in the valley of the St John and on the highlands supposed to overlook Quebec and the St Lawrence, the military experts in Washington were somewhat divided. Scott wanted to keep the British off the crest of the highlands, so as to preserve the Kennebec and Chaudière line of attack upon Quebec, for such an attack, he hoped, would prevent the garrison of that city being allowed to help hold off the main American advance upon Montreal. Colonel Totten, the chief of engineers, thought that this was not very important as the Americans could build works to counter any British forts on the highlands. Colonel Abert, the chief of topographical engineers, considered that the British could not make any advance from these highlands without first securing their flank in the area of Lake Champlain. It was to this area that General Jesup, the quartermaster-general, also turned. He too thought the highlands of little importance since both sides would be too busy with operations elsewhere. What Jesup was referring to was of course the advance against Montreal, and for that all the experts were agreed that the most valuable acquisition for the United States would be the old position at Rouse's Point, of which a more accurate survey had deprived them in October 1818. The other positions at the head of Lake Champlain, at

---

[1] Jones, 'Ashburton and the Maine Boundary', pp. 479–82.

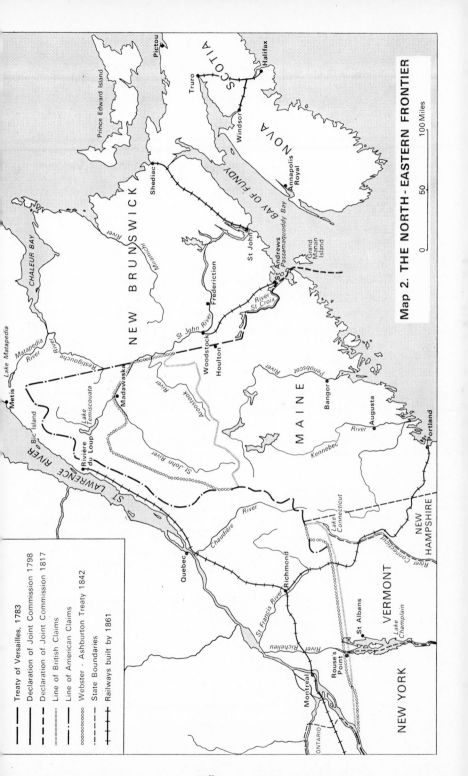

Map 2. THE NORTH-EASTERN FRONTIER

Legend:
- Treaty of Versailles, 1783
- Declaration of Joint Commission 1798
- Declaration of Joint Commission 1817
- Line of British Claims
- Line of American Claims
- Webster - Ashburton Treaty 1842
- State Boundaries
- Railways built by 1861

Scale: 0 — 50 — 100 Miles

NOVA SCOTIA
Pictou
Halifax
Truro
Windsor
Annapolis Royal
BAY OF FUNDY
Prince Edward Island
CHALEUR BAY
NEW BRUNSWICK
Shediac
Miramichi River
St John
St Andrews
Passamaquoddy Bay
Grand Manan Island
Fredericton
River St Croix
St John River
Woodstock
Houlton
Madawaska
Lake Matapedia
Metis
Matapedia River
Restigouche River
Bic Island
Lake Temiscouata
Rivière du Loup
ST LAWRENCE RIVER
Aroostook River
St John River
MAINE
Penobscot River
Bangor
Augusta
Kennebec River
Portland
Quebec
Chaudière River
St Francis River
Richmond
Lake Connecticut
Connecticut River
NEW HAMPSHIRE
VERMONT
St Albans
Lake Champlain
River Richelieu
Rouse's Point
Montreal
ONTARIO
NEW YORK

which they had then been forced to construct alternative works, were much less able to command the ship passage from the lake into the Richelieu River. With Rouse's Point, however, they would have 'the great strategic point on the northern frontier'.

In our hands [Jesup went on] it secures from hostile approach more than two hundred miles of lake coast in New York and Vermont, and not only affords a safe base to an army operating in advance of Lake Champlain; but secures to it, free from interruption, the resources of the whole country bordering on or communicating with, that Lake. It is the only position within or near our line that completely commands the entrance into the lake, and being open to New York it could be readily reinforced on the land side as well as the water by the whole disposable force of that great state.

And though Quebec might be 'the decisive point', the main American attack would have to be first upon Montreal, the key to the upper country and a position too dangerous to be left in the rear of an army marching on Quebec. One force would no doubt march upon Montreal down the St Lawrence, but the main advance would operate from the head of Lake Champlain and would itself hold off the reinforcement from Quebec which Scott had suggested would require the command of the disputed highlands. With this Abert fully agreed. Jesup and Abert, indeed, were categorical in their opinion that it mattered little whether or not the British had their line of communication through the valley of the St John. In wartime this would easily be cut by a force advancing along the road recently constructed from Bangor to Houlton. Rouse's Point was the position of 'positive and decisive' influence. In American hands it would tap the resources of some of the richest and most populous parts of the United States and open to their direct attack first Montreal and then Quebec. But if the position were in British hands not only would this attack be impossible, there would open to the enemy an opportunity of securing the naval command of Lake Champlain and of coming within three days' march of some of the principal American arsenals, including that at Watervliet.[1] The

---

[1] On 13 July 1842 Webster had written to Spencer, asking for these opinions. This letter, Scott's response of the same date, and some notes by Spencer summarizing the opinions of Scott, Totten, and Jesup, are in U.S.N.A., R.G. 107, Secretary of War's in-letters, unregistered series, vol. 33 (1841-44). These refer mostly to the question of the highlands and the valley of the St John, and are somewhat less interesting than some later letters. After the treaty was signed, but presumably to help its passage through the Senate – it passed on 20 Aug. – Spencer sent Webster copies of further papers on Rouse's Point: Jesup to Spencer, 11 Aug., Abert to Spencer, 15 Aug. These are in U.S.N.A., R.G. 76, Records of Boundary and Claims Commissions and Arbitrations, North

Americans had already discovered that the lands to the north of the St John were of little agricultural or commercial value, and in spite of Ashburton's personal preferences they also had a pretty good idea of why the British thought the highlands so important.[1] In July, Ashburton realized he would have to give up the Madawaska settlements to satisfy a jealous Maine, and on 9 August a treaty was at last concluded in which the highlands were virtually exchanged for Rouse's Point.

With the crisis passed and their principal offensive base on the northern frontier secured the Americans could now afford to relax a little. In August 1842 the establishment of the army was again reduced to a little more than 8,500. But the war in the Floridas had now come to an end and released troops for redistribution among the undermanned posts in the west and north. On the frontiers changes of opinion among the military experts as well as altered circumstances made for some delays in the prosecution of fortifications. The principal delay was ironically enough at the head of Lake Champlain where the acquisition of Rouse's Point meant the abandonment once again of the incomplete but nonetheless expensive works that had been started at the inferior alternative positions a year or two before; the new work at Rouse's Point was not begun until 1844. But generally speaking the improvement of the frontier and coastal fortifications was pushed on rapidly for a few more years. Above all, the principal works had been supplied with their proper armament by the end of 1842.

The project of building ships for the lakes, as the British were soon unhappy to discover, also went on. But the general naval programme met

East Boundary miscellaneous papers 1824–1906, envelope 3, folder 11. This folder contains several other interesting papers, among them 'memoranda for the president', 1 July – some notes by Scott on Rouse's Point – and J. D. Graham (a colonel in the topographical engineers, serving as commissioner for the survey of the Maine boundary) to Webster, 18 Aug., referring to his earlier views on the defences of Maine. There are copies of Jesup's letter of 11 Aug. in both collections of his papers in the Library of Congress and the Clements Library.

[1] On the value of the land, see for example a letter of one of the American boundary commissioners, Professor James Renwick, Columbia College, to Webster, 2 April 1842, U.S.N.A., R.G. 76, North East Boundary miscellaneous papers, miscellaneous envelope no. 5: letters and documents relating to the north eastern boundary of the U.S., letter no. 225. So far as the British interest in keeping the Americans out of sight of Quebec was concerned President Van Buren had been told much earlier that 'a gentleman high in office in Lower Canada' had revealed that this was their main anxiety and that they would bargain other territory away to ensure it. He may not, of course, have passed this information on to this successors but it is unlikely that Webster was not equally well informed (E. Harket Derby to Van Buren, 11 Mar. 1839, Van Buren papers in Library of Congress, series ii, vol. 35).

a very disappointing fate. Secretary of the Navy Upshur's gloomy appraisal at the end of 1841 of the vulnerability of American property, its society and its institutions, to predatory attack by an enemy sea power had led him to the conclusion that the danger could be properly fended off only by meeting it on the seas. He had therefore proposed that they should build up a force equal to anything that might be brought against it. On the assumption that no power would be able to spare more than half its navy for an attack, the defending force should be not less than half that of the greatest naval power. It was of course to be achieved gradually and by concentrating on medium sized steamships; but it was nonetheless an impossibly large proposal. As a result Upshur's plans were rejected; and the new administration got even less money for the navy in 1842 than had been voted the previous year. By the end of 1842 the new home squadron, already ridiculously small for the purpose for which it had been voted, had been forced to take over the duties of the old West Indian squadron as well; so that then two large sailing frigates, the two sea-going steam frigates, two sloops, a brig, and a schooner had to cover cruising grounds extending from the banks of Newfoundland to the River Amazon, and including the Caribbean and the Gulf of Mexico.[1]

British generals too could rejoice that the Americans had been pushed back from Quebec and the diplomats that they had left in America a 'good temper . . . and the prospect of a continued peace, with . . . improved friendly relations' which far outweighed 'the value of any additional extent of Pine Swamp'.[2] With this view, however, one important individual at least could not agree. Palmerston, who in office really seemed rather to have neglected American affairs, now roundly turned on both Aberdeen and Ashburton. The surrender of Rouse's Point and the line of the St John was both unjustified and unnecessary, the result far from what its perpetrators claimed.

This Treaty [he told Russell in a letter typical of many at this time], so far from rendering Peace more secure, lays the foundation for future disturbance of Peace by weakening our measures of defence, and by adding to the American means of attack, and thus affording to the United States greater power of annoyance, and giving them greater temptation to annoy. In my opinion it is one of the worst and most disgraceful Treaties that England ever concluded, and this humiliation and sacrifice of real

[1] Report by the secretaries of war and navy, in the president's *Annual Message*, 6 Dec. 1842, House Doc. no. 2, 27th Cong., 3rd sess., vol. i; see also Sprout, pp. 118–24.

[2] Aberdeen to Ashburton, 26 Sept. 1842, cited by Jones, 'Ashburton and the Maine Boundary', p. 489.

interests and established rights, we have submitted to voluntarily and without any necessity; not obliged thereto by unsuccessful war; not compelled thereto by apprehension of impending war, either in America or in Europe, but led thereto by the American propensities and partialities of our citizen negotiator, and by the reckless incapacity, the perverse and wilful ignorance, and the mean spirited timidity of the Government under whom that negotiator acted.[1]

He believed further that the Americans, considering the state of their navy and their finances, had neither the desire nor the means of making war and 'that by a little firmness and some shew of fight we should have obtained terms with which we might have been contented'.[2] And, he argued, so far as 'braying forth that Peace is so good a thing, that any Sacrifice is worth making to secure it', not only was there no question of war, 'if a nation once establishes & proclaims as its Rule of Conduct, that any Sacrifice of Interest is preferable to war, it had better at once abdicate its Independence & place itself under the Protection of some less Quakerlike state'. The territory in question might not be very rich, 'but the Question between the Two Countries was essentially Military & Political, & not agricultural and commercial'. The United States wanted it 'because it intervenes between New Brunswick & Canada; because it affords Strong Military Position for attack against us; because it is a stepping Stone towards the object which they have long avowed as one of their fixed aims, the Expulsion of British authority from the Continent of America'. Thus, he concluded, 'this Treaty is an act of weakness & of Pusillanimity, which both morally & Physically helps them on towards that End; while at the same Time it lowers the Position of England in the opinion of all Foreign Nations, and is a Source of weakness to us in all our Dealings with every other Power'.[3]

Here was a classic exposition of Palmerstonian anti-Americanism but it was more ominous for the future than of much moment as yet; Palmerston did not convince many others and may not yet even have convinced himself. In parliament and among his party Palmerston found himself almost alone in his violent opposition to the treaty. Russell agreed that better terms might have been obtained, 'but there are at the same time such advantages in a settlement of what has been so long unsettled that when the Government have concluded the matter it would be a pity to rip open these sores again'. With this view Melbourne was inclined to agree. It was decided therefore to leave open

[1] Palmerston to Russell, 24 Sept. 1842, Russell papers, P.R.O. 30/22/4c.
[2] Palmerston to Melbourne, 10 Oct. 1842, Broadlands papers.
[3] Palmerston to Monteagle, 28 Oct. 1842, *ibid*.

how far the Opposition would press their criticism until they saw the temper of the country and the House.[1] The result was far from what Palmerston must have hoped and the majority of the Opposition criticized the treaty only with reluctance. But in spite of the tactics agreed to Palmerston insisted on reserving to himself 'freedom of action according to the best judgment I can form of the interests of my country; and that freedom I shall always exercise as long as it may please Heaven to continue to me my Faculties'.[2] Public and parliamentary opinion on the whole then was highly favourable to Ashburton's treaty. Aberdeen of course was convinced that it really had averted war. But privately he too believed that Ashburton could have obtained the line of the St John.[3] Certainly, whatever the chances of the negotiation had been, the fact remained that, with their military experts mesmerized by a newly discovered danger to Quebec and with their diplomats bent on peace and glory, the British had lost a possible opportunity to obtain a radical improvement in their strategic position in North America. With such a dramatic improvement in Anglo-American relations, however, this hardly seemed to matter, and in the course of 1842 the excitement over military preparations on the British side of the frontier too subsided once more into comparative lethargy.

The pace of military preparation on the British side had already begun to slacken as the Maine and McLeod crises gradually receded, but not simply on the change of government in September 1841. Russell had shown how anxious he had become in the summer of 1841 by turning for advice on the defence of Canada to the more aggressive Arthur, then back in England. It was Stanley, however, who received Arthur's memorandum late in September.[4] Arthur's principal objective was to point in some detail to the many areas where he felt it was necessary to take emergency measures. In the event of war he expected the Americans to undertake not one but a number of attacks upon the frontier. Colonel Worth, Scott's northern district commander with headquarters at Buffalo, he believed would lead a considerable portion

[1] Melbourne to Palmerston, 10 Oct., 1842, enclosing Russell to Melbourne, 4 Oct., and Palmerston to Melbourne, 10 Oct., Broadlands papers.

[2] Palmerston to Russell, 14 Nov. 1842, H. L. Bulwer, *Life of Viscount Palmerston* (London, 1874), iii. 113–18. See also Bell, i. 333–6.

[3] Aberdeen to Ashburton, 26 Sept. 1842, cited by Jones, 'Ashburton and the Maine Boundary', p. 489.

[4] Arthur to Lord Fitzroy Somerset (secretary at the Horse Guards), 24 Sept. 1841, enclosing a copy of his private and confidential letter to Stanley and his 'Memorandum upon the Defence of Canada', W.O. 55/1551 (7B). There is another copy of the memo. in Murray's papers, W.O. 80/11; the original is in the Derby papers, microfilms in P.A.C., M.G. 24/A/15 (reel no. 30).

of their regular army and some of the best of the militia across the St Lawrence between Prescott and Cornwall for the purpose of cutting communications between eastern and western Canada. His information was that General Scott had 'personally made a very minute military survey of that part of the river, and had fixed upon a spot for the erection of a strong work'. Simultaneously with this movement he expected attacks on the western frontier by the militia of Michigan, Ohio, and Kentucky under Brigadier-General Brady, who commanded the eastern end of the lake frontier from headquarters at Detroit, and on the Niagara frontier by the militia of New York under Colonel Bankhead. At the same time General Scott himself would advance upon the eastern townships and Montreal with a larger force of militia from Vermont and New Hampshire and with a portion of the regular army.

To meet these dangers Arthur urged immediate attacks upon the Erie canal and the American frontier forts and bases like Fort Gratiot and Sackett's Harbor. But in general he too believed firmly in the necessity of maintaining a defensive attitude. There might arise some unexpected opportunity of demolishing the enemy's army at one blow, but it was more likely that the enemy would avoid meeting British regulars in the field and prefer to sap their strength and draw them on to disaster by attacks upon their flanks and supply routes. An aggressive strategy on the British part would only risk arousing the real strength of the enemy:

We shall have to encounter an enemy of a peculiar character in a People who are enterprizing, reflecting, and very crafty, good Bushmen, and excellent marksmen, and able to endure great fatigue; but then, they are always, more or less, divided by violent Party Spirit; and regard with one common feeling of abhorrence, restraint of every kind, especially that of military discipline, to which they would never long submit, *unless their National Feelings were warmly excited in the cause of warfare, or by circumstances springing out of it.*

Even in the limited attacks he did propose therefore he felt great care should be taken to avoid damage to private property. In his insistence on a defensive policy on the frontier, however, Arthur recognized that a complete system of fortifications would be too expensive where so few natural barriers existed. What he recommended was essentially the reverse of the policy that had dictated defence planning for the last twenty years, the limitation of fortifications and a concentration on naval supremacy on all the lakes, including even Lake Superior. Iron frames and engines should be kept at Niagara and Montreal ready for rapid assembly in the event of war, and the water communications should be improved and guarded so as to allow their ready use for the extension of British naval power throughout the lakes. By this means would be found the most economical method of defending Canada and an effective way of annoying the enemy – a well-organized rather than large force of regulars and militia could move more rapidly to attack an invading force in the rear – and steps could be taken to cripple American trade on the lakes and perhaps even conquer the Michigan territory.

Arthur's paper glossed over many difficulties, not the least, as Stanley pointed out in a marginal comment, how such naval preparations were to be made consistent with the 1817 agreement. An attempt at naval supremacy on all the lakes also ran counter to Wellington's old decision to concentrate on one; but steam power might since have altered the position and the memorandum was therefore passed on to Murray who was also 'engaged in a plan for the defences of the Canadian frontier'.[1] Murray's initial reaction was that it would not be possible to maintain supremacy on all the lakes but that it must be attempted on Lake Ontario and for that the first necessity was the completion of the works for the security of the harbour at Kingston.[2]

Then, early in January 1842, came Murray's general memoranda. The first agreed that Canada 'having, comparatively speaking, so narrow a line of population, it would be a great military error to attempt to defend every point by which an enemy could penetrate. The adoption of such a system of defence would occasion weakness everywhere, and would be the prelude to inevitable, and discreditable defeat.' The emphasis ought to be on the defence of the vital positions and this should be done by putting up permanent fortifications in peacetime and not hastily and badly improvised works in an emergency. The vital positions were Quebec, Montreal, and Kingston, at all of which much work still had to be done. Elsewhere he advised at best rather less ambitious projects than had often been proposed before. The defences of Montreal itself should not be delayed and its garrison drawn off by the works at present being carried out at St John, as recommended by Seaton in March 1839. The communications between these important positions and even the Niagara frontier should be protected by barracks and guardhouses and large mobile forces of militia rather than by extensive fortifications, unlikely ever to be completed and certain to lack proper

[1] Stanley to Murray, private and confidential, 29 Sept. 1841, Murray papers, W.O. 80/11.
[2] Murray to Stanley, confidential, 29 Sept. 1841, Derby papers, microfilms, P.A.C., M.G. 24/A/15, reel no. 2: Section 8 Miscellaneous letters and memoranda, 1838–52.

garrisons. The whole area west of Kingston, which could easily be assailed from the lakes upon which the British had as yet no hope of gaining the ascendancy, should have works only at a few places, like London, which were not too near the frontier and where there was sufficient population to supply useful numbers of militia. Murray's second paper emphasized the defences of Halifax, St John, N.B., and near Rivière du Loup on the St Lawrence for the protection of communications between the United Kingdom and the Canadas, and the opening up of an alternative intercolonial road more distant from the frontier.[1] A few days later, the Niagara frontier apart, these recommendations received the support of the duke of Wellington.[2] Gradually the government's emphasis moved definitely in the direction advocated by Murray.

In September, under the imminent threat of McLeod's execution, the government had shown itself inclined to Arthur's emphasis on the lakes by agreeing to authorize the raising of an additional 100 British seamen for Canada. But this was immediately cancelled when the crisis receded because of American protests about the force already on the lakes. By the summer of 1838 Sandom's force had clearly exceeded the limits of the 1817 agreement, but tacitly conceding the necessity of the increase the American government had not objected to this as a temporary expedient. The construction of so large a vessel as the *Minos* in 1840, however, was rather more alarming. In September 1841 Webster sought renewed assurances, and after McLeod's release, formally demanded a return to the strict terms of the agreement. Aberdeen made no reply until 31 March 1842 and even then said that with the 'utmost reluctance' they would have to keep up the force a little longer. Bagot continued to press for the increases recommended by Sandom; but the September measures had already been cancelled and by April the Admiralty were recommending a return to the 1817 limits. The lack of any further American protests and the continued concern for the security of the frontier held up orders to reduce the force to the agreed

[1] 'Military memorandum upon the defence of the province of Canada by Sir George Murray, sent to Lord Stanley, same day', 8 Jan. 1842, and 'Military memorandum on the defence of the provinces of New Brunswick and Nova Scotia, sent to Lord Stanley, 10 Jan. 1842', in Murray papers, W.O. 80/11, and in W.O. 1/538. On 13 Jan. Murray also sent Stanley a copy of his extensive 'Memorandum respecting Canada, 1815'. There is a very scrappy draft of this in the Murray papers in the National Library of Scotland, Edinburgh, and a good copy in the Derby papers, microfilms in P.A.C., M.G. 24/A/15, reel no. 1: Departmental Memoranda, 1841–45.

[2] Wellington's 'Memorandum on the defence of Canada for Lord Stanley', 12 Jan. 1842, W.O. 55/1551 (7B).

level until February 1843. In the following September Sandom was withdrawn and his force laid up. He claimed, however, to have left the ships in a state which would permit the rapid reforming of the flotilla.[1]

In the meantime attention to the fortifications also showed a change in favour of Murray's approach. At the end of October 1842 work was stopped on the new fort at St John on the Richelieu and the Ordnance directed to concentrate instead on the fortifications at Quebec, Montreal, and Kingston.[2] But now that the immediate crisis was passed resentment at Canadian ingratitude and the Treasury's customary demands for economy began once more to exert their effect. 'Why should we contract the tremendous obligation of having to defend, *on a point of honour*, their territory against American aggression?' asked the prime minister as the Maine boundary negotiations dragged on. 'I say *a point of honour* for I doubt whether any positive gain from the most successful issue of a contest would repay one tenth of the cost of it.' He was prepared to 'fight to the last' if the people of Canada were with them; but the renewed conflict in the Canadian Assembly over the civil list suggested that they were not.

Reflecting on the manifold evils of war with the United States – on the high probability that such a war cannot take place, without involving other parties than the original combatants – seeing that the boundary question involves no principle, I would go as far as we safely can go, in the present sate of the Canadas, in accommodating matters so far as that question is concerned – the prospective evil of a roundabout military communication, between New Brunswick and Quebec is less than the risk of a general war undertaken for such a cause.[3]

The continuation of the state of uncertainty on the frontier allowed the Colonial Office for a while to resist Treasury demands that Canada pay for the militia with the argument that this could not be done while the home government required them to be on a war footing. But in September Stanley wrote privately to Bagot pointing out that they

[1] Callahan, pp. 99–100 and 119–22; Corey, pp. 108–12 and 154–57; C.O. to Adm., 27 April 1842, Adm. 1/5523; Adm. to C.O., 30 April 1842, W.O. 42/499; C.O. to Adm., 18 Feb. 1843, Adm. 1/5534; Sandom to Colchester, 13 Feb. 1846, Colchester papers, P.R.O. 30/9/6, pt. I.

[2] C.O. to Ordnance, 31 Oct. 1842, W.O. 1/538.

[3] Peel to Aberdeen, 16 May 1842, Aberdeen papers, B.M.Add.MS. 40,453 (partly printed in Parker, iii. 388–9). The day before Wellington had been advising Aberdeen to consult the military experts again: *ibid.*, Add.MS.43,060. On 22 May Aberdeen replied that there was no time: 'The matter is now become invested with considerations of the greatest political importance, involving the probability, or rather the certainty of war at no distant period with the United States in the event of Ashburton's failure': *ibid.*, Add.MS.43,060.

could not ask parliament for money for both the militia and the pro-gramme of fortifications contemplated by the previous government. A fortnight later he wrote to Jackson asking him to propose a scheme for the reduction of the regular force and of the programme of works. On 1 December Jackson replied suggesting several large savings in fortifica-tions, especially by the omission of one of the citadels proposed for Montreal and of a new fort on the Niagara frontier. For the moment his proposal seems to have been accepted but the pursuit of economy naturally continued. In September 1843 a cheaper project for the defence of Kingston was being investigated and in the following spring the Ordnance were again required to revise the whole Canadian fortification scheme out of a need for economy.[1]

But substantial progress had been made on the principal forts and this was true too of communications. In the first place the character and outcome of the Maine boundary negotiations naturally emphasized the importance of the intercolonial road. Further investigations of the alternative routes and even of a scheme for a canal from the Bay of Fundy to the Gulf of St Lawrence were carried out in 1842 and 1843 and much was done to improve both the Temiscouata and Kempt roads.[2] At the same time, thanks largely to the pressure exerted by Durham in 1838 and 1839, reviews of the canal system in Canada were carried out and in 1842 work began on the enlargement of the Welland canal locks and the construction of the Beauharnois canal on the St Lawrence above Montreal. In 1843 the Cornwall canal was at last com-pleted and with various other improvements the St Lawrence promised by the late 1840s to open Lake Ontario to large steamboats from the sea. So far as military considerations were involved, however, the Beauharnois already gave concern from its particularly exposed position on the south side of the river.[3]

[1] C.O. to Treasury, 15 April 1842. C.O. 6/86; Stanley to Bagot, private, 19 Sept. 1842, Bagot papers, P.A.C., M.G. 24/A/13, vol. 9; Jackson to Somerset, 1 Dec. 1842, W.O. 1/538; C.O., confidential, to Metcalfe, 14 Sept. 1843, W.O. 1/539; and C.O. to Ordnance, 13 May 1844, W.O. 6/86.
[2] See *passim*, W.O. 1/539, 540 and 541.
[3] Bagot had written home on 19 July 1842 (no. 157, C.O. 42/494) that he had decided to start work on the southern route of the canal, arguing that it was cheaper and of no military significance. If the Americans invaded Canada they would do so from Lake Champlain, and in any case troops could be moved down river without the canal. And if they did capture or destroy the canal they would not have severed Great Britain's strategic connection between the colonies which was by the Ottawa and Rideau system to the rear. In a private letter of the same day he went on to say that, while the northern route would be more secure from the U.S., its supporters really urged it out of vested interests (Bagot to Stanley, private, 19 July 1842, Bagot papers, P.A.C., M.G. 24/A/13,

The most striking improvement was in the establishment of regular troops. By the end of November 1842 Jackson's force of British regulars had fallen from their 1842 peak of nearly 12,500 to a little under 11,000, principally by the withdrawal in August of the two battalions of guards and some of the cavalry. What he proposed in his letter of 1 December was that the remainder of the cavalry, two battalions of infantry, and two companies of artillery should be withdrawn during 1843, followed by a further two battalions of infantry in 1844. This would leave as the permanent garrison ten battalions of British infantry, the Royal Canadian Rifles, and seven companies of artillery, together with three troops of provincial cavalry and two companies of provincial infantry for the special duties of guarding communications and preventing desertion in the Canadian winter – a total of some 7,700 rank and file. In 1843 Bagot failed to get a new militia bill through the Canadian parliament and the Colonial Office felt that any permanent militia at all was too expensive for the British government to maintain. They decided therefore to rely on only the Royal Canadians and a small company of coloured militia to check desertion. Otherwise Jackson's proposals seem to have been accepted. The danger of winter ship-wrecks for a while held up the withdrawal, but by April 1844 the infantry establishment in Canada was shown as eleven battalions, including the Royal Canadians, – a total of 6,400 men.[1] This compared very well with the mere 2,000 which the outbreak of the rebellion had found in the Canadas in 1837. The other garrisons in North America were also kept at or above their former level: in the Maritime Provinces there were still five battalions, a garrison of about 2,500 men; Bermuda, with two battalions (1,140), now had approximately double its former

---

vol. 7). In November the Radical M.P., John Roebuck – who was a Canadian by birth – threatened to challenge this decision in parliament and investigation did reveal that expert opinion was with him. Murray reported that even if the Lake Champlain route were preferred for an attack, the existence of an alter-native line of advance was certainly an advantage since it would compel attention by the defenders and so tend to disperse their resources. The Rideau communi-cation was, of course, greatly inferior in capacity. It was, however, now too late to alter the decision (Peel to Stanley, private, 11 Nov., Peel papers, B.M.Add. MS.40,467; Murray's 'Observations upon that portion of the projected improve-ment of the navigation of the River St Lawrence which consists of the intended Beauharnois canal on the south side of the river', 21 Nov. 1842, Derby papers, microfilms in P.A.C., M.G. 24/A/15, reel no. 1, Departmental Memoranda, 1841–45). For the canal improvements of these years see W. R. Willoughby, *The St Lawrence Waterway* (Madison, 1961), pp. 22–7.

[2] See correspondence between the Horse Guards and the C.O., 7 April 1843, Nov. and Dec. 1843, and return of the army establishments abroad, 1 April 1844, W.O. 1/597.

garrison. Thus the total peacetime strength of the regular force in British North America had risen from 4,500 to just over 10,000.

This was not achieved without some reduction in the other American commands: the infantry establishment in the Jamaica command fell by over 700 men to 2,480, and by more than 1,500 men in the Windward and Leeward Islands command to 3,700.[1] But this was due in part to a growing tendency to concentrate available forces in the more important positions, promising others, like the Bahamas, support only in the event of an emergency.[2] Bermuda, on the other hand, was not neglected. Apparently the alterations recommended by Russell's departmental committee in May 1840 had not been carried out for lack of money and when they came to be re-examined in 1842 naval and military opinion both opposed the alterations on the grounds that additional fortifications would either disperse the garrison in positions which were not vital or force the government to allot to them an inconveniently large number of troops. It was decided therefore to adhere to the original plan of 1826 but to speed up the work by sending out more convict labour.[3]

From the British point of view it was fortunate that pacific gestures had not utterly disposed of increased military precaution. Ashburton's mission to the United States and the settlement of the Maine boundary question were the supreme triumph of Aberdeen's American peace policy. But it was an imperfect and incomplete triumph; and soon, before even Aberdeen had given way again to Palmerston, Anglo-American relations were again to reach a point of apparent explosion.

[1] See correspondence between the Horse Guards and the C.O., 7 April 1843, Nov. and Dec. 1843, and return of the army establishments abroad, 1 April 1844, W.O. 1/597.
[2] Such was the reply which Col. Cockburn got from the C.O. about his weak defences in the Bahamas (2 Oct. 1841, W.O. 1/579). Later Stanley relented and ordered that he be allowed to keep the defences in repair (C.O. to Cockburn, 28 Feb. 1842, *ibid.*).
[3] See *passim*, W.O. 1/538, and especially: Col. W. Reid (governor of Bermuda) to C.O., 1 May; memoranda by Murray, 23 May, and Mulcaster, 7 June; Murray to C.O., confidential, 13 June; C.O. to Adm., 16 July; Adm. to C.O., 26 Oct.; and C.O. to Ordnance, 10 Nov. 1842.

Oregon and Texas, 1843–1846

When Ashburton's most violent critics accused him of incompetence and imbecility, they may or may not have been right; but they were certainly unfair when they accused him of naive affection for the Americans.[1] Ashburton was by no means modest and genuinely believed that he had averted war. But he had done so, he claimed, because the justice of his case and the fairness of his negotiation had so impressed the 'honourable and reasonable portion of the American public'.[2] Of the people in general he had no good opinion and in the permanence of good Anglo-American relations little hope. Of the McLeod case itself he had commented shortly before being invited to undertake the American mission: 'A few days will settle [it] one way or other and upon the whole I am not very fearful for the result *this time*. But there will be no end of boundary questions, sympathizers, and border agitations and some day or other the blow up will come and we shall be disgraced, let who may be at the helm.'[3] With the Anglophil Webster as secretary of state, however, there was some chance of improvement and in his American mission Ashburton had sought to 'improve the present moment by an active attempt to heal all old sores'.[4] But a few minor successes apart, Ashburton's negotiations made virtually no progress beyond the settlement of the Maine boundary question. He failed in particular to make any headway with an agreement over the boundaries

---

[1] In a letter to Russell of which only part has survived but which was probably written in Sept. 1842, Palmerston commented 'never was there imbecility like that of Ashburton if it was nothing worse' (G. P. Gooch, ed., *The Later Correspondence of Lord John Russell, 1840–1878* [2 vols., London, 1925], i. 58–9). When the news of Ashburton's mission broke in London there were 'sly hints' about his financial interest in the U.S. Ashburton insisted, however, that at that time he had no American interests at all, excepting only his wife's inheritance which was administered by trustees (Ashburton to J. W. Croker, 7 Jan. 1842, Croker papers, William Clements Library, Ann Arbor, Michigan).
[2] Ashburton to Bagot, 16 April 1842, Bagot papers, P[ublic] A[rchives of] C[anada], M[anuscript] G[roup] 24/A/13, vol. 2, pt. 1.
[3] Ashburton to Croker, 12 Oct. 1841, Croker papers, Clements Library.
[4] Ashburton to Croker, ? Dec. 1841, *ibid.*

west of the Rockies. According to his own story this was in part because he dared not risk prejudicing the improvement he had made in Anglo-American relations with an open failure on any other important subject; and he did not believe his instructions would allow him to make a settlement satisfactory to the Senate. He also suggested that Webster had been equally lukewarm, perhaps because he wished to repeat the social success of his London visit of 1839 with a diplomatic mission to rival Ashburton's own triumph in Washington.[1] Whatever the truth Ashburton certainly left behind him some of the very 'sores' he believed so dangerous to peace.

The treaty of 1842 had stabilized the Anglo-American frontier in the north and north-east. But on the southern, western, and north-western borders, the Americans felt their strategic security and their pretension to real continental dominion were still threatened. To the south the fate of Texas hung in the balance, its ultimate adherence to the American Union or to a British sphere of influence quite uncertain. In the west they could not even be sure that the erosion of Mexico's rule would not present California to Great Britain rather than to them, and with California would go the glittering prize of San Francisco. In the north-west the pressure of popular opinion, the clash of local commercial interests, and not least the catalytic influence of deteriorating Anglo-American relations, had revived too the long suspended Oregon boundary question. In all these areas, the Americans thought, there were great opportunities for realizing their expansionist dreams, but equally great dangers from the sinister manœuvres of their old rival. The British government, on the other hand, could see only limited opportunities of frustrating and containing American ambitions, and great risks even in those. But though grossly exaggerated, the accusations made openly against the British by nervous Americans in these years were not entirely without foundation.

Following the occasional interest taken in San Francisco Bay in the previous decade local British agents were now stressing the weakness of Mexican authority in California and the danger of the Texan 'game' being repeated. To forestall such a disaster colonization and even protectorates were urged on the British government by consular

---

[1] Ashburton to Croker, 20 Feb. 1843, Croker papers, Clements Library, and to Aberdeen, private, 1 June 1843, Aberdeen papers, B.M.Add.MS.43,123. See also Wilbur Devereux Jones, *Lord Aberdeen and the Americas* (Athens, Ga., 1958), pp. 26–7, and F. Merk,' The Oregon Question in the Webster-Ashburton Negotiations', *Mississippi Valley Historical Review* xliii, (1956–57), 379–404.

officials in August 1841 and September 1843, and about the same time Sir George Simpson, the overseas governor of the Hudson's Bay Company, was pressing for the acquisition of San Francisco. But these proposals met with what seemed to be a very unsympathetic response in London. Generally speaking Conservative and Whig governments alike were anxious to avoid additional colonial burdens, especially if they threatened to provoke new quarrels with foreign powers. Thus Russell had commented on some of the Hudson's Bay Company's suggestions in February 1841, 'we do not contemplate any *new* acquisitions . . . either on the shores, or [in] any of the islands of the Pacific'. His successor, Stanley, was even more scathing when he commented later in the same year about one of the colonization schemes for California: 'I am not anxious for the formation of new and distant colonies, all of which involve heavy direct, and still heavier indirect expense, besides multiplying the possibilities of misunderstandings and collisions with Foreign Powers. Still less am I prepared to recommend the adoption of a plan whereby the soil shall in the first instance be vested in a company of adventurers.' But Stanley did go on to say that he and Aberdeen might be prepared to consider a scheme involving an actual cession of territory to the crown, and similarly, when pronouncing an equally anticolonial verdict on a quite different proposal later in 1841, the prime minister, Peel, had added: 'Still the revolutions that are silently but rapidly effected by the progress of steam navigation, make me pause, before projects, startling at the first mention of them, are at once rejected.'[1]

Certainly there was always good reason to pause in the Pacific where the Royal Navy still lacked any sovereign base whatever; and anticolonial sentiment did not stop the Admiralty and Foreign Office together investigating the utility of acquiring the Galapagos Islands in 1844 and 1845. But nowhere could the Admiralty find a satisfactory site. Pearl Harbor they had long since rashly dismissed as too shallow; if the temporary occupation of Hawaii in 1843 had any ulterior motive beyond the redress of specific grievances, it was to support its independence against others rather than to acquire it for themselves. And what probably put a stop to any government interest in acquiring San

[1] Minutes by Russell, 13 Feb., on Adm. to C.O., 11 Feb. 1841, and by Stanley, 10 Nov., on Pakenham to F.O., no. 91, 30 Aug. 1841, C.O. 42/482; Peel to Stanley, private, 30 Dec. 1841, Peel papers, B.M.Add.MS.40,467. The significant afterthoughts added by Stanley and Peel have usually been quite overlooked; see, for example, E. D. Adams, *British Interests and Activities in Texas, 1838–1846* (Baltimore, 1910), pp. 237–44, and Jones, *Aberdeen and the Americas*, p. 26.

Francisco was the report early in 1842 that it would be indefensible against an attack from the interior.[1]

A few months later Ashburton admitted that his government would probably not now object to the acquisition of California by the United States; but a surprising caution prevented him from seizing the opportunity offered during his Washington mission to bargain away California in exchange for an American agreement on the line of frontier traditionally claimed by the British in Oregon.[2] As the fur trade in the area was now rapidly declining, the principal interest of both governments in this disputed territory was to preserve the good opinion of the public. The Tyler and Peel administrations were both in perilous positions; the Oregon question was fast approaching a climax in American party politics; and Aberdeen well knew that he could ill afford to give Palmerston another opportunity so soon to cry 'capitulation'. For this reason each side tended to cling, though not consistently, to its traditional claim – the United States to the old compromise line of the 49th parallel; Great Britain to access south of that line to the mouth of the Columbia River. In the spring of 1842 Tyler had been willing to think of conceding the British claim in return for California only because it was assumed the United States would still have a great port at the mouth of the Columbia River; but in June Lieutenant Wilkes's exploring expedition returned to the United States with reports of the dangerous bar at the mouth of the river and of the better harbours of Puget Sound. If Wilkes's reports made it essential for the Americans to have the line of 49° giving them access to the waters of Puget Sound, it also made quite pointless any further insistence by the British on the virtually useless possession of the Columbia River.

But what good information and common sense indicated as a worthy compromise at least as early as the summer of 1842, ham-fisted diplomacy and still more the growing fervour of public opinion prevented for nearly another four years. This was particularly the case in the United States where a growing public interest in the Oregon question made compromise increasingly difficult and culminated ultimately in the

[1] For the Galapagos see F.O. to Adm., 30 July and 10 Aug. 1844, Adm. 1/5544; and Adm. to Adm. Sir George Seymour (c.-in-c., Pacific), secret, 5 Sept. 1844, and to Capt. Henry Kellett (commanding the survey frigate *Herald*), 19 May 1845, Adm. 2/1696. For Hawaii see above, p. 67, and R. W. Van Alstyne, 'Great Britain, the United States and Hawaiian Independence, 1850–1855', *Pacific Historical Review*, iv (1935), 15–16. The San Francisco report is cited by Jones, *Aberdeen and the Americas*, p. 26.

[2] Merk, 'The Oregon Question in the Webster-Ashburton Negotiations', pp. 394–401.

Democrats' election manœuvre of the summer of 1844 which linked the two principal expansionist issues so that western votes for the acquisition of Texas might be gained in return for southern votes for Oregon. In both cases it was useful and easy to make wholesale denunciations of British intrigues. For, while in 1842 and 1843 negotiations over Oregon had tended to get bogged down, Aberdeen had been resuming an initiative in Texas that seemed almost Palmerstonian in its daring.

At the end of June 1842 the Texan treaties negotiated by Palmerston and General Hamilton were at last completed by the exchange of ratifications. One of them provided for British mediation with Mexico and before long Aberdeen was intervening energetically to obtain a settlement which would see both Mexico and Texas safely independent of the United States and on especially good terms with Great Britain. At the same time he was in still more earnest pursuit of every opportunity to repair the entente with France that Palmerston's Near Eastern policy had shattered. Texas seemed a promising opportunity for co-operation, and the summer of 1844 found Great Britain and France apparently committed in the defence of Texan independence and Mexican integrity even to the point of war.[1] Whether or not Aberdeen really meant the threat is quite uncertain; in any case the fragility of the new entente with France and the obstinacy of the Mexicans had utterly killed the scheme by the end of October. In the meantime Britain's mediation and anti-slavery activities in Texas had once more aroused American opinion. At the end of 1843 active steps towards annexation were resumed in both Texas and the United States, and although domestic quarrels defeated annexation once again in June 1844 American public opinion was kept at a fever pitch of hostility towards Great Britain. Then in that same summer came the Democrats' election tactics to soften domestic opposition to the annexation of Texas by linking it with the acquisition of Oregon. By the end of the year, it seemed, the British were faced with both a more determined and hostile movement for the annexation of Texas and, as the violent election cry of 'Fifty-Four Forty or Fight' indicated, with an Oregon claim that went far beyond the compromise line of 49°. So far as Oregon was concerned, much depended on the extent to which the public clamour would decline when the election campaign was over and a new administration was safely in office. But in July 1845 the British minister in

[1] Adams, pp. 156–74. Jones, *Aberdeen and the Americas*, is an interesting attempt to discover in Aberdeen's policy a 'grand strategy' designed to keep the United States and France apart while repairing the Anglo-French entente.

Washington missed a golden opportunity to pick up a compromise offer on the line of 49°, and Polk, the new Democratic president, was encouraged instead to continue to use in office the same kind of threatening language towards Great Britain that he had habitually employed at the hustings. By the summer of 1845, then, with Texas at last about to be absorbed into the Union, Anglo-American relations also found themselves at a dangerous impasse over Oregon.

The British government seems to have realized early in 1844 that it was once again approaching the sort of crisis with the Americans that required active military precautions. The first moves in this respect arose casually from the aftermath of the earlier Canadian crisis of 1838–41. As a result of their concern about the ships the British had built on Lake Erie in 1840 the Americans had eventually included in their defence bill of September 1841 an allocation of $100,000 for the construction of two steamers on Lakes Erie and Ontario. In spite of the evaporation of the McLeod crisis and the abandonment of most of the other measures proposed in the bill, they had persisted with this particular plan. Indeed the orders concerning the steamer for Lake Erie had actually been issued during the conversations with Fox about British armaments on the lakes in November 1841. In the following May it was publicly revealed that a contract had been completed. Later in the year building began on the vessel at Pittsburg and in 1843 it was taken in pieces across country and assembled at Erie.[1] Either this entirely escaped the notice of the British government or they assumed that the plan had been dropped with the withdrawal of Captain Sandom in 1843. Towards the end of January 1844, however, a member of the legislative council of Quebec wrote home to the duke of Wellington to point out that the Americans had recently launched a powerful iron steamer on Lake Erie and that another was building on Lake Ontario. Stanley felt it very unlikely that the Americans would break the Rush-Bagot agreement just when the British had reduced their force in response to American protests, but he took the trouble to find out privately from Sir Charles Metcalfe, the new governor-general of Canada, how the matter really stood.[2]

The report, as Metcalfe soon made known, was all too true. The vessel to which it referred to was the famous side-wheel *Michigan*, the first

[1] J. M. Callahan, *The Neutrality of the American Lakes and Anglo-American Relations* (Baltimore, 1898), pp. 123–5.
[2] Stanley to Metcalfe, private, 4 Mar. 1844, enclosing William Walker to Wellington, 24 Jan., and Stanley to Wellington, 26 Feb. 1844, 'Secret and Confidential Despatches from the C.O.', P.A.C., R.G. 7, Governor-General's Office, G 3, vol. i, pt. 2.

iron ship in the United States Navy, of 582 tons and carrying one eight-inch gun. Both in size and armament it broke the 1817 agreement. Metcalfe also pointed out that the Americans had two similar vessels building at Cleveland and Oswego which would enable them to command Lakes Huron and Ontario as well. The available British force, he concluded, was 'totally incompetent' to deal with vessels like these. The British now had three steamers on Lake Ontario (*Mohawk*, *Cherokee*, and *Traveller*), two on Lake Huron (*Experiment* and *Minos*), and a schooner (*Montreal*) on Lake Erie. But the *Traveller* and *Experiment* were old, the *Montreal* of little use as a warship, the *Cherokee* incomplete and laid up, the *Minos* laid up and probably no longer of any use for active service, and the *Mohawk* was a very small iron gunboat carrying only a carronade. Nor in the event of hostilities could they hope to challenge the powerful new American ships by converting merchantmen, and the canals could still pass up to the lakes nothing 'of any considerable size'. Clearly the measures which the Americans took in 1841–44 in response to those of the British threatened to renew what the 1817 agreement had sought to end – competitive warship construction on the lakes in peacetime.[1]

Presumably Stanley had already had independent confirmation of the existence of the *Michigan*, for on 1 April, long before he could have heard from Metcalfe, he had ordered a secret survey of the St Lawrence from Quebec to the lakes. His object was to see how that line of communication could best be protected and exploited in wartime; but no works were to be undertaken without government approval.[2] In the meantime Aberdeen agreed to make representations in Washington about the 1817 agreement. The Americans were to be told that the British action in 1840 did not justify the American breach since that action had been made necessary by the hostile meddling of the American public in Canadian affairs. This was to be put to them 'in the first instance . . . in a friendly and not too formal tone', and only if it became necessary as a formal but still not hostile request. If the Americans still refused to return to the agreement then they should be told that the British would feel obliged to match whatever force they put on the lakes.[3]

[1] Metcalfe to Stanley, no. 66, 18 April 1844, W.O. 1/540.
[2] Stanley to Metcalfe, private and confidential, 1 April 1844, W.O. 6/83. The three men appointed to make the report were Col. Holloway, R.E., Capt. Boxer, R.N., the harbour-master at Quebec, and Mr Killaly, the president of the Canadian Board of Works.
[3] F.O. to Pakenham, no. 24, 3 July 1844, F.O. 5/403.

As it happened Sir Richard Pakenham, the minister in Washington had already raised this matter with the American secretaries of state and of the navy. The ships, they told him, were intended only for revenue purposes. In any case the 1817 limitations of tonnage and weight of guns were inappropriate to iron ships and modern artillery and should now be revised by agreement.[1] This, Pakenham thought, was but a 'feeble justification'; in London they were not so sure. Aberdeen apparently thought that they ought to build up to equality with the Americans and then, as Mason, the secretary of the navy, had suggested, make a new agreement. Stanley, too, admitted that the letter of the old agreement might not cover steamers, but he still thought that the action of the Americans was 'unfriendly', their excuses 'futile'. To build large steam vessels and to supply them with ammunition 'in time of peace', he told Peel in September, 'can hardly be considered consistent with the spirit at least of the agreement'. In any case some steps had to be taken since the government could 'hardly allow our Trade on those Lakes to be left completely at the mercy of the United States'. To contest American supremacy on the lakes in the event of war had long since been dismissed as 'hopeless', and reliance placed instead on Wellington's fortification plan of 1826. About this, 'though much has been said . . . little or nothing has been done'. Stanley believed that the plan involved at present an expenditure of more than £1 million: 'I should very much hesitate about expending such a sum on such an object, in the present state of our connexion with Canada.'[2] He had complained in February of the Canadians' lack of gratitude for defence among other gifts of the mother country, and in May the current programme of fortifications had been modified in the interests of economy.[3] Now in September he was anxious to avoid being driven into vast expenditure on fortifications merely in retaliation to American measures on the lakes. Consequently he tried to separate the two issues, asking the prime minister to make a decision on the general question of the military defences but at the same time proposing a specific way out of the immediate difficulty about the lakes. Back in July the Niagara Harbour and Dock Company, a Canadian shipbuilding firm which had run into financial difficulties with the building of three new vessels for the lakes, had offered, in return for a financial subsidy, to have these

[1] Pakenham to F.O., no. 85, 29 July 1844, F.O. 5/407.
[2] Stanley to Peel, 5 Sept. 1844, printed by Paul Knaplund, 'The Armaments on the Great Lakes, 1844', *American Historical Review*, xl (1934–35), 474–5.
[3] Stanley to Peel, 2 Feb. 1844, Peel papers, B.M.Add.MS.40,468; and C.O. to Ordnance, 13 May, 1844, W.O. 6/86.

vessels constructed in such a manner as would allow them to be readily adapted as powerful war steamers in the event of hostilities. The proposal had met with approval from the Foreign Office and Stanley now put it to the prime minister.[1]

Peel, too, had been impressed with Metcalfe's dismal reports about Canadian behaviour in the continuing constitutional struggles. Great expenditure on land defences, he agreed, would be 'money thrown away so far as Canadian feeling is concerned'. In any case such was the tendency for disagreement among 'Military Men' to slow down the rate of work that anything done was likely by the time it was ready to be utterly useless against new modes of attack. He did not see 'much prospect of controlling effectually the American tendencies to hostility by costly outlays on land fortifications'. So far as the lakes were concerned, if both the letter and the spirit of the 1817 agreements were clear they ought 'temperately but firmly to require adherence to them. That is the proper course, and a more dignified one than retaliation.' If, however, the Americans rejected any remonstrance, or if the British found it impossible to make one, either because the meaning of the agreement was not clear or because they had themselves set an unfortunate precedent, then they would have no alternative but 'counter armament'. And he knew of 'no more economical mode of effecting this' than by accepting the Niagara company's offer. An important consideration in such a contract would be how far it would provide them with a respectable force as compared with that of the Americans. But they would undoubtedly be beaten in a 'mere race of competition for building Vessels of War on the Lakes'. Its 'chief advantage', therefore, would be to lay 'the foundation of a distinct and practicable convention'.[2]

At first the prospects for Peel's attempt to steer a middle course between the rather different approaches of his two senior colleagues seemed very promising. In September came the Americans' formal reply to Pakenham's original protest, and while this merely repeated the 'feeble' and 'futile' excuses of July, it also referred once again to the possibility of a new agreement.[3] Then, towards the end of October, came the Admiralty's acknowledgement that both in their recent shipbuilding and in their suggestion for a new agreement the Americans did have a good case, since the British had broken the 1817 agreement first and the development of iron vessels had made the terms of that old

---

[1] See various enclosures in C.O. to Adm., confidential, 24 Sept. 1844, Adm. 1/5544; and Stanley to Peel, 5 Sept. 1844, Knaplund, pp. 474–5.
[2] Peel to Stanley, 7 Sept. 1844, printed by Knaplund, pp. 475–6.
[3] Enclosed in Pakenham to F.O., no. 102, 12 Sept. 1844, F.O. 5/408.

agreement utterly impractical.[1] But if modern naval technology had made the old agreement impractical, it also promised to make any new agreement relatively ineffective. As Pakenham had already pointed out, a new agreement would presumably still exclude 'dismantled' vessels, and vessels constructed of iron and propelled by steam engines could be dismantled only to a very limited degree. In the event of hostilities, then, such vessels could be prepared all the more rapidly for war. And now James Stephen, the under-secretary at the Colonial Office, added that 'one of the many unexpected results of steam navigation' was the ease with which steamships for commercial purposes could be converted into warships. This after all was the basis of the arrangements recently made by the government with regard to the American and West Indian Mail Packets. The proposed contract with the Niagara Dock Company suggested therefore, not that it would promote a new and more effective agreement about the lakes, but that any agreement would be all too easily evaded. The idea of seeking a new agreement with the United States was quietly dropped. Not so the arrangement with the Niagara company. There might be no point in using it to extract a new agreement from the Americans or any prospect in the long run of it providing an effective force on the lakes. But presumably, as Stanley had suggested earlier, it would serve as a 'demonstration' to 'prevent further armament on the part of the United States'.[2] On 4 November the Admiralty at last approved the proposal and in January 1845 the government's terms were accepted. These provided for three vessels to be built to the Admiralty's specifications at a cost of £11,500 each; the government was to advance £5,000 in respect of each ship; and in the event of taking them over in an emergency was to pay the balance less depreciation.[3]

The plans for increasing the force that would be available for the lakes in an emergency did lead to some additional works being set in hand at Kingston, but these had nothing to do with the general Canadian fortification scheme. Peel and Stanley remained at this stage firmly

[1] Adm. to C.O., 24 Oct. 1844, W.O. 1/541.

[2] For the principal correspondence and minutes on this subject see *passim* W.O. 1/541. The arrangements about the packet steamers to which Stephen referred, were made in 1839–40 with Cunard, the Royal Mail Steam Packet Company, and the P. & O. Company. The Americans began to take an active interest in the scheme in 1841 and similar arrangements were made by them in 1845–46. But naval technology, especially the development of heavy ordnance, rapidly outdistanced such makeshift devices (C. J. Bartlett, *Great Britain and Sea Power, 1815–1853* [Oxford, 1963], pp. 235–7; Harold and Margaret Sprout, *The Rise of American Naval Power, 1776–1918* [Princeton, 1939], pp. 133–5).

[3] Adm. to C.O., 4 Nov. 1844, W.O. 1/541; Metcalfe to Stanley, no 204, 14 Jan. 1845, W.O. 1/552.

opposed to the prosecution of these expensive undertakings, but an 'inferior' naval force, as Stanley described it, would stand in particular need of a well-defended harbour of refuge, and on 23 September he wrote to Sir George Murray, the master-general of the Ordnance, asking if he considered the defences of Kingston satisfactory. Murray began by reminding Stanley that without naval superiority on Lake Ontario, western Canada could only be defended by a large body of militia and that Kingston was also important as the exit of the Rideau communication. Like so many other parts of the 1826 scheme Kingston's defences had never been completed because, as he helpfully put it, of their 'undue magnitude'. What Stanley proposed to the cabinet therefore was that Kingston should be provided with defences capable of resisting a *coup de main* aimed at its destruction, but that until the Canadians 'acted cordially' – presumably by reforming the militia – there was no point in expensive fortifications to hold off a major attack aimed at the permanent occupation of the city. Wellington, of course, again took the opportunity to remind the cabinet of the obligation to defend Canada as a 'point of honour', and the need of field armies and improved communications as well as the fortifications he had so often commended to the government's attention. But Peel came down heavily on Stanley's side, adding with grim sarcasm: 'The reports of the state of defences of almost every important port at home or abroad are most unsatisfactory. . . . It appears to me that there must be something defective in the ordinary system of periodical inspection and in the application of gradual repair and the keeping up of a decent state of defence.' So on 15 January 1845 Murray drew up a modest scheme of local defences for Kingston and on 23 January Stanley ordered its immediate execution.[1]

None of the measures taken up to the beginning of 1845 really reflected any serious preparation for actual war. Stanley had throughout been seeking to avoid a wholesale resumption of the existing fortification scheme and his support of the Niagara Dock Company contract

[1] Stanley's Cabinet Memorandum no. 3, Jan. 1845, 'Defences of Canada; Kingston Harbour' (Derby papers, microfilms in P.A.C., M.G. 24/A/15, reel no. 2, Cabinet Memoranda, 1841–45), includes: Stanley's own memorandum for the cabinet, 29 Nov. 1844; a 'Memorandum for the Master General' (on the defences of Montreal) by Col. E. Fanshawe, 25 Sept; 'Memorandum with regard to the Province of Canada; and particularly with respect to the harbour of Kingston', by Murray, 27 Sept.; a memorandum by Wellington, 2 Dec. 1844; a minute by Peel, Jan. 1845; and Stanley to the master-general, confidential, 23 Jan. 1845. There is a copy of Murray's memorandum of 27 Sept. in the Murray papers, W.O. 80/11.

and the limited defences for Kingston had been intended primarily as a 'demonstration' to the Americans that they would be wiser to suspend any further warship building on the lakes. If the government had any real apprehension of war in the summer and autumn of 1844 it was war with France rather than war with the United States. Even Peel got very heated about an Anglo-French incident over Tahiti and had to be reminded by Aberdeen that war was 'the greatest of all calamities', and ought not to be brought closer by unnecessary preparations. 'There is no more false maxim as applied to Great States,' Aberdeen told him, 'than that we ought to prepare for war, in order to preserve peace. A Small State may perhaps arm for its defence, & to prevent war. A Great State can only prepare for war, in order to make war.'[1] But although Peel had talked for a moment about war with France bringing war with the United States in its train, so far as the Americans alone were concerned in 1844 he thought of defensive measures only as moral weapons designed to control American tendencies to hostility.[2] The same is probably true of Aberdeen's Texan policy in the summer of 1844, when he tried to enlist the aid of France against the new state's annexation by the United States. The collapse of that policy in the autumn left untested Aberdeen's implied threat to meet American 'aggression' against Mexico with force, but in all probability he never really thought that it would come to war. The threat would have been enough.[3] Aberdeen's views in this respect, and those of his government generally, seem in fact to have followed the opinion given by Pakenham in March:

If we cannot definitively settle [the Oregon] question there will be no quarrel – no scandal – to alarm the publick in England or otherwise seriously to embarrass Her Majesty's Government. The fact is the Americans are much more afraid of a rupture than we are, and I am convinced that the bare probability of such a result would cause such a demonstration on the part of the leading interests in this country in favor of peace as would speedily lead to the removal of all difficulties. Nor are the mischievous declarations in Congress which at a distance appear to augur so

[1] Aberdeen to Peel, 22 and 21 Aug. 1844, quoted by Jones, *Aberdeen and the Americas*, p. 38.
[2] Peel to Aberdeen, 21 Aug. 1844, *ibid.*, p. 38, and Peel to Stanley, confidential, 7 Sept. 1844, Knaplund, p. 475.
[3] Opinions have differed on this point. Justin H. Smith, *The Annexation of Texas* (New York, 1911), p. 394, thought that Aberdeen was ready 'to undertake war'; E. D. Adams, *British Interests and Activities in Texas*, p. 172, that he 'never seriously thought that war would result'. Jones, *Aberdeen and the Americas*, pp. 35–6, believes that he 'evidently' did 'contemplate the possibility of a war', but that this did not mean that he 'either wanted or expected' it.

warlike a disposition to be taken at their literal import. A great deal of all this is nothing more than Electioneering manœuvre.[1]

Three months later, after Tyler had tried and failed to get a Texan annexation treaty through the Senate, Pakenham changed his mind, believing that the failure had reduced the president to desperation in the pursuit of re-election: 'Your Lordship may depend upon it,' he told Aberdeen, 'that if he thought that, by bringing about a war with England, on the Oregon question, or by any other manœuvre equally desperate and condemnable, he could add to his prospects of success, he would resort to it at a moment's notice.'[2] But the electioneering tactics of Tyler and his opponent Polk apparently did not change the view of the government in London. With the election over and the new president safely established they expected much of the difficulty over Oregon to evaporate. In this they were to be disappointed and even Peel seems to have sensed that this would be so when news arrived in England early in the new year that the outgoing administration had again refused arbitration. All that had passed he now saw not as so much idle hot air but as making 'compromise and concession . . . ten times more difficult. . . . The point of Honour is now brought into the foreground.' He talked of 'every degree of preparation' now being justified on Great Britain's part; but what most immediately worried him was the position in the disputed territory itself. Aberdeen had assured him that superior numbers of settlers gave Great Britain the upper hand on the banks of the Columbia; but the Americans were now more actively promoting settlement and had begun building fortifications in the area. There was even a bill before Congress to terminate the joint occupation agreement. He suggested therefore that they might at once send out an additional frigate, professedly destined for the Cape or New South Wales, but really with a force of marines and artillery for the mouth of the Columbia.[3] A week later came a letter from Wellington with a gloomy memorandum on the Texas and Oregon questions: 'My conviction is that we have no chance of avoiding disaster excepting in our means and strength. If we should increase these we shall have no occasion to use them. We shall not be insulted, much less attacked.'[4]

[1] Pakenham to Aberdeen, private, 28 Mar. 1844, Aberdeen papers, B.M.Add. MS.43,123.
[2] Pakenham to Aberdeen, private, 13 June 1844, *ibid*. W. D. Jones and J. Chal Vinson, 'British Preparedness and the Oregon Settlement', *Pacific Historical Review*, xxii (1953), 356, note Pakenham's 28 Mar. letter but overlook this change of opinion.
[3] Peel to Aberdeen, 23 Feb. 1845, quoted by Jones, *Aberdeen and the Americas*, pp. 57–8.
[4] Wellington to Aberdeen, 1 Mar., Aberdeen papers, B.M.Add.MS.43,060.

Aberdeen now admitted that it would be 'difficult to avoid a state of actual hostilities' if they failed to arrive at an amicable settlement. But he had understood from Pakenham that the American government would probably kill the occupation bill and British settlers, he believed, still had the local advantage. In any case the termination of the joint occupation agreement required a year's notice and that would give them plenty of time for warlike preparations. In the meantime he would offer arbitration once again. But he had already warned Pakenham that if no agreement was reached they would maintain their rights 'at all hazards', and he hoped when the matter was raised in the House of Commons the next day that 'such an answer may be returned as will afford an ultimatum to the United States of our determination to submit to no insult, and to maintain our rights'.[1] Peel in fact made a rather evasive response in the House of Commons.[2] But Aberdeen got his way about trying arbitration once again.[3] He managed even to persuade Peel to tone down his proposals for secret naval measures off the Oregon coast. 'The proceedings in the United States', the Foreign Office told the Admiralty, 'appear to indicate the necessity of increased vigilance and activity.' But until the Senate's action on the joint occupation bill was known they did 'not think it expedient to direct the adoption of any hostile measure'. What they wanted at this stage was rather to demonstrate their determination to the American 'Government and people in general, and also to that portion of United States citizens who are at this moment established in the Territory in question'. A warship should make frequent appearances off the coast and, 'with a view to give a feeling of security to our own settlers in the Country, and to let the Americans see clearly that Her Majesty's Government are alive to their proceedings, and prepared, in case of necessity, to oppose them', Admiral Seymour, the commander-in-chief in the Pacific, should himself visit Puget Sound as soon as possible. Even this limited demonstration proved impossible. The Foreign Office had already despatched the admiral to Tahiti on a similar mission, and Seymour had to be given orders instead to make the visit to Oregon when he could.[4]

---

[1] Aberdeen to Wellington, 2 Mar., Peel papers, B.M.Add.MS.40,455.
[2] Jones, *Aberdeen and the Americas*, p. 58.　　　　　　　[3] *Idem.*
[4] F.O. to Adm., secret, 5 and 8 Mar. 1845, Adm. 1/5554; Adm. to F.O., 6 Mar., and Adm. to Seymour, 10 Mar., Adm. 2/1696. Apparently misreading the analysis made by E. D. Adams, pp. 248–61, Jones and Vinson, *op. cit.*, p. 358, conclude that these orders were probably never sent to Seymour and that the British were bluffing. But Adams seems rather to say that Seymour never received any direct orders from home about his government's policy towards California. The despatch of the Foreign Office's orders to Seymour on 10 Mar.

In the meantime affairs in the United States were coming to an apparent climax. On 25 January 1845 the Texan annexation bill had passed the House of Representatives; on 27 February it was squeezed through the Senate in an amended form; and on 1 March President Tyler signed it. The last hope of preventing annexation now lay in direct intervention in Mexico and Texas but though Aberdeen went through the motions of mediation and persuasion, with the collapse of the Anglo-French alignment of the previous year he had lost his enthusiasm if not his concern.[1] What aroused both him and his government now was rather the disappointing news that Polk's electioneering fulminations over Oregon had not been dampened by the assumption of office. On 3 March, the same day that Peel had made his statement in the House of Commons, Polk had made his Inaugural Address, and it had been full of bombastic assertions about the American people's 'clear and unquestionable' title to the disputed territory. As the impression grew that Polk's violence was not going to subside, even Aberdeen's attitude began to stiffen. On 29 March Sir George Simpson, the overseas governor of the Hudson's Bay Company, presented him with a memorandum on the company's interests in Oregon and, since he believed they should not give way to the Americans and that war was therefore not improbable, with comprehensive recommendations for the defence of their north-western territories in Oregon and of their settlements on the Red River. The latter, he suggested, were particularly vulnerable to attack from American positions across the border and should have a small force of regulars as well as a company of half-breeds. The Hudson's Bay Company itself would raise another force of two thousand half-breeds and Indians for service in Oregon. But these should be led by regulars and the government, too, ought to send two steamers and two sail warships with a large body of marines to Oregon, and occupy Cape Disappointment to command the entrance of the Columbia River.

Aberdeen at first thought this was all rather overdone. He admitted to Peel that they ought 'without delay' to make what he called 'all reasonable preparations'. But they should still be such as would be 'consistent with the preservation of peace': 'In spite of Mr Polk's address, I cannot believe, that when they see us determined, the American Govt. will drive matters to extremity.' But on 2 April Simpson

---

is properly recorded in Adm. 2/1696, and there is nothing to suggest that Aberdeen was bluffing when he told Pakenham about these orders on 2 April, especially as he referred at the same time to equally martial precautions which certainly were undertaken (Jones, *Aberdeen and the Americas*, p. 59).

[1] Jones, *Aberdeen and the Americas*, pp. 62–7.

was given an opportunity to expound his views before Aberdeen and Peel, and Aberdeen largely gave way. From Polk's language, he now wrote to Pakenham, he expected the Americans would shortly denounce the agreement providing for the joint occupation of Oregon and that if the question were not then settled in the course of the year, 'a local collision must speedily take place, which may too probably involve the Countries in the most serious difficulties, & finally lead to war itself'. 'At all events', he now admitted, 'whatever may be the course of the American Government, the time is come when we must endeavour to prepare for every contingency.' Pakenham was therefore warned that Simpson would be coming out at once to discuss with him such measures 'as may be thought necessary and useful'. The next day, 3 April, orders were also given to the Colonial Office to have a special military investigation made in Oregon. Eventually this was done by sending two young army officers along with Simpson on what was supposed to look like his routine annual visit and ostensibly so that they could hunt. Simpson himself apparently was even authorized to spend £1,000 on forts to protect the company's trade, but with a view too to commanding the entrance of the Columbia.[1]

Replying to an Opposition intervention in the House of Lords on 4 April, Aberdeen declared that while he still considered 'war to be the greatest folly, if not the greatest crime, of which a country could be guilty, if lightly entered into', and his own country's power and position great enough not to be too sensitive about 'questions of national honour', that honour was nevertheless 'a substantial property' which they could never neglect, however painful such a course might be. All this, no doubt, was meant as an 'impressive warning' to the United States, and perhaps also to the Opposition and public opinion generally not to expect him to uphold any exaggerated sense of honour.[2] But what was

[1] Aberdeen to Peel, private, 29 Mar., and to Pakenham, private, 2 April 1845, quoted substantially by Jones, *Aberdeen and the Americas*, pp. 58–9; F.O. to C.O., 3 April, W.O. 1/553. For Simpson's intervention see John S. Galbraith, *The Hudson's Bay Company as an Imperial Factor, 1821–1869* (Berkeley and Los Angeles, 1957), pp. 236–8. C. P. Stacey, 'The Hudson's Bay Company and Anglo-American Military Rivalries during the Oregon Dispute', *Canadian Historical Review*, xviii (1937), 290–1, suggests that Simpson's principal motive was to get help in restoring the company's authority among the Indians of the Red River area. Simpson's memorandum of 29 Mar., and some of the reports of the two engineer officers, are printed in Joseph Schafer, ed., 'Documents Relative to Warre and Vavasour's Military Reconnoissance in Oregon, 1845–46', *Oregon Historical Quarterly*, x (1909), 1–99.

[2] Jones, *Aberdeen and the Americas*, pp. 60–1. See also F. Merk, 'British Government Propaganda and the Oregon Treaty', *American Historical Review*, xl (1934–35), 39.

clearly in the forefront of Aberdeen's calculations was the danger of an accidental 'brush-fire' in the disputed territory itself, leading in turn to a more general conflagration. It was, after all, with a view to boosting the confidence of the local British population and as a warning to the Americans that he had agreed to the orders sent to Seymour early in March. It was with this same limited objective in mind that on 2 April he had consented – reluctantly, perhaps – to Simpson's mission. But even though he was now plainly worried about a local clash, he still hoped to limit the nature and objective of any military preparations, just as, in an admittedly more despondent and half-hearted way, he still searched for a diplomatic solution in both Oregon and Texas. But now in the spring and summer of 1845 the pressure began to build up both in England and in Canada for the rather more extensive prepar- ations which would become necessary if an all-out war with the United States were really in prospect.

In the van of course was the Iron Duke. Stimulated by notice from the leader of the Opposition of an awkward question in the House about Polk's public pronouncements,[1] and feeling that such parliamentary discussions 'render it more difficult to preserve peace by means of diplomatic discussion, and less likely that this object will be attained', Wellington delivered the prime minister a lengthy war memorandum on 8 April 1845. In it he recalled all his old demands – the improvement of the St Lawrence communications; the equipment of a flotilla on the lakes; bringing up the number of regulars to 10,000; and the re- organization of the Canadian militia, and their concentration in four local centres, since even after their loyalty had been ascertained, as he advised it first should, they might otherwise be found 'doing mischief elsewhere'. As for Oregon, he felt it would have to be left to the Pacific squadron. But the duke's apprehensions and consequent demands for preparation were not at all confined to North America. In the second half of his memorandum he elaborated some further awkward, but by no means eccentric, fears:

We must expect however that a war with the United States will not be with that Power alone.

Unfortunately the Democratic Party throughout the World is inimical to this country. The reason is, that our system is essentially conservative: that the freedom of the subject is founded upon law and order; which provides at the same time for the conservation of person, property,

[1] Russell made an aggressive denunciation of Polk's Inaugural in the House of Commons in April (F. Merk, 'British Party Politics and the Oregon Treaty', *American Historical Review*, xxxvii [1931–32], 670–1).

privileges, honor and character; and the institutions of the country. Democracy abroad looks for plunder: which cannot exist with our system.

Wherever a democratical influence or even a democratical Press exists, we must expect to find enemies. But besides the democratical influence, we must expect that the existing manufacturing and commercial spirit throughout Europe will excite many against us, if we should be involved in hostilities with the United States.

The old questions of the Period of the Armed Neutrality will be revived. The United States will of course open their ports to the commerce of all nations of the world; and will employ the ships of all nations each under the flag of its own nation in the carrying on of its commercial intercourse. Thence there will arise the question of free ships and free goods.

We must not expect therefore, that we shall have allies as in the last years of the late war.

And having thus widened the scope of horror, Wellington was able to conclude by dragging in his favourite nightmare of the defenceless state in the age of steam of the United Kingdom itself.[1]

Wellington by now was considered such an alarmist that the government tended to pay little attention to his advice. Still his prestige in the country at large was great and he could easily act as the catalyst for all kinds of criticism against the action – or inaction – of the government. It certainly helped that there was for a time now no further deterioration in relations with America. But much of the summer lull over the Oregon question could be attributed, as Pakenham attributed it, to Polk's fear of trouble with Mexico following upon the imminent annexation of Texas. If Mexico came to acknowledge the independence of Texas – as the British and French were pressing her to do – the Americans would at once become 'more saucy'.[2]

In the meantime disturbing reports were also pouring in from the various expert military investigations initiated during the past year. The most important ones coming in about this time were those from Captain Boxer, the principal member of the group appointed in April 1844 to make a secret survey of the St Lawrence. This investigation had originated in the government's concern in the previous year about the construction of the *Michigan* and the possible revision of the 1817 agreement; but as Boxer had been ordered to report on both the use and the protection of the river in wartime, his reports ultimately amounted to a pretty comprehensive review of the general problem of Canadian defence. By the middle of June the government in London had already

[1] Wellington to Peel, 8 April 1845, Peel papers, B.M.Add.MS.40,461.
[2] Pakenham to Aberdeen, private, 13 May 1845, Aberdeen papers, B.M.Add. MS.43,123.

received from him three major reports as well as a whole series of confidential letters.[1] The situation they exposed – or rather confirmed – was hardly a satisfactory one. There were plenty of naval stores in Canada, he reported, enough naval ordnance for a sudden emergency and the Canadians still had the greater number of large merchant steamers on Lake Ontario. Thus if war broke out in winter – as he expected it would – they would have enough local resources to equip fifty or sixty vessels in the three or four months' grace before the spring, and on that lake at least to establish an initial naval superiority. But in the spring the Americans' better communications would allow them to bring their generally superior strength to bear in that lake too and so to challenge the British fleet 'very soon'. The dockyard at Kingston,where that fleet was supposed to find refuge, was moreover out of date and dilapidated. It was far from safe against a sudden attack, the defences ordered by Stanley in January having made little headway, if indeed they had even been begun. Nor could the defenders expect much if any aid from the sea. In the first place, even with all the recent improvements, the Lachine, on the St Lawrence, and the Welland canal between Lakes Ontario and Erie, were not yet finished and the latter was in any case too small to pass vessels capable of challenging ships like the *Michigan*. In the second place the whole line of river and canal communication with the sea was far too vulnerable to attack. In Boxer's opinion shipping in the St Lawrence would be attacked by American warships coming up from Boston; and since the British fort at Isle aux Noix was made of very poor materials and was therefore quite untenable, Montreal itself was exposed to attacks down the Richelieu River from Rouse's Point. Above Montreal the water route was also insecure, especially at the Beauharnois canal where it passed on the south bank of the river. This was all a rather depressing picture, though Boxer, for reasons that were to become increasingly familiar seems to have accepted a retreat to the last stronghold of Quebec rather cheerfully:

[1] 'First Report from Col. Holloway & Capt. Boxer on the Defences of Canada', (Quebec) 9 Oct. 1844; '2nd Report, "Report on the River Richelieu": being the second of a series of joint reports upon the frontier water & other communications, in connexion with the Defences of Canada', (Montreal) 17 Feb. 1845; '3rd Report upon the Country in the immediate Vicinity of Montreal: being the third of a series of joint reports relative to the Frontier Water and other Communications, in connexion with the Military Occupation and Defence of Canada', (Montreal) 31 May 1845, W.O. 1/553. Adm. 7/626 contains a series of important letters from Boxer to Lord Haddington (the first lord) and to Haddington's successor, Lord Ellenborough, between 26 May 1845 and 28 Jan. 1846.

The Americans themselves [he reflected in his third report], except assisted by money and men from foreign powers, cannot, it is judged, stand a long campaign, and, as by withdrawing a large army from their now country to hold Montreal Island and communications with the frontier of Canada they must weaken their forces on the seaboard materially, all their commercial cities on the Atlantic would become exposed to the attacks of such of our naval and military forces as may be directed from England against them and such diversions would of course not be neglected nor be afforded in doubtful numbers.

A government bent on inaction might have found here, if it had cared to, a convenient justification; but it was hardly an attitude that any government could afford to adopt openly. In any case Boxer asserted just as confidently that they could easily improve the position on the lakes. Some of his remarks about the weakness of the St Lawrence route were certainly exaggerated. Murray, for example, was quite sure that the lower St Lawrence could be adequately protected by batteries in the vicinity of Quebec.[1] But Boxer's suggestions generally made good sense. The most important were: the enlargement of the Welland and the smaller St Lawrence canals; the enlargement of the Grenville canal's three locks on the more secure Ottawa and Rideau route; improvements to the harbour at Kingston and to its fortifications and those at Isle aux Noix; and limited preparations made with a view to assembling a force for the lakes. Among the latter he suggested that before the outbreak of war iron vessels should be sent out in pieces from England, and that as there was no coal in Canada these vessels should have engines capable of burning both coal and wood. In addition engineers should be kept on hand in Canada ready to build and equip a large force for the lakes immediately war began. If all this were done, he maintained, and troops got ready to destroy the American harbours before they were prepared, he was sure they could put a commanding force on the lakes.

Stanley and Lord Haddington, the first lord of the Admiralty, as well as the prime minister, were worried enough about these reports to urge the strictest caution in communicating with Wellington about them.[2] Presumably they threatened to give him too much support in his demands for immediate and warlike action. But the reports themselves could hardly be kept completely from a man who was both a member of the cabinet and commander-in-chief of the army. Suppressing an individual confidential Colonial Office despatch was quite

[1] Murray to Stanley, 26 May 1845, W.O. 1/553.
[2] Haddington to Peel, private, 13 May 1845, Peel papers, B.M.Add.MS.40,458.

another thing. Due warning that an awkward despatch would soon be on its way had already come from the governor-general of Canada. Metcalfe had written home secretly to Stanley on 9 May giving his opinion that the United States government would hardly be so 'misled by a frantic democracy' or 'so mad as to rush into war on account of disputed claims in the Oregon territory, which can be settled by mutual agreement or by arbitration'. If there was to be war it would not be merely for land in Oregon but to drive the British out of all North America for good – a plan that was much more feasible now that increased settlement on the American side of the border made the invasion of Canada possible from three sides. In these circumstances, he warned, 'whenever a war with the United States becomes probable, our preparations and exertions should be on a prodigious and unbounded scale'.[1]

Two months later, and on a singularly inappropriate anniversary – 4 July – he explained in a confidential despatch of very considerable length what he thought these 'preparations and exertions' should be. First of all there must be an end to all prevarication on the part of the home government. Either the loyalty of the Canadian people was to be secured by the immediate application of an adequate system of defence or they must be told without further equivocation what would be the limit of the mother country's military contribution and allowed accordingly to opt if they wished for separation from Great Britain and union with the United States. If, as he presumed and preferred, the government adopted the former course, then, he admitted, 'the means . . . must be vast and the cost enormous'. And he was not referring here only to those old schemes whose cost alone had already been more than enough to depress the martial ardour of administration after administration. The command of the lakes, a massive system of fortifications, large increases in the numbers of both regulars and militia – all these found mention once again. But so too did rather more audacious suggestions. One army of 25,000 men was to defend Lower Canada and New Brunswick by occupying Maine, New Hampshire, and Vermont. Another of the same number was to make up for the absence of effective command of the lakes and defend Upper Canada by seizing the Americans' harbours and dockyards. Above all, yet another 50–100,000 troops were to undertake purely offensive operations. Such operations, he argued, were both necessary and feasible: 'We can only hope to

[1] Metcalfe to Stanley, secret, 9 May 1845, Derby papers, microfilms in P.A.C., M.G. 24/A/15, reel no. 2, section 7, private and confidential correspondence with Metcalfe, 1842–45.

maintain ourselves in British North America, and to cope with the great Continental Power which has swallowed up the greater portion of North America that is not British, by regarding ourselves as a great Continental Power and acting accordingly.' 'The method most likely to secure a speedy and honourable peace' he supposed to be 'by invading the enemy's territory with a force so formidable as to overpower resistance, and to compel submission to the moderate terms which our Country would at all times be ready to grant.' He admitted that the size of the United States and the defensive capabilities of its militia made a very large force absolutely necessary, and prolonged invasion and occupation out of the question. But he had no patience with those who argued that some special or even divine protection made the conquest of the United States impossible:

I presume that war may be carried on in North America on the same principles, and with the same results, as in Continental Europe. I may best perhaps explain my meaning by suggesting the supposition that Napoleon Bonaparte had possession of Canada with the resources of Great Britain, and the command of the ocean. He would, it may be imagined, make short work of a war with the United States, if his object were as moderate as ours would be, namely, an honourable peace. Why might not England do so likewise?

She could, he insisted, if she did not dissipate her offensive forces in

desultory operations on the enemy's coast by landing a force at different points successively . . . experience of past wars, whether in Europe or in America, does not encourage that method of operations. Its result though sometimes brilliant is generally doubtful, and instances of failure are more numerous than those of success, while even success in such operations is rarely productive of permanent benefit.

Thus their secondary value in diverting the enemy's resources – and in the case of an invasion of the western states, the 'salutary measure' of making these 'advocates of war . . . feel that war is no joke' – ought not to distract Great Britain from her principal method of attack – a massive invasion from the north.

The obvious course of proceeding would be to take possession of those States which lie between these Provinces and the southern part of the Union, and especially of those on the sea coast, so as to keep open our communication with our fleet and the Mother Country. As each State of the Union is a separate Sovereign State, it might be practicable to make Treaties of Peace, or armistices to last during the war, with each State separately, as we advanced; a course which would neutralise their hostility, and which they might prefer to our military occupation of their territory, when they found the rest of the Union unable to protect them. It might not be impossible, that this course would facilitate the separation between

141

the Northern and Southern States of the Union, of which, the probability is contemplated, by many of the best portion of their inhabitants. When we had advanced sufficiently far, in sufficient force, to the Southward, the dread of an insurrection of the slaves in the Southern States would probably lead to a speedy peace; and if the war were nevertheless persisted in by the enemy, the reality of that insurrection might lead to the abolition of slavery in that country, as well as to a speedy termination to the war.[1]

England did not have her Bonaparte but she did have her Wellington and it was partly for this reason that Metcalfe's despatch filled his masters in London with horror rather than excitement. Wellington had not abandoned his long-standing scepticism about plans for the large-scale invasion of the United States, and he would probably not have supported its offensive proposals. But its general air of enthusiastic expenditure was sure to inspire him to new heights of prodigality; and for that reason both Peel and Stanley felt it wise not to let the duke see Metcalfe's despatch. In any case they found its arguments as unconvincing as they were inconvenient. Stanley called it a 'very wild letter', and confessed that 'the scheme of offensive operations from Canada, on the scale proposed, or indeed on any scale, in the event of war with the U.S., appears to me not only impracticable, but, if practicable, impolitic'. Peel fully agreed with him: 'I have always had misgivings about the North American Provinces, and feared they might become an onerous possession, but I never dreamed of their being such an encumbrance as they would be if the visions of Metcalfe are to be realised.'[2]

However much he might deplore the particular spirit and terms of Metcalfe's letter Stanley had to admit that the defences in Canada were 'sadly deficient'. This he blamed in part on Wellington's 1826 plan, 'the expense of which was so enormous, that all governments have *deferred* acting upon it, and very little in fact has been done'. He could point to the revised scheme of defences for Kingston and the work still going on at Montreal; but so defenceless were the colonies generally and so numerous therefore the calls for equally expensive projects elsewhere in the world, that he feared even these were not making very rapid progress. In the last resort then everything depended upon Great Britain's naval superiority; and though the force on the North American and West Indian station had been brought down rapidly from its 1842 level of about thirty vessels, it still remained at between thirteen and

[1] Metcalfe to Stanley, confidential, no. 55, 4 July 1845, W.O. 1/552.
[2] Stanley to Peel, 12 Aug. 1845, Peel papers, B.M.Add.MS.40,468; Stanley to Aberdeen, 18 Aug., Aberdeen papers, B.M.Add.MS.43,072; Peel to Stanley, 13 Aug., Peel papers, B.M.Add.MS.40,468.

fifteen vessels, a very respectable force. But in view of the reports from Boxer even Peel now was not content to leave things at that. 'The Americans are overreaching us on the Lakes', he observed to Stanley on 14 August; and he went on to ask some pointed questions. What was the position with regard to increasing the British force? Had there been any recent remonstrance about the 1817 agreement? What was the state of the Canadian militia and how useful could it be in its present condition? Stanley's reply could only expose still further the very casual manner in which they had treated these vital questions and the very unsatisfactory state into which their preparations had fallen. The size of the regular garrison was quite respectable; during the past two years it had been kept pretty well at the level recommended by Jackson in November 1842 and in British North America there were now more than ten thousand regulars. But he had no satisfactory information about the militia in Canada as they had not been mustered since 1837 and Metcalfe had not yet been able to obtain legislation to put them on an efficient footing. The figures of 37,000 for Nova Scotia and Cape Breton, 22,500 for New Brunswick, and 7,000 for Prince Edward Island, were also 'strictly paper strengths'. As for the naval competition on the lakes, he now recalled that though the American reply to the remonstrance of July 1844 had been 'evasive', it had been tacitly agreed by both sides that the agreement was inapplicable to steam vessels. The Niagara company had withdrawn from its contract but had first completed one vessel, the *London*, capable of carrying two 32-pounders and six carronades. Metcalfe had been given discretionary orders to buy it on 3 July. Now another vessel had become available and similar orders for its purchase were going out that night (18 August).[1]

As if all this were not enough Stanley also had to forward to the prime minister the report that had come in on 17 August from the officers privately sent out in April to investigate defences in the northwest. This, Peel noted, made it clear that the Americans had not neglected that quarter either.[2] Probably much to Aberdeen's satisfaction, Simpson had abandoned the idea of erecting a fort at the mouth of the Columbia almost as soon as he had had a chance to consult with Pakenham. It would have looked too much like a forcible occupation of the disputed line and would have made a collision all the more probable. It would be soon enough to take such precautions if and when

---

[1] Stanley to Peel, 12 and 18 Aug. 1845, Peel papers, B.M.Add.MS.40,468; Peel to Stanley, 14 Aug., Jones and Vinson, p. 358.
[2] Peel to Aberdeen, 19 Aug. 1845, Peel papers, B.M.Add.MS.40,455.

the Americans gave notice of the termination of the joint occupation agreement. He did, however, order Ogden, his chief factor in Oregon, to occupy Cape Disappointment, and this Ogden bought from the Americans in his own name. Meanwhile Simpson and the two engineer lieutenants, Warre and Vavasour, had reached the Company's inland settlements on the Red River and found, so they insisted, a 'cordon' of American forts and posts threatening the communications between Canada and Fort Garry (Winnipeg) and the safety of the settlements themselves.[1]

All this was rather worrying, but Warre and Vavasour had yet to move on to the critical area of Oregon itself and Peel thought it best to wait until their full reports came in before authorizing any expenditure on British countermeasures.[2] But then, only a week later, came Wellington's official digest of Boxer and Holloway's first three reports and he made good use of his opportunity once again to parade his old arguments vigorously before his colleagues.[3] By this time too the news had arrived in London that the negotiations with Mexico had finally broken down and that Texas had accepted the American offer of annexation. Soon after followed the report of Pakenham's foolish rejection of a compromise proposal about Oregon. The news from Texas was no surprise, for Aberdeen seems to have been prepared for it as the inevitable consequence of the breakdown of his concert with France in the summer of 1844. But Pakenham's gaffe was an absolute disaster, coming as it did just when a promising effort was being made with the foreign secretary's approval to condition British public opinion to a compromise.[4] Caught off balance and absent with the queen in Germany, Aberdeen momentarily swung in alarm and confusion to the opposite extreme: 'I am decidedly of opinion', he wrote when returning what he called the 'very judicious' Oregon reports to Peel, 'that we ought to make all necessary preparation, both on the Lakes and on our whole frontier where necessary, without delay. There is real danger in that quarter, whether it may arise from Oregon or not.' Apparently he even wrote to Stanley in support of Metcalfe's 'warlike views'.[5]

[1] Pakenham to Aberdeen, private, 28 April 1845, Aberdeen papers, B.M.Add. MS.43,123; Simpson to Warre and Vavasour, 30 May, W.O. 1/552; Warre and Vavasour's Report no. 1, 10 June, W.O. 1/552. See also Galbraith, pp. 239–40.

[2] Peel to Stanley, 19 Aug. 1845, Peel papers, B.M.Add.MS.40,468.

[3] Wellington to Stanley, 25 Aug. 1845, W.O. 1/553.

[4] Merk, 'British Government Propaganda and Oregon', p. 44.

[5] Aberdeen to Peel, 29 Aug. 1845, and Stanley to Peel, 1 Sept., Peel papers, B.M.Add.MSS.40,455 and 40,468.

With a mounting pile of disturbing intelligence reports, with a continuing deterioration in relations with the United States, and now with Aberdeen's apparent desertion to the extremists, the government were at last forced to give to Canadian defence rather more careful attention during the first two weeks of September 1845 than they had hitherto conceded. Peel was still worried about 'the overall financial result of being prepared everywhere'. 'It will make peace so expensive', he complained to Stanley, 'that many will think actual war a more tolerable evil than such a state of burdensome and anxious expense.' But by 5 September he had begun discussions with Haddington, Sidney Herbert, the secretary at war, and Sir James Graham, the home secretary.[1] By 16 September, when detailed instructions went out to Metcalfe, they had probably been extended to a full meeting of the cabinet. But the result was much more modest than the alarmists wanted. This was partly due to the fact that Stanley refused to be panicked. He had admitted to Peel on 1 September that if there were the slightest chance of war they should prepare a 'respectable' force for the lakes, and he had already called Haddington's attention to the task. But on neither this nor the general question of the defence of the Canadian frontier were they yet ready to make a decision. He certainly could not follow Aberdeen's example, and he argued, very sensibly, that an offensive of the kind Metcalfe advocated would have the most undesirable effect of arousing the people of the United States and giving the American militia the opportunity to play the role for which they were designed.[2] Following, rather, the more cautious advice given him by what he called the 'authorities', Stanley prepared for Peel and the cabinet a list proposing:

that they should concentrate on defensive, and not offensive operations in Canada;

that these preparations should be centred on Quebec, Montreal, and Kingston, and that while the defences of Montreal should extend to some new works at Isle aux Noix, St John, and Chambly as well as others for the command of the St Lawrence, no major effort should be made to obtain superiority on the right bank of that river;

that naval superiority on the lakes was vital, and that 'every effort' should be made to secure it, more particularly by investigating the use which could be made of the eighty or ninety British steamers in merchant service on them, by having the Admiralty prepare special iron

---

[1] Peel to Stanley, 5 Sept. 1845, Peel papers, B.M. Add.MS.40,468.
[2] Stanley to Peel, 1 Sept. 1845, *ibid.*

steamboats, and by providing for these boats a more secure passage along the St Lawrence, through the enlarged Grenville locks, and perhaps, by establishing a strong British post to counter the American fort at Sault Ste Marie, even into Lake Superior;

that regular troops should be brought in from the Pacific to operate in the disputed north-west as far as the Rockies; but that since communications were so difficult between those mountains and Sault Ste Marie, the defence of that area might be left, as Murray had suggested, to the local resources of the Hudson's Bay Company;

and that to all these measures the addition of an efficient local militia was 'absolutely indispensable', and Metcalfe should be told at once that 'if the Canadians desire to be protected by Great Britain, and heavy outlay incurred for that purpose, the test of that desire, and the condition of that outlay, must be the organization by the Province, without delay, of an efficient militia force'.[1]

To support his proposals Stanley now secured yet another substantial memorandum from Murray. This new report, dated 8 September, was, Murray admitted, substantially the same as his previous paper of January 1842. It urged once more the provision of adequate defences for Quebec as the point of entry for reinforcements from the mother country or from the Maritime Provinces; for Kingston for whose security against 'the arduous but not impracticable enterprise' of a winter attack, local British naval superiority would not suffice; and above all for Montreal, the seat of government, the principal commercial city, and the centre of communications, whose loss would cut Canada in two. But he again resisted the idea of concentrating the defences of Montreal forward on the line of American advance up the Richelieu from Rouse's Point. Influenced by the reports from Boxer and Holloway Wellington had moved more definitely in support of this idea in his paper of 25 August, but Murray still insisted that they must not so dissipate their limited resources. He did now add, however, some suggestions for posts in this area to support 'desultory warfare' by the militia.[2]

[1] Minute by Stanley, 1 Sept. 1845, forwarded to Peel by Stanley's parliamentary under-secretary, G. W. Hope, 4 Sept., Peel papers, B.M. Add.MS.40,468.
[2] It is interesting to note that in a private letter he had written a few days earlier to Goulburn, the chancellor of the Exchequer, Murray had commented with reference to such posts: '. . . it is very difficult to get Engineers to project or construct anything but Regular Fortifications; and we have for the most part fallen into the opposite error formerly in our military projects for the defence in North America—either that of proposing Fortifications upon too great and extensive a scale, and which are consequently never accomplished—or that of

146

Although he did not draw attention to it, Murray's paper went considerably beyond his earlier recommendations so far as naval efforts were concerned. In 1842 he had admitted that there was no hope of commanding any of the lakes beyond Ontario. Now too he talked of damaging the Beauharnois, as well as the Chambly on the Richelieu, so as to deny them to the enemy, and of ensuring the use of the rearward communication by improving and protecting the Grenville locks on the Ottawa. But he also advocated parity on the lakes generally as being now both necessary and possible. On the question of the local militia there was no argument; without a numerous and well organized force any system of defence must collapse. But what was really welcome to Stanley was the general's conclusion in as much as it utterly repudiated what Aberdeen had unfortunately found so attractive:

With regard to the general character of the war to be carried on in our North American Provinces in the event of hostilities with the United States – it appears to me that it ought to be *Defensive*. But no war of that character ought to be so entirely defensive as to preclude the undertaking of an offensive enterprize of a defined and limited nature. And if, therefore, such an enterprize as the destruction of the American naval establishment at Sackett's harbour should appear at any time to be practicable, it would be right to attempt it. But inroads having no other object than injury to individuals, and to private property, should never be resorted to unless to deter the enemy by retaliation from attempts of this kind, if they should be begun by him.
As for the invasion of the enemy's territory on a large scale, we do not possess the means to undertake it, nor would it be expedient at any rate to do so. We may with considerable confidence, anticipate victory in an encounter between our troops and those of the enemy within our territory; or we may hope to make him tire of the war, if his expectations of conquest are not speedily realized; but if you should attempt to penetrate far into his country, such an enterprize would infallibly terminate in our sustaining a very serious military discomfiture; besides which the attempt would have, politically, the effect of rendering the Americans more unanimous and of stimulating them to greater exertions in the war than might otherwise take place.
There are but two notions upon which the invasion of any considerable State can be based with a probability of advantage. The 1st of these is when there is a tendency to internal convulsion in the invaded country

---

being satisfied with wooden blockhouses, and such other constructions of so perishable a nature that they fall into ruin before the time has arrived when they are wanted. To these errors, it is imputable, I believe, that we are still so much behind in the accomplishment of a system of defence for our North American Provinces; and the accomplishment of such a system is a work of time and perseverance, and is not to be effected on a short notice.' (Murray to Goulburn, private, 3 Sept. 1845, Murray papers, W.O. 80/11.)

which can be promoted by foreign assistance – but even in that case it will be better, in general and particularly with the Americans, to promote it by other means than by the actual introduction of troops.

The 2nd case is when there is some object by a successful attack upon which a great moral effect can be hoped for. But in the United States there exists no such object; for the capture of either the capital itself of the Union, or of any other of the chief cities, would have no greater effect in discouraging the general mass of the population than the taking possession of any one of their remotest villages would produce.

The only means by which the American people, if they engage in a war with us, are likely to be alienated from it is by finding their general commerce on the ocean distressed – their navy crippled – and their efforts to conquer Canada ineffectual. But no one of these ends separately, nor all of them together, would be sufficient to shake the order of the War Party in that country, or undermine its popularity, if we, by an injudicious attempt to penetrate into their territories, should bring discomfiture or disgrace upon our arms, and procure a military triumph for them.[1]

Fortified by all these arguments Stanley repeated his proposals to Peel on 12 September, and concluded: 'This done, I should feel very easy about the defence of Canada, if the Canadians want to be defended.'[2] Stanley's apparent optimism about the effectiveness of such measures seems rather odd, but as a *minimum* precaution at any rate, their need was patent. By 16 September he had secured the cabinet's consent to them and was able at last to send out detailed confidential instructions to Metcalfe. First he disposed of Metcalfe's unwelcome proposals of 4 July, referring in particular to the objections already raised about the absence of a decisive objective, and about the danger of stimulating the defensive qualities of the American militia and the patriotic hostility of the people at large. These were opinions however relating to the *policy* of such a scheme; there was an even more decisive objection as regards *means*. Wellington had stated that 'with proper Naval and Ordnance preparations, Canada may be effectually defended by a force of 10,000 British Troops, if supported by a loyal and well-organized Militia to the extent of 35,000 men'. If, then, the colony herself took 'prompt action' with regard to the militia, the home government would feel able to ask parliament to incur additional expenditure on the most pressing works at Kingston, Montreal, and on the Richelieu, on the preparation of a number of iron screw vessels for the lakes, and on the enlargement of the Grenville canal. But there was no question of

[1] 'Memorandum about the Defence of Canada', 8 Sept., 1845, Murray papers, in P.R.O., W.O. 80/11, and in the National Library of Scotland, Edinburgh, cc. 54–62.
[2] Stanley to Peel, confidential, 12 Sept.1845, Peel papers, B.M.Add.MS. 40,468.

providing the means necessary for the sort of offensive operations Metcalfe had envisaged:

... it is absolutely impossible that this Country could supply an Army of 150,000 men for military operations on the Continent of America. The total amount of the British Army at present is 118,000 men – of whom, in round numbers, there are 53,000 within the British Islands, 26,000 in India, and consequently not above 39,000 available for the service of all the Colonies of the British Empire. Of this number, there are in the North American Colonies between 11,000 and 12,000 men. Independently of the vast expense, it must be a work of no inconsiderable time to raise, from such a foundation, an army of even 100,000 for the service of one Colony, even if every other point were to be left comparatively defenceless. But this is little likely to be the case. Slight as is the control exercised by the United States' Government over their people, I yet believe that they have sufficient power to prevent a declaration of War at a time when, being at peace with all other nations, we should have the means of applying to that single struggle the whole strength of the Empire. I do not therefore anticipate any immediate rupture with the United States; but I as little anticipate the amicable and final settlement of the Oregon question; and whenever we are embroiled with any European Power, I feel perfectly confident that we must be prepared for a war with the United States also. With this expectation, I think that our preparations ought to be quietly, and steadily, made. The opinions of all the Military authorities whom I have consulted, concur with my own, that these preparations must be of a defensive character; and that, in order to ensure success, they must be of a threefold description, and must comprise, first, military fortifications; secondly, the preparation of a Naval Force; thirdly, the organisation of a numerous and effective Militia . . .[1]

The future embroilment with a European power of which Stanley spoke in this despatch, and from which alone he apparently expected actual hostilities with the Americans to arise, was undoubtedly a reference to continued concern about France. In spite of all Aberdeen's efforts, suspicions of French policy persisted, with complications in North Africa and rumours of a French bid for the hand of Isabella of Spain. Wellington kept up his pressure for defensive preparations, and Peel and some of his colleagues remained by no means unaffected.[2] It was perhaps in an attempt to divert attention from France that Aberdeen had suddenly and rather uncharacteristically come round to Metcalfe's 'warlike views' at the end of August. But if this was his intention, it was an unfortunate miscalculation, for his colleagues

[1] Stanley to Metcalfe, confidential, 16 Sept. 1845. There appears to be no copy of this among the Colonial and War Office papers, but the despatch itself is in the archives of the governor-general's office, P.A.C., R.G. 7, G1, vol. 110.
[2] Bartlett, pp. 167–72.

tended to see bad relations with the two states as complementary. Peel himself commented a little later on 'the fruitful germs of War with France which will spring up in the event of War with the United States'.[1] Far from separating the two issues then, when Wellington presented the prime minister with his memorandum on the naval defence of Great Britain on 10 September he demanded adequate forces for operations against the United States as well as in the Mediterranean and for the defence of the English coast.[2] Concerned with his growing isolation in the cabinet Aberdeen denounced Wellington's demands in respect of France as 'childish restlessness', and offered his resignation.[3] But Peel prevailed upon him to remain and he was still there when a few days later the Texan problem presented another opportunity to improve Anglo-French relations.

On 23 September Aberdeen was approached by the Mexican minister who told him that war with the United States was now certain and, in a patent attempt to embroil Great Britain in it, suggested that as Mexico lacked the resources to defend California Great Britain might do it in collaboration with France. After the Texan fiasco in 1844 Aberdeen did not expect the French would now agree to such a scheme and Peel thought that at this late stage it would look particularly selfish and suspicious. Guizot was consulted and his response was much more encouraging than Aberdeen expected but the matter was not pursued. Aberdeen was sure that the United States would resist and he simply did not believe that Guizot and Louis Philippe were really prepared to go to war over California. There was no question of Great Britain intervening alone and so Aberdeen once more confirmed his abandonment of Texas and California by warning the Mexican government that Great Britain would do no more than submit 'sound and useful suggestions'.[4] At the same time, realizing that further trouble in America was not going to help relations with the French, Aberdeen turned once again to the settlement of the Oregon dispute.

On 2 October, the day after Aberdeen sent his warning to Mexico, Peel wrote to him that he thought Pakenham's rejection of the American compromise proposal in July had been 'needlessly harsh and peremptory', but opposed any further concessions to set things right in the belief that the Americans would not let go the diplomatic advantage they had gained. But Aberdeen was assured otherwise by the American

[1] Peel to Aberdeen, 17 Oct. 1845, Jones, *Aberdeen and the Americas*, p. 73.
[2] W.O. 55/1548.
[3] Bartlett, p. 172; Jones, *Aberdeen and the Americas*, p. 76.
[4] Jones, *Aberdeen and the Americas*, pp. 68–71.

minister in London, Louis McLane, and on 3 October he wrote to Pakenham instructing him to try and get the letters on the July exchange withdrawn and the whole matter expunged from the record. What Aberdeen was anticipating was another awkward denunciation by Polk when the president made his first annual address at the beginning of December. He had already been warned to expect a 'strong declaration' from America and even a recommendation to Congress to terminate the joint occupation agreement. But he was not much worried, for he had also been told that American opinion would not unite in support of Polk's more extreme line. He felt therefore that if they pressed arbitration Polk must either accept it or reopen direct negotiations, whatever he said in his Message.[1]

While they awaited news from America, domestic affairs utterly diverted the cabinet's attention. In the first two weeks of December the great corn law crisis exploded, with Stanley's desertion from the ministry and Peel's own resignation on 5 December. Russell's attempt then to form an administration failed and Peel returned to office on 20 December, but with a much weaker government. Almost at once they had to face the news of Polk's aggressive Message of 2 December. Aberdeen, who had returned as foreign secretary, had anticipated what Polk would say and had made his calculations accordingly. Now he continued to strain at optimism. On 25 December he had already written to Peel that he thought Polk's Message 'somewhat more moderate' than he had feared and that he still expected a 'reasonable settlement'. A few days later he professed to find in it even some positive encouragement for British policy, since, as the French press had already noted, its tone was distinctly hostile to France: 'This reference to France in the Message, will produce exactly the effect we most desire, and will greatly promote that policy which I hope may be considered as successful – the separation of France in feeling and interest from the United States.'[2] Aberdeen's information from America, moreover, continued to encourage him in the belief that Polk would secretly welcome an opportunity to break the deadlock. Shortly after making his bombastic address Polk had told a protesting Congressman that 'the only way to treat John Bull was to look him straight in the eye'; but on 13 December his secretary of state had written to McLane that if the British government should make a promising suggestion the

[1] Jones, *Aberdeen and the Americas*, pp. 62 and 77–8.
[2] Aberdeen to Peel, 25 Dec. 1845, Peel papers, B.M.Add.MS.40,455; Aberdeen to Peel, 29 Dec. 1845, C. S. Parker, *Sir Robert Peel from his Private Papers* (London, 1891–99), iii. 411–12.

president would submit it to the Senate for 'their previous advice'.[1] Aberdeen had every reason to suppose, then, that Polk was seeking a way out of the extreme position he had rashly assumed and he put all his faith accordingly in a renewed offer of arbitration. Peel on the other hand, was not so sure. 'Silence and preparation' was the course he advised: 'We shall not reciprocate blustering with Polk but shall quietly make an increase in the Naval and Military and Ordnance Estimates.'[2]

The actual reference to America in the various naval and military measures taken at this time was modest, partly because they did not anticipate any clash of arms until about the end of 1846, when the expected year's notice of the termination of the existing Oregon agreement would have expired. On the other hand, ever since the Tahiti crisis of the summer of 1844 and the exposure at that time of the somewhat disappointing condition of Great Britain's naval and military defences, Peel had been moving in the direction of generally increased expenditure, particularly on steamships and on the defences of the various dockyards at home and abroad. France was foremost in his mind, but as he told the queen, when warning her that he would probably approve such increases, the state of relations with the United States was another good reason. Even Aberdeen saw no harm in impressing upon the American minister on 3 January that the general preparations, though, he said, having 'no direct reference' to a rupture over the Oregon question, would be 'useful and important' in that event.[3]

The one urgent necessity in North America in Peel's view was to find a successor for Metcalfe. Metcalfe's ill-health had forced him to resign at the end of 1845 and Peel wanted to take the opportunity of appointing as his successor a man of high military rank who could combine the civil and military command. But such a man was difficult to find. One eager candidate for the civil office was the earl of Ellenborough. As governor-general of India in 1842–44 he had rescued the British reputation by directing a series of wonderful military victories and astonishing territorial acquisitions; but his audacity had soon outraged the conscience of cabinet and country alike and in 1844 he was

[1] Julius W. Pratt, 'James K. Polk and John Bull', *Canadian Historical Review*, xxiv (1943), 342–3.

[2] Peel to Aberdeen, 26 Dec. 1845, Jones, *Aberdeen and the Americas*, p. 78; Peel to Egerton, 6 Jan. 1846, Parker, iii. 324.

[3] Peel to the queen, 8 Dec. 1845, Peel papers, B.M.Add.MS.40,440; Pratt, p. 343. For Peel's progress towards greater defence expenditure in 1844–46, see Bartlett, pp. 164–83.

recalled. It was perhaps natural then that shortly afterwards he should have commented with some bitterness on the American debates of April 1845:

... our ministers have talked very boldly and ... the Houses have cheered them, but they are very weak if they attach any value to those cheers. The Parliament which would cheer into a War, 'for the Honor of the Country' today, would abandon them in the middle of it, if it lasted a year, and were not altogether successful.

A war with America is obviously a war with France, and I doubt our being prepared for more than one of such wars at a time, if for that.[1]

But now, 'fired with the memory of his exploits in India', as Peel unkindly put it, he offered to go as governor-general to Canada if war seemed probable. His own reason, as he said later, was that he did not 'believe that the Country can be defended without a Napier engrafted on a practical Parliamentary Statesman, and the one man there is not'. Sir Charles Napier had been the lucky instrument of Ellenborough's military triumphs in India but if the earl really expected Peel to repeat that over-energetic combination in Canada he was to be utterly disappointed. Peel's favourite candidate was Lord Fitzroy Somerset, Wellington's one-armed military secretary at the Horse Guards and later, as Lord Raglan, the ill-fated commander-in-chief in the Crimea. But Somerset, on this occasion, had the wisdom to refuse, and the appointment went instead to the man at the bottom of the prime minister's list, Earl Cathcart, whose only merit was that he was already in Canada in command of the military forces.[2] But whatever might have been the case with Somerset, Peel plainly did not intend to supply Cathcart with more aid and assistance than had been envisaged in Stanley's despatch to Metcalfe of 16 September. And very little progress had been made even with that.

Much of Stanley's programme had been made conditional on Canadian action with regard to the militia and the initiative therefore still lay with the colony; but even the most elementary precautionary measures on the British side were still being held up. This was partly owing to the deliberate decision to wait for further news from America, but it was equally the result of considerable gaps in the information

[1] Ellenborough to Sir Henry Hardinge (his successor in India), private, 5 April 1845, Ellenborough papers, P.R.O. 30/12/21.

[2] Peel to the queen, 25 Dec. 1845, Parker, iii. 288; Ellenborough to Gladstone, 15 Jan. 1846, Ellenborough papers, P.R.O. 30/12/4; Peel to Aberdeen, 26 Dec. 1845, Jones, *Aberdeen and the Americas*, p. 78; various Gladstone letters in Gladstone papers, B.M.Add.MSS.44,363 and 44,735.

already in the possession of the service and colonial departments. On 12 September, before even the cabinet had approved Stanley's suggestions, Murray had written to the inspector-general of fortifications asking for plans and estimates of the limited canal and defence works which were being recommended. But as late as 2 January 1846 these could still not be produced, owing, General Burgoyne reported, to the deficiencies of the engineer department in Canada. The best he could do was to supply an abstract of the probable sums needed for the year 1846–47, amounting in all to a little more than half a million pounds.[1]

So far as the lakes were concerned, with such limited local resources, everything depended upon the progress of the various canal improvements undertaken in the 1840s. On the St Lawrence very substantial progress had been made towards creating a passage for vessels up to about 180 feet in length, 44 feet beam, and drawing between 8 and 10 feet of water. When the last of the improvements on the Lachine canal had been completed, first class gunboats would be able to get on to Lake Ontario. But no further than that. The Welland canal was also being enlarged to a depth of 9 feet, but only so as to admit vessels of 150 feet length and $26\frac{1}{2}$ feet beam, that is third and fourth class gunboats which would be helpless against vessels like the *Michigan*. Work on both the Welland and the Lachine canals was proceeding slowly but Metcalfe had insisted that with some pressure he could get the Canadians to accelerate it so as to provide a passage for vessels of 140 feet length, 20 feet beam and $8\frac{1}{2}$ feet draught by the autumn of 1846, when the termination of the provisional Oregon agreement was expected to produce the real crisis. The Admiralty assured Stanley that iron screw-propelled gunboats could be constructed to these dimensions and, according to Metcalfe's instructions of 16 September, they were ordered to prepare some in England, for transportation to the lakes, either whole or in pieces.[2]

At the same time Metcalfe was informed of yet another special mission to investigate the naval position in Canada. Captain Warden's mission was much more extensive than Boxer's – it included instructions to go to the United States, acting 'as far as may be possible as a Person travelling for his own amusement', and to inspect the state of American preparations on the lakes – but otherwise he was to go over much the same ground in examining the prospects for buying and converting

---

[1] Burgoyne to Murray, confidential, 2 Jan. 1846, Murray papers, W.O. 80/11.
[2] Metcalfe to Stanley, 6 Aug. 1845, W.O. 1/552; Stanley to Wellington, 10 Sept. 1845, W.O. 1/553; Stanley to Metcalfe, confidential, 16 Sept. 1845, P.A.C., R.G. 7, G1, vol. 110.

ships on the lakes, the state of the dockyard at Kingston, and the size and defences of the canals.[1] Evidently Stanley was not happy with the information he had so far received from Boxer and Metcalfe. Certainly he was sceptical about the work on the Welland canal being speeded up; the relations between Boxer and his Canadian colleague, Killaly, were so bad that little could be expected from their professional co-operation.[2] No sooner had Warden's mission been decided upon therefore than all material preparations by the Admiralty were ordered to be suspended until the receipt of his report. This was rather an abrupt change from what Metcalfe had first been told, and was probably due to talks which Stanley had at this time with the first sea lord, Sir George Cockburn.[3] For Cockburn must surely have emphasized what Boxer had clearly pointed out, that vessels of the size contemplated were useless. It was probably from this point that the government began once again to limit their plans to a force for Lake Ontario alone, but one composed of rather larger vessels than Stanley had talked of. Freed from the limitation imposed by the Welland canal, they now looked forward to passing up to that lake vessels of the maximum size permitted by the projected improvements to the St Lawrence.[4]

While Warden worked away quietly to check their reports, Boxer and his colleagues were not idle, but went off too to inspect the state of American preparation on the lakes. Their conclusions were inevitably gloomy, predicting that so fast was American commerce expanding that on Lake Ontario too the British would soon be at a disadvantage. Only an immediate offensive to destroy American shipping and ship-building resources at the very outbreak of war could retrieve the lakes for Great Britain and to that end the completion of the canal system, as well as considerable other preparations, was of vital importance.[5] And as Cathcart now pointed out time was slipping by. Machinery should be sent out to be stored ready for placing in converted ships. There was a great need of a large number of British seamen, 'the want of which during the last American war was the occasion of so much calamity'. Above all the improvement of the Lachine canal, on which so

[1] Adm. to Capt. F. Warden, R.N., 16 Sept. 1845, Adm. 2/1696.
[2] C.O. to Adm., 12 Sept. 1845, Adm. 1/5555.
[3] Stanley to Peel, 15 Sept. 1845, Peel papers, B.M.Add.MS.40,468.
[4] Adm. to C.O., 23 Jan. 1846, Adm. 2/1696.
[5] 'Report upon the existing Harbours, Defences, Merchant Steam Vessels, and other resources available to the United States Government on Lakes Ontario, Erie, Huron, and Michigan in the event of Hostilities', by Captain Boxer and Lt. Moody (Holloway's assistant), 12 Dec. 1845, and Boxer's accompanying letter to Haddington, Adm. 7/626.

much depended, should be put in more competent hands since otherwise, it seemed, it would not be finished until the spring of 1847.[1]
Gladstone, the new colonial secretary, was content to put Cathcart
off by saying that the government intended to wait for further news of
the United States real intentions, as well as Warden's report, before
issuing any orders about either fortifications or naval measures. In the
meantime, the governor-general ought to press on with the reorganization of the Canadian militia.[2]

At the Admiralty there had also been a change, and one that did not
promise to emulate such patience. Anxious to keep him out of Canada,
but anxious too to strengthen his administration, Peel had persuaded
Ellenborough instead that 'there would be an ample field for his martial
genius at the Admiralty'. But as the queen pointed out, there was then
the danger that he and Wellington might get together in the cabinet and
press rather too strongly for warlike preparations. This opinion was
one that Aberdeen fully shared, knowing as he did Ellenborough's
'military propensities', and fearing that it might be difficult to resist
those 'duo fulmina belli'.[3] In January Ellenborough and his new department were already at work, bringing forward the preparation of the
'demonstration ships', the first line of reserve battleships, and proposing,
in the event of war, to divert against American shipping some or all of
the twenty-six ships engaged on the anti-slave trade patrol off the West
African coast. So far as Canada was concerned he was naturally far
from happy about all the delay, especially after he had seen Cathcart's
letter and the reports to which it referred. Whatever they were to do,
he told both Gladstone and Peel, it must be done in the coming summer,
so as to be ready to strike the first blow. The canals must be improved
to admit gunboats drawing at least $7\frac{1}{2}$ or 8 feet of water into Lake
Ontario (he had no hope of doing anything on Lake Erie). Blockhouses
must be erected on the canals to guard them against sudden raids, and
to keep the passage open both for the admission of a force on to the
lakes in the first instance and for its return down stream to fend off an
attack upon Montreal. In any case, as advised by Sandom, the precaution should be taken of putting a second force on the river to defend
Montreal. He and Sandom preferred that during the winter they
should send out iron steamers in pieces for assembly by naval artificers

[1] Cathcart to C.O., confidential, 11 Dec. 1845, W.O. 1/552.
[2] Gladstone to Cathcart, private, ? Jan. 1846, Gladstone papers, B.M.Add.
MS.44,363.
[3] Peel to the queen, 25 Dec., the queen to Peel, 27 Dec., and Aberdeen to
Peel, 29 Dec. 1845, Parker, iii. 288 and 411–12.

at Kingston. Even if reliance were placed instead on local building or conversion, it was still necessary to find and send out now not only seamen, but also large guns, since the 32-pounders and 68-pound carronades at present in Canada dated from 1814. And, he warned, there was a shortage of guns as well as powder and gun carriages at Woolwich.[1]

Ellenborough did not get much response from Peel, who was tired enough already of the first lord's constant mention of the Napiers – Ellenborough was now recommending Commodore Sir Charles Napier for the naval command against the United States. Instead the prime minister tried to turn the logic of the situation against him. 'Our relations with the United States are so critical', he replied on 18 January, 'that I advise you to confer with Aberdeen as to the effect of any particular act done at this moment.'[2] But that they now had to make some decisions about preparations, if not the preparations themselves, was clear even to Gladstone. He had not been kept sufficiently informed, he softly complained, to offer an opinion on the likelihood of war; but he had been led to believe that definite news would be brought by the next mail, and they ought to be ready then to issue whatever instructions seemed necessary. With this in view he sent Peel on 22 January a long memorandum for the consideration of the cabinet or, at least, themselves and Wellington, Goulburn, Ellenborough, and Herbert. What he actually proposed went little further than Stanley's instructions to Metcalfe of 16 September. He did suggest, however, that in addition to making any new works conditional on Canadian action on the militia before the end of the summer, they might also ask for a contribution to the expense of those works, like the improvement of the Grenville canals which, Boxer had suggested, would be of real commercial value. So far as naval preparations were concerned, he readily admitted the importance of striking the first blow on the lakes. Nor was he so concerned in this case about the expense of any precautionary measures. It would be much less than that likely to be incurred with fortifications and would in any event be 'retrievable', since any ships got ready could be applied to some other purpose if the crisis passed over. Still he thought it best to wait for Warden's report and the only immediate steps he recommended were negotiations with the Hudson's Bay Company about the cost of the local forces which they

[1] Ellenborough to Gladstone, 15 Jan. 1846, Ellenborough papers, P.R.O. 30/12/4; Ellenborough to Peel, 18 Jan., *ibid.*; Adm. to C.O., 19, 23, and 24 Jan., Adm. 2/1696.

[2] Peel to Ellenborough, 18 Jan. 1846, Peel papers, B.M.Add.MS.40,473.

had offered to raise for the Oregon territory and the Red River settlement.[1]

On 27 January Warden arrived back in London and submitted his report. To the advocates of immediate naval action on the lakes it was a grave disappointment. Some indication of its contents had already filtered through, particularly by way of Cathcart; but its conclusions were still a shock. Not only did Warden confirm Boxer's account of an overwhelming local American superiority in military and merchant steam ships and in shipbuilding resources on the lakes; he also made it clear that there was no hope of the enlargement of the Lachine canal being finished before the spring or even the summer of 1847. In any case so vulnerable was the St Lawrence system, especially of course the Beauharnois, that it could be used only in peacetime, and even then subject to the 1817 agreement. And so far as the safer communication to the rear was concerned, it was all very well to talk of bringing the Grenville locks up to the standard being attained on the St Lawrence system; even after the great expense that would entail there would still be the obstacle of the old works on the Rideau part of the system.[2]

Discouraging though Warden's report was, the news that followed a few days later from the United States was alarming enough to demand action. Contrary to all Aberdeen's information and calculations, it was now discovered that on 3 January Secretary of State Buchanan had rejected a new offer of arbitration from Pakenham. This was too much even for the pacific Aberdeen and calling in the American minister on 3 February he gave him a solemn warning that he would withdraw his opposition to preparations 'founded upon the contingency of war with the United States', including 'offensive operations' as well as measures for the defence of Canada. And these measures would include, so McLane wrote home, 'the immediate equipment of thirty sail of the line, besides steamers and other vessels of war of a smaller class'.[3]

McLane may well have exaggerated this account in order, as he wished, that it might be all the more effective in bringing Polk back to reason. Certainly Aberdeen made no mention of such a force in his

[1] Gladstone to Peel, 22 Jan. 1846, Peel papers, B.M.Add.MS.40,470; a copy of the memorandum accompanying this letter is in the Gladstone papers, B.M.Add.MS.44,735.
[2] 'Captain Warden's Report on Canada', 27 Jan. 1846, Adm. 7/625.
[3] McLane to Buchanan, 3 Feb. 1846, Hunter Miller, *Treaties and Other International Acts of the U.S.A.* (Washington, 1931–42), v. 57–9.

report of the interview to Pakenham; nor were such proposals apparently considered by the government. But active preparations there nevertheless were; for the cabinet had met again on 2 February and a stream of orders followed. So far as Canada was concerned, Gladstone wrote to Cathcart on 3 February, Stanley's despatch of 16 September should still dictate his course of action, though the improvement of the canals and the reorganization of the militia were to be treated now with greater urgency. The canal improvements he was to prosecute 'by any means in his power'; and while doing his best in the new militia bill to preserve the principle of the cost falling upon the colony in time of peace, he was in the end to make the best arrangement possible. The figure the government had in mind for the Canadian militia and the number for which they had already ordered arms was that of 35,000 pressed constantly in recent years by the duke of Wellington. Similar orders went out at the same time about the militia in the Maritime Provinces, and though in this case no firm figure was mentioned, Wellington apparently recommended that 20,000 small arms should be set aside for them. But they could not be supplied immediately with modern weapons, since the Ordnance did not have anything like enough available. They offered instead to issue the militia with flintlocks, of which there were some 70,000 in store in North America. It was agreed, however, that these should be gradually replaced by 'extra-service' percussion muskets identical to those of the United States militia. These were said to be 'equal in efficiency' to those carried by the regulars but costing twenty-two shillings each instead of seventy-eight. Anything better would have caused outcry from the militia in England. On the vital question of naval forces, Gladstone regretted he could still not give any instructions.[1]

This time, however, it did not mean that this question or the matter of land fortifications were being overlooked. Both in fact became the subject of active and serious discussion during the next few days; though in neither case was any action decided upon. Wellington argued that despite the government's financial difficulties 'the preparations must be made which the circumstances require, and the charges must be provided for, as if we were in a state of war'. He did not make the mistake of pressing his old and expensive scheme of permanent

[1] Gladstone to Stephen, 2 Feb. 1846, Gladstone papers, B.M.Add.MS.44,735; Gladstone to Cathcart, confidential, 3 Feb., W.O. 1/552; Wellington to Gladstone, 3 Feb., Peel papers, B.M.Add.MS.40,470; C.O. to governors of Canada and Maritimes, 3 Feb., W.O. 1/543; C.O. to Adm., 3 Feb., W.O. 1/555; Wellington to Gladstone, 7 Feb., Gladstone papers, B.M.Add.MS.44,363; Ordnance to C.O., 13 Feb., W.O. 1/555.

fortifications, but even so he ran into considerable opposition. Arguing once more that they would have before the outbreak of war the year's notice required for the termination of the Oregon agreement, he still insisted that while time was short a great deal could nevertheless be done. Goulburn, the chancellor of the Exchequer, on the other hand, was firmly opposed to the hurried construction of new works which could not possibly be completed in time, but would have advanced only to the point where they would bottle up their own garrisons rather than impede the enemy. It would be far better, he argued, to spend what money they could spare on additional reinforcements of regular troops. On 4 February came a memorandum from General Burgoyne, also arguing that even in an emergency it would be a great mistake to make hurried decisions over such expensive projects, and suggesting instead that for the time being they need only authorize the construction of temporary field works, though these should be designed so far as possible to fit into the planned scheme of permanent fortifications.[1]

So far as naval preparations were concerned Gladstone himself did not expect to be able to make a quick decision, save possibly to authorize the purchase of another vessel which had been offered for sale in Canada. Until some real progress had been made with the canals there was of course no point in discussing what ships might be sent out from England; only whether they might be sent out in pieces or built entirely from local resources. Ellenborough still favoured the former, but was anxious in any case to have at least 250 guns sent out to Kingston. By 7 February he had apparently ordered some large guns for the steamers available on Lake Ontario. On the same day he also wrote to Peel suggesting that they might even look to the American navy to supply Canada's lack of seamen. When the U.S.S. *Columbia* was recently ordered out in view of the Oregon dispute to reinforce the American squadron in the Pacific, he recalled, 'word was passed' while she was still at Norfolk that Englishmen might leave, and some two hundred did, only thirty out of a crew of five hundred being Americans. Now, he suggested, they could send out a 74- and a couple of 50-gun ships to patrol the Chesapeake and lure away the many British sailors who would be glad of the chance to serve in 'a good stout ship', and who might well do to man the lakes squadron.[2]

[1] Wellington to Gladstone, 3 Feb., and Goulburn to Peel, 3 Feb., Peel papers, B.M.Add.MSS.40,470 and 40,445; memorandum by Burgoyne on Canada, 4 Feb., W.O. 1/555.
[2] Ellenborough to Peel, 7 Feb. 1846, Peel papers, B.M.Add.MS.40,473.

By this time Peel had recovered something of his optimism and he was not prepared to encourage Ellenborough any further. McLane apparently was assuring the British government that the combination of Aberdeen's warnings and the queen's moderate speech to parliament on 22 January, would probably be enough to strengthen the American peace party and force Polk to compromise; further menaces and preparations might tip the balance for 'the war party in the United States, a very powerful and reckless party, would fasten on any incident calculated to weaken the advocates of peace'. Peel therefore advised against any orders for building war steamers on the lakes or for the demonstrations Ellenborough had suggested off the American coast until, in about a month's time, they could see more clearly which way things would go.[1] Peel was kept in doubt rather longer than he expected but the signs remained encouraging nonetheless. On 29 January, a few days after receiving news of Aberdeen's first, rather mild warning of 3 January, Buchanan authorized McLane to tell Aberdeen 'cautiously and informally' that while the president still clung to his maximum claim he would nevertheless submit to the Senate any new offer on the lines of the compromise rashly rejected by Pakenham in the previous summer. On 26 February, after the receipt of McLane's account of the more threatening meeting of 3 February, this invitation was repeated, and this time was accompanied by a private letter from Buchanan assuring the minister of a favourable reaction from the Senate.[2] Since Buchanan had first written to McLane on these lines as early as 13 December and since Polk himself had confided to his diary on 23 December that if the British proposed a compromise on the line of 49° he would probably submit it to the Senate, it would be wrong to place too much emphasis on the effect of the news from London.[3] Assuming that it was these hints rather than his bombastic public pronouncements that really counted, the only material change in Polk's position, after the receipt of the threatening news from London, was that much later, in the final settlement in June, he ultimately accepted, at least so far as the Hudson's Bay Company was concerned, what had been ruled out even in the instructions of 26 February – free navigation of the Columbia River for the British south of the 49th parallel. This was an important concession since it helped to salve British pride; but coming so much later, after war had actually broken out with Mexico and when the conciliatory Aberdeen's tenure of the Foreign Office seemed

[1] Peel to Ellenborough, secret, 8 Feb. 1846, Ellenborough papers, P.R.O. 30/12/4. [2] Pratt, pp. 343, 344 and 347.
[3] *Ibid.*, pp. 342–3.

161

to be coming rapidly to an end, it seems rather an exaggeration to suggest that the threats of 3 February were 'probably the decisive factor in breaking the diplomatic deadlock'.[1] They did not of course pass unnoticed, particularly as the Americans had little power to flourish in defiance.

During 1845 the Americans had taken some steps to strengthen their naval forces in the Pacific, but with a view to trouble with Mexico as much as Great Britain. Indeed so far as the latter was concerned the navy's orders were still in the autumn very similar to those given to the British earlier in the year – 'to display the flag of the United States in the Columbia' and to collect information about the prospects and resources of each side in the disputed territory.[2] Generally speaking the Americans appeared to be lamentably unprepared for war with Great Britain. With the increased tension on her southern borders, the United States had by the end of the year only about 480 men left in garrison on the northern frontier; and though a good deal of progress had by now been made with the coastal defences, there was still a considerable gap in the vicinity of New Orleans. Most unsatisfactory of all was the state of the navy. There were ready for service in December only one ship of the line, six frigates, fifteen sloops, six brigs or schooners, four armed store ships, one sea-going steamer, and one other steamer on Lake Erie. Within a year and at an estimated cost of $625,000, they could expect to add another four ships of the line, one razee, and three frigates as well as several smaller vessels; and in about the same time, but with considerably greater expenditure, they could add from ships on the stocks another four ships of the line and three frigates. The real weakness of this force, according to the Board of Naval Commissioners, was its shortage of steamships. Of these, they said, Great Britain now had a total of 141, mounting in all some 698 guns; while the United States had only 7, mounting 39 guns! Without considerable additions of such vessels therefore – and they recommended no less than three large steamers, five steam frigates, and six steam sloops as well as forty coastal steamers – they would not be able to protect their own coasts or commerce, either directly or by diverting the enemy's forces by raids

[1] Jones, *Aberdeen and the Americas*, p. 81. Pratt also emphasizes the importance of these threats in persuading Polk to concede the navigation of the Columbia, but adds the points about the Mexican war and the prospect of having to face a tougher diplomatic opponent in Palmerston when, as was expected, the Peel ministry shortly fell in June.
[2] Secretary of the navy to Commodore Sloat, commanding the U.S. Pacific squadron, 17 Oct. 1845, Naval Records Collection of the Office of Naval Records and Library, U.S.N.A., R.G. 45.

on his merchant marine.[1] Polk had suggested in his Annual Message in December that they ought to have additional steam vessels, and corresponding proposals had been made to the appropriate committees of Congress. As the leader of a party traditionally opposed to the creation of a sea-going navy, however, it was embarrassing for him to make such proposals and he made them very cautiously and tentatively, hoping, as he later told his cabinet, that Congress would act 'in a quiet way without alarming the country at home or attracting unnecessary attention abroad'.[2]

Congress had still not acted when the news arrived of Aberdeen's threats of 3 February. Polk noted in his diary that this news 'was not altogether of so pacific a character as the accounts given in the English newspapers had led me to believe', and the haste with which the cabinet assembled and hurried off another pacifying hint to London, certainly indicates that he was concerned, if not so alarmed as has sometimes been suggested.[3] And if the news no more than reinforced a diplomatic line already embarked upon, even less was there any real change with regard to military precautions. The cabinet met again to consider this question on 28 February, and for once Polk and Buchanan both agreed that the president would have to approach Congress with a special message seeking again the appropriations already asked. But there was still some disagreement in the cabinet and both on that occasion and at another meeting on 7 March, the decision was postponed until the receipt of further news from Great Britain.[4] Only on 24 March did Polk at last send a special message to the Senate drawing attention to the strained relations with both Great Britain and Mexico and the expediency of strengthening the national defences. Even so he was unsuccessful, and it was not until December, when the Mexican war forced the administration once again to approach Congress, that a compromise vote was secured for four additional steam warships and a generous subsidy for companies willing to build merchant vessels readily adaptable for war.[5]

[1] Secretary of war to the chairman of the Senate committee on foreign affairs, 29 Dec. 1845, *Report on Military Defence of Country*, 25 March 1846, Sen. Doc. no. 255, 29th Cong., 1st sess., vol. v; *Report on Naval Power of Maritime Nations*, 2 Mar. 1846, Sen. Doc. no. 187, 29th Cong., 1st sess., vol. iv; Board of Naval Commissioners to secretary of navy, 30 Dec. 1845, in *Report on Naval Force and Supplies*, 8 Jan. 1846, Sen. Doc. no. 263, 29th Cong., 1st sess., vol. iv.
[2] M. M. Quaife, ed., *The Diary of James K. Polk during his Presidency, 1845–1849* (2 vols., Chicago, 1910), i. 257–9.   [3] Pratt, p. 344.
[4] Quaife, i. 257–9 and 270.   [5] Sprout, pp. 132–4.

Although, then, there was considerable talk on the American side too, and even in cabinet, of the great danger of war it is difficult to believe that preparation of the kind Polk was proposing could really have been intended to meet such a contingency. But if, as seems likely, he was bluffing, there is no real sign that the news of the supposed British preparations called that bluff. Rather, he went out of his way only to remind the British of his earlier hints at compromise. At the same time he pressed on with his gestures of military defiance, but probably, as his secretary of war suggested, so as not to allow the British to get too confident and demand what the United States *would* have to resist even to the point of war.[1]

If the British government's naval and military preparations early in 1846 made any real contribution to the progress of the Oregon negotiations, apart from confirming Polk in the course he had already determined upon, it was probably in their effect on that government's own attitude. Together with the success of the approaches being made about the same time to secure the Opposition's support for a compromise, they gave to Peel and Aberdeen, at a time of great parliamentary difficulty, a sense of calm resolution and assurance without which they might not have been able to resist the fire-eaters in the cabinet and the country. As it was Aberdeen patiently awaited the outcome of the congressional debate on the proposal to terminate the joint occupation agreement, and sure enough on 23 April there came the joint resolution authorizing the termination, but at the same time assuring compromise by expressing the hope for 'a speedy and amicable adjustment'. With diplomatic matters going precisely as he had calculated Aberdeen was able in May to send out a new compromise formula to Pakenham for the final settlement of the Oregon question.[2] Meanwhile the extremists in the cabinet had to be prevented from letting military preparations get out of hand. Hence Peel's firm resistance to Ellenborough's excited demands; but the quieter prosecution of rather more limited measures. 'Our belief', wrote Gladstone at the beginning of March, 'is that there

---

[1] Sprout, p. 130, very much doubts that Polk's administration ever 'had any intention of resorting to arms in the Oregon dispute'. On 9 Mar. 1846 W.L. Marcy wrote to General Wetmore: 'Congress are behaving strangely. They will do nothing towards the defences of the country – & some of the members and senators go so strongly on the English side that they will induce the British Government to ask more than can be granted. Their course is well-calculated to bring on ultimately a war' (Library of Congress, Marcy papers, vol. ii). The most recent analysis of Polk's policy, Charles Sellers, *James K. Polk: Continent-alist, 1843–1846* (Princeton, 1966), also concludes that Polk's Oregon policy was mostly bluff; see especially, pp. 244–5, 254–5, and 358–9.

[2] Aberdeen to Pakenham, 18 May 1846, Miller, v. 75–81.

will be no war, although we are not entitled to rely upon it in such a manner as to give up measures of preparation.'[1] But instead of spending the half million that Burgoyne had roughly estimated it would cost to carry out the enlargement of the Grenville locks and the most important of the land works, the cabinet had decided to ask parliament that year for only £133,000 for all military works in Canada. £47,000 of this sum had already been allotted to the urgent works at Kingston and after some special consultations on 2 and 3 March, it was decided that the rest should be spent in descending order of priority on the purchase of land at Quebec so as to clear the ground in front of the defences, on new works at St Helens to protect Montreal, and, if anything remained, on further defences for Kingston.[2] Apart from this the only positive decision made was to send a detachment of regulars to Fort Garry in aid of the Hudson's Bay Company's local efforts. So far as the enlargement of the Grenville locks was concerned, this would have to wait, and so too consequently would any provision for a naval force on the lakes. 'We have not absolutely determined that nothing shall be done during the present year towards strengthening our force upon the Lakes', Gladstone told Cathcart a month later, but the canals not being ready and with 'a gradually growing impression' that there would be no war, there seemed no reason for 'positive action' in that matter.[3]

To the alarmists like Wellington and Cathcart, all this moderation was most unwelcome. The duke's inclination to large expenditure had just been stimulated once again, and in spite of the present lull in the dispute with the United States, by his digestion of Boxer and Holloway's fourth and last report of 29 January. In this they had excelled themselves, with recommendations of blockhouses and gunboats for the Rideau and Welland canals, yet more works at Kingston, and not least the adoption of the duke's old suggestion of a new canal connection with Lake Huron.[4] These recommendations the duke now firmly endorsed on

[1] Gladstone to Cathcart, private, 2 March 1846, Gladstone papers, B.M.Add. MS.44,363.

[2] A special conference was held at the Colonial Office on 2 Mar. to decide this matter and it was attended by Gladstone, Ellenborough, Goulburn, Herbert, and Burgoyne. Murray was ill and sent in his recommendations by letter (Murray to Burgoyne, 2 and 3 Mar. 1846, W.O. 46/39; Gladstone's minute, 2 Mar., W.O. 1/555; Gladstone to Burgoyne, private, 3 Mar., Gladstone papers, B.M.Add.MS.44,363).

[3] Gladstone to Cathcart, no. 9, 3 Mar. 1846, W.O. 1/554, and Gladstone to Cathcart, private, 3 April, Gladstone papers, B.M.Add.MS.44,528. For the Fort Garry expedition see below, p. 173, and C. P. Stacey, 'The Hudson's Bay Company and Anglo-American Military Rivalries during the Oregon Dispute', Canadian Historical Review, xviii (1937), 293–7.

[4] 'Fourth Report', 29 Jan. 1846, W.O. 1/555.

11 April, emphasizing the necessity of a complete interior water communication and taking also the opportunity to remind the government that he had always talked of having four army corps in Canada in addition to the garrisons of Kingston, Montreal, and Quebec:

I request H.M.'s Servants [he concluded] to attend to the importance of H.M. retaining possession of this important Dominion, conquered from the enemy and settled and cultivated by the enterprize, the genius and the labours of her subjects.
If these cannot be maintained, the still, to Great Britain as a naval power, more important Maritime Provinces . . . must be lost; and nothing will remain of the boasted conquests of the Seven Years War and the cessions of the Peace of 1763.[1]

For such a plan of defence as this, the decisions of the conference of 3 March – to which Wellington had not been invited – were disastrously parsimonious, not least in the deliberate postponement of any improvement to the Grenville locks. 'No defence of Canada', the duke continued to insist, 'can be undertaken unless this water communication be completed.'[2] This point too was quickly taken up by Cathcart, who described himself as in general 'exceedingly disappointed', and continued to dispute with what he considered to be Murray's proposal to abandon the area south of the St Lawrence.[3] These complaints Gladstone fended off with further expert advice from the master-general. With most of Wellington's points, Murray admitted on 11 May, he must agree; but not to the extent of approving 'regular systems of fortifications' for towns like Kingston. These would be 'too costly and too tedious', and the proper approach would be to prosecute such limited works as would protect the naval and military positions, not the towns for their own sake. Some of Cathcart's objections, on the other hand, were misconceived. He had never advocated the abandonment of the area south of the St Lawrence, only that they should not undertake a general campaign in that neighbourhood. So far as expenditure generally was concerned the task of the conference had been to allocate what money had already been made available, not to ask for more.[4] Armed with these opinions Gladstone was able to hold off the duke with polite assurances that if the state of affairs required it the government would ask parliament for more money. To Cathcart he was more abrupt: 'I think it quite futile to suppose that under the present or

[1] Wellington to Gladstone, 11 April 1846, W.O. 1/555.
[2] Wellington to Gladstone, 29 April 1846, *ibid*.
[3] Cathcart to Gladstone, confidential, 26 Mar. 1846, W.O. 1/554.
[4] Murray to Gladstone, private, 21 April, and Murray to C.O., 11 May 1846, W.O. 1/555.

any probable circumstance any very large sum will be placed at the disposal of the Government for the purpose of erecting works of defence in Canada.'[1]

Unlike his more optimistic colleagues, Ellenborough could 'as yet see no daylight at all in the difficulty with the United States'. With Hardinge, his successor in India, now being plunged into a great new war with the Sikhs and with the French agitating once more for the strengthening of their navy, he had no intention of being caught by surprise, especially since war with either France or the United States would, he was sure, be followed in six months by war with the other. He too was worried that further enlistment of seamen would force them to exceed the estimates, but in the circumstances he did not see how they could stop. Indeed they might have to go even further. There were not at present enough marines to protect dockyards like Pembroke against American raiders coming round the north coast of Ireland, and if more were not forthcoming they might have to provide military training for the dock workers, as they already had done the previous year at Bermuda.[2] But during his brief tenure of the Admiralty Ellenborough's assault upon the general deficiencies of the navy could make little headway against a man like Peel.

In the middle of March the prime minister replied with a character-istically devastating attack upon new military expenditure. In the first place, he said, it hardly seemed correct to talk of England being taken unprepared and by surprise when such great increases had recently been made in the estimates. The number of seamen for the year 1845–46 had been increased by 4,000 and the estimate raised by nearly £900,000. In the current year a further half million pounds had been added and the ordnance estimate too had risen from £1,850,000 in 1844–45 to £2,550,000 in the present year, most of the increase being taken up by naval armaments and the defences of Portsmouth, Plymouth, and the Thames. And when to all this was added the increase in the current year of 10,000 to the regular infantry and 1,500 to the artillery, it was difficult not to agree with the American alarmists that it was they who were relatively unprepared and the danger of war consequently remote.

Between increased expenditure on the one hand, and reduced Taxation on the other, we are about to incur the serious evil of Deficit in time of Peace. We really had better have war at once – than incur many of the evils of it – by making constantly increasing preparation for it. It is a very

<hr />

[1] Gladstone to Wellington, private, 2 May 1846, and Gladstone to Cathcart, private, 4 May, Gladstone papers, B.M.Add.MSS.44,364 and 44,528.

[2] This scheme was approved and launched in the winter of 1846–47 (Bartlett, pp. 241–4).

good thing no doubt to be prepared at all points – to have twice the naval force of any other Country – to have every colony in a state of complete defence – well garrisoned and the fortifications in good order – to have nothing to fear in the event of hostilities – all this is very desirable if you can afford it – but if you cannot, if in order to secure these advantages you must incur debt in the time of peace – you are crippling your resources (for money and credit are resources) in the event of war.

Such arguments were alien to a man of Ellenborough's temper. 'I fear . . . the character of the Prime Minister is inconsistent with the execution of any grand conception of a military or political nature', he complained to his hero, General Napier, when acknowledging the receipt of a plan of campaign against the United States. More effective, naturally, was 'the sedative effect upon the lovers of war in Washington' which he had to admit would result from the news of quick success against the Sikhs; 'the settlement on the Sutlej may . . . tend to one on the Columbia'. Even so he did not give up his demands entirely. At the beginning of April there was already an excess of 2,000 seamen over the 40,000 voted for the year. But the ships in commission were still 2,500 short of their full complements and by the end of May Ellenborough was again pressing for another 8,000 seamen as well as an additional 3,000 marines. The Oregon difficulty might pass, but the naval preparations the Americans would now have to make against Mexico would still be available against Great Britain when that war was over. On the east coast of Mexico the Americans already had a force far superior to the British, and though they were roughly equal in the Pacific, it was expected that the Americans would shortly be re-inforced by the *Columbus*, which was larger than anything the British had on that station. In an emergency no doubt both deficiencies would have been quickly supplied, as Ellenborough pressed, from the large force tied down in the joint Anglo-French intervention in the River Plate.

The real weakness in the British position was the total absence of a sovereign base in the eastern Pacific. All they had at present was the store ship at Callao, and this, as Ellenborough complained, was hardly a sufficient or secure support in time of peace, let alone war. High tariff duties made its use increasingly expensive and its capture, which would probably be easy to accomplish, would paralyse the whole force. So Ellenborough now made a new attempt to commit the interest of the government to the acquisition of naval bases in the Pacific. To neutralize the French in Tahiti, he claimed, they had found on an American chart an ideal spot in Pago-Pago in the Samoan Islands; but with a view to operations against the Americans in the vicinity of Oregon and Mexico there was more difficulty. One of the best solutions, in the Sandwich

Islands, had unfortunately been ruled out by the government's earlier 'diplomatic transactions', when in 1843, more anxious to counter foreign domination than to acquire them for themselves, they had disavowed the islands' occupation by one of their naval officers, and proclaimed, with France, their legal independence. An alternative among the Revilla Gigedo Islands off the west coast of Mexico, he felt was unlikely to prove any more satisfactory than had the Galapagos Islands two years before. Guadalupe or Cedros, off the coast of lower California, were possibilities and he had ordered them to be investigated. But what he really hoped for was San Francisco itself, firmly believing that it had been quite wrong to dismiss it as defenceless from the land side, and Hawaii too if Aberdeen could recede from the undertakings already made. 'Let us at once obtain possession, if we can, of the key of the north west coast of America', he was urging upon the foreign secretary in May. 'We must look forward to what the obvious course of events is bringing on, the passing of European population to the north west coast of America and to its ultimate consequences on the trade of the Pacific and of China, and take our measures at once.'[1] But with his 'timorous colleagues', as he called them, Ellenborough had no success, and he was not allowed the extra seamen needed for any further reinforcements for either the Pacific or the Gulf of Mexico.

Meanwhile, on 6 June, Aberdeen's new proposal, giving up the line of 49° to the United States, but reserving the whole of Vancouver Island and the free navigation of the Columbia, had arrived in Washington. At the end of June, they heard in London that Polk had indeed passed on this proposal to the Senate for approval and that a treaty had been signed. On 29 June Aberdeen expressed his complete satisfaction to the House of Lords, and immediately afterwards the duke of Wellington announced the resignation of the government following its desertion by the protectionists. All that the disgruntled Ellenborough could do was to leave for the benefit of his successor yet another long paper, pleading for the increases in seamen and marines, and, not least, the acquisition of a Pacific base.[2]

[1] Ellenborough to Peel, 2, 5, 8 Mar. and 29 May 1846, Peel papers, B.M.Add. MS.40,473; Peel to Ellenborough, secret, 17 Mar., Ellenborough papers, P.R.O. 30/12/21; Ellenborough to Hardinge, 3 and 22 April, *ibid.*; Ellenborough to Gen. Sir Charles J. Napier, 3 June, *ibid.*; Ellenborough to Aberdeen, 16 May, Aberdeen papers, B.M.Add.MS.43,198; Adm. to F.O., 10 June, Adm. 2/1696; Ellenborough to Seymour, private, 28 June, Ellenborough papers, P.R.O. 30/12/4. See also Bartlett, pp. 174–83.
[2] 'Paper left by Earl of Ellenborough expressing his views on various subjects connected with Naval Administration', 6 July 1846, Adm. 13/185.

6

Central America and the Collapse of Palmerston's Policy, 1847–1860

The defensive precautions taken by Polk in his diplomatic tussle with Great Britain were negligible, and even the Mexican war made very little permanent contribution to the improvement of the United States military forces. Apart from the small additions to the navy already noted, only the increase of the peacetime regular nucleus of the army to 10,000 men is really worth mentioning. But Polk's contribution to the power and security of the United States was nonetheless immense. The settlement of the Oregon question brought the lion's share of the disputed territory and the possession of the harbours of Puget Sound; the defeat of Mexico not only confirmed the union with Texas, but also brought another vast acquisition of territory on the southern and western frontier, including of course California and the strategic harbour of San Francisco. Establishing as they did beyond dispute the United States pretension to effective continental dominion and striking a colossal if not final blow against any hostile attempt to establish a balance of power in North America, these acquisitions represented a major political victory for the United States.

Nor was this all. Even before the war with Mexico had ended Polk's interest had already turned to Central America and the Caribbean. This policy the milder Whig administration of 1849–53 tempered but did not abandon, least of all in Central America where they too were anxious to find a faster isthmian route to the newly discovered gold fields of California. Then, with the return of the Democrats under President Pierce in 1853, the American drive to power moved rapidly onwards into the Caribbean and the Pacific. Substantially protected though she already was against territorial conquest, the United States sought once again in mid-century to secure too the keys to the ocean approaches by the possession of Hawaii and Cuba – or Samana Bay in Santo Domingo – as well as the control of any future interoceanic communication.

This new round of American expansionism the British viewed with unabated alarm. Most British statesmen were still inimical to the

United States, and utterly disappointed at the American successes of the 1840s. In that period, they knew, they had lost the best chance yet of establishing a territorial balance of power in North America. In Mexico they virtually gave up all hope. Local British representatives continued to resent American policy and to encourage the resistance of their hosts. But their masters in London refused to back them up, and in 1853 the United States marked their diplomatic ascendancy by obtaining the cession of the strip of territory necessary for the construction of a transcontinental railway.[1] But to give up in the face of Mexico's tortuous politics and the United States local advantages was one thing. It was quite another to allow the Americans through the acquisition of strategic islands and communications to challenge Britain's local naval superiority. For in war it was that sea power alone which could compensate for the weakness and vulnerability of Canada. Certainly Palmerston thought in this way, as his criticism of Aberdeen had consistently shown. But once back in the Foreign Office in July 1846 he too showed little inclination to respond with a direct counterattack. Had he made any real attempt to do so diversions in Europe would no doubt soon have forced him to retreat. As it was there were more immediate difficulties – in the persistent problem of Canada's defence and in the uncooperative attitude of the House of Commons – which made him approach relations with America much more cautiously than he probably would have liked.

In Canada the British still hoped to see established at least a symbolic counterweight to the political system of the United States.

The more I see and hear of the state of affairs in the United States [wrote the colonial secretary in 1848], the more convinced I am of the extreme importance of consolidating in British America a system of government really popular and at the same time not so ultra-democratic in principle as that of the great republic. As the effect of the institutions of the United States becomes more and more developed, the more dangerous I think them to the peace of the world, and though otherwise perhaps I would not attach so much value to our possessions in America, I do think it of the utmost consequence that we should at least retain them long enough to raise them to a constitution in which they might maintain their own independence instead of being absorbed in the Union.[2]

But for a while after the suppression of the Canadian rebellion constitutional developments threatened to have precisely the opposite effect.

[1] J. Fred Rippy, *Latin America in World Politics* (New York, 1928), p. 97.
[2] Earl Grey to Lord Elgin (governor-general of Canada), private, 11 Oct. 1848, Elgin papers, microfilms in P[ublic] A[rchives of] C[anada], M[anuscript] G[roup] 24/A/16, reel no. 2 (A397).

Instead of reconciling the population to their imperial connection the 1840 Act of Union and the gradual concession of responsible government tended merely to oust the old loyalists from political power. And when to this political dissatisfaction was added large-scale economic distress following the end of Protection in Britain in 1846, there soon developed, for the first time, an apparently strong movement for annexation to the United States. Fortunately this was not by any means welcome to the South and even for the North there were more immediate practical objectives to be gained, like better access to Canadian waterways and fisheries. Eventually, in June 1854, the British were able to obtain from the Americans a reciprocity treaty which helped to soften the Canadians' economic complaints and promoted the gradual consolidation of a political system which encouraged their permanent separation from the United States. But if the difficulties over the annexation movement were only temporary, the problems of Canadian defence continued to defy resolution.

In contrast to what had been achieved during the Maine and McLeod episodes, the material contribution made to North American defence seemed already to have ground to a virtual halt during the Oregon crisis itself. Considerable progress was being made with Great Britain's general naval and military arrangements, but this was due mostly to the challenge of technological invention and, so far as relations with foreign powers were concerned, to the persistent suspicion of France. Thus the navy continued to experiment with steam and the shell gun, and the army indulged in wholesale schemes of fortification, railway building, and the reform of the militia. But in North America there was little further improvement. Great Britain's naval strength on the Pacific and North American stations remained about the same, each having twelve or thirteen vessels between 1848 and 1852. In Canada a mere dribble of extra money had flowed into the flagging fortification scheme in 1846, and nothing really effective had been done about providing a force for the lakes. Three vessels in all were built under the subsidy scheme, two by the Niagara Dock Company and one by a private individual, but in spite of the considerable sums spent by the Admiralty, the option to purchase was never exercised. One of the Niagara company's vessels was later seized for debt by the United States, and a new proposal from yet another company at the end of 1848 was curtly refused.[1] The garrisons of Canada and the Maritimes even passed

---

[1] Memo. by P. Smith (C.O.), 20 Oct. 1848, Sir Arthur G. Doughty, ed., *The Elgin-Grey Papers, 1846–1852* (4 vols., Ottawa, 1937), iv. 1604–05; W.O. to Elgin, 4 Jan. 1849, W.O. 6/84.

through the new crisis without substantial increase, remaining at about 10,000 men. The only distinct reinforcement was the small detachment of about 350 men who, after much delay, had at length left Cork in June and arrived at Fort Garry in September 1846. But necessary though this outpost seemed even after the passing of the Oregon crisis, it was considered helpless in the event of attack and already in the spring of 1847 arrangements were being made for the withdrawal of the troops in the following year.[1] And in August 1846 the pressure for general reduction had begun again with proposals to withdraw at least two of the British battalions from Canada.[2] Nor was this merely an acknowledgment that the immediate crisis with the United States was over. It was rather the first move in a conscious attempt to extend to defence the implications of the economic and political autonomy now being conceded to the principal colonies.

Self-defence was not a condition of self-government but men like Lord Grey, the colonial secretary in the new Whig government of 1846–52, could not but associate the two. In any case some means of reducing colonial expenditure was vitally necessary, if only to disarm the anti-colonial campaign of the radicals. There was a convenient justification in the current preoccupation with the effects of steam power upon defence. Seaborne invasion forces, it was argued, had been set free from the restrictions hitherto imposed by wind and tide and could now threaten the islands of Great Britain at a multitude of points. Her land forces, rather than being scattered expensively and probably ineffectually about the empire, should be concentrated for the defence of the mother country; and to those who protested that the withdrawals must not be allowed too much to weaken oversea possessions it was pointed out that steam could also be used to despatch reinforcements with unexampled rapidity.

Throughout the lifetime of Lord John Russell's government, from 1846 to 1852, and into those of his successors Derby (1852) and Aberdeen (1852–55), the pressure for reduction in the garrisons of Canada and other colonies was sternly maintained. In 1847 the number of regulars in Canada was reduced from about 8,000 to 6,000, and, after a pause to ride out the inevitable objections, to about 5,000 in 1852; and shortly before the outbreak of the Crimean War forced even greater withdrawals, the government was already proposing to reduce it to a mere 3,000.

[1] Memo. by P. Smith (C.O.) summarizing the correspondence on the Fort Garry question, 11 Jan. 1847, C.O. 537/96.
[2] C. P. Stacey, *Canada and the British Army, 1846–1871; a Study in the Practice of Responsible Government* (Toronto, 1963), p. 66.

During the same period the Maritime Provinces and the West Indies suffered just as severely. In 1849 the office of commander of the forces in North America was abolished in the interests of economy, and the command divided into two, Canada and Nova Scotia. Three years later the garrison in Nova Scotia had been reduced by about 500 men to just over 2,000, though the importance of Halifax as an imperial station saved it from quite such drastic cuts as Canada suffered. In Canada much was made of the wisdom – for security as well as economy – of local concentration and withdrawal from small outlying and exposed posts. In these years at least eight such stations were given up, including Amherstburg on Lake Erie and Penetanguishene on Lake Huron. The same principle was applied even more effectively to the West Indies. Arguing that most of them were now valueless, strategically and politically, and that reinforcements could quickly be rushed by steam vessel to any threatened point, it was proposed in 1853 to withdraw one battalion from the Windward and Leeward command, leaving the rest concentrated mainly on Barbados, but with detachments on Antigua, St Lucia, and Trinidad. But the commander was refused funds to improve the defences at Barbados, and when, early in 1854, he reported that he had already had to squeeze 1,350 men into barracks built for 850 and that new ones would cost £40,000, he was allowed to solve the problem by reducing his force by yet another battalion. Thus his force fell from about 3,700 in March 1853 to 2,500 two years later.[1]

In reducing the garrisons so drastically Whitehall was undoubtedly straining at strategic sense. In consequence some attempt was made to provide or encourage other improvements to the defences. Much was heard again of schemes of assisted military emigration and legions of enrolled pensioners for Bermuda as well as Canada and the Maritimes. Rather more important perhaps was the proposal to improve the weak commercial and strategic communication with Canada by guaranteeing a loan for the construction of an 'intercolonial' railway between Halifax and Quebec. But the railway scheme fell through; only a few hundred 'enrolled pensioners' were settled in Canada, mostly on reserves in the vicinity of abandoned posts; and most disappointing of all was the utter failure to persuade the legislatures of Canada and Nova Scotia to do anything about improving their antiquated and ineffectual militia. Thus while the imperial government did manage between 1847 and 1853 to reduce its expenditure in North America very considerably, largely by reducing the garrisons and transferring other costs to the local authorities,

[1] Newcastle to Wood, 26 Mar. 1853, Wood to Newcastle, 26 May 1853 and 11 Feb. 1854, and C.O. to Horse Guards, 30 Mar. 1854, W.O. 1/591 and 593.

almost nothing was done to make up for the consequential decline in defensive capacity. 'This economy', as the leading authority on the subject therefore concludes, 'had been effected merely by England doing less, without Canada doing more.'[1]

This result could not but have had a cautionary effect upon the British government's policy towards the United States. After all, even before this economical phase, they had hardly been confident about their military position in Canada, and now, they were warned again and again, they were running the risk of driving the Canadians into the arms of the Americans. Palmerston by no means approved the kind of reduction going on; but his opposition was hamstrung by the fact that he was shouting as loudly as anyone about the invasion scare that was largely responsible for the demands for concentration in the United Kingdom. And in spite of his noisy denunciations of Aberdeen's 'surrenders', he seems in any case to have realized on his return to the Foreign Office that he would not be able to confront the Americans any more firmly or directly. His anxiety to resist them always seems to have been rather stronger in opposition than in office. Perhaps it was the almost certain knowledge that he would shortly be returning to the Foreign Office, rather than the pacifying arguments of his senior colleagues, that led him at the end of June 1846 publicly to pronounce the Oregon settlement 'equally favourable to both parties'.[2] So far as Texas was concerned he was, from the beginning in 1836, quite sceptical about the opportunities supposedly presented to Great Britain, and a decade later he had, like Aberdeen, written off California and most of Mexico as well. He consoled himself with the thought that the acquisition of 'a great extent of fine land to the south will render the Americans less anxious to strip us of Canada'. Ultimately, he expected, it would lead to the collapse of the Union. Even if it did not, 'the multitude of conflicting interests which will belong to its various component parts will be an obstacle to any unnecessary war with a great maritime Power and wealthy customer like England'. But effective resistance to the Americans' southward expansion, he believed, could only be maintained by war, and war on behalf of 'such a set of people as the Mexicans would not go down with the House of Commons in the best of times'.[3] In the new phase of American expansionism after

[1] Stacey, p. 88. For this phase of reduction generally see Stacey, pp. 64–88.
[2] Herbert C. F. Bell, *Lord Palmerston* (2 vols., London, 1936), i. 369–70.
[3] Palmerston to Lord Normanby (ambassador in Paris), private, 7 May 1847, Evelyn Ashley, *The Life and Correspondence of Henry John Temple, Viscount Palmerston* (2 vols., London, 1879), ii. 40.

the Mexican war, Palmerston did occasionally profess to hope that the British parliament and public might more readily appreciate the threats that would be presented to their West Indian possessions and to their trade generally by United States control of the Central American isthmus and its interoceanic communications. But even here the same difficulty about arousing serious public attention was bound to intervene. Fortunately for once it was Great Britain who appeared to be operating from a position of relative strength in Central America, and Palmerston clearly hoped by exploiting this advantage to lead the Americans – particularly the moderate Taylor administration – into a convenient compromise and so avoid a showdown in which he might well not be sustained.

American policy in Central America during the first half of the nineteenth century had been unenterprizing and unsuccessful, but the British had acquired a generally predominating influence and, on the east coast, territorial footholds in settlements around Belize and on the Bay Islands, and in the so-called protectorate over the Mosquito Indians. Shortly after Palmerston's return to the Foreign Office in 1846 there was a significant increase in British activity. Originally this probably had little if anything to do with fear of further American advance so far as the government in London was concerned, though local agents may have acted in a very different spirit. More probably it was merely a reaction to local developments and, beyond that, only a normal expression of Palmerston's special interest in the furtherance of British trade.[1] Palmerston also expressed an interest in finding some sort of Pacific naval base, but this was nothing new and was not pressed. The new commander-in-chief of the Pacific squadron was ordered to keep on the lookout for such a station, and about the same time special investigations were made of various islands and positions on the western coast of the isthmus. But nothing came of this interest, largely because even Palmerston was not prepared to approve the high-handed methods

---

[1] Among a large literature on this question, the most important contributions are: M. W. Williams, *Anglo-American Isthmian Diplomacy 1815–1915* (Washington, 1916), pp. 46–66; R. W. Van Alstyne, 'The Central American Policy of Lord Palmerston, 1846–1848', *Hispanic American Historical Review*, xvi (1936), 339–59. For two recent views, see R. A. Naylor, 'The British Role in Central America prior to the Clayton-Bulwer Treaty of 1850', and Mark J. Van Aken, 'British Policy Considerations in Central America before 1850', *Hispanic American Historical Review*, xl (1960), 361–82, and xlii (1962), 54–9. Mario Rodríguez, *A Palmerstonian Diplomat in Latin America: Frederick Chatfield, Esq.* (Tucson, 1964), provides a highly coloured picture and rather exaggerates Palmerston's role.

used by his agent to obtain a base.[1] But whatever the intentions had been Great Britain soon found herself moving into direct conflict with the United States policy in Central America. The key issue here was the control of possible interoceanic routes. Neither side apparently aimed at exclusive control but each feared that this was in fact the other's real intention. By giving actual naval support to the claims of their puppet Mosquito 'king', the British had secured a convenient grip on San Juan del Norte (often called Greytown), the outlet on the Caribbean of one of the most important trans-isthmian routes and also of what was considered one of the most likely canal routes. About the same time, between 1846 and 1849, the Americans, on their part, were securing in one way or another a special hold upon all the other most likely routes – across the isthmus of Tehuantepec, Panama, and Nicaragua.

With the British apparently trying to spread their influence and even their possessions generally throughout Central America, and with the Americans responding to this aggressiveness by making useful bargains with the victims, Anglo-American relations threatened shortly to explode once again. But in 1849 and 1850 neither government wanted such an explosion, and before long they found a compromise formula by which they could skirt the emotional issues of Anglo-American hostility and secure their immediate respective interests. By the Clayton-Bulwer treaty of 19 April 1850 each agreed not to obtain exclusive control of any canal and not to colonize or exercise dominion in any part of Central America; but rather to encourage the construction of a canal and to guarantee its neutrality when built.

Considering that the American administration was a weak one and that they were tackling the British in an area where they were already well entrenched, the Americans appeared to have scored a considerable success in facilitating the construction of the canal free from the threat of British control. Similarly Palmerston could congratulate himself that he had stemmed the tide of American territorial advance and prevented a future canal passing under their exclusive control. He could further reflect that he had avoided the sort of showdown with the United States in which parliamentary and perhaps public opinion would have deserted him. Instead he had achieved his principal ends by precisely the sort of legal undertaking that had been suggested previously for Hawaii and Cuba, but which all his distinguished predecessors had failed to induce the United State to accept. But if Palmerston hoped

---

[1] Earl of Auckland (first lord of the Admiralty) to Palmerston, private, 2 Nov. 1847, Broadlands papers; Rodríguez, pp. 281–316.

to introduce a new era of peaceful containment of American expansion, he was soon to be disappointed.

Between 1849 and 1851 a renegade Spanish officer, General Narciso Lopez, made no less than three attempts, with unofficial American backing, to 'liberate' Cuba from Spanish rule, and though these were all hampered by American law officers and pitifully unsuccessful, the French and British governments were sufficiently impressed with the danger to invite the American government in the spring of 1852 to join yet another 'hands off' convention. But this was too much for President Fillmore. He insisted rather that Cuba was 'mainly an American question' and refused so to restrict the future expansion of his country. Even before this all self-satisfaction over the Clayton-Bulwer treaty itself had rapidly evaporated. A compromise agreement, and particularly one which would satisfy British prestige and yet still pass safely through the Senate, had been found only by obscuring – to some extent deliberately – the meaning and intention of the treaty itself. Almost at once therefore the two sides found themselves squabbling over whether the ban on colonization was prospective or retrospective and, the British possession of Belize being pretty well conceded in any case, whether the British were obliged to withdraw from the Bay Islands and the Mosquito protectorate. Since even Palmerston felt these contravened the spirit if not the letter of the treaty, the whole affair might easily have been settled if only a formula could have been found that safeguarded the access to Greytown and protected the inhabitants from the 'justice' of the Central Americans. For the British and Americans to find a formula was evidently not impossible. In April 1852, less than six months after Palmerston went out of office again, one was found in the Webster-Crampton convention. But this proved unacceptable to Nicaragua.

While the incompatibility of British prestige and Spanish honour kept the fate of the Indians and the self-styled British inhabitants of the Bay Islands undetermined, the Democrats returned to power in Washington in March 1853. More ambitious and less patient than their predecessors, they turned at once upon the imperialist policies of their old enemy. Already, in the election campaign, they had denounced Great Britain's position in Central America as a violation of what was coming to be known as the Monroe Doctrine. Now, in his Inaugural Address of March 1853, President Pierce declared that his policy would 'not be controlled by any timid forebodings of evil from expansion'. Once in office the Pierce administration was inevitably not quite so fierce as it had threatened, but it nevertheless stiffened the United States attitude on the Central American question very considerably, and before long it had also made a series of moves stretching out with an acquisitive grasp into the Pacific and the Caribbean. In April 1854 a supposed insult to the American flag – the *Black Warrior* affair – gave the opportunity to press Spain once again to sell Cuba. In October of the same year came the unauthorized Ostend Manifesto – a rashly worded public statement of American interest and policy with regard to Cuba, issued jointly by the American ministers in London, Paris, and Madrid, and hastily repudiated by their government. Meanwhile draft treaties providing for the annexation of Hawaii and the possession of Samana Bay in Santo Domingo had already been secured in August and September.

What must have given particular encouragement to the Americans was that for the first time in forty years Great Britain was engaged in a major war in Europe and unable therefore to devote so much attention to what was going on in the New World. Certainly this was how it appeared to the British, especially when the impression grew that the Americans were lending considerable support to Russia. But instead of weakening British resistance this feeling tended to make them more obstinate, even where, as in the case of Central America, they would otherwise have been conciliatory. Moreover, while the crisis in the near east did force still further withdrawals of troops from North America, the navy was not nearly so pressed, and warships remained available to reinforce American waters. Indeed, rather than presenting the United States with a real opportunity to exploit a diversion, the Crimean War threatened at last to realize Aberdeen's ambition of an effective Franco-British alliance, containing with equal firmness Russian and American expansionism alike. Britain and France did not declare war on Russia and conclude their alliance until 28 March 1854, but before this they had already begun to concert their action. What is more, an apparently open warning to the United States had already come from London. In a speech on 25 February Lord Clarendon, the foreign secretary, had told the House of Lords that Anglo-French cooperation would not be confined to the eastern question, but rather that 'on the question of policy there is no part of the world in either hemisphere with regard to which we are not entirely in accord'. Pressed on this statement by the American minister, Buchanan, Clarendon shortly afterwards denied that there was any specific Anglo-French understanding about Cuba, though their cooperation did extend to 'the navigation of the Plata, the Paraguay, the Amazon, and other rivers, and to the countries of South America bordering upon them'. Since Buchanan believed British intervention in South America had always been 'fair and liberal' towards the United States, he was not inclined to be worried by Clarendon's speech. But on the other side of the Atlantic they were much more uneasy. At that distance, noted Marcy, the secretary of state, the qualification of Clarendon's speech did not appear 'very satisfactory'. It had been followed by angry letters in *The Times* warning that after humbling Russia the allies would turn on the United States, by speeches from Napoleon III reaffirming Clarendon's original statement, and, not least, by the persistent opposition of the two powers to American policy in the Pacific and the Caribbean.[1]

In spite of all his denials Clarendon certainly dreamed of an Anglo-French combination against the United States, and in some areas there was definitely a most effective coincidence of resistance by the two powers to American expansion. Typical perhaps of the rather extreme view the British were inclined to take of American policy at this time was the analysis submitted to the foreign secretary by John Crampton, Bulwer's successor as minister in Washington. Hawaii, Cuba, and Central America, he argued, were not the only areas of American acquisitiveness; there were too Perry's expedition to Japan and the exploration of the Amur River. Somewhere they must make a stand, and preferably in alliance with France against the Monroe Doctrine itself. Cuba, he suggested, was the key, and it was here that they should join with France in banning American annexation or else acquiesce generally in the expansion of the United States.[2]

So far as Cuba was concerned Clarendon emphatically agreed since, as he said, he cared more about this question than anything else.[3] Here Britain and France had already made a stand together in 1851–52, and although they were not always in agreement over the details of their cooperation, inept American diplomacy in Spain as well as occasional filibuster attempts continued to be totally unsuccessful in their designs upon the island. In Santo Domingo and Hawaii British and French agents intervened together late in 1854 to prevent the

[1] J. Fred Rippy, *The United States and Mexico* (New York, 1926), pp. 200–1; Marcy to Buchanan, 28 May, and Buchanan to Marcy, 15 June 1855, J. B. Moore, ed., *The Works of James Buchanan, Comprising his Speeches, State Papers, and Private Correspondence* (Philadelphia and London, 1908–1911), ix. 345–60.

[2] Crampton to Clarendon, private, 7 Feb. 1853, R. W. Van Alstyne, 'Anglo-American Relations, 1853–1857', *American Historical Review*, xlii (1936–37), 493–5.

[3] Clarendon to Lord Cowley (ambassador in Paris), private, 18 April 1854, Cowley papers, P.R.O., F.O. 519/170.

Americans getting anything but such unfavourable treaties that the projects had to be dropped.[1] But in Central America, where it was the British who were on the defensive and uncertain too of the justice of their present position, there was much less certainty of French support, except against filibusters. In these circumstances Clarendon looked around for advice from statesmen in and out of office about how he should respond to the mounting American pressure for a general British withdrawal from Central America, including, as Buchanan now made clear, Belize as well as the Bay Islands and the Mosquito protectorate. Sir Henry Bulwer, the man most responsible for the negotiation of the ambiguous 1850 treaty, was still inclined to view that arrangement as the best way of regulating the position in Central America. But he admitted that, in view of the connection with Britain's existing possessions in Australia and New Zealand, and with the Chinese empire falling to pieces, it was if anything becoming daily more important to keep the United States out. Apart from Russell who favoured arbitration, Clarendon's advisers were generally inclined to recommend a tough line. For once Palmerston and Aberdeen were as one on American policy, thinking it inexpedient at a moment of weakness to offer arbitration and so invite additional American demands. While the Crimean War lasted, therefore, Clarendon's general line was, without breaking off negotiations, to stand pat on the Central American question.[2] Indeed, under the constant threat of American filibuster raids and with an increasingly aggressive American policy in the isthmus itself, it was necessary even to take further naval precautions.

In 1853 and 1854 United States agents in Central America – whether representing the government or private commercial interests – had become increasingly troublesome. Then in the summer of 1854 came news of an astonishing incident. Earlier in the year what was almost certainly an attempt by the Americans to undermine Mosquito authority at Greytown by exploiting an unpleasant local dispute, had ended

[1] J. M. Callahan, *Cuba and International Relations* (Baltimore, 1899), pp. 221–97; D. Perkins, *The Monroe Doctrine, 1826–1867* (Baltimore, 1933), pp. 268–71; Van Alstyne, 'Great Britain, the United States, and Hawaiian Independence, 1850–1855', *Pacific Historical Review*, iv (1935), 15–24.

[2] Bulwer to Clarendon, private, March 1854, Van Alstyne, 'Anglo-American Relations', pp. 495–6; Van Alstyne, 'British Diplomacy and the Clayton-Bulwer Treaty, 1850–60', *Journal of Modern History*, xi (1939), 175; Clarendon to Russell, private, 17 and 23 April 1854, Russell papers, P.R.O. 30/22/11. The one real sign of weakening which Van Alstyne professed to see in Clarendon's position is based on a wrong attribution of a draft memorandum (cf. Van Alstyne, 'Anglo-American Relations', pp. 496–7 and D. Waddell, 'Great Britain and the Bay Islands, 1821–61', *Historical Journal*, ii (1959), 70, n. 48.

in the bombardment of the town by the U.S.S. *Cyane*, and the burning of what remained by a landing party of marines. Following as it did fast upon the news of American activities in Hawaii and Santo Domingo, Clarendon saw it as yet further confirmation that the Americans were 'becoming a universal nuisance'.[1] No doubt it was all the more offensive inasmuch as in the sheer effrontery of gunboat diplomacy it had out-shone even the best efforts of the British navy. On 31 August he wrote to Crampton describing the affair as an 'outrage without parallel in the annals of modern times'.[2] A few days later he was wisely seeking to found his protests on some more solid basis, like the damage done to the British consulate and property. Palmerston, who was still biding his time at the Home Office and waiting for criticism of the war in the Crimea to sweep him back into power, urged Clarendon to go even further. They ought, he said, to demand an apology and compensation, and take the opportunity of making a firm stand against the United States:

A quarrel with the United States is at all times undesirable, and is especially so when we are engaged in War with another power but though at War, we are crippling effectually the naval means of the power with whom we are at War, and what is of great Importance we are sure at present of not having France against us, as an ally of the United States.

In dealing with Vulgar minded Bullies, and such unfortunately the people of the United States are, nothing is gained by submission to Insult & wrong; on the contrary the submission to an Outrage only encourages the commission of another and a greater one – such People are always trying how far they can venture to go; and they generally pull up when they find they can go no further without encountering resistance of a formidable Character.

In the present Instance we have many advantages on our side.

We are successful in our War against Russia, which the United States Govt. when it sent the *Cyane* to Grey Town thought would hamper & embarrass us, and when we have taken Sebastopol and have knocked down Sweaborg & Cronstadt as we shall do with the Lancaster Guns our naval force will be to a great Degree let free. We have France so bound up with us that she cannot join the United States against us, we have our N. American Provinces now united & loyal, and dissatisfied with the United States, we have public opinion in the United States on our side, we have the United States Govt. itself ashamed of what it has done & not daring to avow its act, though hesitating to disavow & atone for it.

The U.S. have no navy of which we need be afraid, & they might be told that if they were to resort to privateering, we should however reluctantly be obliged to retaliate by burning all their Sea Coast Towns.

---

[1] Clarendon to Cowley, private, 11 Aug. 1854, Cowley papers, F.O. 519/170.
[2] Clarendon to Crampton, no. 191, 31 Aug. 1854, Williams, p. 180.

If we are not firm on this occasion I don't see on what occasion we could ever take our stand. If the Parts had been reversed we should long before this Time have seen Buchanan take his Passage Home unless we had yielded to an imperative Demand for the most ample satisfaction.[1]

Rumours during the same month of September about an American bid to buy a naval base in Europe from the bankrupt prince of Monaco undoubtedly put Clarendon in a very receptive frame of mind. If the prince went ahead with the scheme, he wrote to Paris on 23 September, he should be 'treated as a Common Enemy for having surreptitiously attempted to give an unscrupulous and aggressive maritime power a footing in Europe'. He would even be prepared to sanction forcible occupation by the French or Sardinian armies, since he was

convinced that no necessity can be greater than to exclude those Buccaneers from the Mediterranean. Russian aggressiveness and encroachment would be nothing as compared with theirs and they would be robbing and quarrelling with everybody within six months. The annexation of Piedmont would be their first object and it would be argued and advocated in all the American newspapers until we should have filibustering steamers fitted out to avenge some imaginary Sardinian insult.[2]

Clarendon's despatch to Crampton expressing disappointment that the American government had not yet disavowed the action and suggesting compensation was due went out on 21 September.

Nothing can be worse [he told his ambassador in Paris the next day], than the doings of the United States and they think to make political capital against us in the belief that our hands are full but we mean to dispel that delusion and in order to prevent another attack on Greytown or Ruatan [one of the Bay Islands] which we hear is likely a 90 gun Screw sails shortly to reinforce the West Indian Station, another powerful frigate will follow in a fortnight and if necessary some of the Baltic Screws when the winter sets in . . . These bullies must be shown that we are not afraid of them or they will be hustled into war with us by some of the mob to whose passions they pander.[3]

On 4 December came the president's Message, producing a highly distorted version of the Greytown incident and conveying hardly the least sign of regret. But although Clarendon severely criticized this retort in conversation with Buchanan, the 'firm stand' against the Americans evaporated. In part, perhaps, this was due to the disappointing

[1] Palmerston's 'Memorandum on a Draft of Despatch from Lord Clarendon to Mr Crampton in Washington', 10 Sept. 1854, Broadlands papers.

[2] Clarendon to Cowley, private, 23 Sept. 1854, Cowley papers, F.O. 519/170.

[3] Clarendon to Cowley, private, 22 Sept. 1854, *ibid.*; Clarendon to Crampton, no. 198, 21 Sept. 1854, Williams, p. 182.

news from the east. Following fast upon the landing in the Crimea in September had come the victories of Alma, Balaclava, and Inkerman; but Sebastopol held out and with the onset of winter all the glory threatened to disappear and the allied armies were condemned instead to horrible sufferings. Sobering though this must have been, it might just as easily have tempted both France and Britain to seek consolation in a combined assault upon American pride and arrogance. But the British cabinet had already discovered they were not united even among themselves.

In the middle of October had come the news of the Ostend Manifesto about Cuba and on 24 October Sir James Graham, the first lord of the Admiralty, was again suggesting that France was more likely to give the support thought necessary over that island or Santo Domingo than in Central America. Russell, who had remained in the cabinet after surrendering the Foreign Office to Clarendon in February 1853, was so alarmed that he even suggested a special peace mission to the United States, but this was vetoed by the prime minister. Aberdeen agreed that his country's position in Mosquitia and Greytown was 'questionable', and the title to the Bay Islands 'little better than manifest usurpation'; but he still believed, with Clarendon and Palmerston, that concession now would be taken as weakness, and, moreover, that it would appear as concession 'to Russia, and not to the United States alone'. So while he approved of the naval precautions off the Central American coast, it was rather in the strategic islands of the Caribbean and the Pacific that he stressed firm resistance to the Americans in concert with France. Instead of a firm stand in Central America, he envisaged only a temporizing policy, looking forward to substantial concessions when success in the Crimea made it more expedient. Even Palmerston acquiesced in the wisdom of this strategy.[1] In February 1855 Aberdeen at last gave way to him as prime minister, and the British public looked forward eagerly to a more successful prosecution of the war in the east. This preoccupation perhaps again distracted Palmerston's attention away from the firm stand he had so recently advocated in the west. At the end of July Clarendon, who was still foreign secretary, appealed to him for help since he was at his 'wit's ends about the Grey Town outrage'. The law officers had told him that they could claim compensation only 'upon the ground of our protectorate

---

[1] Graham to Clarendon, 24 Oct. 1854, and Aberdeen to Clarendon, 5 Nov. 1854, Van Alstyne, 'Anglo-American Relations', pp. 497–8. See also Van Alstyne, 'British Diplomacy and the Clayton-Bulwer Treaty', p. 176, and Williams, pp. 183–5.

of Mosquito and John Bull would never stand a quarrel with the United States at this moment for such a cause'. 'Perhaps the least degrading course', he concluded, 'would be to let the matter drop, at least till we have taken Sebastopol, but we are made to feel our non success there in every corner of the world.'[1] Shortly afterwards Crampton was told simply to drop the whole affair.[2]

Throughout 1855, with France and Britain acting in general concert if not in perfect unity, all the efforts of the United States to obtain a naval base in Cuba, Santo Domingo, or Hawaii were persistently frustrated. But though successful in its immediate objective, the allies' anti-American policy never acquired the character of a decisive check to American expansionism, such as Palmerston had certainly dreamed of. Over Central America his administration several times offered arbitration, but very offhandedly it seemed to the Americans, and certainly Clarendon was careful always to maintain his maximum position. But a merely temporizing policy was peculiarly vulnerable to the vagaries of fortune. By the end of 1855 it was clear that in the bombardment affair the British had let slip a vital opportunity and allowed the Americans to seize the moral advantage when an incident of the Crimean War gave them the chance.

Worried by the drain of manpower in the Crimea, the British had begun to turn to the United States as a possible field for the recruitment of British subjects as early as November 1854. In December had come a new Foreign Enlistment Act, and in February 1855 recruiting instructions went out to North America. It does not look as if the government in London had any intention of infringing the American neutrality laws but, carelessly or not, the activities of Crampton and other agents soon managed to offend the Americans. Warned that they were unhappy in July Clarendon brushed their suspicions aside and declared that the instructions had been cancelled. Thinking that this had settled the matter even Buchanan no longer passed on his government's protests, in particular a despatch of 15 July from Marcy, his secretary of state, demanding redress and already hinting at the possible dismissal of the guilty British agents. Clarendon and his colleagues were consequently astonished when they heard from Crampton towards the end of September that the Americans looked like making a serious quarrel out of it. Encouraged by Palmerston's leadership, and still more by the news that Sebastopol had fallen at last, the British government

[1] Clarendon to Palmerston, 31 July, 1855, Broadlands papers.
[2] Williams, p. 186.

began to make the most serious preparations for a showdown since the beginning of 1846.[1]

The preparations began with a suggestion from Palmerston on 24 September that they should send out two battalions to Canada and reinforce the squadron on the North American station.[2] Certainly Canada was in real need of reinforcements if there was going to be trouble with the United States. The reduction to a little more than 3,500 men during 1853 had been followed by even more drastic cuts in the summer of 1854. Faced with the urgent demands to supply the force assembling for the Crimea the colonial secretary in August 1854 had decided to accelerate the process of withdrawal initiated by Grey in 1851. Half the artillery left in North America was to be withdrawn, three battalions of infantry from Canada, and one each from Nova Scotia and the West Indies. By the end of 1854 there were less than 1,900 infantry left in Canada, less than 1,100 in Nova Scotia – and they were allowed that many only in view of the importance of Halifax as an imperial station – and a mere 311 in Newfoundland. On the credit side there had at last been some progress with the militia. In June 1855 a new militia bill passed through the Canadian legislature and preparations were made for the first time to raise a force of 'active militia' or volunteers of up to 5,000 in number. But when the Crampton recruiting crisis loomed up in the autumn of 1855 the organization of this new force had hardly begun and the number of regulars on the mainland of British North America was barely half what it had been at its lowest point after 1814.[3] Even so Palmerston's suggestion about reinforcement was not followed up, probably because the troops could not have been got out of the Crimea in time to reach Canada before the winter severed the St Lawrence route. It was rather on naval reinforcements that the government concentrated, partly no doubt because they would also be useful in keeping a watch on American filibusters in the Caribbean. Ever since early in 1854 these had been threatening to extend their activities into Central America, and in the summer of 1855, after a series of unsuccessful manœuvres, one of them, Colonel Kinney of Philadelphia, did manage to land at Greytown. Kinney's success was shortlived, but the British were seriously concerned that it was all part

---

[1] For this affair see, H. B. Learned, 'William Learned Marcy', in S. F. Bemis, ed., *The American Secretaries of State and their Diplomacy*, vi (New York, 1928), 237–62, and R. W. Van Alstyne, 'John F. Crampton, Conspirator or Dupe?', *American Historical Review*, xli (1935–36), 492–502.

[2] Palmerston to Clarendon, 24 Sept. 1855, Palmerston papers, B.M.Add. MS.48,579.　　　　　　　　　　　　　　　　[3] Stacey, pp. 89–97.

of a plot to oust them from the Mosquito protectorate. Kinney, Clarendon commented late in October before he heard of the colonel's failure, 'is of course acting under secret instruction from the United States government'.[1]

With all this in mind Sir Charles Wood, now first lord of the Admiralty, advised Admiral Fanshawe on the North American station as early as 28 September that in two or three days an additional battleship would be going out to Bermuda since that base was not as well defended as he would have liked, and that more might go out in the autumn. Probably the Americans' 'bullying' would subside when they heard the news from Sebastopol, but in any case 'Brother Jonathan is never the worse for seeing that we are ready'. A few days later he was taking steps to assemble an appropriate force of large ships in home waters and ready to cross the Atlantic 'if Brother Jonathan becomes saucy'. On 1 October Admiral Lyons, commander-in-chief in the Mediterranean, was asked to send home two or three more battleships by next summer, and next day Admiral Dundas, commander-in-chief in the Baltic, a number of screw vessels capable of crossing the Atlantic. On 11 October Fanshawe was told that he would be getting at once two blockships – that is older sailing vessels which had been converted to powerfully armed steam batteries – and a steam sloop for Bermuda, and a sailing battleship for Jamaica, followed shortly by another steam battleship and possibly one or two more ships in the winter. They were not able to spare from the Crimea any of the light draught vessels Fanshawe had wanted for Central American waters, but by the end of October and in spite of having to give leave to some of the crews, all the large ships promised had been sent out save for the second battleship for Jamaica. 'I mean to make a parade of it,' Wood told Fanshawe, 'the object being to show the world, and the people of the United States principally, that we have a spare force after all.'[2]

The 'parade' first seems to have come to Buchanan's attention through a newspaper report on 19 October, and still unaware apparently how seriously his government was treating the recruitment affair, he was inclined to attribute it merely to Kinney's expedition to Greytown.[3] But a few days later, on 25 October, *The Times* started a series of editorials which made the position unmistakably clear. The British were offended and alarmed, it now appeared, by a whole parcel of incidents.

[1] Clarendon to Palmerston, 25 Oct. 1855, Broadlands papers.
[2] Wood to Fanshawe, private, 28 Sept., 11 and 26 Oct., to Lyons, private, 1 Oct., and to Dundas, private, 2 Oct. 1855, Halifax papers, B.M.Add.MS.49,564.
[3] Buchanan to Marcy, private, 19 Oct., Marcy papers, Library of Congress.

There were the various filibuster expeditions, including even a threat to Ireland; there was the recruiting affair and the very offensive language used on that account by the American attorney-general, Caleb Cushing, in particular; there was the suspicious investigation of British positions in the West Indies being made by the U.S.S. *Fulton*; and not least there were the rumours of Russian privateers being fitted out in New York which highlighted the general complaint about the aid and comfort that the Americans appeared to have been giving to the enemy. About the same time Buchanan received another fierce despatch on the recruitment question from Marcy. This he was obliged to read to Clarendon on 1 November, and, since it specifically referred to the earlier despatch of 15 July, Clarendon was belatedly given a copy of that despatch too. Surprised and annoyed though he must have been by this most unfortunate delay, Clarendon apparently preserved a very friendly attitude. On the question of the naval reinforcements he seemed politely firm. Warned by Buchanan that they had better keep 'a respectable distance from our coasts', the foreign secretary retorted that they 'meant only to take care of [themselves] and not to attack or menace others without cause'.[1]

In fact Clarendon was already feeling that his country's position was not a good one and that they might even have fallen into a trap. On 25 September he had confided to Palmerston that he did not feel 'quite easy' about the recruiting affair: 'I am afraid that rather more zeal than prudence has been displayed in procuring recruits, and that they did not bear sufficiently in mind that they were in a hostile country and surrounded by spies.'[2] The next day he had admitted that he was on that account afraid of an impartial enquiry.[3] He went on to express considerable doubts about their grounds for complaint in other matters. Palmerston had suggested that they might answer Marcy by saying that they had thought he would be satisfied by the assurances Clarendon had given in July, and then take the opportunity to add a few well-chosen remarks on the conduct of American neutrality in the war with Russia. Thus they might say:

Her Majesty's Government . . . looked upon those Proceedings as the Acts of a few private Individuals greedy for gain, and by no means as Indications of the general feeling of the American People. For remembering

[1] This interview is described from both sides: by Clarendon in a private letter to Palmerston, 1 Nov. 1855, Broadlands papers; by Buchanan in a private letter to Marcy, 2 Nov., Marcy papers, Library of Congress.

[2] Clarendon to Palmerston, 25 Sept. 1855, Broadlands papers.

[3] Clarendon to Palmerston, 26 Sept. 1855, *ibid*.

the many ties and sympathies which connect the People of the United States with the two Powerful Nations which are engaged in the present contest with Russia, and convinced that a free, enlightened and Generous Race such as the Citizens of the great North American Union must entertain on the important questions at issue sentiments in harmony with those which animate not only the British and French nations but the great mass of the nations of Western Europe, H.M. Gvt. would have passed over in silence the exceptional course thus pursued by a small number of Individuals if it had not been for . . . Mr Marcy's note.

Since the correspondence would be published, Palmerston had concluded, it would be 'worth considering whether some little Flourish of this kind as an appeal to what is probably the dormant sympathy of a large portion of the Americans may not be a set off against the Bunkum vapouring of Marcy'.[1] Clarendon, however, was not so sure.

The opportunity is a good one for saying a word about the pseudo-neutrality of the United States [he admitted], but I doubt if we have any real ground of complaint against the Government on that score, for nothing that I am aware of has taken place which the government has the means of preventing. They can't stop shipments of revolvers to Hamburg or steam engines to Baltic ports, nor can they prevent public meetings of Irishmen; but they can prevent the sailing of an expedition to Ireland and that they will of course say they did do if the improbable attempt were made. We may therefore perhaps expose ourselves to an insolent rejoinder.[2]

Now, in reporting his 1 November interview with Buchanan he had to admit to Palmerston that Marcy 'rather *has us*' in alluding to 'all the guns, swords and pistols we have obtained from the United States and the American ships that have been transporting troops for us and the French – also to the Irish in America not doing more against us than the refugees here do against the countries of their birth in Europe'. And on the recruiting question he was still 'half afraid of taking a very confident tone'.[3] So far as the naval demonstration was concerned he had already begun to hesitate, asking Palmerston before the interview with Buchanan how far he thought 'it would be prudent to admit that our reinforcements of the West Indian fleet are to the address of the United States'.[4] Then when the American minister called on him on 8 and again on 15 November to convey assurances about the 'Russian' privateers and the Irish filibuster, and to suggest that as a gesture of

[1] Palmerston to Clarendon, 25 Sept. 1855, Palmerston papers, B.M.Add. MS.48,579.
[2] Clarendon to Palmerston, 26 Sept. 1855, Broadlands papers.
[3] Clarendon to Palmerston, 1 Nov. 1855, *ibid.*
[4] Clarendon to Palmerston, 27 Oct. 1855, *ibid.*

conciliation before the president's Annual Message of 2 December, they should provide him with a written statement of their intention to withdraw the reinforcements, Buchanan got the impression that this would indeed be done. But though clearly inclined to agree, Clarendon was extremely reserved in conveying all this to Palmerston, and the letter that Buchanan got on 16 November was utterly disappointing to a man who was anxious to return in good odour for the presidential elections of 1856 and wished therefore to dispel the war clouds with a pacifying piece of paper. It made no mention of any withdrawal and merely reiterated that the warships had been sent out as a precaution 'against all dangers which may appear in any part of the horizon', and that no steps had been 'prompted by any hostile feeling or menacing intention on our part towards the United States'. Such hypocrisy, as Buchanan politely inferred, was hardly likely to contribute to the restoration of good relations.[1] Nor was the official reply about the recruiting affair that Clarendon sent out for Marcy on the same day. Unable, apparently, even now to convince the prime minister how weak their position was, on this too he could still make only an evasive and unsatisfactory response.[2]

Unequal though the reply was to the extent of the United States complaints, as well as to the degree of culpability Clarendon himself suspected in his agents, he seems to have thought that the Americans would nevertheless be satisfied with it. Late in November, therefore, it was decided after all not to send out the additional battleship promised to Fanshawe a month before.[3] What rather worried the foreign secretary, and what he thought must be giving distinct satisfaction to the Americans, was the dramatic success being achieved by another filibuster expedition. In 1853 William Walker – 'the grey-eyed man of destiny', as he liked to call himself – had made an attempt upon Lower California and had failed. But in the summer of 1855 he had intervened in a revolution in Nicaragua and by the end of the year had virtually taken over the country. As with the Kinney affair earlier, and this time with even more justification, Clarendon was again inclined to believe that the American government must be involved, but he still did not know what to do. If the British government protested they

[1] Clarendon to Palmerston, 8 and 15 Nov. 1855, Broadlands papers; Buchanan to Marcy, private, 2 Nov., Marcy papers, Library of Congress; Buchanan to Marcy, nos. 101, 9 Nov., 102 and 103, 16 Nov., Clarendon to Buchanan, private, 16 Nov., and Buchanan to Clarendon, private, 16 Nov., Moore, ix. 449–64.

[2] Clarendon to Crampton, 16 Nov. 1855, cited by Learned, pp. 256–7.

[3] Clarendon to Palmerston, 3 Dec. 1855, Broadlands papers; Wood to Fanshawe, private, 23 Nov., Halifax papers, B.M.Add.MS.49,565.

would only get an insolent reply, 'and we must not talk too big unless we are prepared for a quarrel'. He was not thinking of war; only of a suspension of diplomatic relations and forcible intervention against the filibusters. But even in that case, he feared, they would get 'no backing at home if we frightened the Cotton Lords on account of Nicaragua'. They evidently decided therefore to rest content with encouraging the resistance of the Central Americans themselves. They even thought of selling weapons to Costa Rica.[1]

In the meantime, with Clarendon himself increasingly preoccupied with the diplomatic manœuvres of the Russian war's final stages, as well as with his mother's dying illness, the British waited with comparative calmness for news from America of Marcy's reply on the recruiting question and the long awaited Message from the president on Central America. The Message, delivered to Congress rather belatedly on 31 December, did not arrive in England until 15 or 16 January. It was only moderately hostile about the Central American question. It did not recommend abrogation of the Clayton-Bulwer treaty, but pressed rather for Great Britain to fulfil her treaty obligations as the United States saw them. Much more of a bombshell was Marcy's reply of 28 December on the recruiting question. This arrived in London on 18 January, and after reviewing the American case at great length ended by demanding Crampton's recall and the removal of three consuls. Clarendon could not understand why the Americans were not satisfied with the stopping of the recruiting and the explanations they had already received. When Buchanan showed him Marcy's note he cursed Cushing and warned that they would refuse to withdraw Crampton and, if he were dismissed, give Buchanan his passports too. In the meantime he would make no official reply to Marcy's 'pamphlet of a note', but wait and see what Crampton had to say about it.[2]

What made Clarendon hesitate to send back a stiff formal reply at once was no doubt his suspicion that Crampton might not be entirely innocent. In addition there was his feeling that he might not be backed up in parliament. He was particularly concerned that on 30 January 1856, the day before the reassembly of parliament, a sensational article had appeared in the *Morning Post*, denouncing the United States and threatening them with what Buchanan called the 'most

[1] Clarendon to Palmerston, 23 Dec. 1855, Broadlands papers. For British reaction to the Walker incident see Williams, pp. 193–4 and 210–12.
[2] Clarendon to Palmerston, 28 and 30 Jan. 1856, Broadlands papers; Buchanan to Marcy, private, 18 Jan., no. 114, 22 Jan., private, 25 Jan., no. 117, 1 Feb., and no. 119, 5 Feb., Moore, x. 9–34; Clarendon to Cowley, private, 5 Feb., Cowley papers, F.O. 519/173.

atrocious suggestions' about future military operations. Since this article seemed to be based on privy knowledge of the interview Clarendon had had with Buchanan only the day before, and since the paper was notoriously under the influence of Palmerston, Clarendon must have had his tongue in his cheek when he blandly remarked to the prime minister the next day that it would be attributed to him. He was worried most, however, by the prospect of it arousing comment on American affairs in parliament.[1] The next day, when the new parliament met to hear and debate the queen's Address, such a discussion did indeed begin, with Derby, the leader of the Opposition, talking in the Lords about war with the United States being mutually suicidal. But Clarendon was able to fend off criticism of the government's Central American policy by revealing that they had twice recently proposed arbitration and to quieten talk about the Crampton affair by suggesting it could only make things worse.[2] In any case the Commons was preoccupied with the end of the war with Russia and criticism of the government was not pressed so far as Clarendon had feared it might be. That night he wrote to the prime minister, congratulating him upon 'the sober demeanour of the House'. He wished, however, that 'somebody would tread upon that viper Roebuck till he died'.[3]

It was Roebuck who had been largely instrumental in bringing down the previous government over the conduct of the war in the Crimea. He was now pressing the new one about the peace and Clarendon knew too that the radicals were not going to let the government so easily off the hook about American affairs. Sure enough Roebuck was soon attacking them with an American pamphlet full of evidence against Crampton, and Cobden was insisting on the production of the recruitment papers for parliament's scrutiny.[4] When the papers appeared there would undoubtedly be more trouble. For a while, with British opinion generally preoccupied with the peace negotiations with Russia, and with Clarendon himself away in Paris for the congress, Palmerston adroitly held off the pressure of the radicals for the production of the correspondence. Similarly when the new American minister, George Mifflin Dallas, arrived in London in March, the prime minister also refrained from 'uncorking him on the questions', preferring rather to leave them for Clarendon's return.[5] Meanwhile, he was sure, Clarendon's progress

[1] Buchanan to Marcy, no. 117, 1 Feb. 1856, Moore, x. 23–8; Clarendon to Palmerston, 30 Jan., Broadlands papers.   [2] Williams, pp. 204–5.
[3] Clarendon to Palmerston, 31 Jan. 1856, Broadlands papers.
[4] Williams, pp. 205–7.
[5] Learned, pp. 259–60; Palmerston to Clarendon, 18 Mar. and 14 April 1856, Palmerston papers, B.M.Add.MS.48,580.

with the peace negotiations in Paris would 'lower the political baro-
meter at Washington'.[1] Clarendon himself conceded that 'affairs with
the United States were not exactly in a pleasant state', but he too still
did not think that war was imminent. In the delay that would now follow
while each side considered its position, he hoped, 'the good sense or
rather the self interest of the people [in the United States] will put a
check upon their reckless Government who are ready for *any thing* in
order to avert public attention from their despised position'.[2] Still, as
Wood pointed out, a little martial display might strengthen the Americans' pacific disposition. There was also the need to guard against an
accidental collision in the waters off Santo Domingo and Central
America, where British and American warships were jealously watching
each other's movements. With this in mind Wood wrote to Fanshawe
on 1 February to say that although he had originally intended to withdraw the blockships as they were not really seagoing vessels and
their crews had suffered much from yellow fever, he would not now do
so, since they would be useful both for the defence of Bermuda and
for attacks on the American seaboard. On 16 February he also wrote to
the commander-in-chief in the Pacific, Admiral Bruce, asking him to
have Vancouver Island examined with a view to establishing a naval
base there.[3]

Here, for a time, matters rested, while Clarendon busied himself
at the Congress of Paris. Then, convinced that 'Cushing & Co.' would
otherwise seize the chance 'to say that we had made him offer it in
order to save ourselves from being "whipped by the greatest nation on
airth" ',[4] at the end of March the government refused Crampton's
offer to resign and got ready to send a large reinforcement to Canada
with the reopening of the St Lawrence. Preparations had already been
made early in February to have 5,000 rifles sent out to Halifax, and Sir
Edmund Head, the governor-general, had made special arrangements
for their transfer overland to Canada under the code name 'Railroad
Iron'.[5] Now, at the end of March, it was decided to double this number

[1] Palmerston to the queen, 31 Mar. 1856, Bell, ii. 145.
[2] Clarendon to Cowley, private, 5 Feb. 1856, Cowley papers, F.O. 519/173.
[3] Wood to Fanshawe, private, 1 and 16 Feb. 1856, Wood to Bruce, private,
16 Feb., and Adm. Sir George Seymour to Wood, private, 7 Feb., Halifax
papers, B.M.Add.MSS.49,565 and 49,558.
[4] Clarendon (in Paris) to Palmerston, 21 Mar. 1856, Broadlands papers.
[5] D. G. G. Kerr, *Sir Edmund Head: a Scholarly Governor* (Toronto, 1954),
pp. 131–2. For a description of the generally 'inadequate' defences of Canada at
this time, and the 'appalling' and 'irremediable' condition of western Canada
in particular, see Head's memorandum, 'On the defensible condition of Western
Canada', 1 Mar. 1856, *ibid.*, p. 131. In England, however, and in spite of being

and to revive the office of commander-in-chief in North America in the person of Major-General Sir William Eyre, and to give him an extra five battalions of infantry and two batteries of artillery sent out direct from the Crimea. 'This American dispute may, and most likely will, end in smoke,' wrote Palmerston to the secretary of state for war on 30 March, 'but we must be prepared for the case of its ending in gunpowder smoke, and as Peace is now signed, and our troops are disposable, we should be greatly and justly blamed if we lost a day in properly reinforcing the garrison of our North American Colonies.' So by the beginning of May over four thousand men were on their way with ten thousand rifles and other ammunition and equipment to join the small force still in Canada and Nova Scotia and a reinforcement of troops was also on its way to Bermuda.[1] And lest the Americans should think that this was all that could be done, Palmerston went out of his way to persuade the American minister to attend the great naval review held at Portsmouth on 23 April. Dallas refused to be present for the grand intimidation and missed what he claimed with some justice to

---

out of office, Ellenborough seems to have been playing with much the same grandiose ideas as he had pressed on Peel ten years earlier. The year before he had again approached a Napier. General Sir Charles J. Napier had died in 1853, but in the meantime Ellenborough had begun an aquaintance with his younger brother the historian, General Sir William F. P. Napier. On the subject of Canada – as on India – Sir William had responded with appropriate flattery and ardour: 'I . . . think with the addition of 10,000 British troops, the whole under a good head such as yourself if you would become Governor-General, that Canada may be defended, certainly not by negligence if, as you say, everything is neglected, but with energy and providence especially with regard to the command of the lakes for whoever commands the lakes will be master of Canada and the true system of defence will be in taking the offensive. . . . I think myself that if America went to war with us unjustly, a great game might be played with Canada and have long turned it in my thoughts, though this cursed Russian war would greatly cripple our means. Bear in mind always that it will take five years of sharp war to train American militia into good soldiers, and that will not be the case with the Canadian Militia. They will learn better from the English system, being more accustomed to obedience and having better instructors' (Napier to Ellenborough, undated fragment, Ellenborough papers, P.R.O. 30/12, box 6). But by the next summer Napier had become better acquainted with the problems of Canadian defence and he could only put Ellenborough directly in touch with his informant. Col. P. L. Macdougall, who had formerly served in the Royal Canadian Rifles and was now the first commandant of the Staff College, Sandhurst, was convinced that the American constitution was 'more dangerously aggressive than that of Russia', and was therefore only too anxious to seize upon the present opportunity to force a showdown with the Americans before they had had time to create a formidable fleet. But from his personal knowledge of Canada, he had to confess that the militia were unprepared and ill equipped, and the canals unsafe and incapable of passing useful warships (Macdougall to Ellenborough, private, 11 June 1856, *ibid.*, box 28). [1] Stacey, p. 99.

194

have been a ridiculous farce: 'A huge steamer ran down a gunboat. The manœuvring was indistinct and uninteresting, and finally nothing seemed left to comfort the originators of this magnificent turnout, but the certain facts that the number of vessels of war was 240 and their aggregate armament 3,002 guns!'[1]

Mismanaged or not, Britain's display of force was, as Dallas admitted, in size alone imposing enough. Comforted at least to that extent no doubt, Clarendon at last formally rejected Marcy's demands in a conciliatory but nonetheless firm note on 30 April.[2] Then, a month later, he thought they ought to prepare for an offensive American response. Hitherto, Clarendon claimed in a letter to Palmerston on 1 June, he had 'never believed in a rupture with the United States'; but now, after all that Dallas had told him of 'the recklessness of the President and his competitors for the Democratic ticket', he thought it 'probable' and that they ought at all events to be prepared for Crampton's dismissal.[3] By the beginning of June therefore, Clarendon and Palmerston were already exchanging views on what more should be done. Both now indulged in characteristic vituperation of the United States. Palmerston preferred retaliation upon Dallas rather than 'dirt-eating' if Crampton were dismissed. He suggested, too, that the United States were as dependent as the British upon the continuation of the cotton trade and therefore equally reluctant to go to war. Clarendon talked wildly and almost incoherently of the 'rascals who call themselves the Government of the mob which governs them', and warned Cowley, the ambassador in Paris, of the need to keep the French 'up to the mark for that nation of Pirates . . . is every day becoming a more formidable nuisance and there is no country which will not in its turn be exposed to American insolence and encroachment unless the commercial and dollarmaking classes there are made to feel that their Government will end by turning all mankind against them and that there will be a universal league to compel them to observe the usages of civilized nations'.[4]

What was particularly upsetting was that while the Americans were denouncing Crampton's actions, they seemed themselves more clearly than ever to be encouraging the infringement of their neutrality

---

[1] Dallas to Marcy, private, 25 April 1856, George Mifflin Dallas, *Letters from London, 1856–1860* (2 vols., London, 1870), i. 25–6.   [2] Learned, p. 258.
[3] Clarendon to Palmerston, 1 June 1856, Broadlands papers.
[4] Palmerston to Clarendon, 6 and 11 June 1856, Bell, ii. 156; Clarendon to Palmerston, 1 June, Broadlands papers; Clarendon to Cowley, private, 4 and 6 June, Cowley papers, F.O. 519/173.

laws by the filibusters. In June came the news that they had even recognized Walker's government. Walker's followers, Clarendon understood from Dallas, were the 'very scum of the earth', and mostly not Americans at all but 'Germans, French, English, and Irish, and scoundrels attracted by the hope of plunder like any other buccaneers'. And Padre Vijal, the man whom Walker's recognition had now made a member of the *corps diplomatique* in Washington, was not at all the 'venerable ecclesiastic' described by the American newspapers, but a more 'fitting representative of Walker', 'one of the greatest rascals unhung, a disfrocked priest who has committed all manner of enormities'. Since the Americans unfortunately had a perfect right to recognize any government they wished, Europe could hardly protest lest they provoke an insolent reply.[1] Where diplomatic notes would be ineffective and unwise, gunboats might serve very well, but Clarendon was by no means sure even now that public opinion would not desert him. Relatively protected perhaps from the pressure of the radicals and stimulated no doubt by the advice of the French emperor, he had in Paris thought that Crampton's own defence in answer to Marcy would bring British opinion round firmly to the support of the government: 'It will satisfy all lovers of fair play and haters of low malignant dodges and of such happily the great majority of Englishmen is composed.'[2] But even at that time, according to Dallas, America's 'well wishers' were becoming 'loud and more numerous hourly'. By the middle of March he was already in touch with Aberdeen and before long he was being publicly assured by a leading Peelite that the House of Commons would almost certainly 'sustain international rights against any ministry whatever'.[3]

So strongly did Roebuck and Gladstone lead the Opposition in harassing attacks upon the government that Clarendon had no sooner returned to London than he began to suspect he had been wrong. 'The questions with the United States', he wrote back to Cowley on 22 April, 'are now occupying public attention and Parliament more even than the peace [with Russia] and as there is party and political capital to be made out of them it is impossible to say what turn they will take.'[4] By the beginning of June, when Palmerston was pressing for naval reinforcements to go out to Central American waters, his doubts had

[1] Clarendon to Cowley, private, 4 and 6 June 1856, Cowley papers, F.O. 519/173.
[2] Clarendon (in Paris) to Palmerston, 21 Mar. 1856, Broadlands papers.
[3] Dallas, i. 11, 19 and 21.
[4] Clarendon to Cowley, private, 22 April 1856, Cowley papers, F.O. 519/173.

become even stronger and he wanted the backing of the cabinet before risking public censure:

I quite agree with you [he wrote to Palmerston on 4 June] that the conduct of the United States Government renders it necessary to take a decision and that half measures will be both dangerous and undignified. I should not hesitate therefore about sending such a fleet to Central America as would render collision impossible if we could be sure of support at home, but the cowardly feeling with respect to war with the United States is so general that I believe as soon as the orders for sending the ships were given we should have undignified meetings throughout Lancashire, and an expression of opinion in the House of Commons that would upset the Government.

The next day, bowing to Palmerston as the 'better judge' of public opinion, he admitted that his conclusion had 'perhaps been drawn unfairly from the base and lowminded communications which I have so often received respecting the danger of war with the United States and the unlimited amount of dirt which we ought to eat in order to avert that danger'. A day later he even professed to see a better feeling in England.[1]

If Clarendon was inclined to yield to Palmerston, clearly not all his colleagues were quite so compliant. On 7 June the cabinet met to consider its action and two days later Captain Erskine was ordered out with a steam fleet of one battleship, two frigates, two corvettes and three gunboats to Greytown, and Captain Mundy with the battleship *Nile* and a steam corvette to Bermuda. And as soon as the Black Sea fleet returned, it was intended too to assemble a reserve squadron under Admiral Dundas in the Channel or off Lisbon. But this was not as menacing as it looked. At the cabinet meeting the lord privy seal, the duke of Argyll, had put up such a lively resistance to Palmerston's fire-eating proposals that Clarendon's doubts about public support had soon revived. Consequently the measures ordered were not really meant to be threatening but were merely face-saving.[2] So far as Central America was concerned, Wood talked of the reinforcement as tending to deter the Americans from taking liberties and so accidentally clashing with the British. He admitted that the government now had little or no interest even in Greytown. When they had helped expel the Nicaraguans in 1848, there had been some prospect of it becoming the Atlantic terminus of a canal; but this had now disappeared and they were anxious only to extricate themselves honourably from their involvement with the Mosquito Indians. The naval commanders on

[1] Clarendon to Palmerston, 4 and 5 June 1856, Broadlands papers; Clarendon to Cowley, private, 6 June, Cowley papers, F.O. 519/173.
[2] George Douglas [Campbell], eighth duke of Argyll, *Autobiography and Memoirs* (London, 1906), ii. 47.

this coast therefore were given strict orders to use force only for 'the defence of British life and property, and to leave all other matters for the Diplomatists to settle as they best can'. The one exception to this was that if asked by the Americans they might intervene with them to prevent a Nicaraguan occupation of Greytown.[1]

So far as the Central American question was concerned, then, these naval measures did not have quite the threatening character that Palmerston would have liked. On the Crampton question he certainly did not get his way. Instead the cabinet decided to wait for the next move by the Americans. A few days later, on 11 June, Dallas read to Clarendon Marcy's despatch of 27 May accepting the British government's disavowals of evil intentions, but dismissing Crampton and the three consuls with effect from the following day. But the reaction in England was by no means violent. In part this was due to a very temperate despatch on the Central American question which Dallas read to Clarendon at the same meeting, and which suggested that the Americans might accept arbitration on questions of fact, though not on the meaning of the Clayton-Bulwer treaty. But still more important was the fact that virtually all the influential press now joined the radicals in stressing the value of Anglo-American trade and in warning their government against too strong a line on Crampton or Central America.[2] At once the government's resolve weakened. On 12 June Wood managed to put off an awkward question in parliament about the naval reinforcements sent out to the West Indies. But the next day 'a sort of deputation in some fright at the warlike preparations' announced in *The Times* tackled him privately at the House of Commons, and though he managed to soothe their fears by demonstrating the gross exaggeration of the account, he at once approached Palmerston with the suggestion that they might go further still to tone down the alarm, even to the extent of representing the force as a perfectly normal relief.[3] At the same time

[1] Wood to Fanshawe, private, 6 and 10 June 1856, and Wood to Erskine and Mundy, private, 9 June, Halifax papers, B.M.Add.MS.49,566; F.O. to Adm., 9 June, Adm. 1/5677.

[2] For the reaction of the Press, see Williams, pp. 214–15, and Rippy, pp. 103–5.

[3] Wood to Palmerston, 13 June 1856, Broadlands papers. The 'deputation' consisted of four Lancashire radical M.P.s. Their chief spokesman, William Brown, wrote an account of the interview for Dallas, who in turn passed it on to Washington (Brown to Dallas, 13 June, enclosed in Dallas to Marcy, private, 13 June, Marcy papers, Library of Congress). Brown, head of the Liverpool branch of a prominent Anglo-American shipping firm and a partner in the Honduras Railway Company, had kept up a constant correspondence with Wood about naval measures since November 1855 (Halifax papers, B.M.Add. MSS.49,552, 49,564, and 49,565).

even Clarendon had to admit that Marcy's two despatches were 'very friendly and conciliatory in tone'.[1] That they were so soothing in manner if not in substance probably had much to do with the advice Marcy had received from Buchanan. This was in part a warning that in spite of the labour troubles in Manchester, an unsatisfactory financial condition, and the dependence on American markets, there might well be a real danger of war: 'The masses of the British people', Buchanan had told him in November, '. . . are so much under the influence of the governing classes and of the press and are all so ignorant of our country and so arrogantly confident in their own power, that they may be brought up even to this extremity.' But there was also the suggestion that in a moderation of tone might be found the most likely prospect of cultivating the good opinion of America's friends and bringing pressure to bear on Palmerston for peace.[2] Clarendon certainly believed that Marcy had struck the right tone in his note of 27 May: 'The whole is so skilfully done and will so exactly fit the temper of the House of Commons and of the public out of doors that I doubt the possibility of sending Dallas away – at least I have an instinctive feeling that a vote of censure upon such a proceeding would be carried almost unanimously.'[3] On 14 June the cabinet met again and evidently decided to do nothing after all; but to take advantage of the note's making the dismissal personal to Crampton and not to retaliate upon Dallas. 'I have seen Crampton for an hour today', wrote Clarendon on 16 June, 'he is very happy at having left that hell upon earth and agrees that under the circumstances we could not well send Dallas away.'[4] That night the prime minister calmly announced to parliament the determination to avoid a breach. All that was done to convey a hint of injured pride was to delay the appointment of Crampton's successor for ten months.

When, at the end of June and the beginning of July, the House of Commons came to debate the government's American policy, the ministry defeated a vote of disapproval handsomely by 274 to 80, and Clarendon wrote at once to congratulate his chief:

What a capital, most capital speech you made and what a glorious division, and what utter discomfiture of the Tories! I congratulate you upon it all, but no man ever so well deserved success as you do. The majority will do good in the United States and will teach the Cushing gang there *and here*

[1] Clarendon to Cowley, private, 13 June 1856, Cowley papers, F.O. 519/173.
[2] Buchanan to Marcy, no. 105, 23 Nov. 1855, Moore, ix. 466–7.
[3] Clarendon to Cowley, private, 13 June 1856, Cowley papers, F.O. 519/173.
[4] Clarendon to Cowley, private, 16 June 1856, *ibid*.

not to be quite certain of overthrowing your administration whenever they please.[1]

But though the ministry did not fall, the victory so far as policy in America was concerned was quite illusory. Gladstone was much nearer the mark when he commented of the admittedly great parliamentary success Palmerston had scored: 'He not only made the House of Commons drunk, but made them drunk on ginger beer.'[2] On Central America they had tried and failed to make a stand against the Americans; on the recruiting issue they had had a weak case and had been forced to let the initiative slip into the hands of the Americans. Here the Palmerston government had lost more than a mere battle for moral position and prestige. In fumbling for a tougher line they had conjured up the most decisive intervention yet of merchant and radical opinion on American affairs and with Derby, Disraeli, Gladstone and Russell, too, joining with Cobden, Bright, and Roebuck, that intervention was soon to prove of lasting effect. For in the press and parliament alike, not just a passing phase of Anglo-American relations but the whole concept of an anti-American balance of power policy had been challenged and publicly defeated. The damage to British shipping and trade, the cutting off of those vast supplies of cotton and grain upon which the United Kingdom had become so dependent since the tariff reforms of the 1840s – all this would be horrifying enough. But, the critics wondered, surely the policy responsible for the war scare was itself futile and wrongheaded.

In the eye and forecast of the States [*The Times* reminded the country], all North America is theirs excepting only those portions already belonging to European Powers, or [excluding the Mosquito coast] under a recognised European protectorate. . . . For our part we see no reason why we should resist the process except where a British community is established and demands our aid, or where some real interest can be shown to be at stake. . . . It must be for our interest to see North America under strong, civilized, uniform and prosperous government. . . . It does not become us to play the dog in the manger with our fast-growing progeny across the Atlantic.

The Economist spelled it out even more succinctly a fortnight later:

We could not hinder the ultimate absorption by the Anglo-Saxon republicans of the whole of Central America if we would. . . . We can have no interest in upholding the present wretched and feeble governments of

---

[1] Clarendon to Palmerston, 2 July 1856, Broadlands papers.
[2] Gladstone to Sidney Herbert, 12 July 1856, Lord Stanmore (A. H. Gordon), *Sidney Herbert: Lord Herbert of Lea: a Memoir* (London, 1906), ii. 47–8.

Spanish America. Our interest lies all the other way. We wish ourselves for no extension of territory on that continent. We are half inclined to regret that we hold any possession at all there south of the Union. Desiring no territory, we desire only prosperous, industrious, civilized and wealthy customers. . . . Central America peopled and exploited by Anglo-Saxons will be worth to us tenfold its present value.[1]

Clear though the import of this debate of early 1856 was, its immediate effect on the government was limited to a check upon the policy of collision they had hitherto seemed inclined to pursue. Compelled once and for all to give up any idea of a showdown with the Americans, Palmerston and Clarendon sought now not a total surrender to the American advance but only to make the Clayton-Bulwer treaty effective by friendly negotiation over the American complaints. Dignity was preserved by maintaining the force sent out to Central America until the demands of the lorcha *Arrow* war in China forced a reduction in the winter of 1856–57. But the navalists in particular, both Wood and Fanshawe, had cooled off rapidly after the end of June 1856. Before long, indeed, Wood was praising the attitude of the American naval commander off the Central American coast, and reflecting upon the superior management of naval officers over diplomats.[2] At length the diplomats found in the Clarendon-Dallas convention of October 1856, yet another formula for the honourable withdrawal of the British from the Bay Islands and the Mosquito protectorate, only to have the American Senate make further demands in the amendments they introduced with the encouragement of the new president, James Buchanan. Clarendon was inclined to give way. But a few days of instruction from Palmerston again stiffened him.[3] There might even be some advantage to be made out of the news from America. 'I am not sure', the permanent under-secretary at the Foreign Office had commented in February, 'whether it may not have a good effect in this Country, as proving to the Manchester men that there is no good in seeking to be on friendly terms with the United States.'[4]

Deteriorating relations between Spain and Mexico during the same year aroused considerable apprehension once again about Cuba. Spain, Clarendon thought, might take advantage of British and French concern

<hr />

[1] *The Times*, 3 June 1856, and *The Economist*, 14 June 1856, both quoted by Rippy, pp. 103–4.

[2] Wood to Fanshawe, private, 18 and 30 July 1856, Halifax papers, B.M.Add. MS.49,566.

[3] Clarendon to Palmerston, 12, 16, 17 and 18 April 1857, Broadlands papers.

[4] Edmund Hammond to Cowley, private, 25 Feb. 1857, Cowley papers, F.O. 519/186.

about Cuba, to press her quarrel with Mexico too far. War would follow and Buchanan would be sure to make up for the Ostend Manifesto fiasco by taking the opportunity to intervene and somehow secure Cuba. But it is clear that even with this new complication there was no question of adopting a tough line with the Americans. Clarendon, in the first place, had no great faith in the cooperation of the French. The romance of the Crimean alliance had almost disappeared even as peace with Russia was concluded. In the Crampton crisis he had already begun to feel uncertain how far he could rely on their support if matters were pushed to extremes. Now, when the news arrived of a rather too propitiatory speech by the new British minister in Washington, Lord Napier, Napoleon innocently enquired if Britain's old policy of opposition to the United States 'annexing propensities' had changed. Clarendon got quite angry and retaliated by complaining of the French leaving Great Britain alone to cope with affairs in Central America and Cuba. If he was uncertain of French support, he was quite sure of the futility of relying on the Central Americans themselves:

... it is impossible to shut our eyes to that which seems to be inevitable for those wretched mongrels in Central America are absolutely inviting aggression. Their utter inability to do anything but cut each other's throats and the proofs they have recently afforded that neither common danger nor common interest can induce them to unite offer temptations to filibusters which cannot be resisted. It is no business of ours to proclaim this and still less to promote it but unless England and France are prepared to occupy Central America and Mexico with a large land force and to have their fleets to support it in both oceans we may be sure that sooner or later those countries will be overrun and occupied just as have been Louisiana, Texas, and California added to the Union.[1]

To this point of view Palmerston himself was at last coming round. As the Americans appeared constantly to be raising their price for accepting the Clayton-Bulwer treaty, and turning more and more even to threatening its abrogation, many in Britain began to feel that that might well be the best course for them too. It was by now unmistakably clear that the treaty was a total failure from almost every point of view. Rather than removing a major cause of Anglo-American friction it seemed instead to have led to constant bickering since 1850. Most important of all, it promised to be quite ineffective as a barrier to the expansion of American influence, if, as seemed certain, filibusters like Walker's were to continue. The principal merit of accepting abrogation was that the moral responsibility would lie with the Americans. Another was that it would release Great Britain from the awkward

[1] Clarendon to Cowley, private, 21 May 1857, Cowley papers, F.O. 519/175.

obligation to desert the inhabitants of the Bay Islands. Earlier the retention of this 'base' would have represented a return to an aggressively anti-American policy. Certainly this was the view put forward by Bulwer when he propounded his alternative schemes of 1854. It would be best, he had said, to find some way of keeping his treaty; but if all negotiation failed they ought to exploit their possessions and allies in Central America to establish a counterpoise against the United States.[1] But though some of his advisers still clung to such an idea, Palmerston himself did not. He had no doubt that in a hundred years the North Americans would have got 'far down towards Cape Horn', and he conceded that 'commercially no doubt we should gain by having the whole American continent occupied by an active enterprising race like the Anglo-Saxons instead of the sleepy Spaniards'. However, on political grounds – namely the security of the West Indies – he would rather have kept the Clayton-Bulwer treaty as a barrier against the advance of the North Americans. But the Yankees were 'such Rogues and such ingenious Rogues', that, whatever concessions the British made over Mosquitia, the Bay Islands, or Belize, they would find some excuse to circumvent that barrier, or let men like Walker do it for them. So, reluctantly, he too had come by the end of 1857 to approve the idea of throwing over the Clayton–Bulwer treaty and substituting some simple agreement regarding rights of transit across the isthmus. But this did not mean that he any longer envisaged a resumption of direct opposition to the expansion of the United States in Central America. 'These Yankees are most disagreeable Fellows to have to do with about any American question: They are on the Spot, strong, deeply interested in the matter, totally unscrupulous and dishonest and determined somehow or other to carry their Point; We are far away, weak from Distance, controlled, by the Indifference of the Nation as to the Question discussed, and by its Strong Commercial Interest in maintaining Peace with the United States.' The alternative now being pressed would soon bring them therefore into 'Collision with the United States upon Questions such as those of Mosquitia & Grey Town about which the British Nation would not be induced to care at all'.[2]

[1] Bulwer to Clarendon, private, ? Mar. 1854, Van Alstyne, 'Anglo-American Relations', pp. 495–6.

[2] Palmerston to Clarendon, 15, 22 and 31 Dec. 1857, Clarendon papers, Bodleian Library, Oxford. The last of these letters is printed in full in K. Bourne, 'The Clayton-Bulwer Treaty and the Decline of British Opposition to the Territorial Expansion of the United States, 1857–60', *Journal of Modern History*, xxxiii (1961), 290–1, and in part in Van Alstyne, 'Anglo-American Relations', p. 500.

Palmerston's conversion to the inevitable came too late for him to wind up the Central American affair before his government fell over the Conspiracy to Murder bill in January 1858. Then doubt on the part of the Americans and illness and incompetence on the part of the British agents, prolonged the final settlement for another two years. Always suspicious of British motives and frightened lest abrogation leave them too great a territorial foothold in Central America, Buchanan's government retreated from the idea almost as soon as they were told Great Britain would not resent it. Instead they encouraged the progress of such direct negotiations with the various local governments as would extricate the British from their embarrassments in the Bay Islands and Mosquitia. When Palmerston returned as prime minister in June 1859 these negotiations had still not been brought to a successful conclusion. But with Palmerston had come as foreign secretary not Clarendon, but Russell, and Russell, for all his faults, was utterly clear what he should do on this matter. Nor was he to have any trouble from second thoughts of Palmerston's. He came into this cabinet only under a reconciliation conceding him virtually unfettered control over foreign affairs, and in any case, after his conversion in 1857, it is doubtful if Palmerston would again have bothered much with Central America. He did not like lost causes. Within a few weeks of assuming office, therefore, Russell recalled his most unsatisfactory emissary and pressed on rapidly with the negotiations in Central America. In November 1859 and January 1860 agreements were at last made for the transfer of the Mosquito coast and the Bay Islands. Buchanan, in his Annual Message of December 1860, now had to declare himself completely satisfied.

So he ought to have been. Central America, now, was hardly of much material importance to the Americans. The sense of urgency about isthmian routes had died with the discovery that in all canal schemes rogues still abounded while money and engineering talent were lacking. Even the romance with the filibusters was coming to an end as Walker fell out with one of his backers, Commodore Vanderbilt and his Accessory Trust Company, and played havoc with communications across the isthmus. But what the British, including the leaders of the Conservative and Whig parties as well as the radicals, were doing was consciously to give up all real resistance to American expansion on the continent of North America. The radicals apart, this was not by any means a gesture of affection; but rather of frustration and resignation. Malmesbury, the Conservative foreign secretary in 1858–59, as well as Russell, quite agreed with Palmerston

that they should acquiesce in American expansion but not promote it.[1]
In Canada and the West Indies there still remained substantial interests
which would have been stubbornly defended if directly challenged.
But the symbolic importance of what had happened was enormous.
Indeed, in the era of Bismarck's wars, when Britain was feeling isolated
and frustrated in Europe, the rapprochement of 1898–1902 might even
have been anticipated if only the American Civil War had not intervened to disrupt the process of withdrawal.

[1] Malmesbury to Cowley, 28 Sept. 1858, James Howard Harris, third earl
of Malmesbury, *Memoirs of an Ex-minister* (2 vols., London, 1884), ii. 136;
Russell to Lyons, private, 21 Sept. 1859, Russell papers, P.R.O. 30/22/96.
Even Hammond commented on a casual suggestion from Central America
about countering the growth of American influence: 'It is not desirable that we
should be in perpetual conflict with the U.S.' (minute on Marcoleta to Russell,
14 April 1860, F.O. 56/7).

7

The *Trent* Affair, 1861–1862

The reinforcement of 5,000 men sent out to Canada early in the summer of 1856 could hardly have seemed to make much of a contribution to the success of British policy in America. Instead it threatened to halt and reverse the process of colonial reduction and concentration in the United Kingdom to which all parties in Westminster were now firmly committed. Hardly had the measure been announced therefore than it was attacked on this account as well as on the grounds of the inexpediency of quarrelling with the United States. Leading the attack was Lord Elgin, during whose governor-generalship (1847–54) the policy of reduction in Canada had made such substantial progress. When he questioned the secretary for war, Lord Panmure, in the middle of April 1856 he was met with the evasive reply that the reinforcement was merely to restore the garrisons in existence at the beginning of the Crimean War. A few weeks later, at the end of May, Elgin returned to the attack, pointing out that the 1854 withdrawal had really been a continuation of the established policy of reduction, and that this new step would tend to arrest the encouraging beginnings recently made in Canadian contributions to self-defence.[1]

The government in fact were by no means anxious to reverse the process of concentration. Henry Labouchere, the colonial secretary, had already asked Sir Edmund Head, Elgin's successor as governor-general, what effect the reinforcement might have on recruitment for the militia, and had been reassured that if the regulars were concentrated in places like Quebec and Montreal the necessary volunteers for the protection of the country generally would still be forthcoming.[2] The Palmerston government clearly felt, however, that the 1854 reduction in Canada had gone too far, and that it was for this reason,

---

[1] C. P. Stacey, *Canada and the British Army, 1846–1871; a Study in the Practice of Responsible Government* (Toronto, 1963), pp. 99–101.

[2] D. G. G. Kerr, *Sir Edmund Head: a Scholarly Governor* (Toronto, 1954), p. 134; Stacey, p. 101.

as Panmure had put it, that 'Jonathan is bumptious'.[1] With the passing of the American crisis they did withdraw one battalion early in 1857 and later in the year the outbreak of the mutiny in India forced further reductions. But with the encouragement of the new commander-in-chief at the Horse Guards, the duke of Cambridge, they refrained from returning to the very low figures of the summer of 1854. Instead Cambridge insisted on a minimum of two, rather than one, infantry battalions in addition to the Royal Canadian Rifles, and when the Palmerston ministry went out of office in February 1858 the garrison of British North America still numbered more than 5,000. Of these there were about 3,000 in Canada, and rather more than 2,000 in the Maritimes. In addition, there were nearly 1,500 in Bermuda and the Bahamas, and over 2,000 each in the West Indies and Windward and Leeward Islands commands.[2] In spite of changes of government, the renewed dissatisfaction with Canada over the relaxation of her own defence efforts and the raising of the tariff barrier against British products after the economic crisis of 1857, and the Volunteer panic in England, the force in North America still managed to keep above 4,000 during the next three years.[3] But in the same period parliamentary and public pressure for the establishment of imperial defence on an economical and rational basis continued to mount. In 1858 the Derby government appointed an interdepartmental committee to consider the question and the publication of their report in 1860 led in the following year to new debates and the appointment of another parliamentary select committee.

By this time events in North America had overtaken these investigations, but, though argument and disagreement continued, real progress was at last being made towards a true system of imperial defence.

[1] Panmure to General Sir William Codrington (c.-in-c., Sebastopol), 31 Mar. 1856, Sir George Douglas and Sir George Dalhousie Ramsay, eds., *The Panmure Papers* (2 vols., London, 1908), ii. 175. As governor-general Elgin himself had resisted the pace of reduction on much the same grounds: 'I suppose your economists at home do not deign to take into consideration the good effect which Regiments in Canada produce on the American mind. The general notion on the other side of the line being that we are utterly effete, I really believe that the Yankees are much edified by witnessing the manœuvring of a well-disciplined British Regiment. . . . I have no doubt that these spectacles and the civilities they receive from the officers raise us greatly in their estimation and tend insensibly to promote the interests of peace' (Elgin to Grey, private, 25 Oct. 1850, Sir Arthur Doughty, ed., *The Elgin-Grey Papers, 1846–1852* [4 vols., Ottawa, 1937], ii. 726–8).

[2] Appendix to 'Copy of Report of the Committee on Expense of Military Defences in the Colonies', 24 Jan. 1860, *British Parliamentary Papers*, 1860 (282) xli.   [3] Stacey, pp. 107–14.

Since Canada would be to some extent the innocent victim of Britain's quarrels with the United States, there were few suggestions that the principle of colonial self-defence should be carried so far as a total British withdrawal from the interior. But it was generally agreed that a wholesale scheme of fortifications should finally be abandoned and British garrisons concentrated instead in a few strategic fortresses to keep open the lifeline of imperial support, leaving the local population to provide for the police and general defence of the country. Elsewhere the process of withdrawal and the concentration upon a few imperial fortresses was to be more ruthlessly pursued. The West Indies generally were to be written off as 'worthless'; only Jamaica, for its naval dockyard, and the Bahamas, to keep the Florida channel from falling entirely into American hands, were worth defending against anything other than local insurrection. Bermuda and Halifax, however, were admittedly very different. Overall naval superiority was the real basis of Britain's imperial power, and these were the navy's two essential bases in North American waters. So by 1860 the British were apparently moving more rapidly towards a proper appreciation of their real strength and weakness, towards the abandonment – outside the United Kingdom – of general schemes of fortification which drained off their money and dissipated their scarce soldiers, and towards the deployment instead of an overwhelming naval strength based on a few select fortresses.[1]

So far as operations against the United States were concerned this process had the inestimable advantage of playing down to some extent the importance of Canada's vulnerability and emphasizing the value of British naval superiority as the principal defence of the Empire's most vital commercial interests, and the greatest threat to the security of the United States. On the Pacific side admittedly Britain's naval power was still restricted by the lack of any proper base. Admiral Moresby, then commander-in-chief in the Pacific, had suggested that one be established at Esquimalt on Vancouver Island in 1851, and during the crisis of 1856 the first lord, Wood, had again directed attention to the island. But he had done so without much hope that a suitable site

---

[1] See especially: J. F. Burgoyne, the inspector-general of fortifications, 'Memorandum on the Defences of the Foreign Possessions of Great Britain', 28 Nov. 1856, War Office confidential print, W.O. 33/5; Burgoyne's 'On Colonial Defences; the West Indian Islands', 6 Aug. 1858, G. Wrottesley, *Life and Correspondence of Field-Marshal Sir John Fox Burgoyne* (2 vols., London, 1873), ii. 493–4; 'Copy of Report of the Committee on Expense of Military Defences in the Colonies', 24 Jan. 1860, *British Parliamentary Papers*, 1860 (282) xli; and 'Report from the Select Committee on Colonial Military Expenditure', 11 July 1861, *ibid.*, 1861 (423) xiii.

would be found, and sure enough Bruce, the commander-in-chief, replied that though Esquimalt would be better than nothing, the island was so unsafe that the Hudson's Bay Company might as well sell it to the Americans. All that was done here was to set up in 1855 a sort of unofficial hospital and stores depôt, largely through the initiative of the local civilian authorities.[1] Meanwhile, in the bay of Panama for example, the search continued for an island base.[2]

On the Atlantic side, where it was so much more important for Great Britain to be strong, Fanshawe had complained continually during the crisis of the generally 'helpless state' of the West Indies and even of the imperfections of the works at Bermuda and Halifax. While the West Indies, the Maritime Provinces, and even the general frontier defence of Canada languished, it was to bases like Bermuda that the attention of the British turned in the late 1850s.[3] But most important of all was the overall strength of the navy. The Crimean War had still not convinced the Admiralty that sail must go, but with the French setting a threatening example, the British were soon compelled to follow suit with the shell-gun, and with iron and screw battleships. In 1859 they laid down the *Warrior*, the first true ironclad battleship. Even with this magnificent vessel they still clung obstinately to sail combined with steam, but the *Warrior* nevertheless marked the beginning of a fleet which in its day was more than a match for anything else afloat.

Meanwhile the Americans had not been idle either. After the end of the war with Mexico the regular army was again cut down drastically in size and for the next ten years remained at about 10,000 men. Expenditure on the navy rose, but to little purpose at first. Then, beginning in December 1853, a major effort was made to build a considerable number of new steamers. Six first-class frigates were voted at the end of 1853, and since these were of too deep a draught to use southern harbours, five smaller ones were voted in March 1857, seven

[1] Wood to Bruce, private, 16 Feb. 1856, and Bruce to Wood, private, 16 April 1856, Halifax papers, B.M.Add.MSS.49,565 and 49,549. For the early history of the Esquimalt 'base', see Donald C. Davidson, 'The War Scare of 1854: the Pacific Coast and the Crimean War', *British Columbia Historical Quarterly*, v (1941), 243–53; W. Kaye Lamb, 'Correspondence relating to the Establishment of a Naval Base at Esquimalt, 1851–57', *ibid.*, vi (1942), 277–96; and F. V. Longstaff, *Esquimalt Naval Base* (Victoria, 1941).
[2] Adm. Maitland (Pacific) to Adm., no. 63, 22 Feb. 1861, Adm. 1/5761.
[3] Fanshawe to Wood, private, 16 Feb. 1856, Halifax papers, B.M.Add.MS. 49,547; Fanshawe to Mundy, 1 Aug. 1856, enclosed in a W.O. report on the defences of Bermuda, 21 Sept. 1869, Adm. 1/6130; Adm. Houston Stewart's 'General Statement' for his successor on the North American station, Milne, 14 Mar. 1860, Adm. 1/5734; Report on the defences of Newfoundland, 13 Oct. 1859, W.O. 55/1557.

sloops in the summer of 1858, and another seven in February 1861. The friction with Great Britain during this period had a good deal to do with all this naval activity. Much was made of the need to match her forces in the Pacific and the Caribbean, and off the shores of Central and South America. But though useful in showing the flag in Latin America, all these vessels were designed essentially to provide for the coastal defence of the United States themselves. Even in this role they would probably have had little success if war with Britain had broken out. Though powerfully armed, they were slow and made of wood. The Royal Navy may have been reluctant to recognize the lessons of the Crimean War, but they were changing substantially nonetheless; the Americans, apparently, were looking back to the futile legends of success in the War of 1812. 'The steam frigates and sloops, built in the 'fifties', concludes one expert, 'represented a high development of the ship-builder's art, but the entire fleet could scarcely have offered battle to a single one of the sea-going ironclad warships which were beginning to appear in European navies.'[1] It was fortunate, if ironical, for them then, that when they soon proceeded to action it was not to meet a European power but to fight among themselves.

Far from bringing any immediate sense of relief to the old antagonists of the United States in Britain, the outbreak of the American Civil War in April 1861 brought only greater apprehension and concern.[2] As the Union's neighbour to the north and in the West Indies, and as the greatest of the maritime and commercial neutrals, Great Britain was bound to become involved in many difficult and dangerous incidents. Particularly alarming was the evidence that both sides hoped to exploit Britain's difficulties in the most dangerous manner. The South's expectation that dependence on her cotton would force the British government to intervene in her favour to break Lincoln's blockade or even to end the war was already well known. Even more alarming at first was the suspicion about the character and policy of Lincoln's secretary of state, W. H. Seward. Seward, re-called the duke of Newcastle, now colonial secretary in Palmerston's second administration, had told him in 1860 that if he became president he would certainly abuse Great Britain and if necessary find an excuse for war with her. Now, in May and June 1861, the minister in Washington,

[1] Harold and Margaret Spout, *The Rise of American Naval Power, 1776–1918,* (Princeton, 1939), p. 149.

[2] Much of what follows is based upon K. Bourne, 'British Preparations for War with the North, 1861–1862', *English Historical Review,* lxxvi (1961), 600–32.

Lord Lyons, was continually writing home to warn his government that Seward might indeed attempt to reunite the country by conjuring up a patriotic war against Great Britain, France, or Spain. Seward's 'foreign war panacea' was, as historians later discovered, no mere rumour. In the far north-west the Oregon settlement of 1846 had left it quite uncertain who was to have the San Juan Islands in Puget Sound and to avert a clash a joint occupation had begun all over again in this small area. But this time the occupation was by soldiers and early in 1861 the American commandant was indeed thinking of provoking a quarrel.[1] Seward, too, put up a similar scheme, and though this was promptly squashed by Lincoln, he followed it up in May with a particularly offensive and provocative warning to Great Britain which the president only partially softened. It is not surprising therefore that such rumours persisted long after Lincoln had brought his secretary of state to heel. In June, for example, Lyons was reporting a plot by Seward to raise a revolt in Canada. Even if these rumours all proved unfounded or Seward's plots came to nothing, Lyons was inclined to insist, Seward could still be expected to bully Great Britain about maritime rights in the belief that the defenceless state of Canada would make her eat 'any amount of dirt'.[2]

It was certainly true that none of Great Britain's North American and West Indian possessions was now adequately garrisoned. At the end of March 1861 there were rather less than 4,300 regulars in British North America, 2,200 of them in Canada and the rest in Nova Scotia, together with a mere handful of troops in British Columbia and at Fort Garry, and a few weak and scattered garrisons in Bermuda and the West Indies. The militia in North America was still in a most unsatisfactory state and though they could furnish some 10,000 ill-trained volunteers, many of the rifles and much of ammunition sent out in 1856 had since been withdrawn, and in April 1861 there were only some 7,000 Enfields and 10,000 old smooth-bore muskets in store. At the urging of the governor-general of Canada, the commander-in-chief in North America, Lieutenant-General Sir William Fenwick Williams, did what he could with his small force, incomplete fortifications and inadequate artillery – improving works of defence, establishing guard posts on the canals and bridges and concentrating his main strength in the major towns – but to meet the danger properly he would, as he continually wrote home, need considerable reinforcements.[3]

[1] Robin W. Winks, *Canada and the United States; the Civil War Years* (Baltimore, 1960), pp. 35–6.
[2] Lord Newton, *Lord Lyons* (2 vols., London, 1913), i. 39–46.
[3] Head to Newcastle, confidential, 25 May 1861, C.O. 42/626; Stacey, pp. 114 and 118; Kerr, pp. 218–19.

The position at sea was by no means so bad, for Rear-Admiral Sir Alexander Milne had on the North American station a strong fleet of some twenty vessels, including two battleships, two corvettes and seven sloops. But even after he had received a small addition to this force he, too, expressed his dissatisfaction when he heard on 14 June that Lyons did 'not regard a sudden declaration of war against us by the U.S. as an event altogether impossible at any moment'. Milne at once assessed his position and finding that he had only one ship available for 'any special service that may be suddenly required' he asked for reinforcements. All the rest of his force, he explained, was entirely taken up with protecting commerce and defending imperial possessions. Not even the most important of these possessions was properly fortified: the local defences of Antigua Yard were 'utterly *nil*'; at Jamaica the guns were unserviceable and the works 'badly contrived and worse executed'; Barbados was 'not much better than Jamaica'; Bermuda, though extensively fortified, was not wholly protected; St John, New Brunswick, had 'no local defences whatever'; and the Canadian Lakes, Halifax, and the Nova Scotian coal mines all had to be provided for.[1]

These warnings from Lyons and the local commanders did not fall upon deaf ears in London. The colonial secretary, the duke of Newcastle, as well as Russell, the foreign secretary, and Palmerston, the prime minister, were all impressed with the dangers of a clash with the North, especially when they heard, towards the end of May, that Seward was already threatening to make trouble about the 'rebels'' purchase of the Canadian lake steamer, *Peerless*. Not everyone took the rumours about Seward too seriously. Newcastle, for example, argued that they must make allowances for his 'hyper-American use of the policy of bully and bluster'. But incidents like the *Peerless* affair nevertheless seemed to make it utterly clear that 'the swaggering braggadocio style of Mr Seward', as Palmerston put it, 'may at any time create serious discussion'. Even those, like Lord Herbert, the secretary of state for war, who thought the 'American effervescence will pass away', willingly acquiesced in reinforcements being sent for fear that at the end of the Civil War hordes of American soldiers would be set free to turn acquisitive eyes on Canada. It was consequently by general agreement that measures were set on foot in May and June to strengthen the forces in North America. Milne got a reinforcement of six vessels, including two frigates and a corvette; Williams an additional infantry battalion in the middle of May, followed by two more battalions, a field battery of the

---

[1] Milne to Adm., secret, 27 June 1861, Adm. 1/5759.

new Armstrong guns, and some 8,000 rifles, ammunition, and equipment for the militia at the beginning of June.[1]

If war had actually broken out these reinforcements would still have been grossly inadequate, but it proved impossible for a while to do much more. The battalion sent out in May had been intended as a 'quiet' preparation, but at Palmerston's suggestion the rest had followed all together in the *Great Eastern* in a deliberate attempt to overawe the Americans, and particularly that 'vapouring, blustering, ignorant, man', Seward. The dramatic effect of the world's largest ship, carrying over 2,000 troops and large quantities of artillery and small arms, in a record-breaking dash across the Atlantic, must certainly have created a deep impression in North America. But if it was a comforting retort to American bluster and an encouragement to Canadian morale, no one believed that it was really enough to secure the defence of British North America.[2] As the summer advanced, therefore, and Lincoln's blockade of the South and other difficulties caused so much alarm, the prime minister became more and more anxious and wanted in particular to establish a force of at least 10,000 regulars in Canada before the winter cut off communications.[3] But on 11 and again on 24 June the government had already been severely criticized on the grounds that the measures were unnecessary, certain to irritate the United States, and, of particular interest to a parliament currently investigating colonial self-defence, likely to make the Canadians neglect their own efforts.[4] There were strong adherents to such a point of view in the cabinet

[1] Minutes by Russell, 21 May, and Palmerston, 23 May, on Lyons to Russell, private, 2 May 1861, Russell papers, P.R.O. 30/22/35; Palmerston to Russell, 24 May, and Palmerston to Somerset, 11 April 1861, Palmerston papers, B.M.Add.MS.48,582; Newcastle to Palmerston, 25 May, Broadlands papers; Newcastle to Sir Edmund Head, 5 June, John Martineau, *The Life of Henry Pelham, fifth Duke of Newcastle, 1811–1864* (London, 1908), pp. 301–2; Herbert to Cambridge, n.d., W. C. Verner, *The Military Life of the Duke of Cambridge* (2 vols., London, 1905), i. 312; Dundas to Milne, private, 4 May, Milne papers, National Maritime Museum, Greenwich, 107/1; Stacey, p. 118. For the *Peerless* affair, see Winks, pp. 45–7. It was this incident which had led the governor-general to suggest the initial military precautions in Canada mentioned above.
[2] Palmerston to Newcastle, private, 24 May 1861, and to Somerset, private, 26 May, Palmerston papers, B.M.Add.MS.48,582. For an account of the *Great Eastern*'s voyage, see James Dugan, *The Great Iron Ship* (New York, 1953), pp. 96–101, and, more briefly, Winks, pp. 52–3. However, Dugan confuses it all with a Fenian scare, and Winks wrongly describes the whole force as 'Royal Artillery'. Winks also fails to distinguish the earlier 'quiet' reinforcement of one battalion which went out separately to North America.
[3] Palmerston to Russell, 6 July 1861, to Newcastle, 26 Aug., and to Russell, 9 Sept., Palmerston papers, B.M.Add.MS.48,582.
[4] *Hansard's Parliamentary Debates*, 3rd ser., clxiii. 937–8 and 1516–21.

itself. 'It seems incredible', wrote Sir George Cornewall Lewis, then home secretary but soon to succeed Herbert as secretary for war, 'that any Government of ordinary prudence should at a moment of civil war gratuitously increase the number of its enemies, and, moreover, incur the hostility of so formidable a power as England.' He wondered therefore whether the recent reinforcements might not be 'misconstrued, and produce irritation' in America rather than curb Seward's violence.[1] His colleague, Gladstone, as chancellor of the Exchequer, no doubt had economy firmly in mind but he also expressed a neat moral point of view: 'I mistrust the argument about dealing with a bully, because there remains behind the question who *is* the bully, and possibly whether both have not, with the world in general, a good deal of that character.'[2] Such niceties as these were not likely to have much effect on Palmerston who had no doubts about the answer to his colleague's question:

Peace with men who have no sense of Honor and who are swayed by the passions of irresponsible masses, and by a reckless desire to hold their position by all and any means consists in being strong by sea on their coasts and respectable in our military force in our Provinces.

If our precautions are successful and the autumn, winter and spring pass off quietly we may be accused of having taken unnecessary measures, an accusation easily borne, but if in consequence of over-hesitation, we should expose our Provinces to insult and disaster we should justly incur reproaches from which no defence could be pleaded. . . .[3]

There were, however, more practical objections and these the prime minister could not so easily sweep aside.

The most stubborn member of the cabinet at first was the duke of Somerset, the rather unexciting first lord of the Admiralty. At the end of May, when the cabinet was getting ready to order out the troops in the *Great Eastern*, Palmerston was suggesting that a battalion of infantry ought to be sent out to British Columbia from China, and, since he did not expect any trouble from France 'this year', that they might spare some ships from the Channel fleet in order to strengthen still further their naval forces in American waters.[4] Newcastle for the moment at least supported him in this, raising in addition the matter of the garrison at Bermuda and the tricky question of vessels for the Canadian

---

[1] Lewis to Head, private, 24 June 1861, G. F. Lewis, *Letters of Sir George Cornewall Lewis* (London, 1870), pp. 397–8.
[2] Gladstone to Lewis, 21 Sept. 1861, Gladstone papers, B.M.Add.MS.44,532.
[3] Palmerston to Newcastle, 1 Sept. 1861, Palmerston papers, B.M.Add.MS. 48,582.
[4] Palmerston to Somerset, 26 May 1861, *ibid.*

lakes.[1] And someone too seems to have been giving the queen some sensible advice, for she joined in as well with the shrewd observation that with the North engaged in civil war they were less likely to spare troops for an attack upon Canada, 'than that they should commit acts of violence at sea'.[2] But this was all of little avail against Somerset. There was no telling, he said, when the troops might get to British Columbia from China. It would also be too expensive to send them via the Panama railway: the Royal Engineers previously sent out by that route had cost £70 a man for the journey from Colon to Vancouver. In any case the reinforcement was unnecessary, since the colony could best be defended by the Pacific squadron. At present it consisted of three frigates, a sloop, four gunboats, and two storeships. Of these one frigate and the four gunboats were already at Vancouver, and as he understood the Americans had only one small sailing vessel on the station, he was sure this was more than enough. What he was particularly concerned about on these American stations, however, was the temptation to men to desert.[3]

When Palmerston pressed him again about the North American squadron towards the end of June, he pointed out that the battleship *St George* had already lost seventy men at Halifax. Then there was all the expense further reinforcement would entail. The Admiralty already had more than enough to cope with in their current programme to rebuild the fleet with iron ships. Nor did he want to disturb the manœuvres of the Channel squadron by detaching battleships which were in any case too big to be based on Bermuda. On the whole, he thought, the North American squadron too was already big enough. Virtually all of the squadron were steamers, and for those the Union's still largely sailing navy would be no match at all. Nor would anything really be lost by waiting; in the event of an emergency 'a large proportion of the Channel fleet' could be sent out without any appreciable delay. Such was the negative response that Milne received to the urgent pleas he sent out when he got Lyons's alarming message in June. Afterwards Somerset made only a small concession to even his most senior colleagues' anxieties. At the end of July Russell got so alarmed about the blockade that he asked for six battleships and a couple of frigates to go out to Milne as soon as possible. What he got were merely

---

[1] Newcastle to Palmerston, 25 May, 1861, Broadlands papers.
[2] The queen to Palmerston, 30 May 1861, G. E. Buckle, ed., *Letters of Queen Victoria*, first series (3 vols., London, 1907), iii. 562.
[3] Palmerston to Somerset, 23 June 1861, Palmerston papers, B.M.Add.MS. 48,582; Somerset to Palmerston, 25 June, Broadlands papers.

two more frigates which had been held back from Halifax on account of the danger of desertion a few weeks before. Thereafter, exploiting to the full the argument about desertion in particular, Somerset stalled with total success. Even the alarm occasioned by Lincoln's dismissal of the British consuls he had found communicating with the 'rebels', failed to extract a single extra vessel from him. At last in the middle of October three more battleships, a frigate, and a sloop were ordered out, but only to make up for the detachment of the ships destined for the allied expedition to Mexico.[1]

While Russell in particular struggled with little success to persuade Somerset to send some more ships out to Milne, the prime minister turned again at the end of August to the problem of the Canadian garrison. Lyons had already reported that the *Great Eastern's* trip appeared to have had a most salutory effect, and now Palmerston thought it would be wise to show that the British army had yet not shot its bolt. What he wanted was to get at least 10,000 men into Canada before the winter intervened. If they acted quickly and engaged the *Great Eastern* to take another three battalions at once, then there would still be time that year for her to make a third and final trip.[2] This time Lewis put up little resistance, bowing to his prime minister's opinion that there would be no danger in Europe, and reluctantly conceding now that even after their defeat at Bull Run it would be unwise to tempt the 'reckless and unscrupulous' Americans by 'an appearance of unguardedness'.[3] But here too Somerset was at hand to point out that the *Great Eastern* was already engaged on other business and that it was probably unwise in any case to think of entrusting such large forces to the fortunes of a single vessel during the hurricane season.[4] Perhaps it gave him especial satisfaction to hear not long afterwards that the *Great Eastern* had broken down. Infected by his colleague's scepticism, no doubt, Newcastle now intervened to stop any further troop reinforcements at all. Quite probably he shared the sort of civilian prejudice characteristically expressed by one of his own subordinates in the Colonial Office:

[1] Somerset to Palmerston, 25 June, 15 July and 19 Aug. 1861, Broadlands papers; Palmerston to Russell, 25 Aug. and 17 Sept., and Somerset to Russell, 19 and 26 July, Russell papers, P.R.O. 30/22/21 and 24; Russell to Somerset, 26 July, Somerset papers, County Record Office, Aylesbury, Buckinghamshire; Somerset to Milne, private, 12 and 29 July, and 19 Oct., Milne papers, 107/1.
[2] Palmerston to Russell, 25 Aug. 1861, Russell papers, P.R.O. 30/22/21; Palmerston to Lewis, 26 Aug., Broadlands papers.
[3] Lewis to Palmerston, 27 Aug. 1861, Broadlands papers.
[4] Somerset to Palmerston, 30 Aug. 1861, *ibid.*

The weight to be attached to the demands of a general must turn, I suppose, on the general mode and discretion of his applications for assistance. On such a point it would be presumptuous for a civilian to express an opinion in respect of a military man of such fame as Sir Fenwick Williams, but certainly one can hardly have seen the correspondence of the last few years without forming an impression that he has been very fertile of demands and suggestions.[1]

Similarly prejudiced or not, Newcastle maintained that the force already sent had indeed been an encouragement to the Canadians to resist their bullying neighbours; but more would be a plain invitation to neglect their own efforts. Moreover the Union army had hardly shown itself so far to be in any position to menace Great Britain and the coming of winter would be a breathing-space and not, as Palmerston argued, a critical period, because the Americans would hardly dare to repeat 'all the terrors of Moscow'. There was, too, he said, no available winter accommodation for more troops and above all he feared, like Somerset, the awful depredations that the garrisons scattered along the frontiers of Canada, New Brunswick and British Columbia would suffer from the attractions of bounty money offered to deserters by American crimps.[2]

---

[1] Minute of 27 July on W.O. to C.O., 22 July 1861, C.O. 42/630. Such prejudices are made by circumstance. Half a century before Palmerston, as secretary at war, had himself been responsible for military expenditure and, in response to demands for more troops for Canada, had remarked: 'Perhaps there cannot be a better rule on such matters than to give people just half what they ask for' (to Bathurst, 5 Feb. 1816, C.O. 42/166).

[2] Newcastle to Palmerston, 30 Aug. and 3 Sept. 1861, Broadlands papers (part of the second letter is printed in Martineau, pp. 302–3). The important argument about desertion is an interesting example of the sort of difficulty arising out of the British prejudice against conscription. It served not only to hold up reinforcements, but to affect the distribution of those that did go. Williams on one occasion went out of his way to keep a regiment with a high proportion of young men away from the border since young men were considered more likely to succumb to the temptations of American crimps (Williams to Cambridge, private, 24 June and 12 July 1861, Cambridge papers, Royal Archives, Windsor). Special problems were also presented by the Negro West Indian and the Irish regiments, since both were considered unreliable against the North (memo. by de Grey, Lewis papers, National Library of Wales, Aberystwyth, Harpton Court papers, 2948; Palmerston to Herbert, 4 June, Palmerston papers, B.M.Add.MS.48,582). In fact the danger of desertion seems to have been grossly exaggerated in this instance. After discounting those 'recovered', the total net loss by desertion between March and December 1862, when the force in Canada was kept between 11,300 and 12,500 n.c.o.s and men, was only 144 (based on monthly returns in W.O. 17/1566). For the activities of the American crimps during the Civil War see W. F. Raney, 'Recruiting and Crimping in Canada for the Northern Forces, 1861–1865', *Mississippi Valley Historical Review*, x (1923–24), 21–33.

For a while Palmerston kept up a good battle, not hesitating to challenge Newcastle's assertions. When he insisted on an investigation it was found for example that there was enough available accommodation in Canada for another three battalions at least. But, probably with the deliberate intention of whipping up opposition and before even the queen had got to hear of the proposal, someone leaked it to *The Times*. On 2 September that paper came out strongly against any further reinforcements, and Newcastle, blaming it all on 'some clerk in the War Office', suggested that the leak had 'placed the subject in a totally new position' by removing it 'entirely . . . from the province of fair discussion'.[1] Palmerston continued to press on with it for a few days, but at length gave way, professing finally that the argument about desertion had 'shaken [his] previous opinion'. Provided, therefore, that the Americans took the stiff British reply about the dismissed consuls 'quietly', he was prepared to wait till the spring. In the meantime the barrack accommodation should be improved, and another large amount of arms and equipment sent out for the Canadian militia so that the 'encouragement' to self-defence given to them by the absence of a really respectable force of British regulars should not be lost.[2]

Less than a month later the news arrived in London of the gravest incident yet – Captain Wilkes's seizure on 8 November of the Confederate envoys Mason and Slidell from the British mail packet *Trent*. As the news of the incident reached the prime minister on the evening of Wednesday, 27 November, and was published in *The Times* the next day, there was luckily time enough to call the cabinet together before the usual weekend dispersal. At two meetings on 29 and 30 November the only absentee was the lord privy seal, the duke of Argyll, who was on holiday abroad. Assured by the law officers that the Americans had indeed overstepped the bounds of international propriety, the cabinet decided at these meetings to demand that they disavow Wilkes's action and immediately release the prisoners. Largely through the intervention of the queen and the prince consort, the demands were eventually softened in a manner that enabled the Americans to retreat more readily than they might otherwise have done. But even after it had been learned, as it was by 1 or 2 December, that Wilkes's action had been quite unauthorized, such were the accounts of its popularity in the North and such was the general distrust of Seward's intentions in Britain, that war was still thought more likely than not. It seemed

[1] Newcastle to Palmerston, 3 Sept. 1861, Broadlands papers and, in part, in Martineau, pp. 302–3.
[2] Palmerston to Russell, 17 Sept. 1861, Russell papers, P.R.O. 30/22/21.

inevitable indeed if the Union did not back down and, apart from Russell, few had much hope of that – mad though American obstinacy would be at such a time. In any case, the best chance of persuading the Americans to do the right thing probably lay in demonstrating Great Britain's determination to fight if necessary. 'Our only chance of peace', wrote the permanent under-secretary for foreign affairs, 'is to be found in working on the fears of the Government and people of the United States.' Nor were these impressions much modified by the information received in the course of the next three weeks. Only towards the end of December, as the American minister's assurances began to make some impression and even *The Times* had opportunity to reflect on the difficulties of war, did tempers begin to cool. But the dominant spirits in the ministry, like Palmerston, continued to think right up until the very last moment that the chances of peace or war were no better than equal. Seward in fact made a satisfactory, if surly, reply to Lyons's demands on 27 December and the news of this reached England on 8 January 1862.[1] But in the meantime the government in London had been engaged in an absolute torrent of warlike preparations.

It is not clear how soon the cabinet as a whole began to consider military precautions. They did decide on 29 or 30 November to prohibit the export of saltpetre and considered, too, a similar prohibition on the export of arms and ammunition, though the order for the latter was not decided until a subsequent meeting on 4 December.[2] There is a story, derived apparently from the prime minister's private secretary, that Palmerston had opened business by throwing down his hat upon the table, and bluntly telling his colleagues, 'I don't know whether you are going to stand this, but I'll be damned if I do!' But during the meeting Cobden had called twice at Downing Street, and through Lewis, persuaded Palmerston after all not to send out the Channel squadron as he had at first intended.[3] True or not the story is a good clue to the atmosphere of the occasion. Within a week in any case the prime

[1] Palmerston to Lewis, 27 Nov. 1861, Broadlands papers; Stanley of Alderley to Lady Stanley, 29 Nov., 2 and 3 Dec. 1861, Nancy Mitford, ed., *The Stanleys of Alderley* (London, 1939), pp. 319–21; Hammond to Russell, private, 3 Dec. 1861, Russell papers, P.R.O. 30/22/28; Palmerston to de Grey (under-secretary for war), 2 Jan. 1862, Ripon papers, B.M.Add.MS.43,512. The best account of the British reaction to the incident is in E. D. Adams, *Great Britain and the American Civil War* (2 vols., London, 1925), i. 203–43.

[2] Palmerston to Russell, 29 Nov. 1861, Russell papers, P.R.O. 30/22/21; Palmerston's cabinet circular, 30 Nov., Broadlands papers; Stanley of Alderley to Lady Stanley, 4 Dec., Mitford, p. 321.

[3] Sir Horace Rumbold, *Recollections of a Diplomatist* (2 vols., London, 1902), ii. 83–4.

minister and the heads of the two service departments had decided upon sending large reinforcements to North America.

On the evening of 27 November Palmerston had at once got in touch with Lewis to make sure that the small arms and guns which he had insisted the Canadian militia should have before winter did go out in spite of all the objections which were still being raised. On 30 November, having increased the amount and added a battery of regular artillery, the whole was at last ordered out. On 1 December Milne also got general warning orders. Then, on 4 December, the cabinet considered a whole series of proposals about the command and scope of prospective operations and authorized the despatch of a large force to Canada and the provisional preparation of a still larger one. On 6 December reinforcements were ordered for Milne and three days later a special war committee, composed of Palmerston, Somerset, Lewis, Newcastle, Lord Granville, lord president of the council, and the commander-in-chief, the duke of Cambridge, decided to despatch the whole force of troops under orders for Canada.[1] Considering that there were no general staff, no intelligence departments, and no regular procedure for cooperation between the service departments, these quick decisions were no mean achievement. It is true that at the end of December at least two members of the cabinet – Russell and Granville – evidently had very little idea what Somerset's policy was[2]; but even this does not detract from the achievement for the naval position was, on the whole, clear enough.

The question of most immediate difficulty and concern was the defence of Canada. The proposals which Lewis submitted to the cabinet and the war committee were based largely upon the knowledge and wisdom that had been laboriously accumulated in the War and Colonial Offices and fortuitously confirmed – so far as the weak state of Canada was concerned – by the presence in London of the former governor-general, Head, and a group of Canadian ministers seeking to promote the intercolonial railway.[3] But within a few days afterwards, Lewis had assembled a rather more professional body of advice, from

[1] Palmerston to Lewis, 27 Nov. 1861, Broadlands papers; W.O. to Williams, confidential, 30 Nov., P.A.C., R.G. 8 (British Naval and Military Records) I, C. Series, vol. 696; Adm. to Milne, secret, 1 and 6 Dec., Adm. 13/7; Lewis's cabinet agenda, 3 Dec., Lewis papers, 2945 and 2946; Palmerston to the queen, 5 Dec., and Cambridge to the queen, 6 and 9 Dec., Queen Victoria's papers, R[oyal] A[rchives, Windsor], Q 9/32, 36, 37.

[2] Somerset to Granville, 21 Dec. 1861, Granville papers, P.R.O. 30/29/24 pt. II; Russell to Somerset, 28 Dec., Somerset papers; Somerset to Russell, 29 Dec., Russell papers, P.R.O. 30/22/24.

[3] Winks, pp. 78–9; Somerset to Lewis, 5 Dec. 1861, Somerset papers.

Lord Seaton, commander-in-chief in Canada during the rebellion, from General Sir John Fox Burgoyne, the inspector-general of fortifications and the official expert on defence and strategy, and from Colonel P. L. Macdougall, a former commanding officer of the Royal Canadian Rifles, and lately the first commandant of the staff college and an acknowledged military expert.[1] Seaton, who was eighty-three, was apparently consulted only to fend off future criticism, and his paper was certainly brief and thin. But while no written war-plan was finally approved it is easily possible with the help of supporting evidence to reconstruct from the others' papers what were generally the British ideas about the future conduct of a war in Canada.

The first consideration was the size and character of the force the Americans could be expected to apply to the Canadian frontier: in particular whether the Civil War would permit the Americans to mount a major invasion or would confine them to minor operations. By this time the old fear that North and South might reunite in a foreign war had quite passed away: calculations of that kind, Lewis thought, were 'very wild and ill-considered'.[2] With this point of view the military experts largely agreed, Macdougall because 'the feeling of positive hatred entertained by the South towards the North is a passion which infinitely overbears any abstract feeling of patriotism which may once have existed – where patriotism signified devotion to the Union'; Burgoyne because he could not believe that 'the South would commit so suicidal an act, as to engage in a new war of no interest to them, and thus to support and give increased power to those who must always be their antagonists, and who will always have to be dreaded'. They did not, however, agree that Great Britain could rely on the continuation of the war. Macdougall thought it 'by no means impossible that the northern Governt., driven to their wits end for money, & foreseeing no success in their present hopeless undertaking, would be glad of anything which should afford them an excuse in the eyes of their countrymen to put an end to the contest by recognising the seceded States'. Such an excuse they might find in a war for the conquest of Canada. But Burgoyne argued that while the South might accept a Northern offer of peace he did not believe the North would be prepared to make one 'at the sacrifice of establishing a right of secession by other States,

---

[1] Seaton to Lewis, 9 Dec. 1861, J. F. Burgoyne, 'Thoughts on war with the United States, as regards operations by the land forces', 14 Dec., and Col. P. L. Macdougall, 'On the Prospect of War with the United States', 3 Dec., Lewis papers, 2958, 2984 and 2943.
[2] Lewis to Cambridge, 29 Sept., Cambridge papers.

who may happen to find such a course convenient'. Nor were the experts by any means agreed about the effect of the Civil War if it did continue. No official attempt seems to have been made so far to obtain any information about that war and the authorities in London must have relied primarily on newspaper reports. An artillery officer did, however, make some sort of report to Williams on the Union army's rifled cannon, with which he was much impressed, and a very short extract from this was communicated to Lewis.[1] Perhaps the only detailed report was a private one made in November by Sir James Fergusson, an Opposition member of parliament. This had been communicated to Palmerston by Lord Derby a fortnight before the *Trent* crisis but there is no sign that Palmerston passed it on to anyone else. It did, however, express what seems to have been a typical impression of the army of the Potomac:

There can be no doubt that for its size it is one of the best equipped which any nation has set on foot. Its transport is superb, its artillery numerous, well-appointed and of the best description, the physique of its men unsurpassed. . . . But as to the military character of the army my impression and belief is that it lacks as greatly all the qualities of worth and strength which distinguishes the army which England sent to the Crimea as it is rich in those equipments in which that army was deficient.[2]

Seaton was inclined to stress the weakness of the Union army: 'The militia service of the United States, being very oppressive and unpopular, and the Government liable to frequent alarms on the coast, could not venture an incursion into Canada at present, without positive encouragement.' To Macdougall such an army appeared weak or strong according to the continuation or suspension of the Civil War. If the war were suspended Canada would have to face an army of at least 200,000 men; but if it continued the defence of Canada would be 'an easy task'. Burgoyne, however, did not feel that even in the latter event the Americans' strength should be underestimated: 'Although the internal dissensions in the States give us great advantages in now entering upon the war, still the great energy displayed by the North, and the enormous expenditure they are incurring, prove that we must not despise them.'

[1] Williams to Monck, 29 Nov. 1861, enclosed in Monck to C.O., no. 22, 30 Nov., C.O. 42/628; 'Extract from a private letter from Col. J. Eardley-Wilmot, R.A., Washington, 11 Nov.', Lewis papers, 2931. For a study of English observers of the Civil War see J. Luvaas, *The Military Legacy of the Civil War* (Chicago, 1959).
[2] 11 Nov. 1861, enclosed in Derby to Palmerston, 13 Nov., Broadlands papers.

Agreement on this point was unnecessary because their conclusions were the same. They agreed that Canada would have to be prepared to face a major attack – Macdougall because he believed the North might well become free to concentrate her effort against Great Britain, Burgoyne because he thought the Americans could carry on two major campaigns simultaneously. Moreover, as Macdougall was quite well aware, the real difficulty for the British in North America lay not so much in the character of the attacking force as in that of the territory to be defended. A major offensive by a force of any reasonable size and even minor attacks by quite small forces would be extremely dangerous.

The frontier between British North America and the United States extended for over 1,500 miles from the Bay of Fundy to the western lakes, most of it following a line of river and lakes which, being as Macdougall put it 'everywhere vulnerable through its whole length', was less an obstacle than an invitation to attack. And it was still along part of this line that the main area of Canadian settlement, rarely more than fifty miles in depth, was concentrated. The vast length of the exposed frontier alone made it virtually impossible for the British to defend it in its entirety – but, worse, the Americans were peculiarly well placed to attack it. They not only had superior local resources in men and material, they also had excellent communications for concentrating those resources upon the frontier and for reinforcing them from the heart of commercial and industrial America – sufficiently good communications in Macdougall's view to outweigh the difficulties of a winter campaign. To the arsenal near Albany, with its extensive road and rail communications and the Hudson River connection with New York, could be brought without the least difficulty all the materials for mounting a major offensive. From that point a large force could pass by canal into Lake Champlain and, under cover of the fort at Rouse's Point at the head of the lake, it could safely issue for an attack on Quebec, or, more probably, Montreal which lay only forty miles distant. From Albany, too, there were good communications with the Niagara frontier and with Ogdensburg, from which an attempt could be made to cut the St Lawrence. The rich American towns on the lakes could also be expected to supply the resources for at least diversionary attacks on the Detroit frontier and the shores of the lakes.

To cope at all adequately with invasions like these the British had always reckoned that they would need a large force of at least 100,000 militia and 10,000 regulars. The militia would supply scattered garrisons and harass the enemy on his flanks and rear and the regulars

223

would garrison the most vital places like Quebec and Montreal, the gateway to Canada and the centre of communications respectively, and provide a field force capable of meeting the enemy's main thrust. But this was not enough to cover so long a frontier and the task would have to be eased in two further ways – first by an extensive system of fortifications and second by seizing command of the lakes. The second point was of particular importance. With that command the threat of a naval descent upon the towns on the American shores of the lakes would tie down large numbers of the enemy, and allow a large part – two thirds in Macdougall's view – of the force which would otherwise be needed to defend western Canada to be switched to the line of the St Lawrence. Without it the British would have to dispose their available force more thinly along the whole of the frontier, and the Americans would be able to land an invading force at will anywhere on the shores of the lakes where they might turn the flanks of the main British fortifications. If these various conditions – sufficient troops, a system of fortifications and command of the lakes – could be met the British clearly believed that they could defend Canada. Burgoyne indeed stressed the natural advantages of defence when each side was fighting with largely militia forces and when the British would be in prepared positions on their own territory. But not one of these conditions had been established by the autumn of 1861.

None of the earlier fortification schemes had ever been properly carried out and much of what had been done had been allowed to fall into disuse or decay: the important fort at Isle aux Noix, covering the route from Rouse's Point, and the naval base at Penetanguishene had both been turned into juvenile reformatories; old Fort Malden at Amherstburg was being used as a lunatic asylum; and even the citadel at Quebec was by no means secure against modern artillery. Moreover the British had no naval force whatever on the lakes and the troops sent out in May and June had raised the force in Canada to a little less than 5,000. Williams was particularly anxious about his artillery. He had only two batteries of garrison artillery and the only serviceable field guns were the battery of twelve-pounder Armstrongs sent out in June. In August he had been promised another battery of Armstrongs and some more guns for the militia but, through a series of misfortunes, these had still not been despatched by the end of November. He could expect some help from the militia. They had seven batteries of field artillery and there were over a thousand available guns in store. But the field force was said to be in a state of 'sad inefficiency', and the guns in store were old and of small calibre. The militia generally was in a poor state.

After a promising beginning with new legislation in 1855 and 1856 the economic crisis had brought a setback with a new act in 1859 and the militia was still only a paper force. By law the entire male population between eighteen and sixty was liable for service but the vast majority of these, the sedentary militia, had no existence beyond enrolment. The only active force, the volunteers, received a mere six or twelve days' annual training according to the arm of the service, and of the 5,000 authorized there were only some 4,422 in June 1861 – 'a miserably small force! and many of them but ill-trained, unless greatly improved since last year', was Newcastle's comment. This situation was bad enough, but worse was the lack of arms and equipment for the 100,000 militia which the British wanted and which the Canadians now seemed willing to raise. In addition to the 8,000 Enfields sent out in June, Palmerston had insisted on another 25,000 and some artillery going out in October to compensate for the curb on reinforcements of regulars. Unfortunately these were ordered too late to go by the last regular ship to Quebec and the best that could be done was to send 5,000 of them to wait at Halifax. On the eve of the *Trent* incident therefore there were ready for the militia in Canada only 25,000 arms, 10,000 of them smoothbores, and some 13,000 rifles and 7,500 smoothbores in the Maritime Provinces.[1]

The remedies for all these deficiencies – the 5,000 regulars by which Williams's force fell short of the 10,000 winter minimum, the additional arms, ammunition, and equipment for the militia, the guns for whatever works Williams could improvise, and gunboats for the lakes – were readily available in England. But the real difficulty was to get them to Canada for the winter and the Americans would between them completely cut Canada's communications with the sea. Between the Maritime Provinces and Canada there was still no domestic railway link and the only established road lay dangerously close to the Maine frontier. For the passage of troops and equipment then, just as much as for the introduction of a force for the lakes, it was necessary to look to the St

---

[1] Winks, p. 55; Williams to C.O., 23 June 1861, C.O. 42/630; Williams to Monck, 29 Nov., enclosed in Monck to Newcastle, no. 22, 30 Nov., C.O. 42/628; 'Statement of Guns Shot Shell Powder etc. in Store in Canada Halifax and New Brunswick or under orders from England', 'Militia Artillery', 'Small Arms in Store in Canada', 'Return of Mounted Ordnance belonging to the Defences in Canada and Nova Scotia', Nov. 1861, Lewis papers, 2922, 2925, 2926 and 2930; minute on Head to Newcastle, no. 43, 29 June, C.O. 42/627; de Grey to Palmerston, 12 Nov., Broadlands papers. See also Stacey, pp. 119–20, and for the militia C. F. Hamilton, *Canadian Defence Quarterly*, v and vi (1928–29).

Lawrence and canals before the winter or an attack by the Americans on the outbreak of war closed that route too.

The question of getting a naval force on to the lakes in an emergency had not by any means been overlooked in recent months, and in raising the matter of the *Peerless* at the very beginning of the war in April, Seward perhaps had only himself to blame for the British concern. The British on their part no longer had any vessels at all on the lakes; but in spite of occasional protests the Americans had retained the *Michigan* and in 1858 had added six armed revenue cutters. During November 1861 five of the cutters were transferred to other waters and it was hoped too to put the *Michigan* to some warlike use against the South. But she proved too big to pass through the Welland canal, and in spite of renewed protests, the *Trent* crisis found the Americans still with two armed vessels on the lakes. As early as May Newcastle had suggested that the British should also start thinking about a force for the lakes and this suggestion Palmerston had successfully pressed on Somerset's attention.[1] The Admiralty subsequently collected a great deal of relevant information and, on 2 September, Captain R. Collinson, the famous naval surveyor, who was then engaged in examining the naval land reserves in Canada, submitted a paper explaining the problem and making various recommendations.[2] He pointed out the many ways in which the navy could make the defence of Canada easier or even possible at all and stressed in particular the impossibility of keeping the St Lawrence open once war had broken out.

Clearly there could be no hope of securing the command of the lakes unless adequate preparations were made in advance of hostilities. But the time was peculiarly unfavourable for such measures; the whole question of colonial military expenditure had recently been investigated by a committee of the House of Commons whose bias was plainly to encourage greater efforts on the part of the colonists themselves. On 17 October Somerset had concluded that the defence of all the lakes would be 'very difficult' and that the main effort must be left to the Canadians themselves, though 'perhaps with proper arrangements we might defend Lake Ontario and Kingston Dockyard'.[3]

But even for this limited programme no material preparation had

---

[1] Newcastle to Palmerston, 25 May 1861, Broadlands papers; Palmerston to Somerset, 26 May, Palmerston papers, B.M.Add.MS.48,582.

[2] 'Memoranda on the Assistance which can be rendered to the Province of Canada by H.M. Navy in the event of War with the United States', by R. Collinson, 2 Sept. 1861, and 'Memorandum on the American Force on the Lakes', confidential print, Adm. 7/624.

[3] Somerset to Newcastle, secret, 17 Oct. 1861, Adm. 1/5766.

been made by the time Lewis raised the matter at the cabinet of 4 December. Nor was anything done later. On 6 December Somerset said that the Admiralty had been too busy with 'more pressing questions' and while he did then begin to think the problem over he was content to allow the cabinet to postpone a decision until war became 'unavoidable'.[1] In his correspondence with the prime minister he did suggest that they might send an officer, a shipwright and a clerk to help the Canadians acquire, convert and man what suitable ships could be found in Canadian waters, but the large number of gunboats which were ready in the United Kingdom could not now be sent until the spring because of the freezing of the St Lawrence.[2] As almost everyone expected the Americans to have breached the river by the spring it is difficult to understand what Somerset was about. He was certainly concerned about expense: he anticipated, for example, considerable difficulty in exercising any real control over the cost of makeshift measures. But the inevitable effect of his hesitation would have been to surrender the lakes to the Americans. This may have been sheer stupidity but it probably was not. Somerset may well have believed that there had never been any hope of achieving anything on the lakes. The problem could only have been met by large measures in advance of war and as these had not been carried out before winter nothing could now be done. Even if the gunboats had been sent up to the lakes in time they still might not have been of much use. They could only pass the canals because they were light, *wooden* boats and there were no facilities in Canada for protecting them with armour. But wooden gunboats would have been useless against rifled artillery. The Americans, on the other hand, had the means of converting their ships and these, Williams had been told, were 'admirably adapted to carrying rifled cannon seen in such numbers . . . by Col. Eardley-Wilmot'.[3]

The same difficulty about the winter did not so decisively block the provision of the other necessities of Canadian defence – the regulars, guns, arms and ammunition – all of which could, if necessary, be sent overland. The War Office displayed very creditable activity in a series of measures which culminated in the war committee's decision on 9 December to send to North America a reinforcement of 10,000

<hr>

[1] Somerset to Palmerston, 6 Dec. 1861, Broadlands papers.

[2] Somerset to Palmerston, 17 Dec. 1861, *ibid.*

[3] Williams to Monck, 29 Nov., enclosed in Monck to C.O., no. 22, 30 Nov. 1861, C.O. 42/628. For the lakes question see also J. M. Callahan, *The Neutrality of the American Lakes and Anglo-American Relations* (Baltimore, 1898), pp. 132–9, and Winks, pp. 55–6.

men. By 30 November it had been decided to send at once to Canada the guns and rifles hitherto held up by lack of regular transport, a senior engineer officer (Col. J. W. Gordon) to supervise the improvement of the defence works and a deputy adjutant-general (Col. D. Lysons) with a number of officers and non-commissioned officers to organize the expanded militia; recruiting had been resumed in Great Britain and the embarkation ordered of a battalion of infantry to Canada and a further battalion, a battery of field artillery, and a company of engineers to Nova Scotia. By 8 December this force had been raised to two battalions of infantry and a company of engineers each for Canada and Nova Scotia, two batteries of field artillery for Canada and one for Nova Scotia. This was a sufficient demonstration of Great Britain's determination not be be bullied but, if war really had to be faced, many more would have to be sent to make up the winter holding force of 10,000 regulars in Canada before communications became too difficult. Indeed, as the news from America had by no means improved, the war committee at its first – and possibly sole – meeting on 9 December approved the detailed proposals which de Grey and Cambridge had been working out for Lewis. These, after some modification in distribution and a large increase of garrison artillery on 17 December, provided for a reinforcement of over 10,500 rank and file in North America, bringing the total to nearly 12,500 in Canada and over 5,000 in the Maritime Provinces. Moreover in case of an unsatisfactory response to Lyons's representations it was decided to hold ready to embark a further force, including, for the completion of an adequate field army, mounted units which, because of expense, it was thought best to hold back until the last possible moment.[1]

The speed with which the decision to send such a large force was reached to some extent indicates how serious the prospect of war seemed, but it was due at least as much to the familiar difficulties of communications with Canada. The normal route, the St Lawrence, would soon be closed by ice and the War Office could not hope to get into Canada by that route more than the first few units to sail. They could and did save some time by moving into Canada most of the troops already in Nova Scotia but, however quickly they acted, they could not bring the Canadian garrison up to 10,000 while the river remained open. An alternative route had therefore to be found. From the port of St Andrews in New Brunswick a railway passed a short distance inland to Woodstock but for nearly two hundred miles, between that place and the

[1] Cambridge to the queen, 6 Dec. 1861, R.A. Q 9/36; memoranda by de Grey, 8, 13, and 17 Dec. 1861, Lewis papers, 2957 and 2980.

eastern terminus of the Grand Trunk Railway below Quebec at Rivière du Loup, there was no railway link. Only two roads bridged the gap, neither of them very satisfactorily. One, the Matapediac route which struck north to meet the St Lawrence at Metis, hardly existed in more than name and, especially in winter, would first have to be considerably improved. The other, the Temiscouata route, a regular road passing along the St John River valley and the Madawaska settlements, was militarily weak. Until it turned away from the St John northward to Rivière du Loup it passed for more than a hundred of its one hundred and ninety miles within fifteen miles of the American frontier and was utterly exposed to attack.[1]

De Grey, who turned attention to this problem as early as 1 December, felt that the Temiscouata road was dangerous to use in peace because it might tempt the Americans to attack and impossible in war because it could so easily be cut. If it had to be used then there should be established all along the line stockaded posts occupied by detachments of infantry, guards at the railway stations and temporary shelters for the troops. Lewis accepted his recommendations and sent an assistant quartermaster-general and some engineers to see how the road could be made more secure. He also proposed that a spy be sent over the border. But so dubious were all concerned about committing to the road the safety of such troops as the Guards that they gradually increased the number of units who were to try to get up the St Lawrence which, the Admiralty assured them, might well remain navigable until the end of December. By the middle of December it had been decided to send almost all the reinforcement intended for Canada up the river.[2]

Between 12 December 1861 and 4 January 1862 the entire force of over 11,000 officers and men, together with guns, arms and ammunition, and clothing and stores of all kinds, left the British Isles in a variety of ships, ranging from transports to mail packets. All of these had to be hired, for the only Admiralty troop transport, the *Himalaya*, was already taken up with the Mexican expedition. Paget, the secretary of the Admiralty and a devotee of Gladstonian economy, was disgusted that the troops were not sent out in the warships intended for Milne's squadron. Had his advice been taken the men's discomfort would undoubtedly have been acute. As it was their case was bad enough, for comfort and safety seem to have been sacrificed to what would

[1] See Map 2, p. 107.
[2] De Grey's memo., 1 Dec. 1861, and Lewis's consequent instructions, 2 Dec., and agenda for the cabinet, 3 Dec., Lewis papers, 2941, 2942 and 2946; Lewis to Cambridge, 12 Dec., Cambridge papers.

otherwise have been a miracle of despatch. The journey was expected to take about nine days to Halifax or about ten to get up the St Lawrence but that expectation was rarely realized. Some of the unlucky passengers were favourably impressed with neither the stowage nor the sea-worthiness of their transports. Major-General Lord Frederick Paulet, who was to command the Guards Brigade in Canada, complained that in the *Adriatic* there were '75 tons of stores etc., on the Hurricane deck, 90 days provisions below – nothing secured and no room to move' and that if they had run into bad weather outside the Needles they would have had to turn back. Two transports, the *Adelaide* with the 1st battalion, 15th foot and the *Victoria* with the 96th foot and a telegraph section, did in fact have to turn back. Both set out again after repairs but the *Victoria* never reached North America. The most important failure was the fate of the five ships – *Melbourne, Australasia, Persia, Parana* and *Adriatic* – carrying the force intended for Canada via the St Lawrence. These were among the first to leave, between 13 and 20 December, and they were ordered to get as far as Rivière du Loup or, failing that, Bic Island, but if necessary to disembark at Halifax or St John. Only one of them, the *Persia*, got as far as Bic where it managed to unload only part of its cargo and passengers before gales and ice forced it to put back to Halifax. The rest all either had to turn back before reaching Bic or made no attempt at all to run the river and so almost the entire force now had to be carried overland.[1]

If war had broken out, or if it had not been known in North America by this time that the immediate crisis was passed, the reinforcements intended for Canada would have been in a serious position. This would have been particularly true in the case of the staff who had to arrive first to prepare the way. It had been known from the beginning that the *Melbourne* which carried the staff was very slow and the deputy quartermaster-general, Lt.-Col. K. MacKenzie, had asked to be transferred to a ship which, while sailing two or three days later, would yet have arrived earlier but this had apparently been refused so as to give the appearance rather than the fact of speed. The *Melbourne* did indeed make very heavy going. It sailed from Woolwich on 7 December and for some reason took a week to pick up its convoy, *Orpheus*, at Plymouth and reach Queenstown harbour, Cork. It left Cork on 14 December but ran into bad weather, becoming separated from its convoy.

[1] 'Lists showing the force in Canada, etc.', 3 Jan. 1862, W.O. 33/11; Verner, i. 317–19; Paget to Gladstone, 10 Dec. 1861, Gladstone papers, B.M.Add.MS. 44,397; Paulet to de Grey, private, 31 Dec. 1861, Ripon papers, B.M.Add.MS. 43,621.

It then began to run out of coal and, having had to stop to refuel at Sydney, Cape Breton, did not reach Halifax until 5 January. By that time the passage of the St Lawrence was felt to be too much for its engines. To save time the staff were then transferred to a mail steamer, which took them to Boston where, having removed the military labels from their baggage, they travelled to Montreal by the Grand Trunk Railway. But the rest of the force could now safely take the rail and road route through New Brunswick and along it between 11 January and 9 March passed on sleighs some 6,780 men and eighteen guns, including a battery of Armstrongs, in detachments of between fifty and a hundred and fifty, each party taking about a week on the journey. A first hand description of the whole process is provided by Lt.-Col. Garnet Wolseley who, with a medical officer and an assistant commissary-general, was stationed at Rivière du Loup to look after the troops when they arrived:

They come as far as this in sleighs and then are taken by railroad up the country to their several destinations. The 62nd Regt., one Battery of Garrison Artillery and 1/3rd of the Rifle Brigade have already passed on without any accident or even serious frostbite. The papers in England talk so much twaddle about this journey that one would fancy it was a sort of Arctic expedition the men were bound upon, whereas almost all that have gone by it seem to think it a lark and say they have enjoyed themselves immensely. I need scarcely tell you that with such an efficient staff as we have here all possible arrangements have been made along the road for the comfort of the men, and no *expense* spared in providing all that even the doctors wished for them. They take six days coming from Woodstock to this place, a total of 185 miles – 8 men come in each sleigh which is drawn by two horses. . . .

Great care does seem to have been taken for the comfort and safety of the men, both en route and generally for service in Canada, particularly in the way of clothing, blankets, cooking utensils and medical services. The embarkation state shows that each man was provided with a special suit of warm clothing, and there were also sheepskin coats, waterproof capes and 'creepers for walking on snow' for a large proportion of them. No doubt much of this care was in conscious reaction from the inefficiencies of the Crimean campaign and it owed something to special consultations with Florence Nightingale. Not everything was perfect; instead of buying tested equipment locally in North America valuable cargo space was taken up with sleighs bought in England which were found on arrival to be too weak to carry the guns. But on the whole the march across New Brunswick was well done – 'a model of its kind', Paulet called it. Certainly no one in North America or England was sparing of congratulations and the officer in charge, Major-General Sir Charles Hastings Doyle, who had aroused some doubts earlier, Cambridge now felt to have done his work *'right well'*.[1]

There might well have been less cause for self-satisfaction if, in the meantime, war had broken out. Then everything would have depended on the ability of the comparatively small force already in North America to delay the American advance until the reinforcements could arrive and particularly to hamper the American efforts on the lakes and frustrate their attacks on the lines of communication. That Williams would have been successful in all this seems highly unlikely. He made great play of his declared intention of blowing up the bridges over the St Lawrence on the outbreak of war. But the best that he could really be expected to do, Macdougall had argued, would be to guard the most important points and, by making the most of his interior communications, concentrate his force wherever the main threat appeared. Even then he could not really expect to hold off a major attack and presumably it was hoped that the threat to their communications presented by posts on their flanks and rear would deter the Americans from such an attack or, if that failed, make their advance as costly as possible and, above all,

---

[1] G. J. Wolseley, *The Story of a Soldier's Life* (2 vols., Westminster, 1903), ii. 102–15; Wolseley to Biddulph, private, 26 Jan. 1862, H. Biddulph, 'Canada and the American Civil War: More Wolseley Letters', *Journal of the Society for Army Historical Research*, xix (1940), 114–15; Stacey, p. 121; C. Woodham-Smith, *Florence Nightingale* (London, 1950), pp. 382–3; Paulet to de Grey, private, 20 Jan. and 6 Mar. 1862, and Cambridge to de Grey, private, 7 Jan. 1862, Ripon papers, B.M.Add.MSS.43,621 and 43,511. The Q.M.G.'s official record of the march is in W.O. 107/6. There is a story (F. Bancroft, *Life of William H. Seward* [2 vols., New York, 1900], ii. 245) that after a 'vessel with a detachment of troops' had entered Portland harbour and permission had been asked for the troops to cross into Canada, Seward agreed to allow the 'landing and transporting to Canada or elsewhere troops, stores, and munitions of war of every kind without exception or reservation'. The facts are obscure but what evidence there is does not seem to justify the humorous implications of Bancroft's story. The Q.M.G.'s official journal is curiously silent about the last stage of the staff's journey. It ends abruptly with the *Melbourne's* arrival at Halifax and is only taken up again when the staff has arrived in Montreal. There are, however, some later references in it to an intention to pass several other officers and their baggage through U.S. territory. Wolseley's account, moreover, implies that the staff travelled through the U.S. in civilian clothes. Certainly no uniformed 'detachment of troops' was involved. In fact Seward's 'permission' seems to have been a skilful piece of propaganda. When Lyons heard about it he at once instituted enquiries and found that a civilian contractor had quite unnecessarily asked permission to transport some heavy baggage across Maine and Seward had seized the opportunity to reply in the far wider terms quoted. (C.O./F.O. correspondence of Jan. and Feb. 1862, C.O. 42/636. See also J. Mackay Hitsman, 'Winter Troop Movement to Canada, 1862', *Canadian Historical Review*, xliii [1962], 127–35, and Winks, pp. 82–7 and 105–10.)

slow them down. That little more was expected of him is clear from the private instructions he received from Cambridge: he was to scatter his force as little as possible; he was not to attempt too much with so small a force; and he was evidently not expected to hold on to much more than Quebec, Montreal and, 'if possible', Kingston. But to this negative role there was one important exception. On the strongest recommendations of naval and military experts he was ordered to attack Rouse's Point immediately upon the outbreak of war with a view to blocking the Americans' most likely route of advance.[1]

. A successful attack on Rouse's Point would no doubt have been wonderfully effective but it was, as Cambridge admitted, a difficult operation. It would have required naval assistance which was not then available and with such a small force as Williams disposed success would have depended upon the Americans being virtually unprepared – an extremely unlikely circumstance in a war which the British expected to begin with a surprise American attack. And if Williams's superiors really expected such success from his initial efforts, they were curiously remiss for they did not have much confidence in his military capacity. The opinion was strongly expressed at the cabinet meeting of 4 December that a more efficient commander would be needed and Cambridge also found that the sixty-one year-old Nova Scotian, though popular – 'a very handsome old gentleman, with charming manners', Wolseley later called him – did not inspire confidence locally. But the old age or lack of seniority of other candidates for the command and the desire to be tactful made it difficult to replace Williams. Lewis therefore decided that this need not be done until war actually broke out, giving him in the meantime an exceptionally good staff.[2] The decision was

[1] Williams to Cambridge, private, 24 Nov. 1861, and Cambridge to Williams, private, 14 Dec., Cambridge papers. For further details on local preparations see Winks, pp. 72–5; part of the engineer report mentioned by him (p. 73) is in Adm. 7/624: 'Naval Considerations', by Capt. Hatt Noble, R.E., 29 Nov. 1861. There had also been a proposal for a similar attack upon Sackett's Harbor in order to reduce the American advantage on the lakes; but this is not mentioned in the duke's letter, possibly, as Collinson pointed out ('Memoranda on the Assistance which can be rendered to the Province of Canada by H.M.'s Navy in the event of War with the U.S.', Adm. 7/624), because the Americans had several good alternative ports, notably at Oswego and Rochester.

[2] Lewis to Cambridge, private, 4 and 8 Dec. 1861, Cambridge papers; Cambridge to Lewis, private, 7 Dec., Verner, i. 314–15. Williams had come to notice for his brave defence of Kars towards the end of the Crimean War. When, in May 1870, however, he was being considered for governor of Gibraltar, Granville, then colonial secretary, wondered if the 'hero of Kars' were not a bit of a fraud, having shown no 'merit' there but becoming the beneficiary of a 'regular conspiracy' of praise conducted by Humphrey Sandwith, Williams's chief of medical staff at Kars, which had been pressed even to the point of

probably made tolerable by discounting any major attack during the winter.

Macdougall seems to have been alone in his opinion that their good communications would allow the Americans to overcome the difficulties of a winter campaign. More plausible, though stated in rather exaggerated terms, was Newcastle's view about a winter campaign ending in another Moscow. Certainly Burgoyne, shortly after the crisis had ended, and the authors of the two very extensive investigations carried out a few years later concluded that the sort of siege operations that would be required for a successful attack on places like Quebec and Montreal would be impossible in winter.[1] But Williams would still have had to face some grave dangers. Neither the winter nor any efforts on his part could have prevented the Americans cutting Canada's interior communications, particularly by a raid on the Beauharnois canal. Worse still was the prospect of the New Brunswick road also being cut.

Burgoyne had pointed out five years earlier that on such a long exposed frontier as that of New Brunswick forts would be of little use and it would have to be defended by large numbers of troops.[2] But in the context of *Canadian* defence such a method would have been self-defeating for, in the absence of a sufficiently large militia force in the Maritime Provinces, the task would have fallen to the very troops whom it was so important to push into Canada. Probably for this very reason the protection of the road was entrusted to a single battalion of infantry while Doyle had instructions on the outbreak of war to occupy the forts and roads from which the Americans might launch an attack.[3] But even though the country was wild and these counter-measures might have been able to frustrate an advance in force, there must still have remained many points at which comparatively small

---

recommending him for the command in the Crimea. But Sandwith had later changed his mind, and called him 'utterly incompetent'. He was also said to have been considered a 'nincompoop' at Woolwich. Cardwell, the secretary for war, replied that Williams would do for a peacetime command, 'though I own I should not select him for a post of great difficulty, or requiring great power of direction . . .'. (Granville to Cardwell, 21 May 1870, Cardwell to Granville, 23 May 1870, Granville papers, P.R.O. 30/29/53.)

[1] 'Memo by Sir John Burgoyne on the Defence of Canada', 15 Feb. 1862, W.O. 33/11; 'Report of the Commissioners appointed to consider the defence of Canada, 1862', W.O. 33/11; and 'Report on the defence of Canada, made to the Provincial Government on 10 November 1864', by Lt.-Col. Jervois, W.O. 33/15.

[2] 'Memo on the Defences of the Foreign Possessions of Great Britain', 28 Nov. 1856, W.O. 33/5.

[3] Cambridge to Doyle, private and confidential, 14 Dec. 1861, Cambridge papers.

American forces could have so harassed the road as to make it virtually unusable.[1] Certainly no one really felt confident about its safety at the time. The chief of staff in Canada, Col. E. R. Wetherall, stated categorically that it could not have been used in the event of war and both Paulet and Wolseley were of the same opinion. It seems utterly unlikely that the Metis road could have served as an alternative. Work on its improvement had already begun before the crisis and Lewis ordered that this should be accelerated. But the local commanders chose not to divide their staff and resources between two roads and gambled on being able to use the Temiscouata route.[2] The civil authorities did not in fact complete the Metis road until 1867.[3]

That this gloomy picture – of the extreme unlikelihood of the British being able to establish their minimum needs in Canada once war had broken out – was at least implicit in the experts' view is borne out by the apparently unanimous support in the army for one rather desperate scheme – an expedition against Maine. A combined operation, mounted from Nova Scotia, to capture Portland and occupy the greater part of Maine might, it was thought, draw off large numbers of the American soldiers who would otherwise be available for an attack on Canada, and cut the most likely line of attack via Lake Champlain. Still more important, it would also solve the problem of Canada's exterior communications for it would both cover the otherwise vulnerable roads between Nova Scotia and Canada and in the Grand Trunk Railway provide a direct communication with Quebec and Montreal. The Americans themselves certainly thought it a serious threat. When a Canadian newspaper suggested it, the mayor of Portland at once complained of the defenceless state of the forts guarding the harbour and in response got some heavy artillery and permission to retain at Augusta two regiments which had recently been ordered to the front.[4] On their part, Britain's military experts – Burgoyne, Seaton, and Macdougall – all pressed the scheme, and on 3 December Lewis suggested to Palmerston that they give provisional orders to undertake it 'provided that the force at Halifax, military and naval, should render such a step safe and prudent'. He certainly also raised the question in cabinet, the appointment to its command was considered and, as late as 26 December, de

<hr />

[1] Doyle to Horse Guards, 22 Jan. 1863, forwarding a 'Report on the Defences of Nova Scotia and New Brunswick', W.O. 55/1558.

[2] Wetherall to Cambridge, private, 10 Jan. 1862, Lewis papers, 2989; Paulet to de Grey, private, 31 Dec. 1861, and 15 Jan. 1862, Ripon papers, B.M.Add. MS.43,621; Wolseley to Biddulph, private, 10 Dec. 1861, Biddulph, p. 112.

[3] Stacey, p. 121, n. 3.   [4] Winks, pp. 88–9.

Grey was drawing up a list of the troops it would need.[1] But no other preparations at all appear to have been made for a scheme which, if it was to be decisive, had to be attempted at the very outbreak of war. This was probably because the navy, upon whose cooperation it depended, was far from enthusiastic.

There was, in principle, a good deal to be said for offensive operations against the American coastline. The whole question turned, in the first place, upon the proper method, not merely of defending Canada, but generally of waging a successful war against the United States. Whatever the real expectation in Canada it is quite clear that the fate of the province was not considered vital to the conduct of the war – it was the weakest point, not the most important. At best the British might so harass and bleed the enemy in Canada that he would tire of the war; at worst Canada's wealth and British prestige would be severely damaged. The loss of Canada, Palmerston admitted, 'would be a heavy blow to the reputation of England both for sagacity and strength'.[2] But neither the United States nor Great Britain could expect to secure in Canada a victory decisive enough to terminate a war. Canada might not be the useless appendage some thought it to be; but neither was its safety or prosperity vital to the existence of the British Empire. Nor, in turn, was it the base from which the British hoped to advance into the United States. The real battle by which the war would be won and Canada more genuinely defended – or recovered if lost – would be fought elsewhere and that would be where Great Britain was strongest: at sea.

There can be no doubt that in spite of all the fuss made about Canada everyone thought in this way. Williams had, much earlier, written to Cambridge that if war came he hoped the navy would 'punish the maritime cities'.[3] Just before the *Trent* crisis Newcastle had talked of the

---

[1] Lewis to Palmerston, 3 Dec. 1861, Broadlands papers; Lewis's memoranda of 3 Dec. and de Grey's memorandum of 26 Dec., Lewis papers, 2945, 2956, 2988. De Grey's scheme proposed a force of:

8 battalions of infantry	6,400
3 batteries of field artillery	720
2 batteries of garrison artillery	220
2 companies of engineers	300
	7,640

Possibly this was just to form the backbone; Macdougall's paper of 3 Dec. had suggested a large force of 50,000 so as to ensure speedy success, but of these two thirds could be volunteers from Canada together with 10,000 volunteers from England.

[2] Palmerston to Lord Glenelg, 31 Aug. 1861, Palmerston papers, B.M.Add. MS.48,582.

[3] Williams to Cambridge, private, 26 May 1861, Cambridge papers.

regrettable necessity of having to burn New York and Boston.[1] Milne, too, showed just after the crisis that he had basically the same attitude: 'War', he said, 'has no doubt its honours and its evils but to make war felt it must be carried against the enemy with energy and every place must be made to feel what war really is.'[2] That such an attitude was basic to British policy is perhaps best illustrated by the extent to which, with the exception of Canada, the British were determined to avoid merely defensive operations. They did not by any means discount the Americans' ability to strike some dangerous blows at their trade and possessions. There was the usual apprehension of American privateering, and the time limit of seven days for Seward to give way to Lyons's demands was designed not to give the United States too good a chance to prepare suitable ships.[3] Measures were taken to improve the naval defence of the more important harbours in the United Kingdom and there were even plans for coping with a second Paul Jones in the Firth of Forth.[4] The queen, too, had to be reassured that the existing garrison of 800 at Parkhurst Barracks and the two sloops in the Roads would ensure her safety at Osborne.[5]

Warnings went out to distant and isolated colonies but very few of them, apart from North America, received any naval or military reinforcements: the Pacific squadron got no more than an extra corvette and a sloop, the Brazils one corvette, one sloop and two gunboats; only Bermuda received any increase in garrison and that was because of its importance for offensive operations. Even British Columbia which, as Burgoyne pointed out, was both valuable and vulnerable, received very little attention. Rear-Admiral Maitland, the Pacific commander-in-chief, was anxious about the defences of the colony. The Americans had only one or two small revenue cutters on the coast, but he was worried about converted schooners lurking in the fogbanks off San Francisco to prey on British shipping. But his despatches did not arrive in England until the crisis was over and in the meantime Somerset had thought the colony safe enough. The Americans had recently withdrawn their garrison from San Juan Island and it was up

[1] Newcastle to Palmerston, 3 Sept. 1861, Broadlands papers.
[2] Milne to Somerset, private, 24 Jan. 1862, Milne papers, 107/1.
[3] Lord Westbury (lord chancellor) to Palmerston, 3 Jan. 1862, Broadlands papers.
[4] 'The Defence of the East Coast of Scotland in the event of war with the U.S.', Dec. 1861, and memorandum by de Grey, 3 Dec. 1861, Lewis papers, 2952–5 and 2948.
[5] Lewis to Palmerston, 24 Dec. 1861, Broadlands papers; Palmerston to the queen, 24 Dec., Queen Victoria's papers, R.A. R 2/5.

to the North American squadron to see that they got no reinforcements from the Atlantic.[1]

Most illuminating of all was the attitude towards the West Indies. According to all reports, naval and military alike, the local defences were very poor and the garrisons were both small and, the greater part being the Negro West Indian Regiments, possibly unreliable in a war with the North. And an attack, either by roving American ships or by a dash from the squadrons blockading the South, was by no means out of the question. Yet none of them received any increase in garrison at all. Instead they were told bluntly that while they would have the general protection of the fleet they must not expect it to give them absolute protection and for local defence they would have to rely on local resources. Milne was given general instructions to pay particular attention to the defence of British trade and possessions but at the same time he was told not so to disperse his force as to expose it to piecemeal destruction.[2]

Milne's first concern was indeed not to tie down a large part of his force in static defence at the expense of the more aggressive measures he favoured. When he received sufficient reinforcements he intended to have squadrons of cruisers operating from Barbados, St Vincent, Antigua, Jamaica, Demerara, and in the entrance to the St Lawrence; but in the meantime, apart from a few ships needed to protect his bases and to keep open his communications with Washington and Halifax, he kept all his force in two main squadrons at Bermuda and Havana. Great efforts were being made to provide Milne with a force sufficient to carry out the most extensive operations against the Americans. He was advised on 1 December that in the event of an unfavourable reply from the Americans he would get immediate reinforcements of the 'most effective ships', together with smaller vessels particularly suited to the shallow waters of his station. In fact the Admiralty did not wait for the American reply. In the first week of the crisis hurried preparations were made for increasing Milne's force, improving his coal supplies, and engaging shipwrights to make ready the reserves. By 6 December three battleships, a frigate and a corvette from the Mediterranean and Channel fleets and a frigate from the reserve had been ordered to Bermuda, while three more Mediterranean frigates

[1] Circular to the W.I. colonies, 16 Dec. 1861, and 'Circular to officers commanding the garrisons in Hong Kong, Ceylon and Mauritius', 26 Dec., C.O. 323/261; Adm. to Maitland, no. 294, 16 Dec., and to Warren, no. 132, 7 Dec., Adm. 13/7; Maitland to Adm., no. 22, 13 Jan. 1862, Adm. 1/5790.
[2] Adm. to Milne, secret, no. 730, 1 Dec. 1861, Adm. 13/7; Somerset to Milne, private, 1, 15 and 16 Dec. 1861, Milne papers, 107/1.

were to stand by at Gibraltar. Still more went in the course of the month: two of the frigates from Gibraltar to escort the troop ships; and a sloop from the reserve. This gave Milne a very respectable force of about forty vessels, including eight battleships and thirteen frigates and corvettes. A further force of eight vessels, including three battleships, under the command of Rear-Admiral Dacres was held in readiness off Lisbon and Gibraltar to join Milne in case of war. Nor would this have been the maximum possible in a short time; by the beginning of January 1862 there were available in the steam reserve another six frigates, two corvettes and four sloops.[1]

Milne's force by no means equalled the number of American ships – the Americans had some 264 vessels in service by the end of 1861 – but the British still thought it far superior. According to one British estimate Milne's total of 1,273 guns was more than the entire Union navy could muster. This was probably a considerable underestimate of American strength but it was true that most of the American ships were improvised merchantmen. They had also lost several of their finest pre-Civil-War ships and the majority of the remainder were sailing vessels. Milne's force, on the other hand, was composed entirely of steamships and great care had been taken to give him the strongest frigates available. The British, too, thought they had a great advantage in the new Armstrong guns and, though these later proved so faulty that they had to be withdrawn, they now hurriedly pressed on with supplying them to ships in American waters. But if war had broken out the position would soon have changed entirely, for both sides were building new ironclad navies. At the end of 1861 the British had only one of the new ironclads in commission but although the rest emerged slowly in the course of the next few years they could no doubt have been pushed on rapidly if war had broken out. These would have had to meet the American ironclads and turret ships which began to appear in the spring of 1862. The British were not particularly impressed with the *Monitor*'s first appearance in battle: 'We could have done the work of the *Monitor* and *Merrimac* together', was *The Times*'s comment. But

[1] For Milne's plans, see: Milne to Somerset, private, 20 Dec. 1861, and 24 Jan. 1862, Milne to Grey, private, 25 Dec. 1861 and 17 Jan. 1862, memorandum by Milne, 1862, Milne papers, 107/1, 107/2 and 108; and Milne to Adm., no. 182, 15 March 1864, Adm. 1/5871. For details of the reinforcements: Somerset to Milne, private, 1 Dec. 1861, Milne papers, 107/1; Somerset to Palmerston, 2 Dec. 1861, Queen Victoria's papers, R.A. Q 9/28; Adm. to Milne, no. 751, 6 Dec. 1861, Adm. 13/7. There is an excellent contemporary summary of British naval measures in Theseus, late R.N., 'England's Naval Resources', *United Service Magazine*, 1862, i. 215–17.

while the American turret ships were not ocean-going vessels and the British ironclads were stronger ships, the British would still have met with some difficulties. Their ironclads had too deep a draught to use their North American bases or to operate in the shallow waters of the North American coast. Palmerston did suggest sending out the *Warrior*, but this was not done, probably because it could not have entered Bermuda. In these circumstances the American monitors might have played havoc with any attempt by the older wooden frigates to maintain a close blockade.[1]

The emphasis on Milne's squadron and particularly on its offensive qualities owed a good deal to the sense of frustration about Canada, but it was, too, based on a confident contempt for the stability of the American economy and morale, both already severely strained by the Civil War. Indeed for part at least of this belief they had support from Americans themselves, in particular one expert quoted by the Admiralty hydrographer, Captain Washington, in a paper outlining a blockade project:

It may be said of New York . . . that if an enemy succeeded in obtaining command of it, even temporarily, or, what would be nearly the same in its consequences, if he succeeded with his fleet in forcing the entrance to the harbour, and in bringing his guns to bear on the city, such a disaster would result in our buying him off upon any terms he might think it expedient to exact. Attacks upon other great seaport towns, such as Boston or Philadelphia, might indeed be attended with results highly disastrous, but they would tell comparatively little upon the issues of the war. The difference is that between striking a limb and striking the heart, for New York is the true heart of our commerce,– the centre of our maritime resources; to strike *her* would be to paralyse *all* the limbs.[2]

But glittering though the prize appeared to be this sort of attack did not really appeal to the navy. Somerset, though inclined at first to leave such matters to Milne's discretion, later declared himself utterly

[1] Somerset to Adm. Walker (c.-in-c., Cape), private, 5 Dec., and Palmerston to Somerset, 8 Dec. 1861, Somerset papers. See also Theseus, p. 215; C. B. Boynton, *History of the Navy during the Rebellion* (2 vols., New York, 1867), i. *passim*; S. Eardley-Wilmot, *Our Fleet Today* (London, 1900), pp. 172–3; J. P. Baxter, *Introduction of the Ironclad Warship* (Cambridge, Mass., 1933), pp. 311–17.

[2] Major J. G. Barnard, *Dangers and Defences of New York* (New York, 1859), quoted in 'List of the Chief Ports of the Federal Coast of the United States . . . with an approximate Estimate of the Number of Vessels required to blockade the several Ports and Rivers', Admiralty print, 15 Dec. 1861, Milne papers, 105/6. The print is unsigned but that it was by Washington is revealed in his private letter to Milne, 4 Jan. 1862, *ibid.*, 108.

opposed to attacking heavily defended places.[1] This was probably because Washington maintained that the only hope of success in attacking such places as Boston and New York lay in the rather unlikely event of surprising them. 'From the intricacy of the channels and the strength of the forts,' he believed, 'it is probable that Boston could not be attacked with any hope of success.' Nor was he much more optimistic about bombarding New York: 'This might have the effect of putting an end to the war, and if so it might be worth the risk. But the risk would be too great if the intention transpired and time were allowed the enemy to make preparations.' The defences of New York had not yet been made impregnable but could readily be improved; a sudden dash, therefore, would be the 'only hope of success'.[2] Milne, himself, hardly seems to have been much more daring:

The object of the war can of course only be considered to cripple the enemy. That is his trade and of his trade it can only be his shipping. No object would be gained if the Forts alone are to be attacked, as modern views deprecate any damage to a town. If ships are fired upon in a Port the town must suffer; therefore the shipping cannot be fired on. This actually reserves operations to against vessels at sea. If a town is undefended or the defences subdued an embargo might be put on it and a subsidy demanded.[3]

Presumably the last is what he meant when he spoke of acting against 'Boston, etc.'[4] He was certainly doubtful about attempting any operation which, like the Maine scheme, would involve a landing.

There was no question of a general invasion of the United States from the Atlantic coast any more than from Canada. All the experts, naval and military alike, were agreed that the territorial conquest of the United States was a physical impossibility, that 'the very nature of the country', as Williams had put it, 'ensures success to its occupants'.[5] There were considerable doubts about the advisability of making any major attack from the sea. Burgoyne thought it would 'require great caution'. With a good sized force they might gain 'momentary possession', but they would almost certainly be overwhelmed in the end by the 'masses' that would be brought against them – 'a fate that may be fully expected in the end to befall the Federalist expedition to Port

[1] Somerset to Granville, 21 Dec. 1861, Granville papers, P.R.O. 30/29/24 pt. ii; Somerset to Russell, 29 Dec. 1861, Russell papers, P.R.O. 30/22/24.
[2] Washington's 'List of the Chief Ports', 15 Dec. 1861, Milne papers, 105/6.
[3] Memorandum by Milne, 1862, *ibid.*, 108.
[4] Milne to Adm. Sir Frederick Grey (first sea lord), private, 17 Jan. 1862, *ibid.*, 107/2.
[5] Williams to Cambridge, private, 18 Nov. 1861, Cambridge papers.

Royal [South Carolina]'. If the permanent success of that expedition had become apparent at this time, Burgoyne would no doubt have revised his opinion. Still, so far as the Maine scheme was concerned, he did not have the same objection since it was a salient of the enemy's territory, adjoining that of British North America.[1] Washington admitted diffidently that for these reasons the scheme was not utterly impracticable. As Maine was an isthmus, once taken it could probably be held. But, though there was a clear channel for an attack on Portland, as with New York, 'if it were considered desirable to take possession of the place (which seems doubtful)', they would need to act before the Americans improved its defences and even than a strong force, including several battleships, would be needed. But if it were really necessary to occupy Maine both Milne and Washington believed that, rather than risk an attack, they should wait and see whether, as Milne put it, 'that state was inclined to change masters'.[2] This was a reference to a further argument which many of the military experts, recalling 1814, had used to advocate the scheme:

The interests of Maine & Canada are identical. A strong party is believed to exist in Maine in favor of annexation to Canada; and no sympathy is there felt for the war which now desolates the U. States. It is more than probable that a conciliatory policy adopted towards Maine would, if it failed to secure its absolute co-operation, indispose it to use any vigorous efforts against us. The patriotism of the Americans dwells peculiarly in their pockets; & the pockets of the good citizens of Maine would benefit largely by the expenditure and trade we should create in making Portland our base & their territory our line of communication with Canada.[3]

But such confident arguments, dubious though they really were, merely played into the hands of cautious men like Washington: 'Possibly a very strict blockade, without an attack, might induce the people of Maine to consider whether it would not be for their interest to declare themselves independent of the United States, and so profit by all the advantages that would be derived from railway communication with Canada and the Lakes.'[4]

Hesitations of this kind did not apply to attacks on American shipping; provisional orders went out in the first two weeks of the crisis for such operations.[5] For his part Milne intended first of all to destroy the

[1] Burgoyne's 'Thoughts on War', 14 Dec. 1861, Lewis papers, 2984.
[2] Washington's 'List of the Chief Ports', 15 Dec. 1861, Milne papers, 105/6; Milne to Grey, private, 17 Jan. 1862, *ibid.*, 107/2.
[3] Macdougall's 'On the Prospect of War', 3 Dec. 1861, Lewis papers, 2943.
[4] Washington's 'List of the Chief Ports', 15 Dec. 1861, Milne papers, 105/6.
[5] Adm. to Cape of Good Hope, 4 Dec. 1861, to Brazils, 7 Dec., and to Pacific, 16 Dec., Adm. 13/7.

squadrons blockading the South both to break that blockade and also to prevent their sudden descent upon Great Britain's scattered possessions, particularly upon his offensive base at Bermuda where the land defences were not considered sufficient. The Pensacola Bay force he hoped to be able to leave to the squadron which had been assembling at Havana under his commodore, Dunlop, for the Mexican expedition. By the end of December, he expected, it would consist of a battleship, two or three frigates, two corvettes, three sloops, and two gunvessels. By the same time he hoped that he would himself have gathered at Bermuda an even more imposing force of three battleships, two frigates, two sloops, and two gunvessels, and possibly another frigate and three sloops at present engaged in carrying despatches. With this he would dispose of the Union fleet blockading the North Carolina and Virginia coast. He would also apparently have tried to harass the Union capital, cut off communications with Fortress Monroe, and seize a number of positions in order to establish coaling stations for his forces operating off the coast.[1] Somerset also expected him to establish himself in one of the Southern ports to obtain coal and as 'a base for further operations'.[2] But with the possible exception of dislodging the Union from its supposedly tenuous foothold on Port Royal, they did not apparently propose to offer any direct assistance to the South.

The war between the North and South States [Burgoyne argued], so long as it will continue, will greatly relieve our conflict with the former: our proceedings will be in some degree in concert and mutual support with the efforts of the South; but generally it will be well to avoid as much as possible any combined operations on a great scale (except as far as the fleet may be concerned), under any specious project, such as for an attack on Washington or Baltimore; – experience proves almost invariably the great evils of combined operations by armies of different countries; and in this case, the advantage to the enemy of the defensive station will far more than compensate for the union of forces against it.[3]

No doubt, if war had come, the British would gradually have been forced to modify this professional prejudice and to swallow their dislike of being associated with the slave-tainted South. For the time being, however, they confined their contact with the South to collecting information from Confederate officers in England, and even then through 'an

[1] Milne to Somerset, private, 20 Dec. 1861, Milne papers, 107/1; to Grey, private, 25 Dec., *ibid.*, 107/2; Milne's Memorandum, 1862, *ibid.*, 108; and Milne's marginal comments on Washington's 'List of the Chief Ports', 15 Dec., *ibid.*, 105/6.
[2] Somerset to Russell, 29 Dec. 1861, Russell papers, P.R.O. 30/22/24.
[3] Burgoyne's 'Thoughts on War', 14 Dec. 1861, Lewis papers, 2984.

indirect channel'.[1] Breaking the blockade would have been of enormous benefit to the South; so too would have been the blockade it was proposed to apply in turn to some 1,250 miles of the North's own coast. Such a blockade was in fact regarded as the navy's principal offensive role. It was the yardstick by which Somerset had always assessed Milne's needs,[2] and it was for that purpose that Washington had drawn up his paper of 15 December. This proposed a plan of blockade undertaken in two stages, the first employing forty vessels against the principal Atlantic ports, and the second raising it to sixty to cover the minor ports as well. Washington himself admitted that his estimate was a very rough one, and Milne, thinking the amount for the first stage 'utterly inadequate', raised that alone to sixty-five vessels.[3] But on one thing at least all were agreed: it was almost entirely upon the moral and military effectiveness of the blockade that all Great Britain's chances of success seemed to depend.

Fortunately for the course of Anglo-American relations the *Trent* crisis passed without provoking the clash for which all these preparations were intended. It is probably futile to try and estimate what would have been the outcome of a conflict – too much would have depended upon the imponderable fortunes of war. But the state of contemporary British opinion is interesting enough. There seems in the first place to have been very little reluctance to accept a fight. 'There is,' wrote one American observer in England (Thurlow Weed), 'with but few individual exceptions, but one voice here. All are for war, first on account of the Honor of the Flag, and next because they think we want to quarrel with them. All that we have said [and] done in sympathizing with rebellion in Ireland, Canada, etc. and in sending home their minister during the Crimean War, is remembered now.'[4] No doubt this did encourage the tendency to bully a helpless North, but the ministry generally seems to have thought there was serious danger of war. It is difficult to agree with Cobden who thought the prime minister was playing a sort of primitive brinkmanship: 'Palmerston likes to drive the wheel close to the edge, and show how dexterously he can avoid falling over the precipice.'[5]

[1] Washington to Milne, private, 4 Jan. 1862, Milne papers, 108.
[2] Somerset to Palmerston, 6 Dec. 1861, Broadlands papers.
[3] Washington's 'List of the Chief Ports', 15 Dec. 1861, Milne papers, 105/6. For further details of the blockade scheme see Bourne, pp. 627–8.
[4] L. B. Shippee, *Canadian-American Relations, 1849–1874* (New Haven and Toronto, 1939), pp. 126–7.
[5] Cobden to Chevalier, 14 Dec. 1861, J. Morley, *Life of Richard Cobden* (2 vols., London, 1881), ii. 389.

The prime minister and his colleagues may have been wrong but, if so, their mistakes were honest ones. It would indeed be mad for the Union to provoke war at such a time, but this, they thought, was just the sort of insanity to be expected from Americans. Some, like Cobden and Gladstone, deplored the prospect but others showed a distinct tendency, often quite undisguised, to welcome the chance of settling with an old enemy. Cobden certainly thought this was the case. Early in the crisis he wrote to Charles Sumner: 'Formerly England feared a war with the United States as much from the dependence on your cotton as from a dread of your power. *Now* the popular opinion (however erroneous) is that a war would give us cotton. And we, of course, consider your power weakened by your civil war.'[1] The keynote here is one of opportunity; at no time would England be so favourably placed to deal with the United States as during civil war. That advantage might have been countered by fear of French opportunism but the British were soon reassured about that, when the French disapproval of Wilkes's action was officially communicated to Russell on 6 December.[2] The most forceful expressions of this point of view came shortly before the *Trent* incident from Lord Clarendon who, though not in the cabinet, was close to it: 'I don't like the look of things in the U.S.', he wrote to Granville on 14 September, 'The villains seem to be desirous of picking a quarrel with us, wh. as it wd. complete their everlasting & irretrievable ruin I shd. be glad of if I did not feel sure that N[apoleon] wd. instantly leave us in the lurch and do something in Europe wh. we can't stand.'[3] Few were as forthright as Clarendon, who was glad to see that the government was not going to be 'mealy mouthed' about the incident,[4] but the undertones of such sentiments and the apparent confidence that these implied were equally present among the ministers themselves. The queen told her uncle that war would be 'utter destruction to the North Americans',[5] and for this opinion she had the highest possible authority. 'Great Britain', so her prime minister told her, 'is in a better state than at any former time to inflict a severe blow upon and to read

[1] Cobden to Sumner, 29 Nov. 1861, J. Morley, *Life of Richard Cobden* (2 vols., London, 1881), ii. 391–2.
[2] Thouvenel to Mercier, 3 Dec. 1861 (communicated to Russell, 6 Dec.), *British Parliamentary Papers*, 'Correspondence respecting the Seizure of Messrs Mason, Slidell . . .', 1862 [2913] lxii. 6–7.
[3] Clarendon to Granville, 14 Sept. 1861, Granville papers, P.R.O. 30/29/29A.
[4] Clarendon to Cowley (ambassador in Paris), private, 29 Nov. 1861, Cowley papers, P.R.O., F.O. 519/178.
[5] The queen to King Leopold, 7 Dec. 1861, Queen Victoria's papers, R.A. Y 107/23.

a lesson to the United States which will not soon be forgotten.'[1] Even Lewis, whose earlier statements showed that he was not automatically in tune with his chief, believed that 'we shall soon *iron the smile* out of their face'.[2] Equally, when the crisis was over, the British congratulated themselves upon the effectiveness of their preparations both in a diplomatic and a military sense. Lyons himself admitted that his 'diplomacy would have done little toward settling the *Trent* question, had not the military preparations come in aid of it',[3] and Cambridge felt that the whole affair had reasserted Great Britain's military prestige, so badly hit by the Crimean War:

I do not at all regret the demonstration, though we are not as it appears to have war. It will be a valuable lesson to the Americans, and to the World at large, and will prove to all what England can and will do, when the necessity for so doing arises. It also establishes the fact that we are not that insignificant *military Power*, which some people are disposed to make out, and that the military organization of our departments is now such, that at any moment we can be, and are prepared for war, should it suddenly arise. It also proves that we have an able staff to conduct the details of a difficult operation.[4]

This was not all ignorant self-esteem. They were quite well aware how costly even their victories might be. Palmerston's pious gratitude, after the crisis had passed, for avoiding 'a large expenditure of money, ... much embarrassment to commerce and ... painful sacrifices of the lives and blood of brave men'[5] may not mean very much but Newcastle's reflection that the burning of New York and Boston would be as great a blow to England as the destruction of Liverpool and Bristol seems sincere enough.[6] Certainly hardly anyone was confident about Canada. Macdougall thought that its defence during the Civil War would be an 'easy task'[7] but no one else of any importance would go so far. Palmerston, no doubt anxious to rap his colleagues' knuckles for frustrating his earlier demands for reinforcements, thought Canada was 'lamentably unprepared'.[8] Wolseley thought they would have 'toughish work of it', his own private opinion being that they were 'now on the verge

---

[1] Palmerston to the queen, 5 Dec. 1861, H. C. F. Bell, *Lord Palmerston* (2 vols., London, 1936), ii. 295.
[2] Lewis to Edward Twistleton, private, 5 Dec. 1861, Lewis, p. 406.
[3] Lyons to Milne, private and confidential, 27 Feb. 1862, Milne papers, 107/1.
[4] Cambridge to Doyle, private, 22 Feb. 1862, Cambridge papers.
[5] Palmerston to the queen, 12 Jan. 1862, Queen Victoria's papers, R.A. Q 9/66.
[6] Newcastle to Palmerston, 3 Sept. 1861, Broadlands papers.
[7] Macdougall's 'On the Prospect of War', 15 Dec. 1861, Lewis papers, 2943.
[8] Palmerston to Russell, 6 Dec. 1861, Bell, ii. 295.

of the greatest war which has taken place in our days'.[1] Williams, as the local commander, had to put up a brave front – he had even promised the Americans a warm reception if they came in June when he had a miserably small force[2] – but privately he must have realized how difficult his position would have been. These difficulties, however, did not in the least affect the general optimism about the ultimate outcome of the war for, as Palmerston put it, 'we shall have a great advantage by sea, and we must make the most of it'.[3] By making full use of their sea power they might destroy American shipping, institute a severe blockade, harass the Northern coastal cities, and perhaps occupy Maine. It was unlikely that they would be able to secure a decisive military victory by these means. But they would draw off the enemy from hard-pressed Canada and inspire the South morally and materially. Above all, they might so sap the North's moral and economic strength as to bring her government to sue for peace on unfavourable terms. In any case, whatever the cost, the British were less prepared to sacrifice prestige than political or even economic interest:

What a figure . . . we shall cut in the eyes of the world [Clarendon said the day after the crisis broke], if we lamely submit to this outrage when all mankind will know that we should unhesitatingly have poured our indignation and our broadsides into any weak nation . . . and what an additional proof it will be of the universal . . . belief that we have two sets of weights and measures to be used according to the power or weakness of our adversary. I have a horror of war and of all wars one with the U.S. because none would be so prejudicial to our interests, but peace like other good things may be bought too dearly and it never can be worth the price of national honor.[4]

[1] Wolseley to Biddulph, private, 10 Dec. 1861, Biddulph, p. 113.
[2] Williams to Cambridge, private, 30 June 1861, Cambridge papers.
[3] Palmerston to Russell, 6 Dec. 1861, Russell papers, P.R.O. 30/22/21.
[4] Clarendon to Cowley, private, 29 Nov. 1861, Cowley papers, F.O. 519/178.

Part 3

The Withdrawal, 1861–1908

8

The Civil War and its Aftermath
1861-1871

The *Trent* crisis was the most dangerous single incident of the Civil War and perhaps in the whole course of Anglo-American relations since 1815. Its happy termination, however, brought no lasting relief either from the general problem of the defence of British possessions in North America or from fears of further diplomatic clashes with the North. Instead real tension between the two countries continued throughout the war and for some time afterwards to keep the question of war and peace very much in the forefront of Britain's calculations. Some members of the cabinet, of course, continued as before the *Trent* affair to believe that the danger was much exaggerated.

I am not one of those who think that the quarrel with the United States 'is not dead but sleepeth' [protested Sir George Cornewall Lewis early in 1862]. A new ground of quarrel *may* arise – but I do not believe that the Americans will cherish the *Trent* affair in their hearts, and will watch the moment of our weakness to be avenged. If I am not greatly mistaken, they have a gread deal more dirt to eat with respect to the war against the South, the superior dirtiness of which will entirely take the taste of the *Trent* dirt out of their mouths.[1]

Lewis was certainly not alone in this opinion but the majority, like his own deputy at the War Office, de Grey, preferred now more than ever to follow Palmerston's advice on the wisdom of constant vigilance.[2] The *Trent* crisis after all had shown how correct had been his warnings in the summer of the previous year and had quite won over the colonial secretary. 'Even if peace be for the present preserved,' Newcastle admitted as the *Trent* crisis drew to a close, 'I fear we cannot count upon its safe continuance for any length of time in the present temper of the American people, and it is of great importance that our North American possessions should not again allow themselves to be caught in

[1] Lewis to de Grey, 22 Jan. 1862, Ripon papers, B.M.Add.MS.43,533.
[2] De Grey to Lord Frederick Paulet (in command of the Guards Brigade), private, 25 Jan. 1862, Ripon papers, B.M.Add.MS.43,621.

a state of utter unpreparedness.'[1] And as the war went on and Anglo-American relations continued to be plagued by unpleasant incidents, special precautions certainly seemed justified. In July 1862 the *Alabama* escaped from under the cautious scrutiny of the British authorities and began its famous career of destruction; in September Russell narrowly avoided repeating the same mistake by ordering the seizure of the rams which Laird Brothers were building for the South. The end of 1863 saw the beginning of a most dangerous series of raids organized by the Confederates from across the Canadian border: in December 1863 they seized the American coastal steamer *Chesapeake*; a year later they attacked St Albans in Vermont.

With their neutrality in such continual danger, it was only natural that the British should have kept the amount of their naval and military forces in North America up to an unusually high level throughout the war. On the North American station some of the larger ships were withdrawn during 1862 and 1863, but the number of small and medium-sized frigates was actually increased and at the end of the war there were still nearly thirty vessels on the station. The Northern blockade however made rather a special case for the maintenance of so large a force. More significant was the number of British regulars kept in the North American garrisons. By April 1863 that force had fallen by only a little over 2,000 from the peak of 17,600 reached as a result of the *Trent* crisis. Thereafter the reduction continued at a slow pace. At the beginning of 1864 there were still 11,000 British regulars in Canada and another 3,500 in the Maritimes. In May of that year the Schleswig-Holstein crisis among other things forced the withdrawal of the Brigade of Guards but the end of the war still found over 8,000 men in Canada, nearly four times as many as there had been when the war began.[2]

Preoccupied though they were with the immediate incidental dangers of the war, the British were nevertheless quite well aware that the Civil War marked a crucial stage in the development of the Anglo-American balance of power in North America. In the earlier years of the war the collapse of the Union seemed at first sight to offer considerable advantages and opportunities to Great Britain. Such a collapse after all had often been forecast in Britain, especially by those who looked forward to it anxiously as the most effective and permanent solution of all Britain's difficulties of defence and diplomacy in America. Palmerston himself had held up the prospect of 'the Swarms [separating] from the

[1] Newcastle to Monck, private, 4 Jan. 1862, John Martineau, *The Life of Henry Pelham, fifth Duke of Newcastle, 1811–1864* (London, 1908), p. 305.
[2] C. P. Stacey, *Canada and the British Army, 1846–1871* (Toronto, 1963), pp. 149 and 154.

Parent Hive', as the one real consolation for an ultimate acquiescence in American expansion.[1] As prime minister throughout the war he did reveal a certain satisfaction at what most in Britain soon came to regard as the accomplished fact of disunion.[2] And in the anxiety of British opinion generally to condemn the North for refusing to let their brothers go in peace and then in its insistence that the South had successfully established their independence by force of arms, there was undoubtedly some degree of wishful thinking. For once too there was the prospect of securing the almost united support of the cabinet for an active American policy. Even Gladstone was notoriously convinced of the futility of continuing the war once, as he rashly proclaimed in October 1862, the South had 'made a Nation', and he was no prejudiced critic of American democracy. In varying degrees then, professions of humanitarian horror, grief at the disruption of a valuable trade, and the unwelcome dangers of an unaccustomed maritime neutrality all tended to produce an unusual alignment among such argumentative individuals as Palmerston, Russell, and Gladstone and in favour of a diplomatic intervention to secure a peace which could only result in the permanent disunion of the States. Fortunately their opinions never quite agreed at any given moment. Even Palmerston could never really convince himself that the possible benefits of intervention were worth the risks involved. At times, in the summer and autumn of 1862, the cabinet appeared to come very near indeed towards taking some decisive step; but always the fear of being left in the lurch by France and Russia, the danger of becoming directly involved in hostilities, and the hope that a better opportunity lay just around the corner, kept them to a safer course.

Much less dangerous, perhaps, was the opportunity for Great Britain to resume the initiative she had lost in Central America and the Caribbean in the 1840s and 1850s. Here too, however, the government was singularly cautious. The foreign secretary was offered several opportunities in 1862 and 1863 to begin all over again in Central America by purchasing the Bay Islands but all of them he firmly refused.[3] And when at the very beginning of the war Spain succumbed

---

[1] Palmerston to Clarendon, 4 July 1857, R. W. Van Alstyne, 'Anglo-American Relations, 1853–1857; British Statesmen on the Clayton-Bulwer Treaty and American Expansion', *American Historical Review*, xlii (1936–37), 499.

[2] H. C. F. Bell, *Lord Palmerston* (2 vols., London, 1936), ii. 274 and 315.

[3] Russell to Edward Haslewood (a director of the Honduras and Pacific Transit Co; Carlos Gutierrez, the Honduran minister in London, was also a director), 27 Mar. 1862, F.O. 39/14; Russell to Mathew, no. 34, 27 Nov. 1862, F.O. 15/116, and no. 21, 29 June 1863, F.O. 15/119.

at last to the temptation to accept the inhabitants' invitation to reoccupy Santo Domingo, he wrote to Cowley in Paris: 'I suppose Spain will accept Domingo. Those fools they!'[1] Among his many objections to this foolhardy enterprise was the danger of North and South ultimately combining to make it a 'cause of serious diplomatic difference' with Spain.[2] Considering that this incident was indeed foremost in Seward's mind when he pressed upon Lincoln on 1 April his famous 'Thoughts for the consideration of the President', looking for a foreign, patriotic diversion in order to reunite his country, and considering too how great the British suspicions were of just such a scheme, it is all the more surprising that the end of the year should have seen them too about to become involved with France and Spain in Mexico.[3] Perhaps Russell thought that by inviting the participation of the United States, when civil war must certainly prevent her accepting, and then by carefully excluding political intervention from the instrument of cooperation which the three powers signed in London on 31 October, he had removed all possible cause of objection on the part of the Americans. If so he must have been very naive indeed; the signs are that he was not a little dishonest. Russell's personal scepticism about the prospects of political intervention in Central America and Mexico alike seem to have had little to do with genuine approval of American expansion. Rather he thought simply that such adventures were both futile and dangerous. Certainly he greeted almost with contempt the many suggestions made by his own representatives, as well as by the French, that the Mexican people awaited eagerly the humanitarian and stabilizing intervention of European monarchy.

Crampton, now minister at Madrid, thought the chance of the Mexicans being 'able to take advantage of the holiday afforded them by the fight in the U. States to form a government strong enough to hold its own . . . a very unlikely contingency . . . and not one which any archduke that I am acquainted with is likely to bring about'.[4] Palmerston was not quite so sceptical but he felt that it would be a very expensive undertaking, requiring 'a prince of a reigning European family, many

---

[1] Russell to Cowley, private, 27 April 1861, Cowley papers, P.R.O., F.O. 519/199. For British policy in this episode of Spain's abortive colonial renaissance, see C. C. Hauch, 'Attitudes of Foreign Governments towards the Spanish Reoccupation of the Dominican Republic', *Hispanic American Historical Review*, xxvii (1947), 247–68. [2] Hauch, p. 250.
[3] For Britain's involvement in the Mexican affair see W. S. Robertson, 'The Tripartite Treaty of London', *Hispanic American Historical Review*, xx (1940), 167–89.
[4] Crampton to Cowley, private, 13 Nov. 1861, Cowley papers, F.O. 519/203.

millions sterling, and 20,000 European troops'.[1] For this reason, if for no other, he too ruled out any question of political intervention by Great Britain. But a monarchy supported by the great armies of imperial France might be a very different matter. Then the scheme would have a better chance of success and, at no cost to Great Britain, be doubly advantageous to her in Europe as well as in America. 'Would it do any harm to any one', asked the permanent under-secretary at the Foreign Office, 'to have [Prince Napoleon] Emperor of Mexico? The French would be bound to resist the application of the Monroe Doctrine to the prejudice of French aggrandisement.'[2] Later on Palmerston himself commented:

As to the monarchy scheme, if it could be carried out it would be a great blessing for Mexico, and a godsend for all countries having anything to do with Mexico, as far at least, as their relations with Mexico are concerned.

It would also stop the North Americans whether of the Federal or the Confederate States in their projected absorption of Mexico. If the North and South are definitively disunited, and if at the same time Mexico could be turned into a prosperous monarchy I do not know any arrangement that would be more advantageous for us.[3]

And, after the French had captured Mexico City in June 1863, when Russell felt inclined to warn Maximilian off his foolish adventure, Palmerston wrote:

For my part though systematically and on national principle jealous of the ambitious policy of France, I feel no jealousy as to the proceedings of France in Mexico. What she is doing there will not make her more dangerous to us, but on the contrary will have a tendency to fetter her action in Europe by engaging her men and her money for some years to come in supporting an Austrian prince on the other side of the Atlantic.[4]

Intentionally or not, the British, from first to last, placed no real obstacles in the path of Napoleon's ambitions in Mexico. When they signed the convention of London they were already well aware of his

[1] Minute by Palmerston, 18 Oct. 1861, Russell papers, P.R.O. 30/22/56.
[2] Hammond to Cowley, private, 7 Sept. 1861, Cowley papers, F.O. 519/190.
[3] Palmerston to Russell, 19 June 1862, Russell papers, P.R.O. 30/22/22.
[4] Palmerston to Russell, 26 Sept. 1863, Russell papers, P.R.O. 30/22/22, partially quoted by Bell, ii. 352–3. Clarendon, soon afterwards, expressed a similar point of view in rather more colourful language: 'I can't help being very glad that Mexico will require another 20,000 men, first because it is a first rate guarantee against war in Europe and second that it will be the most offensive and effectual way of checking Yankee plots in that country. It amuses me exceedingly to see the Emperor cocking up his leg against their Monroe doctrine which ought long ago to have been *arrosé* in that manner' (Clarendon to Cowley, private, 4 Nov. 1863, Cowley papers, F.O. 519/179).

intentions. Cowley, who supported the idea of 'recommending' monarchy to Mexico, continually warned his government that there was 'no doubt whatever that French influence will be exerted to the utmost endeavour to establish a monarchical form of government in Mexico'.[1] Nor could they have been under any misapprehension when they agreed to the emperor's demand that they drop the article which more specifically limited the objectives of the expedition, and retained instead the one which ultimately allowed Louis Napoleon to plead the support of the people of Mexico for his grander scheme.[2] And in all official instructions it was made quite clear that while British representatives were not to exert any 'influence . . . in the internal affairs of Mexico calculated to prejudice the right of the Mexican nation freely to choose and to establish its own form of Government', any government that respected the rights and well-being of foreigners would secure 'the moral support of the British Government'.[3] Clearly Russell and Palmerston were sufficiently sceptical of the chances of success and possibly so respectful of the power and enmity of even a divided United States, that they had no intention of allowing the British expeditionary force to be dragged by the folly or audacity of their allies into a dangerous monarchical experiment. 'It is true a convention is not a perfect security,' Russell had argued when advising against a mere exchange of notes among the three powers, 'but it is at all events a producable security, and would justify us in the eyes of Parliament.' No doubt he thought, though he did not say so, that it would help too to lull the suspicions of the United States. But he went on to admit that 'in either case France or Spain, if bent on interference, might find grounds to do so in the lamentable state of Mexico'.[4] The London convention was designed only to limit Britain's risks and liabilities, not to hamper Napoleon's scheme.

While the Civil War, then, offered some large opportunities for revolutionizing the balance of power in North America, the British preferred to leave all the work to the French and the Americans themselves.[5] Indeed had the old guard of Palmerstonians attempted anything else their schemes would almost certainly have been nipped in the bud by opposition within the cabinet itself and especially from Gladstone

[1] Cowley to Russell, private, 5 Sept. and 2 Oct. 1861, Russell papers, P.R.O. 30/22/56. [2] Robertson, pp. 176–7.
[3] *Ibid.*, p. 179. [4] Russell memorandum, 2 Oct. 1861, F.O. 50/358.
[5] For a similar view see W. L. Morton, 'British North America and a Continent in Dissolution, 1861–71', *History*, xlvii (1962), 146–7. Morton concludes, however, that the refusal to take active measures to avert the reassertion of United States supremacy in the Americas 'constituted a covert assent to its realization' (p. 148).

and Russell. In any case, whatever long-term hopes some might have had, few believed that the end of the war would bring immediate relief. Russell and Gladstone among cabinet members, and Burgoyne among military experts were all inclined to think that domestic troubles, and the burden of taxation in particular, would continue for a long time to come to divert the attention of the Americans away from their supposed foreign enemies. Gladstone too protested that 'however difficult it may be for Europeans to forecast American judgment and action, yet it must not be too hastily assumed that justice, decency, and prudence go for nothing on the other side of the water'.[1] But most of the diplomats continued to think the worst of the Americans. Lyons, for example, though sometimes more cheerful, often warned, as in April 1864, that 'there can unhappily be no doubt that three quarters of the American people are eagerly longing for a safe opportunity of making war with England'.[2] Even disunion, it was thought, might bring no immediate relief, but for a time at least yet greater danger. 'It is impossible to guess in what shape the different sections of the United States will come out of their present contest,' Crampton admitted, 'but I have no expectation of their assuming a less aggressive shape than before it. On the contrary they will each probably possess a military organisation superior to what they both had when united.'[3] Palmerston, less unwilling to make guesses, expected the war to end in separation and the North to seek compensation in Canada.[4]

Such doubts about the future, in addition to the constant threats to British neutrality during the war, naturally led once again to a general investigation of the whole problem of North American defence. This time, however, it was marked from the first by the determination on the part of the British government to see Canada assume her proper share of the burden. In England the exciting diversion from economy provided by the *Trent* incident evaporated all the more suddenly when the bill was presented to the House of Commons in February 1862. The supplementary naval estimates included £234,000 for the transport

---

[1] 'Memorandum by Sir John Burgoyne, on the Defence of Canada—[15] Feb. 1862', printed as appendix 2 of the 'Report of the Commissioners appointed to consider the Defences of Canada, 1862', W.O. 33/11; Russell to Lyons, private, 21 May 1864, Russell papers, P.R.O. 30/22/97; printed confidential memorandum, 'Defence of Canada', by Gladstone, 12 July 1864, Gladstone papers, B.M.Add.MS.44,599.

[2] Lyons to Russell, private, 19 April 1864, Lord Newton, *Lord Lyons: a Record of British Diplomacy* (2 vols., London, 1913), i. 128–9.

[3] Crampton to Cowley, private, 13 Nov. 1861, Cowley papers, F.O. 519/203.

[4] Palmerston to Lewis, 31 Dec. 1862, Broadlands papers.

of the reinforcements and another £40,000, it was anticipated, would have to be added the following year to cover the whole of the additional naval expenditure. The bill for the army amounted to £609,000 and the Commons was warned that there would be more to come. The immediate result was the passage without division on 4 March of Arthur Mills's resolution that self-governing colonies should assume the 'main responsibility' for their internal defence and 'assist' too in their external defence.[1]

So far as Canada was concerned, the constant threat from the war across the border certainly seemed a most promising encouragement to local efforts. The Canadians had not been idle during the *Trent* crisis. At that time arrangements had been made to increase the number of volunteers and also to call out 38,000 sedentary militia; uniforms, arms, and equipment for 100,000 men had been asked for from England; and John A. Macdonald became the first 'minister of militia affairs'.[2] When the crisis evaporated as suddenly as it had come, some of these measures were soon suspended, but with Monck's encouragement Macdonald was nominated in January 1862 to head a Canadian commission appointed to report on the organization of the provincial forces.[3] Later in the same month Monck and the commander-in-chief of the British forces, General Williams, agreed upon another commission to consider the more general problems of Canadian defence.[4]

Both projects were warmly welcomed by the government in White-hall. For the second they suggested the addition of a naval officer and supplied for its guidance two memoranda by the inspector-general of fortifications. Burgoyne's memoranda went over the familiar ground of fortifications, communications, militia, and naval forces on the lakes, and consequently they were not overburdened with detail. He chose instead to emphasize what was ever most popular in Whitehall, a judicious combination of economy and optimism. He urged, as he had done in the 1850s, a concentration on fieldworks rather than costly and rapidly outmoded permanent fortifications. He also suggested that the Civil War, by ensuring protracted disunion and high taxation in the United States, would make Canada relatively more attractive to immigrants and thus promise her a greater share of power on the North American continent. Even so, he warned, such was her vulnerability in spite of Britain's naval supremacy that if the principle of colonial self-defence were rigidly adhered to no utterly effective defence

<hr>

[1] Stacey, pp. 128–9.   [2] *Ibid.*, p. 122.   [3] *Ibid.*, p. 130.
[4] Monck to Newcastle, no. 23, 1 Feb. 1862, C.O. 42/632.

could be made.[1] Obviously there was no possibility of a complete transfer of the defence burden to Canada. But as the War Office made clear when it approved the defence commission, a new attempt was now going to be made to unload a substantial part of it. The commission was to confine itself to the principal strategic positions and to bear in mind that the execution of its recommendations must 'in the main' be a matter for the consideration of the provincial authorities.[2]

Promising though the circumstances now seemed to be, London was soon to be disappointed. The militia commission reported on 15 March recommending an active trained force of 50,000 and a reserve of another 50,000 and in May a bill to provide these forces was introduced in the provincial legislature. But on 20 May the bill was thrown out and the next day the government resigned. Its successor in June conceded only the amendment of the 1859 act so as to augment the *paid* volunteer force to not more than 10,000. By the beginning of 1863, there were still only about 18,000 volunteers in all. In England press and parliament alike gave themselves up in the summer of 1862 to an orgy of anti-colonial outrage. Even the government only narrowly kept its head. Newcastle confessed that he was strongly tempted to take reprisals for the provincial legislature's 'reprehensible and provoking' conduct.[3] But he agreed with Monck that defence was too serious a matter for such squabbling and decided to set a better example by acceding to the governor-general's request for new arms and guns for the militia. He followed this up towards the end of August 1862, however, with a stern despatch, condemning the feeble defence policy of the Canadian government and expressing the hope that something better might be done before the winter passed.[4]

The only response to Newcastle's firm rebuke was an equally firm rejection from the Canadians at the end of October.[5] Before this there had come another disappointment for the government in London, and this time from their own experts in Canada. Mills's resolution and Burgoyne's memoranda had both agreed that Canada's external defence must still be shared between the home and colonial governments.

[1] Burgoyne's 'Memorandum of General Instructions for the Commission to report on the Defence of Canada', 24 Feb. 1862, and 'Memorandum by Sir John Burgoyne on the Defence of Canada—[15] Feb. 1862', printed as appendices 1 and 2 of the 'Report of the Commissioners appointed to consider the Defences of Canada, 1862', W.O. 33/11.
[2] W.O. to Williams, 15 Feb. 1862, and W.O. to C.O., 22 Feb. 1862, C.O. 42/636.
[3] Minute of 28 June 1862 on Monck to C.O., no. 96, 10 June 1862, C.O. 42/634.
[4] Stacey, pp. 130–46.   [5] *Ibid.*, p. 144.

But how far either government was likely to secure the necessary funds would depend on the amount involved. On 1 September 1862 came the defence commission's report and, in it, recommendations of an expenditure all too reminiscent of the ill-fated schemes supported by the duke of Wellington. It was not surprising that they should have recommended a minimum defence force of 150,000 and have insisted on the necessity of the Canadians also enlarging the canals so as to admit Britain's armoured gunboats on to Lakes Ontario and Erie. But the proposed expenditure of £1,611,000 on fortifications, not including the cost of armament, nor apparently of the land required, was too much.[1]

That the government would be peculiarly unwilling to receive such expensive recommendations they had already made clear in the instructions the colonial secretary had given in the meantime to his 'Defence Committee' – a more or less permanent committee of departmental experts. Following upon the Mills resolution of March, Lewis had ordered the committee to meet with his under-secretary, de Grey, and with the under-secretary of the Colonial Office, and report which of the colonies, apart from Gibraltar and Malta, should have their defences improved and which should have them abandoned or turned over to the local government. They were, moreover, to confine their report to existing positions since the secretary of state was not prepared to entertain plans for entirely new works. Deliberately excluding places of purely local importance, the committee limited its report to what were now conventionally known as imperial forts. These they defined as: places essential to the empire for their commanding positions on the globe or in relation to other countries, like the Mediterranean bases, Halifax, and Bermuda; bases for the command of strategic routes, like the Cape, Mauritius, and Hong Kong; and places of rendezvous for the fleet, as in the West Indies and at Trincomalee. The principal method of promoting efficiency and economy was to be concentration, and so far as the American theatre was concerned considerable reductions were to be achieved in the process. In the two West Indian commands, they found, the resources of defence were still wastefully scattered. Port Royal, Jamaica, they proposed to keep up as 'a secure and spacious harbour, containing a dockyard with extensive store-houses, and a naval hospital'. The Bahamas had some importance in their position at the entrance to the Gulf of Mexico. Barbados and

---

[1] 'Report of the Commissioners appointed to consider the Defences of Canada, [1 Sept.] 1862', confidential print, W.O. 33/11. See also Stacey, pp. 147–8.

Antigua, as seats of government and as additional coal and supply stations, also deserved to be defended against predatory raids. But elsewhere, and even at St Lucia, they recommended that the defences should be altogether abandoned. In view of the investigations then being made by the Canadian defence commission they made no detailed reference to that colony, but in the Maritimes, apart from the works at St John, New Brunswick, the coal mines at Sydney, and a few coastal batteries for St Johns, Newfoundland, they recommended that everything should be abandoned, including Windsor, Annapolis, and even St Andrews as being too close to the United States border.[1]

These were all rather ruthless reductions; even so they promised some not inconsiderable expenditure, since the committee found that most of the works to be retained would need a good deal of attention before they could be deemed secure. Milne had commented adversely on most of them early in the Civil War.[2] And during the *Trent* crisis he had reported so adversely once again on Bermuda that even Somerset readily admitted it deserved the government's special attention.[3] Milne had found that Wellington's old defence scheme of 1826–27 was still not completed. At the end of 1861 there were only one regiment of infantry and a hundred artillerymen on the islands, and so few were the works of defence on land that he had to station several gunboats and launches in position to defend the channels. And though there was a plentiful variety of guns, many of them were old and of inferior calibre. Even so when fired in practice their reverberations had had an alarming effect on the soft stone works of the forts. In the absence of the British fleet, indeed, an attacking force might only have to approach to tempt the fire of the defending guns and see the fortifications reduced to rubble without itself firing a shot.[4] General Doyle, who commanded the military forces in Nova Scotia, could report no better impression when he visited Bermuda a few months later in April 1862. He confirmed the weakness of the stone, pointed to some further gaps in the works of defence, and complained of the unusual drunkenness among the infantry thanks to their idleness and the plentiful supply of cheap liquor.[5] In August the Defence Committee agreed that

[1] Confidentially printed report of the Defence Committee, 6 Aug. 1862, C.O. 323/264. The copy in W.O. 33/11 appears under what is presumably the date of a later printing, 8 Jan. 1863.

[2] Milne to Admiralty, secret, 27 June 1861, Adm. 1/5759.

[3] Somerset to Milne, private, 25 Jan. 1862, Milne papers, 107/1, National Maritime Museum, Greenwich.

[4] Milne to Adm., confidential, no. 640, 31 Dec. 1861, Adm. 1/5787.

[5] Doyle to Cambridge, private, 20 April 1862, Cambridge papers, Royal Archives, Windsor.

Bermuda did indeed require new or modified works – but so too did Port Royal, Antigua, and the Bahamas; Halifax needed some improvements to its outlying defences; and the works at the Sydney coal mines were in a 'ruinous state'.[1]

In spite of the circumstances in which they held their investigations, the committee clearly envisaged a considerable expenditure on works of defence. That such expenditure was necessary was further underlined in a memorandum in which Burgoyne criticized at length the narrow limitations of their instructions, complained of the tendency to rely too much on naval power, and urged particular attention to the bases at Mauritius and Bermuda.[2] The committee itself had not only acknowledged the importance of Bermuda and Halifax as great naval stations, but in spite of the general omission of Canada, had also gone on to stress the importance of maintaining Quebec as a first class fortress through which 'all succours from Great Britain to Canada must pass'.

Since Quebec was still considered the 'imperial' key to the defence of Canada, and since its defences had nevertheless been found to be utterly incapable of withstanding a sustained bombardment by modern artillery, the cabinet turned to consider the problem, separately and even before they had officially received the report of the Canadian Defence Commission. In a paper for the cabinet dated 28 November 1862, de Grey pointed out that for the security of British forces in Canada the matter was of urgent and vital importance. Without the large number of militia thought necessary, the regulars were too few to defend the province; but at the same time too many to be safely sheltered in the present condition of Quebec. Newcastle conceded that the security of Quebec certainly was an *imperial* necessity; but neither Gladstone nor Somerset was much inclined to acquiesce. Gladstone bluntly recorded his opinion that the House of Commons would not vote the money; Somerset pointed out that it was also bad policy to treat Quebec in isolation from the general question of Canadian defence. What the commissioners implied by the Quebec recommendations, the first lord concluded, was the reconquest of Canada from 'a *tête de pont* on the other side of the Atlantic . . . a task, which we could not accomplish except at a cost far beyond its value'. For his part he favoured 'a very different system'. He did not, however, explain what that 'system' was. It was as usual the prime minister's melancholy duty to point out to the cabinet the damage which Canada's loss would do to British

---

[1] Confidentially printed report of the Defence Committee, 6 Aug. 1862, C.O. 323/264.   [2] 30 Sept. 1862, *ibid.*

prestige and to remind them that 'reputation is strength'. The matter ought at least to be referred to a select committee of the House, he concluded, lest the neglect lead ultimately to disaster and the government be blamed for not even having tried to obtain the money: 'I can imagine Dizzy and Derby trampling on our necks on such a topic.'[1] Palmerston continued to plead the danger from the Americans, and Lewis agreed that a decision on Quebec at least was urgently necessary. Evidently they failed to persuade the rest of the cabinet to acquiesce even in a compromise scheme by which parliament was to be asked at first only for four annual instalments of £50,000 each to carry out the improvements recommended for Quebec. Instead the whole report of the commissioners seems to have been rejected as both too ambiguous and too expensive, and yet another investigation ordered to be carried out by Burgoyne's deputy, Lt.-Col. W. F. D. Jervois.[2]

Jervois's report, which came in at last in February 1864, appeared to propose a very much more modest expenditure. Arguing that it was useless to attempt to defend western Canada without command of the lakes, he confined himself to suggesting that the small forces available should be concentrated for the defence of the principal strategic positions commanding communications with Great Britain, namely Montreal and Quebec. If this were done and the fortifications of these two places improved, he believed that the St Lawrence valley could be successfully held until the arrival of reinforcements from England. The total cost of the fortifications, exclusive of armament, he estimated at £200,000 for Quebec and £450,000 for Montreal.[3]

Withdrawal, concentration, and limited fortification – these were welcome expressions in so optimistic a report. In April both the commander-in-chief, Cambridge, and de Grey, who had succeeded Lewis at the War Office in April 1863, recorded their approval and the latter successfully pressed upon the prime minister and upon Cardwell, who now replaced Newcastle as colonial secretary, a scheme by which

[1] 'Memorandum on the Defence of Canada by Lord de Grey', 28 Nov. 1862, together with minutes by Somerset, Gladstone, Newcastle, and Palmerston, 1–2 Dec. 1862, Lewis papers, National Library of Wales, Aberystwyth, 2994 and 2937–40.

[2] Lewis to Palmerston, 26 and 30 Dec., and Palmerston to Lewis, 31 Dec. 1862, Broadlands papers; Palmerston to de Grey, 7 Sept. 1863, Ripon papers, B.M.Add.MS.43,512; Cambridge to de Grey, 7 Jan. 1865, C.O. 42/651.

[3] 'Report on the Defence of Canada and of the British Naval Stations in the Atlantic, by Lt. Col. Jervois . . . Pt. I, Defence of Canada', War Office, Feb. 1864, confidential W.O. print, P[ublic] A[rchives of] C[anada], R[ecord] G[roup] 8, Series II, vol. 20. I have not been able to find a copy of this report in the Public Record Office in London. See also Stacey, pp. 161–2.

Canada should see to the works at Montreal while the United Kingdom looked to those at Quebec.[1]

In pleasant anticipation of success the War Office began at once to reduce the regular force in Canada, pleading economy and 'concentration' as well as the threatening outlook of the Schleswig-Holstein question. The consequent withdrawal of two battalions of Guards and a battalion of military trains reduced the force in Canada to 8,200. Cambridge put up no resistance to the withdrawal of the Guards, 'who found colonial duty tedious', and Williams asked only to be allowed to keep a force at Kingston. Monck protested that concentration was unnecessary in peacetime and, in the event of war, could be rapidly achieved within a week. Hartington, the under-secretary at the War Office, however, doubted if the interior communications were secure enough from American attack, and on 12 July Cardwell ordered that the principle of concentration must be rigidly adhered to, with the temporary exception of a unit at Toronto for the instruction of militia officers.[2] This was in acknowledgement of some recent progress with the militia. In the previous summer new laws had been passed providing for their better organization and training, and authorizing an increase in the number of volunteers up to 35,000. Very much larger sums were voted for the militia, and what is more some $15,000 for the Matapedia road. By the summer of 1864 the effective force of volunteers had risen to nearly 22,000 and though there were serious difficulties with the reorganization of the first line of the ordinary militia, two military schools for the training of officers had at last been opened.[3] In these circumstances Cardwell's gesture, temporarily exempting Toronto alone from the orders for concentration, seemed peculiarly mean. As the news got about protests began to pour in from Canada and they were joined now by complaints from Cambridge too. Much was made of the depressing effect which withdrawal under the guise of 'concentration' would probably have upon Canadian opinion and Canada's efforts to improve the militia. But what was probably much more effective was Cambridge's observation that immediate concentration, by requiring new accommodation at Montreal and Quebec, might actually increase

[1] 'The Duke of Cambridge's Observations on Col. Jervois's Report on the Defence of Canada', April 1864, C.O. 42/646; de Grey to Cardwell, 14 April 1864, and Cardwell to de Grey, 19 April 1864, Ripon papers, B.M.Add.MS. 43,551.
[2] Cambridge to the queen, 22 May 1864, Queen Victoria's papers, R[oyal] A[rchives, Windsor], E14/95; W.O. to Williams, 25 May 1864, Williams to W.O., 13 June, Monck to Cardwell, confidential, 16 June, and Cardwell to Monck, 19 July, Stacey, pp. 155-7. [3] Stacey, pp. 149-51.

expenditure. At length, at the end of September, it was decided that the question would have to be put to the cabinet. In the end only one station, London, was evacuated, and soon that too was reoccupied in order to set up a military school.[1]

In the meantime little progress had been made with a general plan of Canadian defence and the apportionment of costs between the two governments. The cabinet could not even agree among themselves quite what proposal they should make to Canada. They were united only in the conviction that they could not persist in the existing situation, where, as Cardwell put it, '8,000 British troops are left incapable of defending themselves, a temptation to the Federals to attack Canada; no protection but the very opposite'.[2] Gladstone even cast doubt upon Jervois's report as a whole. The 1862 commissioners, he pointed out, had spent seven months preparing their report. It had made no provision for the frontier of New Brunswick or that west of Lake Huron, but for the line from that lake to the mouth of the St Lawrence their plan seemed to him to provide a 'real system of defence', though at what, in spite of their own figures, he reckoned would amount to a real cost of between £6 and £8 million. Now, however, there had come this new report of Jervois's after only three or four weeks in Canada and completely differing from the earlier one without adequate explanation. In the first place, he doubted if they could make Quebec secure even if they spent £400,000, let alone £200,000. Its security ultimately depended on control of the St Lawrence and this Gladstone doubted they could ensure. The Americans had recently demonstrated their ability to build large numbers of ironclads and in spite of their poor sailing qualities these could infiltrate the St Lawrence in overwhelming numbers. Certainly neither report had shown *how* to command the St Lawrence; each had merely assumed it. If even the lower part of the river were insecure the proper place for a retreat would be not Montreal or Quebec, but Halifax! In any case these so-called plans of 'concentration' were not really plans of Canadian defence; a plan which proposed to abandon to the enemy the whole of central and western Canada could hardly be called that!

Looked at in this way Jervois's plan, which was not supported by sufficient military authority, merely demonstrated the unwisdom of

[1] Cambridge to de Grey, 9 Sept. 1864, Col. W. Verner and Capt. E. D. Parker, *The Military Life of H.R.H. George, Duke of Cambridge* (2 vols., London, 1905), i. 360–1; de Grey to Cambridge, 30 Sept. 1864, Cambridge papers; Stacey, p. 160.

[2] Cardwell to Somerset, 11 July 1864, Somerset papers, County Record Office, Aylesbury, Buckinghamshire.

utterly separating the question of Quebec from a general plan of defence. Quebec, it was true, did have to be looked at from the special position of an imperial fortress; but the general defence of Canada still remained an open question and should be examined once again. There was, after all, no hurry: the works recommended for Quebec would take at least five years to complete and since they could not be begun until the spring they had at least the interval of about nine months in which to go over the whole question more carefully. Both Canadian opinion and the British parliament should be given a reasonable opportunity in which to make their views known. Gladstone himself was in general opposed to spending large sums of money on the construction and maintenance of systems of fortification. He doubted if Canada were suitable for the kind of defensive system so favoured by the prime minister. He did not think they ought really to be making any plan at all in this particular case, since it must necessarily have the effect of committing the mother country to at least a limited degree of aid to the colony, and, more probably, to an unlimited amount. 'Concentration' would be no solution in the case of such a vast frontier with an over-whelmingly powerful neighbour. Relief for the British taxpayer would lie, not in that device, but rather in encouraging the inhabitants' own efforts, and the only security for Canada in so organizing and developing the militia that they might usefully act in concert with a force of British regulars, not cooped up in fortresses but actively engaged in the field. Even if it were considered necessary to embark upon some scheme of expensive fortifications, care should be taken to ensure that if Great Britain was committed to the expense at Quebec, then Canada was firmly bound to bear that for Montreal. As an approach to such a bargain, Jervois's plan to abandon most of the province was hardly tempting bait! All in all it would be best to wait, and in particular, upon the outcome of the discussions about the confederation of British North America.[1]

The idea of a union of the various colonies of British North America was nothing new; nor was the assumption that it would benefit defence, especially by promoting the construction of an intercolonial railway and closing the strategic gap in the overland winter route between Halifax and Quebec.[2] The *Trent* incident in particular had drawn

[1] Gladstone's printed memorandum on the 'Defence of Canada', 12 July 1864, Gladstone papers, B.M.Add.MS.44,599.

[2] For a convenient and brief review of the considerable literature on this subject see Robin W. Winks, *Canada and the United States: The Civil War Years* (Baltimore, 1960), pp. 338–9.

attention to the need for united defence and in the early 1860s pressure for it mounted both in Britain and in Canada. For a while the parochialism of colonial politics continued to obstruct all progress, but at length, encouraged by the danger from the south, the inhabitants began to respond in a really positive manner and in June 1864 came a new coalition government, headed by John A. Macdonald and dedicated to the task of confederation. With an intercolonial conference due to meet in September Gladstone's pleas for delay, if not for an immediate decision about cutting down the mother country's defence burden, had much to recommend them. His first objective when the cabinet met to discuss the question towards the end of July was, as he put it, to 'shift the centre of responsibility' for the defence of Canada. Having failed in this he concentrated on getting the cabinet to refrain from making any premature or unilateral commitment before the Canadians had stated what they were prepared to do or before they had got a new report looking this time at the crucial questions of naval strategy on the lakes and in the St. Lawrence.[1] Cardwell, the colonial secretary, put forward a rather different point of view. Had there been no garrisons at present in Canada, he would have had no hesitation in saying to that colony 'no troops of ours shall go to you, till you have built suitable fortifications'. But the British troops were already there, and there were accordingly but two possible courses of action: to withdraw them or take immediate measures to put them in a defensible position. The cabinet did not propose a withdrawal and he did not see how they were to secure any progress with fortifications without putting up specific proposals to the Canadians.[2] Between these opposing views the cabinet found it so difficult to compromise that they could not agree after their first meeting quite which view it was which had prevailed.[3]

At the end of July Cardwell circulated among the cabinet the draft of the despatch he proposed to send to Canada, and this, after considerable amendment in the direction Gladstone desired, went out on 6 August. Here Cardwell's final paragraph proposing the bargain by which Quebec should be strengthened at imperial expense while Canada undertook to see to Montreal was struck out and in its place was put at Russell's suggestion a proposal to hold joint consultations. And Gladstone seemed to have still more of his way in that it was specifically stated that the government must know first how much

[1] Gladstone to Cardwell, 25 July 1864, Gladstone papers, B.M.Add.MS, 44,118.   [2] Cardwell to Gladstone, 27 July 1864, *ibid.*
[3] Gladstone to Argyll, 27 July, and Argyll to Gladstone, 28 July 1864, Gladstone papers, B.M.Add.MS.44,099.

Canada was prepared to spend before themselves approaching Westminster with a scheme requiring further imperial defence expenditure.
Reference was also made to the Canadians widening the scope of their
preliminary investigations of the defence problems, including what
Gladstone had urged in particular – the question of naval means.[1] Thus
was the 'whole subject of defence', as Gladstone later put it, once again
opened up.[2] But his victory was more ambiguous than it looked.
Palmerston insisted that these naval questions were not to delay the
measures necessary for Quebec; Jervois's supposedly objectionable
report was enclosed with the despatch for the guidance of the Canadian
government; and the man chosen to make the new report Gladstone
insisted upon and to advise the Canadians on their reply was Jervois
himself.[3]

Jervois left England for Canada on 3 September 1864. On 10 October
the conference of colonial delegates met at Quebec to consider the
federation of British North America. Preoccupied to some extent as the
conference was with the defence problem, the Canadian ministers soon
presented a series of question to Jervois. On 10 November came his
second report on the defence of Canada, this time addressed formally
to the provincial government of Canada.[4] In stressing once again the
importance of Quebec and Montreal, Jervois naturally followed the
gist of his first report, but this time at the specific request of the
Canadians he did extend his recommendations, as Gladstone had
desired, to the general defence of the country and the contribution
needed from naval means. In this more general context Quebec became
now not merely a place of retreat, but a refuge for the forces who were
to form the nucleus of great offensive armies expanded by reinforcements
from Great Britain and by militia from the surrounding country. And
this time Canada's cooperation in the militia's peacetime training and
equipment and their organization and concentration in wartime were
to be better ensured by extending the commitment of the regular army

[1] Cardwell to Monck, confidential, 6 Aug. 1864, Stacey, pp. 160–1. A copy
of Cardwell's draft, printed confidentially for the cabinet, together with minutes
by Russell, Gladstone, and Palmerston, is in the Russell papers, P.R.O. 30/22/27.
[2] Note by Gladstone, 27 May 1865, Gladstone papers, B.M.Add.MS.44,603.
[3] De Grey to Jervois, 30 Aug. 1864, C.O. 42/646.
[4] Stacey, pp. 165–6. On 16 January 1865 Jervois submitted the report to the
secretary of state for war and it was incorporated in a War Office confidential
print, 'Report on the Defence of Canada (made to the Provincial Government
on 10th November 1864), and of the British Naval Stations in the North
Atlantic; together with observations on the Defence of New Brunswick, etc.',
January 1865, W.O. 33/15. Jervois's covering letter of [16] January, summarizing
his recommendations, was published in *British Parliamentary Papers*, 1865,
xxxvii [3434].

even to the western districts of Upper Canada. For this, Jervois now expressly acknowledged, the improvement of water communications and a real naval effort on the lakes were fundamental necessities, as indeed was also the control of the St Lawrence and its approach by sea for access to both Quebec and Montreal. The expenditure he recommended therefore rose well above that of his earlier report which had been limited to Quebec and Montreal, and even above that of the 1862 defence commission which had not included figures for the cost of land for new works or of any naval measures. Jervois's new figure of £1,754,000 was not unreasonable, including as it did the costs of land and armaments for the new works at Quebec and Montreal, the naval base at Kingston, places of refuge for the militia at Toronto and Hamilton, and, not least, some £300,000 for gunboats to act on the St Lawrence and the lakes. Moreover, while his estimate for works at Quebec remained unchanged at £200,000 plus a sum for armament, the chances of getting the Canadians themselves to undertake the rest seemed more promising than ever. After all the extension of the report to cover the western districts and to include a force of gunboats had been made at their express request.

In the autumn and winter of 1864 came a new series of border scares, culminating in the St Albans raid of 19 October and followed by awful rumours about the sinister activities of the militant Irish-American 'Fenian Brotherhood'. Moreover during the past year the Americans had had to take so many measures on the lakes that in September they had admitted that the lakes agreement was in virtual suspense.[1] Now there came American notice to terminate both the Reciprocity and the Rush-Bagot agreements. In these dangerous and deteriorating circumstances, the Canadians responded by authorizing Monck on 16 November to reply formally to Cardwell's despatch of the previous August. In this reply there were still evasive references to imperial responsibility and some procrastination in suggesting that the principles of federation must be decided first, but it did at least admit the importance of taking a number of precautions at once. The Canadians offered to seek a vote for the works at Montreal as well as $1 million for the militia, if Great Britain saw to Quebec, supplied the armament for both, and guaranteed a Canadian loan.[2]

Armed with a reply from Canada which seemed to commit that colony to a defence expenditure of nearly half a million pounds on

[1] Stacey, pp. 163–5; J. M. Callahan, *The Neutrality of the American Lakes and Anglo-American Relations* (Baltimore, 1898), pp. 145–58; Winks, p. 293.
[2] Monck to Cardwell, confidential, 16 Nov. 1864, Stacey, pp. 167–8.

Montreal and a million dollars on the militia, and with a series of supposedly expert reports, the cabinet in December once again got down to making a decision on their defence policy in North America. At last, it seemed, they might be able to make informed decisions not only about the contributions to fortification but also about the policy of 'concentration' which they had tacitly suspended.[1] But while the Colonial Office had been laboriously collecting papers for the cabinet's confidential print of 10 December, events had not stood still in either Europe or America. The summer of 1863 had brought the ill-concerted interference of the powers in the Polish revolt, and, still worse, the following summer witnessed the collapse of the London conference on the Schleswig-Holstein question. By the end of 1864 it was clear that Anglo-French collaboration was too weak and fragile to cope with Bismarck's challenge to the *status quo* in Europe. And while this new threat arose to the balance of power in Europe, the war in America too was at last approaching its end. First in July 1863 Union victories at Gettysburg and Vicksburg had belatedly thrown the Confederates on the defensive, and now, at the end of 1864, Grant's and Sherman's armies were fast advancing from the north and south to squeeze the Confederacy into final submission.

During 1864, and by the early winter at the latest, it was clear enough even to the most diehard Southern sympathizers in Britain that the Union was going to win. The government therefore now understood that the end of the war would bring, not the relieving prospect of a permanent disunion among the States, but more probably a day of reckoning for all the damage and insults which the Union believed it had suffered at the hands of Great Britain's supposedly unfriendly and even malicious neutrality. Many must have begun to think, as surely Gladstone really did, that so overwhelming was the strength displayed in the American war that Britain had better give up at once all serious idea of resisting the United States by force and instead by diplomacy promote a circumspect improvement in Anglo-American relations. A few, out of fear of that same power, suggested that they should save themselves and their colonies by declaring war while the South still managed to divide the enemy's strength. One who thought there was a good deal to be said for a preventative war against the North was Lieutenant-General Charles Grey, the queen's acting private secretary.

---

[1] 'The Defences of Canada', Colonial Office confidential print for the cabinet, 10 Dec. 1864, in two parts: (i) 'Defence of Canada'; and (ii) 'Question of Keeping a Force in the Western Districts of Canada', C.O. 880/6, no. 44.

Fortunately, and in spite of his influential position at court and the eminence of so many of his relations, Grey made no headway in the face of moral indignation at the thought of contrived association with the slave-tainted South and the memory of the recent collapse of Britain's attempt to present another 'bold front' over Schleswig-Holstein.[1]

To the majority of the cabinet neither immediate withdrawal nor immediate war was an acceptable retort to the progress of the Civil War. This was not in the least due to ignorance of the development of American strength. The Civil War may never have 'exerted a marked influence upon military practices in Europe', and attention there was soon absorbed in Prussia's lightning victories; but this is not to say that the war in America did not attract a stream of visitors from England, official and unofficial, amateur and professional.[2] The official reports made by British officers in particular were preoccupied with technical developments which for the most part were deemed merely to have confirmed the results of experiments carried out at home. But whatever their professional shortcomings these and others supplied the government in London with a wealth of information, especially after the *Trent* crisis had drawn so many experienced and enterprising officers to North America.

In May 1862 General Williams sent out three officers from Canada to inspect the Union army's artillery, and a copy of their report was naturally lodged with the War Office in London.[3] In the autumn an engineer officer, Captain Edward Hewett, and Garnet Wolseley, then on the staff in Canada, went out to have a private look at the two armies.[4] In 1865 Major-General Sir Hastings Doyle, commanding the British forces in Nova Scotia, visited the siege of Richmond, and on his several official visits to North America, Jervois had a close look at American developments in the autumn of 1863 and again in 1865.[5] The principal official report on American military affairs, however, was the one made by two officers, Lt.-Col. Gallwey, R.E., and Captain Alderson, R.A., who had been sent out from London in January

---

[1] Lt.-Gen. Charles Grey to Cardwell, 9 Feb. 1865, Queen Victoria's papers, R.A. Q10/20. Grey wrote again on 13 Feb. (Q10/22), and Cardwell replied on 11 and 26 Feb. (Q10/21 and 35).
[2] Jay Luvaas, *The Military Legacy of the Civil War* (Chicago, 1959), p. 226. Chapter 2 of this book gives a convenient summary of many of these reports and commentaries, both official and unofficial.
[3] Report of Captain Mahon, R.A., Captain Grant, R.E., and Lt. Price, R.A., 1 Aug. 1862, confidential print, W.O. 33/11. See also Luvaas, pp. 23–6.
[4] Luvaas, pp. 26–8 and 46–51.   [5] *Ibid.*, pp. 29–31.

1864.[1] Their report was, like most of the others, principally a technical one, but at the same time Gallwey also prepared a special report in answer to Lord Lyons's enquiries about probable United States operations in the event of war with Great Britain.[2]

Generally speaking these reports and commentaries were not by any means grudging in the respect they accorded to American efforts. This was especially the case with the Americans' technological ingenuity, but even the conscript and volunteer infantry no longer aroused anything like such general contempt as had been the case not long before. Still, in quality of men and material alike, British observers were almost universally convinced of the continuing superiority of their own nation. They could not ignore the existence of such vast numbers of experienced and battle-trained soldiers; but then for a long time now they had expected an almost overwhelming descent of hordes of militia upon the Canadian border. And just as some had nevertheless professed a somewhat optimistic attitude, so now even Gallwey talked in his report to Lyons of frustrating their advance by seizing Rouse's Point with 5,000 men at the very outset of war. A particularly close watch was kept on any American preparations along this frontier. For some mysterious purpose of his own Seward had issued two circulars in the autumn of 1861 recommending the governors of the Northern lake and seaboard states to place their ports and harbours in a state of defence.[3] However, early in February 1862, when the chief of the intelligence department in Canada had toured the frontier west of Lake Ontario, the American defences seemed to him to be in a feeble state. At Buffalo he found the guns had gone and the garrison of 1,100 men a poor lot, composed in the main of raw recruits and even paroled Confederate prisoners. In and around Detroit there were only a hundred Union soldiers, and the guns were few and the defences neglected.

I feel justified in submitting most respectfully the fact from personal observation and from information derived from reliable quarters [he concluded] that there is an entire absence of all preparations for constructing or repairing fortifications from . . . Sault Ste Marie to . . . Niagara, inclusive of Mackinac and the Straits of Lake Michigan; the arsenals have either been removed from their positions for active service at a distance, or pronounced worthless with a few exceptions, and as for

[1] 'Report upon the Military Affairs of the United States of America, by Lt. Col. T. L. Gallwey, R.E., and Captain H. J. Alderson, R.A.', 24 Aug. 1864, confidential print, W.O. 33/14. The report is conveniently summarized in Luvaas, pp. 34–43.
[2] Gallwey to Lyons, 27 May 1864, enclosed in Lyons to F.O., no. 467, F.O. 5/954. [3] Winks, pp. 66–8.

small arms I am confident that 5,000 effective rifles and muskets together could not just now be mustered within the same extent of frontier.[1]

From this low point at the turn of 1861–62, the Union promised as a result of the *Trent* affair to make some better effort to meet the constant dangers from her relations with her neighbour to the north. The secretary of war recommended in his 1861 report to the president that they should give immediate attention to the defences on the lakes, and in his Annual Message Lincoln, though not referring specifically to the *Trent* crisis, had supported Seward's circulars and also recommended improvements on the frontier.[2] Soon afterwards the House of Representatives took up both the questions of lake defence and new canal projects. On 12 February 1862 a select committee reported recommending the construction of new forts and depôts on the lakes and the widening of the Illinois and Michigan Ship Canal. Various canal schemes were brought before Congress in 1862 and 1863 but they were all too clearly more concerned with private profit than national defence and none of them made any progress.

The few minor precautions the Americans took on the northern frontier during the war therefore were hardly of a kind to have alarmed the British. The better informed reports from America merely confirmed the wisdom of the established policy of caution and concentration in Canada. Rather more worrying was the growth of the American navy, for this threatened to undermine the offensive strategy which the British had hitherto so confidently expected to employ at sea.

The Admiralty in London were supplied with plentiful information about American naval developments from officers serving on the North American station and, through the Foreign Office, from British diplomatic and consular officials on the mainland. But by the spring of 1863 at the latest they began to talk of sending out an officer specially to the United States. At that time the foreign secretary advised against the proposal because 'in their present mood' the Americans 'might obstruct and even display hostility'.[3] But at the end of the year a senior naval officer, Captain James G. Goodenough, was sent out to do for the Admiralty what Gallwey and Alderson were about to do for the War Office. Goodenough spent six months in the United States between December 1863 and May 1864, visiting some of the arsenals in the interior as well as the naval yards on the Atlantic coast and making a

---

[1] Thomas Worthington to Captain R. Rollo (the governor-general's military secretary), 14 Feb. 1862, enclosed in W.O. to C.O., [?] March 1862, C.O. 42/636.
[2] Winks, pp. 75–6 and 121–5; Callahan, pp. 140–4.
[3] Russell to Somerset, 6 April 1863, Somerset papers.

series of reports as he went.[1] His reports soon confirmed Lyons's 'impression that the Americans are very seriously preparing for a Foreign War', and the minister suggested that it would be wise to have officers come as something like regular naval and military attachés at the legation, though not in the sort of permanent capacity that would reduce their reports to mere routine.[2] In March 1865 the first regular naval attaché was appointed to Washington, making, after Commodore Hore's in Paris, only the second such post in British service. The officer chosen was Captain Bythesea, V.C., who, appropriately enough, had been the naval member of the Canadian Defence Commission of 1862. Bythesea stayed on until May 1867 and in October 1868 was followed by Captain the Honourable W. J. Ward.[3]

Beginning in late 1863, then, the British government made very special arrangements to watch the progress of the Union navy. It is easily apparent why they should have done so. When the Civil War began the entire United States Navy fit for active service consisted of a mere thirty old sailing vessels, and, in addition to a few under construction, about a dozen new steam cruisers, very heavily armed but utterly without armour. But though some of these fell at once into the hands of the Confederacy, the North, by a most impressive display of energy and ingenuity in conversion and construction, had afloat and building by the end of 1863 a fleet of no less than 588 vessels, three-quarters of them steam propelled and mounting some 4,443 guns, and in spite of losses these figures rose by the end of 1864 to 671 and 4,610 respectively. Most of these, it was true, were former merchant vessels, some of them very hastily and imperfectly converted, but by the end of the war in July 1865 the North had also managed to launch 85 wooden steam vessels and 39 ironclads with another 24 and 29 of each still building.[4]

---

[1] These periodic reports are in Adm. 1/5879, where there are also two consolidated papers, a 'Report on the guns and personnel of the American Navy', 12 April 1864, and a 'Report on the Ships of the United States Navy 1864'.

[2] Lyons to Russell, 19 April 1864, Newton, i. 128–9.

[3] 'Return of Military and Naval Attachés connected with Her Majesty's Diplomatic Service from 1860 to 1871', [C. 338] British Parliamentary Papers, 1871, xxxix. 437.

[4] H. and M. Sprout, The Rise of American Naval Power, 1776–1918 (Princeton, 1939), pp. 151–2; unsigned Admiralty paper, dated 20 Jan. 1865, and entitled 'U.S.N. Return of vessels afloat and building from the Report of the Secretary of the Navy, December 1864', Broadlands papers; and Capt. Bythesea's 'Remarks on the U.S.N.', 25 July 1865, enclosed in F.O. to Adm. 19 Aug., 1865, Adm. 1/5954.

On the British side too these were years of great naval reconstruction, and the fleet of 'Black Ships' that began with the launching of the *Warrior* in 1860, though never tested in battle, would certainly have been more than a match for the Union navy. But compared with the war-forced rate of the Americans, the rebuilding of the Royal Navy proceeded very slowly indeed. Often hastily improvised and even ramshackle though many of the American ships might be there were still from the British point of view periods of awkward disparity between the two fleets. The British were certainly worried for a time about pacing and overtaking the Americans in the production of armoured warships and about the relative merits of their armour and armour-piercing guns. In the spring and summer of 1862 Russell, among others, was warning that the United States might very well get the lead in numbers of ironclads within as little as six months, and to avoid another 1812 he was willing even to support new taxes if an acceleration in shipbuilding required it.[1] Thus the 1860s found the government comparing their ironclad navy as much with the American as with the French. Their investigations certainly exposed considerable discrepancies in the Americans' favour. At the very end of 1864 some seventy-one of the Union navy's 671 vessels building and afloat were ironclads, against a mere thirty in the British steam navy of 417.[2] But these anxieties were temporary and in the ultimate superiority of their new navy the British were justifiably confident.[3] This was true even in respect of the much-vaunted monitors. Of their first appearance in battle *The Times* coolly commented that the *Warrior* would have better done the work of both *Monitor and Merrimac*.[4] Nearer at hand there was rather more alarm, particularly from the governor of Vancouver Island and the Pacific naval commanders, who in 1862–64 reported rumours of the Federal government's intention to build or despatch a number of ironclad monitors for the defence of San Francisco and for possible offensive operations in the Columbia River and off the north-west coast.[5] Somerset was not unsympathetic but he was preoccupied with the problems of the Channel fleet, and soon it was confirmed how

[1] Russell to Palmerston, 31 Mar. 1862, Broadlands papers; Russell to Somerset, 25 and 26 Aug. 1862, Somerset papers.
[2] Unsigned Admiralty paper of 20 Jan. 1865, Broadlands papers, and Bythesea's report of 25 July 1865, Adm. 1/5954.
[3] See, for example, Palmerston to Somerset, 2 Oct. 1863, Somerset papers.
[4] *The Times*, 1 April 1862, quoted by J. P. Baxter, *The Introduction of the Ironclad Warship* (Cambridge, Mass., 1933), p. 313.
[5] Maitland to Adm., no. 235, 9 Aug. 1862, Adm. 1/5790; C.O. to Adm., 6 and 18 Mar. 1863, C.O. 43/129; Denman to Adm. no. 34, 19 Oct. 1864, Adm. 1/5878.

utterly unseaworthy were these American monitors.[1] The comptroller, Admiral Sir Robert Robinson, dismissed them as 'mere rafts'.[2] Even Palmerston, who was not inclined to quiet confidence on such matters, felt by September 1864 that Britain's floating batteries would be able to 'smash and sink the Monitors'.[3]

Much more serious in the British view, since it would probably be a permanent problem, was the threat of increased American commerce-raiding in any future war, in particular on Britain's vulnerable food supplies. The success of the *Alabama* was an ominous enough warning, and when looked at in the light of the North's impressive rate of shipbuilding and conversion it promised, as the prime minister put it, to threaten British sea-borne commerce with 'swarms' of fast and heavily armed if unarmoured American raiders.[4] This problem occupied the Admiralty's active attention to a degree second only to the ironclad race. Ultimately, when the war had ended, they began to build vessels specifically designed to catch and destroy the raiders which they feared so much.[5]

Serious though the commerce-raiding problem was – and it seems the Admiralty never produced an effective answer[6] – it was hardly anything new. Rather it confirmed and heightened the old impression that of all possible wars one with the United States would be perhaps the most damaging to Britain's wealth and the well-being of her people. Much more worrying for the strategists was the contribution made by the Civil War to the development of the United States local defences, on land and on sea; for these threatened to undermine the plan by which Great Britain hoped to compensate for her difficulties in Canada by a wholesale attack by sea upon the trade and cities of the Atlantic coast. Although relatively unseaworthy and therefore powerless to prevent a distant blockade, the American monitors and other craft threatened to realize at last the longstanding ambition of the United States to protect their coasts by large numbers of floating batteries. At the same time, under the stimulus of war and not a little too out of fear of British attacks such as were rumoured at the time of the *Trent* affair, the massive system of fortifications planned at the end of the War of

---

[1] Somerset to Newcastle, 11 Mar. 1863, Somerset papers.

[2] Robinson to Adm., 3 Jan. 1863, Adm. 1/5840.

[3] Palmerston to de Grey, 11 Sept. 1864, Palmerston letter-book, Broadlands papers.

[4] *Idem*, and Palmerston to Somerset, 6 Sept. 1864, Broadlands papers.

[5] See below, pp. 306–7.

[6] See Arthur J. Marder, *The Anatomy of British Sea Power: a History of British Naval Policy in the Pre-Dreadnought Era, 1880–1905* (New York, 1940), pp. 84–104.

1812 was being brought at last to what appeared to Gallwey and Alderson, for example, to be a state of almost utter impregnability so far as attacks by ships were concerned.[1]

Curiously enough, although this certainly confirmed the growing conviction of his immediate superior, General Burgoyne, that rifled artillery had now given land batteries a decisive advantage over warships, and although he was himself very impressed with what he saw of the American fortifications in 1863, Jervois nevertheless clung essentially to the strategy of offensive action against the Atlantic coast by fleets based upon Halifax and Bermuda. Something had been done about the condition of these bases since the adverse comments of Milne and Doyle at the turn of 1861–62. So worried indeed had Doyle been about the state of Halifax that in the spring of 1863 he had on his own authority ordered improvements to the tune of the £15,000 already voted, and so incurred the duke of Cambridge's pleasure but the War Office's disapproval.[2] The Sydney coal mines, too, received considerable attention during 1863 from Milne as well as Doyle.[3] But when he handed over his command to his successor, Admiral Sir James Hope, in March 1864, Milne had to report that the defences of Bermuda were still in a very unsatisfactory state and that although those at Halifax were being improved under the orders given by Doyle, that port too would still have to rely to a great extent upon the presence of the navy.[4] Jervois had visited both these places on his tour of North America in the autumn of 1863 and in February 1864 had already made a report on Bermuda recommending certain changes in the defences to meet the increased threats from ironclad steamers.[5] Now, in January 1865, he elaborated his recommendations on Bermuda, Halifax and the Maritime Provinces and added them as a second part to the War Office's copy of his revised and extended report on Canada.[6] So to Britain's share of £200,000 for

[1] Luvaas, p. 41.
[2] Doyle to Horse Guards, 22 Jan. 1863, W.O. 55/1558; Doyle to Cambridge, private, 30 April and 13 May 1863, Cambridge papers; Cambridge to de Grey, 28 May, and de Grey to Cambridge, 29 May 1863, Ripon papers, B.M.Add. MS.43,511.
[3] Milne to Adm., no. 407, 17 June 1863, forwarding a memo. by Doyle, 6 June, Adm. 1/5820; 'Confidential Report on the Defences of Sydney, Cape Breton', by Lt.-Cols. Westmouth and Clifford, 31 Oct. 1863, W.O. 55/1551 (9).
[4] Milne to Adm., no. 182, 15 Mar. 1864, Adm. 1/5871.
[5] 'Memoranda on the defences of Bermuda and Barbados', 4 Feb. 1864, by Lt.-Col. Jervois, enclosed in Hope to Adm., no. 44, 27 April 1864, Adm. 1/5872.
[6] 'Report on the Defence of Canada (made to the Provincial Government on 10 November 1864) and of the British Naval Stations in the North Atlantic; together with observations on the Defence of New Brunswick, etc.', by Lt.-Col. Jervois, confidential print, Jan. 1865, W.O. 33/15.

Quebec and further sums for armaments at both that place and Montreal, he now proposed to add £260,000 for Bermuda, and, in place of a mere £100,000 in the present parliamentary estimates for the Maritime Provinces, £180,000 for Halifax and £250,000 for St John, New Brunswick, St Johns, Newfoundland, and the Sydney coal mines. And lest the significance of all this be overlooked he commented:

Our proceedings [in Canada and New Brunswick] must necessarily be of a defensive rather than of an aggressive character. . . . Our Navy . . . must perform the principal part of bringing a war . . . to a successful issue. Our offensive operations should be, – the blockade of their sea-ports; the destruction of their commerce; and combined naval and military expeditions, directed, where practicable, against the naval establishments and other places of importance on their sea-board. To undertake and carry out such expeditions, we must have 'points d'appui' possessing good harbours for the fleet, where our naval and military forces may rendezvous in security, and whence they may act readily upon the enemy's shores.[1]

The Admiralty must have been pleased enough that the bases for their fleet were not by any means to be overlooked; but it soon became clear that, unlike Jervois, they did believe that the strategy of naval offensive against the United States had become seriously undermined. This came out clearly, if incidentally, in the careful consideration which they gave at last to the question of the naval defence of the Great Lakes and the St Lawrence after Gladstone had pressed for it in the previous summer and Jervois had obediently responded in his second report. Following upon the investigations he had made about the time of the *Trent* incident, Captain Hatt Noble, R.E., made another report to de Grey on the various canal schemes in April 1863. Milne had passed on his impressions to his successor, and Hope himself, Russell had suggested, should go off with Lyons and the governor-general, Monck, on an extended tour of the St Lawrence and the lakes in the late summer and autumn of 1864.[2] But in spite of all this activity there was still a good deal of disagreement and obscurity about the naval aspects of the interior defence of Canada.

---

[1] 'Report on the Defence of Canada (made to the Provincial Government on 10 November 1864) and of the British Naval Stations in the North Atlantic; together with observations on the Defence of New Brunswick, etc', by Lt.-Col. Jervois, confidential print, Jan. 1865, W.O. 33/35.
[2] Captain Noble to de Grey, 30 April 1863, P.A.C., R.G. 7 (Governor-General's Office), G 21, no. 165, vol. i; Milne to Adm., no. 182, 15 Mar. 1864, Adm. 1/5871; Russell to Lyons, private, 23 July 1864, Newton, i. 132–5. Neither Lyons's nor Monck's report of the tour has come to light, and probably Hope did not in the end join them. Instead he made another tour with the military commander in the summer of the following year (see below, p. 293).

There were, as Gladstone had pointed out, two distinct problems: the command of the lower St Lawrence and its estuary on the one hand, and of the upper part of the river and the lakes on the other. The first appears to have given comparatively little concern. Palmerston had no doubt that they would be able to send across the Atlantic large numbers of floating batteries, with their heavy guns being transported separately if necessary.[1] The more difficult question of the upper St Lawrence and the lakes, however, was still as far from a solution as ever – in spite of the sense of urgency inspired by the Americans' avowed intention of terminating the 1817 agreement and of putting two or three vessels on the lakes to counter Confederate raids.[2] The 1862 Defence Commission had referred continually to the absolute necessity of putting numbers of gunboats and other vessels upon the lakes. They had talked, as had so many others, of keeping vessels ready at Quebec or Montreal, but the success of these or any other schemes depended upon very extensive improvements to the dimensions and to the defences of the canals and locks. Jervois had skirted the problem in his first 1864 report but in the second he had proposed that to supplement locally converted steamers and to impede similar American efforts on Lake Ontario, a force of six armour-plated gunboats should be kept ready at hand for that lake; and that after some improvements to the canal locks gunboats could also be placed in the vicinity of Montreal. Precisely what description of vessel the British could hope to get through to the lakes was still not entirely clear, owing in part perhaps to continued disagreement about the capacity of the canals. But the local naval commanders, Milne and Hope, both seem to have believed that they could place some part of their force there. Milne even thought that, with some manipulation, he could get his eighty horsepower gunvessel, *Nimble*, up on to Lake Ontario.[3] There were also the usual schemes for opening up a better communication by river and canal direct from the St Lawrence to Georgian Bay on Lake Huron: the old scheme via Lake Simcoe and that advocated by both the 1862 Defence Commission and by Captain Noble as less expensive, by the Ottawa River, Lake Nipissing, and the French River.[4] The principal purpose of the Georgian Bay scheme was, of course, commercial – to capture the vast bulk of the trade of the mid-western states, and in

[1] Palmerston to Somerset, 6 and 11 Sept. 1864, Broadlands papers.
[2] Hope, private, to Somerset, 10 Nov. 1864, Somerset papers.
[3] Milne to Adm., no. 182, 15 Mar. 1864, Adm. 1/5871.
[4] 'Report, . . . [1 Sept.] 1862', W.O. 33/11; Noble to de Grey, 30 April 1863, P.A.C., R.G. 7, G 21, no. 165, vol. i.

particular the grain trade – but it would also have some large, and in some ways revolutionary, effects on the military situation too. For by such a canal a safe rear communication would be opened up to put a naval force on Lake Huron; and that force could then be used not only defensively to turn the flanks of an enemy advancing upon western and upper Canada, but also offensively upon the American shore of the lake. But it was still a longterm possibility. The critical question now was how far either side might be able to assemble a fleet in a war in the near future.

As the Erie canal was too small to be of much use for passing up gunboats, the Americans would have to rely on what they could build locally. Milne professed to believe that in the open season Britain could put vessels on the lakes faster than the Americans could build them.[1] But this seems to have disregarded both the limited capacity and the vulnerability of the Canadian canals, and the general opinion, particularly at the Admiralty, was far less optimistic. The Admiralty began an intensive investigation of the problem in December 1864, after the first lord had been presented with yet another warning memorandum, this time from the secretary, W. G. Romaine. With the Confederates trying to embroil Great Britain in the Civil War by their plots and raids from Canada, and with the Union responding by giving notice of the termination of the 1817 agreement and by preparing a large fleet of 'revenue' cruisers, he warned, clashes between Great Britain and the Americans were more likely than ever. He suggested therefore that the time had come for a full-scale review of the position on the lakes and the formation of a special naval command for the inland waters of North America.[2] Somerset was plainly not enthusiastic. 'This suggestion opens up a large question', he noted, ' – a new navy for the lakes of Canada under a new commander in chief. Such a plan could hardly be undertaken without the direct sanction of Parliament. Unless we are quite ready to carry it out the commencement would only mislead the Canadian government as to the extent of aid which this country would give them. Before anything can be done in this direction we must communicate with the Colonial Office.'[3] A few days later, however, Romaine's memorandum was sent to the comptroller for his expert advice; in the meantime Romaine busied himself with yet further papers suggesting how they might organize the proposed command and form a volunteer

[1] Milne to Adm., no. 182, 15 Mar. 1864, Adm. 1/5871.
[2] 'Canadian Defences. Memo. for the Duke of Somerset', initialled by Romaine, 30 Dec. 1864, filed under 9 Jan. 1865, Adm. 1/5931.
[3] Somerset's minute, 1 Jan. 1865, *ibid.*

naval reserve in Canada.[1] Then came the comptroller's report to dash his hopes. They might be able, Admiral Robinson conceded, to send out some of the new twin-screw armour-plated gunvessels they were building, but only in pieces for assembly at Quebec since these could not safely cross the Atlantic. The defence of the St Lawrence between Quebec and Montreal would therefore be quite practicable. But they must have no illusions about being able to challenge American superiority on the lakes. There the United States had an overall superiority of three to one in shipping and shipbuilding and once war had begun the British would not be able to redress the balance by pushing a force through the canals. They could, if they wished, send out parts in peacetime to the lakes for assembly after war had broken out. But he doubted if even that sort of hurried building could be successfully accomplished under the noses of the Americans' initial superiority. Apart from the lower St Lawrence, therefore, he was sure that whatever they did the Americans would still have a superiority of at least two to one on Lake Champlain as well as on the upper lakes. Worse still, he concluded gloomily, 'no one looking at these questions can forget that the naval force possessed by the United States for *defensive* purposes is four or five times larger than that of any European power, and that the possibility of making serious assaults by sea against any of their towns, is in consequence very limited indeed. It is clear that what was in 1861 is no longer so in 1865.'[2]

This highly significant observation clearly made its impression on Romaine. In a new paper he admitted:

The Northern States would suffer little material injury by hostilities with Great Britain. Her [*sic*] commerce has been much curtailed as far as the carrying trade goes, and ships bearing her mercantile flag are comparatively few. Her navy list shews that she has now 35 fast screw and paddle wheel vessels of the classes we call corvettes or sloops. If the war with the South was not concluded when her quarrel with this country began, her blockade of the Southern ports must necessarily cease, and these ships would with all other suitable ships be set free to destroy the commerce of Great Britain all over the world. Very little damage it is apprehended could be done by Great Britain to the coast towns of America by hostile operations. They are defended now by land fortifications and the war with the South has called into existence a large fleet of vessels adapted for the purposes of defence.

[1] Romaine to Robinson, 4 Jan., Romaine's untitled memorandum, 6 Jan., and his 'Naval Command in Canada–Volunteer Reserve', 9 Jan., 1865, Adm. 1/5931.
[2] Untitled memorandum initialled by Robinson, 9 Jan. 1865, *ibid.*

Nevertheless he thought that Britain had some considerable obligation to Canada and her other colonies to help in their defence and even Robinson had shown that much might be accomplished by preparation in advance of war.

It must be conceded [he went on], that in the present state of the military force of the two countries bordering the St Lawrence and the Lakes, it would be impossible to defend the whole territory of the British Provinces, but with due preparation and under able commanders certain positions on land and by water may probably be made impregnable. While such positions are held by a brave enemy [i.e. by the British and Canadians] and the British fleet remains master of the sea, there would be hope that constancy and fortune would make an honourable road to a peace which Great Britain might regard without shame if without great rejoicing.[1]

Such arguments might have appealed to Palmerston, but they did not appeal to Somerset. For a while the investigation continued. In February Robinson and the hydrographer, Captain G. H. Richards, drew up further papers listing the types and number of vessels which might pass the various obstacles on the Canadian waterways. There were a few gunvessels which might be able to pass up the St Lawrence to Lake Ontario if they were lightened; and possibly they could get some of the larger eighty horsepower gunboats up by this route. But the Welland canal would admit into the other lakes only the medium-sized, sixty horsepower boats, and the Ottawa route – which was probably the only one that they would be able to use in the event of war – could pass only the small and 'inefficient' twenty horsepower boats. A list was drawn up of the sixty horsepower boats: there were twenty-six ready for immediate use, two at Malta and the rest in the British Isles, and five more under repair, fourteen in the coastguard service, and nine acting as tenders. But none of them was any good for the purpose. Both they and the eighty horsepower boats were made of wood and would therefore have been quite helpless against the heavy American guns expected to be in service on the lakes. The only possible solution, Robinson suggested, was to store in parts for assembly on the spot a special type of turreted 'monitor'. At this point Somerset brought the discussion to an abrupt conclusion by noting that such vessels would cost £150,000 each to have built in a conventional manner in England, and to that sum would have to be added the costs of trans-

[1] Romaine's 'Memo. on the Defence of Canada by Great Britain for the Duke of Somerset', 9 Jan. 1865, Adm. 1/5931.

portation across the Atlantic and overland to the lakes, and £400,000 for the fortification of the necessary base at Kingston.[1]

If these papers had come into Gladstone's hands he would no doubt have concluded that his pleas for a proper investigation had been utterly vindicated, and, better still, the futility of all Palmerston's proposed expenditure in North America finally exposed to everyone. There is no sign that he ever did get a look at these papers, but the Admiralty's utter inability to make any firm proposals about the naval defence of the lakes must have encouraged him nonetheless. In December 1864, moreover, Cardwell let fall into his hands in mistake for another, a copy of an American report on the defences of their north-eastern frontier which further convinced him of the British experts' unreliability. For it showed him, he believed, that even while they were discussing in July the limited question of Quebec and Montreal, and while their own military advisers were ruling out the possibility of a major attack in the winter, the Americans themselves were making plans to cut off road and rail communications, and to prevent British troops afterwards reaching either of these places.[2] But though logic now seemed clearly on his side he did not get his way. Instead, frightened by the prospect of American revenge at the end of the Civil War, and urged on by the prime minister's patriotic fulminations, his colleagues clung to their age-old thoughts of warlike preparation. Russell thought they had a breathing-space still; but one that should be used in preparation for an awkward future.[3] Palmerston, who had been alarmed by rumours of a new plot to reconcile North and South in an attack upon another power – advance if muddled warning perhaps of the Hampton Roads meeting between Lincoln and the Confederate vice-president in February 1865 – was determined to press on with the defences in North America.[4]

[1] List of the sixty horsepower gunboats available for service, initialled by Robinson, 9 Feb. 1865, Somerset papers. 'Vessels capable of passing through the canals into the North American Lakes', by Robinson, 8 Feb. 1865; a paper by Capt. G. H. Richards, 9 Feb.; and another paper by Robinson, 22 Feb., together with Somerset's final minute: all filed under 17 Oct. 1861, 'Canadian Lakes: Naval Defence of: Papers, 1861–5', Adm. 1/5766.
[2] Gladstone to Cardwell, 21 Dec. 1864, Gladstone papers, B.M.Add.MS. 44,118. The American report referred to was *Report on the Defences of the Northeastern Frontier*, 20 June 1864, House Reports, no. 119, 38th Cong., 1st. sess., vol. II.
[3] Russell to the queen, 23 Dec. 1864, Queen Victoria's papers, R.A., Windsor, I 42/23.
[4] Palmerston to Russell, 14 Dec. 1864, Russell papers, P.R.O. 30/22/15; Palmerston to de Grey, 13 Jan. 1865, Ripon papers, B.M.Add.MS.43,512.

On 16 January the first part of Jervois's revised report on Canada was at last submitted officially to the War Office and on 19 and 20 January the cabinet met to consider it with the army and navy estimates generally. Palmerston's report of the meeting to the queen was, of course, highly prejudiced against the chancellor, who, he casually remarked, was 'as troublesome and wrongheaded as he often is upon subjects discussed in Cabinet'. According to the prime minister Gladstone 'objected strongly to fortifying Quebec and insisted upon a considerable reduction in the number of men for the navy'.[1] But 'the whole Cabinet ... was against him, with the exception of Mr Milner-Gibson who feebly supported him, and the Duke of Argyll who put in a word or two in his favour'. For one who was supposed to have been so nearly isolated in cabinet Gladstone nevertheless won considerable concessions. As Palmerston mentioned, he was 'let down easy' with a cabinet committee to search for reduction in the navy estimates. In addition the only specific decision made about Canada was that of the £200,000 needed for Quebec only the £50,000 which could be spent that summer would be included in the army estimates for the coming year.[2] In two despatches the next day, 21 January, Cardwell was at last able to reply to the fairly favourable reaction that the Canadian government had made the previous November. He reasserted his government's intention to proceed with the defence of Quebec, again expressed the hope that the Canadian government would see to Montreal, and further undertook to supply the armament for both. At the same time he refused to discuss the Canadian proposal for an increase in the number of British troops or to guarantee a loan for the works at Montreal. Thus, 'for the time being', each government

[1] In an interesting letter to Somerset of 13 Dec. 1864 (Somerset papers), Gladstone had summarized firmly the views he had maintained on this subject in recent correspondence and in cabinet, and suggested that while 'the transition to iron ships and new armament is justly urged as a cause for increased charge in building ships . . . I imagine that it may be easily shown that the very same change has brought about an immense economy in point of men'. And in reference to the Foreign Office's demands on account of strained relations, he commented: 'It is surely time that we should prepare, however gently and circumspectly, for modifying our system of *armament all over the world*: a system which, apart from special services requiring to be performed in particular quarters, seems to me, even if it cost nothing, disadvantageous from a tendency to multiply causes of quarrel and dispute: a system which was intelligible in the age of canvass, and of slow & uncertain posts, but which is wholly antiquated in the age of steam, of Mailpackets, of Telegraphs, of rapid, certain, continuous communication all over the world.'

[2] Palmerston to the queen, 20 Jan. 1865, G. E. Buckle, ed., *The Letters of Queen Victoria*, second series, 1862–78 (2 vols., London, 1926), i. 248–9.

was to proceed separately, the general question of defence being post-poned, as the Canadians had suggested, until the end of the negotiations on British North American Confederation.[1] But it was only the special question of the apportionment of the costs of defence that was really postponed. In spite of Gladstone's objections and in spite even of the considerable doubts displayed by other and especially naval experts, Jervois's reaffirmation of the old policy of offensive in the Atlantic to offset the weakness in Canada was clearly approved by the cabinet.

The Colonial Office, at the same time, was proposing yet greater cuts in the defences and garrisons of the West Indies. They recommended the amalgamation of the two military commands and, even more strongly, the reduction or abandonment of many positions. British Guiana and the Windward and Leeward Islands, they stressed, were indefensible by any moderate garrison against hostile expeditions, and some of them – Barbados, British Guiana, and Port of Spain, Trinidad – had no harbours of sufficient value to justify defences even against cruiser or privateer raids. They had found in these possessions therefore a good opportunity to recommend a reduction of over 1,000 men to as little as 700, mainly for purposes of internal order. The Bahamas, too, found little favour, Nassau having too shallow a harbour; but for internal order and as a protection against privateers, it was decided to keep the present garrison of about 430 men. Only Port Royal emerged with more than negative approval, its apparent role as a principal naval depôt requiring the retention of its garrison of nearly 2,000.[2] But while the Colonial Office deprecated and reduced in the West Indies, the cabinet took a very different line over Jervois's recommendations for Halifax and Bermuda. On 7 February they laid Jervois's reports before the House of Commons and asked, not only for the first £50,000 for Quebec, but also to raise the votes for the Maritimes and Bermuda, as Jervois had recommended, to £190,000 and £260,000 respectively. The appropriation passed easily by 275 votes to 40[3]; but the infection of Gladstone's assertions about the inutility of any defence at all was spreading nonetheless.

In the middle of February Cobden launched himself into the attack with two long letters to Gladstone in which he stressed the Americans' local naval superiority. This assured to them the inviolability of their coast as well as the command of the lakes which Wellington had always

---

[1] Cardwell to Monck, no. 14, and confidential, 21 Jan. 1865, C.O. 43/154.
[2] 'Troops and military expenditure in the West Indies, and on the West Coast of Africa', confidential print, 23 Jan. 1865, C.O. 884/2, no. 14.
[3] Stacey, pp. 161, 171 and 173.

insisted Great Britain must have for a successful defence of Canada. He concluded that Canada could not be defended either by land or by sea, and that as what little danger of war there was arose from Britain's position in North America, 'the intangible connection with Canada' should be cut.[1] Gladstone thought Cobden was too indulgent of the Canadians' own idleness, but on most issues he fully agreed and thinking that he ought not to keep such important letters to himself he showed them to other members of the cabinet, beginning with Russell and Milner Gibson.[2] But with the cabinet in general Cobden, like Gladstone, had singularly little success. Naturally Palmerston totally rejected his arguments: 'These Letters of Mr Cobden's are like his Speeches Illustrations of the Saying that shallow Streams run with the most violence and the most Noise . . . the Lakes are not Canada. They are only a Road to Canada, and a less convenient Road than if they were so much Dry Land. To land in Canada is not necessarily equivalent to conquering it.'[3] More surprising perhaps was Argyll's reaction to Cobden's assertion that Canada's indefensibility made its connection with Great Britain a 'powerful temptation' to the United States to attack the mother country. 'Of course it is,' he wrote to Gladstone, 'and therefore, until we *can* cut the connection it is not unreasonable that Canada should be anxious to have two fortified places capable of supporting in some degree, their own forces and ours.'[4] But if Argyll's reaction seemed to show a hardening in the cabinet against both Cobden and Gladstone, the story was very different outside the government. In March the question came out into the open with two House of Commons' debates on Canada's defence on 13 and 23 March in which a group led by Robert Lowe vociferously insisted upon the impossibility of defending Canada.[5] 'Mr Lowe made a very absurd speech', reported Palmerston to the queen.[6]

While in Britain there were by March 1865 some signs that objections were growing to even the limited defence programmes envisaged for the defence of North America, pressure was building up in Canada for urgent action, including even greater contribution on their own part.

[1] Cobden to Gladstone, 14 and 20 Feb. 1865, Gladstone papers, B.M.Add. MS.44,136. [2] Gladstone to Cobden, 22 Feb., *ibid.*
[3] Palmerston to Gladstone, 12 Mar. 1865, Philip Guedalla, ed., *Gladstone and Palmerston, being the Correspondence of Lord Palmerston with Mr Gladstone, 1851–1865* (New York and London, 1928), pp. 325–6.
[4] Argyll to Gladstone, 24 Feb. 1865, Gladstone papers, B.M.Add.MS.44,100.
[5] Stacey, pp. 172–3.
[6] Palmerston to the queen, 13 Mar. 1865, Buckle, *Letters of Queen Victoria,* second series, i. 262–3.

No doubt the illegal Confederate operations, the imminent end of the war, the growth of Fenian activities and probably not least the growing threat of partial or total abandonment by Great Britain were all having their effect. In any event the frequent reference to the American menace in the Canadian debates on federation which had begun in January 1865 led the Canadian government to launch an unusually bold attack upon the defence problem. It offered to undertake the western defences as well as those at Montreal if Britain would make some gunboats available for Lake Ontario and guarantee a loan, and when this was refused, it passed an act to spend $1 million on defence. Then, as the American Civil War drew at last to its end, it proposed to send to London a strong delegation to discuss the various critical Canadian problems, including confederation and relations with the United States, as well as the defence question.[1]

The delegation was to consist of four cabinet ministers – Macdonald, Brown, Cartier, and Galt; but, first, Cartier and Galt, who had arrived before the others, had informal exploratory talks with Cardwell on 26 and 27 April. In these Galt revealed a very different attitude from that of the previous November. The American situation, he argued, made it impossible to await the end of the negotiations on confederation. It would certainly be too dangerous to wait for the completion of Jervois's works. While these fortifications were being constructed therefore, they ought to call out for training a very considerable number of militia, munitions factories should be established, the force of regulars increased, and the naval defence of both lakes and seaboard attended to. The cost of the militia, fortifications, and munitions, it was suggested, should be borne equally by the two governments, but Canada would also pay for the extra expense of keeping regulars in North America, for the improvement of canal communications, and for the construction of a railway between Halifax and Quebec. For all this the two governments would incur a minimum joint expenditure of £8–10 million and Canada alone another £5 million for the partly commercial improvements. To pay her share of £9–10 millions Canada would need an imperial credit. In return for the British expenditure and loan Galt held out the prospect of Canadian self-defence and the reduction of British garrisons within three years.[2]

Brown and Macdonald arrived on 4 May and a committee of the cabinet consisting of Somerset, de Grey, Gladstone, and Cardwell, was

[1] Stacey, pp. 174–6.　　　　[2] *Ibid.*, pp. 183–4.

formed to deal with the full delegation. But no progress was made mainly because Cardwell was decidedly unwilling to consider sharing the cost of anything beyond the fortifications. Even more worrying to the Canadians perhaps was the evidence of widespread pessimism in Britain about the practicability of making any worthwhile defence of Canada at all. Consequently they called upon the British government to provide yet another expert report.[1]

If, as was by no means impossible, the 'Defence Committee' – the panel of experts to whom this problem was put – had unequivocally joined the mounting body of pessimists Gladstone would no doubt have been delighted, but the Anglo-Canadian conference would have ended in consternation and with it would have been imperilled not only British North American Federation but possibly even the connection with Great Britain itself. This the government had no intention of permitting. The day before the defence committee was to meet de Grey, probably without Gladstone's knowledge, wrote a cautionary letter to its chairman, Cambridge. He warned him 'to exercise a careful supervision over the terms in which the Report of the Committee is couched', pointing particularly to the 'difficulties which would arise' if it went back on the earlier opinions already officially adopted and gave the Canadians an opportunity either to press unreasonable demands or retreat from the attitude they had previously assumed. The danger, of course, lay not so much in any wholesale rejection of Jervois's scheme but, as de Grey pointed out, in the Admiralty's pessimism about the naval position on the lakes undermining the whole basis of this or any other scheme.[2] It is hardly surprising that when the committee met on 13 May they pretty well endorsed Jervois's scheme for the land defences, making only one substantial alteration, the addition of 10,000 men to the force recommended for the defence of the area between Quebec and Kingston. The thorny problem of naval assistance they carefully evaded. On it, they admitted, the whole scheme depended, just as much as upon regular and militia forces, fortifications, and improved communications. So too did they admit the advantages possessed by the Americans on the lakes, and the difficulty the British would have in overcoming those advantages by shipbuilding or storing frames upon the spot. But what they did not reveal was that the Admiralty now considered the problem virtually insuperable.[3]

[1] Stacey, pp. 184–5.
[2] De Grey to Cambridge, 12 May 1865, Cambridge papers.
[3] 'Memorandum by the Defence Committee on the Report of Lt. Col. Jervois on the Defence of Canada', 17 May 1865, confidential print, W.O. 33/15.

This manœuvre did not succeed in keeping the Canadian delegates from pressing for a firm commitment on a British naval force for Lake Ontario. This, of course, was what Gladstone, searching for the Achilles' heel of the whole expensive plan of defence, really wanted. 'I think the desire of the Canadian government to arrive at a clear understanding of the intended relations between Canada and England in the event of a war with the United States is to be encouraged and not repressed', he noted on 17 May.[1] But the prime minister was too shrewd a man to fall for Gladstone's spoiling tactics. 'Gladstone, who wants to drive us into undoing and unsaying all we have said and done, while professing that national Duty and Honor require that we should defend Canada, wants to make out by going into all these premature details that it is impossible for us to do so', he warned Cardwell a few days later, 'and the best way of defeating this tortuous Policy is to hold him as far as we can to the practical measures now under consideration.' Thus Gladstone's tactics forced the prime minister into an attitude and policy of quite uncharacteristic restraint:

It would be very desirable [he advised Cardwell], that you should endeavour to confine the Result of your meeting to-morrow as much as possible to things that can immediately be done, such as works at Quebec & the works of the Canadian Govt. at Montreal & elsewhere. . . . It would be not only useless but mischievous to go now into a Discussion of those general measures for the complete Defence of Canada sketched in the Defence Committee's Report. It will be time enough to consider such arrangements when any evidence arises to show that Danger is approaching. It would be even offensive to the United States to be publishing to the world military arrangements for an Invasion from a Power at peace with us & which we may hope will so continue.[2]

Realizing no doubt that his real objective had been discovered, Gladstone quietly abandoned his original approach and instead adopted a compromise line of agreement on principles and postponement of action save on the works at Quebec.[3] Faced, then, with this curious and unusual combination within the British government and the consequent refusal of the British cabinet committee to make any commitment about the lakes or to guarantee a fortification loan until after the Canadian parliament had authorized the works, the Canadian delegates had ultimately no choice but to agree once more that joint

[1] Minute by Gladstone, 17 May 1865, Gladstone papers, B.M.Add.MS.44,603.
[2] Palmerston to Cardwell, 21 May 1865, Broadlands papers.
[3] Gladstone to Cardwell, 23 May 1865, Gladstone papers, B.M.Add.MS. 44,118.

consideration of the whole defence scheme should be postponed until after the achievement of confederation. In the meantime Britain would go ahead with her plans for Quebec, while it was hoped the Canadians might make a start at least on Montreal and other works in the interior.[1]

Before the British and Canadian delegates had begun their work in London the news had arrived of General Lee's surrender at Appomattox courthouse on 9 April, followed with woeful speed by that of Lincoln's assassination five days later. The first opened up at last the dreadful prospect of American revenge; the second smoothed it over at once by generating a friendly air of grief in both Britain and British North America. The Civil War's legacy of conflict, like the *Alabama* claims and the prospective termination of the Reciprocity treaty – though not, after all, the lakes agreement on which Seward had relented just before the war had ended – all these remained to harass the progress of Anglo-American friendship. But the unexpected rapidity with which the United States disbanded her military forces brought much relief. On 1 May the Union army had numbered over a million; by 7 August more than half of these had been disbanded; by 15 November over 800,000 of them. In October death relieved Anglo-American relations of Lord Palmerston's eternal suspicions and helped to open up again in England real prospect of electoral reform. In August 1867 came the second great reform act, and Britain and America seemed to be moving into democratic concord. But no settlement of the Civil War disputes had been reached and in the meantime, unfortunately, there had come too a new round of filibuster activities by the Irish Fenians along the Canadian border to upset any further progress with military economies in British North America and to keep alive the lurking fear of open conflict with the government of the United States.

To meet the Fenian threats beginning in the autumn of 1865 the Canadian government called out a few companies of volunteers in November, 10,000 in the following March, and the whole force of 25,000 in June 1866. In April the Maritimes too called out a part of their militia and volunteers. On their part the British responded by sending out in the spring of 1866 two additional battalions of infantry and more reluctantly in the summer, two more battalions of infantry, a regiment of cavalry, and some engineers and artillery. By 1 April 1867 the number of British officers and men had risen to nearly 12,000 in Canada and over 3,700 in the Maritime Provinces. Meanwhile energetic

---

[1] Stacey, pp. 185–7.

measures were also being taken on the lakes. Beginning in June 1866 the Canadian government hired no less than fifteen vessels to act against the Fenians, and with the prior agreement of the British government these were armed and manned by Admiral Hope.[1] At the same time Monck also asked for some regular British naval vessels to be placed on the lakes.[2]

It happened that the government in London had already been considering this whole question again. Seward had written on 8 March 1865 to say that the United States were not after all going to terminate the Rush-Bagot arrangement but were 'quite willing that the convention should remain practically in force'. To the Canadians this had appeared rather ambiguous. The Americans had not specifically withdrawn their notice to terminate the agreement and Seward's reply might mean that on some future occasion they would not feel bound to give six months' notice again. At the request of the Canadian government, therefore, this matter was taken up by the Foreign Office and satisfactory assurances were received from Seward in June and August 1865.[3] But on 11 September that same year came a report from the naval attaché in Washington, Captain Bythesea, that the Americans were still putting so-called 'revenue' vessels on the lakes in violation of the agreement of 1817.[4]

The Foreign and Colonial Offices at once asked if the Admiralty could reply by putting a similar force on the lakes. The Admiralty's response was unusually encouraging. They confirmed that it was possible to get some types of gunvessels on to Lake Ontario, provided that they were first lightened by the removal of their coal and stores. However, although there were still no less than sixteen of these in service they were old and defective. Fortunately there was now going to be a new class of twin-screw gunvessel, *Plover*, which was strongly built and heavily armed, and was thought to be capable of safely crossing the Atlantic as well as getting up to the lake. Although as yet only the *Plover* itself had been ordered Russell and Cardwell no doubt found this a very promising proposal and the Admiralty was asked to take the necessary steps for placing on the lakes a force of these gunvessels equal in number to whatever the Americans had. But

[1] Stacey, pp. 189–93.   [2] *Ibid.*, p. 191.
[3] Monck to Cardwell, no. 84, 24 Mar. 1865, C.O. 42/648; J. M. Callahan, *The Neutrality of the Lakes and Anglo-American Relations* (Baltimore, 1898), pp. 165–6.
[4] Printed 'Report on United States Revenue vessels on the Lakes', by Captain Bythesea, 11 Sept. 1865, Adm. 1/5766.

they had reckoned without the Admiralty's gift for changing its mind and raising snags. According to the comptroller – who had made the same point in February – it would not after all be a good idea to send these ships across the Atlantic and to have three or four of them built at Montreal and supplied with engines from England would cost between £110,000 and £150,000. Such a sum as this, the Admiralty pointed out, would have to be voted in the estimates and they wondered if Lord Clarendon, who was foreign secretary now that Russell had succeeded Palmerston, would want to risk parliamentary discussion of such a 'great international question'. On this last at least the Admiralty was perfectly correct and when Monck's request for ships to meet the Fenian threat was received in the summer of 1866 nothing had been decided.[1] The government therefore had to fall back on the weak sixty horsepower gunboats. After some holdup out of regard for the 1817 agreement three of these were at length placed on the lakes. In addition the frigate *Aurora* was kept for a while at Quebec, the corvette *Pylades* at Montreal, and in the St Lawrence between Quebec and Montreal from time to time cruised the sloop *Rosario*.[2]

None of the measures taken by the government in London during the Fenian troubles reflected any change in their attitude towards the problem of North American defence. Attempts were still being made to induce a change, notably by the new commanding officer in Canada, Sir John Michel, and by Colonel P. L. MacDougall who shortly before being appointed adjutant-general of the Canadian militia had produced a pamphlet in response to the House of Commons debate on Canadian defence in March 1865. Both rejected, as impolitic and erroneous, the growing conviction that Canada was utterly in-defensible, and both insisted on the need to explain and extend the change in the principal purpose of the fortified positions, already registered in Jervois's second report, from places of refuge to *places d'armes*. Their purpose, they explained, was not in a few select places to trap large bodies of British regulars in futile and probably only temporary security, but to provide a large number of scattered positions from which the militia operating in the vicinity could be supported by

[1] F.O. to Adm., 29 Sept. 1865, Adm. 1/5766; C.O. to Adm., 7 Oct., Adm. to C.O., 9 Oct. 1865, enclosing the comptroller's first report of 4 Oct., C.O. to Adm., 16 Oct., and Adm. to C.O., 26 Oct. 1865, C.O. 42/651; F.O. to Adm., 30 Oct., and Adm. to F.O., 30 Oct. 1865, Adm. 1/5954; F.O. to Adm., 16 Jan. 1866, Adm. 1/5991.

[2] Adm. minute on C.O. to Adm., 31 Aug. 1866, Adm. 1/5990. There is a good deal of information about these measures in the station records for 1866–67, Adm. 128/24.

British troops and supplied with arms and ammunition.[1] Nor did Michel neglect the thorny lakes question. Throughout 1865 and 1866 the Georgian Bay scheme was being pressed again both publicly in Canada and Britain and upon the service departments. Michel brought it continually to the attention of the duke of Cambridge.[2] In the summer of 1865 he and Admiral Hope made a particular inspection of the proposed route during a tour of Canada, and as a result Hope too pressed it on the Admiralty.[3] And on 19 March 1866 Lt.-Col. Millington Synge, a distinguished engineer officer who had probably first drawn Michel's attention to the scheme and had accompanied Michel and Hope on their tour of inspection, spoke warmly in its favour at a meeting of the Royal United Service Institute in London.[4] There was no lack of support in London. Cambridge himself and Sir Richard Airey, the quartermaster-general, both commended it. But an essential feature of the proposal, an imperial loan to finance its construction in return for its specifications meeting Admiralty requirements, found no favour with Cardwell. What they had already promised in May and June 1865, he thought, was quite enough for British public opinion.[5]

Matters did not improve for the protagonists of defences for Canada, when Russell's administration gave way to the Tories in June 1866. Disraeli, who now became chancellor of the Exchequer and the most important man in the cabinet, was still nearer to his 1852 comment that the 'wretched colonies . . . are a millstone round our necks' than to the

[1] 'Memorandum on our Military position in Canada', enclosed in Michel to Cambridge, private, 12 Sept. 1865, Cambridge papers; 'Memorandum on the present military position of Canada, and on the expediency of strengthening her Defences from a Political point of view', by Michel, 31 May 1866, Carnarvon papers, P.R.O. 30/6/171. *Last Thursday's Debate in the House of Commons*, anonymous printed pamphlet of 28 Mar. 1865; MacDougall's authorship is made clear by the duke of Cambridge in forwarding a copy of it to Granville, 27 May 1869, Granville papers, P.R.O. 30/29/72. See also Jay Luvaas, 'General Sir Patrick MacDougall, the American Civil War, and the Defence of Canada', Canadian Historical Association *Annual Report*, 1962, pp. 44–54, and the chapter on MacDougall in the same author's *The Education of An Army: British Military Thought, 1815–1940* (Chicago, 1964), pp. 101–29.

[2] Michel to Cambridge, private, 12 Sept. 1865, enclosing his 'Memorandum on our Military position in Canada', and private, 9 Oct. 1865, Cambridge papers; Michel's 'Memorandum on the present military position of Canada . . .', 31 May 1866, and Michel to Cambridge, private, 17 Nov. 1866, Carnarvon papers, P.R.O. 30/6/171 and 136.

[3] Michel to Cambridge, 22 Aug. 1865, Cambridge papers; Hope to Adm., 28 Sept. 1865, extract in Adm. to C.O., 10 Oct. 1865, C.O. 42/651.

[4] Lt.-Col. Millington Synge, R.E., 'The Lakes and Canals of Canada', Royal United Service Institute, *Journal*, x (1867), 183–208.

[5] Airey to Cambridge, private, 8 Oct., Cambridge to Michel, private, 14 Oct., and Cardwell to Cambridge, 30 Oct. 1865, Cambridge papers.

rediscovery of the empire that he made at the Crystal Palace on 24 June 1872. 'We must seriously consider our Canadian position, which is most illegitimate', he wrote to the prime minister on 30 September 1866. 'An army maintained in a colony which does not permit us even to govern it! What an anomaly! . . . It can never be our pretence or our policy, to defend the Canadian frontier against the U.S. . . . Power and influence we should exercise in Asia; consequently in Eastern Europe, consequently also in Western Europe; but what is the use of these colonial deadweights which we do not govern.' He did not resent the naval and military reinforcement the Fenian scare had forced the government to send out so recently, provided that it was 'not looked upon as a permanent increase of our Canadian establishments'.[1] But with Bismarck's unification of Germany reaching its first climax at the battle of Sadowa, three days after the formation of the Derby administration, it is no wonder that they too should have thought of reduction in America and concentration and reorganization at home.[2] Moreover, although the Fenian border scares had forced the Canadians to maintain a good deal of their newfound enthusiasm for joint if not self defence – bringing up the number of volunteers to nearly 34,000 by the end of 1867, spending unprecedented sums on the defences, and even buying modern rifles from the United States – they had done nothing about the fortifications while the British were busily engaged on the works at Quebec.[3]

Resentful at this and at the petty squabbles about sharing the costs of the Fenian precautions, and gratified by what seemed to be most promising negotiations with the Americans on the *Alabama* and other difficulties, the British government greeted the bill for the Confederation of British North America by hedging over the attached proposal to guarantee a loan for the strategic intercolonial railway and talked instead of further withdrawals of troops.[4] Even before the Act of Confederation had been signed Michel found it necessary to fend off proposals for reduction and a year later, in February 1868, the colonial secretary wrote to warn Monck that he was going to withdraw three battalions of infantry and to suggest that it was about time the new 'Dominion' did something about its share of the defence works.

[1] Disraeli to Derby, 30 Sept. 1866, W. F. Monypenny and G. E. Buckle, *The Life of Benjamin Disraeli* (6 vols., London, 1910–20), iv. 476–7.

[2] The connection between the colonial reductions and events in Europe is ably elaborated by C. P. Stacey, 'Britain's Withdrawal from North America, 1864–1871', *Canadian Historical Review*, xxvi (1955), 185–98.

[3] Stacey, *Canada and the British Army*, pp. 191–7 and 199–200.

[4] *Ibid.*, pp. 196–9.

Belatedly an act was passed in the Canadian parliament, authorizing the loan for the works at St John, New Brunswick, Montreal, and places to the west. At the same time another act reorganized and improved the militia system. But it was too late. When the Canadians applied for the imperial guarantee they thought they had been promised in 1865, the British hedged and the autumn of 1868 found yet another Canadian delegation in London. Before the delegation had made any progress, but not before two more battalions had been ordered home and new garrisons announced of 5,000 for Ontario and Quebec, 2,000 for Nova Scotia, and 1,650 for New Brunswick, the Tory government fell, and Gladstone returned, this time as prime minister, to settle affairs with both Canada and the United States.[1]

Committed as Gladstone's first government was, by the personal conviction of so many of its members as well as by electoral tactics, to a policy of retrenchment and reform, and with Europe still in process of painful transformation, it was clear that the development of imperial and Canadian defence had reached one of its most crucial periods. In a little more than three weeks after taking office Cardwell, now secretary of state for war, was outlining the first of his great army reforms before the cabinet and on 9 January 1869 he presented the prime minister with details of his proposed redistribution of the regular army. Since this aimed at increasing the number of regulars in the British Isles while making a reduction overall, it necessarily provided for a substantial withdrawal from the colonies. Thus the total establishment, excluding the Indian Army, was to be reduced by only 11,500 from 137,500 to 126,000, but the colonial garrisons were to be reduced by nearly half from 50,000 to 26,000. So far as the American colonies were concerned this meant garrisons of only 3,500 for the West Indies and West Africa together, 2,000 for Bermuda, 1,000 for Halifax and Newfoundland, and a mere 2,000 for Canada. Most significant of all Quebec did not even appear among the list of 'imperial stations'.[2]

These proposals naturally met with Gladstone's approval but almost at once the objections to colonial reductions began to come in, led of course by the duke of Cambridge. Cambridge used to the full his royal connection to put pressure on the government, but the queen and General Grey had both already given their broad approval.[3] Neither royal intervention nor the protests of the Canadian delegates therefore

[1] Stacey, *Canada and the British Army*, pp. 197–201.
[2] Cardwell to General Charles Grey (the queen's private secretary), 29 Dec. 1868, and Cardwell to Gladstone, 9 Jan. 1869, Cardwell papers, P.R.O. 30/48, boxes 2 and 6.   [3] Grey to Cardwell, 1 Jan. 1869, *ibid.*, box 1.

could extract more than brief delays from Cardwell, who for once had the enthusiastic support even of the governor-general of Canada. Sir John Young, Monck's successor, felt that Cardwell was withdrawing not a man too many; he had himself drawn up a scheme withdrawing six hundred more![1] With the encouragement given by this opinion and its acceptance by the queen Cardwell stubbornly resisted the continued objections of the duke of Cambridge.[2] On 11 March were moved the revised estimates for 1869–70 which inaugurated the new process of concentration in the United Kingdom and proposed to reduce the garrisons of British North America from 16,185 in 1868–69 to 6,249 in 1869–70.

On 14 April the news went out officially to the governor-general. Now that the Fenian danger had pretty well passed, he was told, the government proposed to make some substantial reductions in the course of the summer. One regiment of cavalry, three batteries of field and three batteries of garrison artillery, and three battalions of infantry were to be withdrawn from Quebec and Ontario. This would still leave a total of 4,000 men, but only as a 'temporary arrangement' since it was intended ultimately to withdraw all but those required for the training of the militia and for the schools of instruction. At the same time two battalions of infantry and one field battery were to be withdrawn from Nova Scotia and New Brunswick, leaving in Halifax about 2,000 men, twice what Cardwell's original plan had envisaged, but again only 'for the present'. The Canadian government was to be expected to pay for the remaining four home service companies of the Canadian Rifles and for any naval force they wished to keep on the lakes. Alternatively they could raise their own naval force under the terms of the Colonial Naval Defence Act of 1865. On the other hand, now that the Canadian parliament had authorized a large defence expenditure, the British government were ready to redeem their promise to guarantee an imperial loan.[3]

In such a large-scale reduction and particularly in the abandonment of Quebec as an imperial station, the government was, as Cambridge recognized, utterly throwing over the minimum precautions of even Jervois's first modest report. Yet in July 1864 Gladstone had professed to find that report inadequate for any serious defence of the colony.

[1] Young to Cardwell, private, 15 Feb. 1869, Cardwell papers *P.R.O.* 30/48, box 1; see also Stacey,*Canada and the British Army*, pp. 210–11.
[2] Cardwell to Grey, 3 and 4 Mar. 1869, Queen Victoria's papers. R.A., E 16/45 and 46.
[3] Stacey, *Canada and the British Army*, pp. 211–15.

Cardwell's proposals therefore were not a scheme for the promotion of colonial self-defence, but the conscious inauguration of a policy of colonial desertion. In these circumstances, and in spite of his almost complete failure at the beginning of the year, Cambridge waged an unrelenting rearguard action throughout 1869 and well into 1870. He even enlisted the support of the ageing Russell, who admitted to having been a protagonist of colonial self-defence since the time of Grey's famous despatch in 1851, but was not a believer in 'holding out a constant temptation to the great Republic to go to war with us by offering them a prospect of carrying Canada and Nova Scotia by a *coup de main*'. The real question, as Cardwell conceded, was whether the proposed garrisons were sufficient and for what purpose. Clearly the duke did not think them adequate for anything, and though there might be other military opinions against him Russell doubted the judgement of Cardwell's principal advisers in this matter, Monck, Young, and Cartier, whom Cardwell cited as having asserted Canada's possession of thirty or forty thousand trained men. 'I would as soon take the opinion of the Lord Chancellor as to the proper complement for one of the new turret ships', Russell avowed.[1]

Encouraged perhaps by the support of the liberal party's elder statesman, on 7 April Cambridge presented to Cardwell his own detailed view of the arrangements necessary for the maintenance of the imperial positions at Quebec, Halifax, and Bermuda. About Bermuda, for which he proposed a peace garrison of 1,700 and a war garrison of 5,900, there was no real dispute as Cardwell himself had allotted it some 2,000 troops in his initial proposals. But Cambridge insisted that both Halifax *and* Quebec were vital to communications between the colonies and Great Britain and as imperial fortresses therefore should have a combined peace strength of 6,200 and a combined war strength of 12,000; of these 4,500 and 7,100 respectively were for Quebec.[2] So conflicting was this with the advice that Cardwell required that he told the duke that his letter's very existence was 'inconvenient', and at length Cambridge agreed to substitute for it a conversation with Cardwell, Granville, the colonial secretary, and Childers, the first lord of the Admiralty.[3] This 'conversation' was held at the Horse Guards on 5 May, and it was apparently agreed to seek expert opinion once again. This time the

<hr>

[1] Russell to Cardwell, 14 and 15 Mar. 1869, enclosed in Cardwell to Granville, 15 Mar., Granville papers, P.R.O. 30/29, box 53.

[2] Cambridge to Cardwell, 7 April 1869, forwarded by Cardwell to Granville, 13 April, *ibid.*, box 53.

[3] Cardwell to Granville, 13 and 25 April 1869, *ibid.*, box 53.

expert was to be Colonel MacDougall, who had just returned from his post as adjutant-general of militia in Canada and was soon to become the chairman of the 'localization committee' which worked out the basis of Cardwell's reorganization of the regular and reserve forces in Britain.[1] Then, at a meeting on 14 May, the cabinet too decided that it would 'shortly' have to consider the matter 'further', and Cardwell apparently decided to consult once more not MacDougall but the government's old standby, Jervois. He now asked for a general report on the importance of Bermuda and the West Indies as well as Canada in the event of war with the United States.[2]

If Cardwell had had any *arrière pensée* in avoiding MacDougall he was soon to be doubly disappointed. Cambridge, suspecting as he politely put it that the decision of 5 May had been 'overlooked', separately extracted a written report from MacDougall. Both this and the reports from Jervois insisted on the importance of keeping British garrisons at Quebec and Halifax as the keys to the connection with Great Britain.[3] None of this budged Cardwell an inch from the determination he had made so early in the life of the ministry. But Cambridge's continual interventions with members of the cabinet and with the queen did have a delaying effect. So too, evidently, did some irritation at the Admiralty. The first lord soon noted a tendency to shrug off colonial protests by references to increased squadrons abroad. Plainly annoyed, Childers protested over a reference of this kind in the case of the withdrawal from New Zealand; Granville tried to soothe him by saying that he had only meant the navy should make an 'ostentatious flourish'.[4] Thus even by the end of 1869 Cardwell was still unable to consider the matter quite closed. On 8 November he was having to suggest a conference with Childers and Granville on the whole question of colonial fortifications when Jervois returned from an investigation of Bermuda he was making for the Colonial Office.[5] Two

[1] Cambridge to Granville, 27 May 1869, Granville papers, P.R.O. 30/29, box 72.
[2] Gladstone to the queen, 14 May 1869, Queen Victoria's papers, R.A., A 38/76.
[3] Cambridge to Granville, 27 May 1869, enclosing MacDougall's memorandum of 22 May, Granville papers, P.R.O. 30/29, box 72; Jervois's printed confidential memorandum, 'Considerations on the military position of Great Britain with respect to the United States', 28 May 1869, W.O. 33/11, and additional manuscript memorandum on Jamaica, 29 May, Granville papers, P.R.O. 30/29, box 53.
[4] Childers to Granville, 27 Oct., and Granville to Childers, 27 Oct. 1869, Granville papers, P.R.O. 30/29, box 54.
[5] Cardwell to Granville, 8 Nov. 1869, *ibid.*, box 53.

days later, on 10 November, the cabinet would still not commit itself to disbanding the Canadian Rifles for which the dominion had refused to pay.[1] For a time, indeed, it looked as if the tide was turning at last against the secretary of war. His plan now was first to concentrate the regulars in Quebec, and then, when the works voted for that place in 1865 were complete, to present the Canadians with an ultimatum: that they should undertake by a parliamentary bill to fortify Montreal before the British government approached Westminster for the loan guarantee, but that the forces would then in any event be withdrawn to Halifax leaving Quebec to be garrisoned by the Canadians.[2] But first protests from the military commander in Canada, General Sir Charles Windham, forced him to postpone the concentration; and then with a new alternative scheme for colonial redistribution Cambridge seemed to be getting rather more support from the queen; he managed to sow doubts even in Granville's mind.[3] But assured as he was of the prime minister's unequivocal support, Cardwell was bound to win ultimately and his success came all the earlier as the result of the rather foolish conduct of the Canadian government in the new Fenian scare of 1869.

In his correspondence about concentration with Windham earlier in the year, Cardwell had only acquiesced very reluctantly and for the time being in the continued dispersal of the troops for political and instructional reasons.[4] But when, almost immediately afterwards, a new Fenian scare seemed to emphasize the justice of Cardwell's fear for the exposed position of detachments of regulars and Windham asked Cartier to call out some 3,000 volunteers for their support, he was met with a cold refusal. Only when he threatened to withdraw the garrison at Toronto did the Canadians comply. With the small British garrison at Prescott, however, threats did not work. There the refusal of the Canadians to keep up the two remaining gunboats or to provide volunteers on land, forced the British government to order an immediate evacuation. Even then the Canadians responded with a force of a mere twenty-four volunteers to replace two hundred regulars. Only in the autumn, when rumours of more serious Fenian activities reached the Canadian government, did they act with more vigour, commissioning the gunboats and calling out volunteer gunners to man them.[5]

[1] Cardwell to Grey, 11 Nov. 1869, Queen Victoria's papers, R.A. E 16/102.
[2] Cardwell to Granville, 9 Dec. 1869, Granville papers, P.R.O. 30/29, box 53.
[3] Stacey, *Canada and the British Army*, pp. 219–20; Cambridge to Cardwell, 14 Dec. 1869, Verner and Parker, i. 396–9; and Granville to Cardwell, 15 and 19 Dec. 1869, Granville papers, P.R.O. 30/29, box 53.
[4] Stacey, *Canada and the British Army*, pp. 219–20.
[5] *Ibid.*, pp. 220–2.

It was probably these irritating evidences of non-cooperation that finally overcame the resistance in Britain. On 12 February 1870 Granville wrote to the governor-general that while the government were still prepared to ask parliament for the guarantee if the Canadians wished it, they proposed in any case to disband the Canadian Rifles, though volunteers from the regulars would be free to accept offers of service from the Canadian government. They would also withdraw all the regulars save for a garrison of 1,500 in the imperial fortress of Halifax and such a 'small body' as the Canadians might wish to have for the instruction of the militia. 'For the present year' only, one battalion of infantry and one battery of garrison artillery would remain all together at Quebec. As a generous gesture to colonial self-defence 44,000 rifles at present on loan were made an outright gift, but it was made clear that there would be no more free loans.[1]

With the decision taken at last the government proceeded to implement it quickly and ruthlessly, neither Secretary of State Fish's talks with the British minister about the 'peaceful' annexation of Canada in January nor another serious Fenian scare and raid in April and May in the least weakening their resolve. The Riel rebellion did elicit a grudging contribution of British regulars to the Red River expedition, but only on condition that the dominion government paid three-quarters of the cost. Against this unhappy background the forthcoming withdrawal brought another Canadian minister in haste once more to London and led Russell in the Lords to denounce wholesale the ministry's entire colonial policy. But the government stood firm. In June Clarendon's death gave the Foreign Office to Granville, and as Kimberley followed Granville at the Colonial Office so the Franco-Prussian war broke out to confirm the apparent wisdom of Cardwell's army redistribution and reforms. During the summer the military establishments at Toronto, Kingston, Ottawa, and Isle aux Noix were all handed over and by September there remained only one battalion of infantry concentrated at Quebec in addition to the garrison of Halifax. In 1871 the various posts in New Brunswick were given up and on 11 November that year the last British troops left Quebec too.[2]

The end of the Civil War in America confirmed the achievement of Manifest Destiny without presenting to Great Britain the expected consolation of a permanent disruption of the Union. The reduction and withdrawal of the garrisons from Canada was a clear recognition of this fact by the Derby and Gladstone governments alike. 'The Northern

[1] Stacey, *Canada and the British Army*, pp. 226–7.   [2] *Ibid.*, pp. 230–53.

300

victory', concludes one of the most recent studies, 'destroyed any remaining possibility of a restoration of the balance of power in North America. Thereafter, Canadian-American relations and British policy with respect to the New World were posited upon the assumption that the United States had the preponderance of power on the continent.'[1] Nothing perhaps so signified the finality of the change as Britain's curt dismissal of the last chance of a French alliance. Late in the summer of 1865 some French and British naval squadrons had mingled in a friendly fashion off Cherbourg, Brest, and Portsmouth, and Palmerston had welcomed the manœuvres as likely not only to improve Anglo-French relations but also 'to produce a wholesome impression upon all other nations and most especially upon the Yankees, who will no doubt see in these meetings even a stronger disposition between the two countries to coalesce against a common enemy than is really at the bottom of the whole thing and the Yankees will be all the less likely to give trouble either in Canada or in Mexico'.[2] A few months later, as the strain of the Mexican expedition began to tell upon him, Louis Napoleon one evening drew the British ambassador quietly into the privacy of his room and suggested an Anglo-French agreement for mutual assistance to discourage an attack by the United States. But now Palmerston was dead and Clarendon could see only danger in the proposal; Napoleon had navy enough to support his intervention in Mexico, while the presence of French troops in Canada might well provoke war with the United States.[3]

Some Americans professed to see in the confederation of British North America a last despairing attempt to restore the balance of power and worked accordingly to counter it by promoting the annexation of British Columbia and squeezing the colony by the acquisition of Alaska.[4] The threat was clear to those Canadians who still dreamed of greatness for the new confederation in the acquisition of a Canadian West, and the British ambassador in St Petersburg warned once more of a sinister Russian-American alliance to challenge British power.[5] But the foreign secretary of the time, Lord Stanley, was singularly unconcerned:

[1] Winks, p. 375.

[2] Palmerston to Somerset, 2 Sept. 1865, Somerset papers.

[3] Cowley to Clarendon, private, 1 Dec. 1865, and Clarendon to Cowley, private, 4 Dec. 1865, Cowley papers, F.O. 519/232 and 179.

[4] Winks, pp. 164–5; T. A. Bailey, 'Why the United States Purchased Alaska', *Pacific Historical Review* iii (1934), 49, n. 30.

[5] Winks, p. 165; Buchanan to Stanley, no. 387, 12 Sept. 1866, F.O. 65/701.

The Americans . . . have bought a large amount of worthless territory. . . .
Their motive is probably twofold: to establish a sort of claim in the
future to British North America, lying as it does between their old and
new possessions; and to gain a victory over us by doing without our
knowledge an act which they probably think will annoy England. In that
expectation they will be disappointed, for I cannot find anyone who cares
about the matter, and the press in general treats it with indifference.[1]

About Mexico, as Maximilian's adventure drew to its tragic conclusion,
he was naturally not worried in the least. He expected the Americans
to 'keep Mexico purposely weak and divided, so as to give them no
trouble: and they will annex a province at a time as they want and can
occupy it'. In any case, Clarendon agreed, it would 'be better employment for them than collecting the *Alabama* debts'.[2]

Although the British clearly and consciously surrendered the
mastery of the North American continent to the United States, it did
not necessarily follow that they had to give up all thought of war.
On 8 May 1871, before the withdrawal of the Canadian garrisons had
been completed, the settlement of the *Alabama* claims and other
difficulties from the Civil War had been provided for at last by the
Treaty of Washington. But the settlement was in doubt right up until
the last minute and before that the American complaints had often
seemed a frightening problem. In May 1869, when news had reached
London of the Senate's rejection of a proposed settlement – the Johnson-
Clarendon convention – and of Sumner's counter-claim to Canada,
the alarm had begun to approach the proportions even of a war
scare. Clarendon reported to the queen: 'It is the unfriendly state of
our relations with America that to a great extent paralyses our action in
Europe. There is not the slightest doubt that if we were engaged in a
Continental quarrel we should immediately find ourselves at war with
the United States.'[3] Withdrawal from Canada seemed the quickest
and most effective way of escaping from this dilemma. It was not an
attempt to solve the problem of Canadian defence, but a way of evading
it. In the era of Gettysburg and Königgrätz, Britain's sense of military
vulnerability in North America and diplomatic weakness in Europe
made a withdrawal from Canada and greater concentration at home
peculiarly attractive. The confederation of British North America and
the reform of the army provided the opportunity; Canada's continued

[1] Stanley to Lyons, 4 April 1867, Newton, i. 168–9.
[2] Stanley to Cowley, private, 12 Dec. 1866, and Clarendon to Cowley,
private, 29 May 1867, Cowley papers, F.O. 519/182 and 181.
[3] Clarendon to the queen, 1 May 1869, G. E. Buckle, ed., *Letters of Queen
Victoria*, second series (2 vols., London, 1926), i. 594–5.

reluctance to contribute her full share gave the excuse. Indeed the government would have been most disappointed if the Canadians had agreed to implement the limited bargains made in the 1860s. On 10 July 1869 Granville had written confidentially to Young asking whether the Canadians really wished to keep the bargain and plainly inviting him to seek some method of withdrawing from it without exposing the home government to accusations of ill faith.[1] And Granville was right to be so suspicious. For the time being the Canadians continued to profess their attachment to the bargain and to press for the fortification guarantee bill to be presented to parliament. But in fact they were not enthusiastic and at length they found a better compromise in the arrangements arising out of the *Alabama* settlement. In that settlement the Canadians agreed to give up their claims against the United States over the Fenian raids and in some sort of recompense the loan guarantee was increased by two and a half million pounds and diverted from fortifications to a transcontinental railway.[2]

Granville did not apparently contemplate what even Lord Grey had suggested in 1851 – that the colonial government might have additional troops if they paid for them. He had declared openly against the idea in the Lords on 7 March 1870, and Cardwell had also discouraged it in the following September.[3] At the same time Granville expressed some of that old anti-colonial sentiment which suggested that he wished to cut the imperial connection with Canada altogether.[4] It may well be that this was a personal attitude rather than that of the ministry as a whole; but it has rightly been observed that the Gladstone government showed themselves singularly unconcerned with making Canada's defence more secure, whether by any contribution from the mother country or by the Canadians' own efforts. They were preoccupied rather with reducing imperial expenditure on defence and with extricating as soon as possible all the regular forces they could.[5] The 'hostage' was not to be released but abandoned.

Once the importance to imperial prestige of remaining in the interior had thus been set aside, the withdrawal of the weak and exposed garrisons could be, and indeed had been, represented as strengthening the British position not only in Europe but also in the event of war with the United States. When Cardwell had presented his policy to parliament in 1869 he had defended it in part by reasserting the old excuse that in spite of withdrawal, 'the true defence of our colonies is that they

---

[1] Stacey, *Canada and the British Army*, pp. 215–16.
[2] *Ibid.*, p. 255. [3] *Ibid.*, p. 228, note 1.
[4] *Ibid.*, p. 216. [5] *Ibid.*, pp. 216–17.

live under the aegis of the name of England, and that war with them is war with England'.[1] But what for the economizing politician was probably an insincere excuse, was an important truth for Britain's naval and military experts. Without much greater efforts than either Canada or Great Britain would ever make in advance of war, a sudden emergency had always been thought likely to catch the British garrisons in a most vulnerable predicament. Their withdrawal first and foremost removed a source of weakness. In any future war with the United States, Britain could now concentrate on exploiting her strength at sea rather than on mitigating her weakness on land. This strength too was dangerously threatened by the effects of the Civil War and the economies of British administrations, but at length neglect on the part of the Americans themselves and the dependence of the British economists upon naval power to justify their reductions to a large extent restored the supremacy of the Royal Navy in American waters.

First Britain's naval supremacy in the western Atlantic had to survive a very dangerous interlude. Even though it presented little threat on the high seas, the United States Navy, as Cobden had pointed out early in 1865, had clearly established local superiority in American coastal waters as a result of its development during the Civil War. It was perhaps for this reason that the British displayed a singular disregard for the security of their naval power in American waters when, in the light of the experience of the Civil War, Seward and his successor searched the seas again for offshore naval bases to supplement nature's niggardly provision on the mainland. Had he succeeded not only would Britain's own bases have been threatened, but also her ability even to maintain distant blockades. But the Conservative foreign minister in particular refused to be disturbed. Of the Sandwich Islands Stanley commented: 'Nothing that we can say will prevent the annexation taking place, if the people of the islands do not themselves object to it, and if the Americans desire it. I am not much disposed to interfere where we cannot possibly do so with effect.'[2] And he took the same line about American ambitions in the Caribbean.[3]

Gladstone, whose ultimate intention it probably was not only to withdraw British land forces from their dangerous entanglement in

---

[1] Stacey, *Canada and the British Army*, p. 212.
[2] Minute by Stanley on Fane (chargé in Paris) to F.O., no. 599, 19 Sept. 1867, F.O. 27/1667.
[3] Minute by Stanley on Lyons (ambassador in Paris) to F.O., no. 121, 6 Feb. 1868, F.O. 27/1701.

Canada, but also to eliminate all reference whatever to the contingency of war with America, equally brought his economizing pressure to bear upon the distribution of British naval power. While Palmerston lived Gladstone's constant criticism brought little more than some famous quarrels. In the era of massive ironclad reconstruction in the 1860s and 1870s it was peculiarly difficult to keep the naval estimates from rising drastically. So before he went out of office in 1866 he was already concentrating his attack upon what he called the 'system of armaments all over the world'.[1] The very limited range of the new battleships also suggested the apparent wisdom of concentrating them in home waters, while leaving the foreign stations to more economical wooden ships, supplemented if possible by a 'flying squadron' of more powerful ships and by whatever coastal warships the colonies might themselves pay for under the Colonial Naval Defence Act of 1865. In the not too long run this policy, though haphazardly pursued, had unfortunate results. The colonies responded very little to the invitation of 1865 and in waters nearer home the concept of 'coastal ironclads' led to the deliberate development of a class of vessel of unnecessarily limited utility. Still, and in spite of the tendency to concede that where foreign nations possessed ironclads so too must the local British squadron, considerable reductions were made on the foreign stations.

The erosion began with the Conservative government of 1866–68. In February 1868 Stanley agreed to some small reductions on the North American and West African stations and when the government went out of office towards the end of 1868 the first lord, under pressure from Disraeli, Gladstone's successor at the Exchequer, was planning a considerable reduction in the estimates.[2] The real attack on the foreign stations, however, came with the first Gladstone government and in parallel with Cardwell's reforms. In January 1869, after consultations with both Clarendon and Granville, Childers arranged for a substantial reduction of about fourteen ships and 2,500 men on the foreign stations.[3] For a time the North American squadron remained untouched, but beginning with the Pacific and South-East Coast of America squadrons, the fleets in American waters underwent considerable reduction between 1869 and 1874. In that period the Pacific squadron fell from thirteen to

---

[1] Gladstone to Somerset, 13 Dec. 1864, Somerset papers.
[2] F.O. to Adm., 20 and 26 Feb. 1868, Adm. 1/6072.
[3] Childers to Granville, 6 Jan. 1869, Granville papers, P.R.O. 30/29, box 25 A; Adm. to F.O., 23 Jan., F.O. to Adm., 25 Jan., and C.O. to Adm., 12 Feb. 1869, Adm. 1/6127. See also Edmund Spencer Eardley Childers, *The Life and Correspondence of the Rt. Hon. Hugh C. E. Childers, 1827–1896* (London, 1901), i. 173.

nine vessels, the South-East Coast squadron from eleven to five, and while the North American still had an ironclad and fifteen other vessels by 1874 that figure, Milne pointed out, included a number of defective vessels.[1]

Paradoxically this gradual reduction reflected not the growth of pessimism about a naval war with the United States, but an apparent recovery of confidence. After the end of the Civil War the British had had a new scare about the monitors when one of the larger ones, the *Miantonomah*, had successfully crossed the Atlantic and apparently upset the Royal Navy's confidence in their inability to operate on the high seas. But the fright was momentary. Captain Bythesea was on that voyage and his report drew attention to the fact that the monitor had had to be towed the whole way![2] Even the British fear of American commerce-raiding declined substantially. During the war Benjamin F. Isherwood, the chief of the United States Navy's Bureau of Steam Engineering, had developed a number of fast steam cruisers specifically designed to cope with any complications with a European power. They were not finished until after the war had ended, but they were first-rate ships. One of them, U.S.S. *Wampanoag*, was apparently the fastest ship afloat.[3] Isherwood's account of the destruction these vessels would commit on British commerce alarmed Russell, who was 'by no means confident that Grant may not throw down his glove', and he wrote at once to Childers suggesting that he should 'see Captain Bythesea, and keep your powder dry!' In reply Childers pointed out that so far as fighting ships were concerned the Americans had no force with which they could cross the Atlantic to attack Great Britain, while Britain's ironclad fleet was 'quite equal to offensive operations on their coast'. And while at the beginning of a war, and especially one with a power which had not accepted the Declaration of Paris, they must expect 'to suffer in . . . commerce', they were better off in that respect than any other country and the danger would not last many months. So far as Isherwood's cruisers were concerned, he had conflicting accounts. In the *Inconstant* the British had a better ship than any of them, and while the Americans had laid down no more the Admiralty were also building the *Volage* and *Active*. Childers's reply gave Russell 'immense relief'. In the circumstances he even professed to be glad that the Americans

[1] Milne's memorandum on the 'North American Station', 15 May 1874, Milne papers, National Maritime Museum, Greenwich, P/B/1(g).

[2] Bythesea to Adm., 20 June 1866, Adm. 1/5992.

[3] H. and M. Sprout, *The Rise of American Naval Power, 1776–1918* (Princeton, 1939), pp. 168–9.

were likely to reject the latest moves for a settlement of the *Alabama* claims: 'we may now insist on honourable conditions, or none at all'.[1]

The *Inconstant* was a fast unarmoured vessel of the type for which Palmerston had agitated during the Civil War to meet the threat of American commerce-raiders.[2] But not until April 1866 were suitable designs submitted by the naval constructor, and the priority of the iron-clad race with France delayed the vessel's laying down until September. She was launched in November 1868 and was followed in the early 1870s by two similar vessels, *Raleigh* and *Shah*. The *Inconstant* in particular was a magnificent ship; in her day she could outsail any warship afloat. But she was very expensive to maintain and the next two vessels built and completed, the *Volage* and *Active*, were made much smaller. No more were built in spite of the continued pleas of the comptroller who commented when he had looked over the United States secretary of the navy's annual report for 1869:

We must never think of going to war with the U.S. until certain classes of our ships are largely increased. I conclude that no one will doubt that at home they are unassailable, and that on the high seas their power of injuring our commerce is enormous. Nothing that we can do will change the former proposition. But it may be in our power to limit considerably their destructive agency on our commerce and I will briefly repeat what is necessary in my opinion to reduce that agency to a minimum. A few ships of the *Triumph* class [a new type of smaller battleship especially suited to service on foreign stations] and a sufficient number of *Inconstants* and improved *Volages* will be required and until provided no one ought to dream of war with the U.S.[3]

But as Childers had pointed out in his letter to Russell, the *Inconstant*'s peculiar method of construction – 'iron frames planked over' – meant that in case of urgent need vessels of this type could be multiplied more readily than the American raiders they were designed to meet. The comptroller's comments were particularly unconvincing inasmuch as they were made on reports from the attaché in Washington showing how far the American navy had already declined and how of their own neglect the Americans had not only weakened the threat to British commerce but once again opened up their coasts to attack.

[1] Russell to Childers, 12 Feb., Childers to Russell, 17 Feb., and Russell to Childers, 19 Feb. 1869, Childers, i. 171–3.

[2] Palmerston to Somerset, 6 Sept. 1864, Broadlands papers.

[3] Minute by Adm. Robinson, 15 Jan. 1870, on Captain Ward (naval attaché in Washington) to Edward Thornton (the minister in Washington), 13 Dec. 1869, Adm. 1/6168. He had already made a similar comment, 11 Jan. 1870, on Ward to Thornton, 27 Dec. 1869, *ibid*. See also Robinson to Adm., 22 Jan. and 9 April 1870, Adm. 1/6177.

The Americans in the late 1860s and 1870s were no less neglectful of the naval strength and experience accumulated from the Civil War than were European powers of its military lessons. In December 1864 the Union navy list included nearly 700 vessels, totalling half a million tons and mounting almost 5,000 guns. By the end of 1870 there were less than 200 vessels in all, mounting about 1,300 guns, and only fifty-two in commission armed with less than 500 guns. Moreover, in type and armament almost all of these were obsolete. Determined to restore their cruising squadrons abroad but lacking coaling stations, the Americans deliberately ignored some of the principal lessons of the war and reverted to sail or a fatal combination of sail and steam. Thus old, prewar vessels and jerry-built wooden vessels from the war were favoured over even the famous monitors, and Isherwood's vaunted commerce-raiders were converted into slow and cumbersome vessels by reducing the capacity of their engines and re-equipping them with full sail. In arms and armour too the navy followed an obsolete policy; and the coast defence monitors soon became worthless even as aids to the land fortifications as the government failed to keep them in repair or to supply them with modern guns. Thus, while possessing no high seas fleet to speak of, the Americans clung obstinately to a policy of commerce-raiding without the ships to carry it out, and to a policy of passive coast defence without the necessary modern weapons or proper maintenance.[1]

In these circumstances and in spite of the comptroller's pessimistic observations it is not surprising that all consideration of war with the United States did not after all totally disappear. While the military bases in the interior of Canada were almost completely run down, the naval bases in American waters continued to maintain their role in prospective operations against the United States. In his plans of January 1865 Jervois had discreetly skirted the fundamental difficulties raised by the development of American sea power and coastal fortifications, though he had directly referred to the 'vast deal' done to improve the coast defences in his February 1864 report. But by May 1869, when Cardwell called upon him for new reports with which to silence the duke of Cambridge's opposition to colonial reduction, he was already able to note with satisfaction the critical weakness that had appeared since on the American side. The monitors, of which they had large numbers, he admitted would be useful for coast defence, 'but built, as most of them were, during the war, when all kinds of jobbing were practised upon the Government of the States, it is exceedingly probable

[1] Sprout, pp. 165–82.

that most of their hulls, which are built of wood, will soon be rotten'. Their turrets and guns could still be used for other purposes, but being built on the Parrott principle, that is of cast iron, most of them burst. On the fortifications he admitted that the Americans had probably spent more than any other nation; but in this case he had some answer to the current preference for forts over ships. Many of them had been designed and built before the development of modern rifled artillery by which he thought they might now 'easily be breached', while their own guns were 'not capable of doing effective damage to the side of iron-plated vessels by which they might be attacked'. There were, therefore, many places which might be attacked 'with good prospect of success'. Newport and the fort at Sandy Hook could be captured and garrisoned to seal off respectively the northern (Long Island) and the southern (Narrows) approaches to New York. Forts which were made of brick like Fort Sumter could also be attacked and San Francisco, though impossible to hold indefinitely against a superior force coming from the interior, could be held long enough to extract a punishing levy.[1]

While Jervois did not in these papers present Cardwell with the view he no doubt wanted on Quebec, his opinions on the naval bases were not unacceptably expensive. He did insist that at Bermuda they must complete the fortifications and station a strong garrison. But Halifax he now believed would soon be safe enough, and the West Indies, including even Port Royal, Jamaica, should be entirely given up. The West Indies generally he thought were of little use and if the Americans attacked them it would only divert their forces from more vital objectives. Port Royal, he conceded, was the best naval base in the western Atlantic but it would cost a great deal to make it secure, and in the weak state of the American defences it would be possible rather to seize one of the enemy's bases such as Key West. Since Cardwell and his colleagues had partly justified their reduction and withdrawal of colonial garrisons by emphasizing the contribution of British sea power to imperial defence, it was fortunate that Jervois's proposals were not so very expensive and even in some cases advocated new economies. Thus while in 1869 and 1870 Cardwell made drastic cuts in the garrisons

---

[1] Jervois's 'Considerations on the military position of Great Britain with respect to the United States', 28 May 1869, confidential print, W.O. 33/20; and his manuscript memorandum on Jamaica, 29 May 1869, Granville papers, P.R.O. 30/29, box 53. Apparently Jervois did not accept the conclusions of Gallwey and Alderson on the resistance of brick and mortar fortifications during the Civil War. See Luvaas, *Military Legacy*, p. 40.

of the West Indies, in Halifax he left a force of nearly 1,600 and in Bermuda over 1,750.

After the *Alabama* settlement and the ludicrous failure of President Grant's pursuit of an island empire, diplomats and statesmen slumbered for twenty years in the peaceful afterglow of the Union's survival. But with the essentials of Britain's naval supremacy miraculously preserved from Gladstonian retrenchment, the very diminution of the American threat, militarily by the decline of her actual, armed power, and politically through the quiescence of Anglo-American relations, had the ironic effect of reviving in pretty full force among the strategists the traditional militants' view of the nature of a war between the two nations. In spite of the Civil War and in spite of all the efforts of postwar British governments, a long period of continuous American neglect of her naval and military power allowed the illusion of victory once again to penetrate even the highest level of British military planning. In a paper of 23 October 1882, specially prepared for the Royal Commission on Imperial Defence, the deputy assistant quartermaster-general, Major L. M. Carmichael, while admitting the familiar immunity of the United States from large-scale invasion and conquest and while acknowledging the rapidly increasing resources of the country, nevertheless predicted certain victory for Britain should war between them ever again break out.

Carmichael did not entirely overlook the lessons of the Civil War. At that time the United States he admitted had dramatically demonstrated that her forces were capable of fantastic improvisation and expansion. In the event of war serious measures would therefore have to be taken to protect such places as Bermuda and Nassau against expeditions of as many as 10,000 or 20,000 men. But potential strength, especially in an increasingly technological age, was not the same as actual strength, 'increased by practice, and combined with skill in the use of certain weapons'. At present the United States Navy was 'contemptible', and for reasons of economy and congressional jealousy of the executive, was likely to remain so. The regular army amounted to no more than 25,000 effectives, scattered throughout the Union, and the militia, theoretically nearly half a million in all, had only 123,000 actually organized and these but inexperienced and ill-disciplined. Britain therefore should be 'free from certain nightmare impressions of the tremendous power of America'. 'The States have money, men, seamen, iron, coal, timber, but, to all appearances they will leave themselves without the one thing necessary – time; time to create fortified depôts, to build ships, forge guns, make torpedoes and torpedo-boats, and to acquire the skill to use them, things which are becoming every day more difficult to improvise.' The problem of Canada, now no longer so much the concern of Whitehall, he glibly glossed over, while remarking

en passant that the position of Canada is somewhat different from that of a European assailant; although the disparity of numbers and resources makes the conquest of the United States by her neighbour very improbable [!], it is possible that Canada, by a superior naval organization on the lakes, and by the employment of a more rapidly mobilized, more homogeneous, and more efficient army, might neutralise superior numbers, capture Chicago, Buffalo, and other important lake and frontier cities, cut off the Peninsula of Michigan, detach the State of Maine, and even advance by Lake Champlain upon the North-eastern States.

Similarly reminiscent of earlier days was the part he envisaged Britain's forces would play; he even found new justification for it in the United States increased resources! Britain might be relatively weaker than she had been in the late eighteenth and early nineteenth centuries, when she had been unable to make much impression on the Americans, but by their very transformation from an agricultural to an industrial society the latter had in turn made themselves more vulnerable. Britain's role therefore might be 'stated broadly to consist of maintaining an exceedingly strict blockade, so as to create the greatest possible discomfort throughout the whole country, and the attack on, and levying contributions from, the whole coast, and as far inland, as small, well-equipped expeditions, acting with rapidity might venture'. The United States, as their writers boasted, might have no single city or state whose conquest alone would be of final effect, but of the utter effectiveness of such attacks in combination from Canada and the sea upon the general wealth of the Union 'the panic which followed Bull's Run and the appearance of the *Merrimac . . .*' seemed to promise much. 'The United States must have wonderful nerve if they would not sacrifice a good deal to save New York and other great coastal cities.' Moreover, in the absence of any real naval power, the territorial and especially overseas expansion of the United States would also be, if anything, to Great Britain's advantage in time of war. For 'populous states, like the United States, France, and Germany, difficult to attack on their main soil, are doing a maritime Power like England a real service, and holding out a limb to be smitten, in every harbour they improve or depôt they establish on the seaboard or beyond their own territory as long as they leave them undefended, or do not increase their fleet'. Thus 'the spasmodic outbreak of American acquisitiveness, or self-assertion', like their recent attempts to acquire naval bases, were 'no danger to England', and she need not therefore trouble herself much about them, 'as long as they are not carried too far' – a reference apparently to the somewhat 'remote danger' of the Americans closing in on the route of the prospective isthmian canal by the acquisition of Mexico. Such weak spots, rather, promised many opportunities for the Royal Navy to establish close places of refuge and supply on or near the American mainland. Given the maintenance of general and local naval supremacy therefore, all that the British needed to pursue an effective course against the United States was the securing of their bases in the immediate vicinity of the country against the raids that even improvised forces might accomplish.

On the Pacific coast the problem was rather more difficult. It was Britain's own trade and possessions that were open to attack rather than the coast of the United States. Her communications were weak and her bases insufficient. The Falkland Islands, Fiji, and Vancouver Island were all very far apart and inferior in position and number to bases actually or potentially under the control of the United States. Here, then, there was some special need to look to the defences of Esquimalt and to watch out for opportunities to acquire bases in Guayaquil, the Galapagos, Guadalupe, and Fonseca Bay. The one chance Britain had of making use of such neutral ports as Callao and Valparaiso was if their owners were too weak to uphold their rights in international law. But Chile was now too powerful for any belligerent to make such forcible use of Valparaiso, and Callao would have been equally immune if Peru had not so recently been defeated in war. Above all the harbours near the isthmus would be denied to the belligerents if the weak states at present holding them were ever united. 'The United States interest in guaranteeing the neutrality of Colombia is obviously connected with the above proposition, and it is equally obvious that until England has secured a harbour of her own on the Pacific side, it is contrary to her interests to allow a powerful state to be consolidated in the immediate vicinity of the Canal.' But generally speaking the solution here lay too in that naval superiority which would in war with the United States allow Britain to defend her trade and possessions by seizing, permanently or only for a time, the ports of San Diego and San Francisco. Thus, Carmichael concluded: 'In the Atlantic, England has only to secure the splendid position she already enjoys. In the Pacific, by the exercise of the most ordinary watchfulness, she may have the ultimate use of all that she requires.'[1]

[1] 'Third and Final Report of the Royal Commission appointed to inquire into the Defence of British Possessions and Commerce abroad', printed confidentially, 1882: appendix ix, 'Intelligence Reports: United States', by Major L. M. Carmichael, D.A.Q.M.G., 23 Oct. 1882, Cab[inet papers, P.R.O.] 7/4.

9

The Era of Rapprochement
1895–1901

So far as overseas defence was concerned, the intention of the naval
and military reform of the late 1860s and 1870s was to concentrate on
an overall naval supremacy, based partly on a 'reserve' of force in the
immediate vicinity of the British Isles and partly on a series of imperial
fortresses with which to guard communications and provide the fleet
with bases. The concept was not by any means new; nor even was the
ruthlessness with which it was applied. But it soon became apparent
that the process of concentration had proceeded much too far. In what
were still the comparatively early days of steam battleships, their range
was severely limited and their coal consumption enormous. The imperial fortresses were too few and too far apart to provide the fleet with the
coal it needed. A casual reference to the weakness of the Cape of Good
Hope in December 1874 led first to some disturbing observations from
the Admiralty and then in January of the following year to a general
review by Jervois.[1] As Jervois pointed out, the defence of British commerce had become both more important and more difficult since the
1860s through the mother country's increased dependence upon it and
through the development of modern commerce-raiders. The only real
protection that commerce could expect must come from the naval
supremacy of Great Britain. But the fourteen coaling stations upon
which the navy must depend had become 'generally neglected' in the
process of concentration upon the United Kingdom and the four
'imperial' fortresses. At present they had a mere 6,400 troops scattered
among them, and some of them, notably Esquimalt and English Harbour, Antigua, had none at all.

Upon this weakness the semi-permanent Defence Committee of the
Colonial Office worked hard during the next three years, with the
Admiralty adding further desirable positions to their list, and with the

---

[1] 'Memorandum by Col. Jervois with reference to the defenceless condition
of our Coaling Stations and Naval Establishments abroad', W.O. confidential
print, 7 Jan. 1875, Adm. 1/6347.

War Office worrying about the insufficiency of available troops.[1] The government managed to find room for additional expenditure in the estimates for 1875–76. But the amount was small. Real progress came only with the Russian crisis of 1877–78 and especially from its supposed threat to the virtually undefended province of British Columbia. First, in February 1878, the special task of recommending the necessary emergency defences was taken from the more leisurely Colonial Office committee and given to an *ad hoc* defence committee under Sir Alexander Milne. Then, when that committee revealed in a series of reports during the summer that Great Britain could not possibly spare all the forces needed to secure the various bases in the absence of the fleet, it was decided to reconstitute the committee with the addition of a former cabinet minister and to have it consider the permanent defences generally.

The Royal Commission on Imperial Defence, or the Carnarvon Commission as it was more commonly known after its chairman, was not allowed to consider home defences or those of the four imperial fortresses; it was torn by internal disagreements and jealousies; and before it had finished its work the election of 1880 had brought back into office a distinctly unsympathetic Gladstone government. The reports of the Commission were never formally adopted by any government: their general tenor, pointing to large expenditure, was quite unacceptable and in many details even military experts, like Sir Andrew Clarke, the inspector-general of fortifications, dissented to no small extent. Nevertheless the mass of evidence and opinions accumulated by the Commission, as well as its own detailed recommendations, helped to provide a framework of reference for the development of imperial defence for some time to come. In particular it distinguished and recommended defences for a whole series of key ports and coaling stations throughout the world. At length, after some modification by the colonial and service departments, some nineteen positions were added to the existing four imperial fortresses. Ten were 'refitting stations and harbours of refuge' in which coal could be stored in large quantities and which were to be made strong enough to resist such attacks as might reasonably be made upon them; and nine were stations at which coal would always be kept but where extensive defences were not necessary. Thus to Halifax and Bermuda there were now added in American waters Port Royal, Jamaica, and St Lucia under the first

[1] 'Reports of a Colonial Defence Committee on the Temporary Defences . . .', C.O. secret and confidential print, June 1878, Cab. 7/1.

category, and Trinidad, Esquimalt, and the Falkland Islands under the second.[1]

Attention to these positions became more systematic in the new era of military bureaucracy as well as under the pressure of revived imperial consciousness. The 1860s and 1870s had seen the general extension of the system of naval and military attachés. In 1873 the War Office established the Military Intelligence Department. In 1886 there followed the Naval Intelligence Department. About the same time an effort was made too to improve the process of consultation with colonial governments and the machinery for interdepartmental cooperation in Whitehall. In April 1887 met the first Colonial Conference, and its main business was an agreement concerning the defence of Australia. Two years earlier a permanent body, the Colonial Defence Committee, had been established at the Colonial Office to take the place of the various *ad hoc* committees to whom specific problems concerning colonial defence had been put from time to time. Further criticism of Whitehall's naval and military planning led in 1891 to the establishment of the Joint Naval and Military Committee of six professional advisers under the parliamentary under-secretary for war. Confined largely, but not entirely, to questions of home and coastal defence, it failed to provide a real policy-making machinery. In 1895 a Cabinet Defence Committee was formed but it too was a total disappointment. At last in 1902 came the Committee of Imperial Defence, a mixed body of cabinet ministers and senior professional advisers which took over the Colonial Defence Committee and the Joint Naval and Military Committee as subcommittees. From 1903 it met under the chairmanship of the prime minister and from 1904 it was provided with a permanent secretariat and tended to meet almost weekly.[2]

None of these developments ever produced a really effective system but at least there gradually arose some established 'principles' and certainly a routine of imperial defence, extending in some cases even

[1] For a brief review of the Royal Commission see Donald C. Gordon, *The Dominion Partnership in Imperial Defense, 1870–1914* (Baltimore, 1965), pp. 61–7. There is a useful summary of the later modification and application of their principal recommendations in the secret printed 'Report on the Defences of British Coaling Stations abroad and of Colonial and Indian Defended Ports by Col. R. A. Vetch, R.E., Deputy Inspector General of Fortifications', 31 Oct. 1894, Cab. 18/14.

[2] For these developments see Franklyn Arthur Johnson, *Defence by Committee; the British Committee of Imperial Defence, 1885–1959* (London, 1960), pp. 11–47. Hereafter the Committee of Imperial Defence will be referred to as the C.I.D., the Colonial Defence Committee as the C.D.C., the naval and military intelligence departments as the N.I.D. and M.I.D., and their directors as the D.N.I. and D.M.I.

to a sort of primitive war-planning. In this period Whitehall's views on the fundamental principles of colonial defence were formally laid down, first in connection with the defence of Australia in the late 1880s, and then at considerable length in a C.D.C. memorandum of May 1896.[1]

The maintenance of sea supremacy [that paper insisted] has been assumed as the basis of the system of Imperial defence against attack from over the sea. This is the determining factor in shaping the whole defensive policy of the Empire, and is fully recognized by the Admiralty, who have accepted the responsibility of protecting all British territory abroad against organized invasion from the sea. To fulfil this great charge they claim the absolute power of disposing of their forces in the manner they consider most certain to secure success, and object to limit the action of any part of them to the immediate neighbourhood of places which they consider may be more effectively protected by operations at a distance.

What they meant was that real security rested fundamentally upon the command of the high seas and that the navy's first task in war must be the destruction of the enemy's fleet. They 'recognized, however, that Her Majesty's ships, engaged in hunting out and destroying the squadrons of an enemy, may not be in a position to prevent the predatory raids of hostile cruisers on British ports'. The nature of such attacks would vary according to 'political combinations' and according to the strength and availability of the enemy's forces, but given the Royal Navy's *general* command of the seas, 'it is in the highest degree improbable that this raiding attack would be made by more than a few ships, nor could it be of any permanent effect unless troops could be landed. In no case could a greater force than a few thousand men be collected and conveyed without such arrangements and preparation as would bring the operations under the category of those which the Navy has undertaken to prevent.' Against such raids, but not against 'organized invasion', appropriate defences were needed and in some cases had already been provided – at the imperial fortresses and coaling stations, and elsewhere by the efforts of the colonies themselves. For the rest, against raids upon commercial ports and other places outside the appointed positions of defence, the colonies ought when considering what defences to provide, to bear in mind first the value their destruction would have to the enemy and their consequent liability to predatory raids and second the available resources for manning them.

[1] C.D.C. confidential printed memorandum 57 M, 'Colonial Defence', 19 May 1896, Cab. 8/1. The C.D.C. issued two main series of printed papers: 'Memoranda' and 'Remarks'. Henceforth these will be referred to by number and letter ('M' or 'R'), together with a title where appropriate. See also Gordon, pp. 104–6, and below, pp. 355–6.

In dealing with places of this nature the Committee have advocated the creation of sufficient fixed defences to prevent their unmolested occupation by hostile cruisers, but more especially the provision of troops sufficient to deal effectively with such forces as an enemy must put on shore to enable him to secure any permanent advantage from his attack. Works without troops are useless and delusive.

Since conditions were bound to vary from place to place the C.D.C. also requested the production of 'schemes of defence' for their annual 'consideration and remarks'. Each scheme was intended to show 'the probable strength and nature of attack on each Colony, and how its existing resources could be utilized to the best advantage for defence'.

Gradually there developed from the old distinction of imperial fortresses, from the recommendations of the Carnarvon Commission, and from the deliberations of the C.D.C. and the service departments a comprehensive list of bases, grouped according to importance and purpose into three general categories. These were: 'Defended Ports', consisting of the principal ports in the United Kingdom and the imperial fortresses of Malta, Gibraltar, Bermuda, and Halifax; 'Coaling Stations'; and 'Ports of Refuge'. To the bases in each group was awarded a 'standard of defence', according to its value and the strength of the attack it might therefore pay an enemy to make upon it. For the first-class fortresses the standard was determined by the possibility of an attack led by modern battleships; the coaling stations were to be defended against cruiser attacks; and the others might at most be prepared to hold off desultory raids. Local defence committees were established to consider the nature of the possible attack and to propose a scheme of defence based on specified standards of works, garrison, and armament. Then their reports were supposed to be reviewed and revised annually by the Colonial Office, usually by the C.D.C. itself.

As a method of dealing with the routine application of the established 'principles' of imperial defence to the individual bases and colonies this machinery seems to have worked rather well. When in 1894 the deputy inspector-general of fortifications came to make a special report on the ten years of progress since the approval of a modified form of the Carnarvon commission's recommendations in 1883, he noted with satisfaction that defence arrangements were nearly completed at all the selected places, save only Esquimalt about which there had been difficulty with the Canadian government.[1]

---

[1] Col. Vetch's 'Report on the Defences of British Coaling Stations abroad, etc.', 31 Oct. 1894, Cab. 18/14. For Esquimalt, see below, pp. 372–7.

While great progress was made with the elaboration and detailed application of the principles of imperial defence laid down in the 1880s, including the defence scheme for Halifax, the last imperial fortress on the mainland of North America, one glaring omission remained in the absence of an overall plan or even minimal material preparations for the defence of Canada generally. The intention of the overhauling of imperial defence since 1865 had certainly not been to leave such a gap but to see that the task of filling it, and the local defence of the self-governing colonies generally, became the responsibility of those colonies. Even more did this become the case as imperial sentiment revived and blossomed in the late 1870s and 1880s and as the pendulum of professional concern swung back again from fear of the invasion of the United Kingdom to concern for the security of imperial communications. 'Where once it had seemed that Britain's interest lay in the direction of the emancipation of the United Kingdom from the burdens of empire by the encouragement of colonial self-reliance,' writes a recent historian, 'now it seemed that the same British interest might be best served by the participation of those same colonies in imperial defense tasks.'[1] In Britain they thought most of some direct and preferably financial contribution to the upkeep of the navy; but internal defence too was by no means overlooked. That such a defence should be attempted in Canada was eminently desirable from both the dominion's and the imperial points of view. It was true that it might not be effective, that it might even fail altogether; but provided that it had not uselessly diverted British resources or dangerously committed British prestige, it would be an important and perhaps essential contribution to the proper prosecution of a war against the United States. At best it might demoralize the Americans; at worst divert and distract their resources from the coast. But since the British withdrawal in 1871 no war-plan had been drawn up and virtually no work had been done on the fortifications. Only at Victoria in British Columbia had a few small earthworks been thrown up and by 1887 the design and armament of almost all the posts handed over by the British were already out of date. In 1880 the Admiralty had been persuaded to lend the Canadians the sloop *Charybdis*, but it was decrepit and unseaworthy and was subsequently returned.[2] The Canadians had also established a Department of Marine and Fisheries and gradually assembled a fleet for the protection of the fisheries. But by 1896 there were still only five vessels, none of them large or built for war, though each had a nine-pounder gun. Their

[1] Gordon, p. 73.   [2] *Ibid.*, p. 69.

combined crews, amounting to only a little more than three hundred men, formed the entire Canadian naval militia. The ships were laid up in winter and the men engaged only for the summer.[1] The position with regard to troops was no less disappointing. In 1883 the Canadian parliament had at last voted a small permanent force, but by 1887 it still amounted to a mere 773 men. In 1893 the infantry was re-named the Royal Canadian Regiment and considerably improved; but the 'active' militia, which had an authorized establishment of 35,000, was still only a paper force. Its actual strength was less than 19,000 and even these were badly neglected, being dispersed among a very large number of sometimes very small units.[2] The C.D.C. had specifically drawn the attention of the dominion government to the matter in November 1886 and had later agreed to the Canadians' rather dilatory reply in January 1888 suggesting the appointment of a local committee to reorganize the militia.[3] But still nothing had been done when at long last towards the end of 1895 Canada found herself threatened once again by a sharp quarrel between Britain and the United States.

When, in the summer of 1895, the United States government inter-vened noisily in the petty boundary quarrel between Great Britain and Venezuela there was certainly no intention of provoking such a crisis as would involve war preparations. Indeed the crisis itself often appears to historians to have been 'somewhat synthetic'.[4] But for a moment, at the very opening of 1896, Salisbury's firm resistance, followed by President Cleveland's blustering, made the crisis appear to be very real. But Cleveland, as a close examination of his special Message shows, was bluffing and, Salisbury apart, the British cabinet had no desire to call that bluff. In these circumstances an honourable compromise was soon found. Yet although in retrospect the crisis seems too silly and even too short to have raised any serious prospect of war, both sides nonetheless did actively consider the possibility.

Caught in their own bluff perhaps the Americans seemed to get the more agitated about a war. Too little has survived of the army's staff and intelligence records of the period to say much about their plans though it is clear from many tantalizing entries in their lists and indexes

[1] Confidential N.I.D. report no. 409, 'Naval Defence of the Canadian Frontier', by Captain R. Custance (naval attaché in Washington), 5 Oct. 1894, Adm. 1/7208 pt. II.
[2] Norman Penlington, *Canada and Imperialism, 1896–1899* (Toronto, 1965), pp. 14–19.
[3] C.D.C. 59 M, 'Canada: Defence of Dominion', 27 Mar. 1896, Cab. 8/1.
[4] J. A. S. Grenville, *Lord Salisbury and Foreign Policy; the Close of the Nineteenth Century* (London, 1964), p. 55.

that they were still thinking of making their main attack upon Montreal from Lake Champlain, while disrupting communications by lightning attacks upon the St Lawrence canals, the intercolonial railway, and the Canadian Pacific Railway.[1] All of this was pretty obvious, though it must have been useful for the British to have confirmation of it from the indiscretions of a member of the Senate Committee on Military Affairs a few years later.[2] How far the Americans believed they might still have to face an expedition against their coasts is not by any means clear.

It is interesting to note however that even as late as 1915 Plan Red – the war-plan with reference to Great Britain which then existed only in outline but had already been approved by the secretary of war – envisaged that New York would still be the enemy's first objective. At this later date the intention was that such an invasion whether by Britain or Germany should be prevented by intercepting the enemy fleet in the West Indies.[3] The United States navy of 1896, however, was hardly up to that task, though the commanders on foreign stations got their warning orders to keep their ships 'fully coaled and in readiness for service' on 29 January.[4] One man perhaps who knew what the navy's principal tasks should be was Captain Mahan. Mahan, of course, was a firm believer in good Anglo-American relations; 'no greater evil can possibly happen to either nation or to the world than such a war', he wrote to an English friend at this very time.[5] But there was a touch of irony, though perhaps unconscious, when he wrote to another: '... if it comes, and I am in it, I think I shall have to request the Admiralty to hoist on your ships some other flag than British – for, save our own, there is none other on which I should be so reluctant to fire.'[6]

The truth is that but a few years earlier Mahan himself had composed

[1] This information is culled from the index and surviving record cards of the Adjutant-General's, Chief of Engineers', and General Staff's files in the U.S. N[ational] A[rchives, Washington], R[ecord] G[roups] 94, 77 and 165. Most of the documents themselves appear to have been destroyed; some I was not allowed to see.   [2] See below p. 377.

[3] U.S.N.A., Records of the War Dept. General Staff, R.G. 165, Record Card 7524–1, 2, 3, 4, 5, 6, and especially 4, 'War College memorandum for the Chief of Staff', 18 Mar. 1915. I was not allowed to see the 'coloured' war-plans themselves, but for further information on them see J. A. S. Grenville, 'Diplomacy and War Plans in the United States, 1890–1917', *Transactions of the Royal Historical Society*, 5th series, ii (1961), 1–21.

[4] U.S.N.A., Naval Records Collection of the Office of Naval Records and Library, R.G. 45, Secretary of the Navy's Correspondence, confidential series.

[5] Mahan to J. Thursfield, 10 Jan. 1896, Mahan papers, Library of Congress, Washington, D.C.

[6] Mahan to Capt. B. F. Clarke, R.N., 17 Jan. 1896, *ibid*.

for the serious consideration of Navy Department a 'Plan for operations in case of war with Great Britain'.[1] Here he turned to the practical problem of what could be done by an inferior navy.[2] Even though the British would have an immense superiority at sea he dismissed an invasion by them 'as unlikely to occur'. Rather he expected the enemy to try and enter an American harbour, or, most likely of all, to resort to a general blockade. To cope with these dangers he suggested that the smaller ships – some of the cruisers and any converted merchantmen – should be scattered about to harass the enemy and relieve the pressure on the coast by forcing the enemy to disperse his fleet in keeping watch upon them. But the main force of American battleships and their attendant cruisers should be concentrated in one port on each ocean, since 'to divide it would be to neutralise wholly whatever power it may possess'. On the Atlantic side this port was, of course, to be New York; but not simply on account of its importance to commerce and prestige. For an inferior fleet it had the immense advantage of having two wide exits over a hundred miles apart. This fact would compel any blockading power to devote a large force to cover each exit, and, what with the constant erosion by night attacks and the necessity of keeping up an adequate reserve nearby, he would probably not be able to make much impression elsewhere. In this way the American coastline generally would be most effectively protected and, quite probably, Britain be forced at length by the strain involved to choose between her interests in Europe and American. In the meantime the army would have been freed sufficiently from merely coast defence to exploit the United States advantages in the north. 'Canada lies at our mercy, unless the British navy by action on our coasts can stay our hand. If our coast defences can hold the enemy in check a month, two months, we may obtain decisive advantages. If for six months, we can overrun Nova Scotia, and hold the enemy's only Atlantic coalfield.' Without this coalfield Britain's fleet would have to rely on coal imported from thousands of miles away and under constant harassment by American raiders. And since coal was 'the controlling element of modern naval strategy' her naval power in the western Atlantic would in consequence be utterly undermined.

[1] U.S.N.A., Records of the Office of the Chief of Naval Operations, R.G. 38, Office of Naval Intelligence, file no. S91/734. The paper is unsigned and undated but the accompanying correspondence makes it clear that it was written by Mahan and shortly before the middle of Dec. 1890.

[2] Cf. Theodore Ropp: 'Mahan never considered the problems of a second-best navy in detail. War with Britain was, to him, unthinkable'. (*War in the Modern World* [Durham, N.C., 1959], p. 193, note 18.)

Coal was the key to America's naval opportunity as well as to Britain's maritime vulnerability. In the first place, Mahan argued, it meant that the United States must not put too much reliance on commerce-raiding. With the war Great Britain would indeed lose the greater part, if not all, of her valuable trade with North America, but 'a glance at the map . . . will show the hopelessness of serious injury to British shipping while we have no assured coal supplies abroad'. But he had not urged that the 'fighting fleets' should be 'kept in being' merely to distract the enemy by their existence. 'Passive defence', he insisted was 'in itself the precursor of ruin.' Instead they must undertake 'offensive operations, by the sagacity and vigour of which, and by them only, can the weaker country validly defend herself. . . . The weaker party must have recourse to action vigorous to desperation. So only can we reverse the odds.' What he meant was that in the early stages of the war, before the enemy had had time to assemble his forces and especially if he were careless, the navy itself might make some daring attack. On the Pacific coast, where it had all the advantages, the American fleet should at once 'so menace her coal and communications as to paralyse her'. On the Atlantic side things were admittedly very different. 'No attempt can be made to carry the war to the other side of the Atlantic, or against a *fortified* island in the West Indies.' But if the opportunity occurred the fleet should attempt a raid and even sacrifice the old battleships in leading a 'forlorn hope' in an attack upon Halifax. The loss of that base would utterly cripple Britain's naval power and cut off Canada from all aid. Even if it were only seriously damaged the British would afterwards be compelled to waste a considerable part of their fleet in its defence. Although it was this raid and the tactics to be employed by the New York fleet which occupied most of Mahan's attention, he also turned to the question of operations on the interior waters of North America. He too expected the major offensive to be made again by the army moving against Montreal; but he suggested that the navy should itself make all sorts of preparation to seize or sever Canada's canal communications and to obtain command of the lakes.

In an exchange of letters with the chief intelligence officer, Commander C. H. Davis, it was suggested that further plans ought to be drawn up in reference to war with other countries and in a postscript Mahan ominously asked for 'a $\frac{1}{2}$ ream of paper like this'. In view of Mahan's productivity there was probably some substantial result.[1]

[1] A decade later Mahan recalled: 'Mr Tracy at one time, in 1890, directed Folger and me to draw up outline plans of operations necessary to be undertaken at once in case of war with foreign nations. I drew up two – that I remember

Mahan had also suggested that 'as soon as matters become threatening' the Navy Department should draw up a schedule of the ships which ought to be retained on the lakes and of the guns and other fittings available for them. In January 1896, as soon as the Venezuela crisis came to a head, the secretary of the navy did give instructions for information to be secretly gathered about the ships suitable for conversion to warlike purposes. The officer chosen for the duty was Commander Charles Gridley, who was two years later to receive Dewey's famous order to open fire on the Spanish fleet in Manila Bay but who in 1896 bore the innocent-sounding title of 'Lighthouse Inspector' at Buffalo. All this information was to be used to perfect a plan then being worked up by Captain Henry C. Taylor, the president of the Naval War College, and Gridley was supplied with an outline of the proposed plan. Unfortunately neither the outline nor the completed plan has come to light. Possibly both were destroyed when the army's refusal to approve them rendered them quite useless. It is clear from the correspondence with Gridley, however, that it was intended to assemble several squadrons, if possible, for operations on Lake Champlain and in the St Lawrence as well as on the upper lakes, and in particular to seize or destroy the Welland canal at the very beginning of war. Possibly it was the prospect of this last proposal diverting too much of their force from the main attack by land upon Montreal which made the army so disapproving. Mahan in 1890 had appreciated that Montreal must be the principal objective and realizing therefore that the navy could not rely on the army to act against the St Lawrence canals or protect their naval bases on the lakes, he had suggested that the marines should

---

– possibly more; in the case of Britain and Spain. I have an impression that those, in which Folger concurred, found their way to the Bureau of Intelligence.' (Mahan to Adm. Luce, 3 Sept. 1901, quoted by John A. S. Grenville and George Berkeley Young, *Politics, Strategy and American Diplomacy: Studies in Foreign Policy, 1873–1917* [New Haven and London, 1966], p. 93.) Capt. W. M. Folger was chief of the Bureau of Naval Ordnance at the time in question. In his correspondence with Davis about the plan Mahan did say that '... in our present condition, the development of material, ordnance among the rest, is a more urgent necessity than these plans as to what to do when we have anything to do it with'. It is also clear from this letter, however, that the paper concerning operations against Great Britain was Mahan's work alone and that he did not propose to wait for Folger's comments before elaborating the plan for Tracy. He ended by suggesting that Davis should consult Folger about taking up next the cases of Germany and Spain. A Spanish war-plan has survived from the cooperation of the Naval War College and the Intelligence Division in 1895–96; but the final draft was the work of another officer and it has been suggested that Mahan probably did not even know of its general outline since he would certainly have disapproved its proposal, adopted in 1898, to divide the battlefleet between the Pacific and the Atlantic (Grenville and Young, p. 292).

be concentrated for this purpose. Gridley's reports moreover were far from encouraging, offering no hope that an effective force could be brought together quickly enough. But by the middle of March the immediate crisis had ended and though Taylor expected it to erupt again very shortly, active preparations soon petered out.[1]

While the Navy Department in Washington was struggling to compensate for inadequate preparation on its part, emergency plans were also being worked up in Canada. These were contained in two papers of 13 January and 29 February 1896 by Captain A. H. Lee, then professor of strategy at the Royal Military College at Kingston.[2] Basically what they advocated was a defensive policy, partly because a war of raids and reprisals on unprotected cities was certain ultimately to arouse bitterness and rebound on Canada as the weaker side, but mainly because of the limited and makeshift forces available. The active Canadian militia at this time in theory numbered 37,000. Of these 10,000 would be needed for garrison duties, principally at Quebec (2,000), Halifax (1,500), Prescott (1,000), and Kingston (1,000), and another 1,000 to watch the New Brunswick frontier. The largest part of the remainder, some 12,000, would form the 'St John Division' for the southern defence of Quebec and Montreal against an invasion by Lake Champlain which new works at Fort Ethan Allen, Plattsburg, and Burlington indicated was still the Americans' favourite route. Otherwise, apart from 'local improvisation' at remote and isolated places like Regina, Calgary, and Winnipeg, Lee proposed to devote what remained of Canada's resources to the command of the lakes and canals 'as the one effective means of defence for the greater frontier of the country'. By this he meant not only Lake Ontario but also Erie and, in order to guard against a flank attack upon Toronto and western Ontario from Georgian Bay, even Lake Huron! This task he assigned principally to

[1] U.S.N.A., R.G. 45/464, subject file OX, box 1, 'Venezuela Incident'. See also Grenville and Young, pp. 171–2. Reference is made to Taylor's plan and its disapproval by the army in Capt. Sperry's evidence before the Taft Board, 25 Apr. 1905, U.S.N.A., Records of the Office of the Chief of Engineers, R.G. 77, file no. 54140, 'National Coast Defence Board–Record of Proceedings of a Certain Committee'.

[2] These are printed as items 3 and 5 in the secret M.I.D. print, 'Defence of Canada: Schedule of papers collated for the use of officers selected to assist the Canadian Government in drawing up a Scheme of Defence', 11 July 1898, Cab. 18/17. Lee, afterwards Viscount Lee of Fareham (1868–1947), was later military attaché with U.S. Army in Cuba and in Washington (1898–99) and he became a good friend of Theodore Roosevelt. Afterwards he entered politics and was civil lord of the Admiralty in 1903–05 and first lord in 1921–22. For his rather different contributions to the interdepartmental debate on strategic planning in America at a later period, see below, pp. 380–3.

the Royal Navy, supplemented by the five vessels of the Canadian Fishery Protection Service. But only one of these was normally kept on the lakes. The rest would have to be brought up to Montreal so that they could be moved into Lake Ontario within thirty-six hours. Communication between the lakes and with the sea would also have to be secured by yet another large part of his scanty force of militia. Thus for the control of the Welland canal and to cover generally the Niagara frontier he had to set aside a force of 5,000, while another 2,000 were to secure the St Clair River and generally protect the London district. To block the Sault Ste Marie canal to American ships from Lake Superior he detached a 'flying column' of another 1,000. And for the protection of the St Lawrence route between Lakes St Francis and Ontario he allocated a force of 5,000 to operate on the American bank. This last was a deliberate departure from his general embargo on offensive operations but it was both necessary and limited in scope. Much more ambitious was his revival of the old idea of a combined invasion of Maine, principally by a British expedition from Halifax, but aided, if the state of their mobilization and the fate of their first defensive measures permitted, by the field force operating to the south of Quebec and advancing down the Richelieu.

The War Office in London, for their part, were by no means totally unprepared for the crisis. Major G. S. Clarke, the secretary of the C.D.C. and later the first secretary of the C.I.D., had gone out to make a report on United States military affairs in 1888, and, largely through the initiative of the D.M.I., Major-General E. F. Chapman, there had been some investigation of the lakes and the frontier generally in 1892, followed by two further reports on Canadian defence in 1893 and 1895.[1] When the crisis reached its supposed danger point in January 1896 therefore, Chapman found himself in a position not only to evaluate and criticize Lee's plan but also to anticipate it with a tentative outline of his own. Chapman's view, in its stress on limited, defensive operations, especially at Montreal, and on guarding the canal and river communications, was fundamentally similar to Lee's. But while he was able to approve the general lines of Lee's scheme, he found it too ambitious

[1] W.O. confidential print A 154, 'Notes on a Tour in the United States in September and October 1888', by Major G. S. Clarke, 4 Dec. 1888, W.O. 33/49; Chapman to Capt. V. Servini, 5 Apr., and to P. Currie (F.O.), 24 June 1892, W.O. 106/16; W.O. confidential print, 'The Military Aspect of the Northern Frontier of the United States, together with notes on matters connected with the naval and military forces of that country', by Major C. Barter, Mar. 1893, W.O. 33/55; and a report made by Major H. J. Foster on the defence of Canada in July 1895 which has not been found (see below, p. 328).

and inclined to stretch the available forces too thinly. He doubted the ability of the militia to make any large offensive southward from Montreal and, indeed, whether 12,000 men were enough even for defensive operations in that area. The Sault Ste Marie 'flying column' he felt was quite pointless, Lake Superior being of no military importance, while an American flank attack via Georgian Bay would be a positive advantage to the defenders by dissipating the enemy's energies. Most serious of all were the doubts he cast in general upon the naval position; for not only did he consider the command of Lakes Huron and Michigan out of the question, he doubted also if the Admiralty contemplated doing anything beyond Lake Ontario.[1]

Evidence of the Admiralty's rather negligent attitude towards the lakes problem was already at hand in their response to the renewal of American agitation over the 1817 agreement. The pressure of American shipbuilding interests on the lakes had led to a formal abrogation proposal by the Senate early in 1892. The motion was not accepted by Congress but Secretary of State Blaine had raised the matter informally with the British minister in May of the same year. Privately the British agreed with the substance of the American complaints – that the agreement limited their shipbuilding enterprise, that its detailed provisions regarding size and weapons had been made completely out of date by modern technology, and that through the superiority of Canada's water communications it tended to favour the British in their ability to despatch vessels from the sea on the outbreak of war. But in view of the Americans' more than compensating advantage in local shipbuilding resources for emergency conversion and construction they very much doubted that this last factor had an unfair effect or that the other two could be adjusted without adding to the American advantage. Indeed the only real utility the Admiralty could see in the agreement was that it freed them from having to meet awkward demands for naval protection which though ineffective they might nevertheless find it difficult to refuse.[2] It was fortunate from the British point of view therefore that knowledge of Canadian opposition led the Americans quietly to drop the subject for the time being. This gave the Admiralty more time to repair a serious omission on their part. Blaine's proposals, they admitted, had caught them totally un-

<hr />

[1] 'Memorandum by D.M.I.', 11 Jan. 1896, and Chapman's 'Remarks', 7 Feb., and 'Memorandum', 17 Mar., on Lee's papers of 13 Jan. and 29 Feb., printed as items 1, 4, and 6 in 'Defence of Canada: Schedule of papers. . .', Cab. 18/17.

[2] See the Admiralty file under 23 Apr. 1897, Adm. 1/7340 B.

prepared and they had petulantly complained of not having had sufficient notice of a question which past precedent and present duty surely required they should already have mastered. Instead they had had to rely on the accidental availability of a recent report by 'a military officer, not writing as an expert'.[1] The naval attaché in Washington, Captain G. C. Langley, had also just quit his post at the crucial moment in 1892 without having made any investigation of the subject, and it was thought unwise to arouse American suspicion and possibly revive agitation for abrogation by abruptly sending him back or too openly sending another officer.[2] The result seems to have been the long delay which now intervened until the arrival of a comprehensive report from the new attaché, Captain R. Custance, towards the end of 1894.[3]

Custance's review of the comparative state of American and British ships, communications, and resources on the frontier was hardly favourable. At best – if the season permitted and the army took the right measures to protect the canals – Britain could expect to match the existing American force (three armed revenue cutters and the old iron steamship *Michigan*) by pushing into Lake Ontario the vessels of the Canadian Fisheries Protection Service and those classes of torpedo boats which could pass the canals. But after that, though the Americans still had no good canal communications of their own, their far superior local resources in shipping and shipbuilding would soon allow them to outclass the British, particularly as the Canadian vessels and almost all the torpedo boats mentioned were poorly armed, old, and virtually useless. When all the projected improvements to the canals were completed, the situation would be very different and the larger, modern classes of torpedo boat would be able to pass into Lake Ontario. The first necessity for the lakes, then, was the improvement of the canals by the Canadian civil authorities.

To the Admiralty the very pessimism of Custance's report probably made it quite welcome, since it seemed to confirm the wisdom of inaction on their part – at least until the Canadians had improved the canals. But to one office of state, the revelation of such weakness implied rather the necessity of action. Thus in acknowledging receipt of a copy of the report on 23 April 1895 the Colonial Office put a series of questions designed to pave the way for a defence scheme by eliciting

---

[1] Minute by Capt. Cyprian Bridge (D.N.I.), 31 May 1892, Adm. 1/7340B.

[2] Minutes by Bridge, 31 May and 14 July 1892, and F.O. to C.O., copy, 22 July 1892, *ibid*.

[3] Confidential N.I.D. report no. 409, 'Naval Defence of the Canadian Frontier', by Capt. R. Custance, 5 Oct. 1894, Adm. 1/7208 Pt. II.

at last from the Admiralty their precise views about naval action on the lakes. So evasive was the Admiralty's reply in asking *first* for the 'Government's opinion' that one Colonial Office official commented: 'One would . . . suppose that it had just dawned upon them that the defence of Canada might involve a certain amount of Imperial assistance.'[1] It is no wonder that when the Venezuelan crisis came and Chapman found himself in some disagreement with Lee on naval measures on the lakes, rather than embark once again on futile approaches to the Admiralty he suggested that the whole question of the defence of Canada should be put to the Joint Naval and Military Committee.

Beyond the brief, formal report itself no record seems to exist of the Committee's deliberations but it is clear what papers were brought to its notice. These included a report on the defence of Canada made by Major Foster in July 1895 as well as two specially prepared papers, one by the D.M.I. and one by Colonel P. Lake, the quartermaster-general of the Canadian militia. Chapman outlined the general problems and Lake, who was in London on a secret mission to arrange for the shipment of arms to the militia in Canada, pinpointed what he considered to be the naval problems. At the same time the Committee was supplied with a draft of a C.D.C. memorandum inspired by the dismal annual report of the Canadian Department of Militia and Defence and recommending the reorganization of the militia and its staff arrangements, attention to the lakes, and the completion of the Soulanges canal on the north bank of the St Lawrence to replace the exposed Beauharnois. All these matters the Committee considered at its meeting at the War Office on 30 March and its printed report appeared on 23 April 1896.[2]

The report itself was pointed and precise, laying down firmly the essential bases of a defence scheme and of the relative contributions to be made by the British and the Canadians. First it approved the general lines of Lee's plans, but confirming on the whole the modifications suggested by Chapman about greater concentration of forces for the defence of Montreal and dropping the idea of an early raid on Sault Ste Marie. The Soulanges canal the Canadian government was urged to complete as soon as possible and the crews of the Fishery

[1] C.O. to Adm., confidential, 23 Apr. 1895, C.O. 537/471.
[2] Chapman's minute for the c.-in-c., 18 Mar. 1896, the papers prepared for the Committee by Chapman, 'Defence of Canada', and by Lake, 'Naval Assistance in the Defence of Canada on the Great Lakes', both dated 28 Mar., together with other minutes and the Joint Naval and Military Committee's printed Report no. XXI, 'Defence of Canada', 23 Apr., are all in W.O. 106/40, file B 1/5. For Lake's mission to London see Penlington, p. 36.

Protection Fleet should be better organized and trained. Equally firm was its attitude towards the imperial contribution. The Royal Navy was to assist by sending what vessels it could into Lakes Ontario and Erie; but the command of Lake Huron was out of the question until the Georgian Bay canal was constructed and the Canadians should therefore prepare to block the St Clair River passage by a submarine minefield. So far as the army was concerned the Committee now went further than almost anyone since 1815 in asserting that 'the safety of Canada could be best ensured (if the state of affairs in Europe admitted of such a course) by landing a British force on American territory, and making a vigorous offensive'. For the better preparation of their tasks the Committee suggested that officers be sent by the Admiralty and War Office respectively to survey the vessels on the lakes and to examine the coasts of Maine and Massachusetts.[1]

The three principal parties to the defence of Canada – the dominion government and the two service departments – now appeared to have the bases of principle necessary to the proper elaboration of a general defence scheme. But the Committee had no executive authority whatever and it still remained for the service department to approve its recommendations and complete their investigations before any scheme could be pressed upon the Canadians. Only one of the departments appears to have acted with any real seriousness and vigour. By 14 May 1896 the War Office had already approved the report and about this time there also began a series of reconnaissances of the Canadian frontier which for many years afterwards were being constantly extended and revised.[2] Conversations between Colonel Lake and the War Office even led to two officers being sent out in the summer of 1896 to recommend field works for the defences of Montreal in the expectation that permanent defences would be held up by political and financial difficulties in Canada.[3] More important, at some time during 1896 or 1897 the War Office sent out Foster once again to report on the proposed expedition against the United States coast. Foster's new report has not come to light but from later summaries and extracts it seems to have been based on the belief that a purely defensive policy would lead inevitably to the loss of Canada. It would be better to exploit the temporary advantage of Great Britain's larger and better organized

---

[1] No direct reference to Maine and Massachusetts was made in the report but apparently their recommendations for the necessary reconnaissance were given verbally: minute by the D.M.I., 13 June 1896, W.O. 106/40, file B 1/5.

[2] W.O. to Adm., 14 May 1896, W.O. 106/40, file B 1/5; Penlington, p. 168.

[3] Penlington, pp. 36–7.

regular army as well as her naval superiority in an offensive operation. This might force the Americans to sue for peace before they had time to summon up vastly superior numbers. Foster estimated that to meet an invasion the United States, with Indian troubles and strained relations with Mexico still tying down part of their forces, could deploy only 10,000 men in the first week, 20–30,000 in two or three weeks, and as much as 60,000 only after about two months. He concluded that for an offensive expedition the British could make do with one brigade for a raid of three or four days, with one division for fourteen days, with one army corps for one month, and two army corps for four or five months. Thus, he argued, two army corps plus sufficient troops to occupy the country could hold out for six months, take Boston, over-run New England, and after joining a force from Canada invest and even capture New York. This report, with the emphasis of the attack shifted from Boston to New York, the commander-in-chief generally approved on 2 February 1898.[1]

Neither the Canadians nor the Admiralty came anywhere near matching this effort. In the apparently critical situation of 1896 the dominion government made a special defence appropriation of $3 million and secured through Lake a large quantity of modern guns and rifles, but with the passing of that ephemeral crisis and in the absence

[1] This summary is drawn from information contained in Capt. W. R. R. Robertson's secret 'Memorandum on the Defence of Canada', 15 Mar. 1901, submitted to the D.M.I. by Col. H. A. Lawrence (deputy assistant quartermaster-general in the M.I.D.) in a secret paper entitled 'War with the United States', 30 Mar. 1901, W.O. 106/40, file B 1/7. Some light is thrown on the absence of Foster's report from the P.R.O. files by the extraordinary secrecy with which it was treated. It was ordered not to be copied or printed and when it was sent to the Admiralty for their opinion in Mar. 1898 it was done privately through the first sea lord. Since he did not return it for some years, when the secretary for war wanted the newly appointed commanding officer at Halifax to acquaint himself with the problems of Canadian defence, that officer, Lt.-General Lord William Seymour, had to go over to the Admiralty to see it. But he only had time for a glance, and learning that Foster was about to be appointed to the headquarters of the Canadian militia he decided to wait until he could approach the author himself. In Canada, however, he found that the British officer commanding the militia, General Hutton, resented and resisted his claim to authority over all British officers serving in the dominion and it does not look as if he ever did see the report. Hutton wrote to the governor-general: 'Foster . . . has only his private draft – no copy – it is in my humble judgement quite certain that Foster has no right to allow his draft to be perused by anyone except Your Excellency. The original is the property of the Secretary of State for War, and is looked upon as of such a confidential and secret character that no copies have ever been allowed to be made.' (Hutton to Minto, 1 July 1899, Public Archives of Canada, Manuscript Group 27 II B 1 [Minto MSS], vol. 15; 'Memorandum by Lord William Seymour', 6 Sept. 1899, *ibid.*, vol. 22; and information from Capt. Robertson's memorandum of 15 Mar. 1901.)

of any positive lead from England, there was little prospect of any substantial action on their part. The pressure was nevertheless kept up, not least by the British officers serving in Canada, who proposed in the summer of 1896 to begin at once with field works for the defence of Montreal and applied to the Colonial Office for no less than £20,000 for the necessary guns. The Canadians, however, refused to share the cost.[1] Then, towards the end of 1897, the two senior British officers in Canada, General Montgomery-Moore, commanding the British garrison at Halifax, and General W. J. N. Gasgoigne, commanding the militia, with the help of a gloomy memorandum from the new D.M.I., Sir John Ardagh, managed to persuade the Canadian and British governments that they should jointly set up a local committee for the purpose of preparing a full-scale defence scheme. Early in 1898 a Canadian Defence Commission was assembled under the presidency of the British officer lately commanding the engineers at Halifax, General E. P. Leach, and including, besides the principal staff officers in Canada and Captain W. G. White, R.N., the two Canadian ministers of Marine and Fisheries and Militia and Defence, Sir Louis Davies and F. W. Borden. The Commission, which sat in Ottawa throughout most of 1898, issued three reports: no. 1, produced in April or May, was the defence scheme proper; no. 2 was 'Recommendations for the Improvement of the Canadian Forces'; and no. 3, produced towards the end of the year, was a final general report.[2]

The Commission's recommendations followed what were by this time very familiar lines: no general defence of the whole frontier but concentration on Montreal, both banks of the St Lawrence, the Niagara frontier and Welland canal, together with naval supremacy on Lakes Erie and Ontario. Its particular contribution was to emphasize the necessity of the defenders taking the initiative from the start and the dependence of such an approach upon the improvement of the Canadian militia, both naval and land. The naval militia was still tiny, the land forces still poorly trained and broken into units which were far too small. There was no proper staff, no transport, no ordnance, pay, or veterinary crops, and no modern heavy or medium guns.

By the end of 1898, with Foster's report and the Commission's recommendations, a plan at last existed for the defence of Canada and in that respect at least the British had reached a level of preparation

[1] Penlington, pp. 33–6 and 75.
[2] *Ibid.*, pp. 78–80 and 149–52. Ardagh's memorandum, 14 Dec. 1897, is in W.O. 106/40, file B 1/5. The Commission's three reports are in Cab. 11/27.

never before approached in this area, and one which embraced in detail the vital dual aspects of defence in Canada and offence by sea. But even a defence scheme was useless without the proper men and material, and these the Canadian government still refused to supply. In 1899 they raised a battalion to free the British regulars at Halifax for service in South Africa; but by 1901 they had still done little more than add some small service and medical units, amalgamate a few of the smaller infantry units, and buy some additional artillery. In view of the long history of neglect the War Office had little right to be surprised and with the Canadians there was always hope of improvement. Much more serious because it threatened to become permanent was the negligent and, later, positively obstructive, attitude at the Admiralty.

The Admiralty had never formally approved the Joint Committee's report no. XXI. All they had done when pressed by the War Office was to express 'general approval', but subject, so far as their own contribution was concerned, to the canal communications being secured by land operations on the south bank of the St Lawrence and to a 'careful consideration' of the proposed operations against the New England coast which the growth of the United States Navy, they casually remarked, now in any case rendered of only 'temporary value'.[1] Yet the Admiralty themselves apparently made no such 'careful consideration'. They were far from energetic or consistent in their handling of the lakes question too. Since all the plans brought to their notice by the army made provision for land operations to cover the canal communications and since, while not guaranteeing their security, they offered, as one D.N.I. privately admitted,[2] a good chance of success, there was no real reason why the Admiralty should not have done its part in this matter at least. Even so they took a whole year to act on the Joint Committee's recommendation about a survey of the lakes shipping and then it was rather in response to a renewal of the American threat to upset the comfortable inactivity supposedly permitted by the Rush-Bagot agreement.

In 1892–93 it had been possible to leave aside the awkward question of revising the lakes agreement largely because the Americans themselves dropped it but partly, too, because American infringements did not seem serious. In 1892 the United States had on the lakes concerned, and in addition to the old *Michigan*, three revenue cutters, *Andrew*

---

[1] Adm. to W.O., secret, 4 June 1896, W.O. 106/40, file B 1/5.
[2] See below p. 334.

Johnson, Commodore Perry, and *W. P. Fessenden,* each armed with from two to four guns. The Canadians then had none and only two vessels of 126 tons each, *Constance* and *Curlew,* building for revenue purposes. Still the American ships were old and even to the Canadians the discrepancy did not at the time seem worth raising a controversy about.[1] But in October 1893 provision was made by Congress for the replacement of the *Andrew Johnson,* and in February 1896 for the construction of two first-class steam revenue vessels of 700–800 tons. The first of these vessels, the *Walter Q. Gresham,* complete with torpedo tubes, was launched in September 1896, and although the *Commodore Perry* had in the meantime been transferred to the Pacific the C.D.C. naturally concluded that with three such vessels on the lakes the Americans would soon have a very respectable force indeed. They did not think that there was any sinister motive involved and they did not recommend any representations about this infringement of the 1817 agreement. They suggested rather that the Canadian government should henceforward consider themselves bound, not by that agreement, but by what force the Americans actually had.[2]

These developments and, perhaps even more, newspaper rumours during the Venezuela scare of an American intention to establish in some lake ports stores of auxiliary arms for placing on converted ships in an emergency, at last stirred the Admiralty to some action. Early in 1897 Captain Lewis Wintz, the new attaché in Washington, and a civilian assistant constructor, E. R. Bates, were ordered to carry out the survey recommended by the Joint Committee.[3] About the same time a particular suggestion arising out of their own 1896 'crisis' preparations led the Admiralty to clarify their attitude and even to come to conclusions that must have seemed promising for the projected Canadian Defence Commission. Because there was no question of absolutely guaranteeing the safety of the canals on which so much depended,

[1] Report of the Committee of the Canadian Privy Council, 28 June 1892, in Admiralty file under 23 Apr. 1897, Adm. 1/7340 B.

Admiralty papers relating to a single subject were frequently collected together and, where not made up into 'case' volumes (e.g. in Adm. 116), filed under a single date in their appropriate series. The location of individual papers cited will in these cases be shown by the Admiralty series and box number, with the date of the file in brackets, thus: Adm. 1/7340 B (23 Apr. 1897).

[2] 30 Oct. 1896, Adm. 1/7340 B (23 Apr. 1897).

[3] Minutes by Capt. Beaumont (D.N.I.) and Adm. Sir Frederick Richards (first sea lord) on C.O. to Adm., 17 Dec. 1896, draft instructions to E. R. Bates, 17 Apr. 1897, and Adm. to C.O., 17 Apr. 1897, Adm. 1/7340 B (23 Apr. 1897). The rumours were well founded: see J. M. Callahan, *The Neutrality of the American Lakes and Anglo-American Relations* (Baltimore, 1898), p. 187.

Captain Lee had been led in 1896 to work out with Sir William Van Horne, the president of the Canadian Pacific Railway, a scheme for the transportation of first class torpedo boats by rail to the lakes. This scheme had been pressed upon the British government by the Navy League and the C.D.C. had passed it on to the Joint Committee in March 1896.[1] What that Committee thought of it is not known but the Admiralty view seems to have been that it was quite practicable but pointless. For in 1897, while the British had two suitable vessels at Halifax and four at Bermuda, the Americans were proposing to make improvements to the Erie canal which would allow them even more easily to place nearly all their force of similar vessels on the lakes, that is to say all but two of the eight already in service and the nine under construction.[2] Even more important than their advantage in numbers was the Americans' better employment for such vessels. In their hands torpedo boats could be used most effectively against any British vessels attempting to enter the lakes; but for the British they would be relatively useless against the shipbuilding resources whose destruction by regular warships alone gave any real prospect of permanently commanding any of the lakes. Rather than experiment with such measures, commented Captain Beaumont, the D.N.I., 'Our best chance, and it does not seem a bad one, considering the smallness of the Regular Army, the slowness of militia forces to take the field and the absence of "defences" along the American bank of the St Lawrence, is to pass on to Lakes Ontario and Erie, under cover of what military force Canada can provide, the largest sized fighting ships the canals will admit and so prevent the formation of an American naval force'.[3] Hence the Admiralty's formal reply to War Office enquiries on 10 March 1897:

Their Lordships cannot look upon the use of Torpedo boats on the Lakes as a substitute, in the event of war, for the largest class of Her Majesty's Ships which the canals would permit.

The resources of the United States, out of which a naval force could be created, are greatly superior to those of Canada, and torpedo boats without adequate support could never acquire or retain naval superiority on the lakes.

In their Lordships' opinion it is most important that the one advantage which this country possesses over America, of being able to pass efficient fighting vessels through the St Lawrence at the very outset of war, should

[1] C.D.C. 60 M, 'Canada: the Navy League and Canadian Defence', 31 Mar. 1896, Cab. 8/1.

[2] In fact these improvements were not begun until 1903 and not completed until 1918.

[3] D.N.I. minutes, 23 Feb. 1897, Adm. 1/7340 B (23 Apr. 1897), and 29 Mar. 1897, Adm. 1/7344 (30 Mar. 1897).

be secured so far as it is possible, by completing the improved canal system and making the best provision for its defence.[1]

Like Cyprian Bridge before him, but for quite different reasons, Beaumont was also opposed to any alteration in the 1817 agreement. The Americans had done little since 1896 to increase their force on the lakes. The U.S.S. *Yantic* placed there in the following year as a training vessel was old and militarily useless; while a Senate proposal to replace the *Michigan* at last was made conditional on the observance of the 1817 agreement. Nevertheless the C.D.C. on 8 March 1898 decided that it would after all be too expensive to match the American force and that, when a suitable opportunity arose, the matter should be raised with the Americans. Such an opportunity came with the conversations between the British ambassador in Washington, Sir Julian Pauncefote, and Secretary of State Day in the summer of 1898 and the question was consequently submitted to the special Joint High Commission which had already been settled upon as a means of disposing of the several awkward differences in Canadian-American relations.[2] Once again it was Canadian opinion which buried the attempt to bring the old agreement up to date; but not before Beaumont had had an opportunity to make plain his opposition to the proposed concessions: 'None of the restrictions will, even if the Americans faithfully observe them, do more than retard for a short time the formation of the war flotilla which the United States will put upon the Lakes in case of war with us.'[3]

Any deduction from the Admiralty's relatively industrious attention to this problem that they were now moving towards effective cooperation with the War Office in the development of a real Canadian warplan would have been a complete illusion. Their apparently satisfactory attitude towards the lakes question may perhaps have been determined by the desire to avoid action; the peculiar merit of the 1817

[1] Adm. to W.O., 10 Mar. 1897, Adm. 1/7340 B (23 Apr. 1897). The main improvement referred to was the Soulanges canal begun in 1891. This was expected to be completed in 1899 and it would then be possible to pass much larger ships into Lake Ontario: C.D.C. 128 M, 'Canada: Canal Communication to the Great Lakes in relation to War', 15 Mar. 1898, Cab. 8/2.

[2] The best general account of the Commission is in Charles S. Campbell, jr., *Anglo-American Understanding, 1898–1903* (Baltimore, 1957), pp. 88–119, but it makes only passing mention of the lakes question. Penlington, pp. 114–17, and Robert Craig Brown, *Canada's National Policy, 1883–1900; a Study in Canadian-American Relations* (Princeton, 1964), pp. 353–6, have some details.

[3] D.N.I. minute, 8 Sept. 1898, on Lord Herschell (head of the British delegation on the Joint Commission) to Salisbury, no. 1, 22 Aug. 1898, Adm. 1/7474 (8 Aug. 1900).

agreement was that it made any action in peacetime – which is all the Admiralty seemed prepared to consider – quite unnecessary, whereas awkward proposals about torpedo boats or allowing the Americans to build warships threatened to require action. Certainly Bridge, Beaumont's predecessor as D.N.I., had harboured a most subversive point of view with which, after a conference with Robert Meade, under-secretary at the Colonial Office, he probably rather rashly associated that office: 'The Colonial Office is not altogether unprepared to find that the enormous change in the conditions of the adjacent country has deprived the naval command of the Lakes of much of the importance which it undoubtedly possessed in the War of American Independence and the War of 1812; and that it may be opposed to sound strategic principles for us to station a squadron on the Lakes.'[1]

Still more significant was the paper which Captain Custance produced for the first lord when he succeeded Beaumont as D.N.I. in the summer of 1899. This showed the extent to which Great Britain's naval position on several stations had deteriorated since 1889. On the North American and West Indian station they were now 'completely outclassed' by the American fleet and on the Pacific station were inferior not only to the United States Navy but also to that of Chile.[2] It was the implications of this observation which, after further ominous silence, led Custance early in 1901 to return at last Foster's 1897 report about an invasion of New England with these comments: 'Events which have happened since it was drawn up have completely altered the conditions, and every day which passes tends to accentuate this change. . . . [Thus] no purpose would be served by making any comments on it.'[3]

The 'events' to which Custance referred were the great strides in naval and military preparation made by the United States in the 1890s. Of the vast American might generated during the Civil War a substantial rump survived only until the French left Mexico. Even while allowing for the policing of the conquered South and the pacification of the Indians, Congress managed to cut back the peacetime strength of the regular army to about 25,000 men in 1869 and it remained at this figure right down to 1898. During the same period the old navy was sold off or rotted away, while until the 1880s new

[1] D.N.I. minute, 14 July 1892, Adm. 1/7340 B (23 Apr. 1897).

[2] Arthur J. Marder, *The Anatomy of British Sea Power; a History of British Naval Policy in the Pre-Dreadnought Era, 1880–1905* (New York, 1940), p. 351.

[3] Quoted in Robertson's 'Memorandum on the Defence of Canada', 15 Mar. 1901, W.O. 106/40, file B 1/7.

warship building clung to a mixture of sail and steam and to merely partial armour; 'an alphabet of floating wash-tubs' was how Representative Long, a future secretary of the navy, described the American fleet in 1885.[1] But as in Britain so too in the United States did the triumphant example of Prussia push the American services into a 'managerial revolution'. By the early 1880s several states were overhauling their militia; in 1884 a Naval War College was established; and 1883 had seen the primitive beginnings of a modern navy – though still mixing sail with steam – and, more successfully, the development of modern artillery. At this time the new navy and the almost complete reconstruction of the coastal fortifications recommended by the Endicott Board in 1885 both indicated an essentially modest and defensive position:

It is no part of our policy [declared President Arthur in December 1883] to create and maintain a Navy able to cope with that [*sic*] of the other great powers of the world.

We have no wish for foreign conquest, and the peace which we have long enjoyed is in no seeming danger of interruption.

But that naval strength should be made adequate for the defense of our harbors, the protection of our commercial interests and the maintenance of our national honor is a proposition from which no patriotic citizen can withhold his assent.[2]

But the Naval War College in August 1886 found itself with Captain Alfred Mahan as president, and by November 1889 his influence already seems to have been sufficiently at work to inspire a new approach in the annual report of the secretary of the navy: 'The country needs a Navy that will exempt it from war, but the only navy that will accomplish this is a navy that can wage war.' So he recommended the rapid construction of two fleets, one for the Atlantic and one for the Pacific, amounting in all to twenty battleships, sixty cruisers, and twenty heavy coast defence monitors. In the event the appropriations of 1890 were rather more modest, providing a mere three 'sea-going coastal battleships'; but it was the real beginning of a bid, if not for seapower, at least for a modern navy. With the publication in May 1890 of Mahan's first great book the American bid for sea-power received its vital impetus. President Harrison, who in his Inaugural Address of 1889 had already warned against too parochial an attitude, in 1892 got a

[1] Quoted by Grenville and Young, p. 10.

[2] Quoted by Walter Millis, *Arms and Men; a Study in American Military History* (New York, 1956), p. 149. This review of the development of American strength is based generally on Millis, pp. 131–98, and H. and M. Sprout, *The Rise of American Naval Power, 1776–1918* (Princeton, 1939), pp. 183–280.

fourth battleship and by the time Cleveland left the White House in March 1897 there was a total of nine built or building. In this process the Venezuelan incident had perhaps played some small part, though the first sea lord undoubtedly exaggerated when he asserted in 1897 that the American government was 'making a supreme effort to fortify the coast Ports (as well as to increase the Navy) before another insult to this country becomes a political necessity to the party in office'.[1]

It was the Spanish-American war of 1898 which most awakened the United States to her need of actual naval and military power. That war strained to the limit the resources of both the National Guard and the regular army. The first was unable to supply the whole of the 125,000 volunteers called for and the army's supply and services completely broke down. Nevertheless the government was able ultimately to raise a force of about 225,000 men. After the war, in March 1899, Congress arranged for a regular army of 65,000 men and 35,000 volunteers for the period until July 1901 when the volunteers were to be disbanded and the regular army was to revert to a strength of 25,000. In February 1901, however, the reduction of the regular army was avoided by a new act empowering the president to maintain at will a regular force of between about 60,000 and 100,000 men. Still more important to British observers was the dramatic increase in the size of the navy in the same period. On the eve of the war there had been only six modern battleships in service and one of those, the *Maine*, had been destroyed even before the war officially began. Five more battleships were completed in 1902–04 and by that time the new enthusiasm had led to the authorization of three more battleships in 1898, three battleships and three armoured cruisers in 1899, and two battleships and three armoured cruisers in 1900. Here Congress decided to rest and in 1901 they refused to vote a single additional ship; but they reckoned without the assassin who at the end of the year disposed of McKinley and so brought Theodore Roosevelt to the presidency. Within four years Roosevelt had pushed and bullied Congress into voting another ten battleships and four armoured cruisers. The whole programme was completed shortly after he left office in 1909 and at that date the United States had a fleet of no less than twenty-seven new battleships and ten new cruisers. Maladministration and a serious shortage of officers and men continued to plague the navy, but by the end of 1908 the United States was second only to Great Britain in first-class capital ships and third in total tonnage built and building.

[1] Sir Frederick Richards's minute on F.O. to Adm., 10 Nov. 1897, Adm. 1/7346 A.

The ascent of the United States to the position of a great naval power was in no sense an unexpected event. The spectre, after all, had haunted naval experts and opinion generally ever since 1812 at least, and it had achieved definite if temporary substance in the Civil War years. More recently it had become one of those nightmares with which William II liked to attempt to frighten the queen, and through her the British government, into friendship with Germany. By the end of 1900 he was warning that the United States would soon have a fleet in the Mediterranean.[1] But he was careless enough to admit that they could not achieve a navy overnight and that Britain could always catch up if she wished. Salisbury's quiet confidence in 1890 was similarly that there was 'no immediate apprehension'.[2] The Venezuelan crisis made it necessary to give the prospect a little more attention. Salisbury was at first convinced that Cleveland was bluffing and that the 'American conflagration will fizzle away'.[3] But soon he was suggesting that 'recent events have introduced a new element into the calculation. A war with America – not this year but in the not distant future – has become something more than a possibility: and by the light of it we must examine the estimates of the Admiralty. It is much more of a reality than the future Russo-French coalition.'[4] With this expensive view even the chancellor of the Exchequer, Sir Michael Hicks Beach, agreed, bracketing American and German hostility together in pressing for increased naval expenditure.[5] Lord Dufferin, formerly governor-general of Canada and now ambassador in Paris, having conjured up every element of Anglo-American enmity he could think of, from the Irish problem to the 'bad blood' produced by 'Lord Dunraven's business [a reference to an unfortunate incident in the Americas Cup race of September 1895] and the squabbles over the other athletic contests in which we have been foolish enough to engage with them', was quite alarmist:

It is to be hoped that the present crisis will be tided over, thanks to the prudence of our Government and to the praiseworthy attitude of the

[1] Major-General Sir Leopold Swaine (military attaché in Berlin) to Sir Arthur Bigge (the queen's private secretary), 28 Dec. 1900, Queen Victoria's papers, Royal Archives, Windsor, I 62/113.
[2] Salisbury to the queen, 28 Feb. 1890, *ibid.*, L 16/39.
[3] Goschen (first lord of the Admiralty) to Salisbury, 19 Dec. 1895, Arthur D. Elliot, *The Life of George Joachim Goschen, First Viscount Goschen* (2 vols., London, 1911), ii. 204.
[4] Salisbury to Hicks Beach, 2 Jan. 1896, J. A. S. Grenville, 'Great Britain and the Isthmian Canal, 1898–1901', *American Historical Review*, lxi (1955–56), 51.
[5] C. J. Lowe, *Salisbury and the Mediterranean, 1886–1896* (London, 1965), pp. 107–8.

English press and of the English nation generally. If this is the case, President Cleveland's action will have rendered us a service, for it will have taught us what we may expect, and what we must be prepared for. Fortunately, in the event of an immediate war, we should be complete masters at sea, and Canada appears to be perfectly loyal, provided of course she can be certain of our support, which Lord Dufferin presumes would be promised. These circumstances will undoubtedly make for peace; but, even if peace is assured for the present, America is sure now to set about strengthening her navy; and, when once she has a powerful fleet, she will be tempted to use it. Consequently, in Lord Dufferin's opinion, England ought to make herself strong enough to confront not two navies, but three, for the best way of discouraging American hostility, is to make them feel that they might get the worst of the contest. Of course, there is a great body of American opinion, probably a large majority, entirely friendly to England, or at all events possessed by a horror of war between the two English-speaking nations, and it is the expression of this opinion, as held by the educated and literary classes, as well as by the churches, of which we hear most. Unfortunately these are not the people who control American politics.[1]

In spite of such windy warnings it is beyond dispute that Anglo-American relations did make giant strides towards real friendship in the years immediately following the first Venezuelan crisis. But that this process was largely irrational and that there was an enormous gulf between it and the hard-headed realism of the school of professional politicians and strategists headed by Salisbury now seems equally clear. In Salisbury there was probably also a lingering trace of the traditional anti-Americanism of his class.[2] But the significant fact of the decade was that in it sentiment and realism made a marriage of convenience. To the realists the dominating factor was that Great Britain's resources were now stretched beyond their limit by the effects of increasing expansionist and naval activity among the European powers as well as in the United States. In Persia and on the frontiers of India the Russian threat by land loomed larger than ever; indeed a full-scale Russian invasion of India promised for the first time to become a practical proposition when the Orenburg-Tashkent railway was completed in 1904.[3] At sea the Franco-Russian alliance of 1894 presented Great Britain with the novel and awful awareness of inferiority in both the Mediterranean and the western Pacific. In the Far East simmered

[1] Dufferin and Ava to the queen, 1 Jan. 1896, Queen Victoria's papers, R.A. J 90/21.
[2] For the 'irrationality' of this period of Anglo-American relations see A. E. Campbell, *Great Britain and the United States, 1895–1903* (London, 1960); for Salisbury's attitude see Grenville, *Salisbury and Foreign Policy*, pp. 55–6.
[3] George Monger, *The End of Isolation: British Foreign Policy, 1900–1907* (London, 1963), p. 4.

an imminent political crisis in the threat to the Open Door made by the powers' scramble for concessions and spheres of influence.

The old policy of Splendid Isolation had been successfully upheld in the South African War but it had appeared to be a close thing. Whether Great Britain could continue to bear the strain of the two-power standard in the face of continued competition in warship building was a matter of some doubt within the cabinet. They were told in January 1901 that the combined French and Russian force of battleships was already forty-three to Britain's forty-five, and was moving towards equality in 1906.[1] There was therefore growing talk of the necessity of concentrating on what was supposed to be the principal threat in Europe and the Far East – the Franco-Russian alliance. In naval terms this meant virtually discounting most navies and applying the two-power standard only to France and Russia; politically it meant the abandonment of isolation in favour of approaches to Germany and Japan. There did not seem much point in an approach to the United States, save possibly over the Far East where there was some identity of interest. Here, at the turn of the century, Germany was the chief hope, but the movement led by Joseph Chamberlain tried also to bring in the United States as a secondary aid in the defence of the Open Door. An unsuccessful approach was made to the Americans in March 1898 but generally speaking actual alliance seemed neither fruitful nor possible to the statesmen of Salisbury's day. Later, when Germany, rather than France and Russia, became the enemy, this would change; but for the time being the growth of American power and expansion was regarded by the realists, first as a major additional strain upon both the political and the naval foundations of splendid isolation, and then as one of those permanent features of world politics with whose potential threat Great Britain could no longer cope, but which could be accepted in due course by a practical rearrangement of priorities.

The statesman's attitude to relations with America, therefore, was in a sense a negative one. His anxiety was not to make an ally of the United States, but to extricate Great Britain from the path of American advance, to see that at such a dangerous time the United States did not again threaten to become an active enemy. It was for this reason among others that the Kaiser's blundering references to the United States utterly failed, and among the 'insuperable' objections which Lansdowne found to an Anglo-German alliance in 1901 was the risk of being entangled in an anti-American policy.[2] By the middle of 1900 it was already clear

---

[1] George Monger, *The End of Isolation: British Foreign Policy, 1900–1907* (London, 1963), pp. 8–12.
[2] *Ibid.*, p. 66.

to at least one German observer that 'England will stand far more from America than from any other Power, and even in purely diplomatic issues it is more difficult to make England take sides against America than to make any other Power do so'.[1] Certainly by the end of 1902, when Salisbury had finally retired, a special attitude towards the United States seems clearly to have been adopted by British statesmen generally.

The growth of American power in the late nineteenth and early twentieth centuries, then, was at first by no means welcome to the policy-makers in Britain; rather its existence had to be accepted in a world where the crucial dangers loomed elsewhere. Sentiment rather than interest made that acceptance at least tolerable and ultimately even welcome; but it was a realistic assessment of priorities that dictated it. This was the direction in which Britain's policy towards the United States moved in the period 1898–1902, particularly in respect to the Spanish-American War and the isthmian canal question. But relatively quick though the transformation was, it was not accomplished overnight even among the statesmen. Nor did they appreciate all its implications or spell it out at once for the benefit of the service departments. This fact seems hard to reconcile with the increasing apparatus of cabinet and interdepartmental planning for defence. But this apparatus, including the C.I.D., never quite came up to expectations. Certainly this new committee did much useful work, and criticism of it has probably been exaggerated, but the fact remains that the coordination of views and action between the service departments and with the new course of foreign policy was far from perfect. No doubt this had much to do with the egocentric professional jealousy of men like Admiral Sir John Fisher and with the fact that the foreign secretary was not by any means a regular member of the C.I.D. until Asquith's premiership. One might also suggest that it took some time to reconcile the forward planning of the C.I.D. and its subcommittees with the traditionally pragmatic approach of British foreign policy.

In spite of the existence of the C.D.C. and later the C.I.D., the service departments did not tamely keep in step with the progress of the famous Anglo-American rapprochement. Indeed there was a prolonged discrepancy between the views of the departments themselves on this subject. The Admiralty, in some ways, may even have been ahead of the statesmen while the War Office tended to cling long after

[1] Memorandum by Count Paul Metternich, summer 1900, printed in Prince von Bülow, *Memoirs, 1897–1903* (London, 1931), p. 422.

1902 to an increasingly inconvenient and eccentric anti-American line. When the Americans began again to build up their actual power in the late 1890s the Admiralty did not at once disavow all consideration of the contingency of war with the United States. It is true that their necessary cooperation in the development of a Canadian defence scheme had always been lukewarm and often downright non-existent. They had equivocated right from the start about the plan to invade the New England coast and their subsequent silence was ominous. In the Venezuelan crisis, moreover, unlike the War Office, they do not seem to have been agitated in the least by any kind of hurried war-plans. This may have been largely because the very brevity of the crisis was altogether too much for their slower pace; but the North American commander-in-chief's request for reinforcements in the event of war met with a revealing response from the Admiralty: 'This contingency would produce entirely exceptional conditions for which no provision can be made even approximately beforehand.'[1]

All this was not simply or even perhaps at all significant of any special goodwill towards the United States. The expansion of the United States in these years, moving towards the acquisition of island naval bases and the construction and control of an isthmian canal, the Admiralty viewed as absolutely antagonistic to Britain's naval interests. Only upon the possibility of an American commitment in the Far East did they look at all favourably. The happy days when they could look upon such acquisitions as choice objects of easy attack had gone with the better development of land fortifications and the growth of the United States Navy. There was, it is true, strong reference to the two peoples' racial affinity, and this had perhaps especially vociferous support in naval circles, probably because of the sense of intimacy engendered by Mahan's fashionable naval theories. But even in the racial arguments there was no real novelty; the 1850s had had their Anglo-American racialist parallel in the then common 'economic' arguments in favour of American expansion – and like that earlier essay the new one also proved fragile in the face of ordinary political crises or professional scruples. The popular movement for Anglo-American naval 'reunion' in the early 1890s and for joint exercises in the early 1900s fell foul respectively of the Venezuelan crisis and the bureaucratic horror of the naval lords.[2] However

[1] Marder, p. 256. Marder also shows (pp. 256–7) that the 'flying squadron' which was first suggested in connection with the Venezuelan scare, was formed in Jan. 1896 with a view to the coincidental crisis in South Africa.
[2] Ibid., pp. 252–5 and 443–9.

much it infected individuals, and however elevated some of those individuals, the sentimental approach failed to capture the process of policy-making even in the Admiralty. Instead the Admiralty generally, like Salisbury, insisted on relating policy not to sentiment but to power and interest. And this, the realistic approach, hardly indicated any particular Anglo-American reconciliation. Rather American expansion, in territory and in naval power, seemed aimed, in the western hemisphere at least, principally at Great Britain, and in a period of growing world tension and increasing strain upon Britain's naval resources. Viewed in this light American expansion seemed to the Admiralty, as to Salisbury, inevitable but unwelcome. That this was so the Admiralty made most clear in its adherence to a traditional attitude towards the United States acquisition of strategic bases.

Active American interest in the acquisition of overseas naval bases had not entirely subsided after Grant's Santo Domingo fiasco. The Americans had, for example, secured the right to the use of a naval base at Pago Pago in Samoa in January 1878. But American acquisitiveness even in this limited sense was revived significantly only with the accession of Blaine to the State Department in 1881. It was part of his programme for hemispheric consolidation to base American leadership firmly on military as well as moral power. For this purpose, as well as with a view to commanding the approaches to an isthmian canal, he accompanied his first moves for an amendment of the impeding Clayton-Bulwer treaty by equally tentative soundings for a number of naval bases and coaling stations. The Galapagos Islands, Chiriqui on the Caribbean coast of Panama, and Chimbote in Peru, as well as Hawaii and Santo Domingo, were thus the subject of a whole series of special and secret missions, negotiations, and reports, brought more or less to an abrupt halt by Blaine's dismissal in 1881 but equally revived with his return in 1889. None of these involved any real question of competition with Great Britain; she had no use for any of them save Samoa, where irritation with Germany overshadowed jealousy of the United States, and the Galapagos, where the Admiralty never managed to convince themselves that they had found a suitable site. Latent opposition to the American intrigues moreover was restrained, partly by the generally sceptical views about the value even to the Americans of some of the positions, and largely by satisfying evidence of domestic American and Latin American opposition. Thus, while the Admiralty was intensely suspicious of American activities in Hawaii, even Pearl Harbor seemed of limited value because of the shallowness of the river channel; and Samana Bay, which the Admiralty and the

War Office alike believed to be one of the world's finest harbours and which there may have seemed to be a genuine opportunity to obtain for themselves, they hoped France, not they, would keep out of American hands.[1]

From this basically disapproving if not actively hostile attitude towards American expansion there was undoubtedly some withdrawal in the warm glow of the Spanish-American War. But the various traditions of Anglo-American naval cooperation in the war are mostly myths, and where official policy went out of its way at all to favour the Americans, it was really for the sake of keeping out of trouble with the more dangerous belligerent.[2] Even Salisbury had learned the wisdom of avoiding quarrels with the United States, so far as Britain's vital interests would permit. Some awareness of the possible utility of an American commitment in the Far East also undoubtedly influenced individual opinions in favour of the annexations of the Philippines and later Hawaii; but there is no sign of positive official encouragement. All that is certain is that the British cabinet, including Salisbury, preferred American acquisition to that of any other power.[3] Nor were even the opinions of senior naval officers all approving. 'The heroics in Oregon are ridiculous', commented Sir Frederick Richards. 'There is not a Spanish vessel of war afloat in the Pacific Ocean nor is it probable that there ever will be again, but it all means trouble for England later on.'[4] That their feelings about American expansion were ambiguous also seems confirmed by the Admiralty's maintenance of a generally antagonistic attitude on the question of new naval bases. Further reviews of possible sites off the Pacific coast in 1898–1900 brought new observations about the 'unscrupulous determination' of the Americans to keep out Great Britain and to have possession themselves.[5]

In the Caribbean the United States felt no reason to be satisfied with the results of the Spanish-American War. With their hold on Cuba

[1] For their attitude towards Hawaii see 'Hawaii and the United States', 12 May 1886, Adm. 1/6813, and especially the D.N.I.'s minute of 13 May. For Santo Domingo see W.O. to Adm., 16 Jan. 1882, forwarding a report of the M.I.D. on Samana Bay, Adm. 1/6640; and for France's involvement Lyons (Paris) to F.O., 8 Nov. 1883, F.O. 55/229.

[2] For the most recent examination of this subject see R. G. Neale, *Britain and American Imperialism, 1898–1900* (St Lucia, Queensland, 1965).

[3] Grenville, *Salisbury and Foreign Policy*, pp. 215–16. Neale, chapter 4, confirms this view.

[4] Minute on F.O. to Adm., 10 June 1898, Adm. 1/7387 B.

[5] Minutes on c.-in-c., Pacific, to Adm., secret, no. 335, 12 Oct. 1898, Adm. 1/7379 B, F.O. to Adm., 30 Nov. 1898, Adm. 1/7389 B, and F.O. to Adm., 14 April 1900, Adm. 1/7471.

extremely tenuous on account of the 1898 Teller Resolution disavowing annexation, until the Platt Amendment in March 1901 assured them a naval base on the island the Americans could count for local supremacy only upon Puerto Rico and Culebra. But the harbour of San Juan in Puerto Rico had insufficient depth of water to accommodate a large squadron of battleships and Culebra, even if as seemed likely its entrance could be deepened at no great cost, would also be rather small. For these reasons the Americans now turned, as had Seward and Grant in the late 1860s, to the Danish West Indian (or Virgin) Islands, one of which, St Thomas, had an excellent strategic position on the Atlantic highway to South America and the isthmus of Panama.[1] Once again, as late as March 1900, expert opinion within the Admiralty could look upon such a consolidation of American power in the Caribbean only with apprehension. 'With Cuba, Puerto Rico and St Thomas in the hands of the Americans,' commented the D.N.I., Custance, 'our position in Jamaica and the Caribbean sea will be precarious, and will be the cause of much anxiety in the event of war with the U.S.' When the negotiations were temporarily suspended in May he minuted his relief and his hope that the Danes would continue to hold out against the transfer.[2] The negotiations were resumed and in 1902 a treaty of cession was signed. But the C.D.C. then decided that it was not important, the island of Culebra being thought to have given the Americans all they needed after all.[3] In any case the treaty was defeated in the Danish parliament and the United States did not gain possession until 1916.

That the Spanish-American War marked no complete or happy acknowledgement of American supremacy in the Caribbean, even among the supposedly indulgent officers of the Royal Navy, seems clearly borne out too by the maintenance of a similar attitude on the central question of an isthmian canal. Fearing the success of de Lesseps's rival scheme and resenting the Clayton-Bulwer treaty's ban on exclusive construction and control by the United States, the Americans had unsuccessfully approached Great Britain for a revision of the treaty in the 1880s. Then, when the experience of the war with Spain and the acquisition of island empires in the Pacific and Caribbean confirmed the inutility of having to divide their naval strength among two separate squadrons, much more urgent approaches were begun at the end of

[1] For the American navy's opinions on this matter see Grenville and Young, pp. 301–2.
[2] Minutes of 3 Mar and 26 May 1900, Adm. 1/7471 (26 Feb. 1900).
[3] C.D.C. 287 M, 'West Indies: Cession of Danish Possessions to the U.S.A.', 19 Dec. 1901, Cab. 8/3.

1898. By 11 January the following year the ambassador in Washington, Sir Julian Pauncefote, and Secretary of State Hay had drawn up the draft of a convention proposing to modify the Clayton-Bulwer treaty. Meanwhile both service departments had been approached by the Foreign Office for an opinion. Apparently only Ardagh replied for the War Office, but it is clear from internal minutes that the Admiralty were in complete agreement with his opinion that the canal's very construction, let alone its control by the Americans, was harmful to British interests. It would confer a vital strategic advantage on the United States, impose an additional strain upon Great Britain's already overstretched naval resources, and increase trade rivalry. But they were all equally in agreement on the inevitability of its construction and the impossibility of ultimate resistance to American wishes. Ardagh therefore suggested and the cabinet decided to accept his suggestion that concession on this matter should be made conditional upon some *quid pro quo* in other, Canadian, issues.[1] It was this tactical course that now preoccupied the Foreign Office and, because of American resistance to even a minor concession in their dispute with Canada over Alaska, prolonged the negotiations for a further two years.

By the beginning of 1901 the British had clearly given way in principle and the issue concerned only the extent of American control and in particular whether the British could concede American fortification of the canal. On this matter the Senate had sought to go somewhat further than had been envisaged and their proposals were again submitted for expert opinion. In their reply the Admiralty still insisted upon the disadvantages of the canal's construction, let alone its fortification by the Americans. In war, they pointed out, it would allow the Americans to unite their naval forces at will. But whether fortified or not its use was unlikely to be available to the British. Once it were fortified Britain would not be able to secure its use to herself, even if she had

---

[1] Ardagh's 'Memorandum respecting the Clayton-Bulwer Treaty', 9 Dec. 1898, is printed in C. S. Campbell, pp. 353–6. A copy of the draft convention and a request for their views, marked 'immediate & confidential', was sent by the F.O. to the Admiralty on 25 Jan. 1899 (Adm. 1/7550 A [9 Jan. 1901]). The hydrographer, Adm. Wharton, and the D.N.I., Adm. Beaumont, both recorded their views in minutes on the letter but according to Beaumont's successor no reply was ever sent to the F.O. (Custance's memorandum on the Nicaraguan Canal, 31 Dec. 1900, *ibid.*). For further views on this question see the confidential memorandum of 14 Mar. 1898 on the 'Panama Canal' by Rear-Adm. Palliser, c.-in-c. Pacific, forwarded to the Adm. in his despatch no. 140, 28 Mar. 1898, Adm. 1/7367; and Wharton's minute on F.O. to Adm., 9 June 1898, Adm. 1/7387 B. For the attitude of the British cabinet and the course of the negotiations, see Grenville, 'Britain and the Isthmian Canal', pp. 48–69.

local naval superiority; she would only be able to deny it to others. But Britain would probably not be able to spare sufficient forces to secure local naval superiority and would therefore be unable to command the use of the canal even if unfortified by land. Even if she could obtain its use, its value to her would not be great as her forces in the Pacific were so small. The Admiralty's reply made it clear that from their point of view the question of fortifications was a comparatively minor matter, that neither these nor any treaty provisions at all but local naval power alone would determine the use of the canal in a war. The Admiralty's paper concluded:

To sum up the situation from a purely naval and strategical point of view, it appears to my Lords that the preponderance of advantage from the canal would be greatly on the side of the United States, and that, in case of war between Great Britain and the United States, the navy of the United States would derive such benefits from the existence of the canal, that it is not really in the interests of Great Britain that it should be constructed.[1]

Since there was no question whatever of stopping the American construction of a canal for much longer the Admiralty's conclusion was quite beside the point. This Lord Lansdowne, who had taken over the Foreign Office from the ageing Salisbury in October 1900, fully understood. The Admiralty's argument that local naval supremacy, not fortification, would dictate control of the canal made the American amendments of comparatively little importance. On Lansdowne's advice, the cabinet decided to reject the amended treaty, but only in the hope of extracting marginally better terms, and to correct any tendency to place Great Britain at a peculiar disadvantage through her unilateral commitment to neutrality. The treaty as ultimately agreed to in November 1901 amounted to a major concession to the growth of American power, without securing any material compensation. To a substantial extent it was undoubtedly a gesture of goodwill. But such goodwill was still more common in social, intellectual, and literary contacts than in the deliberations of the policy-makers; the essential characteristic of the treaty was rather its explicit acknowledgment of hard strategic fact. That this was so owed much to Lansdowne's ingenuity and persistence. According to one view he achieved his purpose 'by skilfully turning upside down the conclusions reached by the Admiralty', that is to say that he thought their reference to Britain's

---

[1] Adm. to F.O., confidential, 5 Jan. 1901, printed in C. S. Campbell, pp. 357–60.

prospective naval weakness in the Caribbean suggested, not opposition to the canal's construction, which would have been both dangerous and futile, but since concession was ultimately inevitable, large and possibly fruitful concession now and in good time.[1] But though Lansdowne's conclusion may seem to contradict that of the Admiralty it did not really do so, as may have been made clear in cabinet. It merely expressed what for some reason the Admiralty, sheltering behind conventional disclaimers of responsibility for 'political' arguments, had themselves concluded but did not choose to communicate.

The Admiralty knew as well as the Foreign Office that the canal's construction was 'inevitable'. Of this they had been well aware when first approached for their opinion in January 1899.[2] Quite possibly they had then failed to make any reply at all, because they saw no way out of the dilemma in which 'manifest destiny' and strategic interest seemed bound to clash head on. Ardagh and Salisbury had then sought consolation but not a solution in a reciprocal American concession on Canadian and other issues. But by the beginning of 1901 even that device had failed. The winter of 1899–1900 had brought war and disaster in South Africa to remind the British of their need for friends, and in October 1900 Salisbury had given up the Foreign Office at last to Lansdowne. Also in November 1900 Lord Selborne succeeded Goschen as first lord of the Admiralty and even before then, in mid 1899, there had been a significant change of personnel in that department. Admiral Lord Walter Kerr, the new first sea lord, and Captain Reginald Custance, the new D.N.I., had no illusions about the growth of American naval power. They may have been too diffident or too sceptical to see to it that the Admiralty's January 1901 reply about the canal expressed precisely the inescapable conclusion, but at least there was a reply and one which gave Lansdowne all the information and opinions he needed in order to come to a real and practical decision. If, in fact, the foreign secretary turned the Admiralty's arguments on end, it was to reach the conclusion that they wished him to reach, in place of that which professional scruples had spuriously contrived. That this was so the comments made on the Foreign Office's enquiry by the first sea lord and the D.N.I. make quite clear. Both of them talked of making concessions in return for 'a friendly settlement of other outstanding questions', but

[1] Grenville, *Salisbury and Foreign Policy*, pp. 385–6. Lansdowne's 15 Jan. 1901 memorandum for the cabinet refuting the Admiralty's arguments is printed in Campbell, pp. 360–3.
[2] See, for example, Beaumont's minute of 6 Feb. 1899 on F.O. to Adm., 25 Jan. 1899, Adm. 1/7550A (9 Jan. 1901).

the most significant comment was Kerr's: 'It seems to me that our policy should be in the direction of meeting the U.S. claims half way, and avoid a *non possumus* attitude. Our interests would be better served if the U.S. carry us with them instead of getting what they are sure to get in spite of us.'[1]

What Lansdowne had done – and done with the aid of the Admiralty, not despite it – was to point out that foreign policy must be adapted to power as much as power to foreign policy. Policies have by nature their own momentum and the paths of power and policy often tend to diverge. In such circumstances the direct and usually sudden, inspirational intervention of a statesman like Lansdowne alone seems able to restore the harmony of purpose. The importance of the treaty has not been exaggerated; it committed Great Britain to naval inferiority in American waters and therefore to friendship with the United States. An alliance still remained only a nebulous possibility; but already some could see practical and beneficial results. Francis Bertie, assistant under-secretary and leader of the anti-German group at the Foreign Office, argued in a memorandum of November 1901 that the British could rely on the United States to protect their interests in the West Indies against hostile European powers.[2] But Bertie's views had not yet captured the government and few perhaps were prepared to go so far. Still the salutary experience of a second brush with Venezuela helped somewhat to define both Anglo-American and Anglo-German relations. Although this new incident began with an alignment of Great Britain and Germany against Venezuelan misbehaviour, it ended with Britain leaving Germany to face American displeasure alone. By the end of 1902 the government was willing to express its approval of the Monroe Doctrine openly before the House of Commons.[3] Two months later Salisbury's successor as prime minister declared in a speech at Liverpool: 'The Monroe Doctrine has no enemies in this country that I know of. We welcome any increase of the influence of the United States of America upon the great Western Hemisphere.'[4]

The Admiralty had not at first entirely appreciated the significance of what was happening in the Americas. But gradually, about the turn

[1] Custance's memorandum on the Nicaraguan Canal, 31 Dec. 1900, and Kerr's minute, 2 Jan. 1901, Adm. 1/7550A (9 Jan. 1901).
[2] *British Documents on the Origins of the War, 1898–1914*, ed. by G. P. Gooch and Harold Temperley, ii (1927), no. 91, 'Memorandum by Mr Bertie', 9 Nov. 1901, p. 75.
[3] Lord Cranborne in the House of Commons, 15 Dec. 1902, *Hansard's Parliamentary Debates*, 4th series, cxvi, col. 1263.
[4] *The Times*, 14 Feb. 1903.

of the century, they had begun to insist upon the realities of naval power and explicitly to require that not only defence but even foreign policy be trimmed accordingly. It cannot be established with any certainty that it was specifically the outcome of their intervention in the Hay-Pauncefote negotiations which first opened their eyes to their need and their opportunity, but 1901 certainly provides some striking evidence of their progress. Only two days after Lansdowne's crucial canal memorandum of 15 January, the first lord was urging before the cabinet the practical necessity of assessing the two-power standard only in relation to France and Russia and altogether dropping the United States Navy from consideration.[1] In April he was writing: 'I would never quarrel with the United States if I could possibly avoid it. It has not dawned on our countrymen yet . . . that, if the Americans choose to pay for what they can easily afford, they can gradually build up a navy, fully as large and then larger than ours and I am not sure they will not do it.'[2] So far as defence planning in the American theatre was concerned there was a striking tendency after 1901, not least in Custance's abrupt return of the Foster report, for the Admiralty to be firm and relatively consistent in a matter upon which they had before been tentative and erratic. Between 1898 and 1901, then, there seems to have been a significant advance in Admiralty opinion from frustrated opposition to realistic tolerance of American assertiveness. Until the signature of the Hay-Pauncefote treaty, however, the supposedly non-political nature of their professional duties impeded any direct expression of this change. From this impediment the government's passive, if not cheerful, acceptance of the treaty's strategic implications now tended to free them. More especially its tacit disregard of the effect of that treaty on the conduct of a war with the United States gave the Admiralty a much easier task in dealing with the inconvenient demands of the War Office.

[1] Monger, p. 11.   [2] *Ibid.*, p. 72, note 1.

IO

The Western Atlantic and the
Great Lakes, 1901–1908

The Admiralty's rejection of the army's plan for the invasion of New England or New York early in 1901 could not have been precisely a bombshell for the War Office since it followed from observations about the growth of American power of which the Military Intelligence Department was just as well aware. Where the two intelligence departments differed, now as in the past, was on whether this implied new plans or no plans at all. The D.N.I.'s rejection of Foster's plan in fact initiated a new and thorough review within the M.I.D.

Active discussion seems to have begun with a paper of 15 March 1901 in which Captain (later Field-Marshal Sir William) Robertson pointed out that the question remained 'in a most unsatisfactory state' because the essential conditions for the offensive strategy of the 1890s were still lacking. In the first place, the Canadians were further than ever from meeting the requirements of the 1898 Defence Commission. The total establishment of the Canadian army was still only just over 38,000 (barely more than 1,000 of them regulars) and the actual strength at the end of 1901 was less than 32,000. In the meantime the forces of the United States had greatly increased, largely as a result of the Spanish-American War. In 1898 a possibly low estimate of 50,000, including 15,000 regulars, had been set upon the American troops expected to be available against imperial forces two months after the outbreak of war. Now, by the act of February 1901, it seemed that it was intended to keep about 50,000 men in the United States as opposed to the 25,000 of three or four years earlier. It was not without significance either that in the Spanish-American War 51,000 volunteers had been concentrated within a month and 216,000 in four months. The doubling of the number of American regulars on the mainland, the virtual elimination of the Indian problem, the Americans' demonstrable ability to concentrate large numbers of volunteers with the utmost speed, and improvements to staff arrangements and coastal defences all tended together to eliminate the opening advantage supposed formerly to belong to Great

Britain's larger and better organized standing army. And whatever temporary military ascendancy which might still have been left to the British was further eroded by the growth of the United States navy and the consequent lack of the local naval command which alone would have enabled the British to exploit that ascendancy. With Custance's view, therefore, Robertson fully agreed: Foster's planned expedition was no longer feasible and the navy would be better employed in the destruction of the enemy's fleet and of his large overseas trade.[1]

This radically new point of view was fully confirmed by two further M.I.D. papers, one in the same month by Lt.-Col. H. A. Lawrence and one a year later by Captain J. A. L. Haldane.[2] Both tended, and Haldane's in particular, to emphasize the insufficiency not only of Canada's own forces but also of the British army. The army's foreign service plans now allowed for a maximum force of three army corps and there was some doubt if these were enough to fulfil even the more strictly defensive strategy of the 1898 commission. Haldane insisted that even if all three were got into Canada in three months they would not be enough to undertake the vital operation on the south bank of the St Lawrence, and that without an increase in the British corps as well as an improvement in the Canadian militia the defence of British North America would end in a 'hopeless fiasco'. Lawrence was not so pessimistic as this, but he was still very cautious. Two army corps introduced in the first month of war would bring the combined Anglo-Canadian force up to about 90,000. This would be 'barely enough' for a successful defence against the 100,000 regulars and volunteers which it was expected the Americans would then have available on the frontier, but he thought that it would still allow for the operation on the right bank of the St Lawrence. With 'good fortune' the defenders would be able to assemble a large mobile force to cover the southern approaches to Montreal and, by advancing along the Lake Champlain route against the manufacturing towns of Springfield, New Haven, and Hartford, harass the enemy's mobilization arrangements and destroy his canal communications. He even thought that similar attacks might be made against Buffalo, Detroit, and Cleveland. For their moral effect

[1] Secret 'Memorandum on the Defence of Canada', by Staff Capt. W. R. Robertson, 15 Mar. 1901, enclosed in the secret paper for the D.M.I., 'War with the United States', by Lt.-Col. H. A. Lawrence, 30 Mar. 1901, W.O. 106/40, file B 1/7.

[2] 'War with the United States', secret memorandum for the D.M.I., by Lt.-Col. H. A. Lawrence, 30 Mar. 1901, W.O. 106/40, file B 1/7; secret 'Memorandum on the policy to be adopted in a war with the U.S.A.', by Staff Capt. A. Haldane, 12 Mar. 1902, *ibid.*, file B 1/1.

Haldane would also have liked any available troops to make limited offensives against outlying possessions like Cuba, Hawaii, and any future canal.

On one vital matter both Lawrence and Haldane were entirely in agreement: that while the main offensive action of the war must clearly be the navy's attacks on the enemy's fleet and trade, the defensive arrangements for Britain's naval bases were inadequate and the local foundations of British naval supremacy therefore insecure. Bermuda was garrisoned not by the scheduled two battalions of infantry but by a mere six companies of the West Indian Regiment of 'inferior physique and intelligence', and her artillery was 50 per cent below strength in officers and 25 per cent in men. In a much worse position was the empire's sole fortified station on the American Pacific seaboard, Esquimalt. Her garrison was too small to oppose a large expedition and her reinforcement was unlikely. The Canadian Pacific Railway would probably be cut and the two battalions which the defence scheme proposed should come from India must now be discounted as the Admiralty had recently renounced responsibility for the safe conveyance of troops.

There was reason enough in these papers why the War Office, before raising directly the general question of Canadian defence, should first approach the Admiralty and the government as a whole about the condition of the various naval bases and coaling stations. This question, indeed, related to a longstanding and fundamental difference of opinion between the two departments which threatened now to reach its climax. Generally speaking, after the reaction against the fortification craze of Palmerston's days, the army had had to concede to the Royal Navy the principal role in the defence of the United Kingdom, the Empire, and overseas trade; but of course it wished nevertheless to preserve for itself a large degree of importance. The opportunity came essentially from the navy's insistence that the proper mode of defence was attack, and its own function therefore not to tie down and dissipate its forces in static, local, and piecemeal defence, but first to pursue and destroy the enemy's fleet so that he could not conceivably make a seaborne attack. In this strategy the army could claim that there still remained the danger of attack and invasion while the fleet was temporarily drawn off in pursuit of a cunning and elusive enemy. Hence the need still for considerable land forces and extensive fortifications. From these differing points of view there arose in the latter part of the century a serious quarrel concerning home defence between what the navalists came to call the 'Blue Water' and 'Blue Funk' schools – or, as the latter was more sympathetically and politely termed, the 'Bolt-from-the-Blue' school. Navy and army officers did not neatly divide into the one school or the other but the Admiralty, though by no means discounting a sudden attack, insisted that the navy was in any event the first line of defence. The quarrel seemed definitely settled in favour of the Blue Water school when the prime minister, Balfour, following the report of a special investigation of 1903, declared in the House of Commons on 11 May 1905 that, provided the navy were efficient, 'serious invasion of these islands is not an eventuality which we need seriously consider'. Led by Field-Marshal Lord Roberts, however, the opposing school continued its agitation and succeeded in getting new investigations in 1907–08 and 1913–14.[1] Essentially the quarrel was one of emphasis rather than principle for both views conceded the primary role to the navy, but the Englishman's persistent dread of invasion lent it passion and bitterness. Though less bitter, the same practical question of the nature and amount of fixed defences and garrisons applied equally to the oversea possessions, and not least to the self-governing colonies. The difficulty sprang from the impossibility of defining precisely the extent of security which the navy's general command of the sea gave to any particular colony and the nature of the attack to which it might therefore be exposed and against which it would have to have adequate land defences.

The colonies themselves found it all very difficult to understand. The C.D.C. had complained in May 1896 that:

proposals are still received based on erroneous conceptions of the true policy of a great State having vast interests to defend in all quarters of the habitable world. Suggestions are, for example, made to station ships of the Royal Navy at individual ports, to utilize Imperial resources for the protection of places that have no importance in the general scheme of the Empire, to increase fortifications and armaments to an extent out of proportion to the personnel that can be made available to man them, and to take measures in war which would inflict certain injury to British commerce without correspondingly increasing the safety of individual places.

In order 'to educate colonial opinion in the right principles of defence' it was decided to produce an elaborate paper, eventually dated 19 May

---

[1] For a convenient summary of the controversy before 1905 see A. J. Marder, *The Anatomy of British Sea Power; a History of British Naval Policy in the Pre-Dreadnought Era, 1880–1905* (New York, 1940), pp. 65–83, and, for the following period, the same author's *From the Dreadnought to Scapa Flow: the Royal Navy in the Fisher Era, 1904–1919*, vol. I, *The Road to War, 1904–1914* (London, 1961), pp. 354–88.

1896, outlining more precisely what was expected in the way of defences. With the concurrence of the service departments this was circulated to colonial governors on 6 July. As it differed in some particulars very little from earlier, secret documents, it was felt wise to mark it 'confidential', and, while intended for 'wide circulation and influence', it was not to be published.[1] But a document for publication would clearly be desirable and a draft of a much reduced version was produced for this purpose by the C.D.C.[2] The Admiralty were far from pleased with this proposal, feeling that it was 'dangerous' to publish expressions which did not precisely describe existing naval policy and which, being released to the public for the first time, would give the impression of novelty. One passage in particular they would have preferred 'materially altered if not omitted altogether'. This was that the navy had 'accepted the responsibility of protecting all British territory abroad against organized invasion from the sea'. To publicize such a statement, thought the first lord, Goschen, would 'give rise to the erroneous impression that their Lordships had entered into some new and solemn obligation; whereas these words were presumably simply intended to embody the time-honoured Naval policy of the country'. But 'the Colonial Office had sold the pass by giving the best of the memorandum to the Duke of Devonshire for use'. What the chairman of the new cabinet Committee of Defence – or the 'Minister of Defence', as Goschen called him – had actually done was to leak the paper in a speech before the British Empire League on 3 December, directly quoting the passage to which the Admiralty referred. All that the Admiralty could do therefore was to hold up approval of the new memorandum, but at length in July 1897 they had to give way.[3] What the Admiralty was registering in these irritable minutes was a growing determination not to allow recorded definitions of their 'obligations' to impede the modification of those obligations, according to changing circumstances and policies. In the desire to concentrate on their principal task of destroying the enemy's fleet their intention was wholly laudable; much less so were their surliness of manner and their almost total unwillingness to explain to other parties who needed to know precisely what the naval policy was in order to fulfil their own obligations. In this respect the War Office had as much to complain of as had the colonies.

[1] C.D.C. 57 M, 'Colonial Defence', 19 May 1896, Cab. 8/1. For the background of the paper see the Admiralty file, 'General Principles affecting Colonial Defence', 2 June 1897, Adm. 1/7340 B.

[2] C.D.C. 90 M, 'Colonial Defence', 31 Dec. 1896, Cab. 8/1.

[3] Various minutes and correspondence in the file of 2 June 1897, Adm. 1/7340 B.

The Admiralty's concern for an unrestricted role on the high seas, and the conclusion that garrison strengths based on the assumption of local naval command might therefore be inadequate, were early apparent in discussions about arrangements for bringing those garrisons up to war strength. The possibility that the navy might not be able to guarantee the safe transportation of such reinforcements after the outbreak of war and that they might therefore have to re-examine their arrangements seems first to have been considered by the C.D.C. in December 1887.[1] On that occasion further concentration and even increases of garrisons, for example in the West Indies, were recommended but the difficulty continued for a long time to agitate the defence experts. The Admiralty insisted that 'the phrase "reinforcing a coaling station" should be regarded as a palpable absurdity', those stations being specifically designed to oppose a 'sudden unexpected attack', and so, even in peacetime, should be ready constantly for war; while the War Office continually proposed consequent adjustments in garrisons and defences.[2]

So far as the western Atlantic was concerned the problem was accentuated as the growth of the United States navy rapidly outdated existing arrangements. This growth and the imminent reorganization of American land forces was noted especially in a C.D.C. memorandum of 12 October 1896:

... at the present time an ironclad squadron of strength far exceeding the British force which is locally available could rapidly concentrate for an attack on Halifax . . . , and might at the outbreak of war be exclusively employed to convoy land forces for so important an object as the only fortified defended station on the Atlantic seaboard of the continent of North America. It may well be anticipated that such an attack in the event of a war with the States might be made before the British North American squadron could be reinforced from home waters. . . . To give real security to Halifax would now involve garrisoning it as a first class coast fortress, liable to immediate and powerful attack from the sea.[3]

Essentially this observation raised very large questions – so large indeed that the committee felt it discreet to leave aside the question of organized attack from the sea and confine itself on this occasion to increases in Halifax's garrison and fortifications and, since that base's increased vulnerability made an alternative one still more important, also in those of Bermuda.[4] Ultimately the larger question could not be evaded. But even the direct investigations of the defence of Canada did not

[1] C.D.C. 31 M, 'Colonial Garrisons', 6 Dec. 1887, Cab. 8/1.
[2] 'Colonial Garrison Reinforcements', 9 July 1896, Adm. 1/7322.
[3] C.D.C. 74 M, 'Colonial Garrisons', 12 Oct. 1896, Cab. 8/1.
[4] *Idem* and C.D.C. 89 M, 'Garrison of Bermuda', 19 Dec. 1896, *ibid.*

at first face it, and the climax came, not with Halifax or Bermuda, but with Port Castries, St Lucia.

Port Castries had had a chequered and tentative history as a defended coaling station. Although the harbour was small it could take the largest ships and in the hurricane season it was considered the safest in the West Indies. It was also strategically well placed to watch the French in Martinique and for the protection of the South Atlantic trade. In 1877 the Admiralty had chosen it as the Windward Islands' coaling station in preference to the existing base, Antigua, which was neglected and far too shallow, and to Barbados which was merely an open road-stead. The choice had been confirmed in 1881 when the Carnarvon Commission recommended that the troops in the West Indies should be concentrated upon Port Castries and upon Port Royal, Jamaica. But this decision was itself apparently the result of a compromise between the conflicting opinions of the service departments and objections in the Windwards and unenthusiasm at home in fact conspired to prevent the decision being fully put into effect. Barbados in particular objected to being left unprotected by British troops, the War Office disliked St Lucia's supposed unhealthiness, and the Treasury hardly welcomed the additional expenditure required to bring the harbour up to standard and to enlarge the barrack accommodation. The Admiralty, on the other hand, stubbornly maintained its choice and the C.D.C. repeatedly confirmed it.[1] But while St Lucia was allowed to raise a loan of £60,000 for harbour improvements, the troop concentration, it was decided, might be gradual so that time could be given for the other colonies to organize local militia and for the construction of barracks at Port Castries. But when the War Office reluctantly signified their approval of this decision, they pointedly warned that other positions, the Cape in particular, had greater priority, and the suspicion this aroused at the Admiralty turned out to be utterly justified: even as late as 1904 there were still British troops in Barbados, though these were supposed to be concentrated in St Lucia in the event of war.

The garrison recommended by the C.D.C. in December 1887 was modest since it was believed that most risk of attack came from the United States rather than France, and American power was then still relatively weak.[2] When the garrison was reviewed in October 1896,

---

[1] C.D.C. 1 M, 'Barbados', 27 April 1885, 23 M, 'Occupation of Port Castries, St Lucia, as a Naval Coaling Station', 12 Aug. 1886, 31 M, 'Colonial Garrisons', 6 Dec. 1887, and 74 M, 'Colonial Garrisons', 12 Oct. 1896, Cab. 8/1. See also Admiralty file, 'Port Castries', 21 April 1884, Adm. 1/6721.

[2] C.D.C. 31 M, 'Colonial Garrisons', 6 Dec. 1887, Cab. 8/1.

the relative state of British and American naval power had changed enough to pose a potential danger to both Port Castries and Port Royal but it was still thought unnecessary to increase either garrison. The Americans would have the advantage only at the beginning of a war and they would then have more important things to do elsewhere, particularly an attempt against Halifax or even Bermuda. They would not have enough forces to mount an attack against Port Castries or Port Royal as well before Britain had reasserted her naval superiority. So the committee recommended increases for both Halifax and Bermuda, but felt that the West Indian bases needed only small revisions to the standards of defence so as to take account of a cruiser raid.[1]

As late as May 1898 the committee still thought in the same way.[2] But on 11 February 1902 the Admiralty wrote to warn the Colonial Office that 'in view of the great development which is taking place in certain Foreign Navies, it has become necessary for strategic reasons to concentrate more than is the case at present the Naval force in commission',[3] and so, when they came to review the revised defence scheme for St Lucia in November 1902, the C.D.C. began at last to display awareness of the changing balance of power in the western Atlantic. First they drew attention to that persistent bugbear, 'the temporary absence of the fleet', and the consequent need to provide against a cruiser raid *and* a landing by troops.[4] Then, on the same day, 10 November 1902, emerged one of the committee's most important memoranda, 'Strategical Considerations in the Caribbean Sea and Western Atlantic', in which they took note of the impending admission of the United States to the ranks of the leading maritime powers.[5] The real implication of this development, they argued, was not that it independently outmoded existing defensive arrangements in American waters; against the United States alone, even with her new power, these would still be sufficient. But 'whether, in the event of uncertain or hostile relations with a European Power at the time of an outbreak of war with the U.S., it would be possible to detach a sufficient naval force from Europe to maintain sea supremacy in the Caribbean Sea and Western Atlantic appears to the C.D.C. to be a question of grave importance which should be submitted for the consideration of the

[1] C.D.C. 74 M, 'Colonial Garrisons', 12 Oct. 1896, Cab. 8/1.
[2] C.D.C. 200 R, 'St Lucia Defence Scheme revised to May 1898', 13 Dec. 1898, Cab. 9/1.
[3] Quoted by Donald C. Gordon, *The Dominion Partnership in Imperial Defense, 1870–1914* (Baltimore, 1965), p. 152, note 22.
[4] C.D.C. 302 R, 'St Lucia: Defence Scheme revised to February 1902', 10 Nov. 1902, Cab. 9/5.   [5] C.D.C. 300 M, 10 Nov. 1902, Cab. 8/3.

Lords Commissioners of the Admiralty'. Thus at once was grave doubt cast upon the standing defence arrangements, not only for Port Castries, but equally for Port Royal, Bermuda, and even Halifax, and, ultimately, upon the whole policy of naval defence in American waters.

This serious matter was put to the Admiralty by the War Office on 21 January 1903 and a month later the Admiralty at length replied.[1] By the end of 1905, they acknowledged, the United States were expected to have a fleet of twenty battleships and eight armoured cruisers, of which only a small part would be kept in the Pacific; while, in view of the growing naval strength of the European powers, it was unlikely that Great Britain would be able to spare more ships than would be needed to protect the grain traffic from Canada and the Argentine, the principal sources of British food supply once the American trade had been suspended. They would probably be unable to blockade the Atlantic portion of the United States navy in its ports and the British bases would therefore have to undertake their own defence. In spite of these large admissions the Admiralty did not believe it necessary to alter the existing standards of defence. It would not be worth the Americans' while to divert against these positions of 'comparatively minor Imperial value' forces more usefully employed against Great Britain's supply line from Canada. Their ultimate fate would depend upon the main issue of the war.

The patent shallowness of the Admiralty's reasoning on this narrower question of revising standards of defence diverted attention from the principal strategic issue for a time, but the result was ultimately to emphasize the main point. First however the War Office had to challenge these clumsy arguments, and they wrote on 4 May questioning what were apparently the fundamental points in the Admiralty's paper. The description of the bases in question as of 'comparatively minor Imperial value' seemed in the first place utterly at odds not only with the report of the Royal Commission of 1882 but also with earlier statements by the Admiralty, asserting that they were essential to the navy for personnel and material as well as for repairs. What, therefore, would be the effect of the loss of Halifax and Bermuda upon the despatch of troop reinforcements from the United Kingdom to Canada; or of Port Castries upon the supply of Argentine wheat? And where, asked the sceptical secretary of state, was this supposed main issue of the

---

[1] W.O. to Adm., 21 Jan., and Adm. to W.O., 24 Feb. 1903, appendices B and C, W.O. 106/40, file B 1/17.

war in which Great Britain could hope for success enough to force the United States to disgorge such prizes as Halifax and Bermuda?[1]

These points the Admiralty wisely did not attempt to deny, but months later, while bringing the issue back to its main point, they were still trying foolishly to evade its full implications.[2] With the possible exception of Halifax's communications with the interior of Canada all the naval operations mentioned – the maintenance of food and troop communications as well as the defence of the bases – depended, the Admiralty insisted, upon general naval superiority in American waters and that superiority Great Britain could not assert in the event of complications in Europe. The importance of the bases was equally dependent upon that naval superiority: 'Without that factor on our side their strategic value disappears, together with our power to protect them.' The Admiralty now were virtually admitting the impossibility of conducting a war against the United States, at least in the event of 'complications in Europe', a condition they probably deemed permanent. Indeed they ended very sensibly by pointing out that the significant conclusion suggested by the C.D.C.'s original questions in November 1902 was not the reconsideration of standards of defence but the necessity of 'preserving amicable relations with the United States'. Unfortunately they also insisted on confusing this vital point by raising new hopes of martial victory over the Americans. As with Great Britain, so also with the United States did the possession of the bases depend upon the general naval command. With the reassertion of British superiority following their victory in Europe, the bases would necessarily return once more to British possession.

The principal fallacy in the Admiralty's final point was at once picked up by the War Office, but they were by now sufficiently disgusted with the Admiralty's incompetent essay in sophistry to bring the entire matter before the newly constituted cabinet Committee of Imperial Defence. In a paper of 17 September 1903 they reviewed the long history of the Port Castries question since 1882 and then went on to refute the Admiralty's main argument. They observed that once the western Atlantic bases were lost Great Britain would have great difficulty in reasserting local naval command and, consequently, in regaining the bases themselves. In the meantime Canada would have had to be abandoned to the Americans and the Canadian and South American

---

[1] W.O. to Adm., 4 May, 1903, appendix D, W.O. 106/40, file B 1/17.
[2] Adm. to W.O., 29 June, 1903, appendix E, *ibid*.

grain trade left to the mercy of the enemy. In the relatively narrow context of Anglo-American relations the implication seemed bad enough. 'Such a condition of affairs', the War Office paper commented, 'might result in our being compelled to sue for peace on humiliating terms.' But probably worse was the apparently radical departure from an assumed general strategy:

Unless, therefore, the War Office has misinterpreted the plan for the strategic distribution of our naval forces, which the Admiralty proposes to adopt in the event of war with the United States coinciding with a time of uncertain relations between this country and a European Power, the conclusion appears to be unavoidable that the present strength of H.M.'s navy would not suffice to defend on the high seas the interests of the Empire; in other words that the two-Power standard, up to which the country has been given to understand the Navy is maintained, no longer exists.

This conclusion so gravely affects the political as well as the military position of the Empire, that it is hoped that the Admiralty will be able to elucidate it. If it be accepted by the Admiralty as correct, the contingency of war with the United States should be avoided at all hazards, unless we are assured of the neutrality of all the European maritime Powers.

Perhaps, they concluded, they had misunderstood the Admiralty's arguments, and it was intended in the case of a war with the United States in alliance with a European power only to concentrate in European waters in the first phase. But if the navy thought of turning in the second phase to the United States and the re-establishment of superiority in the western Atlantic, then at least one of the British bases mentioned should be strengthened so that it could hold out in the meantime, and be available to make the recovery of the naval command easier or even possible at all.[1]

When the Admiralty made out their case on 24 November 1903 they still did not take up directly this apparently important point about the bases required for the recovery of naval superiority; but they did dismiss the idea of increased local defences for all or any of them as useless without command of the surrounding waters. They added however that they felt it unlikely that in the first stage of war – which was the sole concern of the present enquiry – the Americans would bother to attack these bases. They were of minor strategic value compared with, say, an attack on the Canadian grain trade and that trade 'must derive its

[1] War Office 'Memorandum on the standards of defence for the naval bases of Halifax, Bermuda, Jamaica, and St Lucia', 17 Sept. 1903, C.I.D. paper 3c, Cab. 5/1.

protection, not from the bases, but from the fleet'.[1] Here the Admiralty was clearly lifting the argument from the C.D.C.'s papers of the earlier 1890s. But at that time the United States had not had such a large navy. Why should not the Americans now attempt to consolidate their local advantage and make their attack on the grain trade easier by seizing every available base? In any case it was sheer naval heresy to distinguish so between a fleet and its bases; over and over again the Admiralty had themselves admitted that these bases were necessary to their operations in the western Atlantic. Precisely the same ambiguity that the War Office had from the first sought to have elucidated still remained to be explained. It is difficult to avoid the conclusion that the Admiralty, having discovered a valid flaw in current defence planning, was somehow trying to exploit the consequent apprehension in order to get increased naval expenditure – and expenditure on ships for convoying the grain trade, not on the bases necessary to the servicing and maintenance of those ships. Whatever the truth the Admiralty's ambiguous case survived the scrutiny of the C.I.D. when that body met the next day to consider the defences of the bases. Presumably the military members did not simply overlook the continued evasion of their case, nor the political members consciously conspire to promote the Admiralty's selfish interests. Probably the prime minister was content to overlook the weaknesses of an argument he found convenient. Its practical effect would be substantially to lessen talk about plans for war against the United States; to probe deeper would necessarily have raised fundamental political problems for which one of the service departments at least was still apparently unprepared. Thus in the cases of Bermuda, Port Castries, and Port Royal the question of defence against the United States was dismissed as impractical, and that against another naval power as already sufficiently provided. But with Halifax, upon whose link with the mother country and the interior of the continent the entire defence of Canada depended, the problem could not be dismissed so easily. Rather it was sought to evade it by precisely the same method as the government had for a time evaded that of the general land defence of North America immediately after the Civil War – by suggesting that it be passed to the Canadian government.[2]

This suggestion bore all the more striking a resemblance to the manœuvres of the 1860s inasmuch as it seems to have arisen more immediately out of a relatively independent reaction to the continued

[1] Admiralty memorandum, 'Strategic position of British naval bases in the Western Atlantic and West Indies', 24 Nov. 1903, C.I.D. paper 5c, Cab. 5/1.
[2] Minutes of 24th meeting of the C.I.D., 25 Nov. 1903, Cab. 2/1.

delay in the satisfactory development of Canada's own military forces. After the breakdown of the attempts to get the Canadians to act upon the report of the 1898 commission British efforts, outside the planning in the M.I.D., had been concentrated largely in the activities of successive general officers commanding the militia. The efforts of these British officers had been often noisy, sometimes downright offensive, and always unsuccessful. In 1903 General Lord Dundonald still had to report that 'Canada is quite unprepared to carry out schemes of defence and plans of campaign'. For this failure, the Colonial Office insisted, the high-handed attitude of some of the British commanders, including Dundonald, was at least partly responsible. Dundonald's predecessor, General Hutton, had been dismissed for talking too loudly about political interference and Dundonald himself was the next year to commit the same crime and suffer the same fate.[1] In May the colonial secretary suggested that the C.D.C. should consider the advisability of appointing a Canadian officer to the command and of withdrawing the British garrisons. The Committee's interim report of 28 July was far from favourable, the militia still being too inefficient.[2] But on 25 November the controversy between War Office and Admiralty eventually forced from the C.I.D. a decision in favour of withdrawal. Advantage was then taken of the presence in London of the Canadian minister of militia, Sir Frederick Borden. He was appointed a temporary member of the C.I.D. in order to take part in the discussions on the command of the militia. At the Committee's twenty-sixth meeting on 11 December 1903 it was agreed that a Canadian officer might be appointed to command the militia, that Canada would produce a general defence scheme, and that both Esquimalt and Halifax should be handed over, subject to the maintenance of satisfactory armaments and an annual review of the defences by the C.D.C.[3]

With these several decisions relating to the western Atlantic bases, the C.I.D. began at a high level the second stage of that process by which Great Britain withdrew the greater part of her naval and military forces from North America and the West Indies. They were beginning in fact to extricate Great Britain from what many, in the Admiralty in particular, had come to regard both strategically and politically as the

---

[1] Dundonald's 'Remarks on the Defence of Canada', 28 Feb. 1903, printed as appendix 7 to C.D.C. 306 M, 'Canada: Command and Efficiency of Militia', 28 July 1903, Cab. 8/3. For the Hutton and Dundonald dismissals see Gordon, pp. 153–4 and 172–4. [2] C.D.C. 306 M, 28 July 1903, Cab. 8/3.
[3] Minutes of the 25th and 26th meetings of the C.I.D., 4 and 11 Dec. 1903, Cab. 2/1.

impossible task of having to provide for a war against the United States. To that extent the end of 1903 deserves to rank next in significance with Lansdowne's Panama canal decision of 1901; indeed it was the implications of that decision which the C.I.D. now sought to make explicit. But as they were themselves soon to show they were ruling out as yet only the practicability of prosecuting such a war, not the possibility of its outbreak. The distinction was in all common sense a fine one; but then political decisions, properly speaking, were none of their business. Thus the C.I.D.'s initiative, though ultimately decisive, was for a time much less than absolutely effective, perhaps because they really sought to evade a direct and thoroughgoing discussion of such a war. In some important particulars their decisions still seemed vague and this, in turn, gave the army's new General Staff of 1904 many opportunities, especially in the assessment of the standards of defence for the various stations under threat of transfer, to sustain their case well beyond what the C.I.D. must have intended. The quarrel with the Admiralty therefore continued.

In specifically directing the elimination of the United States from consideration in the defence standards of the West Indian bases and in confirming the existing standards against cruiser raids by other powers, the decisions of the C.I.D. seemed conclusive enough. Indeed emphasis here was for even further reduction, and this, by persistently pressing for the clarification and consistent application of the Admiralty's principles, the War Office actually aided, extended, and accelerated. In December 1903 the C.I.D. asked if additional submarine and torpedo defences would permit the withdrawal of one of the battalions in Bermuda's garrison, but both service departments agreed that they would not and the War Office was able to keep both for the time being.[1] Then on 8 July in the following year the C.I.D. referred rather ominously to their defencelessness against the United States making 'very small garrisons desirable' in the western Atlantic bases even for service against other powers, presumably so as to decrease the numbers becoming hostages of the power they were not intended to fight. Bermuda, moreover, was unlikely to be attacked by any other power at all and the arrangements at Port Castries also needed revision.[2]

[1] M.I.D. 'Memorandum on the Defence of Bermuda', 1 Dec. 1903, C.I.D. paper 6c, Cab. 5/1; 'Memorandum of Outstanding Questions now before the Committee of Imperial Defence on which an early decision is urgently needed by the War Office', 25 Mar. 1904, by General J. M. Grierson (director of military operations in the new General Staff of the Army), C.I.D. paper 10c, *ibid.*; and minutes of the 39th meeting of the C.I.D., 20 April 1904, Cab. 2/1.

[2] Minutes of the 48th meeting of the C.I.D., 8 July 1904, Cab. 2/1.

Economizing action in respect of Port Castries was perhaps easier since the defence and concentration arrangements were still not complete: on 1 August 1904 the total garrison was 1,540, about a hundred below the approved 'standard', and some of these were still in Barbados. The C.D.C. began by suggesting a reduction by one British and two West Indian companies so as to give a garrison of only 650 against a cruiser raid. But then, in November, the Admiralty at last agreed that the base was no longer of any use whatever, being indefensible against the United States and, so far as other powers were concerned, having no advantage over Jamaica since it was unable to take large cruisers. On 22 November 1904 the C.I.D. proposed to abandon the base altogether.[1]

In their enthusiastic pursuit of the abandonment of the bases the Admiralty had gone rather further than they had intended, asserting that 'the necessity for a permanently fortified base in the Antilles at all is not now apparent'. On 28 November the Colonial Office wrote to ask if this opinion included Port Royal, Jamaica. Having been put by the Colonial Office the question was probably not a trap, but, with the Admiralty's blundering help, the War Office soon made it one. On 31 December the Admiralty replied that they had meant the Windward Islands in particular but that the same arguments might indeed also apply to Port Royal for it was, like Port Castries, both liable to capture by the Americans and useless against a European power. If this was so, the War Office then commented, the 'obvious course' would seem to be to abandon this base too. But on the same day as the War Office wrote in this sense to the Colonial Office the Admiralty was coolly including Port Royal in a list of 'ports which have special claim to protection on account of the broad national interests involved' and as 'being usefully situated as ports of refuge'. At pretty well the same time they were also observing that 'the sole form of attack to which a commercial port [in which category they were apparently arbitrarily placing Port Royal] is ever remotely likely to be exposed is that of a raiding cruiser'. To the War Office's observation that this conflicted with the decisions of the Joint Naval and Military Committee the Admiralty replied that while there was no reason to retain Port Royal 'on purely strategic grounds', its defence should be continued for the sake of its use as a 'commercial harbour of refuge' and standards of defence applied even for attacks which would be 'strategically wrong'. Then, when the War Office, with the Admiralty's

---

[1] 'St Lucia: Report of the Colonial Defence Committee on the strength of the garrison', 11 Oct. 1904, C.I.D. paper 12c, Cab. 5/1; and minutes of the 58th meeting of the C.I.D., 22 Nov. 1904, Cab. 2/1.

agreement, put the whole confusing situation to the C.I.D.,[1] the Admiralty warned against the War Office's tendency to turn into general principles the isolated opinions which they had extracted from time to time[2] and at last attempted to assert a policy of common sense:

The primary object which a hostile fleet will seek to gain in war will be the destruction of the enemy's ships, and not that of his coast defences.

Under modern conditions ships will not readily engage forts.

To do so would in most cases be a strategic error. Even if successful it would not ensure that which must be the main object of naval operations, *viz.*, the securing and maintaining the command of the sea. If unsuccessful the ships attacking must necessarily lose much of their fighting power and be the less able to cope with their natural adversaries, the enemy's fleet.

They admitted that there might well be exceptions according to local conditions but they were 'averse to the multiplication of distant defended bases', as in a protracted war they could not possibly guarantee the presence of the fleet in every case. The fleet's proper task was the pursuit and destruction of that of the enemy; in its absence no amount of fortification could save an isolated base against a serious and organized attack. But while they consequently deprecated extensive fortifications in distant ports, they most certainly did feel that these should have sufficient local defences to deter an attack and to deny their ready use to the enemy. They were not even prepared to advocate the reduction of existing defences; this 'would be . . . a mistake from other points of view than those connected with naval strategy'. This was probably a reference to local opinion and internal security. Generally therefore they supported the maintenance but not the increase of existing fortifications; and even in the case of Port Castries, which they had recommended should be abandoned, the fortifications should not be dismantled so that they might be reoccupied quickly but temporarily in the event of war.[3] It was decided therefore to keep small peacetime cadres at such places as Port Royal and Port Castries.

[1] Army Council memorandum, 'Scale of defence of Jamaica, Sierra Leone, Mauritius, Colombo, Singapore, and ports of self-governing colonies', 18 April 1905, C.I.D. paper 27c, Cab. 5/1. This paper includes a convenient précis of the earlier correspondence between War Office and Admiralty.

[2] Perhaps it was to this that Admiral Fisher, who had become first sea lord in October 1904, was referring when he wrote a few years later: 'A silly ass at the War Office wrote a paper to prove me inconsistent. Inconsistency is the bugbear of fools. I wouldn't give a d—— for a fellow who couldn't change his mind with a change of conditions! Ain't I to wear a waterproof because I didn't when the sun was shining?' (Marder, *The Road to War*, p. 17).

[3] 'Admiralty Remarks upon the Army Council Memorandum upon the scale of defence of Jamaica, etc.', 15 May 1905, C.I.D. paper 28c, Cab. 5/1.

Throughout 1903 and much of 1904 the War Office had made the Admiralty twist and turn about the naval command in the western Atlantic and the defences of the colonial bases; but given the growing challenge to Britain's naval power and the priority accorded to affairs in Europe this was a game they could not win. Perhaps out of pride and respect for public opinion, the two-power standard was not as formally abandoned as it had been formally adopted in 1889 until Winston Churchill revealed on 28 March 1912 that in '1908 or 1909' – in fact it had been in April 1909 – the government had substituted for it a 60 per cent superiority in dreadnoughts over Germany. In November 1908 the prime minister unequivocally stated in the House of Commons that the standard was one of two powers plus 10 per cent; but on 26 May 1909 he conceded that it was not 'a transcendant dogma, but . . . a convenient rule-of-thumb, to be applied with reference to political and strategical conditions'. The 'crux of the situation', as he put it, was the American navy.[1] But this had been the basis for the Admiralty's attempts to substitute a more sophisticated formula ever since Selborne's complaints of January 1901.[2] Certainly this consideration played its part, and quite undisguisedly, in the redistribution of the fleet in 1904–06. By the end of that period the Anglo-Japanese alliance, Russia's defeat by Japan, the rise of the German naval threat, and the entente with France had transformed the pattern of Britain's naval strategy. In August 1904 there were still a first-class protected cruiser and five other cruisers on the North American station. But on 21 October of that year Admiral Sir John Fisher returned to the Admiralty and this time as first sea lord.

Fisher's views on the United States, as on so many other things, were somewhat mercurial. Certainly it seems something of an exaggeration to say that he 'always worked for close Anglo-American co-operation'.[3] In 1901, for example, he had expressed himself with characteristic vigour on the subject of Anglo-Saxon affinity: 'Only a $\frac{1}{4}$ of the population of the United States are what you may call natives; the rest are Germans, Irish, Italians, and the scum of the earth! all of them hating the English like poison.'[4] Early in 1902 moreover he had included wars against German-American and Russian-American combinations, as well as against the United States alone, in a list of contingencies, 'some . . .

[1] For the two-power standard see Marder, *The Road to War*, pp. 182–5.
[2] See above p. 351.   [3] Marder, *The Road to War*, p. 26.
[4] Fisher to Lord Rosebery, 10 May 1901, *Fear God and Dread Nought; the Correspondence of Admiral of the Fleet Lord Fisher of Kilverstone*, selected and edited by Arthur J. Marder (London, 1959), i. 190.

highly improbable, but none impossible', for which he hoped the Admiralty had plans.[1] He does not seem to have overcome his personal prejudice against the United States until his visit of 1910 but the mesmeric influence of the German naval programme had already led him, persistently if not consistently, to discount the possibility or practicability of a clash with the United States. By the end of 1906 Germany had become 'our only probable enemy' and even 'our only possible foe for years to come'.[2] By the same time it had also become his opinion that the United States was 'a kindred state with whom we may indeed have evanescent quarrels, but with whom, it is scarcely too much to say, we shall never have a parricidal war'.[3] Four years later, when pressing for the adoption of the 'two keels to one' formula as more conveniently applied to Germany, Fisher remarked that its 'inestimable value' was that 'it eliminates the United States Navy, which ought never to be mentioned: criminal folly to do so – '.[4]

While Fisher's later claim never to have accepted the possibility of war with the United States is undoubtedly an exaggeration,[5] it was essentially true at least for the period beginning about the time he returned to the Admiralty in 1904. He may not have had much affection yet for the United States but hard-headed realism made him write off that nation either as a possible enemy or as a possible ally. In August 1904 he wrote that in the search for allies he 'put the United States out of the question, as we ought to clear out from that Hemisphere altogether!'[6] It is no wonder that in the redistribution of the fleet, forced through largely under his dynamic influence in 1904–06, the squadrons in American waters were treated with particular ruthlessness. The old squadrons, apart from that at the Cape, were reorganized into a two-tier system of battle fleets and cruiser squadrons. Three of the four battle fleets, the Channel, Atlantic, and Mediterranean, each with one of the cruiser squadrons, were concentrated in European

---

[1] Fisher (then c.-in-c., Mediterranean) to Capt. Prince Louis of Battenberg, 10 Feb. 1902, *Fear God and Dread Nought; the Correspondence of Admiral of the Fleet Lord Fisher of Kilverstone*, selected and edited by Arthur J. Marder (London, 1959), i. 223.
[2] Fisher to Prince of Wales, 23 Oct. 1906, and to Tweedmouth, 26 Sept. 1906, *ibid.*, ii. 103 and 92.
[3] 'Admiralty Policy: Replies to Criticism', Oct. 1906, Lord Fisher, *Records* (London, 1919), p. 104.
[4] Fisher to Viscount Esher, 5 Aug. 1910, *Fear God and Dread Nought*, ii. 333–4.
[5] Fisher to S. McKenna (first lord of the Admiralty), 12 May 1908, Marder, *The Road to War*, p. 184.
[6] Fisher to Viscount Knollys [late August 1904], *Fear God and Dread Nought*, i. 327.

waters; the fourth, the Eastern fleet, embraced the old China, East Indies, and Australian squadrons. The Pacific and South Atlantic squadrons entirely disappeared and the old North American and West Indies squadron was utterly transformed. From the last it was decided to withdraw all the 'inferior' cruisers, and for reasons of internal security to keep on station only the flagship in the West Indies and one of the new fast *Diamond* class cruisers at Bermuda. Similarly a sloop was to be kept at Esquimalt, mainly to supervise British interests in the Behring Sea fisheries; and a number of other vessels did similar duty with the Newfoundland fisheries from time to time. For the rest the squadron survived only as a polite myth. The 'inferior' cruisers were theoretically replaced by a newly formed training squadron of six large cruisers. This, the 'Fourth Cruiser (Particular Service) Squadron', was formally under the commander-in-chief on the North American station and in the event of war its crews would have been made up with trained men. But in wartime it was destined to join either the Mediterranean or the Channel fleets, and even in peacetime it was not to be permanently on the American station. It was to make three cruises annually, only one of them necessarily in the West Indies, the rest in 'Home and adjacent waters' where it would normally expect to be for at least twenty-two weeks of the year. Its base, moreover, was to be Devonport.[1]

Fisher resented even the rump now left in the West Indies. He loudly objected to what he called 'police work' and successfully resisted the prime minister's gentle pressure late in 1905 that another vessel should join the *Diamond*.[2] In 1906 the absence of British warships was noted with disapproval during the Cuban revolution of February, the earthquakes in Chile in August and September, and a mutiny at Zanzibar in September. In January 1907, when an earthquake caused much damage in Jamaica, there were no British warships on hand and help had to come from the American navy. The flagship was somewhere in the Caribbean, but had only half its agreed complement of marines on board, while the *Diamond* was at Halifax and was said 'never to have been near the islands at all'. In March 1907 the Foreign and Colonial Offices proposed an increase in the number of naval 'police units',

[1] Based on Selborne's two memoranda, 'Distribution and Mobilization of the Fleet', 6 Dec. 1904, and 'Arrangements Consequent on the Redistribution of the Fleet', 15 Mar. 1905, *British Parliamentary Papers*, 1905, xlviii, [Cd. 2335 and 2430]. For the arrangements in the West Indies see also C. D. C. 356 M, 'West Indies: Measures for maintenance of internal order . . .', C.I.D. paper 38c, 21 Dec. 1905, Cab. 5/1.
[2] Minutes of the 81st meeting of the C.I.D., 21 Nov. 1905, Cab. 2/1.

arguing that the risk of their loss at the beginning of a war should be 'faced, for the sake of the world-wide interests of the Empire'. On this occasion Fisher again succeeded with his passionate resistance. But in April riots in St Lucia did lead to the despatch of another cruiser to the West Indies.[1]

The implications of the redistribution of the fleet were unmistakably clear in their relation to the United States. The message was rammed home in the summer of 1905 when Japan and Great Britain came to renew their alliance in the light of the recent defeat of Russia in the Far East. For a time, while the General Staff continued to insist upon the possibility of the United States becoming an enemy, the Admiralty induced the cabinet to talk to the Japanese about excluding the United States fleet from their calculations. At length it was found wiser to withdraw any specific proposal; but the idea remained implicit in the vaguer arrangements eventually adopted. In any case Lansdowne, as foreign secretary, had explained exactly what they had intended:

We had also stipulated that each party should maintain a force superior in strength not to that of any other Power, but to that of any European Power in those seas. This was done in order that we might not be compelled to level our fleets up to the strength of the naval force maintained by the U.S. in or near the Far East. We did not consider it at all likely that we should be at war with the United States and unless this exception were made Great Britain and Japan would each be obliged to maintain a superfluous number of ships.[2]

The wholesale withdrawal from American waters themselves meant that in that area at least there was little point in the War Office continuing its fight over distant colonial garrisons. In July 1905 the chief of the General Staff informed the C.I.D. that in the autumn one battalion would be withdrawn from Bermuda, the white battalion in Jamaica replaced by a West Indian one, and virtually all troops withdrawn from Barbados and St Lucia.[3] There was some delay while the local militias were reorganized but by the beginning of 1907 and in spite of all local protests, there was only a handful of troops in the West Indies in addition to the battalion and depôt of the West Indian Regiment; and in Bermuda only one battalion of infantry, two batteries

[1] Mary Arnold Forster, *The Right Honourable Hugh Oakeley Arnold-Forster: a Memoir* (London, 1910), pp. 321-2; and Marder, *Road to War*, pp. 53-4.
[2] Lansdowne to Sir C. Macdonald (minister in Tokyo), 10 June 1905, *British Documents on the Origins of the War, 1898-1914*, ed. by G. P. Gooch and Harold Temperley, iv (1929), no. 126, p. 137.
[3] Minutes of the 76th meeting of the C.I.D., 20 July 1905, Cab. 2/1.

of artillery, and a company of engineers. Whatever had been the intention of the War Office in so leading the Admiralty by the nose over the West Indian bases, they had failed either to reverse the current trend of withdrawal and reduction or to secure a full consideration of the strategic position with respect to the United States. But there still remained the thorny question of the standards of defence for Halifax and Esquimalt and these had to be fixed before the bases were handed over to the dominion government.

The tendency for the 'evasionists' (at the Admiralty or in Canada) so to neglect the question of defences as to make 'transfer' a euphemism for abandonment had long since been made clear in the case of Esquimalt.[1] Esquimalt's peculiar vulnerability to attack had made it an especial object of the imperial government's determination to exact from the local authorities as great a contribution to the cost of defences as possible. Ever since the 1860s its distance from Great Britain of some 9,000 miles and its proximity to American forces for offence had led to consistent declarations about the impossibility of defending it against the United States. One commander-in-chief of the Pacific squadron went so far as to suggest that it and the colony as a whole should be abandoned.[2] But this was not politically convenient and the Russian scare of 1878 found the base still in British hands but still without any garrison and utterly defenceless. The special Defence Committee of that year belatedly recommended some defences 'in order to protect the small but essential naval establishment, with its stores and workshops for the use of H.M. ships in the Pacific Station, from the risk of capture or destruction in the absence of a naval force'.[3] The armaments suggested, however, were never sent; nor were they, presumably, meant to be an effective answer to an American attack. But the action of the Canadian government in mounting at their own expense in hastily constructed batteries the naval guns held in store, no doubt gave encouragement to the Carnarvon Commission's application in this case of the 'principle' of colonial contribution. That commission

[1] For the history of this base see: Reginald H. Roy, 'The Early Militia and Defence of British Columbia, 1871–1885', *British Columbia Historical Quarterly*, xviii (1954), 1–28; D. M. Schurman, 'Esquimalt Defence Problem, 1865–1887', *ibid.*, xix (1955), 57–69; and F. V. Longstaff, *Esquimalt Naval Base: a History of its Work and its Defences* (Victoria, 1941). There is a useful summary of the official papers relating to the base's history since 1878 in the M.I.D.'s 'Memorandum on the standard of defence at Esquimalt', 24 May 1903, C.I.D. paper 2c, Cab. 5/1.

[2] Adm. Denman to Adm., 15 June and 5 Sept. 1865, Adm. 1/5924.

[3] Printed Report no. 3, 'Naval Station at Esquimalt and the Town and Harbour of Victoria', 1 April 1878, confidential print no. 35B, Cab. 7/1.

bluntly declared that the base could not be held against the United States, that British trade in the area was insignificant, and that the British fleet should be transferred to China. But in view of the importance of the connection with the Canadian Pacific Railway and 'political considerations' – presumably a reference to pro-American feeling in British Columbia – it was suggested that certain limited defences should be established and maintained by the Canadians.

Unfortunately the principal argument in favour of colonial payment, that the base was of no real imperial use, was not one shared either by some of the commissioners or by the Admiralty. Two members, Admiral Sir Alexander Milne and Sir Henry Barkly, the Colonial Office representative, expressly dissented, insisting on the base's importance in relation to powers other than the United States. The Admiralty simply refused to entertain the China idea. The inspector-general of fortifications, moreover, disputed the unimportance of the trade in his paper of 6 June 1883 modifying the commission's recommendations about coaling stations.[1] Inevitably the new Russian scare in 1885 found Esquimalt and Victoria just as defenceless as ever and some works had once again to be hurriedly improvised. Then the C.D.C. reverted to the more favourable view of Esquimalt's value and recommended appropriate standards of defence against a one or two cruiser attack.[2] Canada agreed to provide the garrison and pay for the works, while the British were to supply the armament. As usual, the Canadians were unable to meet their obligations and in 1893 the British had to agree to pay half the cost of the works and to marines sharing the garrison duty with Canadian troops until 1899.[3]

Before the end of the transitional period the growth of actual American power, here as on the eastern seaboard, had thrown very serious doubt once more on the whole defence arrangements, both as to works and garrison. These had been designed to defend the position against a cruiser attack, not against 'a serious assault supported by battleships'. In spite of the pessimistic forecasts of local commanders, the United States had not hitherto possessed on the Pacific coast either the naval force or the secure base from which to launch such an assault. Their fortress in Puget Sound had been armed only with smooth-bore and old-pattern guns and the Pacific squadron in 1887 had still included nothing more than a couple of coast defence ships and six small cruisers.

[1] Memorandum by Sir Andrew Clarke, 6 June 1883, Cab. 7/6.
[2] C.D.C. 2 M, 1 May, and 13 M, 5 Aug. 1885, Cab. 8/1.
[3] See Colonial Office correspondence of October and November 1885 in C.I.D. 2c, Cab. 5/1.

But by 1896 it had one first-class battleship, the *Oregon*, and was later to have a second, and in total numbers was already two or three times as large as the British. Moreover, the fortifications recommended for San Francisco, San Diego, the Columbia River, and Puget Sound by the Endicott Board in 1886 were now being pushed forward. In these circumstances, the C.D.C. calculated in October 1896, the Americans could, within a few days, collect some 2,000 regulars and 4,000 militia at Seattle, the principal fort in Puget Sound, for an attack on Esquimalt which lay only eighty miles away. No British naval reinforcements could arrive in time from China, nor any troops get through by the highly vulnerable Canadian Pacific Railway. The government must therefore decide, the C.D.C. insisted, whether in the event of war the base should be abandoned or overwhelmed, with all the consequent 'bad moral effects', or whether a 'large expenditure on guns' should not be incurred beforehand and its garrison raised to at least 5,000 trained troops. The two service departments after a long delay agreed that on financial, though not strategic, grounds the limited standards of 1893 should be adhered to. To provide against any attack 'reasonably probable' from the United States would require keeping the base on a permanent war footing because of its distance from Great Britain. This would require an initial expenditure of £500,000 on works and barracks and £250,000 per annum thereafter. Such an expenditure was plainly beyond the resources of Canada and would consequently have fallen upon Great Britain. The money would be better spent on the navy. So unsatisfactory was the existing position that Canada should be asked to take over now and not wait until 1899.[1] But the Colonial Office had already in the previous summer approached the dominion government about both Esquimalt and Halifax and having had a distinctly discouraging response now had to ask that the British contribution continue.[2]

The secretary of state for war was to comment later that he viewed 'with some apprehension any proposal which relieves, even temporarily, the Colonies in the performance of specific duties in connection with the defence of the Empire which properly pertain to them'.[3] There was a real danger therefore that the persistent dilatoriness of the Canadians would lead, in this case as it had in others in the past, to some virtually unilateral withdrawal by the British. It was probably for this reason, rather than because of the recent developments that they actually

[1] C.D.C. 79 M, 'Defence of Esquimalt', 26 Oct. 1896, Cab. 8/1.
[2] C.I.D. 2c, Cab. 5/1.   [3] Minute by Lansdowne, 18 Jan. 1899, *ibid.*

cited, that in March 1898 the Admiralty wrote to the Colonial Office proposing an interdepartmental conference in uncharacteristically enthusiastic language:

In the opinion of their Lordships the importance of British Columbia as a province of the Dominion has been much enhanced by the discovery of gold in the northern territories, and boundary disputes in Alaska, together with other causes, may furnish the United States with a pretext for attempting to separate it from the rest of Canada, apart from which the Pacific seaboard is as necessary to the Dominion as it is indispensable to the development of British Columbia; so that not only on one but on many grounds the province deserves a large share of any protection which the Dominion may be able to afford.

To the efficiency of this protection Esquimalt is essential; deprived of their base and coaling station, H.M.'s ships could not be maintained in those waters, and without naval defence, the trade and ports of British Columbia would become a prey to every enemy, and the province be at the mercy of the United States. The Imperial interest in Esquimalt is the use that can be made of it for the protection of Canada as part of the Empire, and the Admiralty would view with favour any equitable course which could hasten the provision of an adequate garrison for the only base on which H.M.'s ships could rely in the event of war.[1]

It is not suprising that a conference of representatives of the service departments, the Colonial Office, and the Treasury on 10 November 1898 recommended that while the defence of Esquimalt was primarily the duty of the dominion government, Canada's present military resources were insufficient and that there must continue to be a 'temporary' arrangement for a further ten years. During that period the provision of the small peacetime garrison of regulars was to remain the responsibility of the War Office, but Canada was to pay half its cost and half that of the barracks. This recommendation the Defence Committee, the Admiralty, the War Office – reluctantly – and the Canadian government accepted at the beginning of 1899.[2] But local feeling, inspired by new threats of Fenian raids as well as the general growth of American power, did not allow the question to be so easily disposed of. In March and April 1900 the Admiralty had to meet a series of proposals arising out of a Fenian scare and in September 1901 the Alaska and isthmian canal disputes led the Pacific commander-in-chief to draw attention once more to the vulnerability of his head-quarters and 'the dangerously weak state of the Squadron'.[3] Apart from improvements in the garrison he wanted a significant increase in

[1] Adm. to C.O., 8 Mar. 1898, C.I.D. 2c, Cab. 5/1.   [2] C.I.D. 2c, Cab. 5/1.
[3] Admiralty file of 7 Sept. 1900, Adm. 1/7491; and Adm. Bickford to Adm., no. 1116, 17 Sept. 1901, Adm. 1/7513.

the squadron generally as a deterrent but also to act offensively if need be. He also wanted some additional destroyers to defend Esquimalt and the coaling depôt of Nanaimo until help could arrive. On this demand the D.N.I. (Custance) merely recorded:'. . . this letter shows, when considered in connection with the calls upon us of other stations, how impossible it is to think of attempting to meet the U.S. on equal terms on the Pacific coast of North America.'

While the Admiralty simply refused these applications, the War Office felt obliged to reopen the whole question:

This decision [of 1898 to keep to the old standard of defence] was given having regard to financial rather than strategic considerations, and the latter aspect of the case was not discussed. The Commander in Chief however, now urges – and the Secretary of State for War concurs in his views – that to enable the defence of the Empire to be duly considered and plans for all contingencies prepared, it would be unwise to eliminate the serious contingency of war with the United States.

They now asked the Admiralty, therefore, whether the loss of Esquimalt would be serious and precisely what naval assistance for its defence might be expected from either the Pacific or the China squadrons.[1] The Admiralty's reply was blunt. There was no prospect of help from either squadron, the navy's 'principle of distribution in war with any power' being 'while leaving in European waters a sufficient force to contain that of any menacing Power, to mass our forces on the decisive points, among which no position in British Columbian waters could be included'. As they did not regard the loss of Esquimalt as serious, they saw 'no reason' for departing from the previous decision.[2] Reference to the weak Cabinet Defence Committee produced no decision, but the institution of what promised to be the more energetic and more effective C.I.D. at the end of 1902 led the M.I.D. to present their case to that committee on 23 May 1903. The Admiralty's arguments of the previous spring, their paper maintained, seemed utterly at odds with those of 8 March 1898 in which they had stressed the importance of British Columbia and insisted that the base at Esquimalt was essential. If, as their new paper seemed to indicate, there was to be no fleet in the area in time of war, then in war Esquimalt would serve no purpose since both it and the Canadian Pacific Railway were indefensible without naval assistance. There were three possibilities: to abandon Esquimalt as a defended port and make it a 'flying squadron

[1] W.O. to Adm., 17 Mar. 1902, C.I.D. 2c, Cab. 5/1.
[2] Adm. to W.O., 12 April 1902, *ibid*.

base' like Wei-hai-wei; to continue the present arrangements but evacuate in the event of war with the United States; or, as the M.I.D. now recommended, since the other alternatives either broke faith with Canada or exposed the garrison to easy capture, to improve the present arrangements 'slightly' so as to give the garrison 'some chance' of holding out against the Americans for at least a short period.[1]

When the C.I.D. agreed with Borden at its meeting of 11 December 1903 to hand over the last British bases in Canada, they did so without having first settled the appropriate standards of defence even among themselves. This was also true of Halifax, though there had been much less fuss about that base than about Esquimalt. The review made of the North American situation in 1896 had led to some new works for Halifax being included in the Army Services Loan of 1897 and to provision being made for a war garrison of a little under 3,500 men. These, so the D.M.I. had reassured his naval colleague as recently as December 1902, were sufficient against any probable attack by the United States, provided that an overland advance from Maine were ruled out and local command of the seas remained in British hands.[2] A major attack from Maine was made highly unlikely by the wooded nature of the frontier and the danger of leaving such places as Boston exposed to attack via the Richelieu valley. But doubt had been cast even in 1896 upon the security of Halifax from organized attack by sea because of the superior ability of the Americans to concentrate their naval forces in that area in the initial stages of a war. This danger was supposed to have been referred to the Canadian Defence Commission of 1898, but there is no sign that they took it seriously into account. Quite possibly they were influenced in this respect by the special information passed on by one of their members, Colonel Lake. Lake had been told by a friend that the Americans' 1896 war-plans had proposed to begin first with an attack on the Canadian canals and an advance on Montreal rather than any attempt on Halifax.[3] The defence arrangements at Halifax in any case remained adequate only against the sort of *coup de main* that Mahan had contemplated in 1890. But, as a M.I.D. paper especially prepared for the C.I.D.'s meeting of 11 December 1903 tried to point out, the Admiralty's warnings about

[1] M.I.D. 'Memorandum on the standard of defence at Esquimalt', 24 May 1903, C.I.D. 2c, Cab. 5/1.
[2] D.M.I. to D.N.I., 22 Dec. 1902, W.O. 106/40, file B 1/1.
[3] Lake to Capt. C. B. Levita, R.A., 4 Oct. 1898, and Levita to Lt.-Col. E. A. Altham (Asst. Q.M.G.), 1 Nov. 1898, W.O. 106/40, file B 1/7. Levita's information was based on talks he had had with Senator Redfield Proctor.

the possible loss of sea command now meant that Halifax must reckon on having to face an organized attack by sea, and for that both garrison and fixed defences would have to be 'greatly improved'.[1] But no decision was made by the C.I.D. at its meeting – perhaps the matter was not even discussed.

On 25 March 1904 the War Office found it necessary to address to the C.I.D. a 'Memorandum of Outstanding Questions now before the Committee of Imperial Defence, on which an early decision is urgently needed by the War Office'.[2] Here, in addition to a final decision on the size of the garrison for Bermuda, they pressed most pointedly for guidance about the defence standards of both Halifax and Esquimalt. The C.I.D. merely turned the matter over to their military members to decide in consultation with the Colonial Office.[3] Shortly afterwards the committee bracketed Halifax with those stations which they thought should have only 'very small garrisons' because of the naval superiority of the United States, and talked of Canada making arrangements for its defence only against 'other powers'.[4] In effect they were inviting the revision of Halifax's standard of defence on an inferior basis. This decision they reaffirmed on 22 November 1904 in spite of continued protests from the War Office that in the event of war with the United States, Halifax must be held and that the existing standards of defence, being adequate in the 'preliminary stages of the war', should be at least maintained.[5]

The C.I.D.'s implicit decision to extend to Halifax the embargo on planning with a view to war with the United States forced the War Office, if they were not altogether to give up the American question, to raise at the end of 1904 the direct question of the defence of Canada itself. For this they were not now unprepared. In the interval since 1901–02 their consciousness of the vast increase in American power had led the M.I.D. or the new General Staff to order Lt.-Col. G. M. Kirkpatrick, the D.A.Q.M.G. at Halifax, and, incidentally, a Canadian, to make a new study of the defence question. This report, which came in some time before 21 September 1904, generally speaking went over much the same ground and came to much the same conclusions as had the M.I.D. memoranda of March 1901. The growth in the

[1] Col. Altham's memorandum on 'The adequacy of the existing garrison and defences of Halifax to resist an attack by land', 11 Dec. 1903, C.I.D. paper 7c, Cab. 5/1.   [2] C.I.D. 10c, *ibid.*
[3] Minutes of the 38th meeting of the C.I.D., 15 April 1904, Cab. 2/1.
[4] Minutes of the 48th meeting of the C.I.D., 8 July 1904, *ibid.*
[5] Minutes of the 58th meeting of the C.I.D., 22 Nov. 1904, and addendum to the minutes of the 48th meeting, 13 July, *ibid.*

naval and military strength of the United States had greatly increased the pressure that they could bring to bear on the traditional invasion routes. Quebec and Montreal now had to face a real threat from the sea as well as from the south and east of the St Lawrence; the Americans were better placed to launch a diversionary attack by way of Georgian Bay; their superior mobilization arrangements might even make it possible for them to launch a winter attack across the frozen St Lawrence. But worst of all the weakness of Britain's naval power in the western Atlantic and the poor condition of her bases would now make it impossible for her to relieve her position in Canada and weaken American morale by mounting diversionary attacks against the Atlantic seaboard. Familiar, too, was the defensive strategy outlined to meet this difficult situation: the abandonment of much of Canada to the enemy as indefensible; the concentration on the defence of Quebec and Montreal; and, of course, special operations like a counterattack across the St Lawrence to cut the relatively weaker American communications, and relieve some of the pressure.

To this conventionally gloomy picture Kirkpatrick added a special emphasis on the naval position, and an emphasis not so much on the western Atlantic as on a naval contribution to the defence of Quebec and Montreal: in the estuary and lower reaches of the St Lawrence to fend off an invasion from the sea or from Lake Champlain; and above Quebec and upon Lake Ontario, to hold off the advance of the Americans' superiority on the other lakes. It was of some help that the completion of the Soulanges canal had at last removed the old difficulty about the vulnerability of the Beauharnois and also allowed somewhat larger vessels to pass into Lake Ontario. But in the centre of the Canadian lifeline there now loomed the threat of an enlargement of the Erie, Oswego, and Champlain canals so as to take barges of 1,000 tons. Funds for this purpose had been voted by the New York State Legislature in November 1903. If completed it would give American warships access to Lake Ontario that would radically alter the situation.[1]

Coming in, as this report did, just when the Admiralty was worrying the War Office most with the far-reaching implications of its new line on the naval situation in the western Atlantic, its special emphasis on the naval contribution to the defence of Canada provided the General Staff with a new and final point of attack. In December 1904 they submitted to the C.I.D. a new paper on the defence of Canada. Its

[1] Lt.-Col. G. M. Kirkpatrick, R.E., 'A Study in the Strategic Conditions existing on the Canadian frontier . . .', 1904, with a preface by the director of military operations, 21 Sept. 1904, Cab. 18/17, paper 6.

immediate purpose was, by highlighting the naval aspects of the question, to get from the committee 'a ruling . . . as to the action to be taken by the Royal Navy to meet a contingency which, however improbable, is not impossible – the contingency of war with the United States'. A land attack on the Maritime Provinces, in view of the difficulties of the terrain, they dismissed as 'most improbable'. Manitoba, the northwest, and the Pacific coast area they wrote off easily in view of their remoteness from British and Canadian resources and their proximity to superior American forces. But Canada proper, they insisted, must be defended in order to avoid 'an Imperial disaster of the very first magnitude'. And this, as Kirkpatrick had emphasized, was more than ever dependent upon the contribution of the navy. To be of any use, in view of the weakness of Canada's water communications, the British must make their preparations in advance of war. But if they could then strike quickly through the Welland canal they might even be able to reverse the balance of advantage upon Lake Erie and thus 'exert enormous moral effect in view of the defencelessness of the great cities of Buffalo and Cleveland and of the quantities of American merchant-vessels which would fall into their hands'. In this way the command of Lake Erie would be worth about 50,000 men to the defenders. Without it they must expect to lose the whole of the western districts of Upper Canada, and if the Americans got through the Welland canal and seized the command on Lake Ontario they would also lose 'the great city of Toronto' and the whole of the 'richest and most populous province of British North America', right up to the River Ottawa.[1]

There was not much that was new in this paper; in tone as well as content it smacked even of the earlier nineteenth century. Its essential significance now was in its reference to the redistribution of naval power. The Port Castries question had led at last to the larger question of the general defence of Canada.

The General Staff's paper succeeded at any rate to the extent that it extracted at last from the Admiralty a comprehensive statement of their view of the defence of Canada and war with the United States. Significantly, the Admiralty's case in reply was prefaced and epilogued by remarks upon the unlikelihood of war with the Americans composed respectively by Selborne, the first lord, and A. H. Lee, now the civil lord. Both stressed the steady growth of Anglo-American friendship since 1898, the extreme remoteness of war, and their utter horror of such a prospect:

[1] General Staff memorandum, 'Defence of Canada', 13 Dec. 1904, C.I.D. paper 15c, Cab. 5/1.

There is no party in the United Kingdom nor even [Selborne believed] in the British Empire which does not contemplate a war with the United States of America as the greatest evil which could befall the British Empire in its foreign relations.

There is no statesman of any party who does not consider cordial friendship with the United States of America as the principal aim and object of British foreign policy.

I know of no statesman who would not rejoice with a great rejoicing if the relations between the British Empire and the United States of America were to ripen into permanent alliance.

Lee for his part was no less passionate:

... I cannot for a moment contemplate the possibility of hostilities really taking place.

I should regard a war between this country and the United States as the supreme limit of human folly, and I cannot conceive that any British statesman is willing to contemplate it under any circumstances, unless it were forced upon us beyond all possibility of avoidance.

In such a war we could not possibly win – no combination of Powers could successfully invade and conquer the United States – and the contest if persisted in could only result in the destruction of the British Empire and the downfall of the English speaking race.

The body of the memorandum, of course, was more at pains to stress the material facts of the relationship, in particular the magnitude of the American naval programme which had begun immediately after the Spanish-American war and which supported the view that the United States was aiming shortly at reaching second place to Great Britain, 'with a possible ultimate bid for first place'. Certainly her current building programme of battleships and armoured cruisers was running very close behind Great Britain's and was almost twice as great as that of the next power.[1] While the American effort rivalled Great Britain's 'gigantic' programme of 1889, in war the United States would have an enormous advantage by being able to concentrate virtually the whole of her force:

The nation which has called into being this prodigious naval force occupies a position, both geographically and politically, unique amongst the Great Powers.

In a sense more true than with ourselves, she 'needs no bulwarks, no towers along the steep'.

[1] Building programmes for 1904–05 were calculated to be:

	Battleships	Armoured cruisers	Total tonnage
Great Britain	12	16	388,000
U.S.A.	14	13	380,000
France	6	9	195,000
Germany	8	3	134,000

Between her and any real threat of foreign aggression lies no mere silver streak of British Channel, but 3,000 miles of storm-swept seas.

The feeble neighbours on her northern and southern boundaries can cause her no serious pre-occupation regarding land frontiers. To these she stands inviolate. And politically thanks to a foreign policy of wise aloofness, she has (at all events until recently) kept free from bitter jealousies and racial hatreds which sunder the nations of the Old World, and which have made the calamities of France, of England, and of Russia, in the past, matters of rejoicing to neighbouring Powers.

If we except the Philippines and Cuba (the loss of either of which she would scarcely feel), she has no distant possessions to be defended.

This happy lack of external causes for pre-occupation has enabled the United States to concentrate her warships upon her own shores, where (in war time) they would find their proper occupation in defending the shores of the Motherland.

To attack her Great Britain, on the contrary, must send her vessels across 3,000 miles of sea.

Centuries of triumphant conflict with her European rivals have left Great Britain the double legacy of world-wide Empire and of a jealousy (of which we had a sad glimpse during the South African war) which would render it hazardous indeed for us to denude our home waters of the battle squadrons, which stand between our own land and foreign invasion.

America, it seems, can employ every ship she possesses in the Western Atlantic, but the conditions under which England could employ her whole naval force in such a distant locality are hardly conceivable. And, as though disparity were not enough, the time is now approaching when, by the completion of the Isthmian Canal, the United States will possess the enormous advantage of moving her war-ships at will from her Pacific to her Atlantic coasts in war by a route some 10,000 miles shorter than that which would be open to the vessels of our own country.

Consolation could be sought no longer in the Americans' former inability to raise sufficient men to man great navies; in the last six years the number of seamen had been raised from under 10,500 to 31,000. Nor, as after the Civil War, was their naval expansion likely to prove a passing phase; manufacturing and shipbuilding facilities alike backed up the Americans' express determination to win and maintain naval predominance in the western hemisphere. But the improvement in Anglo-American relations and the utterings of the American press suggested that not Great Britain but Germany was the prospective antagonist of the United States in the revived pursuit of the Monroe Doctrine.[1] Thus it was felt, 'the flowing tide appears now to be with those who wish well to a cordial Anglo-American Agreement', and

[1] The Admiralty had learnt something, clearly; but they still spelt it 'Munroe'!

even though an alliance might yet be out of the question, still it would be unwise to upset such good feeling by a sudden display of unaccustomed naval activity in Canada:

The view of the Admiralty is that Canada must primarily rely upon her own resources for defence against invasions by the United States: Firstly, because any action on the part of the Mother Country is conditional upon British sea supremacy in the Western Atlantic, which cannot, even now, under all circumstances, be guaranteed in such a war, and, in the near future, in view of the steady increase of the United States' Navy, could probably not be counted on at all. Secondly, because the greatest interest of this country being to maintain friendly relations with the United States, any military preparations for the defence of Canada on the part of Great Britain obviously aimed at that country are greatly to be deprecated; and, Thirdly, because Canada's knowledge that, in a war with the United States, she must rely upon her own resources, must tend to inculcate in her statesmen a wholesome caution.

But however much they tended to disapprove and wanted to dismiss the idea of war with the United States the Admiralty still felt it necessary to consider the possibility of a war arising out of a clash between the United States and Canada. Lee professed to consider this prospect too 'scarcely within the bounds of possibility'; but Selborne felt it necessary to make some reservation about the remoteness of war:

These facts . . . do not release us as trustees for the time being of the future of our country, from considering soberly what steps we should or could take if the people of the United States of America, in a moment of criminal folly were to confront us with the dilemma of having to choose between war with them and the unspeakable disgrace of abandoning our fellow-countrymen in Canada in a righteous quarrel deliberately forced upon them by the American people.

I expect no such criminal folly of the people of the United States of America, any more than of my own people, but history teaches us that peoples, as well as individuals, have attacks of frenzy, and therefore we cannot, in my opinion, absolve ourselves from the duty of contemplating this dim and dire contingency in all its aspects. I have, however, such faith in the innate justice of the American people that I dissent from the verdict of some authorities that in such a war we could not possibly win. Indeed, neither the British Empire nor the whole civilized world could conquer the United States of America, but the British Empire could, in my opinion, enable Canada to make so strenuous and resolute a defence against invasion as to give the American people time to return to righteous sanity and to recoil with horror from a war of aggression, of oppression, of invasion – a war antagonistic to every principle of their own existence.

In that event we should not have conquered the American people, but we should have achieved our sole object in taking up arms, the preservation of Canada from conquest, and of our own honour from disgrace.

For these reasons, then, and in spite of the sweeping statements with which it had begun the memorandum went on to deal in considerable detail with the General Staff's specific proposals – but in such a way as, after all, to grant themselves absolution.

In the first place the navy's present arrangements did not include any special provision for putting a flotilla on the Canadian lakes and it was doubtful if the British taxpayer would consider assuming such an additional burden. The question arose of whether there was some alternative approach. There was some sign that the Canadians themselves were thinking of replacing their fisheries protection fleet – at present virtually useless as a fighting force – with ships discarded by the Royal Navy. The 1817 agreement would preclude their entering the lakes in peacetime, but they could be stationed at Montreal in readiness to go up in the event of war. Indeed, the Admiralty conceded, a fleet of submarines and torpedo boats would greatly strengthen the Canadians' means of defence. But the objections seemed overwhelming. It could hardly be done secretly and it would lead therefore not only to the worsening of American relations with both Canada and Great Britain but also to corresponding preparations on the part of the United States. 'Naval activity on the lakes', as Lee put it, was 'a game that two can play at, and a game in which the Americans hold all the trump cards.' The Americans could easily erect batteries along the shore of the St Lawrence to destroy the light, unarmoured vessels to which any British force for the lakes would still be restricted by the dimensions of the canal locks. They could effectively close the channels by ground mines – in whose use they had become so expert in the Civil War – and they would almost certainly have perfected plans for seizing the Welland canal. Even if they neglected to make peacetime preparations for all these measures, the outbreak of war in winter would give them the breathing-space to do so. Above all there was the likelihood of any Canadian preparations giving the vital impetus to the improvement of the American canals whose dangers the General Staff had themselves referred to. It was true that a Georgian Bay canal would transform the position on the upper lakes radically in Great Britain's favour. This, however, had still to be built.

To ram the moral home the Admiralty memorandum ended with a long review of the familiar points about the Americans' immunity to conquest and their superiority in ships and shipbuilding on the lakes – a superiority which was especially advantageous in winter when they could go on building up their fleet while the ice kept the British out. Even if the British did triumph on the high seas and manage to resume the command in the western Atlantic, 'the victory gained, much as it might humiliate, could hardly have the effect of bringing America to her knees, since it would be very difficult to seriously injure her commerce, in view of the magnitude of her internal trade and resources'. The extinction of her mercantile marine would not be the crushing blow it might first appear because the bulk of her sea-borne trade was carried in neutral bottoms. The only effective way, in view of the Treaty of Paris, of putting a stop to American overseas trade would be by a sweeping declaration regarding contraband or by blockade. But the first would invite more damaging retaliation and offend neutrals; the second was impracticable, since the stipulation that 'blockades to be binding must be effective' would involve the concentration of British efforts upon a very few important seaports and this would leave open thousands of miles of American coast. The food supplies of Great Britain, on the other hand, lay at the mercy of the United States who could simply cut off at source in Canada and North America and otherwise harass and dislocate sea-borne trade. Hence, the Admiralty concluded:

It appears, then, that however unwelcome, the conclusion is inevitable that, in the event of an occurrence so much to be deprecated as the rupture of friendly relations with the United States, the position of Canada is one of extreme danger, and, so far as the navy is concerned, any effective assistance would be exceedingly difficult.

The task of the navy will be to deal with the American fleet on the high seas, and it will be a task that will tax its energies to the utmost.

Generally, the more carefully this problem is considered, the more tremendous do the difficulties which would confront Great Britain in a war with the United States appear. It may be hoped that the policy of the British Government will ever be to use all possible means to avoid such a war.[1]

The arguments used by the Admiralty in their attempt to dismiss permanently the awkward question of war with the United States must have seemed to them to be conclusive; but it was not to this negative end that the War Office had sought so long to extract from them a comprehensive statement of their policy and plans. In any case there were weaknesses of detail which they could not let pass unchallenged. Within a month, therefore, the General Staff had replied with a supplementary paper of their own, picking up not only some points of detail but also the plain question of Canadian defence as a whole. On

---

[1] Admiralty memorandum, 'Defence of Canada', 24 Feb. 1905, C.I.D. paper 21c, Cab. 5/1.

the unlikelihood of war with the United States they admitted they were
in general agreement. They nonetheless called attention to one possible
cause of friction that lay largely outside the control of London, Washington, or even Ottawa: namely, that whenever she wished to embarrass
Great Britain's relations with the United States, France had only to
put up for sale the islands of St Pierre and Miquelon. Perhaps someone
at the War Office recalled that when, in the wake of the Fashoda
incident, the admiral on the North American station had turned to
thoughts of attacking those islands, that admiral had been Sir John
Fisher, now first sea lord.[1] Turning away from such delicate political
matters to the feasibility of passing a flotilla through the canals on the
outbreak of war, the General Staff petulantly complained that this was
a military matter, having 'engaged the attention of officers who, in
addition to being fully acquainted with the local conditions, and who
have carefully examined the ground, combine with their local knowledge
ripe military experience and a practical acquaintance with the art of
war gained in the field'.

But the most worrying feature of the Admiralty's paper, and one
that Kirkpatrick had recently hinted at, was the extension of the general
naval withdrawal to the lower St Lawrence, from the rapids above Montreal to the sea. The exposure of lower Canada to an invasion from the
sea transformed the whole strategical situation. In these circumstances
the General Staff felt obliged to put to the C.I.D. three fundamental
questions:

1. Is the Royal Navy to be held responsible for securing Lake Ontario at
the outbreak of a war with the United States if the Canadian military
forces can safeguard the passage of vessels of suitable class from Montreal
up to the Lake at the outset of hostilities?
2. Is the Royal Navy to be held responsible for commanding the tideway
of the St Lawrence from the open sea up to the rapids immediately
above Montreal?
3. Does the declaration of policy enunciated in paragraph 2 of the C.D.C.
paper, No. 57M, to the effect that the Admiralty had accepted the responsibility of protecting all British territory against oversea invasion, hold
good as regards the Dominion of Canada?[2]

The General Staff had brought the question back to a matter of basic
principle. Since Canada – including the province of British Columbia –
they might also have added the West Indies – now seemed to be excluded

<hr/>

[1] Gordon, p. 123.
[2] General Staff memorandum, 'The Defence of Canada', 17 Mar. 1905,
C.I.D. paper 24c, Cab. 5/1.

from the defence undertakings publicly revealed in 1896, it was time to review the whole subject of the navy's contribution to imperial defence.

In these circumstances the Admiralty wisely reverted to their customary brevity and bluntness. On the first of the General Staff's questions they thought that their previous paper had been explicit enough. On the last they remarked simply that the old undertaking of 1896, contained in C.D.C. 57M, 'must be interpreted in a reasonable sense'. They then proceeded, by way of supposed elaboration of 'reasonable sense', to become quite evasive. Canada was somewhat exceptional in that its vast land frontier made its defence a 'military rather than a naval question'. While the navy would continue to prevent 'organized invasion from the sea', this was not the kind of attack to which Canada was most liable. So far as *its* duties were concerned the navy must be free – that is from specific commitments on the lakes or in the St Lawrence – to distribute the fleet according to strategic necessities: 'The end in view, *viz*, to secure British territory against over-sea invasion, can best be secured by such strategic dispositions of the Naval Forces as may reasonably be expected to leave Great Britain ultimately in command of the seas, and not necessarily by the immediate presence of a British Fleet at every point which can possibly be threatened.'[1]

Having now got as clear statements as they were ever likely to have the War Office added for the C.I.D.'s decision another paper on the still outstanding questions of the standards of defence for Esquimalt and Halifax. On the former, perhaps now seeking to sugar the pill, they were distinctly cooperative. 'It is obvious that the defences are insufficient to repel serious attack from the U.S., but on the other hand they seem excessive against attack from any other quarter. . . . It . . . appears to be generally recognised now that the fortification of Esquimalt was a mistake.' Plainly the War Office was now advocating the base's reclassification as a commercial harbour or even its abandonment altogether. But on Halifax they returned to the attack, suggesting that the C.I.D. had been wrong, not only about its value in the event of war with the United States, but also in regard to its defensive possibilities against an organized expeditionary force. There was moreover, as with the West Indies, the question of public opinion. In Canada secrets had a habit of leaking out and there would be a public outcry if it were learnt that the navy seriously contemplated leaving the Atlantic coast

[1] Admiralty memorandum, 'Defence of Canada', [?] April 1905, C.I.D. paper 25c, Cab. 5/1.

to the mercy of the United States. Even if the strategic arguments behind it were justified there was still good reason to modify the previous decision.[1]

At last, in meetings on 5 and 12 April, the C.I.D. came to discuss the large questions, fundamental both to the defence of Canada and to imperial defence generally, which the passage of arms between the service departments had raised. In the course of the discussions the usual references were made, by the prime minister to Canada's 'right to the support of the whole resources of the Empire' and by the colonial secretary to the existing commitments under Cardwell's despatch of 17 June 1865. On the other hand, were the dangers, mentioned by both Balfour and Fisher, of offending the United States and stimulating counteractivity on their part. It was quite possibly in an attempt to get a real and unequivocal decision without involving the first of these difficulties that the chief of the General Staff, Sir Neville Lyttelton, mentioned at the second meeting that as the Canadian government had never been informed of the nature of the existing defence scheme – by which euphemism he presumably meant the long outmoded projects of 1896–97 – they need not now be informed of any changes in it. But if clarification was his object his tactics were strikingly mistaken for he seems merely to have given the committee yet another golden opportunity to equivocate and evade. On the larger question its conclusions were simply to reaffirm Cardwell's pledge and to declare that 'the general principles of Imperial Defence [formulated in the C.D.C. memorandum of 1896] remain unchanged'. With the defence arrangements for Halifax and Esquimalt, on the other hand, the General Staff did at last seem to have scored some success. For instead of merely reaffirming its earlier decision virtually to discount the possibility of war in these cases, the committee now invited the C.D.C. to reconsider the defence schemes, though it was to do so in the light of 'the recent changes in the distribution of our fleet and in the naval strength of other Powers in neighbouring waters'.[2]

When the C.D.C. produced its report in May, it clearly supported the standpoint adopted by the army. In the event of war with the United States, and especially if the base at Bermuda fell or were destroyed, Halifax would necessarily become the principal naval base in the western Atlantic. In any case it had immense importance as the

[1] General Staff memorandum, 'Defence of Halifax and Esquimalt', 31 Mar. 1905, C.I.D. paper 26c, Cab. 5/1.
[2] Minutes of the 69th and 70th meetings of the C.I.D., 5 and 12 April 1905, Cab. 2/1.

terminus of the intercolonial railway and as the port of disembarkation for military reinforcements for the interior once the St Lawrence was blocked by ice. 'Its defence, then, if practicable, is a matter of great importance both on naval and military grounds.' That defence the committee believed practicable even with local command of the sea in American hands. Against a land attack it could easily be made impregnable by maintaining the present 'moderately small garrison' – that is, one regular and two militia battalions or just over 1,000 men. And as the land defence was so easily obtained it seemed 'justifiable to secure for it a similar immunity against attack from seaward'. This need not entail immense expenditure, for Halifax could be secured by maintaining only sufficient fortifications to present an attacking American fleet with the danger of serious losses; for these the Americans would not risk until they had met the Royal Navy. Before such a meeting deterrent defences would be enough; after it, presumably, the victorious Royal Navy would have local command of the seas. Esquimalt, however, the committee recommended should be completely abandoned: Hong Kong was now the base for the Pacific fleet and if another were needed in British Columbia an alternative should be found further north.[1]

At the end of June the C.I.D. approved the abandonment of the base at Esquimalt and the amendment of Halifax's standards of defence so as to meet an attack either by land or by a fleet including battleships.[2] With these paper decisions settled at last the British prepared to withdraw their remaining troops; though they were anxious that the Canadians should not know that they intended to do so even if the dominion did not itself take over the garrison duty. Fortunately the Canadians were now ready to carry out Borden's promise to provide the garrisons for both bases. By 1906 the last units of British regulars had left Canada, though the navy continued to maintain the dockyard facilities at Halifax until 1910.[3]

To all outward appearances nothing was done in this final withdrawal that abandoned the defence of Canada against the United States. Precise and limited tasks only were handed over to the dominion government. Indeed in first getting the Halifax standards of defence raised the General Staff appeared to have gained a significant victory. But, as they were themselves to admit it was only a paper victory. Assuming that Canada did produce the money and the men to fulfil

[1] C.D.C. 346M, 'Defence of Halifax and Esquimalt', 26 May 1905, C.I.D. paper 29c, Cab. 5/1.
[2] Minutes of the 73rd meeting of the C.I.D., 28 June 1905, Cab. 2/1.
[3] Gordon, pp. 183–6.

her obligations, it only *implied*, it did not enforce, any real modification of Admiralty policy. Only a specific commitment to direct expenditure would have registered a substantial change. They would have been horrified to have it put so bluntly but really both the Admiralty and the Government generally in Whitehall were quite content to indulge, to a small degree at any rate, what they undoubtedly considered to be the General Staff's more fanciful strategic ideas, provided that someone else had to foot the bill. With its transfer to Canada therefore, even Halifax, though essential to any practical defence scheme for Canada, became, as the General Staff recognized, quite irrelevant to the real issue between the two service departments.

The C.I.D.'s reaffirmation of the 'general principles' of colonial defence was accepted by the Army Council at its meeting on 22 May 1905. But as the director of military operations, General Grierson, pointed out: 'For all practical purposes the questions brought forward as to the Defence of Canada remain unanswered. The defences of Halifax and Esquimalt are a side issue. The fundamental principles governing the Defence of the Dominion have still to be fixed by the C.I.D.' In this conclusion the chief of the General Staff concurred and with the encouragement of the secretary of the C.I.D., Sir George Clarke, it was decided to put to the C.I.D. once again the first two of the General Staff's three direct questions of 17 March.[1] Before the committee met, Clarke also made an attempt to 'focus the naval aspect' by direct communication with the two intelligence chiefs. He admitted that an attack upon Montreal across the St Lawrence, in winter, when the river was frozen and Britain could not even attempt to establish her naval supremacy, was, as the president of the United States War College had noted, the Americans' 'best hope of success', and that to overcome the Americans' local advantage on the lakes, which by now would probably extend to Lake Ontario, would require 'previous preparations that would be most marked and located by the U.S.' But, he suggested, this still left the possibility of such lesser naval preparations on the part of the Canadians themselves as could 'be carried out without causing suspicion in the U.S.', and which 'should enable Canada to check any large operations in which the U.S. would require the waters of the Lakes until such time as Great Britain caused a serious diversion elsewhere'. But Clarke extracted from the D.N.I., Captain Ottley, only a general agreement with these 'hypothetical' conclusions and a further reference to the loss of naval command in the

[1] Minutes of 22, 25 and 26 May, and 2 and 5 June 1905, W.O. 106/40, file B 1/4.

western Atlantic being unavoidable at any time of strain in Europe. In passing on these papers to the General Staff Clarke had to confess that he had 'failed apparently to extract any definite opinion from the Admiralty'. He suggested therefore that they should go ahead with their plan to bring their specific questions once more before the C.I.D. He added, however:

I don't myself attach great importance to the matter; because I doubt our being sufficiently free from European embarrassments to exert our whole force in Canada. The U.S. Navy will soon be beyond rivalry *in its own waters* unless we are in a position to divide our battle fleet on this side, which we shall never be able to do.

Any lesser effort, such as an attempt to put a force of gunboats on the lakes, would, he felt sure, 'fail ignominiously'.[1]

With the aid of the advice which Clarke had given the General Staff were able to make their enquiries even more precise, more especially by taking up the point about the utility of a delaying effort on the lakes and in the St Lawrence. Clearly, if Clarke had been right about the Americans being able to mount a winter campaign, the General Staff's whole case would have collapsed – though Clarke himself does not seem to have realized it. But when Kirkpatrick had made a similar point in September 1904 the General Staff had added that the Americans would still not be able to advance on a broad front in winter and would therefore not be able to exploit their advantage in numbers at that time of the year.[2] Now they pointed out that not only would the snow make a winter advance by land slow and difficult, but the ice would also lock up the American vessels on the lakes just as effectively as it would shut British warships out of the St Lawrence. Nor did they really think it likely that there would be any serious attack up the St Lawrence from the sea. What they wanted therefore was a temporary holding force of ships on the vulnerable part of the St Lawrence between Quebec and Montreal and upon Lake Ontario. Hence they now added a new question for the C.I.D.:

Do the Admiralty consider that Canada, without breaking the Rush-Bagot Agreement or without arousing American susceptibilities, could make sufficient preparations in peace to assure to her, during the first three months of a war with the U.S.A., such naval command on Lake

[1] Clarke's 'Notes on the Naval Defence of the Canadian frontier', with a minute by the D.N.I. of 23 June, forwarded to the D.M.O., 26 June 1905, Cab. 17/47.
[2] General Staff memorandum, 'Defence of Canada', 13 Dec. 1904, C.I.D. paper 15c, Cab. 5/1.

Ontario as would prevent the Americans undertaking any military operations across its waters or along its shores?[1]

It would probably be misleading to suggest that when the C.I.D. met to consider the General Staff's question on 13 July, the Admiralty was any more satisfying than it had been on earlier occasions. On the first question, about the navy's responsibility for securing Lake Ontario, Fisher maintained a firm disavowal; on the second, regarding the navy's general commitment to imperial defence, he repeated the rather evasive reference to it being 'interpreted reasonably', but confirmed that it meant the navy would stop a large American expedition but not individual vessels coming up the St Lawrence. The army's emphasis, however, had now shifted from the estuary to the upper St Lawrence and Lake Ontario, and on their third question Fisher merely stated that he could suggest no preparatory measures on these water. But when Grierson mentioned a Canadian contribution to the maintenance of submarines and torpedo boats at Halifax, he got some support from the prime minister, and the conclusions of the committee were not quite so unhelpful as Fisher patently wished. On questions one and two he was simply given his way but on three it was agreed that while the Rush-Bagot agreement prevented any preparatory measures on Lake Ontario, the United States could hardly complain of a torpedo flotilla facing the sea at Halifax.[2]

With this, as with the decisions about the Caribbean bases and about Halifax and Esquimalt, the General Staff had to be content. 'There is no more to be done in this matter as far as the Admiralty are concerned', commented Grierson after the Army Council's meeting on 10 August. 'The discussion has made it clear that the military must take their own measures afloat as well as ashore and I propose to consider the question from this point of view for the future.'[3] They did not then in the least

---

[1] Minutes of 75th meeting of the C.I.D., 13 July 1905, Cab. 2/1.

[2] *Idem.* They were right to tread warily in the matter of naval preparations in Canada. The Americans were always inclined to stress the value rather than the vulnerability of the Canadian waterways. In 1899 one U.S. naval officer, thinking that the British might otherwise prepare in peacetime to rush a force through the river and canals before the Americans could cut them, suggested that the passing of any gunboats through the Lachine should be considered a *casus belli* and the British even warned of the fact. (Lt. A. M. Cook, U.S.N., Naval War College, 'Confidential Notes on the Problem: A Study of the Great Lakes, from a naval point of view', 11 Sept. 1899, U.S.N.A., Naval Records Collection of the Office of Naval Records and Library, R.G. 45/464, subject file ON, box 2.)

[3] Minute of 12 August 1905, W.O. 106/40, file B 1/4; the chief of the General Staff merely added 'Yes, that is so' (15 Aug., *ibid.*).

intend to drop the question permanently. For the time being they would themselves go on considering the matter – in December Kirkpatrick was again at work on the need for Canada to develop a naval policy of her own; but for a new approach to the C.I.D. they would wait upon the change of government that had now become imminent.[1]

During the closing months of Balfour's government the work of the C.I.D. had fallen into considerable disarray – and over more important matters than the defence of Canada[2] – but it is difficult to see why the army should have had any better hopes of its successor. Perhaps, like Balfour himself, Grierson expected the Conservatives to return, and in a better condition to face the problems placed before them. But it was the Liberals who came in at the end of 1905, and they were at least as insistent upon an especially friendly relationship with the United States. This, the new foreign secretary, Sir Edward Grey, had underlined in a speech only a couple of months before: 'There are three cardinal features at the present moment of British policy, not one of which does the Liberal Party wish to see changed. The first is the growing friendship and good feeling between ourselves and the United States, a matter of common ground and common congratulation to all parties in this country.'[3] Richard Haldane, the new secretary for war, in looking forward to substantial economies in defence expenditure had already written to Sir George Clarke: 'It will have to be recognized frankly that the United States will shortly be in such a position that we shall be quite unable to hold our own against them in the Western Atlantic and the Caribbean Sea.'[4] Nevertheless, in January 1906 the General Staff were once again taking every opportunity to raise the question of a war against the United States.

At the height of the Moroccan crisis in the summer of 1905, Clarke had suggested the formation of a C.I.D. subcommittee to look into the possibility of offensive operations of the sort that Admiral Fisher was proposing they should make against the north-west coast of Germany in the event of war. Probably the subcommittee never met; certainly it made no report.[5] But the General Staff nevertheless continued to

[1] Col. Kirkpatrick's 'Memorandum on Canadian Military Policy' [?] Dec. 1905, W.O. 106/40, file B 1/12; General Staff minutes in W.O. 106/40, file B 1/16.

[2] George Monger, *The End of Isolation; British Foreign Policy, 1900–1907* (London, 1963), p. 228, note 7.

[3] 21 Oct. 1905, quoted by G. M. Trevelyan, *Grey of Falloden* (London, 1937), p. 90.

[4] Haldane to Clarke, [?] Feb. 1905, Sir Frederick Maurice, *Haldane, 1856–1915; the Life of Viscount Haldane of Cloan* (London, 1937), i. 139.

[5] Monger, p. 207, and p. 228, note 7.

draw up papers on the subjects it was supposed to consider. One of these was a long memorandum by Grierson on 4 January in which war with the United States still figured among 'the five cases which present themselves as conceivably calling for the employment of large armies in military operations beyond the seas'.[1] Grierson admitted that its likelihood was not properly a question for the General Staff to discuss: 'Everybody recognises that such a conflict is improbable, and that its outbreak would be an overwhelming national calamity to both sides. But', he continued, 'as long as the contingency is at all possible, however remote, it cannot be disregarded by military authorities, in view of the great land frontier of Canada, which would at once become liable to hostile attack.'

With this excuse Grierson went on to demonstrate that a successful defence of Canada was possible with the right kind of assistance from the navy. His strategic assumptions were, first, the impossibility of active winter operations, and, second, the absence of naval command of the western Atlantic for the first six months of war. It was necessary therefore to consider the case of an attack only between the middle of May and the middle of November. If the Americans attacked in the earliest days of this period they would have such an initial superiority that by the end of it they would have occupied a good part of Canada, including, probably, some vitally important positions, and increased their margin of superiority to about 125,000 men. By the time operations were resumed in the spring that margin would have increased again to about 180,000. In the less dangerous case of an attack towards the close of this period there could be no great advance and therefore no significant occupation of Canadian territory and by May the margin of superiority would be about 125,000 men. Taking into account the relative inferiority of American artillery, and assuming that pressure upon the United States coast would have dispersed some of their resources, Grierson reckoned that to win the war in each of these cases would require British reinforcements within six months of 200,000 and 140,000 respectively. But since most of the American forces, unlike the continental armies, would have to be improvised, not all of the British regiments (say only three-quarters of the cavalry for example) need be regulars. On the other hand, such was the capacity of the United States for continual expansion of their forces that the British ought to

[1] Secret 'Memorandum upon the Military Forces required for over-sea warfare', by Major-General J. M. Grierson, 4 Jan. 1906, W.O. 106/44, file E 1/7. The other four 'cases' were: a Boer rising; war with France; war with Russia; and an Anglo-French war with Germany.

add another 25,000 men after three more months and another 50,000 after six months.

Besides glossing over the doubts about the navy's ability now to harass the American coast effectively, Grierson was assuming that the navy would have re-established their command of the western Atlantic within six months and have made it possible for these reinforcements to get to North America. That is to say that they would within that period have disposed both of the United States navy and of any threat from another power. This was a pretty large assumption. Yet the Admiralty, sticking carefully to only the most general question of naval and military cooperation, refused to be drawn on the subject of war with the United States. In a belated reply from the Admiralty Grierson was told merely that the D.N.I. concurred 'throughout so far as naval considerations are touched upon'.[1] In the meantime the General Staff had found another avenue of approach to the C.I.D. in Haldane's request that the committee consider generally 'whether the colonial garrisons in peace are adequate or excessive, and whether they are distributed on a rational plan consistent with modern conditions'.[2] The C.D.C., to whom this matter was referred, merely reiterated the earlier decisions and noted the progress of the withdrawal from the western Atlantic.[3]

This seems to have made the General Staff realize that in concentrating on the Canadian aspect of the problem they had allowed their position on other and equally important points to be seriously undermined. Tactically, perhaps, they had been right to dismiss Halifax as 'a side issue'. But they realized now that if they were ever going to budge the Admiralty on Canada, they must make their attack upon the question of naval command in the western Atlantic. They therefore seized upon the C.D.C.'s casual reference to Bermuda to draw attention to the fact that the loss of this command was what really prejudiced the military defence of Canada, more particularly by hampering the movement of reinforcements across the sea. The present position in Bermuda they insisted was unsatisfactory in any case. With respect to a war with the United States its garrison was either too small or too large; it should be increased by at least one battalion in order to make a worthwhile resistance or its garrison should be cut down or withdrawn altogether so as to reduce the loss from its eventual capture. In any event, the

[1] Capt. G. A. Ballard (Asst. D.N.I.) to Lt.-Col. A. D. Drake (D.A.Q.M.G., W.O.), 11 Dec. 1906, W.O. 106/44, file E 1/7.

[2] Minutes of the 85th meeting of the C.I.D., 9 Mar. 1906, Cab. 2/1.

[3] C.D.C. 364M, 'Colonial Garrisons', 31 May 1906, C.I.D. paper 42c, Cab. 5/2.

argument concluded, care should be taken to conceal the reasons for any changes; for, if the Admiralty's policy was to be the approved one, it was inexpedient so to inform either the United States or Canada, neither of whom seemed to see things in the same light as the Admiralty.[1] Clarke, in preparing the matter for the C.I.D., attempted once again to focus attention on what the General Staff clearly regarded as the main point and he ended by asking precisely: 'Is war with the U.S. a possibility which must be taken into account in the scheme of national preparations? If so, could we, at the onset of such a war, man the dockyard and reinforce the garrison of Bermuda?' Clarke opened the way to the Admiralty by giving his own opinion that it would be impracticable to transfer forces from home waters for the purpose of restoring command in the western Atlantic: 'Unless a great change occurs, which we have no right to expect, it seems clear that public opinion in this country which is being led to believe in increasing danger from Germany, would never tolerate any considerable weakening of the fleet in close vicinity to our shore.'[2]

In spite of the opportunity Clarke had given them, the Admiralty still refused to be drawn on the major question, preferring to repeat their familiar generalizations about imperial prestige and undefined 'naval considerations' requiring limited garrisons against *coups de main*. True they could not guarantee reinforcement after the commencement of war, but the despatch of additional dockyard workers by fast steamer was another matter.[3] Thus this new manœuvre too failed to secure the General Staff's object. Later in the year they tried again, bringing the Treasury in as a powerful ally by proposing that the island should bear more of the cost of defence. The Treasury insisted that it could not go on paying after 1908–09, but once again the matter foundered, this time on the General Staff's own arguments that for the sake of the dockyard and so as not to alarm Canadian opinion by revealing the essence of the navy's attitude, a garrison must be maintained.[4] In the spring of 1908 the General Staff was still complaining of the situation of the island's garrison.[5]

[1] General Staff memorandum, 'The Garrison of Bermuda', 14 Dec. 1906, C.I.D. paper 43c, Cab. 5/2.
[2] Clarke's note, 'Garrison of Bermuda', 3 Jan. 1907, C.I.D. paper 45c, *ibid*.
[3] Admiralty memorandum, 'Garrisons of defended stations abroad', 2 Feb. 1907, C.I.D. paper 46c, *ibid*.
[4] General Staff memorandum, 'Maintenance of the Bermuda Militia Artillery and Rifle Volunteer Corps', 13 April 1908, C.I.D. paper 51c, *ibid*.
[5] Capt. A. Grant Duff (G.S.O.2), secret memorandum, 'The Defence of the Bermudas', 8 May 1908, W.O. 106/40, file B 1/20.

In the meantime the General Staff had shifted their line of attack. The question of modifying the Rush-Bagot agreement had been raised again by Secretary of State Root in 1906, but after a discouraging response from Canada had been allowed to sleep once more. But the Americans continued, as they had done ever since 1890, to move vessels between the lakes and the sea. The Canadian government reluctantly acquiesced, finding it 'inexpedient' to refuse lest the United States again give notice to terminate the existing agreement. On 17 January 1908 the General Staff approached the C.I.D. with a paper asking that the agreement should neither be modified nor the Americans allowed to go on breaking it as they had done ever since 1890. For, with the effects of the Admiralty's new attitude to the naval defence of Lake Ontario, its impediment to the Americans and the Canadians' supposed advantage in canal communications had become all the more vital.[1] When the C.I.D. met on 14 May 1908 and considered this and the question of Bermuda the General Staff at last got a more definite expression of policy perhaps because the month before Herbert Asquith had succeeded the ailing Campbell-Bannerman as prime minister. But it was hardly the answer they had wanted.

Lord Morley, secretary of state for India, began by stating that he could not understand why the matter had been raised at all in the C.I.D. since their earlier decisions about both Canada and Bermuda appeared to him to be a clear 'declaration of opinion that war with the U.S. was a contingency so remote that it might for defensive purposes be neglected. . . . Apart from the . . . remoteness of the contingency, it was clear that we should not be able to defend 3,000 miles of the Canadian frontier in such a war.' He was unaware that anything had happened to require any modification of these decisions and it followed 'that the question before the Committee is not a military question at all, but a question of policy in its widest sense, for it affects not only our relations with Canada and the United States, but also the mutual relations of the two latter'. In this opinion Morley had the outspoken support of the foreign secretary: 'Sir Edward Grey explained . . . that he had no desire to discuss the question of what action could be taken by us in the event of war with the United States. On the contrary he agreed with Lord Morley in being strongly opposed to that subject being discussed at all in connection with this question.' Nevertheless both agreed that the narrower question of 'American wishes about the lakes agreement

[1] General Staff memorandum, 'Warships on the Great Lakes of North America', 17 Jan. 1908, C.I.D. paper 50c, Cab. 5/2/1.

had to be discussed as it was necessary to regard Canadian opinion; and that this did involve a simple strategic assessment of the interior waters of North America. Lord Tweedmouth, no longer first lord of the Admiralty, but still in the cabinet, now revealed that he had already been in correspondence with the Canadian prime minister on this subject and that Laurier, while 'opposed to taking any special measures for defence against the United States . . . was anxious about the position on the Great Lakes'. He had therefore asked and been given the services of an English naval officer.

The conclusion of the committee was simply that there was no reason to alter the decisions of the earlier meeting of 13 July 1905 in which the Admiralty's withdrawal from any commitment on the lakes had been confirmed and the army fobbed off instead with the suggestion that the Canadians might establish a torpedo boat force at Halifax. With regard to Bermuda, however, they admitted that the position had changed somewhat. With the closing down of Port Castries, the reduction of Port Royal, and the transfer of Halifax to Canada, Bermuda would remain the only imperial naval dockyard in North American waters. The committee therefore recommended that the home government should continue to pay for the upkeep of the local defence forces.[1]

With this decision, amounting to an explicit instruction that so remote was the contingency of war with the United States that it need not be taken into account in assessing standards of defence, the General Staff had at last to face defeat, though the attempt to get a redefinition of general overseas defence policy continued. In November 1908 the Foreign Office did produce, for the benefit of a special subcommittee of the C.I.D. on the 'Military needs of the Empire', a list of possible wars which dealt mainly with Germany but also included ones against Russia and the United States. But the Foreign Office themselves added that this last was considered 'so improbable at present' that it was not put forward for discussion 'though circumstances are conceivable in which it would come to pass'. The C.I.D. subcommittee in fact did not trouble to consider either of these additional possibilities.[2]

References to war against the United States continued to recur in the General Staff's planning. Perhaps they still do. As late as 1920 even the Admiralty's Plans Division was seeking to advise the

---

[1] Minutes of the 99th meeting of the C.I.D., 14 May 1908, Cab. 2/2/1.

[2] 'Possible sphere of action for the British Army. Memorandum by the Foreign Office', 11 Nov. 1908, C.I.D. paper E 2, Cab. 16/5; 'Report of the Sub-Committee . . . on the Military Needs of the Empire', 24 July 1909, C.I.D. paper 109b, Cab. 4/3/1.

Canadians how they might best defend the lakes against an American attack.[1] But after 1908 they all appeared to be very much more casual and patently lacked any overall seriousness of purpose. An apparent exception was perhaps the 1910 report of Sir John French, the inspector-general of the forces, who had been invited by the now more energetic Canadians to make a report on the reorganization of their forces. French's report stressed, among other things, the vital necessity of commanding the lakes and assumed also a substantial contribution of British troops to help oppose the regular forces of the United States. All this was carefully noted by the secretary of the C.I.D., but though these assumptions ran counter to everything that had been decided in the past few years, the C.I.D. seem to have kept silent. Instead they took advantage of the Canadians' newfound enthusiasm to help and encourage them in the reorganization of their staff arrangements following French's report.[2] On the eve of the great European war in May 1914, the C.I.D. were repeating that 'in considering the question of the defence of British islands in the Western Atlantic, there is no need to take into account the scale of attack that might be brought to bear against the islands by the United States'.[3]

On the other hand, and rather ironically, part of the very development which had compelled and at the same time allowed the naval withdrawal from the Americas had in the meantime brought a new reference to war with the United States back even into the calculations of the Admiralty. In 1906–07 a secret three-man committee, meeting at the 'Naval War College' at Portsmouth under the chairmanship of the assistant D.N.I., Captain G. A. Ballard, had produced at last for the Admiralty an elaborate set of so-called war-plans.[4] Significantly but not surprisingly, all of them were concerned with war with Germany, but one of them, W/4, envisaged a war against Germany in alliance with the United States. This plan was based upon the not uncommon assumption that Britain's special regard for Japan and Japanese-American friction over the immigration question in particular might expose the Achilles' heel of Anglo-American friendship and open up a great opportunity for a German-American rapprochement. A similar idea

[1] James Eayrs, 'Arms Control on the Great Lakes', *Disarmament and Arms Control*, ii (1964), 388.
[2] Note by the secretary of the C.I.D., 20 Sept. 1910, Cab. 18/24; Gordon, p. 276.
[3] Minutes of the 126th meeting of the C.I.D., 14 May 1914, Cab. 2/3/3.
[4] The 'college' was more properly a 'War Course' of the Royal Naval College, and had been begun at Greenwich late in 1900 (Marder, *The Road to War*, pp. 32–3). The 'plans' themselves are in Case 0073, Adm. 116/1043B, Pt. I.

had naturally occurred to the M.I.D.[1] and of course it fitted with some of Fisher's observations about the racial composition of the United States. But it is doubtful if he wasted much time on them at this stage. It is true that in October 1907 he did write to the king that 'the only *one* thing in the world that England has to fear is Germany and the United States combining against England', and mistakenly went on to suggest that the recent Hague and Algericas conferences had brought this 'nearer than ever before'.[2] But as the rest of the letter seems to show, it was probably only in order to press his own view of the respective requirements of the army and navy. Considering his continual references since 1904 to war with the United States being out of the question, it is more likely that he fully approved – even if, as its style might suggest, he did not actually compose – the Admiralty paper of June 1907 specifically refuting the awful possibility referred to in the war-plans.[3] Before long, too, the Japanese complication had been pretty well disposed of by the improvement in American-Japanese relations following the conclusion of the Root-Takahira agreement in November 1909. To make quite sure that the alliance with Japan could not automatically bring Britain into conflict with the United States, Grey nevertheless added a clause when the treaty was renewed in 1911, which ruled out any obligation to join Japan in a war against a power with whom Great Britain happened to have a general arbitration treaty.

So far as the so-called war-plans of 1907 or 1908 were concerned, they were expressly designed for instructional purposes and were, as a note on their title page states, 'not in any way to be considered as those definitely adopted'. The plan in question envisaged no naval assistance to Canada, and on the outbreak of war three second class cruisers only would proceed to Barbados to act as a deterrent to American attacks by merchant cruisers on British commerce and to 'filibustering expeditions' against British possessions. There would be no special protection for trade on the North Atlantic route to Canada, though the Cape and other cruiser squadrons would 'do their best' to cover the main South Atlantic route. With these exceptions there would instead be a concentration in home waters to meet the German and United States fleets: 'Neither the German nor the United States Fleet

---

[1] For example Capt. A. Grant Duff's paper, 'The Conditions of a War between the British Empire and the United States', Dec. 1907, W.O. 106/40, file B 1/20.
[2] Fisher to King Edward, 4 Oct. 1907, *Fear God and Dread Nought*, ii. 142.
[3] Cited by Marder, *The Road to War*, p. 183.

alone stand [*sic*] a chance against ours, and not much chance even if
united, especially remembering the inevitable difficulties and dangers of
co-operation of two Fleets of different nationalities', commented a note,
possibly by Fisher himself, at the front of the first volume of plans.
'One might almost wish the United States would join Germany!'
This was a far cry from the usual Admiralty gloom about the United
States navy; perhaps the eccentric fantasy of the plan may be judged
accordingly.

Conclusion

It is a common belief, even among historians, that General Staffs and Intelligence Departments are crammed with war-plans for every possible contingency and that these plans therefore have little or no political significance. This is a delusion. It might be nearer the truth to say of Germany in 1914, for example, that she had only one plan and Europe suffered accordingly. 'Plans' that are mere exercises, for instructional purposes or for testing theory or efficiency, belong to staff colleges. The various papers produced by the General Staff or the M.I.D. which figure so largely in the last part of this book were in no sense definitive; certainly they were not meant to be brought into automatic operation in the event of war. But in the continuous reappraisal of imperial defence they had real and meaningful objectives. Not only did they suggest the improvement of fortifications and the disposition of forces, they also guided the reform and reorganization of those forces. These plans, then, were bound to affect immediate expenditure and ultimate security. Of this the planners were well-aware and their work consequently had a very serious purpose indeed – even in peacetime. Certainly their plans were not supposed to be divorced from political realities, whether foreign or domestic. In the former, moreover, General Staffs could make a crucial contribution; of this the famous Anglo-French staff talks beginning in December 1905 are as much a proof as is the Schlieffen plan itself for Germany. These were undoubtedly unusual – but only to a degree. British governments and even the British Foreign Office were not in the habit of spelling out in a definitive and permanent form the supposed ingredients of the country's foreign interests. Their appraisal and pursuit was a continuing process in which many could play a part. Thus it is probably misleading to say of the naval withdrawal from the western Atlantic that 'what the diplomatists began the admirals finished'.[1] Given, in the crisis of 1895–96, the former's very mixed views and the Admiralty's unwillingness to consider war with the United States, one might well deduce that it had all been begun by the navy. Given too that, the defence of India apart, Great Britain's naval interests were so prominent in any attempt to define her principles of foreign policy it was inevitable that statesmen and admirals should reach similar conclusions at pretty well the same time.

[1] L. M. Gelber, *The Rise of Anglo-American Friendship* (London, 1938), p. 95.

In an era in which Great Britain could no longer aim at supremacy everywhere upon the seas the service departments' strategical and statistical calculations necessarily made an independent contribution to the identification of the power who was potentially most dangerous and the power with whom Great Britain could least afford to clash. But which powers should fall into which category, why first France and Russia and then Germany should be put in the former and the United States consistently in the second, involved a choice of enemies and friends according to criteria which lay outside their professional terms of reference. A proper evaluation of interest, not by any means unmixed with sentiment and even affection, dictated what that choice should be. But the calculations of the principal departments of state did not lead to exactly the same conclusions and if it is significant that the Admiralty had one view, it is only somewhat less so that the War Office had another. That department's plans cannot be written off as merely 'bizarre' and belonging to the 'lunatic fringe'.[1]

There was not really so deep-rooted a difference between Admiralty and War Office as interdepartmental jealousies made it appear. There was no fundamental difference in their regard for good Anglo-American relations. Both accepted the existence or the desirability of a 'special' relationship and both believed it was to some extent vulnerable. Each in fact provided choice examples of a direct inheritance from the anti-democratic prejudices of the middle and early nineteenth century statesmen. 'War between the British Empire and the United States of America would be a calamity', commented one General Staff paper in 1907, 'not only for both victor and vanquished, but for the whole world.' Yet having made the arrogant but then conventional tribute to the merits of the Anglo-Saxon race, the author felt compelled to proceed: 'Sensible as is the General Staff of this fact, it cannot ignore the possibility of such a conflict. With the progress of democratic institutions the governments of states become more and more influenced by popular passions and less under the control of responsible rulers.'[2]

A similar prejudice held its place at the Admiralty too. In Selborne's February 1905 statement arguing against a British naval contribution to the defence of Canada, for example, the first lord had actually admitted the duty of considering the possibility of a war provoked by 'the people of the United States of America, in a moment of criminal

[1] J. A. S. Grenville, *Lord Salisbury and Foreign Policy: the Close of the Nineteenth Century* (London, 1964), pp. 422 and 389.
[2] Capt. A. Grant Duff, 'The Conditions of a War between the British Empire and the United States', Dec. 1907, W.O. 106/40, file B 1/20.

folly'.[1] But related though they were to the General Staff's and older British prejudices, Selborne's remarks suggest some interesting contrasts to the conventional arguments of the mid-nineteenth century. Earlier, whatever material interest or common sense might seem to recommend, such 'criminal folly' had to be faced as characteristic of the Americans; in 1905 it was 'not expected'. There is a similar advance in the optimists' reflections on how Great Britain would 'win' a war in which she could not 'conquer': in the earlier period massive retaliation would bring the Americans to sue for peace by eroding their pockets, their morale, and their loyalty; in Selborne's day dignified resistance would give the American people time to come to their senses. The whole perhaps reveals more about the British character than the American.

In contrast to the War Office the Admiralty even in the early twentieth century lagged far behind with war-plans. It would be a gross exaggeration to say that the War Office stuffed full a bag left empty by the Admiralty, but in the Agadir crisis of July 1911 the cabinet was shocked to find that the Admiralty, unlike the General Staff, could produce no plan for war. Fisher had often complained in the past of the navy's neglect of war-plans, but as first sea lords both he and his successor claimed that they thought it best not to have them on paper but in as few heads as possible. The suspicion must remain that these heads were empty or dazed with fuzzy projects. This complacent and self-deluding attitude curiously survived the investigation of Admiral Beresford's famous complaints in March 1909, and not until about 1912 do the Admiralty seem to have started their plans in earnest.[2] The evasiveness of an overweening Admiralty, riding on the crest of popular indulgence, contrasted blatantly with the apparently superior professional expertise of the General Staff in the aftermath of the Boer War. Clearly the War Office needed to have the Admiralty's guidance in the proper definition of the principles governing the distribution of forces. But their irritation and annoyance also helped to carry their attention to war with the United States beyond the point which in normal circumstances they would themselves have viewed as reasonable. These circumstances tended to exaggerate the difference between the two departments. The essence of that difference is less fantastic and more illuminating. It explains why the Admiralty were so far ahead of the War Office in spite

---

[1] Selborne's preface to the Admiralty memorandum, 'Defence of Canada', 24 Feb. 1905, C.I.D. paper 21c, Cab. 5/1. See also p. 383 above.
[2] A. J. Marder, *From the Dreadnought to Scapa Flow: the Royal Navy in the Fisher Era, 1904–1919*, vol. I, *The Road to War, 1904–1914* (London, 1961), pp. 197–9 and 244–7.

of their incompetent planning, why indeed they may even have anticipated the Foreign Office and the cabinet as a whole. By 1902 it was clear
to British statesmen at large, and by 1906 even to the War Office, that
Anglo-American relations had improved so much that war could
virtually be discounted; but it was the Admiralty who first saw in the
late 1880s that so imminent and so overwhelming was the growth of
American naval power that those relations had better be improved as
soon as possible.

The Admiralty had always had a special apprehension about the
United States. To the arguments of the economizers, democrats,
racialists, and mere sentimentalists, the navy had long since added their
own contribution to the definition of the 'special relationship': an
inheritance from the wars of 1775–83 and 1812–14 of a sense of real
strategic weakness in respect to the United States. But right up to the
end of the century this did not result in any adjustment in policy that
was accommodating to the United States. Nothing would be further
from the truth. But it may well be that the vast gulf of planning and
effort that separated the Admiralty from the War Office, a gulf which
existed long before the classic period of supposed 'rapprochement',
meant that they had never really believed in the utility of attempting to
confront the United States, let alone actually counterbalancing Canada's
position as hostage. This feeling, however, they never dared make
utterly explicit until the very end of the century. Their nagging doubts
lay hidden in silence and inaction. Cabinet and public alike probably
interpreted this as the silent service's traditional way of expressing a
supreme confidence in the apparently overwhelming strength of the
fleet. With the possible exception of the brief period in and after the
Civil War British opinion continued to delude itself about the vulnerability of the United States to British sea-power.

The illusion of American vulnerability was undoubtedly heightened
by the consistent attitude of the army. India and Canada presented the
British Empire with its only two great land frontiers to defend. The
magnitude and inconvenience of the problem was all the greater for a
defensive system based on island security and sea-power abroad. It
was therefore the special difficulty of wars on these peripheries that so
attracted the attention of the army and in the case of Canada even
beyond the point when the War Office itself admitted that war with the
United States had become 'unlikely'.[1] The army too had more than
reason enough for pessimism and despair. India was nearly as remote

[1] General Staff memorandum, 'Defence of Canada', 13 Dec. 1904, C.I.D.
paper 15c, Cab. 5/1.

405

from the armies of her expected invader as from the resources of Great Britain; and in the Himalayas she had a magnificent natural barrier. But Canada was flanked by a far more powerful neighbour immediately to the south, and was, as Wellington once put it, 'all frontier and nothing else'.[1] Still they were used to difficult problems. What puzzled them was the Admiralty's attitude. 'If distance from the base of operations, where it is the ocean, is to be an insuperable obstacle', complained one engineer officer in reference to the defence of Canada, 'then farewell imperial greatness and possession.'[2] The army's answer to the problem was continually to insist on proper preparation; the navy's to evade it – an interesting contrast.

While the schemes of massive preparation advocated by the army were never properly completed it is important to remember that with the aid of the repeated Anglo-American crises in the middle of the century they did nevertheless manage to expend a very large amount of public money in anticipation of a war which never occurred and which British public opinion is supposed always to have abhorred.[3] Clearly expenditure on such a scale was more significant than the composition of scores of plans and could not have been achieved without the indulgence and approval of the government. Even Peel and Aberdeen in the end tended to give way before the combined offensive of the army's demands and of American bluster.

Yet even in the first half of the nineteenth century there was a curious discrepancy between the attention of the military planners and that of the makers of foreign policy. While the former linked India and Canada together as their two greatest problems outside the United Kingdom, the latter always tended to subordinate American to European interests. It is true that many of them were already well aware that the future would one day bring a more strictly global struggle for power, with Russia on the one side and the United States on the other.[4] But the fact

[1] Wellington to Lord Hill, 31 Mar. 1841, printed in 'Papers relative to the Fortifications and Defences of Canada', confidential print, W.O. 1/536.

[2] Lt.-Col. Millington Synge, R.E., 'The Lakes and Canals of Canada', Royal United Service Institute, *Journal*, x (1867), 183–208.

[3] For some indication of the amount see C. P. Stacey, *Canada and the British Army, 1846–1871* (Toronto, 1963). In 1846–47 imperial military expenditure on the province of Canada alone was £474,789 out of a total of less than £3,000,000 for all the colonies except India; in 1857–58 the figures were £261,000 and £3,590,000 respectively. In the first year of its existence the Dominion of Canada cost the British £1,250,000 and most of that was still for military defence.

[4] See Geoffrey Barraclough, 'Europe and the Wider World in the Nineteenth and Twentieth Centuries', *Studies in Diplomatic History and Historiography in honour of G. P. Gooch*, ed. by A. O. Sarkissian (London, 1961), pp. 364–82.

remains that until the transformation was actually realized British foreign policy remained firmly fixed on the European powers and European rivalry overseas. Purely American affairs, though by no means unimportant, were always subordinate. Canning 'called a New World into existence in order to redress the balance of the old'; in the Texan question Aberdeen had his calculations fixed firmly upon France; and even Palmerston could hardly be bothered to turn in 1839 from the Near East to Maine or in 1850 from Don Pacifico and the Hungarian refugees to Central America. Thus there was a persistent discrepancy between a pragmatic foreign policy on the one hand, and abstract war-planning on the other. The one dealt with the actual, the other with the merely prospective. By withdrawing the garrisons and drastically cutting down imperial expenditure on fortifications the Gladstone government of 1868–74 removed the most serious evidence of this discrepancy. But it persisted in military planning nonetheless and in spite of all the committees established to promote interdepartmental cooperation and the better integration of strategic and political calculations.

The C.I.D. itself failed to become the centre of strategic planning.[1] Indeed after its establishment the calculations made by the M.I.D. and the General Staff with regard to North America seem to be utterly out of touch with the views held by the majority of British statesmen and applied with such effect to foreign policy. The development of a modern military bureaucracy was in some respects defeating its own purpose. This new professionalism and the increasing technological complexity of war at length proved too much for the honest endeavours of the statesmen. Whereas formerly men with such conflicting views as Palmerston and Gladstone could quickly muster enough naval and military expertise to keep strategic needs constantly under review, their successors could find time in the early twentieth century only to keep track of what was most important, like the defence of India or the United Kingdom itself. Such neglect did not impede professional planning; it allowed it to flourish undisturbed. It was only the General Staff's determined pursuit of their quarrel with the Admiralty which in 1908 brought the American question finally into the open and their planning for war with the United States face to face at last with the new course of Anglo-American friendship long since adopted by the makers of foreign policy.

[1] On this question see John P. Mackintosh, 'The Role of the Committee of Imperial Defence before 1914', *English Historical Review*, lxxvii (1962), 490–503.

The transformation in British foreign policy in which the role of the United States changed from that of a likely enemy to that of a useful and necessary friend was a long and difficult process. The 1850s had brought a presentiment of the 'rapprochement' of 1898–1902, but it had been reluctantly conceded and brought to a most abrupt conclusion by the outbreak of the Civil War. For the most part the United States remained an enemy in Britain's calculations right up to the end of the war and, in a quieter way, in the long aftermath until 1895–96. Until after the Venezuelan affair any increase in the territory and strength of the United States was regarded as a direct threat to British possessions and British power and influence in the western hemisphere. This followed naturally from the isolationist philosophy which insisted that Britain had no permanent friends but only permanent interests. Throughout most of the first half of the century the British therefore tried to contain the United States by erecting fortifications on the frontier and by intervening with diplomacy wherever they could. But in the long run both methods proved too difficult, too expensive, and too unpopular. Of course there remained the hope that if Britain alone could not afford to maintain the balance of power against the United States someone else might help. There was also the faint hope that if only she could survive in the interval, Canada herself might one day rival her neighbour to the south. But when confederation finally came in 1867 it served rather to free Great Britain to some extent from an embarrassing dispersal of her forces and contributed more to her power in Europe than to her strength in America. Ultimately the collapse of the Union itself would be the most effective means of preserving Britain's interests. Some thought the opportunity had come with the American administration's rejection of Texan annexation in 1838. Few doubted its accomplishment in 1861, genuinely regretful though they usually were of the circumstances of the Civil War, and certainly disappointed that it should come in a way that threatened to involve Great Britain in the hostilities.

The Union victory also brought to an end the only other real prospect of effective aid in the establishment of a balance of power in America – the involvement of another European power, and preferably one who unlike Britain could bring to bear an imposing land army. The possibility of getting France to help on the American continent had played some part in Aberdeen's calculations and had come right to the forefront with the Crimean alliance of 1854. But on both occasions common hostility towards the United States had foundered on the rock of a preeminent mutual suspicion between France and Britain. In the Mexican affair of 1862–67 hostility to the United States and fear of France had curiously combined to secure some degree of tacit approval from the British. But the end of the Civil War had soon brought an end to that experiment too. The approval that some British statesmen gave to Napoleon's involvement in Mexico, moreover, was largely due to the exceptional circumstances of the time in both America and Europe. In America the dangers of a clash with the United States had rarely seemed so great; while in Europe France had not been so power- ful since 1815. There was little likelihood of an active Anglo-French alliance in America because it would have run absolutely counter to one of the fundamental principles of Great Britain's American policy – the exclusion of rival European influence.

The support that Britain gave to some of the implications if not to the letter of the Monroe Doctrine helped British interests by substantially exempting the American continent from the rivalries of the European great powers. But paradoxically by shielding the continent with her naval power Great Britain also ensured that the United States could grow more easily and that Britain alone had American interests and possessions to defend against that growing power. And in defence of hostage Canada against the new Leviathan, the naval strength which kept out the European military powers could only hope to harass and demonstrate on and off the coast. For this problem there was no ultimate solution. Fortunately it had only a secondary importance in Britain's calculations. The greatest danger the British thought they faced from their difficulties in North America was an alignment between their enemies in the old and in the new worlds. Even more likely, so they thought, was a stab in the back from one side while engaged in a violent struggle with the other. 'Our means of maintaining ourselves in Europe with permanent advantage', one colonial secretary had long ago insisted, 'depends in no small degree upon our being *free from danger of attack* in *that* quarter [North America], and I have not suffici- ent confidence in any American, of any description to make me believe that they would overlook a good opportunity of giving us a heavy blow.'[1]

In the neutrality of the French and Russians few Englishmen had any greater faith. With the possible exception of the quieter interlude of 1871–95 they lived for a century in almost constant fear of a repetition of 1778 or 1812, the occasions on which they believed the French had taken advantage of Britain's troubles in America and the United States of her crusade against Napoleon. By the beginning of the twentieth century they had decided they could no longer bear the strain of splendid

[1] Lord Goderich to Palmerston, 24 Jan. 1831, Broadlands papers.

isolation. Rather they had then to concentrate their strength against their principal enemies, and in distinguishing enemies they also had to choose friends. Almost the first of those friends was the United States. Yet in a real sense the appeasement of the United States at the end of the nineteenth century was the natural if belated conclusion of a policy which Great Britain had long since adopted in the interest of her security. As long ago as 1803 the British had helped the Americans buy Louisiana in order to keep France out. Perhaps one ought even to go back to 1783. The success of the rebels was probably assured in any case; but the British acquiesced all the more readily for fear of complications in Europe. The settlements of 1842, 1846, and 1871 were but further episodes in the same story. Still the final act of appeasement was a long time in coming. In part, of course, it had to wait upon the agonizing reappraisals made by the British themselves. But it was also dependent upon developments in Europe and America. Between 1846 and 1871 events had conspired on both continents to push Great Britain towards a decision. The result was considerable: the confederation of Canada, the withdrawal of the legions, and the Geneva arbitration. But there she stopped short of final withdrawal and rapprochement in North America. In the weary aftermath of war the United States had relaxed her pressure on Britain by dispersing her military power and turning to internal expansion. In Europe, too, the old fears had been considerably relieved by Cardwell's reforms and the defeat of France by Prussia. But the relief was illusory. Gradually the strain on Britain's security system revived and not only in Europe and America, but in Asia and Africa too. At length it became intolerable as it had never been before.

The American assertiveness that helped push Great Britain into finally dropping the idea of the United States as a potential enemy was not without its compensations. The ablest of the statesmen on both sides recognized that an actual alliance was out of the question. But, just as had the protagonists of the abortive Central American rapprochement in the late 1850s, so at the turn of the century did strong bodies of opinion on either side, rightly or wrongly, assume an identity of interests in many parts of the world. To the extent that this was true an actual alliance was unnecessary.

While security dictated Britain's decision to appease the United States and to withdraw her naval as well as her military forces from North America and the West Indies in the decade after 1895, her trading interests confirmed the wisdom of the choice involved and sentiment made it tolerable to a great empire. To put these and other 'peace' factors properly in their context in the history of Anglo-American relations must belong to another historian. It is enough to say here that they did play their part in promoting good relations and that their importance in this respect was noted by contemporary statesmen as well as by the 'Manchester Men' in England. It was always ackowledged that in a war with the United States the loss of trade and supplies would be distressing. But so long as the war did not spread the damage was unlikely to be any more fatal than it had been in 1812. Moreover, as Britain became more and more dependent on supplies from North America, so also did naval doctrine more and more insist that the inferior naval power could not win a war by commerce-raiding. To be really effective in the days before the advent of the submarine and the sea mine, such a strategy would need the command of the seas. But the value of Anglo-American trade certainly was a factor which made these two governments and peoples – the *'joint tenants . . .* of the commerce of the world', as Croker described them[1] – pause to wonder if a war would be worth while. It would be 'like breaking your neighbour's windows with doubloons', commented one American in the crisis of late 1855.[2]

Probably sentiment was no less of a deterrent. There had always been a general feeling that war with the United States would involve a special kind of horror – 'some of the unnatural horror of a civil war', as Balfour put it at the time of the Venezuelan crisis.[3] But there had also been men like Palmerston and Salisbury at hand to suggest that interest and prestige must both set limits to such a point of view. With his arguments about interest perhaps Palmerston never made out a sufficiently plausible case to overcome the general resistance of British public opinion; but if it had ever become really necessary there are convincing signs that he would have had more success with pride. To Palmerston prestige was not a mere matter of self-respect but a factor of material value in the attitude of other powers. This others would dispute. The Cobdenites naturally considered it a false god, comparable in its evil effects only with that other 'foul idol', the Balance of Power. But of one fact there seems little doubt: that simple self-esteem in the McLeod and *Trent* crises was what most threatened to

[1] Quoted in David Paul Crook, *American Democracy in English Politics, 1815–1850* (London, 1965), p. 119.
[2] Commander Charles Henry Davis to Caleb Cushing (then U.S. attorney-general), 10 Nov. 1855, Cushing papers, Library of Congress, Washington, D.C.
[3] Blanche E. C. Dugdale, *Arthur James Balfour* (2 vols., London, 1936), i. 226.

rally public opinion behind the warlike party. On both occasions it was only the retreat of the Americans that saved the peace.

When the spirit of manifest destiny faltered the Americans, too, were inclined to reflect that war would not be worth while. In 1895 Wall Street collapsed with remarkable suddenness after Cleveland's Venezuelan Message. Perhaps Canada did now lie at their mercy, but the invasions of 1775 and 1812 had been ghastly failures, and they would certainly suffer enormously at sea and on the coast. It was safer to exploit their local advantage by peaceful means. 'They have gained and wrested from us by the Pen', Palmerston complained of Ashburton's treaty, 'districts which they never could have acquired by the Sword.'[1] If the essence of Britain's difficulties was that she could not readily bring her enormous power to bear against the United States, it was the Americans' that they had not yet secured the stature of a great military power. 'I hope however for Peace', wrote the British military commander in Canada in 1840. 'We have had sufficient experience of the horrors of war in this part of the World, and the impossibility of turning the Events to the advantage of either Party.'[2] The McLeod and *Trent* affairs may have shown how fickle mere sentiment might be as a peace factor in Anglo-American relations, but they also showed, in common with the other crises of that relationship, that it takes two sides to make a war if only one to preserve the peace. And a war in which even the militarists on both sides are unable to forecast total victory is singularly unlikely to occur.

[1] Palmerston to Monteagle, 28 Oct. 1842, Broadlands papers.
[2] Sir Richard Jackson to Sir George Arthur, 9 Jan. 1840, Charles R. Sanderson, ed., *The Arthur Papers* (3 vols., Toronto, 1943–59), ii. 376.

Index

de Grey—*contd.*
  and colonial defence, 260;
  and defence of Canada, 262, 263–4,
    278, 287–8;
  and *Trent* preparations, 228, 229,
    235–6
de Lesseps, Ferdinand (1805–94), 346
Decatur, Capt. Stephen, U.S.N.
  (1779–1820), 10
Demerara (Georgetown, B.G., map 3),
  238
Derby, 14th earl of, *see* Stanley,
  Edward George Geoffrey Smith
Derby, 15th earl of, *see* Stanley,
  Edward Henry Smith
Desertion,
  from British army, 88 n. 5, 118, 217,
    218;
  from British ships, 215–16;
  from U.S. ships, 160
Detroit (map 1), 3, 80, 98, 113, 223,
  272, 353
Devonshire, Spencer Compton
  Cavendish (Lord Hartington),
  8th duke of (1833–1908: under-
  secretary for war, 1863–66; secretary for war, 1866, 1882–85;
  president of council, 1895–1903),
  264;
  and colonial defence, 356
Dewey, Commodore (later Adm.)
  George, U.S.N. (1837–1917: commanding Asiatic squadron, 1898–
  99), 323
Diamond, 370
Dickens, Charles (1812–70), 70 n. 2
Disraeli, Benjamin (earl of Beacons-
  field, 1804–81: chancellor of
  Exchequer, 1852, 1858–59, 1866–
  68; prime minister, 1868, 1874–
  80),
  and colonies, 293–4;
  and defence of Canada, 263, 294;
  and naval distribution, 305;
  and recruiting crisis, 200
Dominica, B.W.I. (map 3), 87
Dominican Republic (map 3), 63;
  Spanish reoccupation, 254;
  U.S. interest in, 170, 179, 180–1,
    182, 184, 185, 193, 344–5
Doyle, Maj.-Gen. (later Gen.) Sir
  Charles Hastings (1805–83:
  G.O.C., Nova Scotia, 1861, lt.-
  gov., Nova Scotia, 1867–73),
  and Bermuda defences, 262;

and Halifax defences, 277;
and New Brunswick road, 232, 235;
  visits siege of Richmond, 271
Drummond Island (map 1), 59
Dufferin and Ava, Frederick Temple
  Hamilton - Temple - Blackwood,
  1st marquis of (1826–1902: gov.-
  gen. of Canada, 1872–78; am-
  bassador in Paris, 1891–96),
  on Venezuelan crisis, 339–40
Dundas Rear Adm. (later Vice-Adm.)
  Sir Richard Saunders, R.N.
  (1802–61: c.-in-c., Baltic, 1855–
  56), 187, 197
Dundas, Robert Saunders, *see* Mel-
  ville,
Dundonald, Maj.-Gen. (later Lt.-
  Gen.) Douglas Mackinnon Baillie
  Hamilton Cochrane, 12th earl of
  (1852–1935: commanding Cana-
  dian militia, 1902–04), 364
Dunlop, Commodore (later Rear-
  Adm.) Hugh, R.N. (1812–87),
  243
Dunraven and Mount-Earl, Windham
  Thomas Wyndham-Quin, 4th
  earl of (1841–1926), 339
Durham, John George Lambton, 1st
  earl of (1792–1840: gov.-in-chief,
  Canada, 1838), 117

Eardley-Wilmot, Col. J., R.A.,
  report on Union artillery, 222, 227
Economist, The,
  on Central American question,
    200–1
Elgin, James Bruce, 8th earl of (1811–
  63: gov.-in-chief, Canada, 1847–
  54), 206, 207 n. 1
Ellenborough, Edward Law, earl of
  (1790–1871: gov.-gen. of India,
  1841–44; 1st lord of Admiralty,
  1846), 138 n. 1, 152–3, 156–7,
  160–1, 164, 165 n. 2, 167–9, 193
  n. 5
Elphinstone-Holloway, *see* Holloway
Endicott Board, 337, 374
English Harbour (Antigua, map 3),
  313
Erie (map 1), 24, 32 n. 3, 125
Erie, Lake (maps 1 and 3), 38, 174;
  access into, 4, 30, 46, 89, 138;
  battle of, 6;
  naval bases, 22, 24–5, 26, 32 n. 3;

Lake of the Woods (map 3), 61
Lamb, Sir Frederick James (later Baron Beauvale and 3rd Viscount Melbourne, 1782–1853 : ambassador at Vienna, 1831–41), 57 n. 1
Lamb, William, see Melbourne
Lambton, John George, see Durham
Langley, Capt. (later Adm.) G. C., R.N. (1848–1914), 327
Lansdowne, Henry Charles Keith Petty-FitzMaurice, 5th marquis of (1845–1927 : secretary for war, 1895–1900; foreign secretary, 1900–05),
   and Anglo-American relations, 341, 371;
   and colonial defence, 374;
   and isthmian canal question, 348–50, 351, 365
Laurier, Sir Wilfrid (1841–1919 : prime minister of Canada, 1896–1911), 398
Law, Edward, see Ellenborough
Lawrence, Lt.-Col. (later Gen. Sir) Herbert Alexander (1861–1943), paper on war with U.S., 330 n. 1, 353–4
Leach, Gen. (later Sir) Edward Pemberton (1847–1913), 331
Lee, Arthur Hamilton, (later Viscount Lee of Fareham, 1868–1947; professor of military science, R.M.C., Kingston, 1893–98; military attaché, Cuba and Washington, 1898–1900; civil lord of Admiralty, 1903–05; first lord of Admiralty, 1921–22),
   Canadian defence plan, 1896, 324–5, 328, 334;
   and war with U.S., 380–1, 383, 384
Leeward Islands, see Windward and Leeward Islands
Lennox, Charles Gordon, see Richmond
Leveson-Gower, Granville George, see Granville
Levita, Capt. (later Lt.-Col. Sir) Cecil Bingham, R.A. (1867–1953),
   forwards information on U.S. war plans, 377
Lewis, Sir George Cornewall (1806–63 : home secretary, 1859–61; secretary for war, 1861–63),
   on chances of war, 214, 216, 251;

and Civil War, 221;
   and colonial defence, 260;
   and defence of Quebec, 263;
   and *Trent* war-preparations, 219, 220, 227, 228, 229, 233, 235, 246
Lewiston (map 1), 80
Lincoln, Abraham (1809–65: U.S. president, 1861–65), 210, 211, 213, 216, 254, 273, 283, 290
Liverpool, Robert Banks Jenkinson, 2nd earl of (1770–1828 : prime minister, 1812–27), 6, 7 n. 2, 17 n. 3, 64–5
London, Ontario (map 1), 265, 325
London, 143
Londonderry, see Castlereagh
Long, John Davis (1838–1915 : U.S. secretary of navy, 1897–1902), 337
Long Island (map 3), 39, 309
Lopez, Gen. Narciso, 178
Louis Philippe, King of the French (1773–1850), 150
Louisiana Purchase (map 3), 62, 202, 410
Lowe, Robert (later Viscount Sherbrooke, 1811–92 : vice-president of board of education, 1859–64; chancellor of Exchequer, 1868–73; home secretary, 1873–74), 286
Lyons, Rear-Adm. (later Vice-Adm.) Sir Edmund (later Baron Lyons, 1790–1858), 187
Lyons, Richard Bickerton Pemmell, 1st Earl (1817–87 : minister in Washington, 1859–65; in Paris, 1867–87), 272;
   on danger of war, 210–11, 212, 215, 216, 257, 274;
   tour of Canada, 278;
   and *Trent* affair, 219, 228, 232 n. 1, 237, 246
Lysons, Col. (later Gen. Sir) Daniel (1816–98), 228
Lyttelton, Lt.-Gen. (later Gen.) Sir Neville Gerald (1845–1931 : chief of General Staff, 1904–08), 388, 390

Mackinac (map 1), 272
Macdonald, Sir John Alexander (1815–91 : prime minister of Canada, 1857, 1867–73, 1878–91), 258, 267, 287

Mediterranean, 260;
fleet, 150, 187, 238, 340, 369, 370;
U.S. in, 10, 103, 183, 339
Mehemet Ali, *see* Mahomet Ali
Melbourne, William Lamb, 2nd
Viscount (1779–1848: prime
minister, 1835–41), 82–3, 93, 111
Melbourne, 230–1, 232 n. 1
Melville, Robert Saunders Dundas,
2nd Viscount (1771–1851: 1st
lord of Admiralty, 1812–27), 14,
17, 20, 29, 31, 49
Merrimac, 239, 275, 311
Metcalfe, Sir Charles Theophilus
(later Baron Metcalfe, 1785–
1846: gov.-in-chief, Canada,
1843–45), 128, 152;
on canals, 154, 155;
defence instructions, 145, 148–9,
153, 155;
and lakes warships, 125–6, 143;
and militia laws, 143;
warlike despatch, 140–2, 144, 145
Metis (map 2), 229, 235
Mexico (map 3), 61, 68, 168, 169, 202,
209, 312;
Anglo-American rivalry in, 55–6,
65, 71, 121, 171, 175, 202;
European intervention, 202, 216,
229, 243, 254–6, 301, 302, 336,
408–9;
and Texan question, 75, 76–8, 124–
5, 131, 134, 137, 144, 150, 161–2,
163, 170
Miantonomah, 306
Michel, Lt.-Gen. (later Field-Marshal)
Sir John (1804–86: c.-in-c.,
Canada, 1865–67),
on defence of Canada, 292–3;
and garrison, 294
Michigan (map 1), 24, 113, 114, 311
Michigan, Lake (maps 1 and 3), 272,
326
Michigan, 125–6, 137, 138, 154, 226,
327, 332, 335
Militia, *see under* British North
America, Canada, *etc.*
Mills, Arthur (1816–98),
resolution on colonial defence, 258,
259, 260
Milne, Adm. (later Adm. of the fleet)
Sir Alexander, R.N. (1806–96:
c.-in-c., North America, 1860–
63; 1st naval lord, 1866–68, 1872–
76),

and colonial defences, 211, 238, 261,
277;
and 1878 Defence Committee, 314;
and Esquimalt, 373;
and lakes defences, 211, 278, 279;
and North American squadron, 211,
212, 215–16, 220, 229, 238–9,
306;
and proposed operations in *Trent*
affair, 237, 238, 240–4
Milne, Rear-Adm. (later Adm.) Sir
David, R.N. (1763–1845: c.-in-c.,
North America, 1816–19), 10–11,
15, 16, 23, 28, 53
Milner-Gibson, Thomas (1806–84:
president of Board of Trade,
1859–66), 284, 286
Minos, 89, 115, 126
Miquelon Island (map 3), 386
Miramichi River (map 2), 45
Mississippi, 100, 102
Mississippi River (map 3), 61, 62
Missouri, 100, 102
Mohawk, 89 n. 2, 126
Monaco,
rumour about U.S. interest in, 183
Monck, Charles Stanley, 4th Viscount
(1819–94: gov.-gen. of Canada,
1861–68), 258, 259, 264, 269, 278,
291, 292, 294, 296, 297
Monitor, 239, 275
Monitors, 239–40, 275–6, 306, 308–9
Monroe, James (1758–1831: U.S.
secretary of state, 1811–17; secretary of war, 1814–15; president,
1817–25), 12, 14, 17, 18, 21, 37,
64
Monroe Doctrine, 37, 64, 68, 178, 180,
255, 350, 382, 409
Montgomery-Moore, Lt.-Gen. (later
Sir) Alexander George (1833–
1919: G.O.C., Halifax, 1893–98),
331
Montreal (maps 1, 2, and 3), 46, 47,
59, 233, 234, 265, 281;
communications with, 4, 39, 45,
231, 235, 269;
garrison and defences, 35, 36, 38,
44, 90–1, 92, 114, 116, 117, 142,
145, 146, 148, 165, 166, 206, 224,
263, 264, 266, 267, 269, 278, 283,
284, 289, 290, 295, 299, 325, 328,
329, 331, 353, 379;
importance of, 90, 108, 114, 146,
263;

429

431

Robinson, George Frederick Samuel, *see* de Grey
Robinson, Rear-Adm. (later Adm.) Sir Robert Spencer, R.N. (1809–89: comptroller of the navy, 1861–71),
on lakes force, 280–3;
on monitors, 276, 282;
on comparative naval strength, 307
Rochester (map 1), 232 n. 1
Rocky Mountains (map 3), 61, 146
Roebuck, John Arthur (1801–79),
and Beauharnois canal, 117 n. 3;
and recruiting crisis, 192, 196, 200
Romaine, William Govett (1815–93: secretary of Admiralty, 1857–69),
and lakes force, 280–2
Rome, N.Y. (map 1), 102
Roosevelt, Theodore (1858–1919: U.S. assistant secretary of navy, 1897–98; president, 1901–09), 324 n. 2;
and U.S. navy, 338
Root, Elihu (1845–1937: U.S. secretary of war, 1899–1904; secretary of state, 1905–09),
and Rush-Bagot agreement, 397;
and Japan, 400
Rosario, 292
Rouse's Point (maps 1 and 2), 22, 50, 59–60, 106–9, 110, 138, 146, 223, 224, 233, 272
Royal Canadian Rifles, 88, 118, 207, 221, 296, 299, 300
Royal Commission on Imperial Defence, 1879–1882, 310, 314, 317, 358, 360, 372–3
Royal Mail Steam Packet Company, 129
Ruatan (map 3), 183; *see also* Bay Islands
Rush, Richard (1780–1859: U.S. secretary of state, 1817; minister in London, 1817–25), 19, 64
Rush-Bagot agreement, 27, 32, 292, 391, 392;
breaches of, 26, 89, 115–16, 125–7, 128, 137, 143, 226, 269, 332–3;
effects of, 30, 114, 335–6, 384, 387;
negotiation, 12–14, 17–19;
revision, 127, 128–9, 137, 326–7, 332–3, 335, 397–8;
termination threatened, 269, 279, 280, 291, 326

Russell, Lord John (1st Earl Russell, 1792–1878: home secretary, 1835–39; secretary for war and colonies, 1839–41; leader of Opposition, 1841–46; prime minister, 1846–52, 1865–66; foreign secretary, 1852–53, 1859–65), 151, 293;
and acquisitions in the Pacific, 122;
and Central America, 181, 184, 200, 204–5, 253, 254;
and chances of war, 86, 112, 212, 215, 219, 283;
and Civil War, 212, 215–16, 219, 245, 252, 254, 257, 283;
and colonial defences, 87–92, 112, 119, 278, 285, 291–2, 297, 300;
and France, 85–6;
and Mexican expedition, 254–6;
and north-eastern boundary question, 84 n. 2, 85–6, 111;
and Oregon question, 136 n. 1;
and Santo Domingo, 253–4;
and *Trent* affair, 219, 245;
and U.S. expansion, 204–5, 253–4;
and U.S. navy, 274, 275, 306–7;
and war-preparations, 93, 112, 215–16, 220, 283
Russia, 3, 66, 179, 180, 182, 183, 192, 196, 202, 314, 339, 340, 341, 368, 371, 372, 373, 382, 398, 403, 406, 409;
and Anglo-American relations, 46, 62, 184, 188–9, 253, 301

Sabine River (map 3), 51
Sackett's Harbor (map 1), 12, 24, 32 n. 3, 35, 97, 98, 113, 147, 233 n. 1
St Albans (maps 1 and 2), 252, 269
St Aldwyn, Earl, *see* Hicks Beach
St Andrews, New Brunswick (map 2), 41, 228, 261
St Bartholomew Island, 67 n. 2
St Clair Lake (map 1), 16
St Clair River (map 1), 16, 24, 26, 38, 325, 329
St Francis, Lake (map 1), 325
St George, 215
St George's Island (Bermuda, map 3), 49
St Helens Island (Montreal, map 1), 36, 165
St John, Lower Canada (map 1), 34, 92, 114, 116, 145, 324

141-142